Reading Across the Disciplines

College Reading and Beyond

Second Edition

Kathleen T. McWhorter
Niagara County Community College

PEARSON
Longman

New York   San Francisco   Boston
London   Toronto   Sydney   Tokyo   Singapore   Madrid
Mexico City   Munich   Paris   Cape Town   Hong Kong   Montreal

Vice President and Editor-in-Chief: Joseph Terry
Acquisitions Editor: Susan Kunchandy
Development Manager: Janet Lanphier
Development Editor: Leslie Taggart
Senior Marketing Manager: Melanie Craig
Senior Supplements Editor: Donna Campion
Media Supplements Editor: Nancy Garcia
Production Manager: Joseph Vella
Project Coordination, Text Design, and Electronic Page Makeup: Thompson Steele, Inc.
Design Manager/Cover Designer: John Callahan
Cover Photos: Getty Images, Inc.
Photo Researcher: Photosearch, Inc.
Manufacturing Buyer: Roy L. Pickering, Jr.
Printer and Binder: R.R. Donnelley/Crawfordsville
Cover Printer: Phoenix Color Corporation

For permission to use copyrighted material, grateful acknowledgment is made to the copyright holders on pp. 743–745, which are hereby made part of this copyright page.

Library of Congress Cataloging-in-Publication Data

McWhorter, Kathleen T.
    Reading across the disciplines : college reading and beyond / Kathleen T. McWhorter.-- 2nd ed.
        p. cm.
    Includes index.
    ISBN 0-321-14248-9 (student : alk. paper) -- ISBN 0-321-14251-9 (instructors)
1. College readers. 2. Reading (Higher education) 3. Interdisciplinary approach in education. I. Title.
PE1122.M37 2005
428.6--dc22

                                                                    2004000170

Please visit us at http://www.ablongman.com/mcwhorter.

ISBN 0-321-14248-9 (Student Edition)
ISBN 0-321-14251-9 (Annotated Instructor's Edition)

1 2 3 4 5 6 7 8 9 10—DOC—07 06 05 04

Brief Contents

Detailed Contents

v

Preface

This high-interest, four-color book is designed to improve college students' reading and thinking skills through brief skill instruction and extensive guided practice with academic discipline–based readings. The text is structured around 13 academic disciplines. The 39 readings—all of which aim to motivate students—are selected from college textbooks as well as from books, periodicals and popular magazines, newspapers, and Internet sources. The objective is to show the relevance of college studies to events and issues in everyday life through the use of engaging readings.

PURPOSE

The primary purposes of the text are to teach essential college reading skills and to guide their application in each of 13 academic disciplines. The text develops basic vocabulary and comprehension skills, as well as inferential and critical-reading and -thinking skills. In addition to developing overall reading skills, the text also introduces students to content-specific reading skills. Each chapter in Part Two, "Readings for Academic Disciplines," begins with a tip list for applying reading and thinking skills to text with the unique characteristics of the discipline. Questions and activities that precede and follow each reading demonstrate the application of vocabulary, comprehension, and critical-reading and -thinking skills to the particular discipline.

Another important goal of the text is to demonstrate to students the relevance and utility of college courses to their daily lives. The book attempts to answer the long-standing question frequently asked by students, "Why do I have to take a course in history, biology, etc.?" The book presents readings that show students how academic disciplines embrace and investigate topics of interest and concern to everyday human experience.

CONTENT OVERVIEW

The book is organized into three parts:

- **Part One, "A Handbook for Reading and Thinking in College,"** presents a brief skill introduction. Written in handbook format (1a, 1b, etc.), this part introduces students to essential vocabulary, comprehension, critical-reading, and reading-rate skills.

- **Part Two, "Readings for Academic Disciplines,"** has 13 chapters, each containing readings representative of a different academic discipline. Each chapter has three reading selections. The readings in each chapter are chosen from textbooks, books, periodicals, newspapers, and Internet sources that contain material relevant to the discipline. The readings in each chapter vary in length as well as difficulty. Within each chapter, readings are arranged from least to most difficult, providing students with the opportunity to strengthen their skills, experience success, and build positive attitudes toward reading. Two chapters include a pair of readings on the same topic to encourage synthesis and integration of ideas. Each reading is accompanied by an extensive apparatus that guides student learning.
- **Part Three, "Textbook Chapter Readings,"** contains two complete textbook chapters, one from a psychology textbook and one from a history textbook. These chapters enable students to practice skills on larger pieces of writing and to apply the skills they have developed in the preceding parts. Apparatus is provided for each major section of the chapters.

FEATURES

Reading Across the Disciplines guides students in learning reading and thinking skills essential for college success.

Students Approach Reading as Thinking

Reading is approached as a thinking process—a process of interacting with textual material and sorting, evaluating, and reacting to its organization and content. The apparatus preceding and following each reading focuses, guides, and shapes the students' thought processes.

Students Develop Active Reading Skills

Students learn to approach reading as a process that requires involvement and response. In doing so, they are able to master the skills that are essential to college reading. The reading apparatus provides a model for active reading.

Students Learn Essential Reading Skills

Vocabulary, comprehension, and critical-reading skills are presented concisely in Part One, "A Handbook for Reading and Thinking in College," and are accompanied by several exercises.

Students Learn Discipline-Specific Reading Skills

The high-interest readings in Part Two are grouped according to academic discipline. Each chapter begins with a brief list of tips for reading and learning within the particular discipline. Students are encouraged to apply these techniques as they read the selections within the chapter.

Students Learn as They Work

Unlike many books, which simply test students after they have read a selection, this text teaches students as they work. Some of the apparatus provides new material on vocabulary, methods of organizing information, transitions, and reading/study strategies.

Students Understand the Importance of Academic Disciplines to Their Daily Lives

Through the high-interest topics selected, students will come to understand the relevance of various academic disciplines to their daily lives, careers, and workplace.

Students Learn Visually

Increasingly, college students are becoming visual learners, and visual literacy is critical to success in today's world. To promote visual learning, this text is four-color and contains numerous photographs, graphics, graphic organizers (maps), charts, and diagrams.

Students Appreciate Consistent Format

Because students often need structure and organization, this text uses a consistent format for each reading selection. Students always know what to expect and what is expected of them.

Students Can Build Success by Progressing from Less to More Difficult Readings

The readings within each chapter are organized conceptually from less to more difficult. Instructors may choose a starting level that is appropriate for their classes. By starting with a relatively easy reading, students can build confidence and success before approaching more challenging readings.

Students Refer to Part One, "A Handbook for Reading and Thinking in College," to Get Help Answering Questions

The activities following each reading are parallel to the topics in Part One of the book, which presents a brief skill overview in a handbook format. For example, if students have difficulty answering inferential questions, they may refer to the section in Part One that explains how to make inferences. The handbook also includes a section on reading and evaluating electronic sources.

Format of the Apparatus

The apparatus for each reading selection follows a consistent format. The sections vary in the number of questions and the specific skills reviewed. Each reading selection has the following parts:

- **Headnote.** A headnote introduces the reading, identifies its source, provokes the students' interest, and most important, establishes a framework or purpose for reading.
- **Previewing the Reading.** Students are directed to preview the reading using the guidelines provided in Part One and to answer several questions based on their preview.
- **Making Connections.** This brief section encourages students to draw connections between the topic of the reading and their own knowledge and experience.
- **Reading Tip.** The reading tip is intended to help students approach and work through the reading. A different reading tip is offered for each reading. For example, a reading tip might suggest how to highlight to strengthen comprehension or how to write annotations to enhance critical thinking.
- **Reading Selection/Vocabulary Annotation.** Most reading selections contain difficult vocabulary words that are essential to the meaning of the selection. Often these are words that students are unlikely to know and cannot figure out from context. These words are highlighted, and their meanings are given as marginal annotations. Preferable to a list of words preceding the reading, this format allows students to check meanings on an as-needed basis, within the context of the selection. Annotations are also used occasionally to provide necessary background information that students may need to grasp concepts in a reading.
- **Understanding the Thesis and Other Main Ideas.** This section helps students figure out the thesis of the reading and identify the main idea of selected paragraphs.
- **Identifying Details.** This section focuses on recognizing the relationship between main ideas and details, as well as distinguishing primary from secondary details. The format of questions within this section varies to expose students to a variety of thinking strategies.
- **Recognizing Methods of Organization and Transitions.** This part of the apparatus guides students in identifying the overall organizational pattern of the selection and in identifying transitional words and phrases within the reading. Prompts are provided that serve as teaching tips or review strategies.
- **Reviewing and Organizing Ideas.** Since many students are proficient at literal recall of information but have difficulty seeing relationships and organizing information into usable formats for study and review, this section emphasizes important review and organizational skills such as paraphrasing, mapping, outlining, and summarizing.
- **Figuring out Inferred Meanings.** The ability to think inferentially is expected of college students. This section guides students in making inferences based on information presented in the reading selection.
- **Thinking Critically.** This section covers essential critical-thinking skills including distinguishing fact from opinion, identifying the author's purpose, recognizing bias, evaluating the source, identifying tone, making judgments, and evaluating supporting evidence.

- **Building Vocabulary.** The first part of this section focuses on vocabulary in context, while the second is concerned with word parts. Using words from the reading selection, exercises are structured to encourage students to expand their vocabulary and strengthen their word-analysis skills. A brief review of the meanings of prefixes, roots, and suffixes used in the exercise is provided for ease of reference and to create a meaningful learning situation. The third vocabulary section focuses on a wide range of interesting features of language, drawing upon unusual or striking usage within the reading. Topics such as figurative language, idioms, and connotative meanings are included.
- **Selecting a Learning/Study Strategy.** College students are responsible for learning and studying what they read; many use the same study method for all disciplines and all types of material. This section helps students to choose appropriate study methods and to adapt their study methods to suit particular academic disciplines.
- **Exploring Ideas Through Discussion and Writing.** Questions provided in this section are intended to stimulate thought, provoke discussion, and serve as a springboard to writing about the reading.
- **Beyond the Classroom to the Web.** These activities draw on the skills students have learned by directing them to the Internet, where they are asked to read particular articles. These activities also demonstrate the relevance of the academic discipline beyond the classroom and provide guidance in using Web sources.

FEATURES OF THE SECOND EDITION

The goals of the revision were to increase the coverage of culturally diverse topics and authors, to increase the number of practice exercises in Part One, to introduce more readings from the physical sciences and mathematics, and to address more contemporary concerns.

Greater Emphasis on Cultural Diversity. New readings examine cultural differences in marriage ceremonies, the protection of sacred Native American burial sites, biracial self-identity, preschool education of Hispanic children, and the plight of refugees coming to America. A short story by Panos Ioannides, a native of Cyprus, is also included, as is a work by Linda Hogan, a Native American poet. Culturally diverse readings carried over from the first edition include neurosurgeon Ben Carson's description of racial discrimination he has experienced, a discussion of Native American art, a story of a child's search for her Korean birth mother, and a report on Hispanic Americans as an important business marketing segment.

Double the Number of Exercises in Part One. The first edition contained 84 exercises. The second edition contains more than twice as many. For most skills, two exercises are now provided. One activity may be completed in class; the second can be assigned for completion outside of class. Exercises remain brief to reinforce use of Part One as reference material.

New Physical Sciences/Mathematics Chapter. This chapter increases the book's coverage of the hard sciences and adds coverage of mathematics. The readings demonstrate the practical application of topics studied. Probability theory yields information on the fairness of lotteries. A physics textbook discussion of the effects of radiation demonstrates our frequent exposure to its various forms. A reading on the exploration and exploitation of outer space brings new relevance to the study of astronomy.

Expansion of Literature Coverage. The Arts/Humanities chapter has been expanded to include literature. The short story "Gregory" by Panos Ioannides is dramatically compelling as it examines moral issues related to wartime and obeying orders. In the poem "The Truth," biracial poet, Linda Hogan, confronts self-identity issues.

New Full-Length History Chapter. Part Three now contains a full-length history chapter from *The American People: Creating a Nation and a Society,* replacing the health chapter in the first edition. The chapter covers the post–Cold War period from 1992 to 2002. The chapter reports the September 11 terrorist attacks, demonstrating to students how recent events become part of our historical record.

New Chapter on Public Policy/Contemporary Issues. Regrouping readings from other chapters, this chapter provides a new emphasis on issues important to contemporary living. The chapter includes a pair of readings that examine the issues of euthanasia. Another reading describes an adopted child's search for her birth mother.

New Anthropology Chapter. Anthropology helps students understand the world they live in as they learn how people interact in different cultures. The reading "To Love and to Cherish" examines the tradition of a marriage ceremony in a variety of religious groups. "Stand Off Begins to Protect Sacred Sites" focuses on the issue of preservation of Native American burial sites. The reading "Apes and Language" deals with the biological question of whether apes can acquire a uniquely human trait—language.

More Logical Flow of Chapters in Part Two. Chapters in Part Two have been rearranged so that chapters progress from the academic world to the world of work, concluding with a chapter on workplace topics.

BOOK-SPECIFIC ANCILLARY MATERIALS

- **Annotated Instructor's Edition.** The Annotated Instructor's Edition is identical to the student text, but it includes answers printed directly on the pages where questions and exercises appear. ISBN 0-321-14251-9
- **Test Bank.** This supplement contains numerous tests for each chapter, formatted for easy distribution and scoring. It includes content review

quizzes and skill-based mastery tests for Part One and a discipline-based test and two discipline-based mastery tests for Part Two. ISBN 0-321-08966-9

- **Instructor's Manual.** The manual includes teaching suggestions for each section of Part One. For each reading in Part Two, the manual provides numerous suggestions for introducing the reading and offers a variety of follow-up activities designed to review and reinforce skills. ISBN 0-321-08967-7

- *Vocabulary Simplified.* Instructors may choose to shrink-wrap *Reading Across the Disciplines* with a copy of *Vocabulary Simplified.* This book, written by Kathleen McWhorter, works well as a supplemental text providing additional instruction and practice in vocabulary. Students can work through the book independently or units may be incorporated into weekly lesson plans. Topics covered include methods of vocabulary learning, contextual aids, word parts, connotative meanings, idioms, euphemisms, and many more interesting and fun topics. The book concludes with vocabulary lists and exercises representative of eleven academic disciplines. To preview this book, contact your Longman sales consultant for an examination copy.

- *The Longman Reader's Journal.* This free supplement, prepared by Kathleen T. McWhorter, is available free with *Reading Across the Disciplines.* The journal offers students a place to respond to and think critically about their reading materials, as well as keep track of their progress. It is an excellent tool for any course with a portfolio component. For an examination copy, contact your Longman sales representative.

- **Companion Website.** For additional exercises, readings, and Internet activities, be sure to visit this book's Companion Website at http://www.ablongman.com/mcwhorter.

THE LONGMAN DEVELOPMENTAL READING PACKAGE

In addition to the book-specific ancillaries described above, Longman offers many other supplements to instructors and students. All of these supplements are available either free or at greatly reduced prices.

For Additional Reading and Reference

The Dictionary Deal. Two dictionaries can be shrink-wrapped with any Longman Reading title for a nominal fee. *The New American Webster Handy College Dictionary* is a paperback reference text with more than 100,000 entries. *Merriam Webster's Collegiate Dictionary,* Eleventh Edition, is a hardback reference with a citation file of more than 14.5 million examples of English words drawn from actual use. For more details on ordering a dictionary with this text, please contact your Longman sales representative.

Penguin Quality Paperback Titles. A series of Penguin paperbacks is available at a significant discount when shrink-wrapped with any Longman title. Some titles available are Toni Morrison's *Beloved*, Julia Alvarez's *How the Garcia Girls Lost Their Accents*, Mark Twain's *Huckleberry Finn*, Frederick Douglass's *Narrative of the Life of Frederick Douglass*, Harriet Beecher Stowe's *Uncle Tom's Cabin*, Dr. Martin Luther King, Jr.'s *Why We Can't Wait*, and plays by Shakespeare, Miller, and Albee. For a complete list of titles or more information, please contact your Longman sales representative.

The Longman Textbook Reader. This supplement, for use in developmental reading courses, offers five complete chapters on computer science, biology, psychology, communications, and business from Addison Wesley/Longman textbooks. Each chapter includes additional comprehension quizzes, critical-thinking questions, and group activities. For information on how to bundle the free *Longman Textbook Reader* with *Reading Across the Disciplines*, please contact your Longman sales representative. (This is available in two versions, with and without answers.)

***Newsweek* Alliance.** Instructors may choose to shrink-wrap a 12-week subscription to *Newsweek* with any Longman text. The price of the subscription is 59 cents per issue (a total of $7.08 for the subscription). Available with the subscription is a free *Interactive Guide to Newsweek*, a workbook for students who are using the text. In addition, *Newsweek* provides a wide variety of instructor supplements free to teachers, including maps, skill builders, and weekly quizzes. For further information on the *Newsweek* Alliance, please contact your Longman sales representative.

Florida Adopters: *Thinking Through the Test*, by D. J. Henry. This special workbook, prepared specially for students in Florida, offers ample skill and practice exercises to help students prepare for the Florida State Exit Exam. To shrink-wrap this workbook free with your textbook, please contact your Longman sales representative. Also available are two laminated grids (one for reading, one for writing) that can serve as handy references for students preparing for the Florida State Exit Exam.

Texas Adopters: The Longman THEA Study Guide, by Jeannette Harris (Student ISBN: 0-321-20271-6). Created specifically for students in Texas, this study guide includes straightforward explanations and numerous practice exercises to help students prepare for the reading and writing sections of THEA Test.

New York Adopters: Preparing for the CUNY-ACT Reading and Writing Test, edited by Patricia Licklider (Student ISBN: 0-321-19608-2). This booklet, prepared by reading and writing faculty from across the CUNY system, is designed to help students prepare for the CUNY-ACT exit test. It includes test-taking tips, reading passages, typical exam questions, and sample writing prompts to help students become familiar with each portion of the test.

Electronic and Online Offerings

My Skills Lab (www.ablongman/myskillslab) (Student Pin Card ISBN: 0-321-26323-5 or Instructor Pin Card ISBN: 0-321-26322-7). This website houses all media tools for developmental English (reading, writing, and study skills) in one place: Avoiding Plagiarism, Exercise Zone, Research Navigator, Longman Writer's Warehouse, Reading Roadtrip, Longman Vocabulary Website, and Longman Study Skills Website. This site is free when packaged with any Longman Textbook. Please contact your Longman sales representative for further details.

Reading Road Trip 3.0 Multimedia Software (Student Pin Card: ISBN: 0-321-14962-9 or Instructor Pin Card: ISBN: 0-321-14961-0). Taking students on a tour of 16 cities and landmarks throughout the United States, each of the 16 modules corresponds to a reading or study skill (for example, finding the main idea, understanding patterns of organization, thinking critically). All modules contain a tour of the location, instruction and tutorial, exercises, interactive feedback, and mastery tests. This new release includes all-new additional exercises and tests; additional exercises at the lowest level; and a brand-new module of longer readings that help students integrate all the skills and prepare for exit exams. An Instructor's Manual for Reading Road Trip 3.0 (Instructor ISBN: 0-321-16195-5) is available free with adoption. Please contact your Longman sales representative for further details.

Teaching Online Internet Research, Conversation, and Composition, **Second Edition.** Ideal for instructors who have never surfed the Net, this easy-to-follow guide offers basic definitions, numerous examples, and step-by-step information about finding and using Internet sources. Free to adopters. ISBN 0-321-01957-1

Research Navigator Guide for English, H. Eric Branscomb & Doug Gotthoffer (Student ISBN: 0-321-20277-5). Designed to teach students how to conduct high-quality online research and to document it properly, Research Navigator guides provide discipline-specific academic resources; in addition to helpful tips on the writing process, online research, and finding and citing valid sources. Free when packaged with any Longman text, Research Navigator guides include an access code to Research Navigator™—providing access to thousands of academic journals and periodicals, the New York Times Search by Subject Archive, Link Library, Library Guides, and more.

For Instructors

[NEW] Electronic Test Bank for Reading. This electronic test bank offers more than 3,000 questions in all areas of reading, including vocabulary, main idea, supporting details, patterns of organization, language, critical thinking, analytical reasoning, inference, point of view, visual aids, and textbook reading. With this easy-to-use CD-ROM, instructors simply choose questions from the electronic test bank, then print out the completed test for distribution. (CD-ROM: 0-321-08179-X; Print version: 0-321-08596-5)

CLAST Test Package, Fourth Edition. These two 40-item objective tests evaluate student readiness for the CLAST exams. Strategies for teaching CLAST preparedness are included. Free with any Longman English title. (Reproducible sheets: 0-321-01950-4; Computerized IBM version: 0-321-01982-2; Computerized Mac version: 0-321-01983-0)

TASP Test Package, Third Edition. These 12 practice pre-tests and post-tests assess the same reading and writing skills covered in the THEA examination. Free with any Longman English title. (Reproducible sheets: 0-321-01959-8; Computerized IBM version: 0-321-01985-7; Computerized Mac version: 0-321-01984-9)

ACKNOWLEDGMENTS

I wish to express my gratitude to my reviewers for their excellent ideas, suggestions, and advice on the preparation and revision of this text:

Jennifer Britton, Valencia Community College; Mary Lou Coleman, Rose State College; Christopher Fauske, Newbury College; Mamie Griffin, Fayetteville Technical Community College; Tami Hale, Northwestern State University; Bernadette Henry, Essex Community College; Margaret Inman, University of North Carolina, Pembroke; Caren Kessler, Blue Ridge Community College; Julie King, University of Wisconsin, Parkside; Karen Nelson, Craven Community College; Elva Peña, Del Mar College; Teresa Reed, Southern Illinois University; Mary Reeves, Miami Dade Community College; Catherine Seyler, Palm Beach Community College; Lynn Wright, Pasadena City College; Rose Yesu, Massosoit Community College; Janet Yu, Santa Monica College

I also wish to thank Leslie Taggart, my developmental editor, for her creative vision of the project, her helpful suggestions, and her assistance in preparing and organizing the manuscript. I am particularly indebted to Susan Kunchandy, acquisitions editor, for her enthusiastic support, valuable advice, and expert guidance in the revision of this book.

KATHLEEN T. MCWHORTER

PART ONE

A Handbook for Reading and Thinking in College

1 Active Reading and Thinking Strategies

What does it take to do well in biology? In psychology? In history? In business? In answer to these questions, college students are likely to say:

- "Knowing how to study."
- "You have to like the course."
- "Hard work!"
- "Background in the subject area."
- "A good teacher!"

Students seldom mention reading as an essential skill. In a sense, reading is a hidden factor in college success. When you think of college, you think of attending classes and labs, completing assignments, studying for and taking exams, and writing papers. A closer look at these activities, however, reveals that reading is an important part of each.

Reading stays "behind the scenes" because instructors rarely evaluate it directly. Grades are based on production: how well you express your ideas in papers or how well you do on exams. Yet reading is the primary means by which you acquire your ideas and gather information.

Throughout this handbook you will learn numerous ways to use reading as a tool for college success.

1a ACTIVE READING: THE KEY TO ACADEMIC SUCCESS

Reading involves much more than moving your eyes across lines of print, more than recognizing words, and more than reading sentences. Reading is thinking. It is an active process of identifying important ideas and comparing, evaluating, and applying them.

Have you ever gone to a ball game and watched the fans? Most do not sit and watch passively. Instead, they direct the plays, criticize the calls, encourage the players, and reprimand the coach. They care enough to get actively involved in the game. Just like interested fans, active readers get involved. They question, challenge, and criticize, as well as understand. Table 1.1 on page 4 contrasts the active strategies of successful readers with the passive ones of less successful readers. Not all strategies will work for everyone. Experiment to discover those that work particularly well for you.

TABLE 1.1 ACTIVE VERSUS PASSIVE READING

ACTIVE READERS . . .	PASSIVE READERS . . .
Tailor their reading to suit each assignment.	Read all assignments the same way.
Analyze the purpose of an assignment.	Read an assignment because it was assigned.
Adjust their speed to suit their purpose.	Read everything at the same speed.
Question ideas in the assignment.	Accept whatever is in print as true.
Compare and connect textbook material with lecture content.	Study lecture notes and the textbook separately.
Skim headings to find out what an assignment is about before beginning to read.	Check the length of an assignment and then begin reading.
Make sure they understand what they are reading as they go along.	Read until the assignment is completed.
Read with pencil in hand, highlighting, jotting notes, and marking key vocabulary.	Read.
Develop personalized strategies that are particularly effective.	Follow routine, standard methods. Read all assignments the same way.

➤ NOW PRACTICE . . . ACTIVE READING

Consider each of the following reading assignments. Discuss ways to get actively involved in each assignment.

1. Reading two poems by Maya Angelou for an American literature class.

   <u>annotate as you read, compare and contrast the poems' subject matter,</u>

   <u>language, and meaning</u>

2. Reading the procedures for your next biology lab.

   <u>underline key steps, visualize the process, focus on overall purpose</u>

   <u>of the lab</u>

3. Reading an article in *Newsweek* magazine assigned by your political science instructor in preparation for a class discussion.

   <u>underline, write summary notes, discover how the article relates to</u>

   <u>course content</u>

1b   PREVIEWING

Previewing is a means of familiarizing yourself with the content and organization of an assignment *before* you read it. Think of previewing as getting a "sneak preview" of what a chapter or reading will be about. You can then read the material more easily and more rapidly.

How to Preview Reading Assignments

Use the following steps to become familiar with a textbook chapter's content and organization.

1. **Read the title.** The title indicates the topic of the article or chapter; the subtitle suggests the specific focus of, or approach to, the topic.
2. **Check the author and the source of articles and essays.** This information may provide clues about the article's content or focus.
3. **Read the introduction or the first paragraph.** The introduction or first paragraph serves as a lead-in to the chapter, establishing the overall subject, and suggesting how it will be developed.
4. **Read each boldface (dark print) heading.** Headings label the contents of each section and announce the major topic covered. If there are no headings, read the first sentence of each paragraph. The first sentence of the paragraph is often the topic sentence, which states the main idea of the paragraph. By reading first sentences, you will encounter most of the key ideas in the article.
5. **Read the first sentence under each major heading.** The first sentence often states the central thought of the section. If the first sentence seems introductory, read the last sentence; often this sentence states or restates the central thought.
6. **Note any typographical aids.** Italics are used to emphasize important terminology and definitions, distinguishing them from the rest of the passage. Material that is numbered 1, 2, 3; lettered a, b, c; or presented in list form is also of special importance.
7. **Note any graphic aids.** Graphs, charts, photographs, and tables often suggest what is important in the chapter. Be sure to read the captions of photographs and the legends on graphs, charts, or tables.
8. **Read the last paragraph or summary.** This provides a condensed view of the chapter, often outlining the key points of the chapter.
9. **Read quickly any end-of-article or end-of-chapter material.** This might include references, study questions, discussion questions, chapter outlines, or vocabulary lists. If there are study questions, read them through quickly because they tell you what is important to remember in the chapter. If a vocabulary list is included, rapidly skim through it to identify the terms you will be learning as you read.

A section of an interpersonal communication textbook chapter discussing the breakup of a relationship is reprinted here to illustrate how previewing is done. The portions to focus on when previewing are shaded. Read only those portions. After you have finished, test how well your previewing worked by answering the questions that follow, titled, "What Did You Learn from Previewing?"

Ending a Relationship

1   Some relationships, of course, do end. Sometimes there is simply not enough to hold the couple together. Sometimes there are problems that cannot be resolved. Sometimes the costs are too high and the rewards too few, or the relationship is recognized as destructive and escape is the only alternative. As a relationship ends, you're confronted with two general issues: (1) how to end the relationship, and (2) how to deal with the inevitable problems that relationship endings cause.

The Strategies of Disengagement

2   When you wish to exit a relationship you need some way of explaining this—to yourself as well as to your partner. You develop a strategy for getting out of a relationship that you no longer find satisfying or profitable. The table identifies five major disengagement strategies (Cody 1982). As you read down the table, note that the strategies depend on your goal. For example, you're more likely to remain friends if you use de-escalation than if you use justification or avoidance (Banks, Altendorf, Greene, and Cody 1987). You may find it interesting to identify the disengagement strategies you have heard of or used yourself and see how they fit in with these five types.

Dealing With a Breakup

3   Regardless of the specific reason, relationship breakups are difficult to deal with; invariably they cause stress. You're likely to experience high levels of distress over the breakup of a relationship in which you were satisfied, were close to your partner, had dated your partner for a long time, and felt it would not be easy to replace the relationship with another one (Simpson 1987, Frazier and Cook 1993).

4   Given both the inevitability that some relationships will break up and the importance of such breakups, here are some suggestions to ease the difficulty that is sure to be experienced. These suggestions apply to the termination of any type of relationship—between friends or lovers, through death, separation, or breakup.

Break the Loneliness-Depression Cycle

5   The two most common feelings following the end of a relationship are loneliness and depression. These feelings are significant; treat them seriously. Realize that depression often leads to serious illness. In most cases, fortunately, loneliness and depression are temporary. Depression, for example, usually does not last longer than three or four days. Similarly, the loneliness that follows a breakup is generally linked to this specific situation and will fade when the situation changes. When depression does last, is especially deep, or disturbs your normal functioning, it's time for professional help.

FIVE DISENGAGEMENT STRATEGIES

Think back to relationships that you have tried to dissolve or that your partner tried to dissolve. Did you or your partner use any of the strategies listed here? These strategies are taken from research by Michael Cody (1982).

STRATEGY	FUNCTION	EXAMPLES
Positive tone	To maintain a positive relationship; to express positive feelings for the other person	I really care for you a great deal but I'm not ready for such an intense relationship.
Negative identity management	To blame the other person for the breakup; to absolve oneself of the blame for the breakup	I can't stand your jealousy, your constant suspicions, your checking up on me. I need my freedom.
Justification	To give reasons for the breakup	I'm going away to college for four years; there's no point in not dating others.
Behavioral de-escalation	To reduce the intensity of the relationship	Avoidance; cut down on phone calls; reduce time spent together, especially time alone.
De-escalation	To reduce the exclusivity and hence the intensity of the relationship	I'm just not ready for so exclusive a relationship. I think we should see other people.

Source: Joseph A. DeVito. *The Interpersonal Communication Book,* Ninth Ed. New York: Longman, 2001, pp. 278–281.

Take Time Out

6   Resist the temptation to jump into a new relationship while the old one is still warm or before a new one can be assessed with some objectivity. At the same time, resist swearing off all relationships. Neither extreme works well.

7   Take time out for yourself. Renew your relationship with yourself. If you were in a long-term relationship, you probably saw yourself as part of a team, as part of a couple. Now get to know yourself as a unique individual, standing alone at present but fully capable of entering a meaningful relationship in the near future.

Bolster Self-Esteem

8   When relationships fail, self-esteem often declines. This seems especially true for those who did not initiate the breakup (Collins and Clark 1989). You may feel guilty for having caused the breakup or inadequate for not holding on to the relationship. You may feel unwanted and unloved. Your task is to regain the positive self-image needed to function effectively.

9   Recognize, too, that having been in a relationship that failed—even if you view yourself as the main cause of the breakup—does not mean that you are a failure. Neither does it mean that you cannot succeed in a new and different relationship. It does mean that something went wrong with this one relationship. Ideally, it was a failure from which you have learned something important about yourself and about your relationship behavior.

Remove or Avoid Uncomfortable Symbols

10   After any breakup, there are a variety of reminders—photographs, gifts, and letters, for example. Resist the temptation to throw these out. Instead, remove them. Give them to a friend to hold or put them in a closet where you'll not see them. If possible, avoid places you frequented together. These symbols will bring back uncomfortable memories. After you have achieved some emotional distance, you can go back and enjoy these as reminders of a once pleasant relationship. Support for this suggestion comes from research showing that the more vivid your memory of a broken love affair—a memory greatly aided by these relationship symbols—the greater your depression is likely to be (Harvey, Flanary, and Morgan 1986).

Seek Support

11   Many people feel they should bear their burdens alone. Men, in particular, have been taught that this is the only "manly" way to handle things. But seeking the support of others is one of the best antidotes to the unhappiness caused when a relationship ends. Tell your friends and family of your situation—in only general terms, if you prefer—and make it clear that you want support. Seek out people who are positive and nurturing. Avoid negative individuals who will paint the world in even darker tones. Make the distinction between seeking support and seeking advice. If you feel you need advice, seek out a professional.

Avoid Repeating Negative Patterns

12   Many people repeat their mistakes. They enter second and third relationships with the same blinders, faulty preconceptions, and unrealistic expectations with which they entered earlier ones. Instead, use the knowledge gained from your failed relationship to prevent repeating the same patterns.

13   At the same time, don't become a prophet of doom. Don't see in every relationship vestiges of the old. Don't jump at the first conflict and say, "Here it goes all over again." Treat the new relationship as the unique relationship it is. Don't evaluate it through past experiences. Use past relationships and experiences as guides, not filters.

➤ WHAT DID YOU LEARN FROM PREVIEWING?

Without referring to the passage, answer each of the following true/false questions.

___T___ 1. To end a relationship you need to find a way to explain the breakup to yourself and to your partner.

___T___ 2. The breakup of a relationship almost always causes stress.

___F___ 3. The two most common feelings following the end of a relationship are anger and fear of desertion.

___F___ 4. After a breakup occurs, it is important to keep letters and photographs as reminders of the relationship at its best.

___T___ 5. One mistake people often make after a breakup is to enter into a new relationship too soon.

You probably were able to answer all (or most) of the questions correctly. Previewing, then, does provide you with a great deal of information. If you were to return to the passage from the textbook and read the entire section, you would find it easier to do than if you hadn't previewed.

Why Previewing Is Effective

Previewing is effective for several reasons:

- Previewing helps you to make decisions about how you will approach the material. On the basis of what you discover about the assignment's organization and content, you can select the reading and study strategies that will be most effective.

- Previewing puts your mind in gear and helps you start thinking about the subject.

- Previewing also gives you a mental outline of the chapter's content. It enables you to see how ideas are connected, and since you know where the author is headed, your reading will be easier than if you had not previewed. Previewing, however, is never a substitute for careful, thorough reading.

> NOW PRACTICE . . . PREVIEWING

Assume you are taking a biology course. Your instructor has assigned the following article from U. S. News and World Report. *Preview the article using the procedure described in this section. When you have finished, answer the questions that follow.*

Animal Emotions

Sheer joy. Romantic love. The pain of mourning. Scientists say pets and wild creatures have feelings, too.

By Laura Tangley

1   Swimming off the coast of Argentina, a female right whale singles out just one of the suitors that are hotly pursuing her. After mating, the two cetaceans linger side by side, stroking one another with their flippers and finally rolling together in what looks like an embrace. The whales then depart, flippers touching, and swim slowly side by side, diving and surfacing in perfect unison until they disappear from sight.

2   In Tanzania, primatologists studying chimpanzee behavior record the death of Flo, a troop's 50-year-old matriarch. Throughout the following day, Flo's son, Flint, sits besides his mother's lifeless body, occasionally taking her hand and whimpering. Over the next few weeks, Flint grows increasingly listless, withdrawing from the troop—despite his siblings' efforts to bring him back—and refusing food. Three weeks after Flo's death, the formerly healthy young chimp is dead, too.

Who's Happy? Some animals, like cats, keep their feelings to themselves. Many biologists maintain that all mammals feel joy.

3   A grief-stricken chimpanzee? Leviathans in love? Most people, raised on Disney versions of sentient and passionate beasts, would say that these tales, both true, simply confirm their suspicions that animals can feel intense, humanlike emotions. For their part, the nation's 61 million pet owners need no convincing at all that Fido and Fluffy can feel angry, morose, elated—even jealous or embarrassed. Recent studies, in fields as distant as ethology and neurobiology, are supporting this popular belief. Other evidence is merely anecdotal, especially for pets—dogs that become depressed, or even die, after losing a beloved companion, for instance. But the anecdote—or case study in scientific parlance—has now achieved some respectability among researchers who study animal behavior. As University of Colorado biologist Marc Bekoff says, "The plural of anecdote is data."

4   Still, the idea of animals feeling emotions remains controversial among many scientists. Researchers' skepticism is fueled in part by their professional aversion to anthropomorphism, the very nonscientific tendency to attribute human qualities to nonhumans. Many scientists also say that it is impossible to prove animals have emotions using standard scientific methods—repeatable observations that can be manipulated in controlled experiments—leading them to conclude that such feelings must not exist. Today, however, amid mounting evidence to the contrary, "the tide is turning radically and rapidly," says Bekoff, who is at the forefront of this movement.

5   Even the most strident skeptics of animal passion agree that many creatures experience fear—which some scientists define as a "primary" emotion that contrasts with "secondary" emotions such as love and grief. Unlike these more complex feelings, fear is instinctive, they say, and requires no conscious thought. Essential to escape predators and other dangers, fear—and its predictable flight, fight, or freeze response—seems to be hard-wired into many species. Young geese that have never before seen a predator, for example, will run for cover if a hawk-shaped silhouette passes overhead. The shape of a non-predatory bird, on the other hand, elicits no such response.

6   But beyond such instinctual emotions and their predictable behavioral responses, the possibility of more complex animal feelings—those that entail mental process-

Who's Happy? Obviously this playful orangutan.

ing—is difficult to demonstrate. "I can't even *prove* that another human being is feeling happy or sad," says Bekoff, "but I can deduce how they're feeling through body language and facial expression." As a scientist who has conducted field studies of coyotes, foxes, and other canines for the past three decades, Bekoff also believes he can accurately tell what these animals are feeling by observing their behavior. He adds that animal emotions may actually be more knowable than those of humans, because they don't "filter" their feelings the way we do.

7   Yet because feelings are intangible, and so tough to study scientifically, "most researchers don't even want to talk about animal emotions," says Jaak Panksepp, a neuroscientist at Bowling Green State University in Ohio and author of *Affective Neuroscience.* Within his field, Panksepp is a rare exception, who believes that similarities between the brains of humans and other animals suggest that at least some creatures have true feelings. "Imagine where we'd be in physics if we hadn't inferred what's inside the atom," says Panksepp. "Most of what goes on in nature is invisible, yet we don't deny that it exists."

8   The new case for animal emotions comes in part from the growing acceptability of field observations, particularly when they are taken in aggregate. The latest contribution to this body of knowledge is a new book, *The Smile of a Dolphin,* which presents personal reports from more than 50 researchers who have spent their careers studying animals—from cats, dogs, bears, and chimps to birds, iguanas, and fish. Edited by Bekoff, who says it will finally "legitimize" research on animal emotions, the volume already has garnered scientific attention, including a Smithsonian Institution symposium on the subject this week.

9   **Beastly joy.** One of the most obvious animal emotions is pleasure. Anyone who has ever held a purring cat or been greeted by a bounding, barking, tail-wagging dog knows that animals often appear to be happy. Beastly joy seems particularly apparent when the animals are playing with one another or sometimes, in the case of pets, with people.

Maternal Mourning. Many species, from polar bears to chimps, have been observed grieving their losses. Like depressed humans, some stop eating and wither.

10   Virtually all young mammals, as well as some birds, play, as do adults of many species such as our own. Young dolphins, for instance, routinely chase each other through the water like frolicsome puppies and have been observed riding the wakes of boats like surfers. Primatologist Jane Goodall, who has studied chimpanzees in Tanzania for four decades, says that chimps "chase, somersault, and pirouette around one another with the abandon of children." In Colorado, Bekoff once watched an elk race back and forth across a patch of snow—even though there was plenty of bare grass nearby—leaping and twisting its body in midair on each pass. Though recent research suggests that play may help youngsters develop skills needed in adulthood, Bekoff says there's no question that it's also fun. "Animals at play are symbols of the unfettered joy of life," he says.

11   Grief also seems to be common in the wild, particularly following the death of a mate, parent, offspring, or even close companion. Female sea lions witnessing their pups being eaten by killer whales are known to actually wail. When a goose, which mates for life, loses its partner, the bird's head and body droop dejectedly. Goodall, who saw the young chimp Flint starve after his mother died, maintains that the animal "died of grief."

12   Elephants may be nature's best-known mourners. Scientists studying these behemoths have reported countless cases of elephants trying to revive dead or dying family members, as well as standing quietly beside an animal's remains for many days, periodically reaching out and touching the body with their trunks. Kenyan biologist Joyce Poole, who has studied African elephants since 1976, says these animals' behavior toward their dead "leaves me with little doubt that they experience deep emotions and have some understanding about death."

13   But there's "hard" scientific evidence for animal feelings as well. Scientists who study the biology of emotions, a field still in its infancy, are discovering many similarities between the brains of humans and other animals. In animals studied so far, including humans, emotions seem to arise from ancient parts of the brain that are located below the cortex, regions that have been conserved across many species throughout evolution.

14   The most important emotional site identified so far is the amygdala, an almond-shape structure in the center of the brain. Working with rats, neuroscientists have discovered that stimulating a certain part of the amygdala induces a state of intense

Petting and Fretting. Biochemistry may explain lions in love (left). Looks can deceive, though. This dolphin (right) may appear to be enjoying itself, but it's actually in distress.

fear. Rats with damaged amygdalas, on the other hand, do not show normal behavioral responses to danger (such as freezing or running) or the physiological changes associated with fear—higher heart rate and blood pressure, for example. . . .

15   **No movie version?** "A whale may behave as if it's in love, but you can't prove what it's feeling, if anything," says neuroscientist LeDoux, author of *The Emotional Brain.* He maintains that the question of feelings boils down to whether or not animals are conscious. And though animals "may have snapshots of self-awareness," he says, "the movie we call consciousness is not there." Richard Davidson, a neuroscientist at the University of Wisconsin–Madison, agrees that higher primates, including apes and chimps, are the only animals that have demonstrated self-consciousness so far. Still, he believes that there are other creatures that "may at least have antecedents of feelings."

16   Or probably more, say Bekoff and his colleagues. Their most convincing argument, perhaps, comes from the theory of evolution, widely accepted by biologists of all stripes. Citing similarities in the brain anatomy and chemistry of humans and other animals, neuroscientist Siviy asks: "If you believe in evolution by natural selection, how can you believe that feelings suddenly appeared, out of the blue, with human beings?" Goodall says scientists who use animals to study the human brain, then deny that animals have feelings, are "illogical."

17   In the end, what difference does it really make? According to many scientists, resolving the debate over animal emotions could turn out to be much more than an intellectual exercise. If animals do indeed experience a wide range of feelings, it has profound implications for how humans and animals will interact in the future. Bekoff, for one, hopes that greater understanding of what animals are feeling will spur more stringent rules on how animals should be treated, everywhere from zoos and circuses to farms and backyards.

18   But if there is continuity between the emotional lives of humans and other animals, where should scientists draw the line? Michel Cabanac, a physiologist at Laval University in Quebec, believes that consciousness arose when animals began to experience physical pleasure and displeasure. In experiments with iguanas, he discovered that the animals show physiological changes that are associated with pleasure

in mammals—a rise in body temperature and heart rate—whereas frogs and fish do not. He proposes that emotions evolved somewhere between the first amphibians and reptiles. Yet even enthusiasts don't ascribe emotions to the very bottom end of the food chain. Says Bekoff: "We're not going to talk about jealous sponges and embarrassed mosquitoes."

1. What is the overall subject of this article?

   animal emotions

2. List at least four animals that are likely to be discussed in the article.

   a. cats   Answers will vary

   b. polar bears

   c. orangutans

   d. whales

3. List at least three emotions that you expect to be discussed in the reading.

   a. happiness   Answers will vary

   b. joy

   c. mourning

4. On a scale of 1 to 5 (1 = easy, 5 = very difficult), how difficult do you expect the article to be? Answers will vary

---

1c   ACTIVATING BACKGROUND KNOWLEDGE

After previewing your assignment, you should take a moment to think about what you already know about the topic. Whatever the topic, you probably know *something* about it: this is your background knowledge. For example, a student was about to read an article titled "Growing Urban Problems" for a sociology class. His first thought was that he knew very little about urban problems because he lived in a rural area. But when he thought of a recent trip to a nearby city, he remembered seeing the homeless people and crowded conditions. This recollection helped him remember reading about drug problems, drive-by shootings, and muggings.

Activating your background knowledge aids your reading in three ways. First, it makes reading easier because you have already thought about the topic. Second, the material is easier to remember because you can connect the new information with what you already know. Third, topics become more interesting if you can link them to your own experiences. Here are some techniques to help you activate your background knowledge.

- *Ask questions, and try to answer them.* If a chapter in your biology textbook titled "Human Diseases" contains headings such as "Infectious diseases," "Sexually transmitted diseases," "Cancer," and "Vascular diseases," you might ask and try to answer such questions as the following: What kinds of infectious diseases have I seen? What caused them? What do I know about preventing cancer and other diseases?
- *Draw on your own experience.* If a chapter in your business textbook is titled "Advertising: Its Purpose and Design," you might think of several ads you have seen and analyze the purpose of each and how it was constructed.
- *Brainstorm.* Write down everything that comes to mind about the topic. Suppose you're about to read a chapter in your sociology textbook on domestic violence. You might list types of violence—child abuse, rape, and so on. You might write questions such as "What causes child abuse?" and "How can it be prevented?" Alternatively, you might list incidents of domestic violence you have heard or read about. Any of these approaches will help to make the topic interesting.

> **NOW PRACTICE ... ACTIVATING BACKGROUND KNOWLEDGE**

Use one of the three strategies listed above to discover what you already know about animal emotions.

1d   CHECKING YOUR COMPREHENSION

What happens when you read material you can understand easily? Does it seem that everything "clicks"? Do ideas seem to fit together and make sense? Is that "click" noticeably absent at other times?

Table 1.2 on page 16 lists and compares common signals to assist you in checking your comprehension. Not all the signals appear at the same time, and not all the signals work for everyone. But becoming aware of these positive and negative signals will help you gain more control over your reading.

> **NOW PRACTICE ... CHECKING YOUR COMPREHENSION**

Read the article titled "Animal Emotions" that appears on page 9. Be alert for positive and negative comprehension signals as you read. After reading the article, answer the following questions.

1. On a scale of 1 to 5 (1 = very poor, 5 = excellent), how would you rate your overall comprehension? _____

TABLE 1.2 COMPREHENSION SIGNALS

POSITIVE SIGNALS	NEGATIVE SIGNALS
You feel comfortable and have some knowledge about the topic.	The topic is unfamiliar, yet the author assumes you understand it.
You recognize most words or can figure them out from context.	Many words are unfamiliar.
You can express the main ideas in your own words.	You must reread the main ideas and use the author's language to explain them.
You understand why the material was assigned.	You do not know why the material was assigned and cannot explain why it is important.
You read at a regular, comfortable pace.	You often slow down or reread.
You are able to make connections between ideas.	You are unable to detect relationships; the organization is not apparent.
You are able to see where the author is leading.	You feel as if you are struggling to stay with the author and are unable to predict what will follow.
You understand what is important.	Nothing (or everything) seems important.

2. What positive signals did you sense? List them below.

_____

_____

_____

3. What negative signals did you experience, if any? List them below.

_____

_____

_____

4. In which sections was your comprehension strongest? List the paragraph numbers. _____

5. Did you feel at any time that you had lost, or were about to lose, comprehension? If so, go back to that part now. What made it difficult to read?

_____

_____

1e   STRENGTHENING YOUR COMPREHENSION

Here are some suggestions to follow when you realize you need to strengthen your comprehension.

1. **Analyze the time and place in which you are reading.** If you've been reading or studying for several hours, mental fatigue may be the source of the problem. If you are reading in a place with distractions or interruptions, you might not be able to understand what you're reading.
2. **Rephrase each paragraph in your own words.** You might need to approach complicated material sentence by sentence, expressing each in your own words.
3. **Read aloud sentences or sections that are particularly difficult.** Reading out loud sometimes makes complicated material easier to understand.
4. **Reread difficult or complicated sections.** In fact, at times several readings are appropriate and necessary.
5. **Slow down your reading rate.** On occasion, simply reading more slowly and carefully will provide you with the needed boost in comprehension.
6. **Write guide questions next to headings.** Refer to your questions frequently and jot down or underline answers.
7. **Write a brief outline of major points.** This will help you see the overall organization and progression of ideas.
8. **Highlight key ideas.** After you've read a section, go back and think about and underline what is important. Underlining forces you to sort out what is important, and this sorting process builds comprehension and recall. (Refer to 7a for suggestions on how to highlight effectively.)
9. **Write notes in the margins.** Explain or rephrase difficult or complicated ideas or sections.
10. **Determine if you lack background knowledge.** Comprehension is difficult, or at times impossible, if you lack essential information that the writer assumes you have. Suppose you are reading a section of a political science text in which the author describes implications of the balance of power in the Third World. If you do not understand the concept of balance of power, your comprehension will break down. When you lack background information, take immediate steps to correct the problem:
    - Consult other sections of your text, using the glossary and index.
    - Obtain a more basic text that reviews fundamental principles and concepts.
    - Consult reference materials (encyclopedias, subject or biographical dictionaries).
    - Ask your instructor to recommend additional sources, guidebooks, or review texts.

2 Vocabulary Building

Your vocabulary can be one of your strongest assets or one of your greatest liabilities. It defines and describes you by revealing a great deal about your level of education and your experience. Your vocabulary contributes to that all-important first impression people form when they meet you. A strong vocabulary provides both immediate academic benefits and long-term career effects. This section describes two methods of strengthening your vocabulary: using context clues and word parts.

2a USING CONTEXT CLUES

Read the following brief paragraph in which several words are missing. Try to figure out the missing words and write them in the blanks.

Rate refers to the _____ at which you speak. If you speak too _____ , your listeners will not have time to understand your message. If you speak too _____ , your listeners' minds will wander.

Did you insert the word <u>speed</u> in the first blank, <u>fast</u> in the second blank, and <u>slowly</u> in the third blank? Most likely you correctly identified all three missing words. You could tell from the sentence which word to put in. The words around the missing words—the sentence context—gave you clues as to which word would fit and make sense. Such clues are called **context clues.**

While you probably won't find missing words on a printed page, you will often find words that you do not know. Context clues can help you to figure out the meanings of unfamiliar words.

Example:

Phobias, such as fear of heights, water, or confined spaces, are difficult to eliminate.

From the sentence, you can tell that *phobia* means "fear of specific objects or situations."

18

Here's another example:

> The couple finally **secured** a table at the popular, crowded restaurant.

You can figure out that *secured* means "got or took ownership of" the table.

There are four types of context clues to look for: (1) definition, (2) example, (3) contrast, and (4) logic of the passage.

Definition Clues

Many times a writer defines a word immediately following its use. The writer may directly define a word by giving a brief definition or a synonym (a word that has the same meaning). Such words and phrases as *means, is, refers to,* and *can be defined as* are often used. Here are some examples:

> **Corona** refers to *the outermost part of the sun's atmosphere.*
>
> A **soliloquy** is *a speech made by a character in a play that reveals his or her thoughts to the audience.*

At other times, rather than formally define the word, a writer may provide you with clues. Punctuation is often used to signal that a definition clue to a word's meaning is to follow. Punctuation also separates the meaning clue from the rest of the sentence. Three types of punctuation—commas, parentheses, and dashes—are used in this way. In the examples below, notice that the meaning clue is separated from the rest of the sentence by punctuation.

1. Commas

> *Five-line rhyming poems,* or **limericks,** are among the simplest forms of poetry.
>
> **Equity,** *general principles of fairness and justice,* is used in law when existing laws do not apply or are inadequate.

2. Parentheses

> **Lithium** (*an alkali metal*) is so soft it can be cut with a knife.
>
> A leading cause of heart disease is a diet with too much **cholesterol** (*a fatty substance made of carbon, hydrogen, and oxygen*).

3. Dashes

> Our country's **gross national product**—*the total market value of its national output of goods and services*—is increasing steadily.
>
> Ancient Egyptians wrote in **hieroglyphics**—*pictures used to represent words.*

> **Facets**—*small flat surfaces at different angles*—bring out the beauty of a diamond.

➤ NOW PRACTICE . . . USING DEFINITION CLUES 1

Read each sentence and write a definition or synonym for each boldfaced word or phrase. Use the definition context clue to help you determine word meaning.

1. The judge's **candor**—his sharp, open frankness—shocked the jury.

   frankness of expression

2. A **chemical bond** is a strong attractive force that holds two or more atoms together.

   a strong attractive force that holds atoms together

3. Hearing, technically known as **audition,** begins when a sound wave reaches the outer ear.

   hearing

4. A **species** is a group of animals or plants that share similar characteristics and are able to interbreed.

   a group of animals or plants that share similar characteristics and are able

   to interbreed

5. Many diseases have **latent periods,** periods of time between the infection and the first appearance of a symptom.

   periods of time between an infection and appearance of a symptom

➤ NOW PRACTICE . . . USING DEFINITION CLUES 2

Read the following paragraph and use definition clues to help you determine the meaning of each boldfaced word or phrase.

During **adolescence** (the period of growth from childhood to maturity), friendship choices are directed overwhelmingly to other students in the same school. Adolescent students may be involved in an informal network of friendship subsystems that operate primarily within the boundaries of the school world.

Cliques are relatively small, tightly knit groups of friends who spend considerable and often exclusive time with each other. Although cliques are the most common and important friendship structure for adolescents, not everyone belongs to one; in fact, fewer than half of adolescents do. About 30 percent of students are **liaisons**—individuals who have friends from several different cliques but belong to none. The remaining students are **social isolates**—individuals with few friends. Schools also contain **crowds**, which are loose associations of cliques that usually get together on weekends.

—adapted from Rice and Dolgan, *The Adolescent: Development, Relationships, and Culture*, pp. 250–251

1. adolescence the period of growth from childhood to maturity

2. cliques small, closely knit groups of friends who spend most or all of their

   time together

3. liaisons individuals who have friends from several cliques but belong to none

4. social isolates individuals with few friends

5. crowds: loose associations of cliques that usually meet on weekends

Example Clues

Writers often include examples that help to explain or clarify a word. Suppose you do not know the meaning of the word *toxic,* and you find it used in the following sentence:

> **Toxic** materials, such as arsenic, asbestos, pesticides, and lead, can cause bodily damage.

This sentence gives four examples of toxic materials. From the examples given, which are all poisonous substances, you could conclude that *toxic* means "poisonous."

Examples:

> Forest floors are frequently covered with **fungi**—molds, mushrooms, and mildews.

Fungi, then, are types of molds, mushrooms, and mildews.

> **Legumes,** such as peas and beans, produce pods.

Legumes, then, are vegetable plants that produce pods.

> Many **pharmaceuticals,** including morphine and penicillin, are not readily available in some countries.

From the examples of morphine and penicillin, you know that *pharmaceuticals* are drugs.

> **NOW PRACTICE . . . USING EXAMPLE CLUES 1**

Read each sentence and write a definition or synonym for each boldfaced word or phrase. Use the example context clue to help you determine word meaning.

1. The child was **reticent** in every respect; she would not speak, refused to answer questions, and avoided looking at anyone.

   reserved; restrained
   _____

2. Instructors provide their students with **feedback** through test grades and comments on papers.

   information about performance or results
   _____

3. Clothing is available in a variety of **fabrics,** including cotton, wool, polyester, and linen.

   materials
   _____

4. **Involuntary reflexes,** like breathing and beating of the heart, are easily measured.

   natural, necessary unconscious bodily activities
   _____

5. The student had a difficult time distinguishing between **homonyms**—words such as *see* and *sea, wore* and *war,* and *deer* and *dear.*

   words with identical pronunciations but different spellings
   _____

> **NOW PRACTICE . . . USING EXAMPLE CLUES 2**

Read the following paragraphs and use definition and example clues to help you determine the meaning of each boldfaced word or phrase.

Freshwater lakes have three life zones. The **littoral zone,** nearest to shore, is rich in light and nutrients and supports the most diverse community—from cattails and bulrushes close to shore, to water lilies and algae at the deepest reaches of the zone. Inhabitants include snails, frogs, minnows, snakes, and turtles, as well as two categories of the microscopic organisms called plankton: photosynthetic **phytoplankton,** including bacteria and algae, and nonphotosynthetic **zooplankton,** such as protists and tiny crustaceans.

The **limnetic zone** is the open-water region of a lake where enough light penetrates to support photosynthesis. Inhabitants of the limnetic zone include cyanobacteria, zooplankton, small crustaceans, and fish. Below the limnetic zone lies the **profundal zone,** which is too dark for photosynthesis. This zone is inhabited primarily by decomposers and detritus feeders, such as bacteria, snails, and insect larvae, and by fish that swim freely among the different zones.

—adapted from Audesirk, Audesirk, and Byers, *Life on Earth,* pp. 622–624, 632

1. littoral zone <u>a lake zone near the shore in which abundant light and</u>
   <u>nutrients support a diverse plant and animal community</u>

2. phytoplankton <u>photosynthesizing, microscopic organisms present in a</u>
   <u>lake's littoral zone</u>

3. zooplankton <u>nonphotosynthesizing, microscopic organisms present in a</u>
   <u>lake's littoral zone</u>

4. limnetic zone <u>an open-water lake zone that allows enough light for photo-</u>
   <u>synthesis; it is inhabited by bacteria, zooplankton, crustaceans, and fish</u>

5. profundal zone <u>a deep, dark lake zone that does not support photosyn-</u>
   <u>thesis; it is inhabited by decomposers, detritus feeders, and fish</u>

Contrast Clues

It is sometimes possible to determine the meaning of an unknown word from a word or phrase in the context that has an opposite meaning. Notice, in the following sentence, how a word opposite in meaning from the boldfaced word provides a clue to its meaning:

> One of the dinner guests **succumbed** to the temptation to have a second piece of cake, but the others resisted.

Although you may not know the meaning of *succumbed,* you know that the one guest who succumbed was different from the others who resisted. The word *but* suggests this. Since the others resisted a second dessert, you can tell that one guest gave in and had a piece. Thus, *succumbed* means the opposite of *resist*; that is, to give in to.

Examples:

> Most of the graduates were **elated,** though a few felt sad and depressed.
> (The opposite of "sad and depressed" is joyful.)

> The old man acted **morosely,** whereas his grandson was very lively.
> (The opposite of "lively" is quietly and sullenly.)

> The gentleman was quite **portly,** but his wife was thin.
> (The opposite of "thin" is heavy or fat.)

➤ **NOW PRACTICE . . . USING CONTRAST CLUES 1**

Read each sentence and write a definition or synonym for each boldfaced word. Use the contrast clue to help you determine word meaning.

1. Some city dwellers are **affluent;** others live in or near poverty.

   wealthy; well-to-do

2. I am certain that the hotel will hold our reservation; however, if you are **dubious,** call to make sure.

   doubtful

3. Although most experts **concurred** with the research findings, several strongly disagreed.

   agreed

4. The speaker **denounced** certain legal changes while praising other reforms.

   condemned; spoke against

5. When the couple moved into their new home they **revamped** the kitchen and bathroom but did not change the rest of the rooms.

   renovated; changed; updated

➤ **NOW PRACTICE . . . USING CONTRAST CLUES 2**

Read the following paragraph and use contrast clues to help you determine the meaning of each boldfaced word. Consult a dictionary, if necessary

The Whigs chose General William Henry Harrison to run against President Martin Van Buren in 1840, using a **specious** but effective argument: General Harrison is a plain man of the people who lives in a log cabin. Contrast him with the suave Van Buren, **luxuriating** amid "the Regal Splendor of the President's Palace." Harrison drinks ordinary hard cider with his hog meat and grits, while Van Buren **eschews** plain food in favor of expensive foreign wines and fancy French cuisine. The general's furniture is **unpretentious** and sturdy; the president dines off gold plates and treads on carpets that cost the people $5 a yard. In a country where all are equal, the people will reject an **aristocrat** like Van Buren and put their trust in General Harrison, a simple, brave, honest, public-spirited common man. (In fact, Harrison came from a distinguished family, was well educated and financially comfortable, and certainly did not live in a log cabin.)

—adapted from Carnes and Garraty, *The American Nation*, p. 267

1. specious   misleading, deceptive

2. luxuriating   living in luxury, indulging in fancy tastes

3. eschews __rejects, turns away from__

4. unpretentious __modest, plain, simple__

5. aristocrat: __someone from high society, far from the "common man"__

Logic of the Passage Clues

Many times you can figure out the meaning of an unknown word by using logic and reasoning skills. For instance, look at the following sentence:

> Bob is quite **versatile;** he is a good student, a top athlete, an excellent car mechanic, and a gourmet cook.

You can see that Bob is successful at many different types of activities, and you could reason that *versatile* means "capable of doing many things competently."

Examples:

> When the customer tried to pay with Mexican **pesos,** the clerk explained that the store accepted only U.S. dollars.

Logic tells you that customers pay with money; *pesos,* then, are a type of Mexican currency.

> We had to leave the car and walk up because the **incline** was too steep to drive.

Something that is too steep must be slanted or have a slope; *incline* means a slope.

> Since Reginald was nervous, he brought his rabbit's foot **talisman** with him to the exam.

A rabbit's foot is often thought to be a good luck charm; *talisman* means a good luck charm.

> ➤ NOW PRACTICE . . . USING LOGIC OF THE PASSAGE CLUES 1

Read each sentence and write a definition or synonym for each boldfaced word. Use information provided in the context to help you determine word meaning.

1. The foreign students quickly **assimilated** many aspects of American culture.

   __incorporated; absorbed__

2. The legal aid clinic was **subsidized** by city and county funds.

   <u>financially supported</u>

3. When the bank robber reached his **haven,** he breathed a sigh of relief and began to count his money.

   <u>place of safety</u>

4. The teenager was **intimidated** by the presence of a police officer walking the beat and decided not to spray-paint the school wall.

   <u>frightened; deterred</u>

5. If the plan did not work, the colonel had a **contingency** plan ready.

   <u>future emergency</u>

▶ NOW PRACTICE . . . USING LOGIC OF THE PASSAGE CLUES 2

Read the following paragraph and use logic of the passage clues to help you choose the correct meaning of each boldfaced word or phrase.

The map of the geography of languages is not **static.** The use of some languages is expanding because the speakers of those languages are **diffusing** around the world, are gaining greater power and influence in world affairs, or are winning new **adherents** to their ideas.

For international **discourse,** English is the world's leading **lingua franca,** partly because of its widespread use in science and business. Many multinational corporations have designated English their corporate language, whatever the languages of their home countries might be.

—adapted from Bergman and Renwick, *Introduction to Geography,* p. 263

1. static
   a. difficult
   b. unchanging
   c. unfit
   d. unlikely

2. diffusing
   a. spreading
   b. revealing
   c. being eliminated
   d. causing confusion

3. adherents
   a. opponents
   b. meanings
   c. supporters
   d. power

4. discourse
   a. communication
   b. problems
   c. currency exchange
   d. society

5. lingua franca
   a. international currency
   b. form of negotiation
   c. language held in common by many countries
   d. corporate policy

SUMMING IT UP

CONTEXT CLUES

CONTEXT CLUE	HOW TO FIND MEANING	EXAMPLE
Definition	1. Look for words that announce that meanings are to follow (*is, refers to, means*).	Broad, flat noodles that are served with sauce or butter are called **fettucine.**
	2. Look for parentheses, dashes, or commas that set apart synonyms or brief definitions.	Psychologists often wonder whether **stereotypes**—the assumptions we make about what people are like—might be self-fulfilling.
Example	Figure out what the examples have in common. (Peas and beans both are vegetables and both grow in pods.)	Most **condiments,** such as pepper, mustard, and catsup, are used to improve the flavor of foods.
Contrast	Look for a word or phrase that is the opposite in meaning of a word you don't know.	Before their classes in manners, the children were disorderly; after "graduation" they acted with much **decorum.**
Logic of the Passage	Use the rest of the sentence to help you. Pretend the word is a blank line and fill in the blank with a word that makes sense.	On hot, humid afternoons, I often feel **languid.**

2b   LEARNING PREFIXES, ROOTS, AND SUFFIXES

Suppose that you came across the following sentence in a human anatomy textbook:

> Trichromatic plates are used frequently in the text to illustrate the position of body organs.

If you did not know the meaning of *trichromatic*, how could you determine it? There are no clues in the sentence context. One solution is to look up the word in a dictionary. An easier and faster way is to break the word into parts and analyze the meaning of each part. Many words in the English language are made up of word parts called **prefixes, roots,** and **suffixes.** These word parts have specific meanings that, when added together, can help you determine the meaning of the word as a whole.

The word *trichromatic* can be divided into three parts: its prefix, root, and suffix.

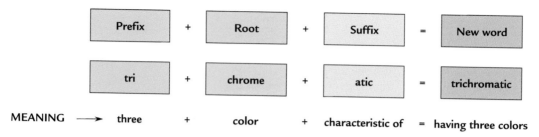

You can see from this analysis that *trichromatic* means "having three colors."

Here are two other examples of words that you can figure out by using prefixes, roots, and suffixes:

> The parents thought the child was **unteachable.**
>
> un- = not
>
> teach = help someone learn
>
> -able = able to do something
>
> unteachable = not able to be taught

> The student was a **nonconformist.**
>
> non- = not
>
> conform = go along with others
>
> -ist = one who does something
>
> nonconformist = someone who does not go along with others

The first step in using the prefix-root-suffix method is to become familiar with the most commonly used word parts. The prefixes and roots listed in Tables 2.1 and 2.2 (pages 30–33) will give you a good start in determining the meanings of thousands of words without looking them up in the dictionary. Before you begin to use word parts to figure out new words, there are a few things you need to know:

1. In most cases, a word is built upon at least one root.
2. Words can have more than one prefix, root, or suffix.
   a. Words can be made up of two or more roots (*geo/logy*).
   b. Some words have two prefixes (*in/sub/ordination*).
   c. Some words have two suffixes (*beauti/ful/ly*).
3. Words do not always have a prefix and a suffix.
   a. Some words have neither a prefix nor a suffix (*read*).
   b. Others have a suffix but no prefix (*read/ing*).
   c. Others have a prefix but no suffix (*pre/read*).
4. The spelling of roots may change as they are combined with suffixes. Some common variations are included in Table 2.2.

5. Different prefixes, roots, or suffixes may have the same meaning. For example, the prefixes *bi-, di-,* and *duo-* all mean "two."

6. Sometimes you may identify a group of letters as a prefix or root but find that it does not carry the meaning of that prefix or root. For example, the letters *mis* in the word *missile* are part of the root and are not the prefix *mis-,* which means "wrong; bad."

Prefixes

Prefixes appear at the beginnings of many English words. They alter the meaning of the root to which they are connected. For example, if you add the prefix *re-* to the word read, the word *reread* is formed, meaning to read again. If *pre-* is added to the word *reading,* the word *prereading* is formed, meaning before reading. If the prefix *post-* is added, the word *postreading* is formed, meaning after reading. Table 2.1 lists 62 common prefixes grouped according to meaning.

▶ NOW PRACTICE . . . USING PREFIXES 1

Read each of the following sentences. Use your knowledge of prefixes to fill in the blank and complete the word.

1. A person who speaks two languages is _____bi_____lingual.

2. A letter or number written beneath a line of print is called a _____sub_____script.

3. The new sweater had a snag, and I returned it to the store because it was _____im_____ perfect.

4. The flood damage was permanent and _____ir_____reversible.

5. I was not given the correct date and time; I was _____mis_____informed.

6. People who speak several different languages are _____multi_____lingual.

7. A musical _____inter_____lude was played between the events in the ceremony.

8. I decided the magazine was uninteresting, so I _____dis_____continued my subscription.

9. Merchandise that does not pass factory inspection is considered _____sub_____standard and is sold at a discount.

10. The tuition refund policy approved this week will apply to last year's tuition as well; the policy will be _____retro_____active to January 1 of last year.

TABLE 2.1 COMMON PREFIXES

PREFIX	MEANING	SAMPLE WORD
Prefixes referring to amount or number		
mono-/uni-	one	monocle/unicycle
bi-/di-/du-	two	bimonthly/divorce/duet
tri-	three	triangle
quad-	four	quadrant
quint-/pent-	five	quintet/pentagon
dec-/deci-	ten	decimal
centi-	hundred	centigrade
homo-	same	homogenized
mega-	large	megaphone
milli-	thousand	milligram
micro-	small	microscope
multi-/poly-	many	multipurpose/polygon
nano-	extremely small	nanoplankton
semi-	half	semicircle
equi-	equal	equidistant
Prefixes meaning "not" (negative)		
a-	not	asymmetrical
anti-	against	antiwar
contra-/counter-	against, opposite	contradict
dis-	apart, away, not	disagree
in-/il-/ir-/im-	not	incorrect/illogical/ irreversible/impossible
mal-	poorly, wrongly	malnourished
mis-	wrongly	misunderstand
non-	not	nonfiction
un-	not	unpopular
pseudo-	false	pseudoscientific
Prefixes giving direction, location, or placement		
ab-	away	absent
ad-	toward	adhesive
ante-/pre-	before	antecedent/premarital
circum-/peri-	around	circumference/perimeter

(continued on next page)

(continued from previous page)

PREFIX	MEANING	SAMPLE WORD
com-/col-/con-	with, together	compile/collide/convene
de-	away, from	depart
dia-	through	diameter
ex-/extra-	from, out of, former	ex-wife/extramarital
hyper-	over, excessive	hyperactive
hypo-	below, beneath	hypodermic
inter-	between	interpersonal
intro-/intra-/in-	within, into, in	introduction
post-	after	posttest
pre-	before	preview
re-	back, again	review
retro-	backward	retrospect
sub-	under, below	submarine
super-	above, extra	supercharge
tele-	far	telescope
trans-	cross, over	transcontinental

▶ NOW PRACTICE . . . USING PREFIXES 2

Read the following paragraph and choose the correct prefix from the box below to fill in the blank next to each boldfaced word part. One prefix will not be used.

multi	uni	pseudo
tri	bi	sub

Neurons, or nerve cells, can be classified structurally according to the number of axons and dendrites that project from the cell body. (1) ___Uni___ **polar** neurons have a single projection from the cell body and are rare in humans. (2) ___Bi___ **polar** neurons have two projections, an axon and a dendrite, extending from the cell body. Other sensory neurons are (3) ___pseudo___ **-unipolar** neurons, a (4) ___sub___ **class** of bipolar neurons. Although only one projection seems to extend from the cell body of this type of neuron, there are actually two projections that extend in opposite directions. (5) ___Multi___ **polar** neurons, the most common neurons, have multiple projections from the cell body; one projection is an axon, all the others are dendrites.

—adapted from Germann and Stanfield, *Principles of Human Physiology*, p. 174

TABLE 2.2 COMMON ROOTS

COMMON ROOT	MEANING	SAMPLE WORD
anthropo	human being	anthropology
archaeo	ancient or past	archeology
aster/astro	star	astronaut
aud/audit	hear	audible
bene	good, well	benefit
bio	life	biology
cap	take, seize	captive
cardi	heart	cardiology
chron(o)	time	chronology
corp	body	corpse
cred	believe	incredible
dict/dic	tell, say	predict
duc/duct	lead	introduce
fact/fac	make, do	factory
graph	write	telegraph
geo	earth	geophysics
gyneco	woman	gynecology
log/logo/logy	study, thought	psychology
mit/miss	send	permit/dismiss
mort/mor	die, death	immortal
neuro	nerve	neurology
path	feeling	sympathy
phono	sound, voice	telephone
photo	light	photosensitive
port	carry	transport
pulmo	lungs	pulmonary
scop	seeing	microscope
scrib/script	write	inscription
sen/sent	feel	insensitive
spec/spic/spect	look, see	retrospect
tend/tent/tens	stretch or strain	tension
terr/terre	land, earth	territory
theo	god	theology

(continued on next page)

(continued from previous page)

COMMON ROOT	MEANING	SAMPLE WORD
ven/vent	come	convention
vert/vers	turn	invert
vis/vid	see	invisible/video
voc	call	vocation

Roots

Roots carry the basic or core meaning of a word. Hundreds of root words are used to build words in the English language. Thirty-seven of the most common and most useful are listed in Table 2.2. Knowledge of the meanings of these roots will enable you to unlock the meanings of many words. For example, if you know that the root *dic/dict* means "tell or say," then you have a clue to the meanings of such words as *dictate* (to speak for someone to write down), *diction* (wording or manner of speaking), or *dictionary* (book that "tells" what words mean).

▶ NOW PRACTICE . . . USING ROOTS 1

Use the list of common roots in Table 2.2 to determine the meanings of the following words. Write a brief definition or synonym for each, checking a dictionary if necessary.

1. photocopy

   a duplicate copy or reproduction

2. visibility

   ability to be seen

3. credentials

   written evidence of one's qualifications

4. speculate

   to guess, reflect, take a risk

5. terrain

   a tract of land; the character or quality of land

6. audition

   a trial or hearing; a presentation of something heard

7. astrophysics

   a study of the physics of the stars

8. chronicle

   a record of events in time order or sequence

9. autograph

   a person's signature

▶ NOW PRACTICE . . . USING ROOTS 2

Read the following paragraph and choose the correct root from the box below to fill in the blank next to each boldfaced word part. One root will not be used.

graph	scope	mit
astro	photo	logy

You might think that the easiest way to discover extrasolar planets, or planets around other stars, would be simply to (1) ___photo___ **graph** them through a powerful (2) **tele**___scope___. Unfortunately, current observational (3) **techno** ___logy___ cannot produce such images. The primary problem arises from the fact that any light that an orbiting planet might (4) **trans**___mit___ would be overwhelmed by light from the star it orbits. For example, a Sun-like star would be a *billion times* brighter than the reflected light from an Earth-like planet. Because even the best telescopes blur the light from stars at least a little, finding the small blip of planetary light amid the glare of scattered starlight would be very difficult. For now, (5) ___astro___**nomers** must rely on techniques that observe the star itself to find indirect evidence of planets.

—adapted from Bennett, Donahue, Schneider, and Voit,
The Cosmic Perspective, p. 218

Suffixes

Suffixes are word endings that often change the part of speech of a word. For example, adding the suffix *y* to the noun *cloud* forms the adjective *cloudy*. Accompanying the change in part of speech is a shift in meaning (*cloudy* means "resembling clouds; overcast with clouds; dimmed or dulled as if by clouds").

Often, several different words can be formed from a single root word by adding different suffixes.

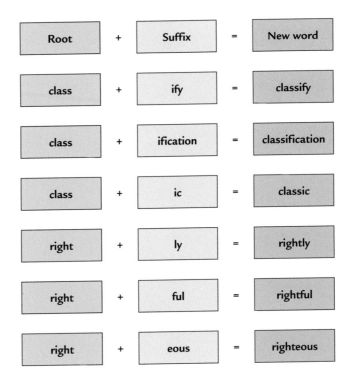

Root	+	Suffix	=	New word
class	+	ify	=	classify
class	+	ification	=	classification
class	+	ic	=	classic
right	+	ly	=	rightly
right	+	ful	=	rightful
right	+	eous	=	righteous

If you know the meaning of the root word and the ways in which different suffixes affect the meaning of the root word, you will be able to figure out a word's meaning when a suffix is added. A list of common suffixes and their meanings appears in Table 2.3.

You can expand your vocabulary by learning the variations in meaning that occur when suffixes are added to words you already know. When you find a word that you do not know, look for the root. Then, using the sentence the word is in, figure out what the word means with the suffix added. Occasionally you may find that the spelling of the root word has been changed. For instance, a final *e* may be dropped, a final consonant may be doubled, or a final *y* may be changed to *i*. Consider the possibility of such changes when trying to identify the root word.

TABLE 2.3 COMMON SUFFIXES

SUFFIX	SAMPLE WORD
Suffixes that refer to a state, condition, or quality	
-able	touchable
-ance	assistance
-ation	confrontation
-ence	reference
-ible	tangible
-ic	chronic
-ion	discussion
-ish	girlish
-ity	superiority
-ive	permissive
-less	hopeless
-ment	amazement
-ness	kindness
-ous	jealous
-ty	loyalty
-y	creamy
Suffixes that mean "one who"	
-an/-ian	Italian
-ant	participant
-ee	referee
-eer	engineer
-ent	resident
-er	teacher
-ist	activist
-or	advisor
Suffixes that mean "pertaining to or referring to"	
-ac	cardiac
-al	autumnal
-ary	secondary
-ship	friendship
-hood	brotherhood
-ward	homeward

Examples:

> The article was a **compilation** of facts.
>
> root + suffix
>
> compil(e) + -ation = something that has been compiled, or put together into an orderly form
>
> We were concerned with the **legality** of our decision to change addresses.
>
> root + suffix
>
> legal + -ity = pertaining to legal matters
>
> Our college is one of the most **prestigious** in the state.
>
> root + suffix
>
> prestig(e) + -ious = having prestige or distinction

➤ **NOW PRACTICE . . . USING SUFFIXES 1**

For each of the words listed, add a suffix so that the new word will complete the sentence. Write the new word in the space provided. Check a dictionary if you are unsure of the spelling.

1. converse

   Our phone _____conversation_____ lasted ten minutes.

2. assist

   The medical _____assistant_____ labeled the patient's blood samples.

3. qualify

   The job applicant outlined his _____qualifications_____ to the interviewer.

4. intern

   The doctor completed her _____internship_____ at Memorial Medical Center.

5. eat

   We did not realize that the blossoms of the plant could be _____eaten_____.

6. audio

   She spoke so softly that her voice was not _____audible_____.

7. season

   It is usually very dry in July, but this year it has rained constantly. The weather isn't very _____seasonable_____.

8. permit

The professor granted her _____permission_____ to miss class.

9. instruct

The lecture on Freud was very _____instructive_____.

10. remember

The wealthy businessman donated the building in
_____memory_____ of his deceased father.

▶ NOW PRACTICE . . . USING SUFFIXES 2

Read the following paragraph. For each pair of words in parentheses, circle the word that correctly completes each sentence.

How do new species form? Most evolutionary (1) (biologists / biological) believe that the most common source of new species, especially among animals, has been geographic isolation. When an (2) (impassable / impassor) barrier physically separates different parts of a population, a new species may result. Such physical separation could occur if, for example, some members of a population of land-dwelling organisms drifted, swam, or flew to a remote (3) (oceany / oceanic) island. Populations of water-dwelling organisms might be split when (4) (geological / geologist) processes such as volcanism or continental drift create new land barriers that divide previously (5) (continuous / continuation) seas or lakes. You can probably imagine many other scenarios that could lead to the geographic subdivision of a population.

—adapted from Audesirk, Audesirk, and Byers, *Life on Earth*, p. 237

SUMMING IT UP

WORD PARTS

WORD PARTS	LOCATION	HOW TO USE THEM
Prefixes	Beginnings of words	Notice how the prefix changes the meaning of the root or base word. (How does meaning change when *-un* is added to the word reliable?)
Roots	Beginning or middle of words	Use roots to figure out the basic meaning of the word.
Suffixes	Endings of words	Notice how the suffix changes the meaning of the root or base word. (How does meaning change when *-ship* is added to the word friend?)

3

Thesis, Main Ideas, Supporting Details, and Transitions

Most articles, essays, and textbook chapters contain numerous ideas. Some are more important than others. As you read, your job is to sort out the important ideas from those that are less important. For exams your instructors expect that you have discovered and learned what is important in assigned chapters. In class, your instructors expect you to be able to discuss the important ideas from an assignment. In this section you will learn to identify the thesis of a reading assignment and to distinguish main ideas and supporting details. You will also learn about transitions that writers use to link ideas together.

3a   IDENTIFYING THE THESIS

The **thesis** is what the entire reading selection is about. Think of it as the one most important idea that the entire article or assignment is written to explain. In articles and essays the thesis is quite specific and is often stated in one sentence, usually near the beginning of the article. In textbook chapters the thesis of the entire chapter is much more general. Individual sections of the chapter may have more specific theses. A psychology textbook chapter on stress, for example, may have as its thesis that stress can negatively affect us, but there are ways to control it. A section within the chapter may discuss the thesis that there are five main sources of stress. A magazine article on stress in the workplace, because it is much shorter, would have an even more specific thesis. It might, for instance, express the thesis that building strong relationships with coworkers can help to alleviate stress.

Now reread the article from *U.S. News & World Report* magazine on the topic of animal emotions that appears on p. 9. Do not continue with this section until you have read it.

The thesis of this reading is that recent research supports the popular belief that animals do have emotions. The remainder of the article describes evidence that supports this thesis.

➤ NOW PRACTICE . . . IDENTIFYING THESIS STATEMENTS

Underline the thesis statement in each group of sentences.

1. a. Monotheism is a belief in one supreme being.

   b. Polytheism is a belief in more than one supreme being.

   c. <u>Theisms are religions that worship supernatural beings.</u>

   d. Monotheistic religions include Christianity, Judaism, and Islam.

2. a. <u>Vincent Van Gogh is an internationally known and respected artist.</u>

   b. Van Gogh's art displays an approach to color that was revolutionary.

   c. Van Gogh created seventy paintings in the last two months of his life.

   d. Van Gogh's art is respected for its attention to detail.

3. a. The Individuals with Disability Education Act offers guidelines for inclusive education.

   b. <u>The inclusive theory of education says that children with special needs should be placed in regular classrooms and have services brought to them.</u>

   c. The first movement toward inclusion was mainstreaming—a plan in which children with special needs were placed in regular classrooms for a portion of the day and sent to other classrooms for special services.

   d. Families play an important role in making inclusive education policies work.

4. a. Stress can have a negative effect on friendships and marital relationships.

   b. Stress can affect job performance.

   c. <u>Stress is a pervasive problem in our culture.</u>

   d. Some health problems appear to be health related.

3b   FINDING MAIN IDEAS

A paragraph is a group of related sentences that express a single idea about a single topic. This idea is called the **main idea.** All the other sentences in the paragraph support this main idea. These sentences are called **supporting details.** Not all details in a paragraph are equally important.

In most paragraphs the main idea is expressed in a single sentence called the **topic sentence.** Occasionally, you will find a paragraph in which the main idea is not expressed in any single sentence. The main idea is **implied**; that is, it is suggested but not directly stated in the paragraph.

You can visualize a paragraph as shown in the accompanying diagram.

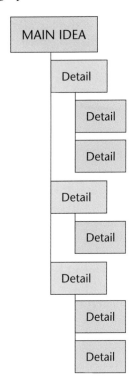

How to Find the Main Idea

We have defined a paragraph as a group of related ideas. The sentences are related to one another, and all are about the same person, place, thing, or idea. The common subject or idea is called the *topic*—what the entire paragraph is about. As you read the following paragraph, you will see that its topic is elections.

> Americans elect more people to office than almost any other society. Each even year, when most elections occur, more than 500,000 public officials are elected to school boards, city councils, county offices, state legislatures, state executive positions, the House of Representatives and the Senate, and of course, every fourth year, the presidency. By contrast with other countries, our elections are drawn-out affairs. Campaigns for even the most local office can be protracted over two or three months and cost a considerable amount of money. Presidential campaigns, including the primary season, last for at least ten months, with some candidates beginning to seek support many months and, as noted earlier, even years before the election.

—Baradat, *Understanding American Democracy*, p. 163

Each sentence of this paragraph discusses or describes elections. To identify the topic of a paragraph, then, ask yourself: *"What or who is the paragraph about?"*

The *main idea* of a paragraph is what the author wants you to know about the topic. It is the broadest, most important idea that the writer develops throughout the paragraph. The entire paragraph explains, develops, and supports this main idea. A question that will guide you in finding the main idea is *"What key point is the author making about the topic?"* In the paragraph above, the writer's main idea is that elections in the United States are more numerous and more drawn-out than in other countries.

The Topic Sentence

Often, but not always, one sentence expresses the main idea. This sentence is called the *topic sentence.*

To find the topic sentence, search for the one general sentence that explains what the writer wants you to know about the topic. A topic sentence is a broad, general statement; the remaining sentences of the paragraph provide details about or explain the topic sentence.

In the following paragraph, the topic is the effects of high temperatures. Read the paragraph to find out what the writer wants you to know about this topic. Look for one sentence that states this.

> Environmental psychologists have also been concerned with the effects that extremely high temperatures have on social interactions, particularly on aggression. There is a common perception that riots and other more common displays of violent behaviors are more frequent during the long, hot days of summer. This observation is largely supported by research evidence (Anderson, 1989; Anderson & Anderson, 1984; Rotton & Frey, 1985). C. A. Anderson (1987, 1989) reported on a series of studies showing that violent crimes are more prevalent in hotter quarters of the year and in hotter years, although nonviolent crimes were less affected. Anderson also concluded that differences in crime rates between cities are better predicted by temperature than by social, demographic (age, race, education), and economic variables. Baron and Ransberger (1978) point out that riots are most likely to occur when the outside temperature is only moderately high, between about 75° and 90°F. But when temperatures get much above 90°F, energy (even for aggression) becomes rapidly depleted, and rioting is less likely to occur.
>
> —Gerow, *Psychology: An Introduction,* p. 553

The paragraph opens with a statement and then proceeds to explain it by citing research evidence. The first sentence of the paragraph functions as a topic sentence, stating the paragraph's main point: High temperatures are associated with aggressive behavior.

The topic sentence can be located anywhere in the paragraph. However, there are several positions where it is most likely to be found.

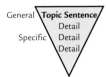

Topic Sentence First.   Most often the topic sentence is placed first in the paragraph. In this type of paragraph, the author first states his or her main point and then explains it.

> There is some evidence that colors affect you psychologically. For example, when subjects are exposed to red light respiratory movements increase; exposure to blue decreases respiratory movements. Similarly, eye blinks increase in frequency when eyes are exposed to red light and decrease when exposed to blue. This seems consistent with intuitive feelings about blue being more soothing and red being more arousing. After changing a school's walls from orange and white to blue, the blood pressure of the students decreased while their academic performance improved.
>
> —DeVito, *Interpersonal Communication*, p. 182

Here the writer first states that there is evidence of the physiological effects of color. The rest of the paragraph presents that evidence.

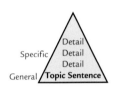

Topic Sentence Last.   The second most likely place for a topic sentence to appear is last in the paragraph. When using this arrangement, a writer leads up to the main point and then directly states it at the end.

> Is there a relationship between aspects of one's personality and that person's state of physical health? Can psychological evaluations of an individual be used to predict physical as well as psychological disorders? Is there such a thing as a disease-prone personality? Our response is very tentative, and the data are not all supportive, but for the moment we can say yes, there does seem to be a positive correlation between some personality variables and physical health.
>
> —Gerow, *Psychology: An Introduction*, p. 700

In this paragraph, the author ponders the relationship between personality and health and concludes with the paragraph's main point: that they are related.

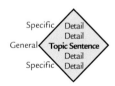

Topic Sentence in the Middle.   If it is placed neither first nor last, then the topic sentence appears somewhere in the middle of the paragraph. In this arrangement, the sentences before the topic sentence lead up to or introduce the main idea. Those that follow the main idea explain or describe it.

> There are 1,500 species of bacteria and approximately 8,500 species of birds. The carrot family alone has about 3,500 species, and there are 15,000 known species of wild orchids. Clearly, the task of separating various living things into their proper groups is not an easy task. Within the insect family, the problem becomes even more complex. For example, there are about 300,000 species of beetles. In fact, certain species are disappearing from the earth before we can even identify and classify them.
>
> —Wallace, *Biology: The World of Life*, p. 283

In this paragraph, the author first gives several examples of living things for which there are numerous species. Then he states his main point: Separating living things into species is not an easy task. The remainder of the paragraph offers an additional example and provides further information.

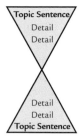

Topic Sentence First and Last. Occasionally the main idea is stated at the beginning of a paragraph and again at the end, or elsewhere in the paragraph. Writers may use this organization to emphasize an important idea or to explain an idea that needs clarification. At other times, the first and last sentences together express the paragraph's main idea.

> Many elderly people have trouble getting the care and treatment they need for ailments. Most hospitals, designed to handle injuries and acute illness that are common to the young, do not have the facilities or personnel to treat the chronic degenerative diseases of the elderly. Many doctors are also ill-prepared to deal with such problems. As Fred Cottrell points out, "There is a widespread feeling among the aged that most doctors are not interested in them and are reluctant to treat people who are as little likely to contribute to the future as the aged are reputed to do." Even with the help of Medicare, the elderly in the United States often have a difficult time getting the health care that they need.
>
> —Coleman and Cressey, *Social Problems*, p. 277

The first and last sentences together explain that many elderly people in the United States have difficulty obtaining needed health care.

▶ NOW PRACTICE . . . FINDING MAIN IDEAS 1

Underline the topic sentence(s) of each of the following paragraphs.

Paragraph 1

> Evidence suggests that groups given the right to vote do not immediately exercise that right. In recent elections, young people have not voted at a high rate—always well below 50 percent. Since the passage of the Twenty-sixth Amendment in 1971, the addition of 18- to 20-year-olds to the electorate has contributed to a lower turnout. After the passage of the Nineteenth Amendment in 1920, many women were slow to use their new right. The difference in turnout between men and women has not been significant in recent decades, though. By the 1988 presidential election, it was fairly easy for most Americans to register and vote; yet only about 50 percent turned out to vote. What causes low turnout? How serious is it?
>
> —Keefe et al., *American Democracy*, p. 178

Paragraph 2

> The symbols that constitute language are commonly referred to as words—labels that we have assigned to concepts, or our mental representations. When we use the word *chair* as a symbol, we don't use it to label just one specific instance

of a chair. We use the word as a symbol to represent our concept of chairs. As symbols, words need not stand for real things in the real world. We have words to describe objects or events that cannot be perceived, such as *ghost* or, for that matter, *mind*. With language we can communicate about owls and pussycats in teacups and a four-dimensional, time-warped hyperspace. Words stand for cognitions, or concepts, and we have a great number of them.

—Gerow, *Psychology: An Introduction,* p. 250

Paragraph 3

Body mass is made up of protoplasm, extracellular fluid, bone, and adipose tissue (body fat). One way to determine the amount of adipose tissue is to measure the whole-body density. After the on-land mass of the body is determined, the underwater body mass is obtained by submerging the person in water. Since water helps support the body by giving it buoyancy, the apparent body mass is less in water. A higher percentage of body fat will make a person more buoyant, causing the underwater mass to be even lower. This occurs because fat has a lower density than the rest of the body.

—Timberlake, *Chemistry,* p. 30

Paragraph 4

Early biologists who studied reflexes, kineses, taxes, and fixed action patterns assumed that these responses are inherited, unlearned, and common to all members of a species. They clearly depend on internal and external factors, but until recently, instinct and learning were considered distinct aspects of behavior. However, in some very clever experiments, Jack Hailman of the University of Wisconsin showed that certain stereotyped behavior patterns require subtle forms of experience for their development. In other words, at least some of the behavior normally called instinct is partly learned.

—Mix, *Biology, The Network of Life,* p. 532

Paragraph 5

On election day in 1972, at 5:30 p.m. Pacific Standard Time, NBC television news declared that Richard Nixon had been reelected president. This announcement came several hours before the polls were closed in the western part of the United States. In 1988, polls in a dozen western states were still open when CBS and ABC announced that George Bush had been elected president. These developments point to the continuing controversy over the impact of election night coverage on voter turnout.

—Keefe et al., *American Democracy,* p. 186

Paragraph 6

According to economic data, a tiny segment of the American population owns most of the nation's wealth. The wealthiest 1 percent (900,000 households with about $6 trillion net worth) own more than the least affluent 99 percent of Americans (84 million households with about $5 trillion net worth). Or, from another angle, the top 1 percent of the population owns about 38 percent of all wealth in the United States while the bottom 80 percent of the population accounts for about 17 percent of the national wealth (Mishel et al., 2001). To give you a more personalized view of the gap between rich and poor consider this: Bill Gates owns "more wealth than America's 100 million poorest people" (Greider et al., 1998:39).

—Thompson and Hickey, *Society in Focus,* p. 198

Paragraph 7

A gunnysack is a large bag, usually made of burlap. <u>As a conflict strategy, gunnysacking refers to the practice of storing up grievances so we may unload them at another time.</u> The immediate occasion for unloading may be relatively simple (or so it might seem at first), such as someone's coming home late without calling. Instead of arguing about this, the gunnysacker unloads all past grievances. As you probably know from experience, gunnysacking begets gunnysacking. When one person gunnysacks, the other person often reciprocates. Frequently the original problem never gets addressed. Instead, resentment and hostility escalate.

—DeVito, *Human Communication,* 9th edition, p. 217

Paragraph 8

As just about everyone today knows, e-mail has virtually become the standard method of communication in the business world. Most people enjoy its speed, ease and casual nature. <u>But e-mail also has its share of problems and pitfalls, including privacy.</u> Many people assume the contents of their e-mail are private, but there may in fact be any number of people authorized to see it. Some experts have even likened e-mail to postcards sent through U.S. mail: They pass through a lot of hands and before a lot of eyes, and, theoretically, many different people can read them.

—adapted from Ebert and Griffin, *Business Essentials,* p. 64.

Paragraph 9

Patrescence, or becoming a father, usually is less socially noted than matrescence. The practice of **couvade** is an interesting exception to this generalization. <u>Couvade refers to "a variety of customs applying to the behavior of fathers during the pregnancies of their wives and during and shortly after the births of their children"</u> (Broude 1988:902). The father may take to his bed before, during, or after the delivery. He may also experience pain and exhaustion during and after the delivery. More common is a pattern of couvade that involves a set of prohibitions and prescriptions for male behavior. Couvade occurs in societies where paternal roles in child care are prominent. One interpretation views couvade as one phase of men's participation in parenting: Their good behavior as expectant fathers helps ensure a good delivery for the baby. Another interpretation of couvade is that it offers support for the mother. In Estonia, a fold belief is that a woman's birth pains will be less if her husband helps by taking some of them on himself.

—adapted from Miller, *Cultural Anthropology,* pp. 144–45

Paragraph 10

Everything moves. Even things that appear at rest move. The move relative to the sun and stars. As you're reading this you're moving at about 107,000 kilometers per hour relative to the sun. And you're moving even faster relative to the center of our galaxy. When we discuss the motion of something, we describe motion relative to something else. If you walk down the aisle of a moving bus, your speed relative to the floor of the bus is likely quite different from your speed relative to the road. When we say a racing car reaches a speed of 300 kilometers per hour, we mean relative to the track. <u>Unless stated otherwise, when we discuss the speeds of things in our environment we mean relative to the surface of the earth; motion is relative.</u>

—adapted from Hewitt, *Conceptual Physics,* p. 39

➤ **NOW PRACTICE . . . FINDING MAIN IDEAS 2**

Underline the topic sentence(s) of each of the following paragraphs.

Symbols and Superstitions On the surface, many marketing images have virtually no literal connection to actual products. What does a cowboy have to do with a bit of tobacco rolled into a paper tube? How can a celebrity such as basketball star Michael Jordan enhance the image of a cologne? <u>The meanings we impart to these symbols are largely influenced by our culture, so marketers need to take special care that the symbol they use in a foreign market has the meaning they intended.</u> Even the same product may be used quite differently and take on a different meaning to people. In parts of rural India, for example, the refrigerator is a status symbol, so people want a snazzy-looking one that they can keep in the living room to show off to visitors.

<u>For assistance in understanding how consumers interpret the meanings of symbols, some marketers are turning to a field of study known as **semiotics,** which examines how people assign meanings to symbols.</u> For example, although the American cowboy on packs of Marlboro cigarettes is a well-known symbol of the frontier spirit in many countries, people in Hong Kong see him as a low-status laborer. Philip Morris has to make sure he's always pictured riding a white horse, which is a more positive symbol in that country. Even something as simple as a color takes on very different meanings around the globe. Pepsodent toothpaste found this out when it promised white teeth to people in Southeast Asia, where black or yellow teeth are status symbols.

<u>Marketers also need to be concerned about taboos and superstitions.</u> For example, the Japanese are superstitious about the number four. *Shi,* the word for "four," is also the word for "death," so Tiffany sells glassware and china in sets of five in Japan. In some Arab countries, alcohol and pork are forbidden to Islamic consumers (even stuffed pig toys are taboo), and advertisers may refrain from showing nudity or even the faces of women in photos, which some governments prohibit.

—Solomon and Stuart, *Marketing: Real People, Real Choices,* p. 108

3c   FINDING THE IMPLIED MAIN IDEA

Although most paragraphs do have a topic sentence, some do not. This type of paragraph contains only details or specifics that, taken together, point to the main idea. The main idea, then, is implied but not directly stated. In such paragraphs you must infer, or reason out, the main idea. This is a process of adding up the details and deciding what they mean together or what main idea they all support or explain. Use the following steps to grasp implied main ideas.

- Identify the topic by asking yourself, "What is the one thing the author is discussing throughout the paragraph?"
- Decide what the writer wants you to know about the topic. Look at each detail and decide what larger idea each explains.
- Express this idea in your own words.

Here is a sample paragraph; use the above questions to identify the main idea.

> Severe punishment may generate such anxiety in children that they do not learn the lesson the punishment was designed to teach. Moreover, as a reaction to punishment that they regard as unfair, children may avoid punitive parents, who therefore will have fewer opportunities to teach and guide the child. In addition, parents who use physical punishment provide aggressive models. A child who is regularly slapped, spanked, shaken, or shouted at may learn to use these forms of aggression in interactions with peers.
>
> —Newcombe, *Child Development*, p. 354

The topic of this paragraph is the punishment. The author's main point is that punishment has negative effects. You can figure out this writer's main idea even though no single sentence states this directly. You can visualize this paragraph as follows:

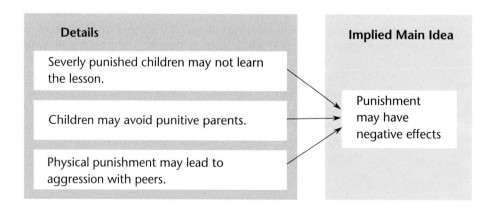

Details	Implied Main Idea
Severly punished children may not learn the lesson.	
Children may avoid punitive parents.	Punishment may have negative effects
Physical punishment may lead to aggression with peers.	

> **NOW PRACTICE . . . UNDERSTANDING IMPLIED MAIN IDEAS 1**

After reading each of the paragraphs, complete the diagram that follows by filling in the missing information.

Paragraph A

The average American consumer eats 21 pounds of snack foods in a year, but people in the West Central part of the country consume the most (24 pounds per person) whereas those in the Pacific and Southeast regions eat "only" 19 pounds per person. Pretzels are the most popular snack in the mid-Atlantic area, pork rinds are most likely to be eaten in the South, and multigrain chips turn up as a favorite in the West. Not surprisingly, the Hispanic influence in the Southwest has influenced snacking preferences—consumers in that part of the United States eat about 50 percent more tortilla chips than do people elsewhere.

—adapted from Solomon, *Consumer Behavior*, p. 184

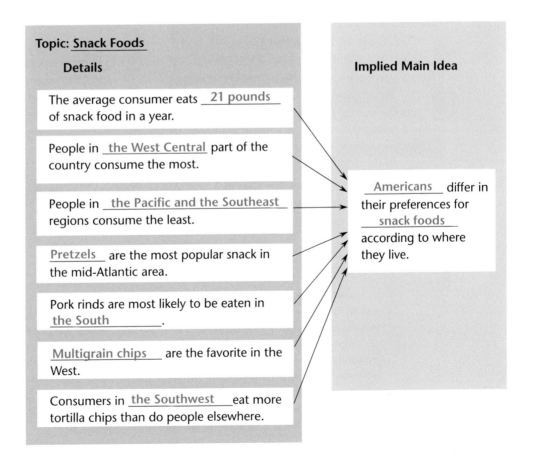

Paragraph B

The constellation [group of stars] that the Greeks named Orion, the hunter, was seen by the ancient Chinese as a supreme warrior called *Shen*. Hindus in ancient India also saw a warrior, called *Skanda*, who rode a peacock. The three stars of Orion's belt were seen as three fishermen in a canoe by Aborigines of northern Australia. As seen from southern California, these three stars climb almost straight up into the sky as they rise in the east, which may explain why the Chemehuevi Indians of the California desert saw them as a line of three sure-footed mountain sheep.

—adapted from Bennett et al., *The Cosmic Perspective*, p. 40

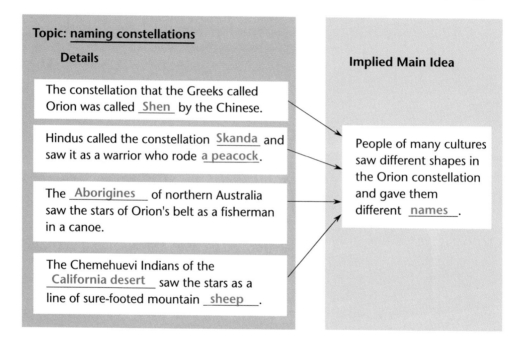

Topic: naming constellations

Details

The constellation that the Greeks called Orion was called Shen by the Chinese.

Hindus called the constellation Skanda and saw it as a warrior who rode a peacock .

The Aborigines of northern Australia saw the stars of Orion's belt as a fisherman in a canoe.

The Chemehuevi Indians of the California desert saw the stars as a line of sure-footed mountain sheep .

Implied Main Idea

People of many cultures saw different shapes in the Orion constellation and gave them different names .

Paragraph C

Initially, many computers entered homes as children's games. But the trend spread fast, from simple games to more sophisticated ones. Soon they became a favorite pastime both for children and young adults. This group of people showed an almost natural ability to adapt to computers; software developers saw the opportunity for the market and developed increasingly challenging games as well as educational programs. Many parents were then tempted to buy computers for home use and this, in turn, led to a situation where people of all ages and backgrounds saw the benefit of computers not only for young people but also for adults who used them for personal and business purposes.

—Bandyo-padhyay, *Computing for Non-specialists*, p. 4

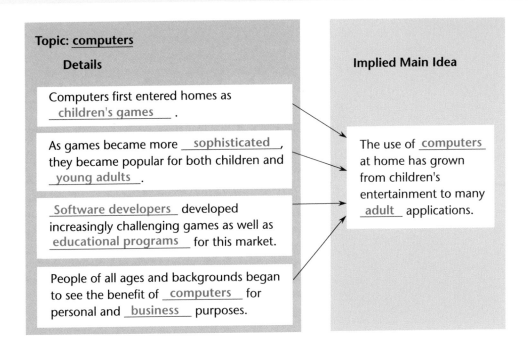

Topic: computers

Details

Computers first entered homes as children's games .

As games became more sophisticated , they became popular for both children and young adults .

Software developers developed increasingly challenging games as well as educational programs for this market.

People of all ages and backgrounds began to see the benefit of computers for personal and business purposes.

Implied Main Idea

The use of computers at home has grown from children's entertainment to many adult applications.

> **NOW PRACTICE . . . UNDERSTANDING IMPLIED MAIN IDEAS 2**

Write a sentence that states the main idea for each of the following paragraphs.

Paragraph 1

During the 1960s, police went from walking "beats" [regular routes] to riding in squad cars. While squad cars provided a faster response to emergency calls, they also changed the nature of social interaction between police officers and the public. Much police work had been highly personal, as officers strolled the sidewalks talking to storekeepers and homeowners, but it became much more impersonal, with less contact between officers and citizens. Since the 1960s, technological advances have provided more elaborate means of communication and surveillance, better-equipped squad cars, and more sophisticated weaponry. Unfortunately criminals have benefited from increased technology as well. This increased technology and other developments have led many city leaders to question contemporary policing practices and some to accentuate the need to reemphasize police–community relations.

—Thompson and Hickey, *Society in Focus*, p. 162

Main idea: Changes in police work since 1960 have had mixed results.

Paragraph 2

When a homemaker is killed in an auto accident, that person's family can often sue for the value of the services that were lost. Attorneys (who rely on economists) are often asked to make an attempt to estimate this value to present to the court. They add up the cost of purchasing babysitting, cooking, housecleaning, and tutoring services. The number turns out to be quite large, often in excess of $30,000 a year. Of course one of the problems in measuring the value of unremunerated housework in such a way is that we could often purchase the services of a full-time live-in housekeeper for less money than if we paid for the services of the various components of housekeeping. And what about quality? Some homemakers serve fabulous gourmet meals; others simply warm up canned and frozen foods. Should they be valued equally? Another problem lies in knowing when to stop counting. A person can hire a valet to help him or her get dressed in the morning. Should we therefore count the time spent in getting dressed as part of unpaid work? Both men and women perform services around the house virtually every day of the year. Should all of those unremunerated services be included in a "new" measure of GDP [Gross Domestic Product]? If they were, measured GDP would be increased dramatically.

—Miller, *Economics Today*, p. 185

Main idea: It is difficult to estimate the value of a homemaker's services.

Paragraph 3

In 1970 the federal government passed the Comprehensive Drug Abuse, Prevention and Control Act (also known as the Controlled Substance Act). That act did not contain a rigid penalty system but rather established only upper bounds for the fines and prison terms to be imposed for offenses. In 1984 the act was amended in order to impose fixed penalties, particularly for dealers. For anyone caught with more than 1 kilogram of heroin, 50 grams of cocaine base, or 1,000 kilograms of marijuana, the applicable penalty was raised to imprisonment from 10 years to life plus a fine of $4 million. A variety of other prison penalties and fines were outlined in that amendment. Another amendment passed in 1988 included the death penalty for "drug kingpins."

—Miller, *Economics Today*, p. 513

Main idea: Since 1970, the penalties for drug dealing have increased.

Paragraph 4

As recently as 20 years ago, textbooks on child psychology seldom devoted more than a few paragraphs to the behaviors of the neonate—the newborn through the first 2 weeks of life. It seemed as if the neonate did not do much worth writing about. Today, most child psychology texts devote substantially more space to discussing the abilities of newborns. It is unlikely that over the past 20 years neonates have gotten smarter or more able. Rather, psychologists have. They have devised new and clever ways of measuring the abilities and capacities of neonates.

—Gerow, *Psychology: An Introduction,* p. 319

Main idea: Coverage of neonates in psychology textbooks has increased

as psychologists have learned more about them.

➤ **NOW PRACTICE . . . FINDING STATED AND IMPLIED MAIN IDEAS**

Turn to the article titled "Animal Emotions" on p. 9. Using your own paper, number the lines from 1 to 18, to correspond to the 18 paragraphs in the article. For each paragraph number, if the main idea is stated, record the sentence number in which it appears (first, second, etc.). If the main idea is unstated and implied, write a sentence that expresses the main idea.

3d   RECOGNIZING SUPPORTING DETAILS

Supporting details are those facts and ideas that prove or explain the main idea of a paragraph. While all the details in a paragraph do support the main idea, not all details are equally important. As you read, try to identify and pay attention to the most important details. Pay less attention to details of lesser importance. The key details directly explain the main idea. Other details may provide additional information, offer an example, or further explain one of the key details.

Figure A shows how details relate to the main idea and how details range in degree of importance. In the diagram, more important details are placed toward the left; less important details are closer to the right.

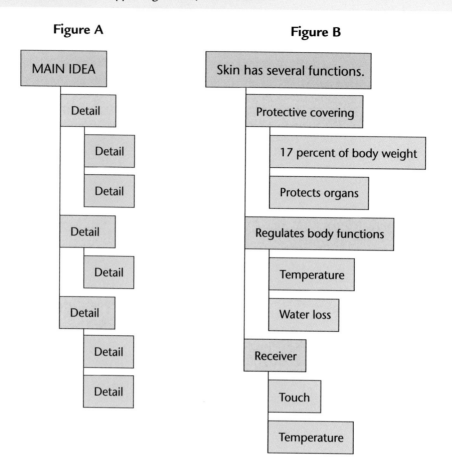

Figure A

Figure B

Read the following paragraph and study Figure B.

> The skin of the human body has several functions. First, it serves as a protective covering. In doing so, it accounts for 17 percent of the body weight. Skin also protects the organs within the body from damage or harm. The skin serves as a regulator of body functions. It controls body temperature and water loss. Finally, the skin serves as a receiver. It is sensitive to touch and temperature.

From this diagram you can see that the details that state the three functions of skin are the key details. Other details, such as "protects the organs," provide further information and are at a lower level of importance.

Read the following paragraph and try to pick out the more important details.

> Many cultures have different rules for men and women engaging in conflict. Asian cultures are more strongly prohibitive of women's conflict strategies. Asian women are expected to be exceptionally polite; this is even more important when women are in conflict with men and when the conflict is public. In the United

States, there is a verbalized equality; men and women have equal rights when it comes to permissible conflict strategies. In reality, there are many who expect women to be more polite, to pursue conflict in a nonargumentative way, while men are expected to argue forcefully and logically.

This paragraph could be diagrammed as follows (key details only):

Many cultures have different rules for men and women engaging in conflict.

Rules in Asian cultures

Rules in the United States

▶ NOW PRACTICE . . . FINDING SUPPORTING DETAILS 1

Each of the following topic sentences states the main idea of a paragraph. After each topic sentence are sentences containing details that may or may not support the topic sentence. Read each sentence and put an "S" beside those that contain details that support the topic sentence.

1. Topic Sentence: It is expected that most U.S. cities will continue to see population declines in the next ten or twenty years.

   __S__ a. White, middle class people will continue to leave inner cities.

   __S__ b. Population will continue to shift to suburbs and rural areas.

   _____ c. Those left behind in cities will be primarily African American, poor, and elderly.

   __S__ d. Businesses will continue to move to the suburbs where most service and management workers live.

   _____ e. The federal government will continue to cut funding for cities.

2. Topic Sentence: *Mens rea*, a term that refers to person's criminal intent when committing a crime, or his or her state of mind, can be evaluated in several ways.

   __S__ a. Confessions by criminals are direct evidence of their criminal intent.

   __S__ b. Circumstantial evidence can be used to suggest mental intent.

   _____ c. *Actus rea* is a person's actions that make up a crime.

   _____ d. A person may unknowingly commit a crime.

   __S__ e. Expert witnesses may offer an opinion about a person's criminal intent.

3. Topic Sentence: Food irradiation is a process in which food is treated with radiation to kill bacteria.

    _____ a. Gamma radiation is made up of radioactive cobalt, cesium, and x rays.

    __S__ b. The radioactive rays pass through the food without damaging it or changing it.

    __S__ c. The newest form of irradiation uses electricity as the energy source for irradiation.

    __S__ d. Irradiation increases the shelf life of food because it kills all bacteria present in the food.

    _____ e. E. coli, salmonella, and listeria cause many illnesses each year.

4. Topic Sentence: Overtraining is the most common type of fitness-related injury, and it can be easily avoided.

    _____ a. A physical fitness program will improve your health and well-being.

    __S__ b. Our bodies usually provide warning signs of potential muscle damage.

    __S__ c. People often injure themselves by doing too much too soon when they exercise.

    __S__ d. To avoid injury, do not rely solely on repetitive motion activities like running or step aerobics.

    __S__ e. Varying an exercise program can allow muscles time to rest and recover from strain.

5. Topic Sentence: Frank Lloyd Wright was a radically innovative architect.

    _____ a. Wright believed that buildings fit their surroundings.

    __S__ b. He popularized the use of steel cantilevers in homes at a time when they were only used commercially.

    __S__ c. He built the Kaufmann Residence over a waterfall without disturbing it.

    __S__ d. Wright had plans to build a mile-high skyscraper but died before he could do so.

    _____ e. Wright designed the Guggenheim Museum.

➤ NOW PRACTICE . . . FINDING SUPPORTING DETAILS 2

Underline only the most important details in each of the following paragraphs.

Paragraph 1

Physical dependence is what was formerly called addiction. It is characterized by *tolerance* and *withdrawal*. *Tolerance* means that more and more of the drug must be taken to achieve the same effect, as use continues. *Withdrawal* means that if use is discontinued, the person experiences unpleasant symptoms. When I quit smoking cigarettes, for example, I went through about five days of irritability, depression, and restlessness. Withdrawal from heroin and other narcotics is much more painful, involving violent cramps, vomiting, diarrhea, and other symptoms that continue for at least two or three days. With some drugs, especially barbiturates, cold-turkey (sudden and total) quitting can result in death, so severe is the withdrawal.

—Geiwitz, *Psychology*, p. 512

Paragraph 2

The two most common drugs that are legal and do not require a prescription are caffeine and nicotine. *Caffeine* is the active ingredient in coffee, tea, and many cola drinks. It stimulates the central nervous system and heart and therefore is often used to stay awake. Heavy use—say, seven to ten cups of coffee per day—has toxic effects, that is, it acts like a mild poison. Prolonged heavy use appears to be addicting. *Nicotine* is the active ingredient in tobacco. One of the most addicting of all drugs and one of the most dangerous, at least when obtained by smoking, it has been implicated in lung cancer, emphysema, and heart disease.

—Geiwitz, *Psychology*, p. 513

Paragraph 3

Hypnosis today is used for a number of purposes, primarily in psychotherapy or to reduce pain, and it is an acceptable technique in both medicine and psychology. In psychotherapy, it is most often used to eliminate bad habits and annoying symptoms. Cigarette smoking can be treated, for example, by the suggestion that the person will feel nauseated whenever he or she thinks of smoking. Sufferers of migraine headaches treated with hypnotic suggestions to relax showed a much greater tendency to improve than sufferers treated with drugs; 44 percent were headache-free after 12 months of treatment, compared to 12 percent of their drug-treated counterparts.

—Geiwitz, *Psychology*, p. 229

Paragraph 4

There are four main types of sunglasses. The traditional *absorptive* glasses soak up all the harmful sun rays. *Polarizing* sunglasses account for half the market. They're the best buy for knocking out glare, and reflections from snow and water, but they may admit more light rays than other sunglasses. *Coated* sunglasses usually have a metallic covering that itself reflects light. They are often quite absorptive, but a cheap pair of coated glasses may have an uneven or nondurable coating that could rub off after a short period of time. New on the market are the somewhat more expensive *photochromatic* sunglasses. Their chemical composition causes them to change color according to the brightness of the light: in the sun, they darken; in the shade, they lighten. This type of sunglasses responds to ultraviolet light only, and will not screen out infrared rays, so they're not the best bet for continual exposure to bright sun.

—George, *The New Consumer Survival Kit*, p. 14

Paragraph 5

In simplest outline, how is a President chosen? First, <u>a candidate campaigns within his party for nomination at a national convention.</u> After the convention comes a <u>period of competition with the nominee of the other major party and perhaps the nominees of minor parties.</u> The showdown arrives on Election Day. <u>The candidate must win more votes than any other nominee in enough states and the District of Columbia to give him a majority of the electoral votes.</u> If he does all these things, he has won the right to the office of <u>President of the United States.</u>

—"ABC's of How a President is Chosen," *US News and World Report,* p. 45

> **NOW PRACTICE . . . FINDING SUPPORTING DETAILS 3**

Reread the article "Animal Emotions" on p. 9 and underline the most important supporting details in each paragraph.

3e   RECOGNIZING TRANSITIONS

Transitions are linking words or phrases used to lead the reader from one idea to another. If you get in the habit of recognizing transitions, you will see that they often guide you through a paragraph, helping you to read it more easily.

In the following paragraph, notice how the underlined transitions lead you from one important detail to the next.

The principle of rhythm and line also contributes to the overall unity of the landscape design. This principle is responsible for the sense of continuity between different areas of the landscape. <u>One</u> way in which this continuity can be developed is by extending planting beds from one area to another. <u>For example,</u> shrub beds developed around the entrance to the house can be continued around the sides and into the backyard. Such an arrangement helps to tie the front and rear areas of the property together. <u>Another</u> means by which rhythm is given to a design is to repeat shapes, angles, or lines between various areas and elements of the design.

—Reiley and Shry, *Introductory Horticulture,* p. 114

Not all paragraphs contain such obvious transitions, and not all transitions serve as such clear markers of major details. Often, however, transitions are used to alert you to what will come next in the paragraph. If you see the phrase *for instance* at the beginning of a sentence, then you know that an example will follow. When you see the phrase *on the other hand,* you can predict that a different, opposing idea will follow. Table 3.1 lists some of the most common transitions used within a paragraph and indicates what they tell you.

TABLE 3.1 COMMON TRANSITIONS

TYPES OF TRANSITIONS	EXAMPLES	WHAT THEY TELL THE READER
Time or Sequence	first, later, next, finally	The author is arranging ideas in the order in which they happened.
Example	for example, for instance, to illustrate, such as	An example will follow.
Enumeration	first, second, third, last, another, next	The author is marking or identifying each major point (sometimes these may be used to suggest order of importance).
Continuation	also, in addition, and, further, another	The author is continuing with the same idea and is going to provide additional information.
Contrast	on the other hand, in contrast, however	The author is switching to a different, opposite, or contrasting idea than previously discussed.
Comparison	like, likewise, similarly	The writer will show how the previous idea is similar to what follows.
Cause and Effect	because, thus, therefore, since, consequently	The writer will show a connection between two or more things, how one thing caused another, or how something happened as a result of something else.

▶ NOW PRACTICE . . . RECOGNIZING TRANSITIONS 1

Select the transitional word or phrase from the box below that best completes each of the following sentences.

another	however	more important
for example	because	

1. The function of taste buds is to enable us to select healthy foods. ___Another___ function is to warn us away from food that is potentially dangerous, such as those that are sour or bitter.

2. Michelangelo considered himself to be primarily a sculptor; ___however___, the Sistine Chapel ceiling painting is one of his best known works of art.

3. Failure to floss and brush teeth and gums can cause bad breath. ___More important___, this failure can also lead to periodontal disease.

4. Businesses use symbols to stand for a product's qualities; ___for example___, the golden arches have come to represent the McDonald's chain.

5. In the 1800s the "wild west" was made up of territories that did not belong to states. ___Because___ there was no local government, vigilantes and out-laws ruled the land, answering only to U.S. marshalls.

▶ NOW PRACTICE ... RECOGNIZING TRANSITIONS 2

Using the article "Animal Emotions" on p. 9, list at least five transitions and the number of the paragraph in which each appears. For each transition you list, indicate what type it is and the kind of information it gives you.

1. _____

2. _____

3. _____

4. _____

5. _____

▶ NOW PRACTICE ... RECOGNIZING TRANSITIONS 3

Each of the following beginnings of paragraphs uses a transitional word or phrase to tell the reader what will follow in the paragraph. Read each, paying particular attention to the underlined word or phrase. Then, in the space provided, describe as specifically as you can what you would expect to find next in the paragraph.

1. Price is not the only factor to consider in choosing a pharmacy. Many provide valuable services that should be considered. <u>For instance</u> . . .

   an example of the valuable services that pharmacies provide

2. There are a number of things you can do to prevent a home burglary. <u>First,</u> . . .

   one suggestion for preventing a home burglary

3. Most mail order businesses are reliable and honest. <u>However,</u> . . .

   information that suggests some mail order businesses are not honest

   and reliable

4. One advantage of a compact stereo system is that all the components are built into the unit. <u>Another</u> . . .

   a second advantage of a compact stereo system

5. To select the presidential candidate you will vote for, you should examine his or her philosophy of government. <u>Next</u> . . .

   the next step in choosing a candidate you will vote for

4 Organizational Patterns

Most college students take courses in several different disciplines each semester. You may study psychology, anatomy and physiology, mathematics, and English composition all in one semester. During one day you may read a poem, solve math problems, and study early developments in psychology.

What few students realize is that a biologist and a psychologist, for example, think about and approach their subject matter in similar ways. Both carefully define terms, examine causes and effects, study similarities and differences, describe sequences of events, classify information, solve problems, and enumerate characteristics. The subject matter and language they use differ, but their approaches to the material are basically the same. Researchers, textbook authors, and your professors use standard approaches, or **organizational patterns,** to express their ideas.

In academic writing, commonly used organizational patterns include definition, classification, order or sequence, cause and effect, comparison and contrast, and listing/enumeration. Other important patterns include statement and clarification, summary, generalization and example, and addition.

These patterns can work for you in several ways:

- Patterns help you anticipate the author's thought development and thus focus your reading.
- Patterns help you remember and recall what you read.
- Patterns are useful in your own writing; they help you organize and express your ideas in a more coherent, comprehensible form.

The following sections describe each pattern listed above. In subsequent chapters, you will see how these patterns are used in specific academic disciplines.

4a DEFINITION

Each academic discipline has its own specialized vocabulary. One of the primary purposes of introductory textbooks is to introduce students to this new language. Consequently, definition is a commonly used pattern throughout most introductory-level texts.

61

Suppose you were asked to define the word *comedian* for someone unfamiliar with the term. First, you would probably say that a comedian is a person who entertains. Then you might distinguish a comedian from other types of entertainers by saying that a comedian is an entertainer who tells jokes and makes others laugh. Finally, you might mention, by way of example, the names of several well-known comedians who have appeared on television. Although you may have presented it informally, your definition would have followed the standard, classic pattern. The first part of your definition tells what general class or group the term belongs to (entertainers). The second part tells what distinguishes the term from other items in the same class or category. The third part includes further explanation, characteristics, examples, or applications.

You can visualize the definition pattern as follows:

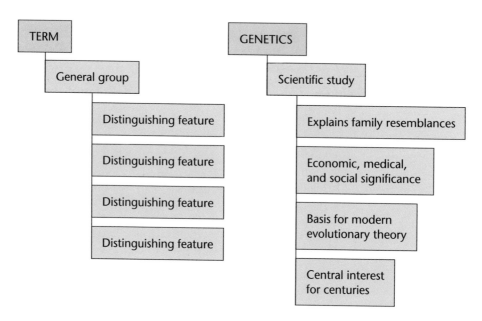

See how the term *genetics* is defined in the following paragraph, and notice how the term and the general class are presented in the first sentence. The remainder of the paragraph presents the distinguishing characteristics.

Genetics is the scientific study of heredity, the transmission of characteristics from parents to offspring. Genetics explains why offspring resemble their parents and also why they are not identical to them. Genetics is a subject that has considerable economic, medical, and social significance and is partly the basis for the modern theory of evolution. Because of its importance, genetics has been a topic of central interest in the study of life for centuries. Modern concepts in genetics are fundamentally different, however, from earlier ones.

—Mix, Farber, and King, *Biology, The Network of Life,* p. 262

Writers often provide clues called **transitions** that signal the organizational pattern being used. These signals may occur within single sentences or as connections between sentences. (Transitional words that occur in phrases are italicized here to help you spot them.)

TRANSITIONS FOR THE DEFINITION PATTERN

genetics *is* . . .
bureaucracy *means* . . .
patronage *refers to* . . .
aggression *can be defined* as . . .
deficit is *another term* that . . .
balance of power *also means* . . .

➤ **NOW PRACTICE . . . USING DEFINITION**

Read each of the following paragraphs and answer the questions that follow:

A. A **Pidgin** is a contact language that emerges when different cultures with different languages come to live in close proximity and therefore need to communicate. Pidgins are generally limited to highly functional domains, such as trade, since that is what they were developed for. A pidgin therefore is no one's first language. many pidgins of the Western hemisphere developed out of slavery, where owners needed to communicate with their slaves. A pidgin is always learned as a second language. Tok Pisin, the pidgin language of Papua New Guinea, consists of a mixture of many languages, some English, Samoan, Chinese, and Malayan. Tok Pisin has been declared one of the national languages of Papau New Guinea, where it is transforming into a **creole,** or a language descended from pidgin with its own native speakers and involving linguistic expansion and elaboration. About two hundred pidgin and creole languages exist today, mainly in West Africa, the Caribbean, and the South Pacific.

—Miller, *Cultural Anthropology*, pp. 308–309

1. What term is being defined?

   pidgin _____

2. Explain the meaning of the term in your own words.

   It is a language that develops when people who speak different languages

   live near one another. _____

3. Give an example of the term. Tok Pisin _____

B. The **integumentary** system is the external covering of the body, or the skin. It waterproofs the body and cushions and protects the deeper tissues from injury. It also excretes salts and urea in perspiration and helps regulate body temperature. Temperature, pressure, and pain receptors located in the skin alert us to what is happening at the body surface.

—Marieb, *Essentials of Human Anatomy and Physiology*, p. 3.

4. Define the integumentary system in your own words.

It is the skin that covers the body.

5. List three things the integumentary system does.

waterproofs the body, protects tissue, excretes salts and urea, regulates

body temperature, serves as a sensor for the body surface

4b   CLASSIFICATION

If you were asked to describe types of computers, you might mention mainframes, minicomputers, and microcomputers. By dividing a broad topic into its major categories, you are using a pattern known as *classification*.

This pattern is widely used in many academic subjects. For example, a psychology text might explain human needs by classifying them into two categories: primary and secondary. In a chemistry textbook, various compounds may be grouped and discussed according to common characteristics, such as the presence of hydrogen or oxygen. The classification pattern divides a topic into parts, on the basis of common or shared characteristics.

Here are a few examples of topics and the classifications or categories into which each might be divided.

- Movies: comedy, horror, mystery
- Motives: achievement, power, affiliation, competency
- Plants: leaves, stem, roots

Note how the following paragraph classifies the various types of cancers.

The name of the cancer is derived from the type of tissue in which it develops. Carcinoma (carc = cancer; omo = tumor) refers to a malignant tumor consisting of epithelial cells. A tumor that develops from a gland is called an adenosarcoma (adeno = gland). Sarcoma is a general term for any cancer arising from connective tissue. Osteogenic sarcomas (osteo = bone; genic = origin), the most frequent type of childhood cancer, destroy normal bone tissue and eventually spread to other areas of the body. Myelomas (myelos = marrow) are malignant tumors, occurring in middle-aged and older people, that interfere with the blood-cell-producing function of bone marrow and cause anemia. Chondrosarcomas (chondro = cartilage) are cancerous growths of cartilage.

—Tortora, *Introduction to the Human Body*, p. 56

You can visualize the classification pattern as follows:

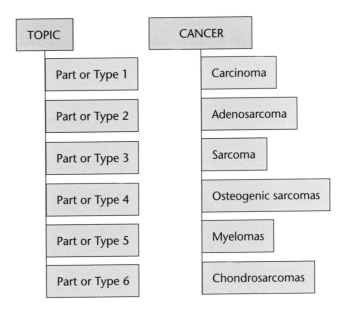

TRANSITIONS FOR THE CLASSIFICATION PATTERN

There are *several kinds* of chemical bonding . . .
There are *numerous types of* . . .
Reproduction can be *classified as* . . .
the human skeleton is *composed of* . . .
muscles *comprise* . . .
one type of communication . . .
another type of communication . . .
finally, there is . . .

▶ **NOW PRACTICE . . . USING CLASSIFICATION**

Read each of the following paragraphs and answer the questions that follow.

A. The reptiles made one of the most spectacular adaptive radiations in all of Earth history. One group, the pterosaurs, took to the air. These "dragons of the sky" possessed huge membranous wings that allowed them rudimentary flight. Another group of reptiles, exemplified by the fossil *Archaeopteryx*, led to more successful flyers: the birds. Whereas some reptiles took to the skies, others returned to the sea, including fish-eating plesiosaurs and ichthyosaurs. These reptiles became proficient swimmers, but retained their reptilian teeth and breathed by means of lungs.

—Tarbuck and Lutgens, *Earth Science,* p. 309.

1. List the classification of reptiles included in this paragraph.

   pterosaurs, archaeopteryx, plesiosaurs and ichthyosaurs

2. Highlight the transitional words used in the paragraph.

   One group, another group

B. From the hundreds of billions of galaxies, several basic types have been identified: spiral, elliptical, and irregular. The Milky Way and the Great Galaxy in Andromeda are examples of fairly large **spiral galaxies.** Typically, spiral galaxies are disk-shaped with a somewhat greater concentration of stars near their centers, but there are numerous variations. Viewed broadside, arms are often seen extending from the central nucleus and sweeping gracefully away. One type of spiral galaxy, however, has the stars arranged in the shape of a bar, which rotates as a rigid system. This requires that the outer stars move faster than the inner ones, a fact not easy for astronomers to reconcile with the laws of motion. Attached to each end of these bars are curved spiral arms. These have become known as **barred spiral galaxies.** The most abundant group, making up 60 percent of the total is the **elliptical galaxies.** These are generally smaller than spiral galaxies. Some are so much smaller, in fact, that the term dwarf has been applied. Because these dwarf galaxies are not visible at great distances, a survey of the sky reveals more of the conspicuous large spiral galaxies. As their name implies, elliptical galaxies have an ellipsoidal shape that ranges to nearly spherical, and they lack spiral arms. Only 10 percent of the known galaxies lack symmetry and are classified as **irregular galaxies.** The best-known irregular galaxies, the Large and Small Magellanic Clouds in the Southern Hemisphere, are easily visible with the unaided eye.

   —Tarbuck and Lutgens, *Earth Science*, pp. 620–21

3. What are the three primary classifications of galaxies?

   spiral, elliptical, irregular

4. What determines how a galaxy is classified?

   shape

5. Highlight transitional words used in the paragraph.

   several basic types, one type, are classified as

4c   ORDER OR SEQUENCE

If you were asked to summarize what you did today, you probably would mention key events in the order in which they occurred. In describing how to write a particular computer program, you would detail the process step-by-step. In each case, you are presenting information in a particular sequence or order. Each of these examples illustrates a form of the organizational pattern known as *order* or *sequence*. Let's look at several types of order.

Chronology

Chronological order refers to the sequence in which events occur in time. This pattern is essential in the academic disciplines concerned with the interpretation of events in the past. History, government, and anthropology are prime examples. In various forms of literature, chronological order is evident; the narrative form, used in novels, short stories, and narrative essays, relies on chronological order.

You can visualize the chronological order pattern as follows:

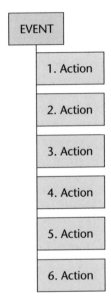

The following paragraph uses chronology to describe how a conflict in Kosovo developed into an allied operation in Europe.

In 1999, a smoldering conflict in Kosovo, another of the provinces of the former Yugoslavia, led to war. In an effort to stop Slobodan Milosevic, the Serbian leader responsible for the devastation of Bosnia, from squelching a movement for autonomy in Kosovo, NATO, now 50 years old, launched an American-led bombing campaign. Milosevic responded with an even more violent "ethnic cleansing" campaign that drove hundreds of thousands of Kosovars from their homes. Even without the introduction of ground troops, this ultimately successful air assault was the largest allied operation in Europe since World War II.

—Nash et al. *The American People*, p. 1099

TRANSITIONS FOR CHRONOLOGICAL ORDER

in ancient times . . .
at the start of the battle . . .
on September 12 . . .
the *first* primate species . . .
later efforts . . .
Other chronological transitions are *then, before,*
during, by the time, while, afterward, as, after, thereafter,
meanwhile, and *at that point.*

➤ NOW PRACTICE . . . USING ORDER OR SEQUENCE

Read each of the following textbook excerpts and answer the questions that follow.

A. **Railroads: Pioneers of Big Business**

Completion of efficient and speedy national transportation and communications networks encouraged mass production and mass marketing. Beginning in 1862, federal and state governments vigorously promoted railroad construction with land grants from the public domain. Eventually, railroads received lands one and a half times the size of Texas. Local governments gave everything from land for stations to tax breaks.

With such incentives, the first transcontinental railroad was finished in 1869. Four additional transcontinental lines and miles of feeder and branch roads were laid down in the 1870s and 1880s. By 1890, trains rumbled across 165,000 miles of tracks. Telegraph lines arose alongside them.

—Nash et al., *The American People,* pp. 611–13

1. What events does the excerpt detail?

   railroad construction
   _____

2. What is the importance of these events?

   The building of the railroads encouraged businesses to grow and develop.
   _____

3. Highlight the transitional words used in the excerpt.

   Beginning in 1862, in 1869, by 1890
   _____

B. The pretext for full-scale intervention in Vietnam came in late July 1964. On July 30 South Vietnamese PT (patrol torpedo) boats attacked bases in the Gulf of Tonkin inside North Vietnamese waters. Simultaneously, the *Maddox,* an American destroyer, steamed into the area to disrupt North Vietnamese communication facilities. On August 2, possibly seeing the two separate missions as a combined maneuver against them, the North Vietnamese sent out several PT boats to attack the destroyer. The *Maddox* fired, sinking one of the attackers, then radioed the news to Washington. Johnson ordered another ship into the bay. On August 3 both destroyers reported another attack, although somewhat later, the commander of the *Maddox* radioed that he was not sure. Nonetheless, the president ordered American planes to retaliate by bombing inside North Vietnam.

—Wilson et al., *The Pursuit of Liberty,* p. 493

4. What events in history does this paragraph describe?

The events leading up to the bombing inside North Vietnam and the

full-scale intervention in Vietnam

5. Highlight the transitional words used in the paragraph.

in late July 1964, on July 30, simultaneously, on August 2, on August 3,

although somewhat later

Process

In disciplines that focus on procedures, steps, or stages by which actions are accomplished, the process pattern is often employed. These subjects include mathematics, natural and life sciences, computer science, and engineering. The pattern is similar to chronology, in that the steps or stages follow each other in time. Transitional words and phrases often used in conjunction with this pattern are similar to those used for chronological order. You can visualize the process pattern as follows:

Note how this pattern is used in a paragraph explaining what occurs in the brain during sleep.

Let us track your brain waves through the night. As you prepare to go to bed, an EEG records that your brain waves are moving along at a rate of about 14 cycles per second (cps). Once you are comfortably in bed, you begin to relax and your brain waves slow down to a rate of about 8 to 12 cps. When you fall asleep, you enter your *sleep cycle,* each of whose stages shows a distinct EEG pattern. In Stage 1 sleep, the EEG shows brain waves of about 3 to 7 cps. During Stage 2, the EEG is characterized by *sleep spindles,* minute bursts of electrical activity of 12 to 16 cps. In the next two stages (3 and 4) of sleep, you enter into a very deep state of relaxed sleep. Your brain waves slow to about 1 to 2 cps, and your breathing and heart rate decrease. In a final stage, the electrical activity of your brain increases; your EEG looks very similar to those recorded during stages 1 and 2. It is during this stage that you will experience REM sleep, and you will begin to dream.

—Zimbardo and Gerrig, *Psychology and Life,* p. 115

➤ NOW PRACTICE . . . USING PROCESS

Read each of the following textbook excerpts and answer the questions that follow.

A. Should you eat less fat? Scientists doing medical research think you probably should; they recommend no more than 30% fat in our diets, whereas the average American diet is estimated to contain 34% fat. Perhaps you're convinced that you should cut down on fatty foods, but you can't imagine watching the Super Bowl without a big bag of chips at your side. The chemists at Procter & Gamble have been trying to resolve your dilemma by developing an edible substance with the rich taste and smooth texture of fat molecules but without the calories. Olestra seems to meet these criteria.

Fat digestion is an enzyme-mediated process that breaks fat molecules into glycerol and fatty acids, which are then able to enter the bloodstream. Olestra is a hexa-, hepta-, or octa-ester of fatty acids (derived from vegetable oil, such as soybean oil or cottonseed oil) and sucrose. Because the body contains no digestive enzymes that convert Olestra's fat-like molecules into their smaller components of sucrose and fatty acids, and because Olestra is too large to enter the bloodstream undigested, the compound passes through systems unchanged.

—Bishop, *Introduction to Chemistry,* p. 749

1. What process does this passage explain?

   how Olestra creates the taste of fat without the calories

2. Why is Olestra not digested?

   because the body cannot convert Olestra's molecules into sucrose and fatty

   acids and the molecules are too large to enter the bloodstream undigested

B. BMI [body mass index] is an index of the relationship of height and weight. It is one of the most accurate indicators of a person's health risk due to excessive weight, rather than "fatness" per se. Although many people recoil in fright when they see they have to convert pounds to kilograms and inches to meters to calculate BMI, it really is not as difficult as it may seem. To get your kilogram weight, just divide your weight in pounds (without shoes or clothing) by 2.2. To convert your height to meters squared, divide your height in inches (without shoes) by 39.4, then square this result. Sounds pretty easy and it actually is. Once you have these basic values, calculating your BMI involves dividing your weight in kilograms by your height in meters squared.

$$BMI = \frac{\text{Weight (in lbs) 2.2 (to determine weight in kg)}}{(\text{Height [in inches] 39.4})^2 \text{ (to determine height in meters squared)}}$$

Healthy weights have been defined as those associated with BMIs of 19 to 25, the range of the lowest statistical health risk. A BMI greater than 25 indicates overweight and potentially significant health risks. The desirable range for females is between 21 and 23; for males, it is between 22 and 24. A body mass index of over 30 is considered obese. Many experts believe this number is too high, particularly for younger adults.

—Donatelle, *Access to Health,* p. 264

3. What process is being described in this paragraph?

the calculation of BMI

4. How do you convert height in inches to meters squared?

Divide your height in inches by 39.4, then square the result.

5. What does BMI measure and why is it useful?

It measures the relationship of height and weight; it predicts health risks

due to being overweight.

Order of Importance

The pattern of ideas sometimes expresses order of priority or preference. Ideas are arranged in one of two ways: from most to least important, or from least to most important. In the following paragraph, the causes of the downward trend in the standard of living are arranged in order of importance.

The United States' downward trend in standard of living has many different causes, of which only a few major ones can be identified here. Most important is probably deindustrialization, the massive loss of manufacturing jobs as many U.S. corporations move their production to poor, labor-cheap countries. But deindustrialization hurts mostly low-skilled manufacturing workers. Most of the well-educated, high-skilled employees in service industries are left unscathed. Deindustrialization alone is therefore not enough to explain the economic decline. Another major factor is the great increase in consumption and decrease in savings. Like their government, people spend more than they earn and become deeply in debt. Those who do practice thrift still have an average rate of savings significantly lower than in countries with fast-growing economies. The habits of high consumption and low saving may have resulted from the great affluence after the Second World War up until the early 1970s (Harrison, 1992).

—Thio, *Sociology*, p. 255

Order of importance is used in almost every field of study.

> **TRANSITIONS FOR ORDER OF IMPORTANCE**
>
> is *less* essential than . . .
> *more* revealing is . . .
> of *primary* interest is . . .
> Other transitions that show the order of importance are *first, next, last, most important, primarily,* and *secondarily.*

➤ **NOW PRACTICE . . . USING ORDER OF IMPORTANCE**

Read the following paragraph and answer the questions that follow.

A. Media resources are being reassembled in a new pattern, with three main parts. The first is the traditional mass media that will continue to be for a long time the most important element in the pattern in terms of their reach and influence. The second consists of the advanced electronic mass media, operating primarily within the new information utility, and competing increasingly with older media services. Finally, there are newer forms of personal electronic media, formed by clusters of like-minded people to fulfill their own professional or individual information needs. Internet chat rooms and personalized Web pages are fast-expanding examples of this development. Each of these parts of the evolving mass-communications pattern deserves separate scrutiny.

—Dizard, *Old Media, New Media*, p. 179

1. What does this paragraph describe?

   the three main types of resources that are currently important

2. Highlight the transitional words used in the paragraph.

   first, the most important, second, finally,

3. Why is traditional mass media the most important type of resource?

because of its reach and influence

4. Which type of media resource competes the most with the traditional mass media?

advanced electronic mass media

5. What are some examples of personal electronic media?

Internet chat rooms, personalized Web pages

Spatial Order

Information organized according to its physical location, or position or order in space, exhibits a pattern that is known as *spatial order*. Spatial order is used in academic disciplines in which physical descriptions are important. These include numerous technical fields, engineering, and the biological sciences.

You can see how the following description of a particular type of blood circulation relies on spatial relationships.

> Pulmonary circulation conducts blood between the heart and the lungs. Oxygen-poor, CO_2-laden blood returns through two large veins (venae cavae) from tissues within the body, enters the right atrium, and is then moved into the right ventricle of the heart. From there, it is pumped into the pulmonary artery, which divides into two branches, each leading to one of the lungs. In the lung, the arteries undergo extensive branching, giving rise to vast networks of capillaries where gas exchange takes place, with blood becoming oxygenated while CO_2 is discharged. Oxygen-rich blood then returns to the heart via the pulmonary veins.
>
> —Mix, Farber, & King, *Biology: The Network of Life*, pp. 663–664

Diagramming is of the utmost importance in working with this pattern; often, a diagram accompanies text material. For example, a diagram makes the functions of the various parts of the human brain easier to understand. Lecturers often refer to a visual aid or chalkboard drawing when providing spatial descriptions.

TRANSITIONS FOR SPATIAL ORDER
the *left side* of the brain . . .
the *lower* portion . . .
the *outer* covering . . .
beneath the surface . . .
Other spatial transitions are *next to, beside, to the left, in the center,* and *externally.*

> **NOW PRACTICE . . . SPATIAL ORDER**

Read the following passage and answer the questions that follow.

A. **Skeletal muscle tissue** is named for its location—attached to bones. Skeletal muscle tissue is also *voluntary* because it can be made to contract by conscious control. A single skeletal muscle fiber (cell) is cylindrical and appears *striated* (striped) under a microscope; when organized in a tissue, the fibers are parallel to each other. Each muscle fiber has a plasma membrane, the **sarcolemma,** surrounding the cytoplasm, or **sarcoplasm.** Skeletal muscle fibers are multinucleate (more than one nucleus), and the nuclei are near the sarcolemma.

—Tortora, *Introduction to the Human Body,* p. 77

1. Briefly describe skeletal muscle tissue.

    Skeletal tissue is tissue that is attached to bones and is voluntary

    (can be controlled).

2. Highlight the transitional words in the paragraph.

    attached to, parallel, surrounding, near

3. How are skeletal muscle fibers or cells arranged in a tissue?

    The fibers are arranged parallel to each other.

4. Where can the sarcolemma (or plasma membrane) be found in muscle fibers?

    They surround the sarcoplasm (or cytoplasm).

5. Where are the nuclei in the skeletal muscle fibers located?

    They are located near the sarcolemma.

4d   CAUSE AND EFFECT

The cause-and-effect pattern expresses a relationship between two or more actions, events, or occurrences that are connected in time. The relationship differs, however, from chronological order in that one event leads to another by *causing* it. Information that is organized in terms of the cause-and-effect pattern may:

- explain causes, sources, reasons, motives, and action
- explain the effect, result, or consequence of a particular action
- explain both causes and effects

You can visualize the cause and effect pattern as follows:

Cause and effect is clearly illustrated by the following passage, which gives the sources of fashions or the reasons why fashions occur.

> Why do fashions occur in the first place? One reason is that some cultures, like ours, *value change:* what is new is good, even better. Thus, in many modern societies clothing styles change yearly, while people in traditional societies may wear the same style for generations. A second reason is that many industries promote quick changes in fashion to increase sales. A third reason is that fashions usually trickle down from the top. A new style may occasionally originate from lower-status groups, as blue jeans did. But most fashions come from upper-class people who like to adopt some style or artifact as a badge of their status. But they cannot monopolize most status symbols for long. Their style is adopted by the middle class, maybe copied or modified for use by lower-status groups, offering many people the prestige of possessing a high-status symbol.
>
> —Thio, *Sociology,* p. 534

The cause-and-effect pattern is used extensively in many academic fields. All disciplines that ask the question "Why" employ the cause-and-effect thought pattern. It is widely used in the sciences, technologies, and social sciences.

Many statements expressing cause-and-effect relationships appear in direct order, with the cause stated first and the effect following: "When demand for a product increases, prices rise." However, reverse order is sometimes used, as in the following statement: "Prices rise when a product's demand increases."

The cause-and-effect pattern is not limited to an expression of a simple one-cause, one-effect relationship. There may be multiple causes, or multiple effects, or both multiple causes and multiple effects. For example, both slippery road conditions and your failure to buy snow tires (causes) may contribute to your car sliding into the ditch (effect).

In other instances, a chain of causes or effects may occur. For instance, failing to set your alarm clock may force you to miss your 8:00 A.M. class, which in turn may cause you not to submit your term paper on time, which may result in a penalty grade.

TRANSITIONS FOR THE CAUSE-AND-EFFECT PATTERN

stress *causes* . . .
aggression *creates* . . .
depression *leads to* . . .
forethought *yields* . . .
mental retardation *stems from* . . .
life changes *produce* . . .
hostility *breeds* . . .
avoidance *results in* . . .
Other cause-and-effect transitions are *therefore,*
consequently, hence, for this reason, and *since.*

➤ **NOW PRACTICE . . . USING CAUSE AND EFFECT**

Read each of the following paragraphs and answer the questions that follow.

A. All objects continually radiate energy. Why, then, doesn't the temperature of all objects continually decrease? The answer is that all objects also continually absorb radiant energy. If an object is radiating more energy than it is absorbing, its temperature does decrease; but if an object is absorbing more energy than it is emitting, its temperature increases. An object that is warmer than its surroundings emits more energy than it receives, and therefore it cools; an object colder than its surroundings is a net gainer of energy, and its temperature therefore increases. An object whose temperature is constant, then, emits as much radiant energy as it receives. If it receives none, it will radiate away all its available energy, and its temperature will approach absolute zero.

—Hewitt, *Conceptual Physics,* p. 272

1. Explain why not all objects that radiate energy drop in temperature.

   All objects continue to absorb radiant energy, and some objects absorb

   more than they radiate.

2. What happens to an object that radiates energy but does not absorb any?

   Its temperature will approach absolute zero.

3. Highlight the transitional words used in the paragraph. Why, therefore

4. What causes an object's temperature to remain constant?

   emitting as much radiant energy as it receives

5. What is the effect of an object radiating away all of its available energy?

   Its temperature will approach absolute zero.

B. It's the end of the term and you have dutifully typed the last of several papers. After hours of nonstop typing, you find that your hands are numb, and you feel an intense, burning pain that makes the thought of typing one more word almost unbearable. If you are like one of the thousands of students and workers who every year must quit a particular task due to pain, you may be suffering form a **repetitive stress injury (RSI).** These are injuries to nerves, soft tissue or joints that result from the physical stress of repeated motions. One of the most common RSIs is **carpal tunnel syndrome,** a product of both the information age and the age of technology in general. Hours spent typing at the computer, flipping groceries through computerized scanners, or other jobs "made simpler" by technology can result in irritation to the median nerve in the wrist, causing numbness, tingling, and pain in the fingers and hands.

—Donatelle, *Access to Health,* p. 516

6. What is the cause of RSIs?

   repetitive motion

7. What kind of damage causes carpal tunnel syndrome?

   irritation to the median nerve in the wrist

8. What do students often do that can cause RSIs?

   typing

9. What kinds of symptoms can result from RSI?

   numbness, tingling, and pain in the fingers and hands

10. Highlight the transitional words used in the passage.

   result from, result in

4e COMPARISON AND CONTRAST

The comparison organizational pattern is used to emphasize or discuss similarities between or among ideas, theories, concepts, or events, whereas the contrast pattern emphasizes differences. When a speaker or writer is concerned with both similarities and differences, a combination pattern is used. You can visualize these three variations of the pattern as follows:

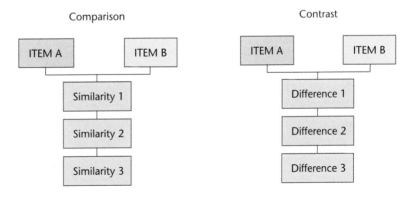

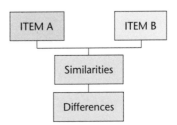

The comparison-and-contrast pattern is widely used in the social sciences, where different groups, societies, cultures, or behaviors are studied. Literature courses may require comparisons among poets, among several literary works, or among stylistic features. A business course may examine various management styles, compare organizational structures, or contrast retailing plans.

A contrast is shown in the following paragraph, which describes the purchasing processes of small and large businesses.

> Small businesses are likely to have less formal purchasing processes. A small retail grocer might, for example, purchase a computer system after visiting a few suppliers to compare prices and features, while a large grocery store chain might collect bids from a specified number of vendors and then evaluate those bids on pre-established criteria. Usually, fewer individuals are involved in the decision-making process for a small business. The owner of the small business, for example, may make all decisions, and a larger business may operate with a buying committee of several people.
>
> —Kinnear, Bernhardt, and Krentler, *Principles of Marketing*, p. 218

Depending on whether a speaker or writer is concerned with similarities, differences, or both similarities and differences, the pattern might be organized in different ways. Suppose a professor of American literature is comparing the work of two American poets, Walt Whitman and Robert Frost. Each of the following organizations is possible:

1. Compare and then contrast the two. That is, first discuss how Frost's poetry and Whitman's poetry are similar, and then discuss how they are different.
2. Discuss by author. Discuss the characteristics of Whitman's poetry, then discuss the characteristics of Frost's poetry, then summarize their similarities and differences.
3. Discuss by characteristic. For example, first discuss the two poets' use of metaphor, next discuss their use of rhyme, and then discuss their common themes.

TRANSITIONS THAT SHOW CONTRAST

unlike Whitman, Frost . . .
less wordy *than* Whitman . . .
contrasted with Whitman, Frost . . .
Frost *differs from* . . .
Other transitions of contrast are *in contrast, however, on the other hand, as opposed to,* and *whereas.*

TRANSITIONS THAT SHOW COMPARISON

similarities between Frost and Whitman . . .
Frost is *as* powerful *as* . . .
like Frost, Whitman . . .
both Frost and Whitman . . .
Frost *resembles* Whitman in that . . .
Other transitions of comparison are *in a*
like manner, similarly, likewise, correspondingly, and
in the same way.

▶ NOW PRACTICE . . . USING COMPARISON AND CONTRAST

Read each of the following paragraphs and answer the questions that follow.

A. When considering the relationship of Congress and the president, the basic differences of the two branches must be kept in mind. Members of Congress are
elected from narrower constituencies than is the president. The people usually expect the president to address general concerns such as foreign policy and economic prosperity, while Congresspersons are asked to solve individual problems.
There are structural differences as well. Congress is a body composed of hundreds
of independent people, each with a different power base, and it is divided along
partisan lines. Thus, it is difficult for Congress to act quickly or to project unity
and clear policy statements.

—Baradat, *Understanding American Democracy,* p. 300

1. What two branches of the government are discussed?

   Congress, presidency

2. Does this paragraph mainly use comparison, contrast, or both?

   contrast

3. Explain how the two branches are similar and/or different.

   Differences: constituencies from which elected, types of concerns expected

   to address, structure, speed of action, and unity

4. Why is it difficult for Congress to act quickly?

   because Congress is composed of hundreds of people divided along party lines

5. Highlight the transitional words in the paragraph.

   basic differences, structural differences

B. What are the main characteristics of this new postindustrial society? Unlike the industrial society from which we are emerging, its hallmark is not raw materials and manufacturing. Rather, its basic component is *information*. Teachers pass on knowledge to students, while lawyers, physicians, bankers, pilots, and interior decorators sell their specialized knowledge of law, the body, money, aerodynamics, and color schemes to clients. Unlike the factory workers in an industrial society, these workers don't *produce* anything. Rather, they transmit or use information to provide services that others are willing to pay for.

—Henslin, *Social Problems*, p. 154

6. What two things are being compared or contrasted?

   postindustrial and industrial societies

7. What is the postindustrial society based upon?

   information

8. What did most workers in industrial society do at their jobs?

   produce things

9. How is information connected to money in postindustrial society?

   People are willing to pay for information or services based on information.

10. Highlight the transitional words used in the paragraph.

    unlike, rather, unlike, rather

4f   LISTING/ENUMERATION

If asked to evaluate a film you saw, you might describe the characters, plot, and technical effects. These details about the film could be arranged in any order; each detail provides further information about the film, but they have no specific relationship to one another. This arrangement of ideas is known as *listing* or *enumeration*—giving bits of information on a topic by stating them one after the other. Often there is no particular method of arrangement for those details. You can visualize the listing/enumeration patterns as follows:

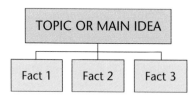

The following list of managers' difficulties in problem solving could have been presented in any order without altering the meaning of the paragraph.

Although accurate identification of a problem is essential before the problem can be solved, this stage of decision making creates many difficulties for managers. Sometimes managers' preconceptions of the problem prevent them from seeing the situation as it actually is. They produce an answer before the proper question has ever been asked. In other cases, managers overlook truly significant issues by focusing on unimportant matters. Also, managers may mistakenly analyze problems in terms of symptoms rather than underlying causes.

—Pride, Hughes, and Kapoor, *Business,* p. 189

This pattern is widely used in college textbooks in most academic disciplines. In its loosest form, the pattern may be simply a list of items: factors that influence light emission, characteristics of a particular poet, a description of an atom, a list of characteristics that define poverty.

Somewhat tighter is the use of listing to explain, support, or provide evidence. Support may be in the form of facts, statistics, or examples. For instance, the statement, "The incidence of white collar crime has dramatically increased over the past ten years" would be followed by facts and statistics documenting the increase.

TRANSITIONS FOR LISTING

one aspect of relativity . . .
a second feature of relativity . . .
also, relativity . . .
there are *several characteristics of* . . .
(1) . . . , *(2)* . . . , *and (3)* . . . ,
(a) . . . , *(b)* . . . , *and (c)* . . . ,
Other transitional words and phrases are *in addition, first, second, third, finally,* and *another.*

> **NOW PRACTICE . . . USING LISTING**

Read the following paragraphs and answer the questions that follow.

Minorities come into existence, then, when, due to expanded political boundaries or migration, people with different customs, languages, values or physical characteristics come under control of the same state organization. There, some groups who share physical and cultural traits discriminate against those with different traits. The losers in this power struggle are forced into minority group status; the winners enjoy the higher status and greater privileges that their dominance brings. Wagley and Harris noted that all minorities share these five characteristics: (1) They are treated unequally by the dominant group. (2) Their physical or cultural traits are held in low esteem by the dominant group. (3) They tend to feel strong group solidarity because of their physical or cultural traits—and the disabilities these traits bring. (4) Their membership in a minority group is not voluntary but comes through birth. (5) They tend to marry within their group. Sharing cultural or physical traits, having similar experiences of discrimination, and marrying within their own group create a shared identity—sometimes even a sense of common destiny. These shared experiences, however, do not mean that all minority groups have the same goals.

—Henslin, *Social Problems*, p. 252

1. What does this paragraph list?

    the characteristics of minority groups

2. How do minority groups come into existence?

    They come into existence when, due to expanded boundaries or migration,

    people with different customs, languages, values, or physical characteristics

    come under the control of the same state organization.

B. Voters make two basic decisions at election time. The first is whether to vote. Americans' right to vote is well established, but in order to do so citizens must go through the registration process. America's unique registration system is one major reason why turnout in American elections is much lower than in most other democracies. The 1996 election was another in a long string of low-turnout elections. Second, those who choose to vote must decide for whom to cast their ballots. Over a generation of research on voting behavior has helped political scientists understand the dominant role played by three factors in voters' choices: party identification, candidate evaluations, and policy positions.

—Edwards, *Government in America*, p. 330

3. What does this paragraph list?

    the decisions voters make at election time and the factors that influence

    voter choice

4. Highlight the transitional words used in the paragraph.

    two basic decisions, the first, second, three factors

5. What is the major reason why voter turnout is low in America?

    Voter turnout is low due to the registration system.

4g   MIXED PATTERNS

Organizational patterns are often combined. In describing a process, a writer may also give reasons why each step must be followed in the prescribed order. A lecturer may define a concept by comparing it to something similar or familiar. Suppose an essay in your political science textbook opens by stating, "The distinction between 'power' and 'power potential' is an important one in considering the balance of power." You might expect a definition pattern (where the two terms are defined), but you also might anticipate that the essay would discuss the difference between the two terms (contrast pattern).

> **NOW PRACTICE . . . USING ORGANIZATIONAL PATTERNS 1**

For each of the following topic sentences, anticipate what organizational pattern(s) the paragraph is likely to exhibit. Record your prediction in the space provided.

1. The Enlightenment celebrated the power of reason; however, an opposite reaction, Romanticism, soon followed.

   Pattern: comparison and contrast or cause and effect

2. Psychogenic amnesia—a severe and often permanent memory loss—results in disorientation and the inability to draw on past experiences.

   Pattern: cause and effect / definition

3. Several statistical procedures are used to track the changes in the divorce rate.

   Pattern: process or listing

4. The GNP (gross national product) is an economic measure that considers the total value of goods and services that a country produces during a given year.

   Pattern: definition

5. Large numbers of European immigrants first began to arrive in the United States in the 1920s.

   Pattern: order or sequence

6. There are sources of information about corporations that might help an investor evaluate them. One of the most useful is the Value Line Investment Survey.

   Pattern: order of importance

7. Diseases of the heart and blood vessels—cardiovascular diseases—are the leading cause of death in the United States today.

   Pattern: cause and effect

8. The spinal cord is located within the spinal column; it looks like a section of rope or twine.

   Pattern: spatial

9. Think of the hardware in a computer system as the kitchen in a short-or-der restaurant: It's equipped to produce whatever output a customer (user) requests, but sits idle until an order (command) is placed.

    Pattern: comparison and contrast

10. The purpose of a résumé is to sell the qualities of the person writing it; it should include several important kinds of information.

    Pattern: listing/enumeration

➤ NOW PRACTICE . . . USING ORGANIZATIONAL PATTERNS 2

Read each of the following paragraphs and identify the primary organizational pattern used in each.

Paragraph 1

Ours is an ethnically, religiously, and racially diverse society. The white European Protestants, black slaves, and Native Americans who made up the bulk of the U.S. population when the first census was taken in 1790 were joined by Catholic immigrants from Ireland and Germany in the 1840s and 1850s. In the 1870s, Chinese migrated to America, drawn by jobs in railroad construction. Around the turn of the twentieth century, most immigration was from eastern, central, and southern Europe, with its many ethnic, linguistic, and religious groups. Today, most immigration is from Asia and Latin America.

—Greenberg and Page, *The Struggle for Democracy*, p. 71

Pattern: order or sequence

Paragraph 2

Anthropology is the study of human beings from their origins to the present time. It is concerned with humans as both natural and social beings, and, as such, overlaps with other academic disciplines such as sociology, psychology, biology, and history. Because the field of anthropology is so complex and diverse, it is commonly divided into four branches. Cultural anthropology focuses on the be-havior of human beings in social groups. Archaeology is the study of people who lived in the past; it concentrates on material goods that humans left behind. Physical anthropology studies the biological development of human beings. Anthropological linguistics is the study of human language, both historical and modern and focuses on the development, change, and use of language.

—Tortora, *Introduction to the Human Body*, p. 77

Pattern: classification

Paragraph 3

Once you know someone's e-mail address, you're ready to send a mail mes-sage. If you want to experiment without risking embarrassment, try sending a test message to yourself before you send a message to someone else. Just put your own user ID in the To: field; the mail will be sent to you. All mailers have a command that puts you in a mode for creating and sending your own mail messages. Look for a New Message command in a pull-down menu or perhaps a special "new message" icon on a tool bar. After issuing the command for starting a new message, you will be put into a mode for constructing an e-mail message. You'll be given an opportunity to enter the To: header, the Subject: header, and the optional Cc: header. The From: header will be filled in for you automatically. You will probably be given a window display in which all of these items can be filled by moving your mouse around and clicking the field you want to complete. If you don't want to put something in a given field, just press Return or Enter to leave it blank. The only header field that can't be left blank is the To: field.

—Lehnert, *Light on the Internet, Essentials of the Internet and the World Wide Web*, 1999, p. 34.

Pattern: process

Paragraph 4

By far the most important committees in Congress are the standing committees. Currently 16 standing committees in the Senate and 22 in the House receive the bills that are introduced in Congress. The standing committees are assigned subject-matter jurisdiction by the rules of their respective house, and their titles reflect their general area of expertise. Hence, we have the Senate Finance Committee, the House Agriculture Committee, the Senate Budget Committee, the House Judiciary Committee, and so on. The authority of the standing committees includes the power to study legislation, to subpoena witnesses or information, to remand bills to subcommittees, to vote bills dead, to table bills (putting them aside, thus allowing them to die quietly at the end of the congressional term), to amend bills, to write bills (amending a bill or writing an entirely new version of a bill is called **marking-up**), or to report the bill to the floor.

—Baradat, *Understanding American Democracy*, p. 202

Pattern: listing/enumeration

Paragraph 5

When considering the relationship of Congress and the president, the basic differences of the two branches must be kept in mind. Members of Congress are elected from narrower constituencies than is the president. The people usually expect the president to address general concerns such as foreign policy and economic prosperity, while Congresspersons are asked to solve individual problems. There are structural differences as well. Congress is a body composed of hundreds of independent people, each with a different power base, and it is divided along partisan lines. Thus, it is difficult for Congress to act quickly or to project unity and clear policy statements.

—Baradat, *Understanding American Democracy*, p. 300

Pattern: comparison and contrast

4h   OTHER PATTERNS OF ORGANIZATION

Although the patterns presented in the previous sections are the most common, writers do not limit themselves to these six patterns. Especially in academic writing, you may also find statement and clarification, summary, generalization and example, and addition. Transitions associated with these different patterns are listed in the "Summing It Up" table on pages 91–92.

Statement and Clarification

Many writers make a statement of fact and then proceed to clarify or explain that statement. For instance, a writer may open a paragraph by stating that "The best education for you may not be the best education for someone else." The remainder of the paragraph would then discuss that statement and make its meaning clear by explaining how educational needs are individual and based on one's talents, skills, and goals. Here is a sample paragraph about sex ratios.

> Sex ratios in the poor countries do not show a consistent pattern. In some poor countries men outnumber women, but in others, in tropical Africa, for example, women outnumber men. In fact, variations in sex rations can be explained only by a combination of national economic and cultural factors. In the countries of North America and Europe and in Japan, women may suffer many kinds of discrimination, but they are not generally discriminated against when it comes to access to medical care.
>
> —Bergman and Renwick, *Introduction to Geography*, p. 185

Notice that the writer begins with a statement about sex ratios in poor countries and then goes on to clarify this fact. The author uses the transitional phrase "in fact."

Summary

A summary is a condensed statement that provides the key points of a larger idea or piece of writing. Frequently, summaries at the end of each chapter provide a quick review of the chapter's contents. Often writers summarize what they have already said or what someone else has said. For example, in a psychology textbook you will find many summaries of research. Instead of asking you to read an entire research study, the textbook author will summarize the study's findings. Other times a writer may repeat in condensed form what he or she has already said as a means of emphasis or clarification.

In the following paragraph about the magazine industry, the author uses the summary method of organization.

> In summary, the magazine industry is adapting to the new world of electronic multimedia information and entertainment, with formats that will be quite different from the familiar ones. Computer-generated publishing has become the norm

in the magazine business, expanding beyond its uses in producing newsletters and other specialized publications. Most general circulation magazines already rely heavily on desktop computers, interacting with other electronic equipment to produce high-quality, graphics-filled products.

—Dizard, *Old Media, New Media,* p. 169

Notice that the author summarizes many facts about how the magazine industry uses electronic multimedia information and that the transitional phrase "in summary" is used.

Generalization and Example

Examples are one of the best ways to explain something that is unfamiliar or unknown. Examples are specific instances or situations that illustrate a concept or idea. Often writers make a general statement, or generalization, and then explain it by giving examples to make its meaning clear. In a social problems textbook, you may find the following generalization: Computer theft by employees is on the increase. The section may then go on to offer examples from specific companies in which employees insert fictitious information into the company's computer program and steal company funds.

In the following paragraph about dreams, the writer uses generalization and example.

Different cultures place varying emphases on dreams and support different beliefs concerning dreams. For example, many people in the United States view dreams as irrelevant fantasy with no connection to everyday life. By contrast, people in other cultures view dreams as key sources of information about the future, the spiritual world, and the dreamer. Such cultural views can influence the probability of dream recall. In many modern Western cultures, people rarely remember their dreams upon awakening. The Parintintin of South America, however, typically remember several dreams every night (Kraeke, 1993) and the Senoi of Malaysia discuss their dreams with family members in the morning (Hennager, 1993).

—Davis and Palladino, *Psychology,* p. 210

Notice that the author begins with the generalization that different cultures place different emphases on dreams and then goes on to give examples of the way specific cultures treat dreams. Note the use of the transitional phrase "for example."

Addition

Writers often introduce an idea or make a statement and then supply additional information about that idea or statement. For instance an education textbook may introduce the concept of home schooling and then provide in-depth information about its benefits. This pattern is often used to expand, elaborate, or discuss an idea in greater detail.

In the following paragraph about pathogens, the writer uses addition.

> Some pathogens [disease-causing organisms] evolve and mutate naturally. Also, patients who fail to complete the full portion of their antibiotic prescriptions allow drug-resistant pathogens to multiply. The use of antibiotics in animal feed and sprayed on fruits and vegetables during food processing increases opportunities for resistant organisms to evolve and thrive. Furthermore, there is evidence that the disruption of Earth's natural habitats can trigger the evolution of new pathogens.
>
> —Bergman and Renwick, *Introduction to Geography*, p. 182

Notice that the writer states that some pathogens mutate naturally and then goes on to add that they also mutate as a result of human activities. Note the use of the transitional words "also" and "furthermore."

▶ NOW PRACTICE . . . USING ORGANIZATIONAL PATTERNS 3

For each of the following statements, identify the pattern that is evident and write its name in the space provided. Choose from among the following patterns: process, statement and clarification, summary, generalization and example, addition, and spatial order.

1. If our criminal justice system works, the recidivism rate—the percentage of people released from prison who return—should decrease. In other words, in a successful system, there should be a decrease in the number of criminals who are released from prison and become repeat offenders.

   Pattern: statement and clarification

2. Students who are informed about drugs tend to use them in greater moderation. Furthermore, they tend to help educate others.

   Pattern: addition

3. A successful drug addiction treatment program would offer free or very cheap drugs to addicts. Heroin addicts, for example, could be prescribed heroin when under a physician's care.

   Pattern: generalization and example

4. In conclusion, it is safe to say that crime by women is likely to increase as greater numbers of women assume roles traditionally held by men.

   Pattern: summary

5. The pollutants we have just discussed all involve chemicals; we can conclude that they threaten our environment and our well-being.

   Pattern: summary

6. Sociologists study how we are socialized into sex roles, the attitudes expected of males and females. Sex roles, in fact, identify some activities and behaviors as clearly male and others as clearly female.

   Pattern: statement and clarification

7. Patients often consult a lay referral network to discuss their medical problems. Cancer patients, for instance, can access Internet discussion groups that provide both information and support.

   Pattern: generalization and example

▶ NOW PRACTICE ... USING ORGANIZATIONAL PATTERNS 4

Read each of the following paragraphs and identify the predominant organizational pattern used. Write the name of the pattern in the space provided. Choose from among the following patterns: statement and clarification, summary, generalization and example, and addition.

1. **Managing Emotional Responses**

   Have you gotten all worked up about something you thought was happening only to find that your perceptions were totally wrong or that a communication problem had caused a misrepresentation of events? If you're like most of us, you probably have. We often get upset not by realities but by our faulty perceptions. For example, suppose you found out that everyone except you is invited to a party. You might easily begin to wonder why you were excluded. Does someone dislike you? Have you offended someone? Such thoughts are typical. However, the reality of the situation may have absolutely nothing to do with your being liked or disliked. Perhaps you were sent an invitation and it didn't get to you.

   —Donatelle, *Access to Health*, p. 81

   Pattern: generalization and example

2. A serious problem with some drugs is **addiction, or drug dependence.** That is, people come to depend on the regular consumption of a drug in order to make it through the day. When people think of **drug addiction,** they are likely to think of addicts huddled in slum doorways, the dregs of society who seldom venture into daylight—unless it is to rob someone. They don't associate addiction with "good," middle-class neighborhoods and "solid citizens." But let's look at drug addiction a little more closely. Although most people may think of heroin as the prime example of an addictive drug, I suggest that nicotine is the better case to consider. I remember a next-door neighbor who stood in his backyard, a lit cigarette in his hand, and told me about the operation in which one of his lungs was removed. I say "I remember," because soon after our conversation he died from his addiction.

   —Henslin, *Social Problems*, p. 93

   Pattern: statement and clarification

3. In short, the view that a drug is good or bad depends not on objective conditions but on subjective concerns. It is a matter of how people define matters. People's definitions, in turn, influence how they use and abuse drugs, whether or not a drug will be legal or illegal, and what social policies they want to adopt. This is the central sociological aspect of drug use and abuse, one that we shall stress over and over in this chapter.

—Henslin, *Social Problems*, p. 91

Pattern: <u>summary</u>

4. Human migration has by no means come to an end. Large-scale migrations still make daily news. The United Nations' Universal Declaration of Human Rights affirms anyone's right to leave his or her homeland to seek a better life elsewhere, but it cannot guarantee that there will be anyplace willing to take anyone. As in the past, the major push and pull factors behind contemporary migration are economic and political. Also, people are trying to move from the poor countries to the rich countries and from the politically repressed countries to more democratic countries. In addition, millions of people are fleeing civil and international warfare. Pressures for migration are growing, and in coming years they may constitute the world's greatest political and economic problem.

—Bergman and Renwick, *Introduction to Geography*, p. 197

Pattern: <u>addition</u>

5. Be careful not to evaluate negatively the cultural differences you perceive. Be careful that you don't fall into the trap of ethnocentric thinking, evaluating your culture positively and other cultures negatively. For example, many Americans of Northern European descent evaluate negatively the tendency of many Hispanics and Southern Europeans to use the street for a gathering place, for playing Dominoes, and for just sitting on a cool evening. Whether you like or dislike using the street in this way, recognize that neither attitude is logically correct or incorrect. This street behavior is simply adequate or inadequate for *members of the culture.*

—DeVito, *Human Communication*, p. 103

Pattern: <u>generalization and example</u>

SUMMING IT UP

Patterns and Transitions

PATTERN	CHARACTERISTICS	TRANSITIONS
Definition	Explains the meaning of a word or phrase	Is, refers to, can be defined as, means, consists of, involves, is a term that, is called, is characterized by, occurs when, are those that, entails, corresponds to, is literally
Classification	Divides a topic into parts based on shared characteristics	Classified as, comprises, is composed of, several varieties of, different stages of, different groups that, includes, one, first, second, another, finally, last
Chronological Order	Describes events, processes, procedures	First, second, later, before, next, as soon as, after, then, finally, meanwhile, following, last, during, in, on, when, until
Process	Describes the order in which things are done or how things work	First, second, next, then, following, after that, last, finally
Order of Importance	Describes ideas in order of priority or preference	Less, more, primary, first, next, last, most important, primarily, secondarily
Spatial Order	Describes physical location or position in space	Above, below, beside, next to, in front of, behind, inside, outside, opposite, within, nearby
Cause and Effect	Describes how one or more things cause or are related to another	*Causes:* because, because of, for, since, stems from, one cause is, one reason is, leads to, causes, creates, yields, produces, due to, breeds, for this reason *Effects:* consequently, results in, one result is, therefore, thus, as a result, hence
Comparison and Contrast	Discusses similarities and/or differences among ideas, theories, concepts, objects, or persons	*Similarities:* both, also, similarly, like, likewise, too, as well as, resembles, correspondingly, in the same way, to compare, in comparison, share

(continued on next page)

(continued from previous page)

PATTERN	CHARACTERISTICS	TRANSITIONS
		Differences: unlike, differs from, in contrast, on the other hand, instead, despite, nevertheless, however, in spite of, whereas, as opposed to
Listing/Enumeration	Organizes lists of information: characteristics, features, parts, or categories	The following, several, for example, for instance, one, another, also, too, in other words, first, second, numerals (1., 2.), letters (a., b.), most important, the largest, the least, finally
Statement and Clarification	Indicates that information explaining an idea or concept will follow	In fact, in other words, clearly, evidently, obviously
Summary	Indicates that a condensed review of an idea or piece of writing is to follow	In summary, in conclusion, in brief, to summarize, to sum up, in short, on the whole
Generalization and Example	Provides examples that clarify a broad, general statement	For example, for instance, that is, to illustrate, thus
Addition	Indicates that additional information will follow	Furthermore, additionally, also, besides, further, in addition, moreover, again

5 Making Inferences

Look at the photograph below, which appeared in a psychology textbook. What do you think is happening here? What is the man's occupation? What are the feelings of the participants?

In order to answer these questions, you had to use any information you could get from the photo and make guesses based on it. The facial expression, body language, clothing, and other objects present in this photo provided clues. This reasoning process is called "making an inference."

5a MAKING INFERENCES FROM THE GIVEN FACTS

An **inference** is a reasoned guess about what you don't know made on the basis of what you do know. Inferences are common in our everyday lives. When you get on an expressway and see a long, slow-moving line of traffic, you might predict that there is an accident or roadwork ahead. When you see a puddle of water under the kitchen sink, you can infer that you have a plumbing problem. The inferences you make may not always be correct, even though you based them on the available information. The water under the sink might have been the result of a spill. The traffic you encountered on the expressway might be normal for that time of day, but you didn't know it because you aren't normally on the road then. An inference is only the best guess you can make in a situation, given the information you have.

> **NOW PRACTICE . . . MAKING INFERENCES 1**

Read each of the following statements. Place a check mark in front of each of the sentences that follow that is a reasonable inference that can be made from the statement.

1. Twice as many couples seek marriage counseling as they did twenty years ago.

   _____ a. There are more married people now than twenty years ago.

   ✓ b. There has been an increased demand for licensed marriage counselors.

   _____ c. Marriage is more legalistic than it used to be.

   ✓ d. Couples are more willing to discuss their differences than they were twenty years ago.

2. More than half of all Americans are overweight.

   ✓ a. Many Americans are at high risk for heart disease.

   ✓ b. Teaching children about nutrition and exercise should be a high priority in public schools.

   _____ c. Americans place great emphasis on appearance.

   ✓ d. The weight-loss industry is an important sector of business.

3. Many courts now permit lawyers to file papers and handle some court work over the Internet.

   _____ a. Courtrooms will no longer be needed.

   ✓ b. Attorneys will be able to check the status of their cases from their home computers.

   ✓ c. Some cases may proceed more quickly now.

   ✓ d. More lawyers will carry laptops.

5b   MAKING INFERENCES FROM WRITTEN MATERIAL

When you read the material associated with your college courses, you need to make inferences frequently. Writers do not always present their ideas directly. Instead, they often leave it to you to add up and think beyond the facts they present. You are expected to reason out or infer the meaning an author intended (but did not say) on the basis of what he or she did say. In a sense, the inferences you make act as bridges between what is said and what is not said, but is meant.

5c   HOW TO MAKE INFERENCES

Each inference you make depends on the situation, the facts provided, and your own knowledge and experience. Here are a few guidelines to help you see beyond the factual level and make solid inferences.

Understand the Literal Meaning

Be sure you have a firm grasp of the literal meaning. You must understand the stated ideas and facts before you can move to higher levels of thinking, which include inference making. You should recognize the topic, main idea, key details, and organizational pattern of each paragraph you have read.

Notice Details

As you are reading, pay particular attention to details that are unusual or stand out. Often such details will offer you clues to help you make inferences. Ask yourself:

- What is unusual or striking about this piece of information?
- Why is it included here?

Read the following excerpt, which is taken from a business marketing textbook, and mark any details that seem unusual or striking.

Marketing in Action

Dressing Up the Basics in Idaho

In almost any grocery store across the United States, consumers can purchase ten pounds of Idaho-grown potatoes for less than $5.00. Despite this fact, Rolland Jones Potatoes, Incorporated, has been extremely successful selling a "baker's dozen" of Idaho potatoes for $18.95. The potatoes are wrapped in a decorative box that uses Easter grass.

The Baker's Dozen of Idaho potatoes is only one example of a growing phenomenon. Laura Hobbs, marketing specialist for the Idaho Department of Agriculture, reports that more than 200 Idaho farms produce specialty or value-added products. These goods typically consist of basic farm commodities that have been "dressed-up" with packaging. Consumers can choose from these products: microwave popcorn that comes on the cob and pops right off the cob, a bag of complete chili ingredients that makers claim won't cause embarrassing side-effects, and chocolate-covered "Couch Potato Chips."

Idaho farmers are supported by two groups, the Idaho Specialty Foods Association and Buy Idaho, whose goals are to help producers market and promote unique items. With the help of the groups, Idaho farmers are getting quite savvy. The marketers have discovered, for example, that packaging certain items together can increase their attractiveness. Hagerman's Rose Creek Winery found that sales of its wines soared when they were packaged in gift baskets with jars of Sun Valley brand mustard.

According to Hobbs, consumers attracted to the unique packaging provide a market for an endless variety of products, all of which are standard commodities transformed into new products through packaging. The value added through the unique packaging also provides opportunities to charge prices in ranges far above the prices of standard products—like $18.95 for 12 potatoes!

—Kinnear, Bernhardt, and Krenther, *Principles of Marketing*, p. 301

Did you mark details such as the price of $18.95 for potatoes, corn that pops right off the cob, and chocolate-covered potato chips?

Add Up the Facts

Consider all of the facts taken together. To help you do this, ask yourself such questions as the following:

- What is the writer trying to suggest from this set of facts?
- What do all these facts and ideas seem to point toward or add up to?
- Why did the author include these facts and details?

Making an inference is somewhat like assembling a complicated jigsaw puzzle; you try to make all the pieces fit together to form a recognizable picture. Answering these questions will require you to add together all the individual pieces of information, which will enable you to arrive at an inference.

When you add up the facts in the article "Dressing Up the Basics in Idaho," you realize that the writer is suggesting that people are willing to pay much more than a product is worth if it is specially packaged.

Be Alert to Clues

Writers often provide you with numerous hints that can point you toward accurate inferences. An awareness of word choices, details included (and omitted), ideas emphasized, and direct commentary can help you determine a textbook author's attitude toward the topic at hand. In the foregoing excerpt, the authors offer clues that reveal their attitude toward increased prices for special packaging. Terms such as *dressed-up* and the exclamation point at the end of the last sentence suggest that the authors realize that the products mentioned are not worth their price.

Consider the Author's Purpose

Also study the author's purpose for writing. If an author's purpose is to convince you to purchase a particular product, as in an advertisement, as you begin reading you already have a clear idea of the types of inferences the writer hopes you will make. For instance, here is a magazine ad for a sound system:

If you're in the market for true surround sound, a prematched system is a good way to get it. The components in our system are built for each other by our audio engineers. You can be assured of high performance and sound quality.

Verify Your Inference

Once you have made an inference, check that it is accurate. Look back at the stated facts to be sure that you have sufficient evidence to support the inference. Also, be certain that you have not overlooked other equally plausible or more plausible inferences that could be drawn from the same set of facts.

▶ NOW PRACTICE . . . MAKING INFERENCES 2

Read each of the following statements. Place a check mark in front of each of the sentences that follow that is a reasonable inference that can be made from the statement.

1. Political candidates must now include the Internet in their campaign plans.
   - ✓ a. Political candidates may host online chats to assess voter opinion.
   - ✓ b. Informal debates between candidates may be conducted online.
   - ____ c. Internet campaigning will drastically increase overall campaign expenditures.
   - ____ d. Television campaigning is likely to remain the same.

2. Half of the public education classrooms in the United States are now hooked up to the Internet.
   - ✓ a. Children are more computer literate than their parents were when they were in school.
   - ✓ b. Students now have access to current world news and happenings.
   - ✓ c. Books are no longer considered the sole source of information on a subject.
   - ____ d. Teachers have become better teachers now that they have Internet access.

3. The Internet can make doctors more efficient through the use of new software and databases that make patient diagnosis more accurate.
   - ____ a. The cost of in-person medical care is likely to decrease.
   - ✓ b. Doctors may be able to identify patients with serious illness sooner.
   - ____ c. Doctors are likely to pay less attention to their patients' descriptions of symptoms.
   - ✓ d. Information on the symptoms and treatment of rare illnesses is more readily available.

> **NOW PRACTICE . . . MAKING INFERENCES 3**

Read each of the following passages. Using inference, determine whether the statements following each passage are true or false. Place a checkmark next to each untrue statement.

1. The United Nations Population Division predicts that by 2025, world population will increase to about 9 billion people. More disturbing, whereas the United Nations earlier predicted that the world population would stabilize at around 10 billion, it has revised its estimate to close to 11 billion, or even as high as 14 billion. These projections have prompted concerns that overpopulation and food scarcity are the principal threats to the planet's future. The United Nations sponsored an International Conference on Population and Development held in Cairo in 1994. There, a World Programme of Action was developed to shift the focus of dismal demographic projections toward concern about a gender-sensitive, humanistic approach to population control.

—Thompson and Hickey, *Society in Focus*, p. 544

_____ a. If the projections are inaccurate, the world community no longer needs to be concerned about overpopulation.

✓ b. Previous approaches to population control have not been gender sensitive.

✓ c. If population increases more rapidly than predicted, there will be even greater food shortages.

_____ d. The United Nations has developed adequate responses to food scarcity.

_____ e. By 2050 world population will have increased to 20 billion.

2. Blowfish is one of the most prized delicacies in the restaurants of Japan. This fish is prized not only for its taste, but for the tingling sensation one gets around the lips when eating it. In blowfish TTX (a neurotoxin) is concentrated in certain organs, including the liver and gonads. Its preparation takes great skill and can only be done by licensed chefs who are skilled at removing the poison-containing organs without crushing them, which can lead to contamination of normally edible parts. The toxin cannot be destroyed by cooking. Lore has it that the most skilled chefs intentionally leave a bit of the poison in, so that diners can enjoy the tingling sensation caused by blockage of nerve signals from the sense receptors on the lips.

—Germann and Stanfield, adapted from *Principles of Human Physiology*, p. 185

✓ a. TTX has potentially dangerous consequences.

_____ b. The United States has strict rules about the preparation of blowfish.

✓ c. Japanese diners enjoy blowfish partly because of the sense of danger involved.

_____✓_____ d. TTX causes blockage of signals from nerves.

_____ e. Blowfish is always unsafe to eat.

3. Through your parents, teachers, and the media, your culture instills in you a variety of beliefs, values, and attitudes—about success (how you define it and how you should achieve it); the relevance of a person's religion, race, or nationality; the ethical principles you should follow in business and in your personal life. These teachings provide benchmarks against which you can measure yourself. Your ability to, for example, achieve what your culture defines as success, will contribute to a positive self-concept. Your failure to achieve what your culture teaches (for example, not being married by the time you're thirty) will contribute to a negative self-concept.

—DeVito, *Essentials of Human Communication*, pp. 36–37

_____✓_____ a. People with positive self-concepts often have achieved their culture's notion of success.

_____ b. Most cultures do not believe that race or religion are relevant.

_____ c. People often ignore their culture's beliefs about ethical principles.

_____✓_____ d. Self-concept is affected by both success and failure.

_____ e. Your self-concept can never change.

▶ NOW PRACTICE . . . MAKING INFERENCES 4

Read the following paragraph. A number of statements follow it; each statement is an inference. Label each inference as either:

PA—Probably accurate—there is substantial evidence in the paragraph to support the statement.

IE—Insufficient evidence—there is little or no evidence in the paragraph to support the statement.

A. While working for a wholesale firm, traveling to country stores by horse and buggy, Aaron Montgomery Ward conceived the idea of selling directly to country people by mail. He opened his business in 1872 with a one-page list of items that cost one dollar each. People could later order goods through a distributed catalog and the store would ship the merchandise cash on delivery (COD). The idea was slow to catch on because people were suspicious of a strange name. However, in 1875 Ward announced the startling policy of "satisfaction guaranteed or your money back." Contrasting with the former retailing principle of caveat emptor (Latin for "buyer beware"), this policy set off a boom in Ward's business.

—Frings, *Fashion: From Concepts to Consumer*, p. 11

_PA_   1. Aaron Ward had experience in sales before he began his own business.

_IE_   2. Country people were targeted because they do not have access to stores in cities.

_IE_   3. Ward's mistake was to give every item on the list the same price.

_PA_   4. Other stores in operation at the time did not offer money back guarantees.

_IE_   5. Other mail order businesses quickly followed Ward's success.

B. Artist Georgia O'Keefe was born in Sun Prairie, Wisconsin, and spent her childhood on her family's farm. While in high school, she had a memorable experience that gave her a new perspective on the art-making process. As she passed the door to the art room, O'Keefe stopped to watch as a teacher held up a jack-in-the-pulpit plant so that the students could appreciate its unusual shapes and subtle colors. Although O'Keefe had enjoyed flowers in the marshes and meadows of Wisconsin, she had done all of her drawing and painting from plaster casts or had copied them from photographs or reproductions. This was the first time she realized that one could draw and paint from real life. Twenty-five years later she produced a powerful series of paintings based on flowers.

—adapted from Preble and Preble, *Artforms*, p. 34

_PA_   6. O'Keefe's artistic style was influenced by her high-school art teacher.

_IE_   7. O'Keefe's paintings from plaster casts were unsuccessful.

_PA_   8. O'Keefe was deeply influenced by nature.

_IE_   9. O'Keefe was not influenced by modern art.

_IE_   10. O'Keefe never copied flowers from other paintings.

> ## NOW PRACTICE . . . MAKING INFERENCES 5

Read the following paragraphs and the statements following them. Place a check mark next to statements that are reasonable inferences.

August Vollmer was the chief of police of Berkeley, California, from 1905 to 1932. Vollmer's vision of policing was quite different from most of his contemporaries. He believed the police should be a "dedicated body of educated persons comprising a distinctive corporate entity with a prescribed code of behavior." He was critical of his contemporaries and they of him. San Francisco police administrator Charley Dullea, who later became president of the International Association of Chiefs of Police, refused to drive through Berkeley in protest against Vollmer. Fellow California police chiefs may have felt their opposition to Vollmer was justified, given his vocal and strong criticism of other California police departments. For example, Vollmer publicly referred to San Francisco cops as "morons," and in an interview with a newspaper reporter, he called Los Angeles cops "low grade mental defectives."

Because of his emphasis on education, professionalism, and administrative reform, Vollmer often is seen as the counterpart of London's Sir Robert Peel and is sometimes called the "father of modern American policing." Vollmer was decades ahead of his contemporaries, but he was not able to implement significant change in policing during his lifetime. It remained for Vollmer's students to implement change. For example, O.W. Wilson, who became chief of police of Chicago, promoted college education for police officers and wrote a book on police administration that reflected many of Vollmer's philosophies. It was adopted widely by police executives and used as a college textbook well into the 1960s.

Vollmer is credited with a number of innovations. He was an early adopter of the automobile for patrol and the use of radios in police cars. He recruited college-educated police officers. He developed and implemented a 3-year training curriculum for police officers, including classes in physics, chemistry, biology, physiology, anatomy, psychology, psychiatry, anthropology, and criminology. He developed a system of signal boxes for hailing police officers. He adopted the use of typewriters to fill out police reports and records, and officers received training in typing. He surveyed other police departments to gather information about their practices. Many of his initiatives have become common practice within contemporary police departments.

—Fagin, *Criminal Justice,* p. 195

_____ a. Vollmer did not have a college degree.

___✓___ b. Most police officers of Vollmer's time had limited educations.

___✓___ c. Vollmer believed police should be held accountable for their actions.

___✓___ d. Sir Robert Peel dramatically changed policing procedures in England.

_____ e. Vollmer received support from most police officers on the street.

___✓___ f. Vollmer would support technological advances in policing.

_____ g. Police departments of Vollmer's time were run with a careful eye toward accuracy.

_____ h. Vollmer outlawed billy clubs.

6 Critical Reading

In college you will be reading many new kinds of material: research articles, essays, critiques, reports, and analyses. Your instructors expect you to be able to do much more than understand and remember the basic content. They often demand that you read critically, interpreting, evaluating, and reacting to assigned readings. Specifically, an instructor may expect you to do all of the things listed above. To meet these expectations, you'll need to distinguish facts from opinions, identify the author's purpose, recognize the author's tone, detect bias, evaluate data and evidence, understand connotative language, and interpret figurative language.

6a IS THE MATERIAL FACT OR OPINION?

When working with any source, try to determine whether the material is factual or an expression of opinion. **Facts** are statements that can be verified—that is, proven to be true or false. **Opinions** are statements that express feelings, attitudes, or beliefs and are neither true nor false. Below are examples of each:

Facts

1. More than one million teenagers become pregnant every year.
2. The costs of medical care increase every year.

Opinions

1. Government regulation of our private lives should be halted immediately.
2. By the year 2025, most Americans will not be able to afford routine health care.

Facts, once verified or taken from a reputable source, can be accepted and regarded as reliable information. Opinions, on the other hand, are not reliable sources of information and should be questioned and carefully evaluated. Look for evidence that supports the opinion and indicates that it is reasonable. For example, opinion 2 above is written to sound like a fact, but look closely. What basis does the author have for making that statement?

Some authors are careful to signal the reader when they are presenting an opinion. Watch for words and phrases such as:

Apparently	This suggests	In my view
One explanation is	Presumably	Possibly
It is likely that	According to	In my opinion
It is believed that	Seemingly	

In the following excerpt from a social problems textbook, notice how the author carefully distinguishes factual statements from opinion using qualifying words and phrases (shown here underlined).

Economic Change, Ideology, and Private Life

It seems clear that there has been a major change in attitudes and feelings about family relationships since the eighteenth century. It is less clear how and why the change came about. One question debated by researchers is: In what social class did the new family pattern originate—in the aristocracy, as Trumbach (1978) believes, or in the upper gentry, as Stone (1977) argued, or in the working class, as Shorter (1975) contended? Or was the rise of the new domesticity a cultural phenomenon that affected people in all social categories at roughly the same time? Carole Shammas (1980) has found evidence of such a widespread cultural change by looking at the kinds of things people had in their homes at various times in the past, as recorded in probate inventories. She found that in the middle of the eighteenth century all social classes experienced a change in living habits; even working-class households now contained expensive tools of domesticity, such as crockery, teapots, eating utensils, and so on. Thus, according to Shammas, the home was becoming an important center for social interaction, and family meals had come to occupy an important place in people's lives.

—Skolnick, *The Intimate Environment: Exploring Marriage and the Family*, p. 96

Other authors do just the opposite; they try to make opinions sound like facts, as in opinion 2 above, or they mix fact and opinion without making clear distinctions. This is particularly true in the case of *expert opinion,* which is the opinion of an authority. Ralph Nader represents expert opinion on consumer rights, for example. Textbook authors, too, often offer expert opinion, as in the following statement from an American government text.

Ours is a complex system of justice. Sitting at the pinnacle of the judicial system is the Supreme Court, but its importance is often exaggerated.

—Lineberry, *Government in America*, p. 540

The author of this statement has reviewed the available evidence and is providing his expert opinion as to what the evidence indicates about the Supreme Court. The reader, then, is free to disagree and offer evidence to support an opposing view.

The article, "Animal Emotions," reprinted in Chapter 1, contains numerous examples of expert opinion, as well. The opinions of Bekoff, Panksepp, and Goodall, experts in their fields, are given as evidence that animals do have emotions.

➤ NOW PRACTICE . . . DISTINGUISHING FACT AND OPINION 1

Read each of the following statements and identify whether it is fact (F), opinion (O), or expert opinion (EO).

___F___   1. United Parcel Service (UPS) is the nation's largest delivery service.

___O___   2. United Parcel Service will become even more successful because it uses sophisticated management techniques.

___F___   3. Americans spend $13.7 billion per year on alternative medicine.

___O___   4. The best way to keep up with world news is to read the newspaper.

___EO___ 5. A community, as defined by sociologists, is a collection of people who share some purpose, activity, or characteristic.

___F___   6. The Bill of Rights comprises the first ten amendments to the Constitution.

___EO___ 7. Archaeologists believe that the stone monument known as Stonehenge was built to serve a religious purpose.

___EO___ 8. According to Dr. Richard Sobol, a communication specialist, conflict in interpersonal relationships is not only inevitable, it can also be beneficial.

___O___   9. The finest examples of landscape photography can be found in the work of Ansel Adams.

___F___ 10. The symbol of Islam—a crescent and star—appears on the flags of nations that have a Muslim majority, such as Turkey and Pakistan.

➤ NOW PRACTICE . . . DISTINGUISHING FACT AND OPINION 2

Each of the following paragraphs contains both fact and opinion. Read each paragraph and label each sentence as fact, opinion, or expert opinion.

A. 1. Almost half of all Americans drink coffee every day, making it the most widely consumed drug in the United States. 2. Some people believe its popularity can be explained by the "wake-up" effect of caffeine, a critical element of many people's morning ritual. 3. A five-ounce cup of coffee contains between 65 and 115 milligrams of caffeine, depending on the brand of coffee and the strength of the brew. 4. In addition to enhancing mental alertness and reducing fatigue, the stimulant effects of caffeine include increases in urinary output, insomnia, irregular heartbeat, and indigestion. 5. Apparently, these rather unpleasant side effects are not enough to deter millions of Americans from their daily caffeine "fix."

—adapted from Donatelle, *Health: The Basics*, p. 215

Sentences: 1. ___fact___ 2. ___opinion___ 3. ___fact___ 4. ___fact___ 5. ___opinion___

B. 1. Harriet Tubman was born a slave in Maryland in 1820 and escaped to Philadelphia in 1849. 2. Her own escape presumably required tremendous courage, but that was just the beginning. 3. Through her work on the Underground Railroad, Harriet Tubman led more than 300 slaves to freedom. 4. During the Civil War, Tubman continued her efforts toward the abolition of slavery by working as a nurse and a spy for the Union forces. 5. Today, Americans of all races consider Harriet Tubman one of the most heroic figures in our country's history.

Sentences: 1. ___fact___ 2. ___opinion___ 3. ___fact___ 4. ___fact___ 5. ___opinion___

C. 1. Smokeless tobacco is used by approximately 5 million U.S. adults, most of whom are young males. 2. One explanation for the popularity of smokeless tobacco among young men is that they are emulating professional athletes who chew tobacco or use snuff. 3. In any major league baseball game, more than a few players with chewing tobacco bulging in their cheeks apparently believe the myth that smokeless tobacco is less harmful than cigarettes. 4. In reality, smokeless tobacco contains 10 times the amount of cancer-producing substances found in cigarettes and 100 times more than the Food and Drug Administration allows in foods and other substances used by the public. 5. Smokeless tobacco has been banned from minor league baseball, a move that should be extended to all professional sports to help discourage the use of smokeless tobacco products.

—adapted from Donatelle, *Access to Health*, pp. 372–373

Sentences: 1. ___fact___ 2. ___opinion___ 3. ___opinion___ 4. ___fact___ 5. ___opinion___

D. 1. Managed care plans have agreements with certain physicians, hospitals, and health care providers to give a range of services to plan members at a reduced cost. 2. There are three basic types of managed care plans: health maintenance organizations (HMOs), point-of-service plans (POSs), and preferred provider organizations (PPOs). 3. The PPO, in my opinion, is the best type of managed care plan because it merges the best features of traditional health insurance and HMOs. 4. As in traditional plans, participants in a PPO pay premiums, deductibles, and co-payments, but the co-pay under a PPO is lower (10 percent or less compared to the 20 percent co-pay under a traditional plan). 5. The best part of a PPO, though, is its flexibility: participants may choose their physicians and services from a list of preferred providers, or they may go outside the plan for care if they wish.

—adapted from Pruitt and Stein, *HealthStyles*, pp. 572–573

Sentences: 1. ___fact___ 2. ___fact___ 3. ___opinion___ 4. ___fact___ 5. ___opinion___

E. 1. Some sociologists believe that if any nation deserves the "pro-family" label, it is Sweden. 2. The typical Swedish family today consists of two working parents, with the majority of women working part-time and more than 90 percent of men working full-time. 3. To support women's and men's dual roles in the family and work, the state has devised a benefit package that *all* families receive, regardless of class or income. 4. Benefits include public-supported child care, parental leave insurance for both men and women, a basic child allowance per year of around $900, and a housing allowance that is based on income and number of children in the family. 5. Despite deficiencies (for example, women occupy only 5 percent of upper management positions), the way Sweden combines family and employment appears to be far superior to the situations in most other countries.

—adapted from Thompson and Hickey, *Society in Focus*, p. 364

Sentences: 1. ___expert opinion___ 2. ___fact___ 3. ___fact___ 4. ___fact___
          5. ___opinion___

<table>
<tr><td>6b</td><td></td></tr>
</table>

WHAT IS THE AUTHOR'S PURPOSE?

Writers have many different reasons or purposes for writing. Read the following statements and try to decide why each was written:

1. About 14,000 ocean-going ships pass through the Panama Canal each year. This averages to about three ships per day.
2. *New Unsalted Dry Roasted Almonds.* Finally, a snack with a natural flavor and without salt. We simply shell the nuts and dry-roast them until they're crispy and crunchy. Try a jar this week.
3. Man is the only animal that blushes. Or needs to. (Mark Twain)
4. If a choking person has fallen down, first turn him or her face up. Then knit together the fingers of both your hands and apply pressure with the heel of your bottom hand to the victim's abdomen.
5. If your boat capsizes, it is usually safer to cling to the boat than to try to swim ashore.

Statement 1 was written to give information, 2 to persuade you to buy almonds, 3 to amuse you and make a comment on human behavior, 4 to explain, and 5 to give advice.

In each of the examples, the writer's purpose is fairly clear, as it is in most textbooks (to present information), newspaper articles (to communicate daily events), and reference books (to compile facts). However, in many other types of writing, authors have varied, sometimes less obvious, purposes. In these cases, an author's purpose must be inferred.

Often a writer's purpose is to express an opinion indirectly. The writer may also want to encourage the reader to think about a particular issue or problem. Writers achieve their purposes by manipulating and controlling what they say and how they say it.

Writers may vary their styles to suit their intended audiences. A writer may write for a general-interest audience (anyone who is interested in the subject but is not considered an expert). Most newspapers and periodicals, such as *Time* and *Newsweek,* appeal to a general-interest audience. The article "Animal Emotions," reprinted from *U.S. News & World Report,* seems to be written for the general public. It does not assume the readers have a scientific background and it mentions household pets, something the general public is familiar with.

On the other hand, a writer may have a particular interest group in mind. A writer may write for medical doctors in the *Journal of American Medicine,* for skiing enthusiasts in *Skiing Today,* or for antique collectors in *The World of Antiques.* A writer may also target his or her writing to an audience with particular political, moral, or religious attitudes. Articles in the *New Republic* often appeal to those interested in a particular political viewpoint, whereas articles in the *Catholic Digest* appeal to a specific religious group.

Depending on the group of people for whom the author is writing, he or she will change the level of language, choice of words, and method of presentation. One step toward identifying an author's purpose, then, is to ask yourself the question: Who is the intended audience? Your response will be your first clue to determining why the author wrote the article.

▶ NOW PRACTICE . . . IDENTIFYING THE AUTHOR'S PURPOSE 1

Read each of the following statements, find the author's purpose for each statement in the box below, and write it in the space provided.

to persuade	to entertain	to inform
to advise	to criticize	

<u>to advise</u>   1. If you are looking for specialized information on the Internet, the best approach is to use a metasearch engine such as ProFusion.

<u>to entertain</u>   2. Good judgment comes from experience, and a lot of that comes from bad judgment. (Will Rogers)

<u>to inform</u>   3. The Constitution of the United States prescribes a separation of powers among the executive, legislative, and judicial branches of government.

<u>to persuade</u>   4. Members of the art gallery enjoy benefits such as free admission and discounts on special gallery exhibits.

<u>to criticize</u>   5. The governor's ill-advised plan to attach a "sin tax" to sales of tobacco and alcohol can only have a negative effect on tourism in our state.

➤ NOW PRACTICE . . . IDENTIFYING THE AUTHOR'S PURPOSE 2

Read each of the following statements and identify the author's purpose. Write a sentence that describes the intended audience.

1. Chances are you're going to be putting money away over the next five years or so. You are hoping for the right things in life. Right now, a smart place to put your money is in mutual funds or bonds.

   <u>This was written for people with enough income to invest money.</u>

   _____

2. Think about all the places your drinking water has been before you drink another drop. Most likely it has been chemically treated to remove bacteria and chemical pollutants. Soon you may begin to feel the side effects of these treatments. Consider switching to filtered, distilled water today.

   <u>This was written for environmentally conscious people who are concerned</u>

   <u>about their health.</u>

3. Introducing the new, high-powered Supertuner III, a sound system guaranteed to keep your mother out of your car.

   <u>This was written for teenagers who own cars.</u>

   _____

4. Bright and White laundry detergent removes dirt and stains faster than any other brand.

   <u>This is intended for people who do laundry.</u>

   _____

5. As a driver, you're ahead if you can learn to spot car trouble before it's too late. If you can learn the difference between drips and squeaks that occur under normal conditions and those that mean that big trouble is just down the road, then you'll be ahead of expensive repair bills and won't find yourself stranded on a lonely road.

This is intended for car owners who are unfamiliar with a car's trouble signs

and maintenance.

6c   WHAT IS THE TONE?

The tone of a speaker's voice helps you interpret what he or she is saying. If the following sentence were read aloud, the speaker's voice would tell you how to interpret it: "Would you mind closing the door?" In print you cannot tell whether the speaker is polite, insistent, or angry. In speech you could tell by whether the speaker emphasized the word _would, mind,_ or _door._

Just as a speaker's tone of voice tells how the speaker feels, a writer conveys a tone, or feeling, through his or her writing. **Tone** refers to the attitude or feeling a writer expresses about his or her subject. The tone of the article "Animal Emotions" is informative. The author presents informed opinion and other evidence to support her thesis that animals do have emotions.

A writer may adopt a sentimental tone, an angry tone, a humorous tone, a sympathetic tone, an instructive tone, a persuasive tone, and so forth. Here are a few examples of different tones. How does each make you feel?

■ **Instructive**

> When purchasing a piece of clothing, one must be concerned with quality as well as with price. Be certain to check for the following: double-stitched seams, matched patterns, and ample linings.

■ **Sympathetic**

> The forlorn, frightened-looking child wandered through the streets alone, searching for someone who would show an interest in helping her find her parents.

■ **Persuasive**

> Child abuse is a tragic occurrence in our society. Strong legislation is needed to control the abuse of innocent victims and to punish those who are insensitive to the rights and feelings of others.

■ **Humorous**

> Those people who study animal behavior professionally must dread those times when their cover is blown at a dinner party. The unfortunate souls are sure to be seated next to someone with animal stories. The conversation will invariably be about some pet that did this or that, and nonsense is the *polite* word for it. The worst stories are about cats. The proud owners like to talk about their ingenuity, what they are thinking, and how they "miss" them while they're at the party. Those cats would rub the leg of a burglar if he rattled the Friskies box. (Marge Thielman Hastreiter, "Not Every Mother Is Glad Kids Are Back in School." *Buffalo Evening News,* 1991)

■ **Nostalgic**

> Things change, times change, but when school starts, my little granddaughter will run up the same wooden stairs that creaked for all of the previous generations and I will still hate it when the summer ends. (Hastreiter)

In the first example, the writer offers advice in a straightforward, informative style. In the second, the writer wants you to feel sorry for the child. This is accomplished through description. In the third example, the writer tries to convince the reader that action must be taken to prevent child abuse. The use of such words as *tragic, innocent,* and *insensitive* establish this tone.

To identify an author's tone, pay particular attention to descriptive language and shades of meaning. Ask yourself: "How does the author feel about his or her subject and how are these feelings revealed?" It is sometimes difficult to find the right word to describe the author's tone. Table 6.1 lists words that are often used to describe the tone of a piece of writing. Use this list to provoke your thinking when identifying tone. If any of these words are unfamiliar, be sure to check their meanings in a dictionary.

▶ NOW PRACTICE . . . RECOGNIZING TONE 1

Read each of the following statements, choose a word from the box that describes the tone it illustrates, and write it in the space provided.

optimistic	angry	admiring	cynical/bitter
excited	humorous	nostalgic	disapproving
formal	informative	sarcastic	

<u>disapproving</u>   1. Taking a young child to a PG-13 movie is inappropriate and shows poor judgment on the part of the parents.

<u>informative</u>   2. The brown recluse spider has a dark, violin-shaped marking on the upper section of its body.

<u>admiring</u>   3. The dedication and determination of the young men and women participating in the Special Olympics were an inspiration to everyone there.

<u>nostalgic</u>   4. The first tomato of the summer always makes me think fondly of my grandfather's garden.

<u>humorous</u>   5. Nobody is ever a complete failure; he or she can always serve as a bad example.

<u>sarcastic</u>   6. The councilman once again demonstrated his sensitivity toward the environment when he voted to allow commercial development in an area set aside as a nature preserve.

<u>optimistic</u>   7. The success of the company's youth mentoring program will inspire other business groups to establish similar programs.

<u>cynical/bitter</u>   8. Professional athletes have no loyalty toward their teams or their fans anymore, just their own wallets.

<u>excited</u>   9. We were thrilled to learn that next year's convention will be held in San Antonio—we've always wanted to see the Alamo!

<u>formal</u>   10. To be considered for the president's student-of-the-year award, an individual must demonstrate academic excellence as well as outstanding community service, and the individual must furnish no fewer than four letters of reference from faculty members.

▶ **NOW PRACTICE . . . RECOGNIZING TONE 2**

Read each of the following statements, paying particular attention to the tone. Then write a sentence that describes the tone. Prove your point by listing some of the words that reveal the author's feelings.

1. No one says that nuclear power is risk-free. There are risks involved in all methods of producing energy. However, the scientific evidence is clear and obvious. Nuclear power is at least as safe as any other means used to generate electricity.

   The tone of this statement seems logical and persuasive.

   words: scientific evidence, clear and obvious, at least as safe as

2. The condition of our city streets is outrageous. The sidewalks are littered with paper and other garbage—you could trip while walking to the store. The streets themselves are in even worse condition. Deep potholes and crumbling curbs make it unsafe to drive. Where are our city tax dollars going if not to correct these problems?

The author of this statement is angry and disturbed.

words: outrageous, littered, unsafe, problems

3. I am a tired American. I am tired of watching criminals walk free while they wait for their day in court. I'm tired of hearing about victims getting hassled as much or more than criminals. I'm tired of reading about courts of law that even accept a lawsuit in which a criminal sues his or her intended victim.

The author of this statement seems disgusted with the legal system.

words: tired, victims, hassled

4. Cross-country skis have heel plates of different shapes and materials. They may be made of metal, plastic, or rubber. Be sure that they are tacked on the ski right where the heel of your boot will fall. They will keep snow from collecting under your foot and offer some stability.

This statement is intended to be instructive.

words: different shapes and materials, Be sure that, on the ski right where

5. In July of 1986 my daughter, Lucy, was born with an underdeveloped brain. She was a beautiful little girl—at least to me and my husband—but her disabilities were severe. By the time she was two weeks old we knew that she would never walk, talk, feed herself, or even understand the concept of mother and father. It's impossible to describe the effect that her five-and-a-half-month life had on us; suffice it to say that she was the purest experience of love and pain that we will ever have, that she changed us forever, and that we will never cease to mourn her death, even though we know that for her it was a triumphant passing.

—Armstrong, "The Choices We Made," p. 165

The tone of this statement is one of deep emotion, conveying a feeling of

tragedy and sorrow.

words: beautiful little girl, impossible to describe the effect, changed us

TABLE 6.1 WORDS FREQUENTLY USED TO DESCRIBE TONE

abstract	condemning	formal	joyful	reverent
absurd	condescending	frustrated	loving	righteous
amused	cynical	gentle	malicious	sarcastic
angry	depressing	grim	melancholic	satiric
apathetic	detached	hateful	mocking	sensational
arrogant	disapproving	humorous	nostalgic	serious
assertive	distressed	impassioned	objective	solemn
awestruck	docile	incredulous	obsequious	sympathetic
bitter	earnest	indignant	optimistic	tragic
caustic	excited	indirect	outraged	uncomfortable
celebratory	fanciful	informative	pathetic	vindictive
cheerful	farcical	intimate	persuasive	worried
comic	flippant	ironic	pessimistic	
compassionate	forgiving	irreverent	playful	

6d   IS THE AUTHOR BIASED?

Bias refers to an author's partiality, inclination toward a particular viewpoint, or prejudice. A writer is biased if he or she takes one side of a controversial issue and does not recognize opposing viewpoints. Perhaps the best example of bias is in advertising. A magazine advertisement for a new car model, for instance, describes only positive, marketable features—the ad does not recognize the car's limitations or faults. In some material the writer is direct and outright in expressing his or her bias; other times the bias is hidden and left for the reader to discover through careful analysis.

Read the following description of the environmental protection group Greenpeace. The author expresses a favorable attitude toward the organization and a negative one toward whale hunters. Notice, in particular, the <u>underlined</u> words and phrases.

Greenpeace is an organization <u>dedicated</u> to the preservation of the sea and its great mammals, notably whales, dolphins, and seals. Its ethic is <u>nonviolent</u> but its aggressiveness in <u>protecting</u> our oceans and the life in them is becoming <u>legendary.</u> In their roving ship, the *Rainbow Warrior,* Greenpeace volunteers have <u>relentlessly hounded</u> the <u>profiteering</u> ships of any nation harming the resources Greenpeace deems to be the property of the world community. Whales, they believe, belong to us all and have a right to exist no matter what the demand for shoe-horns, cosmetics, and machine oil.

—Wallace, *Biology: The World of Life,* p. 518

To identify bias, use the following suggestions:

1. **Analyze connotative meanings.** Do you encounter a large number of positive or negative terms used to describe the subject?
2. **Notice descriptive language.** What impression is created?
3. **Analyze the tone.** The author's tone often provides important clues.
4. **Look for opposing viewpoints.**

▶ NOW PRACTICE . . . DETECTING BIAS 1

Read each of the following statements, and place a check mark in front of each one that reveals bias.

✓ 1. Testing the harmful effects of cosmetics on innocent animals is an outrage.

___ 2. Judaism, Christianity, and Islam share a common belief in an all-powerful creator.

✓ 3. One of Shakespeare's wittiest and most delightful romantic comedies is *The Taming of the Shrew*.

___ 4. Each fall, thousands of greater sandhill cranes leave their nesting grounds in Idaho and fly south to the Rio Grande.

___ 5. A laissez-faire policy asserts that businesses should be able to charge whatever they want for their goods and services without interference from the government.

✓ 6. Campaign finance reform is essential to restoring both the integrity of the election process and the faith of Americans in our political system.

___ 7. The longest siege of the Civil War took place in Petersburg, Virginia, when Union troops blocked Confederate supply lines from June 1864 to April 1865.

✓ 8. Students should not waste their time joining fraternities and sororities; they should concentrate on their academic coursework.

✓ 9. Bicycling is the only way to fully experience the beautiful scenery of southern France.

___ 10. The hardware in a computer system includes the physical system itself, which may consist of a keyboard, a monitor, a central processing unit (CPU), and a printer.

▶ NOW PRACTICE . . . DETECTING BIAS 2

Read the following passage and underline words and phrases that reveal the author's bias.

Not unlike drugs or alcohol, the television experience allows the participant to blot out the real world and enter into a pleasurable and passive mental state. The worries and anxieties of reality are as effectively deferred by becoming absorbed in a television program as by going on a "trip" induced by drugs or alcohol. And just as alcoholics are only inchoately aware of their addiction, feeling that they control their drinking more than they really do ("I can cut it out any time I want—I just like to have three or four drinks before dinner"), people similarly overestimate their control over television watching. Even as they put off other activities to spend hour after hour watching television, they feel they could easily resume living in a different, less passive style. But somehow or other while the television set is present in their homes, the click doesn't sound. With television pleasures available, those other experiences seem less attractive, more difficult somehow.

—Winn, *The Plug-In Drug*

6e HOW STRONG ARE THE DATA AND EVIDENCE?

Many writers who express their opinions or state viewpoints provide the reader with data or evidence to support their ideas. Your task as a critical reader is to weigh and evaluate the quality of this evidence. You must examine the evidence and assess its adequacy. You should be concerned with two factors: the type of evidence being presented, and the relevance of that evidence. Various types of evidence include:

- personal experience or observation
- expert opinion
- research citation
- statistical data
- examples, descriptions of particular events, or illustrative situations
- analogies (comparisons with similar situations)
- historical documentation

Each type of evidence must be weighed in relation to the statement it supports. Acceptable evidence should directly, clearly, and indisputably support the case or issue in question.

▶ NOW PRACTICE . . . EVALUATING DATA AND EVIDENCE

Refer to the article "Animal Emotions" on page 9. For each of the following paragraphs, identify the type(s) of evidence the author provides.

1. Paragraph 1 examples
2. Paragraph 7 expert opinion

3. Paragraph 10 examples, expert opinion _____

4. Paragraph 14 research citation _____

5. Paragraph 15 expert opinion _____

6f   HOW IS CONNOTATIVE LANGUAGE USED?

Which of the following would you like to be a part of: a crowd, mob, gang, audience, congregation, or class? Each of these words has the same basic meaning: "an assembled group of people." But each has a different *shade* of meaning. *Crowd* suggests a large, disorganized group. *Audience,* on the other hand, suggests a quiet, controlled group. Try to decide what meaning each of the other words in the list suggests.

This example shows that words have two levels of meanings—a literal meaning and an additional shade of meaning. These two levels of meaning are called denotative and connotative. A word's **denotative meaning** is the meaning stated in the dictionary—its literal meaning. A word's **connotative meaning** is the additional implied meanings, or nuances, that a word may take on. Often the connotative meaning carries either a positive or negative, favorable or unfavorable impression. The words *mob* and *gang* have a negative connotation because they imply a disorderly, disorganized group. *Congregation, audience,* and *class* have a positive connotation because they suggest an orderly, organized group.

Here are a few more examples. Would you prefer to be described as "slim" or "skinny"? As "intelligent" or "brainy"? As "heavy" or "fat"? As "particular" or "picky"? Notice that each pair of words has a similar literal meaning, but that each word within the pair has a different connotation.

Depending on the words they choose, writers can suggest favorable or unfavorable impressions of the person, object, or event they are describing. For example, through the writer's choice of words, the two sentences below create two entirely different impressions. As you read them, notice the underlined words that have a positive or negative connotation.

> The <u>unruly</u> crowd <u>forced</u> its way through the restraint barriers and <u>ruthlessly attacked</u> the rock star.
>
> The <u>enthusiastic</u> group of fans <u>burst</u> through the fence and <u>rushed</u> toward the rock star.

When reading any type of informative or persuasive material, pay attention to the writer's choice of words. Often a writer may communicate subtle or hidden messages, or he or she may encourage the reader to have positive or negative feelings toward the subject.

▶ **NOW PRACTICE . . . USING CONNOTATIVE LANGUAGE 1**

For each of the following pairs of words, underline the word with the more positive connotation.

1. <u>request</u>   demand

2. <u>overlook</u>   neglect

3. ridicule   <u>tease</u>

4. <u>display</u>   expose

5. garment   <u>gown</u>

6. gaudy   <u>showy</u>

7. <u>artificial</u>   fake

8. <u>costly</u>   extravagant

9. <u>choosy</u>   picky

10. sieze   <u>take</u>

▶ **NOW PRACTICE . . . USING CONNOTATIVE LANGUAGE 2**

For each of the following sentences, underline the word in parentheses that has the more appropriate connotative meaning. Consult a dictionary, if necessary.

1. The new superintendent spoke (<u>extensively</u> / enormously) about the issues facing the school system.

2. The day after we hiked ten miles, my legs felt extremely (rigid / <u>stiff</u>).

3. Carlos thought that he could be more (<u>productive</u> / fruitful) if he had a home office.

4. The (stubborn / <u>persistent</u>) ringing of the telephone finally woke me up.

5. The investment seemed too (perilous / <u>risky</u>) so we decided against it.

6g   HOW IS FIGURATIVE LANGUAGE USED?

Figurative language is a way of describing something that makes sense on an imaginative level but not on a literal or factual level. Many common expressions are figurative:

The exam was a piece of cake.

Sam eats like a horse.

He walks like a gazelle.

In each of these expressions, two unlike objects are compared on the basis of some quality they have in common. Take, for example, Hamlet's statement "I will speak daggers to her, but use none." Here the poet is comparing the features of daggers (sharp, pointed, dangerous, harmful) with something that can be used like daggers—words.

Figurative language is striking, often surprising, even shocking. This reaction is created by the unlikeness of the two objects being compared. To find the similarity and understand the figurative expression, focus on connotative meanings rather than literal meanings. For example, in reading the lines

A sea

Harsher than granite

from an Ezra Pound poem, you must think not only of rock or stone but also of the characteristics of granite: hardness, toughness, impermeability. Then you can see that the lines mean that the sea is rough and resistant. Figurative words, which are also called figures of speech, are used to communicate and emphasize relationships that cannot be communicated through literal meaning. For example, the statement by Jonathan Swift, "She wears her clothes as if they were thrown on by a pitchfork," creates a stronger image and conveys a more meaningful description than saying "She dressed sloppily."

The three most common types of figurative expressions are similes, metaphors, and symbols. Similes make the comparison explicit by using the word *like* or *as*. Metaphors, on the other hand, directly equate the two objects. Here are several examples of each.

■ **Similes**

We lie back to back.
Curtains lift and fall,
like the chest of someone sleeping.

—Kenyon

Life, like a dome of many-colored glass,
stains the white radiance of Eternity.

—Shelley

■ **Metaphors**

> My Life has stood—a Loaded Gun—
> In Corners—till a Day
> The Owner passed—identified—
> And carried Me away—
>
> > —Emily Dickinson
>
>
> ...his hair lengthened into sunbeams ...
>
> > —Gustave Flaubert

▶ NOW PRACTICE . . . USING FIGURATIVE LANGUAGE 1

Each of the following sentences uses figurative language. For each figurative expression, circle the choice that best explains its meaning.

___a___ 1. Craig looked <u>like a deer caught by headlights</u> when I found him eating the last piece of pie.

    a. startled into immobility

    b. worried he would be injured

    c. comfortable in the spotlight

    d. ready to be admired

___b___ 2. Rosa was <u>walking on air</u> after she learned that she had made the dean's list.

    a. hurrying

    b. happy and lighthearted

    c. unable to get her footing

    d. numb

___c___ 3. Throughout my grandmother's life, her church has been her <u>rock</u>.

    a. hard

    b. unfeeling

    c. source of strength

    d. heavy weight

___d___ 4. Our computer is <u>a dinosaur</u>.

    a. very large

    b. frightening

    c. unique

    d. outdated

_b_ __ 5 The food at the sales meeting tasted <u>like cardboard</u>.

   a. artificial

   b. tasteless

   c. stiff

   d. sturdy

➤ NOW PRACTICE . . . USING FIGURATIVE LANGUAGE 2

Study the figurative expression in each of the following statements. Then, in the space provided, explain the meaning of each.

1. Hope is like a feather, ready to blow away.

    A feather is light and whimsical, and can blow away easily. The author is

    suggesting that hope is changeable and unsteady, undependable.

    _____

2. Once Alma realized she had made an embarrassing error, the blush spread across her face like spilled paint.

    Spilled paint is messy and splotchy; it spreads fast and unevenly. The author

    is suggesting that the woman's blushed face was obvious and somewhat

    unattractive.

3. A powerboat, or any other sports vehicle, is a hungry animal that devours money.

    A powerboat uses money in a way similar to how a hungry animal eats

    food. A powerboat is a vehicle that requires a great deal of money to

    support.

4. Sally's skin was like a smooth, highly polished apple.

    Sally's skin was shiny and clear with a reflective quality.

    _____

    _____

5. Upon hearing the news, I took shears and shredded my dreams.

The speaker destroyed her dreams in a sharp, deliberate, and forceful .

manner.

SUMMING IT UP

CRITICAL-READING QUESTIONS	BENEFITS
Is the material fact or opinion?	Facts are verifiable statements; you can determine whether they are true or false. Opinions express attitudes, feelings, or personal beliefs. By distinguishing statements of fact from opinions you will know what ideas to accept or verify and which to question.
What is the author's purpose?	Authors usually address specific audiences. Depending on their purpose, authors adjust content, language, and method of presentation to suit their audience. Recognizing the author's purpose will help you to grasp meaning more quickly and evaluate the author's work.
What is the tone?	Tone refers to the attitude or feeling an author expresses about his or her subject. Recognizing tone will help you evaluate what the writer is attempting to accomplish through his or her writing.
Is the author biased?	Bias refers to an author's partiality toward a particular viewpoint. Recognizing tone will help you evaluate whether the author is providing objective, complete information or selectively presenting information that furthers his or her purpose.
How strong are the data ions, and evidence?	Data and evidence are used to support statements, opin- and viewpoints. By evaluating the data and evidence, you will be able to decide whether to accept a writer's position.
How is connotative language used?	Connotative language refers to a word's implied meanings or nuances. By analyzing connotative language you will uncover writers' efforts to create favorable or unfavorable impressions of their subjects.
How is figurative language used?	Figurative language is a way of describing something that makes sense on an imaginative level but not on a literal level. It compares two unlike things that have some quality in common. By understanding figurative language you will more fully appreciate the writer's use of language and gain a fuller understanding of how the writer views his or her subject.

7 Organizing Ideas

Have you ever wondered how you will learn all the facts and ideas from your textbooks and instructors? The key to handling the volume of information presented in each course is a two-step process. First, you must reduce the amount to be learned by deciding what is most important, less important, and unimportant to learn. Then you must organize the information to make it more meaningful and easier to learn. This section describes three strategies for reducing the information—textbook highlighting, annotating, and paraphrasing—and three means of organizing the information—outlining, mapping, and summarizing.

7a HIGHLIGHTING

Highlighting is an excellent way to improve your comprehension and recall of textbook assignments. Highlighting forces you to decide what is important and sort the key information from less important material. Sorting ideas this way improves both comprehension and recall. To decide what to highlight, you must think about and evaluate the relative importance of each idea. To highlight most effectively, use these guidelines.

1. **Analyze the assignment.** Preview the assignment and define what type of learning is required. This will help you determine how much and what type of information you need to highlight.
2. **Assess your familiarity with the subject.** Depending on your background knowledge, you may need to highlight only a little or a great deal. Do not waste time highlighting what you already know.
3. **Read first, then highlight.** Finish a paragraph or self-contained section before you highlight. As you read, look for signals to organizational patterns (See Chapter 4). Each idea may seem important as you first encounter it, but you must see how it fits in with the others before you can judge its relative importance.
4. **Use the boldface headings.** Headings are labels that indicate the overall topic of a section. These headings serve as indicators of what is important to highlight.

5. **Highlight main ideas and only key supporting details.** Avoid highlighting examples and secondary details.

6. **Avoid highlighting complete sentences.** Highlight only enough so that your highlighting makes sense when you reread it. In the following selection, note that only key words and phrases are highlighted. Now read only the highlighted words. Can you grasp the key idea of the passage?

Biomes

By using imagination, we can divide the earth's land into several kinds of regions called biomes, areas of the earth that support specific assemblages of plants. As would be expected, certain kinds of animals occupy each type of biome, since different species of animals are dependent on different sorts of plant communities for food, shelter, building materials, and hiding places. . . .

Tropical rain forests are found mainly in the Amazon and Congo Basins and in Southeast Asia. The temperature in this biome doesn't vary much throughout the year. Instead, the seasons are marked by variation in the amount of rainfall throughout the year. In some areas, there may be pronounced rainy seasons. These forests support many species of plants. Trees grow throughout the year and reach tremendous heights, with their branches forming a massive canopy overhead. The forest floor, which can be quite open and easy to travel over, may be dark and steamy. Forests literally swarm with insects and birds. Animals may breed throughout the year as a result of the continual availability of food. Competition is generally considered to be very keen in such areas because of the abundance of species.

—Wallace, *Biology: The World of Life*, pp. 708, 710

7. **Move quickly through the document as you highlight.** If you have understood a paragraph or section, then your highlighting should be fast and efficient.

8. **Develop a consistent system of highlighting.** Decide, for example, how you will mark main ideas, how you will distinguish main ideas from details, and how you will highlight new terminology. Some students use a system of single and double highlighting, brackets, asterisks, and circles to distinguish various types of information; others use different colors of ink or combinations of pens and pencils.

9. **Use the 15–25 percent rule of thumb.** Although the amount you will highlight will vary from course to course, try to highlight no more than 15 to 25 percent of any given page. If you exceed this figure, it often means that you are not sorting ideas as efficiently as possible. Other times, it may mean that you should choose a different strategy for reviewing the material. Remember, the more you highlight, the smaller your time-saving dividends will be as you review. The following excerpt provides an example of effective highlighting.

Temperate deciduous forests once covered most of the eastern United States and all of Central Europe. The dominant trees in these forests are hardwoods. The areas characterized by such plants are subject to harsh winters, times when the trees shed their leaves, and warm summers that mark periods of rapid growth and rejuvenation. Before the new leaves begin to shade the forest floor in the spring, a variety of herbaceous (nonwoody) flowering plants may appear. These wildflowers are usually perennials, plants that live and produce flowers year after year. In the early spring, they don't have time to manufacture the food needed to grow and bloom suddenly. Instead, they draw on food produced and stored in underground parts during the previous year. Rainfall may average 75 to 130 centimeters or more each year in these forests and is rather evenly distributed throughout the year.

—Wallace, *Biology: The World of Life*, pp. 712–713

➤ NOW PRACTICE . . . HIGHLIGHTING 1

Read the following paragraphs, which have been highlighted two different ways. Look at each highlighted version, then write your answers to the questions that follow in the spaces provided.

Example A

Murders, especially mass murders and serial murders, fascinate the public and criminologists. Murder is the least committed crime but receives the most attention. Murder trials often capture the attention of the entire nation. The O. J. Simpson murder trial was one of the most watched television programs in the history of network Nielson ratings.

—Fagin, *Criminal Justice*, p. 89

Example B

Murders, especially mass murders and serial murders, fascinate the public and criminologists. Murder is the least committed crime but receives the most attention. Murder trials often capture the attention of the entire nation. The O. J. Simpson murder trial was one of the most watched television programs in the history of network Nielson ratings.

1. Is Example A or Example B the better example of highlighting?   B

2. Why isn't the highlighting in the other example effective?

   Example A contains too much highlighting. Too many details are

   highlighted, and the highlighting will not save much time in reviewing.

Example C

Air pollution results when several factors combine to lower air quality. Carbon monoxide emitted by automobiles contributes to air pollution, as do smoke and other chemicals from manufacturing plants. Air quality is usually worst in certain geographic locations, such as the Denver area and the Los Angeles basin, where pollutants tend to get trapped in the atmosphere. For this very reason, the air around Mexico City is generally considered to be the most polluted in the entire world.

—Ebert and Griffin, *Business Essentials*, p. 71

Example D

Air pollution results when several factors combine to lower air quality. Carbon monoxide emitted by automobiles contributes to air pollution, as do smoke and other chemicals from manufacturing plants. Air quality is usually worst in certain geographic locations, such as the Denver area and the Los Angeles basin, where pollutants tend to get trapped in the atmosphere. For this very reason, the air around Mexico City is generally considered to be the most polluted in the entire world.

1. Is Example C or Example D the better example of effective highlighting?

    C

2. Why isn't the highlighting in the other example effective?

    Important key words and phrases are not highlighted in Example D.

▶ NOW PRACTICE . . . HIGHLIGHTING 2

Highlight the article "Animal Emotions" on page 9.

7b   ANNOTATING

In many situations, highlighting alone is not a sufficient means of identifying what to learn. It does not give you any opportunity to comment on or react to the material. For this, you might want to use annotation. Annotating is an active reading process. It forces you to keep track of your comprehension as well as react to ideas. The figure on page 126 suggests various types of annotation used in marking a political science textbook chapter.

Marginal Annotation

TYPES OF ANNOTATION	EXAMPLE
Circling unknown words	. . . redressing the apparent (asymmetry) of their relationship
Marking definitions	*def* ⌐To say that the balance of power favors one party over another is to introduce a ⌐disequilibrium.
Marking examples	*ex* ⌐. . . concessions may include negative sanctions, trade ⌐agreements . . .
Numbering lists of ideas, causes, reasons, or events	components of power include ①self-image, ②population, ③natural resources, and geography ④
Placing asterisks next to important passages	* ⌐Power comes from three ⌐primary sources . .
Putting question marks next to confusing passages	? ⟶ war prevention occurs through institutionalization of mediation . . .
Making notes to yourself	*Check def in soc text* power is the ability of an actor on the international stage to . . .
Marking possible test items	*T* There are several key features in the relationship . . .
Drawing arrows to show relationships	. . . natural resources . . . , . . . control of industrial manufacture capacity
Writing comments, noting disagreements and similarities	*Can terrorism be prevented through similar balance?* war prevention through balance of power is . . .
Marking summary statements	*sum* ⌐the greater the degree of conflict, the more intricate will be . . .

► **NOW PRACTICE . . . ANNOTATING 1**

Add annotations to the reading "Animal Emotions" on page 9.

► **NOW PRACTICE . . . ANNOTATING 2**

Add annotations to the reading "Economic Change, Ideology, and Private Lives" on page 103.

7c   PARAPHRASING

A **paraphrase** is a restatement of a passage's ideas in your own words. The author's meaning is retained, but your wording, *not* the author's, is used. We use paraphrasing frequently in everyday speech. For example, when you relay a message from one person to another you convey the meaning but do not use the person's exact wording. A paraphrase can be used to make a passage's meaning clearer and often more concise. Paraphrasing is also an effective learning and review strategy in several situations.

First, paraphrasing is useful for portions of a text for which exact, detailed comprehension is required. For example, you might paraphrase the steps in solving a math problem, the process by which a blood transfusion is administered, or the levels of jurisdiction of the Supreme Court. Below is a paraphrase of a paragraph from "Animal Emotions."

A Sample Paraphrase

PARAGRAPH	PARAPHRASE
Still, the idea of animals feeling emotions remains controversial among many scientists. Researchers' skepticism is fueled in part by their professional aversion to anthropomorphism, the very nonscientific tendency to attribute human qualities to nonhumans. Many scientists also say that it is impossible to prove animals have emotions using standard scientific methods—repeatable observations that can be manipulated in controlled experiments—leading them to conclude that such feelings must not exist. Today, however, amid mounting evidence to the contrary, "the tide is turning radically and rapidly," says Bekoff, who is at the forefront of this movement.	Scientists do not agree about the existence of animal emotions. Researchers are careful to avoid anthropomorphism—assigning human characteristics to other species. As a result, researchers are doubtful of the existence of animal emotions. Research scientists also say that they cannot prove that animals have emotions using the scientific method. That is, they cannot create experiments that prove animal emotions exist. Consequently, many scientists decide that emotions do not exist. Given contrary evidence, Bekoff says that opinion is changing rapidly.

Paraphrasing is also a useful way to be certain you understand difficult or complicated material. If you can express the author's ideas in your own words, you can be certain you understand it, and if you find yourself at a loss for words—except for those of the author—you will know your understanding is incomplete.

Paraphrasing is also a useful strategy when working with material that is stylistically complex, poorly written, or overly formal, awkward, or biased. Use the following suggestions to paraphrase effectively.

1. **Read slowly and carefully.**
2. **Read the material through entirely before writing anything.**
3. **As you read, pay attention to exact meanings and relationships among ideas.**
4. **Paraphrase sentence by sentence.**
5. **Read each sentence and express the key idea in your own words.** Reread the original sentence; then look away and write your own sentence. Then reread the original and add anything you missed.
6. **Don't try to paraphrase word by word. Instead, work with ideas.**
7. **For words or phrases you are unsure of** or that are not words you feel comfortable using, check a dictionary to locate a more familiar meaning.
8. **You may combine several original sentences into a more concise paraphrase.**

> ### NOW PRACTICE . . . USING PARAPHRASING 1

Read each paragraph and the paraphrases following them. Answer the questions about each paragraph.

Paragraph A

The use of silence can be an effective form of communication, but its messages and implications differ cross culturally. In Siberian households, the lowest status person is the in-marrying daughter, and she tends to speak very little. However, silence does not always indicate powerlessness. In American courts, comparison of speaking frequency between the judge, jury, and lawyers shows that lawyers, who have the least power, speak most, while the silent jury holds the most power.

—Miller, *Cultural Anthropology,* p. 302

Paraphrase 1

Silence carries a message as well as serves as a form of communication. Young married Siberian women speak very little, lawyers (who are powerless) speak a great deal, and the jury (which is most powerful) is silent.

Paraphrase 2

Silence is a way to communicate, but its meaning varies from culture to culture. In Siberia, women have low status in their husband's family and speak very little. In American courts, however, the most powerful group, the jury, is silent, while the least powerful—attorneys—speak the most.

Paraphrase 3

Silence has many meanings. Siberian women speak very little, indicating their low status. Lawyers speak a great deal, while a jury is silent.

1. Which is the best paraphrase of the paragraph? _____2_____

2. Why are the other paraphrases not as good? Answers will vary

Paraphrase 1 does not contain the important idea that silence varies cross

culturally. Paraphrase 3 is inaccurate (not all Siberian women are silent)

and it does not explain that silence is a form of communication that

varies cross culturally. It does not explain that silence does not always

indicate powerlessness.

Paragraph B

Today, the dominant family form in the United States is the child-free family, where a couple resides together and there are no children present in the household. With the aging of the baby boomer cohort, this family type is expected to increase steadily over time. If current trends continue, nearly three out of four U.S. households will be childless in another decade or so.

—Thompson and Hickey, *Society in Focus*, p. 355

Paraphrase 1

A child-free family is one where two adults live together and have no children. It is the dominant family form.

Paraphrase 2

The child-free family is dominant in the U.S. Baby boomers and their cohorts are having fewer children. Three out of four homes do not have children in them.

Paraphrase 3

The child-free family is dominant in the U.S. As baby boomers get older, there will be even more of these families. Three quarters of all U.S. homes will be childless ten years from now.

3. Which is the best paraphrase of the paragraph? _____3_____

4. Why are the other paraphrases less good?

Paraphase 1 does not contain enough information. Paraphrase 2 is

inaccurate; it states the projected statistic as a fact.

➤ NOW PRACTICE . . . PARAPHRASING 2

Write a paraphrase of paragraph 8 in the reading "Animal Emotions" on p. 9.

7d   OUTLINING TO ORGANIZE IDEAS

Outlining is a writing strategy that can assist you in organizing information and pulling ideas together. It is also an effective way to pull together information from two or more sources—your textbook and class lectures, for example. Finally, outlining is a way to assess your comprehension and strengthen your recall. Use the following tips to write an effective outline.

1. **Read an entire section and then jot down notes.** Do not try to outline while you are reading the material for the first time.
2. **As you read, be alert for organizational patterns** (See Chapter 4). These patterns will help you organize your notes.
3. **Record all the most important ideas in the briefest possible form.**
4. **Think of your outline as a list of the main ideas and supporting details of a selection.** Organize it to show how the ideas are related or to reflect the organization of the material.
5. **Write in your own words; do not copy sentences or parts of sentences from the selection.** Use words and short phrases to summarize ideas. Do not write in complete sentences.
6. **Use a system of indentation to separate main ideas and details.** As a general rule, the greater the importance of an idea, the closer it is placed to the left margin. Ideas of lesser importance are indented and appear closer to the center of the page. Your notes might follow a format such as this:

TOPIC
Main Idea
    Supporting detail
        fact
        fact
    Supporting detail
Main Idea
    Supporting detail
    Supporting detail
        fact
        fact

To further illustrate the techniques of outlining, study the notes shown in the sample outline below. They are based on a portion (paragraph 1 and the table included in the reading) of the textbook excerpt "Ending Relationships" on page 6.

A Sample Outline

I. Ending Relationships

    A. How to Break Up (Disengage)

        1. Five Strategies

            a) use a positive tone and express positive feelings

            b) blame the other person (negative identity management)

            c) give reasons for breakup (justification)

            d) reduce the strength of the relationship by avoiding the person or spending less time with him or her (behavioral de-escalation)

            e) reduce exclusivity (de-escalation)

        2. Strategy used depends on a person's goal

➤ NOW PRACTICE . . . OUTLINING 1

Read the following passage and complete the outline.

Gender Characteristics

Masculinity refers to attributes considered appropriate for males. In American society, these traditionally include being aggressive, athletic, physically active, logical, and dominant in social relationships with females. Conversely, femininity refers to attributes associated with appropriate behavior for females, which in America include passivity, docility, fragility, emotionality, and subordination to males. Research conducted by Carol Gilligan and her students at Harvard's Gender Studies Department indicate that children are acutely aware of and feel pressure to conform to these powerful gender traits by the age of 4. Some people insist that gender traits such as male aggressiveness are innate characteristics linked to sex and do not depend on cultural definitions. However, the preponderance of research indicates that females and males can be equally aggressive under different social and cultural conditions and that levels of aggression vary as widely within the sexes as between them.

—adapted from Thompson and Hickey, *Society in Focus*, p. 285

Gender Characteristics

A. Masculinity

    1. attributes society believes appropriate for males

    2. includes <u>aggresiveness, athleticism, being physically active, being logical,</u>
    <u>and dominance over females in social relationships</u>

B. Femininity

    1. <u>attributes society believes appropriate for females</u>

    2. includes <u>passivity, docility, fragility, emotionality,</u>
    and subordination to males

C. <u>Children</u> are aware of and feel pressure to conform to gender
expectations by <u>age 4</u>

D. Link to Sex

    1. some people believe linked to sex

    2. research shows both sexes can be equally aggressive and levels of
    <u>aggression vary widely within the sexes and between them</u>

> **NOW PRACTICE . . . OUTLINING 2**

Finish outlining the textbook excerpt "Ending Relationships" on page 6.

7e   MAPPING TO SHOW RELATIONSHIPS

Mapping is a way of drawing a diagram to describe how a topic and its related ideas are connected. Mapping is a visual means of learning by writing; it organizes and consolidates information.

    This section discusses four types of maps: conceptual maps, process diagrams, part and function diagrams, and time lines.

Conceptual Maps

A conceptual map is a diagram that presents ideas spatially rather than in list form. It is a "picture" of how ideas are related. Use the following steps in constructing a conceptual map.

1. **Identify the topic and write it in the center of the page.**
2. **Identify ideas, aspects, parts, and definitions that are related to the topic.** Draw each one on a line radiating from the topic.
3. **As you discover details that further explain an idea already recorded, draw new lines branching from the idea that the details explain.**

A conceptual map of Part One of this book is shown below. This map shows only the major topics included in Part One. Maps can be much more detailed and include more information than the one shown, depending on the purpose for drawing it.

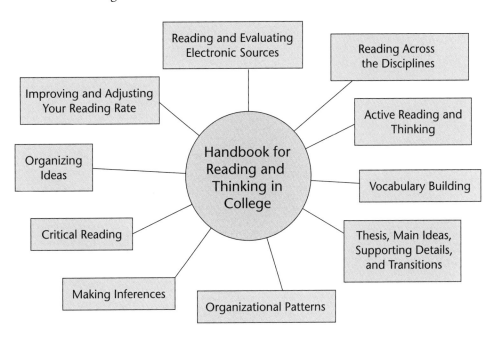

> **NOW PRACTICE . . . DRAWING A CONCEPTUAL MAP 1**

Read the following paragraph about social institutions. Complete the conceptual map that presents the ideas contained in this paragraph.

Society cannot survive without social institutions. A social institution is a set of widely shared beliefs, norms and procedures necessary for meeting the basic needs of society. The most important institutions are family, education, religion, economy, and politics. They have stood the test of time, serving society well. The family institution leads countless people to produce and raise children to ensure that they can eventually take over from the older generation the task of keeping society going. The educational institution teaches the young to become effective contributors to the welfare—such as the order, stability, or prosperity—of society. The religious institution fulfills spiritual needs, making earthly lives seem more meaningful and therefore more bearable or satisfying. The economic institution provides food, clothing, shelter, employment, banking, and other goods and services that we need to live. The political institution makes and enforces laws to prevent criminals and other similar forces from destabilizing society.

—Thio, *Sociology: A Brief Introduction,* pp. 35–36

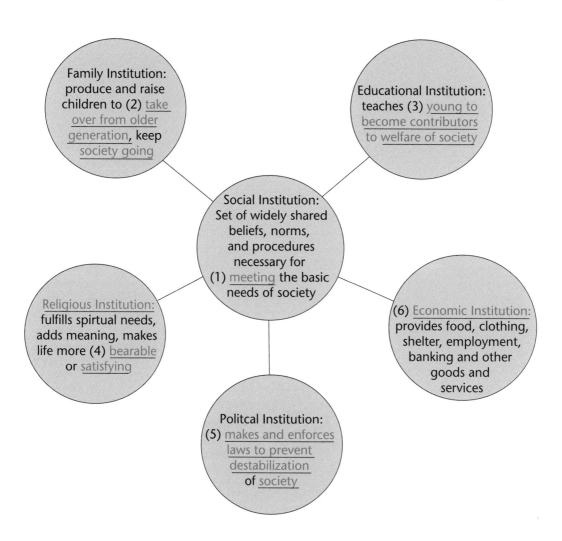

NOW PRACTICE . . . DRAWING A CONCEPTUAL MAP 2

Draw a conceptual map for the textbook excerpt "Ending a Relationship" on page 6.

Process Diagrams

In the technologies and the natural sciences, as well as in many other courses, *processes* are an important part of the course content. A diagram that visually describes the steps, variables, or parts of a process will make learning easier. For example, the diagram below visually describes the steps in the search process for using library sources.

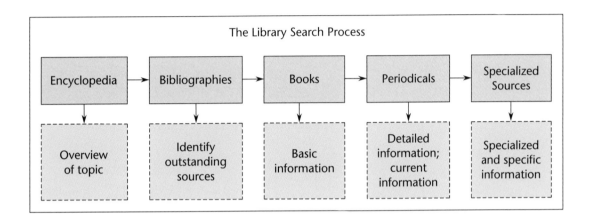

> ## NOW PRACTICE . . . DRAWING A PROCESS DIAGRAM 1

The following paragraph describes how a bill becomes a law. Read the paragraph and then complete the process diagram that describes this procedure.

Federal criminal laws must originate in the House of Representatives or the U.S. Senate. A senator or representative introduces a proposal (known as a bill) to create a new law or modify an existing law. The merits of the bill are debated in the House or Senate and a vote is taken. If the bill receives a majority vote, it is passed on to the other house of Congress where it is again debated and put to a vote. If any changes are made, the amended bill must be returned to the house of Congress where it originated and voted on again. This process continues until the House and Senate agree on a single version of the bill. The bill is then forwarded to the president, who can sign the bill into law, veto it or take no action, in which case the bill dies automatically when Congress adjourns. If the president vetoes a bill, Congress can pass the law over the president's veto by a two-thirds vote of both houses. Whether approved by the president and the Congress or by the Congress alone, a bill becomes a law when it is published in the *U.S. Criminal Codes.*

—Fagin, *Criminal Justice*, p. 107

Drawing a Process Diagram – 1

The Making of Federal Criminal Laws

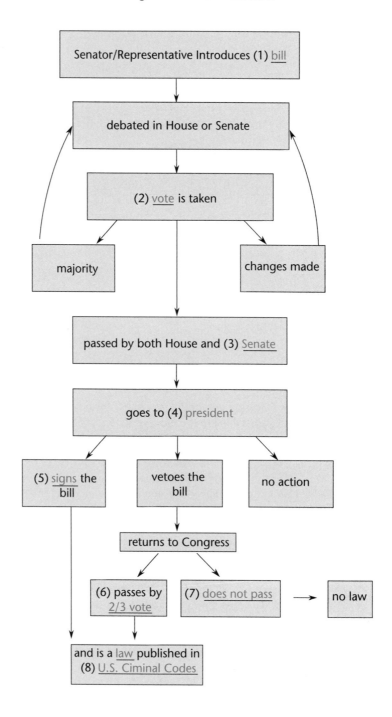

> **NOW PRACTICE . . . DRAWING A PROCESS DIAGRAM 2**

The following paragraph describes the sequential effects of taking the psychedelic drug LSD. Read the paragraph and then draw a process diagram that describes this response sequence. Compare your diagram with those of several other students.

Psychedelics are . . . a group of drugs that produce hallucinations and various other phenomena that very closely mimic certain mental disorders. These drugs include lysergic acid diethylamide (LSD), mescaline, peyote, psilocybin, and various commercial preparations such as Sernyl and Ditran.

Of these, LSD is probably the best known, although its use has apparently diminished since its heyday in the late 1960s. LSD is synthesized from lysergic acid produced by a fungus (ergot) that is parasitic on cereal grains such as rye. It usually produces responses in a particular sequence. The initial reactions may include weakness, dizziness and nausea. These symptoms are followed by a distortion of time and space. The senses may become intensified and strangely intertwined—that is, sounds can be "seen" and colors "heard." Finally, there may be changes in mood, a feeling of separation of the self from the framework of time and space, and changes in the perception of the self. The sensations experienced under the influence of psychedelics are unlike anything encountered within the normal range of experiences. The descriptions of users therefore can only be puzzling to nonusers. Some users experience bad trips or "bummers," which have been known to produce long-term effects. Bad trips can be terrifying experiences and can occur in experienced users for no apparent reason.

—Wallace, *Biology: The World of Life*, pp. 632–633

Time Lines

When you are studying a topic in which the sequence or order of events is a central focus, a time line is a helpful way to organize the information. Time lines are especially useful in history courses. To map a sequence of events, draw a single line and mark it off in year intervals, just as a ruler is marked off in inches. Then write events next to the correct year. For example, the time line on page 138 displays major events during the presidency of Franklin D. Roosevelt. The time line shows the sequence of events and helps you to visualize them more clearly.

Sample Time Line

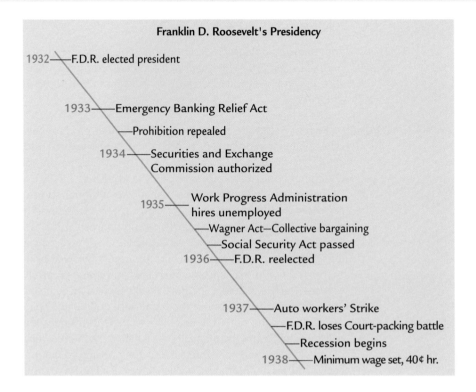

Franklin D. Roosevelt's Presidency

1932——F.D.R. elected president

1933——Emergency Banking Relief Act
        ——Prohibition repealed
    1934——Securities and Exchange
        Commission authorized
        Work Progress Administration
    1935——hires unemployed
        ——Wagner Act–Collective bargaining
        ——Social Security Act passed
    1936——F.D.R. reelected

    1937——Auto workers' Strike
        ——F.D.R. loses Court-packing battle
        ——Recession begins
    1938——Minimum wage set, 40¢ hr.

➤ NOW PRACTICE . . . DRAWING A TIME LINE

The following passage reviews the chronology of events in public school desegregation. Read the selection and then draw a time line that will help you to visualize these historical events.

Desegregating the Schools

The nation's schools soon became the primary target of civil-rights advocates. The NAACP concentrated first on universities, successfully waging an intensive legal battle to win admission for qualified blacks to graduate and professional schools. Led by Thurgood Marshall, NAACP lawyers then took on the broader issue of segregation in the country's public schools. Challenging the 1896 Supreme Court decision (*Plessy* v. *Ferguson*) which upheld the constitutionality of separate but equal public facilities, Marshall argued that even substantially equal but separate schools did profound psychological damage to black children and thus violated the Fourteenth Amendment.

A unanimous Supreme Court agreed in its 1954 decision in the case of *Brown* v. *Board of Education of Topeka*. Chief Justice Earl Warren, recently appointed by President Eisenhower, wrote the landmark opinion which flatly declared that "separate educational facilities are inherently unequal." To divide grade-school children "solely because of their race," Warren argued, "generates a feeling of inferiority as to their status in the community that may affect their hearts and minds in a way unlikely ever to be undone." Despite this sweeping language, Warren realized that it would be difficult to change historic patterns of segregation quickly. Accordingly, in 1955 the Court ruled that implementation should proceed "with all deliberate speed" and left the details to the lower federal courts.

The process of desegregating the schools proved to be agonizingly slow. Officials in the border states quickly complied with the Court's ruling, but states deeper in the South responded with a policy of massive resistance. Local White Citizen's Councils organized to fight for retention of racial separation; 101 congressmen and senators signed a Southern Manifesto in 1956 which denounced the *Brown* decision as "a clear abuse of judicial power." School boards, encouraged by this show of defiance, found a variety of ways to evade the Court's ruling. The most successful was the passage of pupil-placement laws . . . .

Southern leaders mistook Ike's silence for tacit support of segregation. In 1957, Governor Orville Faubus of Arkansas called out the national guard to prevent the integration of Little Rock's Central High School on grounds of a threat to public order. . . .

Despite the snail's pace of school desegregation, the *Brown* decision led to other advances. In 1957, the Eisenhower administration proposed the first general civil-rights legislation since Reconstruction. Strong southern resistance and compromise by both the administration and Senate Democratic leader Lyndon B. Johnson of Texas weakened the bill considerably. The final act, however, did create a permanent Commission for Civil Rights, one of Truman's original goals. It also provided for federal efforts aimed at "securing and protecting the right to vote." A second civil-rights act in 1960 slightly strengthened the voting-rights section.

—Divine, *America Past and Present,* pp. 890–891

Part and Function Diagrams

In courses that deal with the use and description or classification of physical objects, labeled drawings are an important learning tool. In a human anatomy and physiology course, for example, the easiest way to learn the parts and functions of the brain is to draw it. To study, sketch the brain and test your recall of each part and its function.

▶ NOW PRACTICE . . . DRAWING A PART AND FUNCTION DIAGRAM

The following paragraph describes the layers of the earth. Read the paragraph and then draw a diagram that will help you to visualize how the earth is structured.

Outer Layers of the Earth

The Earth's crust and the uppermost part of the mantle are known as the *lithosphere.* This is a fairly rigid zone that extends about 100 km below the Earth's surface. The crust extends some 60 km or so under continents, but only about 10 km below the ocean floor. The continental crust has a lower density than the oceanic crust. It is primarily a light granitic rock rich in the silicates of aluminum, iron, and magnesium.

In a simplified view, the continental crust can be thought of as layered: On top of a layer of igneous rock (molten rock that has hardened, such as granite) lies a thin layer of sedimentary rocks (rocks formed by sediment and fragments that water deposited, such as limestone and sandstone); there is also a soil layer deposited during past ages in the parts of continents that have had no recent volcanic activity or mountain building.

Sandwiched between the lithosphere and the lower mantle is the partially molten material known as the *asthenosphere*, about 150 km thick. It consists primarily of iron and magnesium silicates that readily deform and flow under pressure.

—Berman and Evans, *Exploring the Cosmos*, p. 145

7f   SUMMARIZING TO CONDENSE IDEAS

Like outlining, summarizing is an excellent way to learn from your reading and to increase recall. A **summary** is a brief statement that reviews the key points of what you have read. It condenses an author's ideas or arguments into sentences written in your own words. A summary contains only the gist of the text, with limited explanation, background information, or supporting detail. Writing a summary is a step beyond recording the author's ideas; a summary must pull together the writer's ideas by condensing and grouping them. Before writing a summary, be sure you understand the material and have identified the writer's major points. Then use the following suggestions:

1. **As a first step, highlight or write brief notes on the material.**
2. **Write one sentence that states the writer's overall concern or most important idea.** To do this, ask yourself what one topic the material is about. Then ask what point the writer is trying to make about that topic. This sentence will be the topic sentence of your summary.
3. **Be sure to paraphrase, using your own words rather than those of the author.**
4. **Review the major supporting information that the author gives to explain the major idea.**
5. **The amount of detail you include, if any, depends on your purpose for writing the summary.** For example, if you are writing a summary of a television documentary for a research paper, it might be more detailed than if you were writing it to jog your memory for a class discussion.
6. **Normally, present ideas in the summary in the same order in which they appeared in the original material.**
7. **If the writer presents a clear opinion or expresses an attitude toward the subject matter, include it in your summary.**
8. **If the summary is for your own use only and is not to be submitted as an assignment, do not worry about sentence structure.** Some students prefer to write summaries using words and phrases rather than complete sentences.

A sample summary of the article "Ending Relationships" which appears on page 6 is shown below.

A Sample Summary

> It is inevitable that some relationships do end. As a relationship ends, there are two concerns: how to end it and how to deal with the breakup. There are five ways to end a relationship, called disengagement strategies. They are: use a positive tone, blame the other person, give reasons for the breakup, reduce the intensity of the relationship, and reduce the exclusivity of the relationship. Breakups always cause stress. Six ways to deal with a breakup are to avoid loneliness and depression, avoid jumping into a new relationship, build self-esteem, get rid of hurtful reminders, seek help and support from family and friends, and avoid repeating the same mistakes.

➤ NOW PRACTICE . . . SUMMARIZING 1

Complete this summary of the passage about psychedelic drugs on page 137.

Psychedelic drugs cause _____hallucinations_____ and can cause reactions mimicking _____mental disorders_____. Examples include _____mescaline, peyote, and psilocybin_____. LSD is the best known and was most popular in _____the late 1960s_____. It is created from _____lysergic acid_____ which comes from a _____fungus that lives on cereal grain_____. Initially, it causes weakness, _____dizziness_____ and _____nausea_____ and later a distortion of time and space. It causes senses to be _____stronger and mixed up with each other_____. The drug affects _____people's moods_____, creates a feeling of distance, and creates changes in _____self-perception_____. The sensations resulting are outside _____the normal range of experiences_____. _____Bad trips_____ can have _____long-term_____ consequences and the reason for them is not understood.

—Donatelle, *Health: The Basics,* p. 179

➤ NOW PRACTICE . . . SUMMARIZING 2

Write a summary of the section titled "Beastly Joy" (paragraphs 9–14) of the article "Animal Emotions" on page 9.

8 Improving and Adjusting Your Reading Rate

The speed at which you read, called your reading rate, is measured in words per minute (WPM). What should your reading rate be? Is it better to be a fast or slow reader? You should be able to read at 100, 200, 300, and even 400 words per minute, depending on what you are reading and why you are reading it. You should be both a slow and a fast reader; when you are reading difficult, complicated material you should read slowly. When reading easy material or material that you do not have to remember for a test, you can afford to read faster. This section will offer some suggestions for improving your reading rate and explain how to adjust your reading rate.

8a IMPROVING YOUR READING RATE

Here are a few suggestions for improving your overall reading rate.

1. **Try to read a little faster.** Sometimes by just being conscious of your reading rate, you can improve it slightly.
2. **Be sure to preview** (see Chapter 1, Section 1b). Previewing familiarizes you with the material and allows you to understand what you are reading more easily, thereby enabling you to read slightly faster.
3. **Improve your concentration.** If your mind wanders while you are reading, it will cost you time. Eliminate distractions, read in a place conducive to study, use writing to keep you mentally and physically alert, and alternate between different types of reading assignments.
4. **Set time goals.** Before you begin an assignment, decide approximately how much time it should take. Without a time goal, it is easy to drift and wander through an assignment rather than working straight through it efficiently.

8b ADJUSTING YOUR RATE TO MEET COMPREHENSION DEMANDS

Do you read the newspaper in the same way and at the same speed at which you read a biology textbook? Do you read an essay for your English class in the same way and at the same speed at which you read a mystery novel? Surprisingly, many people do.

If you are an efficient reader, however, you read the newspaper more quickly and in a different way than you read a biology textbook. The newspaper is usually easier to read, and you have a different purpose for reading it. Efficient readers adapt their speed and comprehension levels to suit the material.

Rate and comprehension are the two main factors that you must keep in balance; as your reading rate increases, your comprehension may decrease. Your goal is to achieve a balance that suits the nature of the material and your purpose for reading it. The following steps will help you learn to vary your reading rate.

1. **Assess how difficult the assignment is.** Factors such as the difficulty of the vocabulary, length, and organization all affect text difficulty. Usually, longer or poorly organized material is more difficult to read than shorter or well-organized material. Numerous typographical aids (italics, headings, etc.) can make material easier to read. As you preview an assignment, notice these features and estimate how difficult the material will be to read. There is no rule to use when adjusting your speed to compensate for differing degrees of difficulty. Instead, use your judgment to adjust your reading rate and style to the material.

2. **Assess your familiarity with and interest in the subject.** Your knowledge of and interest in a subject influence how fast you can read it. Material you are interested in or that you know something about will be easier for you to read, and you can increase your speed.

3. **Define your purpose.** The reason you are reading an assignment should influence how you read it. Different situations demand different levels of comprehension and recall. For example, you can read an article in *Time* magazine assigned as a supplementary reading in your sociology class faster than you can read your sociology text, because the magazine assignment does not require as high a level of recall and analysis.

4. **Decide what, if any, follow-up activity is required.** Will you have to pass a multiple-choice exam on the content? Will you be participating in a class discussion? Will you summarize the information in a short paper? The activities that follow your reading determine, in part, the level of comprehension that is required. Passing an exam requires a very high level of reading comprehension, whereas preparing for a class discussion requires a more moderate level of comprehension or retention.

Table 8.1 shows the level of comprehension required for various types of material and gives approximate reading rates that are appropriate for each level.

TABLE 8.1 LEVELS OF COMPREHENSION

DESIRED LEVEL OF COMPREHENSION	TYPE OF MATERIAL	PURPOSE IN READING	RANGE OF READING RATES
Complete, 100%	Poetry, legal documents, argumentative writing	Analysis, criticism, evaluation	Less than 200 WPM
High, 80–100%	Textbooks, manuals, research documents	High comprehension, recall for exams, writing research reports, following directions	200–300 WPM
Moderate, 60–80%	Novels, paperbacks, newspapers, magazines	Entertainment, enjoyment, general information	300–500 WPM

➤ NOW PRACTICE . . . ADJUSTING YOUR READING RATE

For each of the following situations, define your purpose and indicate the level of comprehension that seems appropriate.

1. Reading a credit card agreement or an insurance policy before signing it.

    Purpose: understand all clauses and aspects of the agreement or policy.

    _____

    Comprehension level: complete

2. Reading a critical essay that analyzes a Shakespearean sonnet you are studying in a literature class.

    Purpose: analyze and interpret the sonnet

    _____

    Comprehension level: high

3. Reading an encyclopedia entry on poverty to narrow down a term paper assignment to a manageable topic.

    Purpose: obtain a general overview of the topic

    _____

    Comprehension level: moderate

4. Reading a newspaper article on a recent incident in the Middle East for your political science class.

Purpose: understand sequence and relationship of events; consider political implications

Comprehension level: high

5. Reading an excerpt from a historical novel set in the Civil War period for your American history class.

Purpose: note historical events; get a general sense of the times and the culture

Comprehension level: moderate

9 Reading and Evaluating Electronic Sources

Most of today's college students and teachers learned to read using print text. We have been reading print text much longer than electronic text; consequently our brains have developed numerous strategies or "work orders" for reading traditional printed material.

Electronic text has a wider variety of formats and presents us with more variables than traditional text. Because electronic text is a relatively new form of text, our brains need to develop new strategies in order to understand Web sites. And because Web sites vary widely in both purpose and reliability, it is important that your reading be critical.

9a DEVELOPING NEW WAYS OF THINKING AND READING

The first step in reading electronic text easily and effectively is to understand how it is different from print text. A print source is linear—it goes in a straight line from idea to idea. Electronic sources, in contrast, tend to be multidirectional. Using links, you can follow numerous paths. (See the accompanying figure.) Therefore, reading electronic sources demands a different type of thinking than reading print sources.

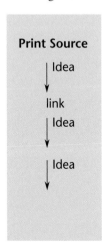
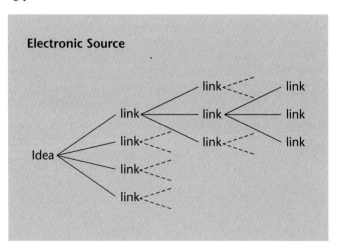

Using electronic text also requires new reading strategies. You need to change and adapt how you read. To do this, focus on your purpose, get used to a site's design and layout, pay attention to how information is organized, and use links to find the information you need.

Focus on Your Purpose

Focus clearly on your purpose for visiting the site. What information do you need? Because you must create your own path through the site, fix in your mind what you are looking for. If you don't, you may wander aimlessly, waste valuable time, or even become lost, following numerous links that lead you farther and farther away from the site at which you began.

Get Used to the Site's Design and Layout

Each Web site has unique features and arranges information differently. Use the following suggestions to help you get used to a site's design and layout.

1. **When you reach a new site, spend a few minutes getting used to it and discovering how it is organized.** Scroll through it quickly to determine how it is organized and what information is available. Ask yourself the following questions:

   - What information is available?
   - How is it arranged on the screen?
   - Can I search the site using a search option or box?
   - Is there a site map?

   Especially on large and complex sites, you will have a number of different choices for locating the information you need. Be sure to spend time exploring your choices before choosing a particular path for your search. The Web site for MEDLINEplus shown in the figure on page 148 is a good example.

   Suppose you are searching for information on laser surgery. On the MEDLINEplus site there are a number of different ways of locating information. One choice is to perform a keyword search by entering "laser surgery" into the search box and clicking "Go." This results in almost 50 hits on various laser surgery topics. Another choice is to click on "Health Topics" and then on the letter "L." This leads to a great deal of well-organized information, but on laser eye surgery only. A third choice would be to click on "Dictionaries" where you can pick a place to search for laser surgery to receive basic information that explains the process and uses of laser surgery. Under "Other Resources," you can search MEDLINE, which is an enormous database of research articles from medical journals. A search for laser surgery here brings back thousands of hits. You would need to do a carefully planned refined search to find the exact information desired.

**MEDLINEplus
Web Site**

MEDLINEplus®
Health Information

A service of the U.S. NATIONAL LIBRARY OF MEDICINE
and the NATIONAL INSTITUTES OF HEALTH

Search   About | Site Map | FAQs | Contact Us | español

▶ Health Topics
Start here with over 600 topics on conditions, diseases and wellness

▶ Drug Information
About your prescription and over-the-counter medicines

▶ Medical Encyclopedia
Includes pictures and diagrams

▶ Dictionary
Spellings and definitions of medical words

▶ News
Health News from the past 30 days

▶ Directories
Find doctors, dentists and hospitals

▶ Other Resources
Local libraries, health organizations, international sites and more

Current Health News
▶ Chimp, Human Genomes Aligned
▶ Human Papillomavirus Tied to Oral Cancer
▶ Hypertension May Be Inflammatory Disease
▶ More news

Featured Site

News from the National Eye Institute on Retinopathy of Prematurity

In the Spotlight 📖

It's flu season. Learn more:

▶ Influenza Health Topic Page
▶ Latest news on Influenza

Interactive Tutorials
Over 165 slideshows with sound and pictures

ClinicalTrials.gov
Studies for new drugs and treatments

NIHSeniorHealth
Health information for older adults

▶ What's new on MEDLINEplus?

Sign up now! ✉

▶ Add MEDLINEplus to your site
▶ Take a tour of the site

Copyright | Privacy | Accessibility | Freedom of Information Act | Selection Guidelines
U.S. National Library of Medicine | National Institutes of Health | Department of Health & Human Services
Page last updated: 11 December 2003 | URL for this page: http://medlineplus.gov

2. **Expect the first screen to grab your attention and make a main point.**
Web site authors know that many people (up to 90 percent) who read a Web page do not scroll down past the first screen. Therefore, they try to make their first screen interesting and memorable.

3. **Get used to the colors, flashing images, and sounds before you attempt to obtain information from the site.** Your eye may have a tendency to focus on color or movement, rather than on print. Because Web sites are highly visual, they require visual as well as verbal thinking. The author intends you to respond to photos, graphics, and animation.

4. **Consider both the focus of and limitations of your learning style.** Are you a spatial learner? If so, you may have a tendency to focus too heavily on the graphic elements of the screen. If, on the other hand, you tend to focus on words, you may ignore important visual elements or signals. If you focus *only* on the words and ignore color and graphics on a particular screen, you probably will miss information or may not move through the site in the most efficient way.

Pay Attention to How Information Is Organized

Because you can navigate through a Web site in many different ways, it is important to have the right expectations and to make several decisions before you begin. Some Web sites are much better organized than others. Some have clear headings and labels that make it easy to discover how to proceed; others do not and will require more thought before you begin. For example, if you are reading an article with as many as 10 or 15 underlined words (links), there is no prescribed order to follow and these links are not categorized in any way. Below are some suggestions on how to stay organized when using a Web site.

1. **Use the site map, if provided, to discover what information is available and how it is organized.** A sample site map for the *Consumer Reports* Web site is shown on page 150. Notice that the links are categorized according to the types of information (ratings, safety alerts, recalls, etc.) a consumer may need.
2. **Consider the order in which you want to take in information.** Choose an order in which to explore links; avoid randomly clicking on link buttons. Doing so is somewhat like randomly choosing pages to read out of a reference book. Do you need definitions first? Do you want historical background first? Your decision will be partly influenced by your learning style.
3. **Consider writing brief notes to yourself as you explore a complicated Web site.** Alternatively, you could print the home page and jot notes on it. You can also save Web pages on to a disk or save them on your computer, as a text file.
4. **Expect shorter, less detailed sentences and paragraphs.** Much online communication tends to be briefer and more concise than in traditional sources. As a result, you may have to mentally fill in transitions and make inferences about the relationships among ideas. For example, you may have to infer similarities and differences or recognize cause-and-effect connections on your own.

Use Links to Find the Information You Need

Links are unique to electronic text. The suggestions below will help you use links to find the information you need.

1. **Plan on exploring links to find complete and detailed information.** Both remote links (those that take you to another site) and related links (within a site) are intended to provide more detailed information on topics introduced on the home page.
2. **As you follow links, be sure to bookmark your original site and other useful sites you come across so you can find them again.** Bookmarking is a feature of your Internet browser that allows you to record Web site addresses and access them later by simply clicking on the site name. Different search engines use different terms for this function. Netscape Communicator uses the term *Bookmarks*, Microsoft Explorer calls it *Favorites*. In addition, Netscape Communicator has a *History* or "Back" feature that allows a user to retrace the steps of the current search.

Consumer Reports Web Site Map

3. If you use a site or a link that provides many pages of continuous paragraphs, print the material and read it offline.
4. If you find you are lacking background on a topic, use links to help fill in the gaps, or search for a different, less technical Web site on the same topic.

▶ **NOW PRACTICE . . . NEW WAYS OF THINKING AND READING 1**

Visit one of the following Web sites. Locate the information needed and take brief notes to record what you find.

URL	Information to Locate
1. **http://www.consumer.gov**	List three tips for buying a used car.

1. Inspect the car carefully. 2. Take the car for a test drive in traffic, on the

open road, and up hills. 3. Examine the repair and maintenance records

for the car. 4. Ask the previous owner about the car. 5. Hire your own

mechanic to look over the car.

2. **http://www.bls.gov.oco/**	What is the job outlook for designers?

Job growth in this area will be "faster than average."

3. **http://thomas.loc.gov/home/ lawsmade.toc.html**	Why are lights and ringing bells used in parts of the Capitol Building and U.S. House and Senate Office Buildings?

The system of lights and ringing bells is used to inform members of

Congress of certain events taking place in the House and Senate

chambers while these members are away on other business in the

Capitol building or office buildings.

▶ **NOW PRACTICE . . . NEW WAYS OF THINKING AND READING 2**

For one of the Web sites you visited above or a new site of your choice, follow at least three links and then answer the following questions. Answers will vary.

1. What type of information did each contain?

2. Was each source reliable? How do you know?

3. Which was the easiest to read and follow? Why?

TABLE 9.1 TYPES OF WEB SITES

TYPE	PURPOSE	DESCRIPTION	URL EXTENSION
Informational	To present facts, information, and research data	May contain reports, statistical data, results of research studies, and reference materials	.edu or .gov
News	To provide current information on local, national, and international news	Often supplements print newspapers, periodicals, and television news programs	.com
Advocacy	To promote a particular cause or point of view	Usually concerned with a controversial issue; often sponsored by nonprofit groups	.org
Personal	To provide information about an individual and his or her interests and accomplishments	May list publications or include the individual's résumé	URL will vary; may contain .com or .org or may contain a tilde (~)
Commercial	To promote goods or services	May provide news and information related to their products	.com

9b DISCOVERING THE PURPOSE OF WEB SITES

There are thousands of Web sites and they vary widely in purpose. Table 9.1 summarizes five primary types of Web sites.

9c EVALUATING WEB SITES

Once you have become familiar with the organization of a Web site and determined its purpose, you should evaluate it. To do this, consider its content, accuracy, and timeliness.

Evaluating the Content of a Web site

When evaluating the content of a Web site, evaluate its appropriateness, its source, its level of technical detail, its presentation, its completeness, and its links.

Evaluate Appropriateness. To be worthwhile a Web site should contain the information you need. It should answer one or more of your search questions. If the site only touches upon answers to your questions but does not address them in detail, check the links on the site to see if they will lead you to more detailed information. If they do not, search for a more useful site.

Evaluate the Source. Another important step in evaluating a Web site is to determine its source. Ask yourself "Who is the sponsor?" and "Why was this site put up on the Web?" The sponsor of a Web site is the person or organization who paid for it to be created and placed on the Web. The sponsor will often suggest the purpose of a Web site. For example, a Web site sponsored by Nike is designed to promote its products, while a site sponsored by a university library is designed to help students learn to use its resources more effectively.

If you are not sure who sponsors a Web site, check its URL, its copyright, and the links it offers. The ending of the URL often suggests the type of sponsorship. The copyright indicates the owner of the site. Links may also reveal the sponsor. Some links may lead to commercial advertising while others may lead to sites sponsored by nonprofit groups.

Another way to check the ownership of a Web site is to try to locate the site's home page. You can do this by using only the first part of its URL—up to the first slash (/) mark. For example, suppose you found a student paper about Amy Tan on the Internet and you wanted to track its source. Its URL is **http://www.msu.edu/~shoopsar/joyluck.htm** If you shorten it to **http://www.msu.edu/**, this URL takes you to the home page for Michigan State University, the author's school. Further checking reveals that the essay was written by an undergraduate student for a course on writing, women, and America.

Evaluate the Level of Technical Detail. A Web site should contain a level of technical detail that is suited to your purpose. Some sites may provide information that is too sketchy for your search purposes; others assume a level of background knowledge or technical sophistication that you lack. For example, if you are writing a short, introductory-level paper on threats to the survival of marine animals, information on the Web site of the Scripps Institution of Oceanography (**http://www.sio.ucsd.edu**) may be too technical and contain more information than you need. Unless you already have some background knowledge in that field, you may want to search for a different Web site.

Evaluate the Presentation. Information on a Web site should be presented clearly and should be well written. If you find a site that is not clear and well written, you should be suspicious of it. If the author did not take time to present ideas clearly and correctly, he or she may not have taken time to collect accurate information, either.

Evaluate Completeness. Determine whether the site provides complete information on its topic. Does it address all aspects of the topic that you feel it should? For example, if a Web site on important twentieth century American poets does not mention Robert Frost, then the site is incomplete. If you discover that a site is incomplete, search for sites that provide a more thorough treatment of the topic.

Evaluate the Links. Many reputable sites supply links to other related sites. Make sure that the links work and are current. Also check to see if the sites to which you were sent are reliable sources of information. If the links do not work or the sources appear unreliable, you should question the reliability of the site itself. Also determine whether the links provided are comprehensive or only present a representative sample. Either is acceptable, but the site should make clear the nature of the links it is providing.

➤ NOW PRACTICE . . . EVALUATING CONTENT

Evaluate the content of two of the following sites. Explain why you would either trust or distrust the site for reliable content.

1. **http://www.geocities.com/RainForest/6243/index.html**

   The site presents many good points about environmental conservation.

   However, it does not cite any sources or openly reveal the author's

   credentials. There are some broken links that need to be fixed.

2. **http://www1.umn.edu/ohr/ecep/resume/index.htm**

   The site is sponsored by the University of Minnesota. The site makes

   explicit statements that this is a tutorial only and explains clearly what the

   site will and will not do. All of the contributors are identified and contact

   information is provided.

3. **http://home.inreach.com/dov/tt.htm**

   This site sells a product that carries no warranty or guarantee and makes

   unsubstantiated claims for the product.

Evaluating the Accuracy of a Web site

When using information on a Web site for an academic paper, it is important to be sure that you have found accurate information. One way to determine the accuracy of a Web site is to compare it with print sources (periodicals and books) on the same topic. If you find a wide discrepancy between the Web site and the printed sources, do not trust the Web site. Another way to determine the accuracy of the information on a site is to compare it with other Web sites that address the same topic. If discrepancies exist, further research is needed to determine which site is more accurate.

The site itself will also provide clues about the accuracy of its information. Ask yourself the following questions:

1. **Are the author's name and credentials provided?** A well-known writer with established credentials is likely to author only reliable, accurate information. If no author is given, you should question whether the information is accurate.
2. **Is contact information for the author included on the site?** Often, sites provide an e-mail address where the author may be contacted.
3. **Is the information complete, or in summary form?** If it is a summary, use the site to find the original source. Original information is less likely to contain errors and is usually preferred in academic papers.
4. **If opinions are offered, are they clearly presented as opinions?** Authors who disguise their opinions as facts are not trustworthy. (See the section on fact and opinion, page 102.)
5. **Does the site provide a list of works cited?** As with any form of research, sources used to put information up on a Web site must be documented. If sources are not credited, you should question the accuracy of the Web site.

It may be helpful to determine whether the information is available in print form. If it is, try to obtain the print version. Errors may occur when the article or essay is put up on the Web. Web sites move, change, and delete information, so it may be difficult for a reader of an academic paper to locate the Web site that you used in writing it. Also, page numbers are easier to cite in print sources than in electronic ones.

► **NOW PRACTICE . . . EVALUATING ACCURACY**

Evaluate the accuracy of two of the following Web sites.

1. **http://gunscholar.com/**

   Complete credentials and contact information of experts on gun use are

   included. The mission and purpose are clear. There are no dates to use

   in verifying the information.

2. **http://gecko.gc.maricopa.edu/~ssburd/tv.htm**

   There is no indication of what this is supposed to be. By shortening the

   URL, you can Discover that this is on the site of a student at a community

   college, but we do not know if it was written by that student. Works are

   cited in the text, but no reference list is given.

3. **http://www.theonion.com**

Although the user may not realize it immediately, this site is

for entertainment purposes only. Its "news" is based on real events but then

elaborated upon with humor and sarcasm.

Evaluating the Timeliness of a Web site

Although the Web is well known for providing up-to-the-minute information, not all Web sites are current. Evaluate a site's timeliness by checking:

- the date on which the Web site was posted (put on the Web).
- the date when the document you are using was added.
- the date when the site was last revised.
- the date when the links were last checked.

This information is usually provided at the end of the site's home page or at the end of the document you are using.

➤ NOW PRACTICE . . . EVALUATING TIMELINES

Evaluate the timeliness of two of the following Web sites, using the directions given for each site.

1. **http://www.state.gov/r/pa/ei/bgn/** Choose a geographic region, such as Africa, and evaluate whether information is up-to-date.

   Answers will vary.

2. **http://www.netcat.org/trojan.html** Evaluate whether this paper as a whole and the references within it are timely.

   The article shown here is from almost ten years ago. Some of the

   information may still be useful, but without

   updates, the user cannot be sure of its value.

3. **http://www.trailmix.ca/parks/parksupdateval.shtml** Evaluate whether this site contains up-to-date information and discuss why current information on this topic is crucial.

   The information is several years old and does not reflect any changes

   that might have been made to these recreational areas. This lack of

   information could cause safety problems.

10 Reading Across the Disciplines

Each academic discipline is a unique branch of knowledge, and each takes a specialized approach to the study of the world around us. To illustrate, let's take the example of a house pet—the dog—and consider how various disciplines might approach its study.

An artist might consider the dog as an object of beauty, focusing on its flexible muscular structure or meaningful facial expressions. A zoologist would be concerned with the animal's health, living habits, and bodily functions. A historian might research the historical significance of dogs and focus on their use as guard dogs in warfare or their role in herding sheep. Finally, an economist might focus on the supply and demand of dogs as it influences cost and consider the amount of business they generate (kennels, supplies, dog food, etc.).

Because each course you will take is different, you have to read and think differently in each. A national research study titled "Understanding University Success"[*] was conducted in 2003; it identified the critical thinking skills essential to success in various academic disciplines. Table 10.1, intended to demonstrate that different disciplines require different types of thinking, includes many of these skills identified by the study. Study the table to get an idea of the types of thinking involved in each disciplinary grouping. As you work through Part Two of this book, you will sample each of these disciplines and learn specific tips for reading skillfully in each.

---

[*] Conley, D.T. (Ed.) (2003). *Understanding University Success: A Report from Standards for Success.* A project of the American Association of American Universities and The Pew Charitable Trust. Eugene, OR: Center for Educational Policy Research, University of Oregon.

TABLE 10.1 ADAPTING YOUR THINKING TO ACADEMIC DISCIPLINES

DISCIPLINE	SPECIALIZED TYPES OF THINKING REQUIRED	EXAMPLES
Social Sciences (sociology, psychology, anthropology, economics)	Evaluate ideas, make generalizations, be aware of bias, follow and evaluate arguments	Studying patterns of child development, examining causes of age discrimination, comparing cultures
Mathematics	Think sequentially, reason logically, evaluate solutions	Solving word problems, understanding theorems
Natural and Life Sciences (biology, chemistry, physiology, physics, astronomy, earth science)	Grasp relationships, ask questions, understand processes, evaluate evidence	Studying the theory of evolution, examining the question of life in outer space.
Arts (music, painting, sculpture)	Evaluate the work of others, express your own ideas, critique your own work	Evaluate a sculpture, revise a musical score.
Applied Fields (career fields, technology, business)	Follow processes and procedures, make applications, make and evaluate decisions	Evaluate a patient (nursing). Find a bug in a computer program (computer technology)

PART TWO

Readings for Academic Disciplines

11

Social Sciences

The social sciences are concerned with the study of people, their history and development, and how they interact and function together. These disciplines deal with the political, economic, social, cultural, and behavioral aspects of people. Social scientists study how we live, how we act, how we dress, how we get along with others, and how our culture is similar to and different from other cultures. By reading in the social sciences, you will learn a great deal about yourself and those around you. In "Urban Legends" you will learn about a type of story that people share with each other. "The New Flirting Game" examines a much more personal form of human interaction—flirtation. "Coming Into My Own" considers a social problem—racial discrimination—and shows how a black neurosurgeon dealt with it. Use the following tips when reading in the social sciences.

TIPS FOR READING IN THE SOCIAL SCIENCES

- **Pay attention to terminology.** The social sciences use precise terminology to describe their subject matter. Learn terms that describe behavior, name stages and processes, and label principles, theories, and models. Also learn the names of important researchers and theorists. As you read, highlight new terms. You can transfer them later to index cards or a vocabulary log for that course.
- **Understand explanations and theories.** The social sciences are devoted, in part, to explaining how people behave as they do. In this chapter you will read an explanation of how people flirt and why people tell stories, for example. As you read theories and explanations, ask these questions: What behavior is being explained? What evidence is offered that it is correct? Of what use is the explanation?
- **Look for supporting evidence.** As you read, look for details, examples, anecdotes, or research evidence that demonstrates that the writer's explanations are reasonable or correct. When reading "Urban Legends" look for and study the author's examples of urban legends, for instance. Often, too, in the social sciences, the examples and applications are highly interesting and will help you remember the theories they illustrate.
- **Make comparisons and connections.** Try to see relationships and make comparisons. Draw connections between topics. Draw charts or maps that compare different explanations, for example.
- **Make practical applications.** As you read, consider how the information is useful to you in real-life situations. Make marginal notes of situations that illustrate what you are reading about. Write comments, for example, about what you have observed about flirting or about stories friends share among themselves.

161

SELECTION
1

Urban Legends
James M. Henslin

This reading was taken from a sociology textbook titled Sociology: A Down-to-Earth Approach. *It discusses a new phenomenon in storytelling—urban legends.*

▶ PREVIEWING THE READING

Using the steps listed on page 5, preview the reading selection. When you have finished, complete the following items.

1. Write a question you expect to be able to answer after you have read the article.

   What are urban legends?

2. This textbook excerpt probably defines the term _____urban legends_____.

 ## MAKING CONNECTIONS

NetSquirrel.com

THE URBAN LEGEND COMBAT KIT
AT NETSQUIRREL.COM

Is SULFNBK.EXE a virus? NO! It is an essential Windows utility that restores long file names. DO NOT DELETE SULFNBK.EXE!

If you accidentally deleted SULFNBK.EXE and want instructions on how to restore the file, visit http://netsquirrel.com/msconfig/sulf.html

Older Urban Legends and Myths

- The TRUTH about the "Forward an Email to All of Your Friends and Something Great Will Happen" Stories
- Should You Be Worried about the New Virus Warning Your Friend Just Sent You? (Maybe, maybe not. Probably not. Here are six rules that will help you protect yourself from all sorts of viruses ... and virus hoaxes)

- Are Crayons Really A Health Threat Because They Contain Asbestos? (No.)
- Are People Really "Harvesting" Kidneys? (No.)
- Are People Really Putting HIV-Infected Needles in Gas Pump Handles? (No!)
- Are People Really Putting HIV-Infected Needles in Theatre Seats and Pay Phone Coin Returns? (No.)
- Does Dialing 9-0-# Really Open Up Your Telephone Lines to Criminals? (Maybe, but only at work.)
- Have Gang Members Been Placing LSD and Strychnine on Pay Phone Number Pads? (No.)
- Have Asbestos and Rayon Been Added to Tampons to Make Women Bleed More? (No.)

Have you heard any of the stories (the urban legends) this Web page refers to? Did you believe any of them? Why or why not?

▶ READING TIP

Highlight this textbook excerpt as if you were preparing for an exam in a sociology class. Highlighting will focus your attention and help you remember what you read.

CHECKING YOUR READING RATE

If you plan to compute your reading rate, be sure to record your starting time in the box at the end of the exercises before you begin reading.

Urban Legends

1   Did you hear about Katie and Paul? They were parked at Echo Bay, listening to the radio, when the music was interrupted by an announcement that a rapist-killer had escaped from prison. Instead of a right hand, he had a hook. Katie said they should leave, but Paul laughed and said there wasn't any reason to go. When they heard a strange noise, Paul agreed to take her home. When Katie opened the door, she heard something clink. It was a hook hanging on the door handle!

2   For decades, some version of "The Hook" story has circulated among Americans. It has appeared as a "genuine" letter in "Dear Abby," and some of my students heard it in grade school. **Urban legends** are stories with an ironic twist that sound realistic but are false. Although untrue, they usually are told by people who believe that they happened.

3   Another urban legend that has made the rounds is the "Kentucky Fried Rat."

4   One night, a woman didn't have anything ready for supper, so she and her husband went to the drive-through at Kentucky Fried Chicken. While they were eating in their car, the wife said. "My chicken tastes funny."

5   Her husband said, "You're always complaining about something." When she insisted that the chicken didn't taste right, he put on the light. She was holding fried rat—crispy style. The woman went into shock and was rushed to the hospital.

6   A lawyer from the company offered them $100,000 if they would sign a release and not tell anyone. This was the second time this happened.

7   Folklorist Jan Brunvand (1981, 1984, 1986) reported that urban legends are passed on by people who think that the event happened just one or two people down the line of transmission, often to a "friend of a friend." The story has strong appeal and gains credibility from naming specific people or local places. Brunvand views urban legends as "modern morality stories"; each one teaches a moral lesson about life.

morality story
a story that is intended to teach a lesson

8   If we apply Brunvand's analysis to these two urban legends, three major points emerge. First, these morals serve as warnings. "The Hook" warns young people that they should be careful about where they go, with whom they go, and what they do. The world is an unsafe place, and "messing around" is risky. "The Kentucky Fried Rat" contains a different moral: Do you *really* know what you are eating when you buy food from a fast-food outlet? Maybe you should eat at home, where you know what you are getting.

9   Second, each story is related to social change: "The Hook" to changing sexual morality, the "Kentucky Fried Rat" to changing male–female relationships, especially to changing sex roles at home. Third, each is calculated to instill guilt and fear: guilt—the wife failed in her traditional role of cooking supper, and she was punished; and fear—we should all be afraid of the dangerous unknown, whether it lurks in the dark countryside or inside our bucket of chicken. The ultimate moral of

these stories is that we should not abandon traditional roles or the safety of the home.

10   These principles can be applied to an urban legend that made the rounds in the late 1980s. I heard several versions of this one; each narrator swore that it had just happened to a friend of a friend.

11   Jerry (or whoever) went to a nightclub last weekend. He met a good-looking woman, and they hit it off. They spent the night in a motel. When he got up the next morning, the woman was gone. When he went into the bathroom, he saw a message scrawled on the mirror in lipstick: "Welcome to the wonderful world of AIDS."

12   What moral and aspects of social change does this legend illustrate?

➤ A.   UNDERSTANDING THE THESIS AND OTHER MAIN IDEAS

Select the best answer.

__d__ 1. The term "urban legends" can be defined as

a. ordinary people making extraordinary contributions to their communities.

b. stories about modern-day heroes in urban settings.

c. traditional American folktales passed on from one generation to the next.

d. stories with an ironic twist that sound realistic but are false.

__b__ 2. The central thesis of "Urban Legends" is that

a. most urban legends are based on actual incidents.

b. urban legends provide moral lessons about life.

c. the people who create urban legends should be prosecuted.

d. people who believe in urban legends are gullible and will believe anything you tell them.

__b__ 3. The statement that best supports the author's central thesis is

a. "For decades, some version of 'The Hook' story has circulated among Americans." (paragraph 2)

b. "Brunvand views urban legends as 'modern morality stories'; each one teaches a moral lesson about life." (paragraph 7)

c. "The world is an unsafe place, and 'messing around' is risky." (paragraph 8)

d. "Maybe you should eat at home, where you know what you are getting." (paragraph 8) _c_ 4. The topic of paragraph 2 is

    a. "The Hook" story.

    b. letters to "Dear Abby."

    c. urban legends.

    d. people who believe urban legends.

_b_ 5. The main idea of paragraph 8 is expressed in the

    a. first sentence.

    b. second sentence.

    c. third sentence.

    d. last sentence.

➤ B. IDENTIFYING DETAILS

Select the best answer.

_c_ 1. According to Jan Brunvand, urban legends are often passed on by

    a. the individuals who were part of the actual event.

    b. the writers and folklorists who made them up.

    c. people who believe the event happened to a friend of a friend.

    d. older people who want to teach teenagers a lesson.

_b_ 2. In the story of "The Hook," the hook refers to the

    a. line that Paul uses to get Katie to go to Echo Bay with him.

    b. hook of an escaped rapist-killer with no right hand.

    c. catchy way urban legends draw the listener in.

    d. song that was playing on the radio while Katie and Paul were parked.

_d_ 3. After the woman tasted the fried rat in the story of the "Kentucky Fried Rat," she

    a. sent her husband into the restaurant to complain.

    b. immediately called the police to report the incident.

    c. died from eating the rat.

    d. went into shock and was rushed to the hospital.

_a_ 4. According to the reading, urban legends are

    a. untrue.

    b. possibly true.

    c. unlikely but possible.

    d. exaggerations of actual events.

___a___ 5. According to the reading, urban legends gain credibility by

    a. naming specific people or local places.

    b. being repeated several times.

    c. being reported in the newspaper.

    d. appearing on the local news.

➤ C.   RECOGNIZING METHODS OF ORGANIZATION AND TRANSITIONS

Complete the following statements by filling in the blanks.

In paragraphs 8 and 9, the phrase "three major points emerge" indicates the organizational pattern called ___enumeration___. The transitional words that identify the organizational pattern in the paragraphs are ___first___, ___second___, and ___third___.

➤ D.   REVIEWING AND ORGANIZING IDEAS: MAPPING

Complete the following map, "The Function of Urban Legends," by filling in the blanks.

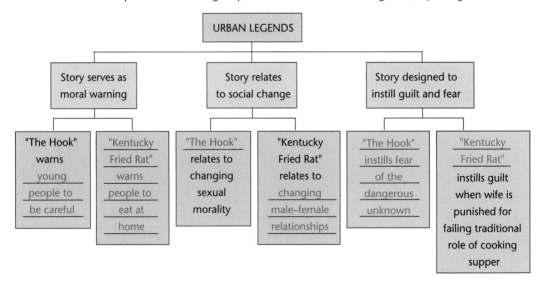

➤ E.   FIGURING OUT INFERRED MEANINGS

Indicate whether each statement is true (T) or false (F).

___F___ 1. The fact that "The Hook" appeared in a "Dear Abby" newspaper column means that it probably is true.

___T___ 2. The author of "Urban Legends" seems to have researched the topic of urban legends.

_F_ 3. The author of "Urban Legends" made up the stories in the article.

_F_ 4. Kentucky Fried Chicken sued the person who started the urban legend about the fried rat.

_T_ 5. The author of "Urban Legends" is applying Jan Brunvand's analysis to various urban legends.

➤ **F. THINKING CRITICALLY**

Select the best answer.

_a_ 1. The author supports the thesis of "Urban Legends" in all of the following ways *except*

    a. providing statistics.

    b. citing an expert.

    c. giving examples.

    d. giving definitions.

_b_ 2. The author's tone throughout the article can best be described as

    a. disgusted.

    b. informative.

    c. concerned.

    d. humorous.

_c_ 3. In paragraph 6, the statement "This was the second time this happened" was included in the story because

    a. it proves that the story was true.

    b. the incident had happened many times before.

    c. it adds credibility by making the story sound like it was not an isolated incident.

    d. the author had heard another, similar version of the story.

_d_ 4. In paragraph 10, the statement "I heard several versions of this one; each narrator swore that it had just happened to a friend of a friend" means that the

    a. person telling the story to the author was able to prove that it was true.

    b. woman in the story had done the same thing to several different men.

    c. same person was spreading around different versions of the story.

    d. person telling the story believed it to be true, but the author knew it was an urban legend.

➤ G.   BUILDING VOCABULARY

➤ Context

Using context and a dictionary, if necessary, determine the meaning of each word as it is used in the selection.

__d__ 1. morality (paragraph 7)

    a. dishonor

    b. individuality

    c. faith

    d. set of values

__a__ 2. analysis (paragraph 8)

    a. interpretation

    b. therapy

    c. modification

    d. lesson

__a__ 3. lurks (paragraph 9)

    a. hides

    b. observes

    c. realizes

    d. follows/returns

➤ Word Parts

A REVIEW OF ROOTS, PREFIXES, AND SUFFIXES

CRED- means *believe*
MIS- means *send*
DEC- means *ten*
TRANS- means *across*
-ION refers to a *condition*
-IST means *one who*
-ITY refers to a *quality*

Using your knowledge of word parts, write a definition for each of the following words.

1. decades (paragraph 2) _____ tens of years _____

2. folklorist (paragraph 7) _____ one who studies folklore _____

3. transmission (paragraph 7)

the condition of sending across/communication

4. credibility (paragraph 7) _____ _the quality of believing/believability_

> **Unusual Words/Unusual Meanings**
> *Select the best answer.*

_____ _b_ _____ When the author states that an urban legend has "circulated"
(paragraph 2) or "made the rounds" (paragraphs 3 and 10), both
phrases mean that the legend has been

a. published.

b. passed along or repeated.

c. proven false.

> **H. SELECTING A LEARNING/STUDY STRATEGY**

*Assume you were to take an essay exam on the sociology textbook chapter of
which this reading is part. Predict an essay question that might be asked on this
excerpt, and outline your answer to it.*

> **I. EXPLORING IDEAS THROUGH DISCUSSION AND WRITING**

1. Have you ever heard an urban legend? How far down the "line of transmission" from you were the people named in the event?

2. Give an example of a traditional "morality story." What moral lesson about life does it teach?

> **J. BEYOND THE CLASSROOM TO THE WEB**

Visit the Urban Legends Combat Kit at **http://www.netsquirrel.com/combatkit/index.html**.

*The selection you have just read suggests that urban legends are "modern
morality stories." Choose one of the stories at the Urban Legends Combat Kit, and
explain in a few sentences what morals it seems to support.*

✔ **Tracking Your Progress**

Selection 1

Section	Number Correct		Score
A. Thesis and Main Idea (5 items)	_____	x 5	_____
B. Details (5 items)	_____	x 4	_____
C. Organization and Transitions (4 items)	_____	x 3	_____
E. Inferred Meanings (5 items)	_____	x 4	_____
F. Thinking Critically (4 items)	_____	x 4	_____
G. Vocabulary			
1. Context (3 items)	_____	x 1	_____
2. Word Parts (4 items)	_____	x 1	_____

TOTAL SCORE _____%

CHECKING YOUR READING RATE

Words in Selection 1: 630

Finishing Time:	_____	_____	_____
	(hour)	(minutes)	(seconds)
Starting Time:	_____	_____	_____
	(hour)	(minutes)	(seconds)
Total Reading Time:		_____	_____
		(minutes)	(seconds)

Words Per Minute Score (page 735) _____ WPM

SELECTION 2

The New Flirting Game
Deborah A. Lott

This article first appeared in *Psychology Today* in February 1999. Read it to discover how pyschologists study the age-old custom of flirtation.

> **PREVIEWING THE READING**

Using the steps listed on page 5, preview the reading selection. When you have finished, complete the following items.

1. The subject of this reading is ___flirting___.

2. List at least three questions you expect to be able to answer after reading the article:

   a. What is the "flirting game"? or Why do people flirt?

   b. Who takes the lead in flirting?

   c. What are sexual semaphores? or Who is submissive in flirting?

 MAKING CONNECTIONS

Are these people flirting with each other? How can you tell?

➤ READING TIP

As you read, look for and highlight the qualities and characteristics of flirting. Highlighting will make it easier to review the reading and find information you need.

 CHECKING YOUR READING RATE

If you plan to compute your reading rate, be sure to record your starting time in the box at the end of the exercises before you begin reading.

The New Flirting Game

1   We flirt with the intent of assessing potential lifetime partners, we flirt to have easy, no-strings-attached sex, and we flirt when we are not looking for either. We flirt because, most simply, flirtation can be a liberating form of play, a game with suspense and ambiguities that brings joys of its own. As Philadelphia-based **social psychologist** Tim Perper says, "Some flirters appear to want to prolong the interaction because it's pleasurable and erotic in its own right, regardless of where it might lead."

2   Here are some of the ways the game is currently being played.

Taking the Lead

3   When it comes to flirting today, women aren't waiting around for men to make the advances. They're taking the lead. Psychologist Monica Moore, Ph.d. of Webster University in St. Louis, Missouri, has spent more than 2000 hours observing women's flirting maneuvers in restaurants, singles bars and at parties. According to her findings, women give nonverbal cues that get a flirtation rolling fully two-thirds of the time. A man may think he's making the first move because he is the one to literally move from wherever he is to the woman's side, but usually he has been summoned.

4   By the standards set out by **evolutionary psychologists**, the women who attract the most men would most likely be those with the most symmetrical features or the best hip-to-waist rations. Not so, says Moore. In her studies, the women who draw the most response are the ones who send the most signals. "Those who performed more than 35 displays per hour elicited greater than four approaches per hour," she notes, "and the more variety the woman used in her techniques, the more likely she was to be successful."

Sexual Semaphores

5   Moore tallied a total of 52 different nonverbal courtship behaviors used by women, including glancing, gazing (short and sustained), primping, preening, smiling, lip licking, pouting, giggling, laughing and nodding, as if to nonverbally indicate, "Yes! yes!" A woman would often begin with a room-encompassing glance, in actuality a casing-the-joint scan to seek out prospects. When she'd zeroed in on a target she'd exhibit the short darting glance—looking at a man, quickly looking away, looking back and then away again. There was something shy and indirect in this initial eye contact.

social psychologist
a person who studies how groups behave and how individuals are affected by the group

evolutionary psychologist
a person who tracks how human behavior and psychological traits have developed and changed over the course of history

semaphores
visual, nonverbal systems for sending information or signals

6   But women countered their shy moves with other, more aggressive and overt tactics. Those who liked to live dangerously took a round robin approach, alternately flirting with several different men at once until one responded in an unequivocal fashion. A few women hiked their skirts up to bring more leg into a particular man's field of vision. When they inadvertently drew the attention of other admirers, they quickly pulled their skirts down. If a man failed to get the message, a woman might parade, walking across the room towards him, hips swaying, breasts pushed out, head held high.

Who's Submissive?

7   Moore observed some of the same nonverbal behaviors that Eibl Eibesfeldt and other ethologists had deemed universal among women: the eyebrow flash (an exaggerated raising of the eyebrows of both eyes, followed by a rapid lowering), the coy smile (a tilting of the head downward, with partial averting of the eyes and, at the end, covering of the mouth), and the exposed neck (turning the head so that the side of the neck is bared.

ethologist
a person who
studies behavior
patterns

8   But while many ethologists interpret these signs as conveying female submissiveness, Moore has an altogether different take. "If these behaviors serve to orchestrate courtship, which they do, then how can they be anything but powerful?" she observes. "Who determined that to cover your mouth is a submissive gesture? Baring the neck may have a lot more to do with the neck being an erogenous zone than its being a submissive posture." Though women in Moore's sample used the coy smile, they also maintained direct eye contact for long periods and smiled fully and unabashedly.

9   Like Moore, Perper believes that ethologists have overemphasized certain behaviors and misinterpreted them as signifying either dominance or submission. For instance, says Perper, among flirting American heterosexual men and women as well as homosexual men, the coy smile is less frequent than direct eye contact and sustained smiling. He suggests that some cultures may use the coy smile more than others, and that it is not always a sign of deference.

10   In watching a flirtatious couple, Perper finds that a male will perform gestures and movements that an ethologist might consider dominant, such as sticking out his chest and strutting around, but he'll also give signs that could be read as submissive, such as bowing his head lower than the woman's. The woman may also do both. "She may drop her head, turn slightly, bare her neck, but then she'll lift her eyes and lean forward with her breasts held out, and that doesn't look submissive at all," Perper notes.

11   Men involved in these encounters, says Perper, don't describe themselves as "feeling powerful." In fact, he and Moore agree, neither party wholly dominates in a flirtation. Instead, there is a subtle, rhythmical and playful back and forth that culminates in a kind of physical synchronization between two people. She turns, he turns; she picks up her drink, he picks up his drink.

synchronization
happening at the
same time

12   Still, by escalating and de-escalating the flirtation's progression, the woman controls the pace. To slow down a flirtation, a woman might orient her body away slightly or cross her arms across her chest, or avoid meeting the man's eyes. To stop the dance in its tracks, she can yawn, frown, sneer, shake her head from side to side as if to say "No," pocket her hands, hold her trunk rigidly, avoid the man's gaze,

stare over his head, or resume flirting with other men. If a man is really dense, she might hold a strand of hair up to her eyes as if to examine her split ends or even pick her teeth.

Learning the Steps

13   If flirting today is often a conscious activity, it is also a learned one. Women pick up the moves early. In observations of 100 girls between the ages of 13 and 16 at shopping malls, ice skating rinks and other places adolescents congregate, Moore found the teens exhibiting 31 of the 52 courtship signals deployed by adult women. (The only signals missing were those at the more overt end of the spectrum, such as actual caressing.) Overall, the teens' gestures looked less natural than ones made by mature females: they laughed more boisterously and preened more obviously, and their moves were broader and rougher.

14   The girls clearly modeled their behavior on the leader of the pack. When the **alpha female** stroked her hair or swayed her hips, her companions copied quickly. "You never see this in adult women," says Moore, "Indeed, women go to great lengths to stand out from their female companions."

alpha female the "first" female in a group, the leader whose behavior is copied by the others in the group

15   Compared with adults, the teens signaled less frequently—7.6 signs per hour per girl, as opposed to 44.6 per woman—but their maneuvers, though clumsy, were equally effective at attracting the objects of their desire, in this case, teen boys.

16   Some of the exhilaration of flirting, of course, lies in what is hidden, the tension between what is felt and what is revealed. Flirting pairs volley back and forth, putting out ambiguous signals, neither willing to disclose more than the other, neither wanting to appear more desirous to the other.

17   To observers like Moore and Perper, flirtation often seems to most resemble the antics of children on the playground or even perhaps the ritual peek-a-boo that babies play with their caregivers. Flirters jostle, tease and tickle, even sometimes stick out a tongue at their partner or reach around from behind to cover up their eyes. As Daniel Stern, researcher, psychiatrist, and author of *The Interpersonal World of the Infant* (Karnac, 1998), has pointed out, the two groups in our culture that engage in the most sustained eye contact are mothers and infants, and lovers.

18   And thus in a way, the cycle of flirting takes us full circle. If flirting sets us off on the road to producing babies, it also whisks us back to the pleasures of infancy.

A.   UNDERSTANDING THE THESIS AND OTHER MAIN IDEAS

Select the best answer.

___d___ 1. The author's primary purpose in "The New Flirting Game" is to

a. expose the shallowness and superficiality of flirting behavior.

b. teach women and men the modern methods of flirting.

c. compare flirting behaviors of today with those of previous generations.

d. describe how and why women and men flirt.

_____d_____ 2. The main idea of paragraph 1 is that women and men flirt

    a. to find lifetime partners.

    b. to have uncomplicated sex.

    c. as a game.

    d. for many different reasons.

_____a_____ 3. The main idea of paragraph 3 is expressed in the

    a. first sentence.

    b. third sentence.

    c. fourth sentence.

    d. last sentence.

_____c_____ 4. The topic of paragraph 6 is

    a. risky behavior.

    b. male responses.

    c. flirting tactics.

    d. flirting mistakes.

_____d_____ 5. The main idea of paragraph 8 is that

    a. nonverbal flirting behaviors convey female submissiveness.

    b. women use both a smile and eye contact when flirting.

    c. the neck is an erogenous zone.

    d. nonverbal flirting behaviors are often powerful rather than submissive.

_____a_____ 6. The statement that best expresses the main idea of paragraph 13 is

    a. "If flirting today is often a conscious activity, it is also a learned one."

    b. "Women pick up the moves early."

    c. "The only signals missing were those at the more overt end of the spectrum."

    d. "Overall, the teens' gestures looked less natural than ones made by mature females."

_____b_____ 7. The main idea of paragraph 17 is that

    a. flirters are immature.

    b. flirtation resembles play.

    c. eye contact is important to mothers and infants.

    d. the eye contact between lovers is like that between mothers and infants.

➤ B.   IDENTIFYING DETAILS

Select the best answer.

____c____ 1. According to Dr. Moore's research, the women who attract the most
men are those

    a. with the most symmetrical features.

    b. with the best hip-to-waist ratios.

    c. who send the most signals.

    d. who are least interested in attracting men.

____b____ 2. All of the following courtship behaviors are considered "sexual semaphores" *except*

    a. glancing and gazing.

    b. using suggestive language.

    c. primping and preening.

    d. smiling and laughing.

____d____ 3. As described in the reading, one way that a woman can slow the pace
of a flirtation is by

    a. staring directly into the man's eyes.

    b. nodding as if in agreement.

    c. orienting her body toward him.

    d. crossing her arms across her chest.

____c____ 4. Nonverbal flirting behaviors that are considered universal among
women include all of the following *except* the

    a. eyebrow flash.

    b. coy smile.

    c. wink.

    d. exposed neck.

____c____ 5. As compared to the flirting behavior of adult women, the adolescent
girls observed by Dr. Moore did all of the following *except*

    a. exhibit many of the same courtship
signals.

    b. look less natural in their gestures.

    c. go to greater lengths to stand out from their female
companions.

    d. signal less frequently.

___c___ 6. According to Dr. Moore's findings, women give nonverbal cues that begin a flirtation

   a. one-third of the time.

   b. half of the time.

   c. two-thirds of the time.

   d. three-fourths of the time.

➤ C.   RECOGNIZING METHODS OF ORGANIZATION AND TRANSITIONS

Complete the following statements by filling in the blanks.

1. Locate a phrase in paragraph 9 that indicates an example is to follow.

   _____ For instance _____

2. In paragraphs 13–15, Dr. Moore's observations of adult women and adolescent girls are discussed using an organizational pattern called ___comparison and contrast___. A transitional phrase that helps identify the organizational pattern in this section is ___Compared with adults___.

➤ D.   REVIEWING AND ORGANIZING IDEAS: PARAPHRASING

Complete the following paraphrase of paragraph 8 by filling in the blanks with the correct words or phrases.

Paragraph 8: Although many ___ethologists___ believe these ___signs___ convey female ___submissiveness___, Dr. Moore disagrees. She says that since these ___behaviors___ seem to promote ___courtship___, they must be ___powerful___. She also disagrees that ___covering your mouth___ is a ___submissive___ gesture and states that ___baring the neck___ may have more to do with it being an ___erogenous zone___ than a ___submissive___ posture. Women in Moore's ___sample___ used the ___coy smile___ but they also maintained ___direct eye contact___ for extended periods and ___smiled___ fully and openly.

➤ E.   FIGURING OUT INFERRED MEANINGS

Indicate whether each statement is true (T) or false (F).

___T___ 1. Some people enjoy flirting simply for the fun of it.

___F___ 2. The people in the studies mentioned in the reading knew they were being observed.

___F___ 3. Evolutionary psychology and social psychology are the same thing.

___F___ 4. Flirting behaviors are the same in all cultures.

___T___ 5. Teenage girls learn most of their flirting behaviors from watching adult women.

➤ F. THINKING CRITICALLY

Select the best answer.

___b___ 1. The author supports the thesis of "The New Flirting Game" primarily with

    a. cause and effect relationships.

    b. research evidence.

    c. personal experience.

    d. statistics.

___d___ 2. The author's tone throughout the article can best be described as

    a. serious and concerned.

    b. judgmental and opinionated.

    c. pessimistic and depressing.

    d. light and factual.

___c___ 3. Another appropriate title for this reading would be

    a. "The Modern Moral Decline."

    b. "Commitment in the Twenty-First Century."

    c. "The Art and Science of Flirting."

    d. "Nonverbal Communication between Women and Men."

___d___ 4. In paragraph 3, the phrase "but usually he has been summoned" means that the man

    a. is usually the one who makes the first move.

    b. is expected to move from his location to the woman's.

    c. has been waved at from across the room.

    d. doesn't realize that he is responding to the woman's nonverbal invitation.

___a___ 5. The author ends the reading with

    a. a pleasing comparison.

    b. a warning.

    c. an appeal to action.

    d. a sympathetic note.

➤ **G.   BUILDING VOCABULARY**

➤ **Context**

Using context and a dictionary, if necessary, determine the meaning of each word as it is used in the selection.

___b___ 1. elicited (paragraph 4)

    a. expected from

    b. brought forth

    c. directed at

    d. returned to

___d___ 2. encompassing (paragraph 5)

    a. avoiding

    b. emptying

    c. filling

    d. including

___a___ 3. overt (paragraph 6)

    a. obvious

    b. secret

    c. friendly

    d. private

___a___ 4. dominance (paragraph 9)

    a. control

    b. stubbornness

    c. outgoing

    d. extrovert

___b___ 5. culminates (paragraph 11)

    a. fears

    b. concludes

    c. recovers

    d. begins

___d___ 6. congregate (paragraph 13)

    a. depart

    b. arrange

    c. plan

    d. gather

➤ **Word Parts**

> ### A REVIEW OF PREFIXES MEANING "NOT"
> Each of the following prefixes means *not*.
> DE-
> IN-
> MIS-
> NON-
> UN-

Match each word in Column A with its meaning in Column B. Write your answers in the spaces provided.

	Column A		Column B
	Prefix + Root		**Meaning**
d	1. nonverbal		a. not on purpose
e	2. indirect		b. not understood correctly
f	3. unequivocal		c. without embarrassment
a	4. inadvertently		d. not spoken
c	5. unabashedly		e. not straightforward
b	6. misinterpreted		f. without doubt or misunderstanding

➤ **Unusual Words/Unusual Meanings**
Indicate whether each statement is true (T) or false (F).

___T___ 1. In paragraph 1, the phrase "no-strings-attached sex" means sex that is uncomplicated by expectations of commitment.

___T___ 2. In paragraph 12, the phrase "to stop the dance in its tracks" means to bring an end to the flirtation.

➤ **H.   SELECTING A LEARNING/STUDY STRATEGY**

Discuss how visualization might help you learn the characteristics of flirting presented in this article.

➤ **I.   EXPLORING IDEAS THROUGH DISCUSSION AND WRITING**

1. The author uses terms that imply games or sports, such as the phrases "a round robin approach" (paragraph 6) and "volley back and forth" (paragraph 16). How do these phrases support her central thesis?
2. What images do the words "maneuvers" (paragraph 3) and "deployed" (paragraph 13) bring to mind?
3. Why is the reading called "The *New* Flirting Game"? What do you think the old flirting game consisted of?

➤ **J.   BEYOND THE CLASSROOM TO THE WEB**

Visit *"Developing Flirt-Ability"* at **http://www.askheartbeat.com**.
    Skim several articles. Compare the reliability of the articles on this Web site with Lott's article. Which is more likely to provide helpful information on dating and relationships? Why?

✔ **Tracking Your Progress**

Selection 2

Section	Number Correct		Score
A. Thesis and Main Idea (7 items)	_____	x 4	_____
B. Details (6 items)	_____	x 3	_____
C. Organization and Transitions (3 items)	_____	x 2	_____
E. Inferred Meanings (5 items)	_____	x 3	_____
F. Thinking Critically (5 items)	_____	x 3	_____
G. Vocabulary			
1. Context (6 items)	_____	x 2	_____
2. Word Parts (6 items)	_____	x 1	_____
		TOTAL SCORE	_____%

CHECKING YOUR READING RATE

Words in Selection 2: 1,358

Finishing Time:	_____ (hour)	_____ (minutes)	_____ (seconds)
Starting Time:	_____ (hour)	_____ (minutes)	_____ (seconds)
Total Reading Time:		_____ (minutes)	_____ (seconds)

Words Per Minute Score (page 735) _____ WPM

SELECTION 3

Coming Into My Own

Ben Carson

This reading was taken from an autobiography titled *Gifted Hands: The Ben Carson Story,* published in 1990. In his book, Carson, a well-known neurosurgeon, describes his journey from his childhood in inner-city Detroit to a position as director of pediatric neurosurgery at Johns Hopkins Hospital.

> ### PREVIEWING THE READING

Using the steps listed on page 5, preview the reading selection. When you have finished, answer the following questions.

1. What is the setting of the first half of the reading?

   A hospital

2. What is the subject's profession in this reading?

   A medical doctor

 ### MAKING CONNECTIONS

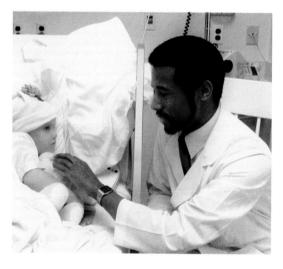

Dr. Benjamin Carson at Johns Hopkins Hospital. What do you suppose Dr. Carson is doing in this photo?

> **READING TIP**

As you read, notice situations that reveal racial discrimination or prejudice and how the author responded to them.

 CHECKING YOUR READING RATE

If you plan to compute your reading rate, be sure to record your starting time in the box at the end of the exercises before you begin reading.

Coming Into My Own

1   The nurse looked at me with disinterest as I walked toward her station. "Yes?" she asked, pausing with a pencil in her hand. "Who did you come to pick up?" From the tone of her voice I immediately knew that she thought I was an **orderly**. I was wearing my green scrubs, nothing to indicate I was a doctor.

orderly
an attendant
who does routine,
nonmedical work
in a hospital

2   "I didn't come to pick up anyone." I looked at her and smiled, realizing that the only Black people she had seen on the floor had been orderlies. Why should she think anything else? "I'm the new **intern**."

3   "New intern? But you can't—I mean—I didn't mean to" the nurse stuttered, trying to apologize without sounding prejudiced.

intern
a recent medical
school graduate
undergoing
supervised
practical training

4   "That's OK," I said, letting her off the hook. It was a natural mistake. "I'm new, so why should you know who I am?"

5   The first time I went into the **Intensive Care Unit**, I was wearing my whites (our monkey suits, as we interns called them), and a nurse signaled me. "You're here for Mr. Jordan?"

6   "No, ma'am, I'm not."

7   "You sure?" she asked as a frown covered her forehead. "He's the only one who's scheduled for respiratory therapy today."

**Intensive Care
Unit**
a specialized
section of a
hospital
containing the
equipment,
medical and
nursing staff,
and monitoring
devices necessary
to provide care
of extremely ill
patients

8   By then I had come closer and she could read my name badge and the word *intern* under my name.

9   "Oh, I'm so very sorry," she said, and I could tell she was.

10   Although I didn't say it, I would like to have told her, "It's all right because I realize most people do things based on their past experiences. You've never encountered a Black intern before, so you assumed I was the only kind of Black male you'd seen wearing whites, a respiratory therapist." I smiled again and went on.

11   It was inevitable that a few White patients didn't want a Black doctor, and they protested to Dr. Long. One woman said, "I'm sorry, but I do not want a Black physician in on my case."

12   Dr. Long had a standard answer, given in a calm but firm voice. "There's the door. You're welcome to walk through it. But if you stay here, Dr. Carson will handle your case."

13   At the time people were making these objections, I didn't know about them. Only much later did Dr. Long tell me as he laughed about the prejudices of some patients. But there was no humor in his voice when he defined his position. He was adamant about his stance, allowing no prejudice because of color or ethnic background.

14   Of course, I knew how some individuals felt. I would have had to be pretty insensitive not to know. The way they behaved, their coldness, even without saying anything, made their feelings clear. Each time, however, I was able to remind myself they were individuals speaking for themselves and not representative of all Whites. No matter how strongly a patient felt, as soon as he voiced his objection he learned that Dr. Long would dismiss him on the spot if he said anything more. So far as I know, none of the patients ever left!

15   I honestly felt no great pressures. When I did encounter prejudice, I could hear Mother's voice in the back of my head saying things like, "Some people are ignorant and you have to educate them."

16   The only pressure I felt during my internship, and in the years since, has been a self-imposed obligation to act as a role model for Black youngsters. These young folks need to know that the way to escape their often dismal situations is contained within themselves. They can't expect other people to do it for them. Perhaps I can't do much, but I can provide one living example of someone who made it and who came from what we now call a disadvantaged background. Basically I'm no different than many of them.

17   As I think of Black youth, I also want to say I believe that many of our pressing racial problems will be taken care of when we who are among the minorities will stand on our own feet and refuse to look to anybody else to save us from our situations. The culture in which we live stresses looking out for number one. Without adopting such a self-centered value system, we can demand the best of ourselves while we are extending our hands to help others.

18   I see glimmers of hope. For example, I noticed that when the Vietnamese came to the United States they often faced prejudice from everyone—White, Black, and Hispanics. But they didn't beg for handouts and often took the lowest jobs offered. Even well-educated individuals didn't mind sweeping floors if it was a paying job.

entrepreneurs
businesspeople

19   Today many of these same Vietnamese are property owners and **entrepreneurs**. That's the message I try to get across to the young people. The same opportunities are there, but we can't start out as vice president of the company. Even if we landed such a position, it wouldn't do us any good anyway because we wouldn't know how to do our work. It's better to start where we can fit in and then work our way up.

➤ A.   UNDERSTANDING THE THESIS AND OTHER MAIN IDEAS

Select the best answer.

___c___ 1. The writer of "Coming Into My Own" can best be described as

a. a black respiratory therapist.

b. a white female nurse.

c. a black male doctor.

d. the white patient of a black doctor.

_c_ 2. The statement from the reading that best supports the writer's primary thesis is

    a. "From the tone of her voice I immediately knew that she thought I was an orderly." (paragraph 1)

    b. "It was inevitable that a few White patients didn't want a Black doctor." (paragraph 11)

    c. "I can provide one living example of someone who made it and who came from what we now call a disadvantaged background." (paragraph 16)

    d. "I see glimmers of hope." (paragraph 18)

_a_ 3. According to the writer, the only pressure he felt during and after his internship has been from

    a. himself as he strives to be a role model for black youngsters.

    b. white nurses and doctors who treat him as less than equal.

    c. his parents and other family members because of their high expectations for him.

    d. members of other ethnic groups who resent his success.

_a_ 4. The statement that best expresses the main idea of paragraph 17 is

    a. People should look to themselves rather than others to improve their situations.

    b. Adopting a self-centered value system is the only way to succeed in our culture.

    c. The racial problems in our society are primarily caused by misunderstanding.

    d. Extending help to others is not as important as getting ahead.

_b_ 5. The topic of paragraph 18 is

    a. low-paying jobs.

    b. Vietnamese immigrants.

    c. prejudice among ethnic groups.

    d. education levels of immigrants.

_d_ 6. The main point of paragraph 19 is expressed in the

    a. first sentence.

    b. second sentence.

    c. fourth sentence.

    d. last sentence.

➤ B. IDENTIFYING DETAILS

Indicate whether each statement is true (T) or false (F).

__T__ 1. The writer/intern was mistaken for both an orderly and a respiratory therapist.

__F__ 2. The white patients who were prejudiced were careful to hide their feelings.

__F__ 3. Many patients left the hospital immediately rather than be treated by a black doctor.

__F__ 4. The writer came from a privileged background.

__T__ 5. Many Vietnamese immigrants who started in low-paying jobs now own property.

➤ C. RECOGNIZING METHODS OF ORGANIZATION AND TRANSITIONS

Select the best answer.

__b__ 1. In paragraphs 1–10, the writer describes the prejudice he has faced. The organizational pattern used in these paragraphs is

    a. cause and effect.   c. enumeration.

    b. time sequence.   d. comparison and contrast.

__c__ 2. A phrase in paragraph 18 that indicates that the writer will illustrate his ideas is

    a. But   c. For example

    b. Even   d. If

➤ D. REVIEWING AND ORGANIZING IDEAS: SUMMARIZING

Complete the following summaries of paragraphs 5–10 and 11–13 by filling in the missing words and phrases.

Paragraphs 5–10: The nurse assumed that the writer was a __respiratory therapist__, not a __doctor__. The writer understood that the nurse's assumption was based on her __past experiences__.

Paragraphs 11–13: Some __white__ patients did not want to be treated by a __black__ doctor. When they __complained/protested__ to Dr. Long, his response was that __they could either leave or stay and be treated by a black doctor__. Dr. Long later __laughed__ about the patients' __prejudices__, but he also made it clear that he would not tolerate __prejudice based on color or ethnic background__.

➤ **E.   FIGURING OUT INFERRED MEANINGS**

Indicate whether each statement is true (T) or false (F).

___F___ 1. From the situation described in paragraphs 1–4, it can be inferred that all orderlies are black males.

___T___ 2. From the description of the writer's mother, it can be inferred that she believed that her son could change people's attitudes toward blacks.

___F___ 3. From paragraphs 18–19, it can be inferred that the writer believes that immigrants are taking jobs away from blacks.

➤ **F.   THINKING CRITICALLY**

Select the best answer.

___b___ 1. The writer's primary purpose in writing this article is to

a. expose prejudice in the medical profession.

b: persuade others, especially black youth, that it is possible to succeed in spite of prejudice and a disadvantaged background.

c. discourage black males from becoming doctors.

d. argue against affirmative action programs that offer "handouts" to minorities.

___a___ 2. The writer supports his ideas primarily by

a. describing his personal experience.

b. reporting statistics.

c. defining terms.

d. citing facts.

___b___ 3. By stating in paragraph 2 that he looked at the nurse "and smiled," the writer indicates that he

a. was being sarcastic.

b. understood the nurse's error and forgave her.

c. was incredulous at being treated that way.

d. thought the nurse was joking.

___c___ 4. The writer's tone throughout the article can best be described as

a. bitter.   c. encouraging.

b. angry.   d. grateful.

➤ **G.   BUILDING VOCABULARY**

➤ **Context**
Using context and a dictionary, if necessary, determine the meaning of each word as it is used in the selection.

___b___ 1. prejudiced (paragraph 3)

    a. confused   c. inconsiderate

    b. biased   d. distracted

___c___ 2. inevitable (paragraph 11)

    a. unfortunate   c. unavoidable

    b. disappointing   d. unexpected

___a___ 3. adamant (paragraph 13)

    a. uncompromising   c. easygoing

    b. angry   d. humorous

___b___ 4. pressing (paragraph 17)

    a. pushy   c. unnecessary

    b. urgent   d. minor

➤ **Word Parts**

> **A REVIEW OF PREFIXES**
>
> **DIS-** means *not*
> **IN-** means *not*

Using your knowledge of word parts, choose the answer that best defines the underlined word in each sentence.

___d___ 1. "The nurse looked at me with <u>disinterest</u> as I walked toward her station." (paragraph 1)

    a. fascination   c. fear

    b. approval   d. indifference

___b___ 2. "I would have had to be pretty <u>insensitive</u> not to know." (paragraph 14)

    a. concerned   c. unhappy

    b. not aware   d. emotional

___c___ 3. ". . . I can provide one living example of someone who made it and who came from what we now call a <u>disadvantaged</u> background." (paragraph 16)

    a. wealthy   c. poor

    b. privileged   d. unlimited

➤ Unusual Words/Unusual Meanings

Use the meanings given below to write a sentence using the underlined phrase.

1. The expression <u>letting someone off the hook</u> (paragraph 4) means to release someone from an embarrassing situation or to forgive someone for an embarrassing mistake.

   Your sentence: _____

2. The phrase <u>looking out for number one</u> (paragraph 17) means to be concerned only with yourself or your own wants and needs.

   Your sentence: _____

H. SELECTING A LEARNING/STUDY STRATEGY

Assume this reading will be tested on an upcoming exam. Evaluate the usefulness of the summaries you completed above. Which other paragraphs would be useful to summarize?

I. EXPLORING IDEAS THROUGH DISCUSSION AND WRITING

1. Do you think the writer's response to prejudice was typical? How do you think you would react in a similar situation?

2. Have you observed or experienced situations in which someone revealed prejudice? How did you or the person handle the situation?

J. BEYOND THE CLASSROOM TO THE WEB

Visit the Gallery of Achievers Web page at http://www.achievement.org/frames.html.

Read the profile or interview of Dr. Ben Carson in the Hall of Science and Exploration. If you have the capability, view the video clips in the interview. After reading this additional information, how does your view of Ben Carson change, if at all?

✔ **Tracking Your Progress**

Selection 3

Section	Number Correct		Score
A. Thesis and Main Idea (6 items)	_____	x 5	_____
B. Details (5 items)	_____	x 4	_____
C. Organization and Transitions (2 items)	_____	x 2	_____
E. Inferred Meanings (3 items)	_____	x 4	_____
F. Thinking Critically (4 items)	_____	x 4	_____
G. Vocabulary			
1. Context (4 items)	_____	x 3	_____
2. Word Parts (3 items)	_____	x 2	_____

TOTAL SCORE _____ %

CHECKING YOUR READING RATE

Words in Selection 3: 860

	(hour)	(minutes)	(seconds)
Finishing Time:	_____	_____	_____
Starting Time:	_____ (hour)	_____ (minutes)	_____ (seconds)
Total Reading Time:		_____ (minutes)	_____ (seconds)

Words Per Minute Score (page 735) _____ WPM

12 Communication/Speech

The field of communication is concerned with the exchange of information between individuals and groups through speaking, writing, or nonverbal communication (body language, such as gestures). Communication may be interpersonal, such as communication between two persons; may occur within a small group, such as a group of friends or a class discussion; and may also be public, in which a speaker addresses an audience. Communication skills are important for success in college, for finding and keeping a rewarding job, and for building and maintaining healthy, strong relationships with family, friends, and coworkers.

By studying communication, you will come to understand those around you and exchange ideas with them more effectively. In "Can True Love Be Only 480 Seconds Away?" you will learn how people assess others as potential dates in an amazingly short amount of time. "Reading People: Actions Speak Louder Than Words" describes how to understand people by studying how they act, rather than what they say. In "Lovers" you will discover a method of classifying types of interpersonal love relationships and take a quiz to find out which type of love best describes your important relationships. Use the following tips when reading in the communication field.

TIPS FOR READING IN COMMUNICA-TION/SPEECH	■ **Pay attention to processes.** The field of communication is often concerned with how communication works. In "Can True Love Be Only 480 Seconds Away?" notice how the speed dating process works. ■ **Pay attention to principles—rules that govern how communication works.** The article "Reading People: Actions Speak Louder Than Words" is based on the principle that nonverbal signs and signals reveal a great deal about a person's attitudes. ■ **Notice theories (explanations that attempt to describe how or why something happens).** In "Lovers" you read one researcher's theory of how love can be classified. ■ **Be alert for cultural differences.** Not all cultures and ethnic groups follow the same conventions and theories. Do you think the classifications of love presented in "Lovers" would work in India or in Saudi Arabia, for instance? ■ **Pay attention to terminology.** In "Lovers," for example, you will find six new terms that are used to classify love.

- **Think critically.** As you read theories, ask challenging questions, such as "Does this information fit with what I already know and have experienced?" For example, when reading "Reading People: Actions Speak Louder Than Words," have you observed similar or different behaviors from those the author describes at family dinners and in the workplace?

SELECTION 4	Can True Love Be Only 480 Seconds Away?

This article first appeared in a July 2000 issue of *The Christian Science Monitor*. Read it to discover one of the newest trends in dating.

PREVIEWING THE READING

Using the steps listed on page 5, preview the reading selection. When you have finished, complete the following items.

1. What is the subject of this selection?

   speed dating
   _____

2. What is the time frame specified for each "date"?

   eight minutes
   _____

3. List one reason given in the selection for the popularity of speed dating.

   It's a safe way to meet people or It's a fast way to meet a partner.
   _____

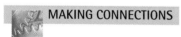 MAKING CONNECTIONS

From the SpeedDating logo, what can you infer about this new form of dating?

READING TIP

As you read this article, create a list of the pros and cons of speed dating.

CHECKING YOUR READING RATE

If you plan to compute your reading rate, be sure to record your starting time in the box at the end of the exercises before you begin reading.

Can True Love Be Only 480 Seconds Away?

1   Eight minutes. That's about the time it takes for the sun's light to reach Earth. It's also roughly the time it takes to wolf down a McDonald's cheeseburger. Or bake a batch of chocolate-chip cookies. Or meet your soul mate. Yep, short-on-time singles say that's how long it takes to size up a potential love interest in today's lightning-speed world. After all, why waste an entire evening on someone they deemed incompatible in the first few minutes?

2   It's no wonder so many singles are embracing the newest trend in relationships: speed dating. Supporters say it offers a chance to meet lots of new people in less-charged circumstances. But others lament what it says about the rushed nature of American lives, that people can't savor getting to know one another. To say nothing of a superficial society able to dismiss someone in the time it takes to boil an egg.

3   The evening begins with an equal number of men and women pairing off to chat for exactly eight minutes. The bell rings, the chairs rotate, and it's on to the next prospect. At the end of the evening, tallies are made and phone numbers given out—but only if both sides agree.

4   SpeedDating is the creation of Aish HaTorah, an international Jewish educational resource center. Its intent is to preserve the Jewish heritage by encouraging marriage within the faith. It was launched last year in Los Angeles and has swept into Jewish communities across the United States, Australia, Britain, Canada, South Africa, even the Ukraine. Now the **secular** community has grabbed hold of the idea.

secular
not related to religion or a religious organization

Safer Way to Meet

5   "It's got all the safety of **the personals** with more of the interaction," says Eden Cloud, SinglesScene coordinator at the Philadelphia Weekly who runs a secular version of SpeedDating, called Nanodates. "Everyone can be interesting for eight minutes. I can talk about baseball for eight minutes and I don't know the first thing about it." Nanodates began in Philadelphia earlier this month and is already booked (with long wait lists) through September.

the personals
the personal advertisements placed in a newspaper

6   Ms. Cloud says it's too early for any of her speed daters to be walking down the aisle. But she recently ran into a participant who, smiling from ear to ear, said she had already been on several dates with her match. "It's all about first impressions. And eight minutes is enough time to decide if you want to see someone again," Cloud says.

7   Some may disagree. Others claim to need even less time. "I think you can tell in the first five minutes, or at least you can eliminate someone in the five minutes," says Laura Lieberman, a communications consultant from Philadelphia who participated in a Nanodates session. "I was a little hesitant at first, thinking, how is this going to be? But it turned out to be a lot of fun," Ms. Lieberman says. "Everybody was in the same boat, everybody was nervous."

8   Her first question to every man sitting in front of her was: "How was your day?" The rapid-fire conversation moved to jobs, free time, families. She had one match and is going on a date with him this week. Impressed with her success, her friends

are now signing up for future sessions. "I'm not surprised that it's spreading. It's a brilliant idea," says Rabbi Micha Turtletaub, director of education of Aish HaTorah, Boston, which will begin SpeedDating this fall. He and other Jewish leaders hope that the secular version's success doesn't overshadow SpeedDating's original purpose—though perhaps the spread was inevitable.

Time's A-Wasting

9   "People feel their time is limited and to do the bar scene or simply wait until they meet someone somewhere feels to them a waste of time," says Mr. Turtletaub. Not only do people feel they have less time to meet their perfect partner, the anxiety created by those feelings is at an all-time high. "The collective unconscious fear that we are never going to meet anybody, that everyone is gay or married, makes people nervous, and they withdraw even further," says Judy Kuriansky, a clinical psychologist and author of "Complete Idiot's Guide to Dating."

collective unconscious a concept from Jungian psychology in which a part of each person's mind contains the unconscious feelings shared by a society or all humankind

10   SpeedDating and similar concepts like Internet dating have their pros and cons, she says. One pro is the ability to meet a wide variety of people in a short time. "I totally agree that we need to expose ourselves to many different types of people, to see what our instinctive reaction is to them," Dr. Kuriansky says. "Eight minutes is long enough to see how conversation goes, to see if you are comfortable, to see if he asks about you and shares about himself." But it is not long enough to get a good grasp on someone, she says. Three dates is her benchmark.

11   But some research shows that it only takes 15 seconds to make a first impression, and that that impression remains important throughout the relationship. "So eight minutes is already a lot more data than most people start with," Kuriansky says. Back in Philadelphia, Jerod (not his real name) saw the Nanodates ad and decided to give it a try. He came away with two matches. But he does have some reservations about the time limit. "My gut feeling is that eight minutes isn't long enough," says Jerod. "We all see ourselves as complex and varied. How can somebody express their personality in eight minutes?"

12   At a local restaurant, Jerod talked for almost two hours to eight different women about buying a house, his job, his likes and dislikes, his family. But he says he was more interested in finding out about the woman sitting across from him. "I felt like I was under the gun to find out what made that other person tick, what they were passionate about," he says. "Most of the time I would just ask them, 'what would you be doing if you weren't here?'"

➤ A. UNDERSTANDING THE THESIS AND OTHER MAIN IDEAS

Select the best answer.

___c___ 1. The central thesis of the selection is that
  a. the Jewish community created speed dating.

  b. speed dating is an indication of how superficial society has become.

  c. speed dating is a recent trend among single people looking for a relationship.

  d. the secular community has adopted many programs that were originally religion-based.

___b___ 2. The author's primary purpose is to

    a. promote speed dating.

    b. describe speed dating.

    c. criticize people who participate in speed dating.

    d. compare Jewish speed dating programs to secular programs.

___c___ 3. The question that is answered in paragraph 3 is

    a. Who created speed dating?

    b. Why do people speed date?

    c. How does speed dating work?

    d. What are the advantages of speed dating?

___d___ 4. The topic of paragraph 4 is

    a. Aish HaTorah.

    b. Jewish educational resource centers.

    c. Jewish heritage.

    d. the origin of speed dating.

___d___ 5. The main idea of paragraph 9 is that speed dating is becoming popular because

    a. it costs less than traditional dating services.

    b. people are more interested in marrying within their own religion.

    c. it eliminates people who are gay or married.

    d. people are anxious to meet a partner quickly.

▶ B. IDENTIFYING DETAILS

Indicate whether each statement is true (T) or false (F).

___T___ 1. A speed dating session begins with equal numbers of men and women.

___T___ 2. Speed dating was launched in Los Angeles.

___F___ 3. Nanodates is geared to Christian singles.

___F___ 4. Dr. Kuriansky believes that eight minutes is long enough to get a good sense of what someone is like.

___F___ 5. The first question Jerod asked each woman he met during his Nanodates session was "What do you do for a living?"

➤ **C.   RECOGNIZING METHODS OF ORGANIZATION AND TRANSITIONS**

Complete the following statements by filling in the blanks.

1. In paragraph 2, the author uses the ___comparison and contrast___ organizational pattern to compare supporters' views of speed dating with the views of those who criticize the idea. The transitional word that indicates this pattern is ___but___.

2. The transitional words in paragraph 4 that suggest a sequence in time are ___last year___ and ___now___.

➤ **D.   REVIEWING AND ORGANIZING IDEAS: SUMMARIZING**

Complete the following summary of paragraphs 7–8 by filling in the missing words or phrases.

Paragraphs 7–8: People disagree on whether ___eight___ minutes is long enough to decide about seeing someone again. One participant in ___Nanodates/speed dating___ thinks ___five___ minutes is long enough. She felt nervous at first, but she enjoyed her session, which began with a ___question___ about each date's ___day___ and quickly moved on to other subjects. She made a ___date___ with one person she met, which has encouraged her ___friends___ to sign up. A ___rabbi___ whose congregation will soon begin a speed dating program believes the idea will continue to spread, although he and other ___Jewish leaders___ hope that ___secular___ speed dating doesn't diminish its original purpose.

➤ **E.   FIGURING OUT INFERRED MEANINGS**

Indicate whether each statement is true (T) or false (F).

___T___ 1. It can be inferred that speed daters are not always successful in finding someone they want to date.

___F___ 2. It can be inferred that Jews are forbidden to marry outside their faith.

___F___ 3. People believe that speed dating is not as safe as placing a personal advertisement.

___F___ 4. It can be inferred that Nanodates is struggling to find clients.

___F___ 5. First impressions do not really matter in relationships.

➤ **F.   THINKING CRITICALLY**

Select the best answer.

___a___ 1. The author supports the central thesis of the selection primarily with

   a. descriptions and examples.

   b. facts and statistics.

   c. personal experience.

   d. cause and effect relationships.

____c____ 2. In the beginning of the article the author captures the reader's attention by

   a. quoting a person who has participated in speed dating.

   b. quoting a person who runs a speed dating service.

   c. describing a variety of actions that require only eight minutes to happen.

   d. describing a typical speed dating session.

____b____ 3. The description of the speed dating environment as "less-charged" (paragraph 2) means that, in comparison to traditional methods of meeting people, participants do not

   a. feel they have to charge as much on their credit cards.

   b. experience as much emotional pressure or anxiety.

   c. feel as obligated to ask for another date.

   d. worry about being accused of inappropriate behavior.

____d____ 4. The author includes the quotes from Eden Cloud at Nanodates (paragraphs 5–6) in order to

   a. imply that Nanodates is unsuccessful because none of the participants have gotten married.

   b. endorse Nanodates as the best speed dating organization mentioned in the selection.

   c. point out the superficiality of speed dating.

   d. explain the appeal of speed dating.

____a____ 5. When Judy Kuriansky mentions "the collective unconscious fear" (paragraph 9), she is referring to the

   a. feelings shared by many people that they will never be able to find a mate.

   b. idea that most people are unaware of what they truly want in a mate.

   c. theory that most people are afraid of revealing their fears.

   d. fear of Jewish leaders that their heritage will be lost.

G. BUILDING VOCABULARY

Context

Using context and a dictionary, if necessary, determine the meaning of each word as it is used in the selection.

__b__ 1. lament (paragraph 2)

    a. discuss   c. consider

    b. regret   d. admire

__c__ 2. savor (paragraph 2)

    a. wait   c. enjoy

    b. believe   d. decide

__a__ 3. heritage (paragraph 4)

    a. tradition   c. style

    b. rules   d. obligation

__c__ 4. benchmark (paragraph 10)

    a. replacement   c. standard

    b. opinion   d. prediction

Word Parts

> **A REVIEW OF PREFIXES**
>
> **IN-** means *not*
> **NANO-** means *extremely small*
> **SUPER-** means *above, upon*

Use the review of prefixes above to fill in the blanks in the following sentences.

1. If you are *incompatible* (paragraph 1) with another person, the two of you are _____not_____ compatible, or not right for each other.

2. To describe society as *superficial* (paragraph 2) is to say that it dwells on what is ___above or upon___ the surface; in other words, society is shallow rather than in-depth or profound.

3. The name of the speed dating company, *Nanodates* (paragraph 5), refers to the ___extremely small___ amount of time allotted for each meeting or "date" within a speed dating session.

➤ **Unusual Words/Unusual Meanings**
Use the meanings on the next page to write a sentence using the underlined word or phrase.

1. To <u>size up</u> someone (paragraph 1) is to evaluate the person's worth or form an opinion about the person; you can also size up a problem or task by evaluating it.

   Your sentence: _____

2. The term <u>rapid-fire</u> (paragraph 8) applies to something that happens very rapidly and continually, as in shots being fired from a gun.

   Your sentence: _____

3. To be <u>under the gun</u> (paragraph 12) is to feel pressure to accomplish something within a limited amount of time or by a deadline.

   Your sentence: _____

➤ **H.   SELECTING A LEARNING/STUDY STRATEGY**

Select the best answer.

   __d__   Which of the following strategies would be most useful in preparing to answer the following essay question: "Define speed dating and discuss its advantages and disadvantages."?

   a. reread the article

   b. visualize a speed dating session

   c. use index cards to record facts about speed dating

   d. write a paragraph summarizing its pros and cons

➤ **I.   EXPLORING IDEAS THROUGH DISCUSSION AND WRITING**

1. Did the selection convince you that speed dating is a good way to find a mate? Why or why not?

2. What question would you use to get the conversation going in a speed dating situation?

3. Tell how much time you think is necessary to get a "good grasp" on someone's personality. Do you think you could express your personality in eight minutes?

4. How significant are first impressions? Describe an experience in which your first impression of someone or something turned out to be wrong.

➤ **J.   BEYOND THE CLASSROOM TO THE WEB**

Visit "The Dating Dilemma—A Brief History of Dating" at **http://www
.geocities.com/Heartland/Prairie/5894/datinghistory.html**.

Contrast speed dating with two or three of the other methods used throughout
U.S. history to meet potential marriage partners. Write a paragraph explaining how
speed dating is different from these other ways of interacting.

✔ **Tracking Your Progress**

Selection 4

Section	Number Correct		Score
A. Thesis and Main Idea (5 items)	_____	x 5	_____
B. Details (5 items)	_____	x 4	_____
C. Organization and Transitions (2 items)	_____	x 2	_____
E. Inferred Meanings (5 items)	_____	x 4	_____
F. Thinking Critically (5 items)	_____	x 4	_____
G. Vocabulary			
1. Context (4 items)	_____	x 2	_____
2. Word Parts (3 items)	_____	x 1	_____
		TOTAL SCORE	_____%

CHECKING YOUR READING RATE

Words in Selection 4: 985

Finishing Time:	_____	_____	_____
	(hour)	(minutes)	(seconds)
Starting Time:	_____	_____	_____
	(hour)	(minutes)	(seconds)
Total Reading Time:		_____	_____
		(minutes)	(seconds)

Words Per Minute Score (page 735) _____ WPM

SELECTION 5

Reading People: Actions Speak Louder Than Words

Jo-Ellan Dimitrius and Mark Mazzarella

This reading was taken from a book titled *Reading People: How to Understand People and Predict Their Behavior—Anytime, Anyplace.* Dimitrius, Ph.D., is a jury consultant who helps attorneys select jurors. Mazzarella is a practicing trial lawyer. Read this article to find out how you can learn to read people, not by what they say but by what they do.

➤ PREVIEWING THE READING

Using the steps listed on page 5, preview the reading selection. When you have finished, complete the following items.

1. What is the topic of this selection?

   <u>understanding people</u>

2. List four places the author suggests for people-watching.

   a. <u>family dinners</u>

   b. <u>a workplace other than your own</u>

   c. <u>company picnics</u>

   d. <u>crowded rooms</u>

 MAKING CONNECTIONS

From this photo, can you guess what this woman is feeling?

How much does having the rest of the context help you determine what she is probably feeling? Why would this be so?

➤ **READING TIP**

Draw a vertical line down the middle of a sheet of paper. Draw another line horizontally across the middle of the page. (Your paper should look like this: ⊞ .) Write one of the following words or phrases in each box: "family dinner," "workplace," "company picnic," and "crowded room." As you read the article, make notes about what behaviors to look for in each place.

CHECKING YOUR READING RATE

If you plan to compute your reading rate, be sure to record your starting time in the box at the end of the exercises before you begin reading.

Reading People: Actions Speak Louder Than Words

1   Certain situations are tailor-made for people-watching. In these settings you can observe how someone deals with people he likes, people he can't stand, family, co-workers, and strangers. You've been a participant in scenes like these many times, but the next time you're there, take a moment not only to watch the people around you but to read them.

The Family Dinner

2   In many famous films, the crucial scene takes place around the family dinner table. It's the perfect forum for drama, and it's fun and informative to watch, especially if the family isn't your own.

3   The family dinner can be extremely revealing, especially if it's attended by someone's parents, spouse, siblings, and children. For one thing, you can get a good feel for the person's background. Someone's background is a key predictive factor. How someone was raised, and by whom, will have a tremendous influence on the type of person she is. Psychologists often point out that when it comes to child-rearing, what goes around comes around: those who are raised with criticism become critical, those who are raised with love become caring, and those who are raised with encouragement become supportive. By watching how someone's parents treat her and her siblings, and how she treats them, you can get a good feel for the way she was raised and how she's likely to treat others.

4   A person's relationship with his spouse is also very telling. Does he expect to be waited on, or is he quick to offer to fill empty glasses, set and clear the table, and wash the dishes? Does he lead the discussion, or passively sit by and watch? Is he affectionate or distant?

5   The dinner table is also a good place to watch how a person treats her children. Does she draw them into the conversation? Does she keep an eye on their manners? Is she warm and affectionate? Is she relaxed and comfortable around her kids, or critical and tense? Patient or quick-tempered? Take note of the subtleties, and how the children behave toward their parents. Are they timid or confident? Polite or disrespectful?

6   If you spend time with the family before or after the meal, keep your eyes open. Is there laughter and playfulness in the home? Does the family sit motionless in front of the television until dinner is served, or do they chat? If so, what about? Can you spot evidence of family projects—a jigsaw puzzle, art projects, a plate of kid-decorated cookies? Are there any pets, and if so, how do the family members interact with them?

7   The first time you have a meal with the family of someone important to you—a prospective mate, a new friend, a business associate—you're often too nervous about the impression you'll make to notice much of what's going on. If you can summon your concentration and really look around, you'll get a priceless preview of what's in store should your relationship grow.

A Workplace, Not Your Own

8   I love going to my dentist's office. It's not that I have a masochistic streak that attracts me to Novocain and dental drills. It's just that I always feel uplifted in that environment. My dentist and his assistant, hygienist, and receptionist have all been together for years. There is constant laughter, joking, and friendly inquiries about the events in one another's lives. I'm inspired by the competence, good cheer, and kindness with which the people in the office interact with one another and with patients. This is how all dentists' offices would be in a perfect world.

9   Even before I learned more about the individual personalities in my dentist's office, I could guess a lot about them just because of the environment they have created together and the way they treat one another. The laughter tells me they're friendly, open, and don't take life too seriously. It also suggests that they're content with their jobs and with life in general. I've never heard any of them gossip, about anyone. While all of them are very professional and competent, no one appears oppressed or fixed, nose to the grindstone, at his or her station. The overall feel is one of ideal equality, respect, and teamwork. In fact, if I didn't know that in a dentist's office the dentist is typically the boss, I would probably pick the receptionist as the one in charge, since she's always directing traffic.

10   What can I tell from a workplace like this? The person whom it reflects most strongly is the dentist. He picked the staff, and he nurtures the environment. While the other members of the team are equally dedicated and cooperative, he gets credit for creating and maintaining this atmosphere, because he has the most control over it. The fact that his staff has stayed with him for many years indicates not only that he's a nice person and good manager, but also that he probably pays them a fair wage. He's generous not only with his praise but with his pocketbook—an all too uncommon trait.

11   You can learn several important things when you enter someone's workplace. First, the atmosphere will tell you what kind of person is running the show. This can be an important clue about the person you're evaluating: Why did he choose this workplace, and this boss? Does he enjoy the atmosphere, or dread coming to work each day? Are the other workers cheerful or grouchy? Are they tired and overworked, or energetic? After sizing up the atmosphere, take a look at how your "readee" fits in. If it's a healthy atmosphere, does he appear to be contributing to it, or cynically staying on the sidelines? If it's a tense, unpleasant atmosphere, does he seem to notice and mind, or does he shrug and say, "That's life in the big city"?

12   When someone is willing to work in a tense, high-pressure atmosphere, it's essential that you look for reasons. For instance, many large law firms have reputations for being **sweatshops**. The attorneys, particularly the young ones, work incredibly long hours and have little time for themselves or their families. If the only thing I know about someone is that he works in one of these firms and is happy and satisfied there, I know he is probably aggressive, hard-charging, confident, intelligent, and strong-willed. I can also reasonably assume that his family is not his highest priority; he's ambitious and probably self-centered. Once again, there are always exceptions, but this is my bias, and it has been borne out many times as I've gotten to know people who thrive in this environment.

sweatshops
shops or factories in which employees work many hours for low pay under poor conditions

The Company Picnic

13   A company party or picnic is an excellent occasion to watch your co-workers. Maybe you see them every day at the water cooler or in staff meetings, but larger events can give you a different, and often more revealing, view. Frequently those in attendance are so busy partying they don't spend much time people-watching. But where else can you see someone interact with his boss, colleagues, subordinates, friends, spouse, and children (other people's as well as his own)?

14   Watch to find out who organizes games and who joins in. Who are the socialites and who are the recluses? Do people spend their time mingling comfortably with superiors, co-workers, and subordinates alike, or do they keep to their own? How do they relate to the children present? How do they treat their spouse? Who spends time with his mate, and who abandons her in favor of other pursuits?

15   You'll be able to pinpoint the leaders, the followers, and the loners. You'll find out who is confident and who's insecure; who is happy and who's discontented; who's friends with whom, and who is no one's friend. So don't back out of the next company event. Go to it, watch, and learn.

The Crowded Room

16   If you've never gone to a party, wedding, or other big event where you don't know most people, and played the observer with the intent to read them, try it. A bash like this is a great opportunity to try to peg different types.

17   Find the person with the loudest voice and watch how he moves around the room. How closely does he approach the people he talks to? How frequently does he sit down with them? Does he dominate discussions? Observe the observer. Watch how she reacts when someone approaches her. See how she holds her drink, and whether she sips it nervously or takes long, slow sips as she peers over the glass across the room. Watch the line at the bar or the buffet table, and see who pushes in and who graciously makes room for others. Identify who's taking the lead by organizing activities, making toasts, introducing people, or assuring that everyone's needs are met.

18   Practiced observation will reveal much about the personalities you study in a crowded room. Some people will seem intent on dominating the group. They will position themselves at the head of the table, or wherever the most people are. They will be loud and control virtually any discussion in which they participate. These people, while seemingly confident, may actually be the most insecure. Undeniably, they are seeking attention.

19   There are also observers. They will typically position themselves at the edge of the room, where they can watch everything. They usually speak with people one on one, and while talking they continue to survey the environment. Observers may withdraw to their observation posts because they are uncomfortable in large groups. It's just as likely, however, that they are perfectly comfortable but would rather sit on the sidelines. I can usually tell which: If an observer is approached and withdraws at the first opportunity, he reveals that he's uncomfortable and has staked out his observation post for that reason. If, on the other hand, he engages in conversation for a reasonable period of time, but then graciously excuses himself to find another secluded post, he shows that he is not particularly uncomfortable with large groups but for whatever reason has chosen on that evening to remain on the sidelines.

20   Those who are generally uncomfortable in large groups will typically shift nervously and change locations frequently. They will avoid contact with others. They will resist when someone attempts to draw them into whatever activities are under way. I know a man who frequently seeks out a television to watch, even when he's a guest in someone else's home. Others will disguise their retreat as an excursion to look at the art down the hall or check out the landscaping in the yard. This type of reaction in a group environment may reveal a number of different things. Perhaps the person is preoccupied with other matters and simply wants to be alone for a while. He may also be very uncomfortable and trying to escape.

21   I know one very well-known attorney who has the disconcerting habit of looking over people's shoulders as he greets them in a crowded room. He's scanning for anyone more worthwhile on whom to focus his attention. This obviously reflects arrogance and earns him a poor score on my personal "hardness scale."

22   Other people will quickly attach themselves to someone and spend hours without mingling at all. Maybe these two have a lot of catching up to do. But if not, they probably feel uncomfortable in groups.

23   Still others will work the room, going from person to person as if prizes were being awarded to whoever shakes the most hands. Generally speaking, more confident and outgoing people will be much more sociable in large groups but won't feel the need to flit from person to person.

24   You never need to evaluate these interactions in isolation. The general observations I've offered here may be confirmed by physical appearance, body language, voice, and other clues. But if those other clues persuade you that the person's interaction in a crowd doesn't fit his overall pattern, you may choose to give it little weight. But make sure you add it to the mix.

➤ A.   UNDERSTANDING THE THESIS AND OTHER MAIN IDEAS

Select the best answer.

___c___ 1. The central thesis of "Reading People" is that

  a. the best way to evaluate a potential friend or mate is to watch the person around his or her family.

  b. body language is an important means of communicating with other people.

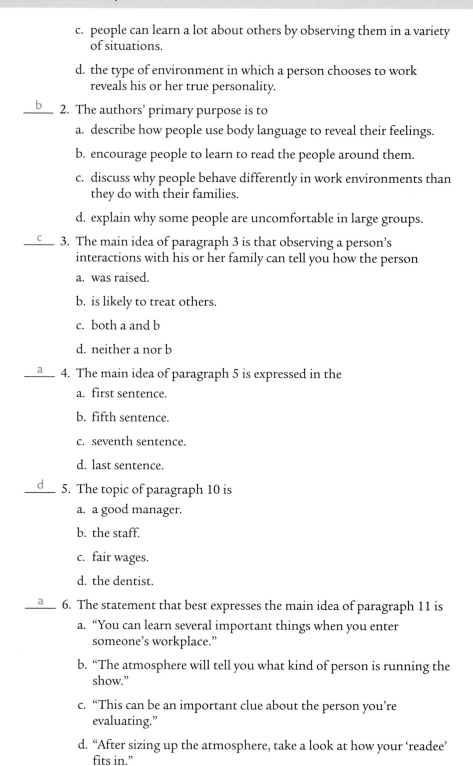

       c. people can learn a lot about others by observing them in a variety of situations.

       d. the type of environment in which a person chooses to work reveals his or her true personality.

___b___ 2. The authors' primary purpose is to

       a. describe how people use body language to reveal their feelings.

       b. encourage people to learn to read the people around them.

       c. discuss why people behave differently in work environments than they do with their families.

       d. explain why some people are uncomfortable in large groups.

___c___ 3. The main idea of paragraph 3 is that observing a person's interactions with his or her family can tell you how the person

       a. was raised.

       b. is likely to treat others.

       c. both a and b

       d. neither a nor b

___a___ 4. The main idea of paragraph 5 is expressed in the

       a. first sentence.

       b. fifth sentence.

       c. seventh sentence.

       d. last sentence.

___d___ 5. The topic of paragraph 10 is

       a. a good manager.

       b. the staff.

       c. fair wages.

       d. the dentist.

___a___ 6. The statement that best expresses the main idea of paragraph 11 is

       a. "You can learn several important things when you enter someone's workplace."

       b. "The atmosphere will tell you what kind of person is running the show."

       c. "This can be an important clue about the person you're evaluating."

       d. "After sizing up the atmosphere, take a look at how your 'readee' fits in."

___d___ 7. The focus of paragraph 17 is on observing how

    a. loud people often dominate conversations at parties.

    b. people-watchers react to those who approach them at parties.

    c. some people naturally take the lead at parties.

    d. people interact with others at parties.

___b___ 8. The focus of paragraph 19 is on people who

    a. tend to dominate conversations.

    b. observe rather than participate.

    c. watch television during parties.

    d. make excuses to leave parties.

➤ B. IDENTIFYING DETAILS

Complete the following statements by filling in the blanks.

1. According to psychologists, people who are raised with criticism become _____critical_____, while those raised with love become _____caring_____ and those raised with ____encouragement____ become supportive.

2. One author's _____dentist_____ and his staff have been together for years.

3. According to the authors, many large _____law_____ firms have reputations for being sweatshops.

4. According to the authors, the people who try to dominate a group are often the most _____insecure_____.

5. The _____attorney_____ described in the selection has a habit of looking over people's shoulders as he greets them in a crowd.

➤ C. RECOGNIZING METHODS OF ORGANIZATION AND TRANSITIONS

Select the best answer.

___b___ 1. In paragraph 3, the authors, in describing how a person's background influences who that person becomes, use the organizational pattern called

    a. problem and solution.

    b. cause and effect.

    c. definition.

    d. time sequence.

___d___ 2. In paragraph 11, the authors, in describing several important things you can learn about someone from his or her workplace, use the organizational pattern called

    a. definition.

    b. comparison and contrast.

    c. problem and solution.

    d. enumeration.

___a___ 3. The transitional word in paragraph 11 that indicates the pattern above (question #2) is

    a. first.

    b. clue.

    c. or.

    d. after.

___b___ 4. The transitional word or phrase that indicates the authors are going to illustrate their ideas in paragraph 12 is

    a. when.

    b. for instance.

    c. particularly.

    d. once again.

___d___ 5. In paragraph 19, the authors use the comparison and contrast organizational pattern to compare

    a. people who dominate conversations and those who prefer to listen.

    b. people who prefer one-on-one conversations and those who prefer large groups.

    c. social personalities and antisocial personalities.

    d. two types of observers, comfortable and uncomfortable.

___c___ 6. The transitional word or phrase in paragraph 19 that indicates the authors are making a contrast is

    a. also.

    b. usually.

    c. on the other hand.

    d. then.

D.   REVIEWING AND ORGANIZING IDEAS: PARAPHRASING

Use the following list of words to complete the paraphrase of paragraph 13.

children	superiors	interacting	perspective
at work	enjoying themselves	party or picnic	co-workers
subordinates	friends		

Paragraph 13: A good place to observe your ___co-workers___ is at a company ___party or picnic___. Even if you see these people ___at work___ every day, seeing them at a social function can give you a different ___perspective___. The people attending the party are often too busy ___enjoying themselves___ to people-watch. However, this is where you can observe your coworkers ___interacting___ with others, including their ___superiors___ and their ___subordinates___, their coworkers, their ___friends___, their families, and any ___children___ at the party.

E.   FIGURING OUT INFERRED MEANINGS

Indicate whether each statement is true (T) or false (F).

__F__ 1. An unmarried person's relationship with his or her parents is unrelated to the kind of parent he or she will become.

__T__ 2. The author probably recommends his or her dentist to other people.

__T__ 3. Lawyers who make their families their highest priority probably do not do well in the type of law firm described in paragraph 12.

__T__ 4. Many hospital interns willingly work long hours for little pay. The author would assume the interns are confident and strong-willed.

__F__ 5. At a company picnic, a person who organizes raffles and group entertainment is probably not a leader in his or her department.

F.   THINKING CRITICALLY

Select the best answer.

__c__ 1. The tone of the selection can best be described as

a. formal and overbearing.

b. concerned and urgent.

c. informative and helpful.

d. critical and objective.

___a___ 2. The authors support the thesis primarily by

    a. describing examples and personal experience.

    b. reporting facts and statistics.

    c. quoting experts.

    d. making analogies.

___d___ 3. The reason that the dinner table is the "perfect forum for drama" (paragraph 2) is that

    a. people tend to act their best at the dinner table.

    b. a dining room makes the ideal setting for a dramatic scene in a movie.

    c. families typically discuss emotional issues while they are eating dinner.

    d. dining together as a family presents many opportunities for interaction and observation.

___d___ 4. The authors include the description of lawyers who work for certain large law firms (paragraph 12) in order to

    a. argue that such law firms are harmful to families.

    b. criticize lawyers who put their jobs ahead of their personal lives.

    c. express admiration for the intelligence and dedication it takes for a lawyer to succeed in an environment like that.

    d. show that you can find out about someone's personality and priorities by the type of workplace in which that person thrives.

___a___ 5. At a large party, if a woman flits from person to person, the authors would assume that she

    a. lacks confidence.

    b. is flirting.

    c. wants to make new friends.

    d. wants to avoid serious relationships.

___b___ 6. The authors' "hardness scale" (paragraph 21) is their way of describing how

    a. difficult it is to observe certain people without being noticed.

    b. arrogant or tough some people are.

    c. hard it is to get to know certain people well.

    d. complicated some relationships can be.

_____c_____ 7. The statement that "You never need to evaluate these interactions in isolation" (paragraph 24) means that you should

   a. always ask other people whether their own observations confirm yours.

   b. only make observations in a crowded room where your people-watching will go unnoticed.

   c. consider other aspects of a person's appearance and personality in addition to your observations of how the person interacts with others.

   d. talk to the person you have observed and ask him or her to confirm or deny your observations.

➤ **G. BUILDING VOCABULARY**

➤ **Context**
Using context and a dictionary, if necessary, determine the meaning of each word as it is used in the selection.

_____c_____ 1. crucial (paragraph 2)

   a. dramatic   c. important/critical

   b. questionable   d. beginning

_____b_____ 2. forum (paragraph 2)

   a. excuse   c. action

   b. setting   d. design

_____c_____ 3. prospective (paragraph 7)

   a. considerate   c. potential

   b. similar   d. attractive

_____d_____ 4. masochistic (paragraph 8)

   a. one who abuses drugs

   b. one who complains a lot

   c. one who enjoys hurting others

   d. one who enjoys being abused

_____a_____ 5. pinpoint (paragraph 15)

   a. identify   c. ignore

   b. accuse   d. greet

_____c_____ 6. secluded (paragraph 19)

   a. crowded   c. isolated

   b. comfortable   d. nervous

➤ **Word Parts**

A REVIEW OF PREFIXES

DIS- means *not*
IN- means *not*
PRE- means *before* or *in advance*
SUB- means *below* or *under*
UN- means *not*

Match each word in Column A with its meaning in Column B. Write your answers in the spaces provided.

Column A

Prefix + Root

Column B

Meaning

___e___ 1. insecure

___a___ 2. discontented

___b___ 3. undeniably

___c___ 4. predictive

___d___ 5. subordinates

a. not satisfied

b. without doubt

c. revealing information in advance

d. those under another's authority

e. not self-confident

➤ **Unusual Words/Unusual Meanings**

Use the meanings given below to write a sentence using the underlined word or phrase.

1. To <u>read</u> someone (paragraph 1) means to look carefully and closely at a person in order to learn more about his or her personality.

   Your sentence: _____

2. A <u>priceless preview</u> (paragraph 7) is an extremely valuable indication of what will come at some later point; in this case, the preview is of how a person will probably behave further on in a relationship.

   Your sentence: _____

3. A person who has his or her <u>nose to the grindstone</u> (paragraph 9) is working extremely hard at a task or job (not necessarily one involving an actual grindstone!).

   Your sentence: _____

4. Someone who prefers to <u>sit on the sidelines</u> (paragraph 11) would rather not participate in an activity or get involved in a situation because of cynicism or shyness or simply a desire to observe rather than participate.

   Your sentence: _____

5. To give something <u>little weight</u> (paragraph 24) is to decide that it does not influence you very much; in this case, an *observation* that has little weight is one that does not seem as significant as other clues about someone's personality.

Your sentence: _____

➤ **H.   SELECTING A LEARNING/STUDY STRATEGY**

Select the best answer.

____d____   Which of the following techniques would be most useful in preparing a study sheet for review purposes?

    a. Write a list of the author's experiences.

    b. Try out the observational techniques yourself and record your results.

    c. Write a list of what you observe in a crowded room.

    d. Divide your review sheet into four sections and record what to look for at (1) the family dinner, (2) the workplace, (3) the company picnic, and (4) a crowded room.

➤ **I.   EXPLORING IDEAS THROUGH DISCUSSION AND WRITING**

1. In paragraph 2, why does the author say the family dinner is fun and informative "especially if the family isn't your own"? Describe an experience, either at your own home or someone else's, when the family dinner was the scene of "drama."

2. Do you plan to start people-watching in the situations suggested by the author? If you are already a people-watcher, describe some of your favorite places or situations to observe people.

➤ **J.   BEYOND THE CLASSROOM TO THE WEB**

Visit the Amazon.com Web site at **http://amazon.com**.

In the Search box, type in the title of the book from which this reading selection was taken. (See page 201.) On the page for the book, scroll down and read all the editorial reviews of the book. Do the reviews suggest the book might be helpful to you? Why or why not?

✔ **Tracking Your Progress**

Selection 5

Section	Number Correct		Score
A. Thesis and Main Idea (8 items)	_____	x 4	_____
B. Details (5 items)	_____	x 3	_____
C. Organization and Transitions (6 items)	_____	x 1	_____
E. Inferred Meanings (5 items)	_____	x 3	_____
F. Thinking Critically (7 items)	_____	x 3	_____
G. Vocabulary			
1. Context (7 items)	_____	x 1	_____
2. Word Parts (5 items)	_____	x 1	_____

TOTAL SCORE _____ %

CHECKING YOUR READING RATE

Words in Selection 5: 2,008

Finishing Time:	_____	_____	_____
	(hour)	(minutes)	(seconds)
Starting Time:	_____	_____	_____
	(hour)	(minutes)	(seconds)
Total Reading Time:		_____	_____
		(minutes)	(seconds)

Words Per Minute Score (page 735) _____ WPM

SELECTION 6

Lovers

Joseph A. DeVito

This reading is taken from a college textbook, *The Interpersonal Communications Book*. Read the article to discover what kind of lover you are and learn about the different types of love.

 MAKING CONNECTIONS

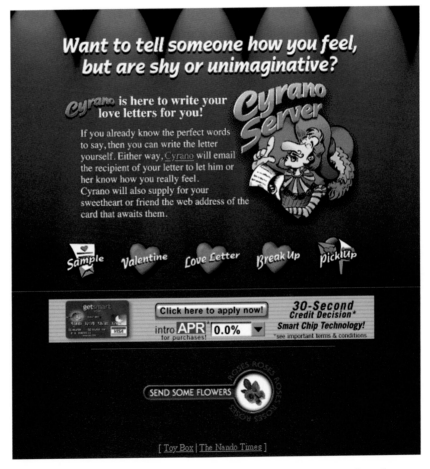

Cyrano will write and e-mail a love letter "from" you to someone else whose e-mail address you provide. If you wanted to write a love letter to someone you cared about, would you consider using this service from Cyrano Server? Why or why not?

➤ **PREVIEWING THE READING**

Using the steps listed on page 5, preview the reading selection. When you have fin-ished, complete the following items.

1. What is the subject of this selection? __types of love__

2. List at least three types of love described in the selection.

   a. __Eros, Pragma__

   b. __Ludus, Mania__

   c. __Storge, Agape__

➤ **READING TIPS**

1. *As you read, highlight key words that describe each type of love.*

2. *As you read, try associating each type of love with a particular person you know. For example, when reading about compassionate love, think of a person who is compassionate.*

 CHECKING YOUR READING RATE

If you plan to compute your reading rate, be sure to record your starting time in the box at the end of the exercises before you begin reading.

Lovers

1   Of all the qualities of interpersonal relationships, none seem as important as love. "We are all born for love," noted famed British prime minister Disraeli; "It is the prin-ciple of existence and its only end." It's also an interpersonal relationship developed, maintained, and sometimes destroyed through communication.

Types of Love

2   Although there are many theories about love, the one that has captured the at-tention of interpersonal researchers was one proposing that there is not one but six types of love (Lee 1976). View the descriptions of each type as broad characteriza-tions that are generally but not always true. As a preface to this discussion of the types of love, you may wish to respond to the self-test "What Kind of Lover Are You?"

Test Yourself: What Kind of Lover Are *You?*

3   Respond to each of the following statements with *T* for true (if you believe the statement to be a generally accurate representation of your attitudes about love) or *F*

for false (if you believe the statement does not adequately represent your attitudes about love).

_____ 1. My lover and I have the right physical "chemistry" between us.

_____ 2. I feel that my lover and I were meant for each other.

_____ 3. My lover and I really understand each other.

_____ 4. I believe that what my lover doesn't know about me won't hurt him or her.

_____ 5. My lover would get upset if he or she knew of some of the things I've done with other people.

_____ 6. When my lover gets too dependent on me, I want to back off a little.

_____ 7. I expect to always be friends with my lover.

_____ 8. Our love is really a deep friendship, not a mysterious, mystical emotion.

_____ 9. Our love relationship is the most satisfying because it developed from a good friendship.

_____ 10. In choosing my lover, I believed it was best to love someone with a similar background.

_____ 11. An important factor in choosing a partner is whether or not he or she would be a good parent.

_____ 12. One consideration in choosing my lover was how he or she would reflect on my career.

_____ 13. Sometimes I get so excited about being in love with my lover that I can't sleep.

_____ 14. When my lover doesn't pay attention to me, I feel sick all over.

_____ 15. I cannot relax if I suspect that my lover is with someone else.

_____ 16. I would rather suffer myself than let my lover suffer.

_____ 17. When my lover gets angry with me, I still love him or her fully and unconditionally.

_____ 18. I would endure all things for the sake of my lover.

4   This scale, from Hendrick and Hendrick (1990), is based on the work of Lee (1976), as is the following discussion of the six types of love. The scale is designed to enable you to identify those styles that best reflect your own beliefs about love. The statements refer to the six types of love that we discuss below: eros, ludus, storge, pragma, mania, and agape. "True" answers represent your agreement and "false" answers represent your disagreement with the type of love to which the statements refer. Statements 1–3 are characteristic of the eros lover. If you answered "true" to these statements, you have a strong eros component to your love style. If you answered "false," you have a weak eros component. Statements 4–6 refer to ludus love, 7–9 refer to storge love, 10–12 to pragma love, 13–15 to manic love, and 16–18 to agapic love.

One research program has identified love as a combination of intimacy, passion, and commitment (Sternberg 1986, 1988). Intimacy is the emotional aspect of love and includes sharing, communicating, and mutual support; it's a sense of closeness and connection. Passion is the motivational aspect and consists of physical attraction and romantic passion. Commitment is the cognitive aspect and consists of the decisions you make concerning your lover. When you have a relationship characterized by intimacy only, you have essentially a liking relationship. When you have only passion, you have a relationship of infatuation. When you have only commitment, you have empty love. When you have all three components to about equal degrees, you have complete or consummate love. What do you think of this position?

Eros: Beauty and Sexuality

Narcissus
a figure in Greek mythology who fell in love with his own reflection and subsequently was transformed into a flower

5   Like Narcissus, who fell in love with the beauty of his own image, the erotic lover focuses on beauty and physical attractiveness, sometimes to the exclusion of qualities you might consider more important and more lasting. Also like Narcissus, the erotic lover has an idealized image of beauty that is unattainable in reality. Consequently, the erotic lover often feels unfulfilled. Not surprisingly, erotic lovers are particularly sensitive to physical imperfections in the ones they love.

Ludus: Entertainment and Excitement

6   Ludus love is experienced as a game, as fun. The better he or she can play the game, the greater the enjoyment. Love is not to be taken too seriously; emotions are to be held in check lest they get out of hand and make trouble; passions never rise to the point where they get out of control. A ludic lover is *self*-controlled, always aware of the need to manage love rather than allow it to be in control. Perhaps because of this need to control love, some researchers have proposed that ludic love tendencies may reveal tendencies to sexual aggression (Sarwer, Kalichman, Johnson, Early, et al. 1993). Not surprisingly, the ludic lover retains a partner only as long as the partner is interesting and amusing. When interest fades, it's time to change partners. Perhaps because love is a game, sexual fidelity is of little importance. In fact, recent research shows that people who score high on ludic love are more likely to engage in "extradyadic" dating and sex than those who score low on ludus (Wiederman and Hurd 1999).

Storge: Peaceful and Slow

7   Storge love lacks passion and intensity. Storgic lovers don't set out to find lovers but to establish a companionable relationship with someone they know and with whom they can share interests and activities. Storgic love is a gradual process of unfolding thoughts and feelings; the changes seem to come so slowly and so gradually that it's often difficult to define exactly where the relationship is at any point in time.

Sex in storgic relationships comes late, and when it comes, it assumes no great importance.

Pragma: Practical and Traditional

8   The pragma lover is practical and seeks a relationship that will work. Pragma lovers want compatibility and a relationship in which their important needs and desires will be satisfied. They're concerned with the social qualifications of a potential mate even more than with personal qualities; family and background are extremely important to the pragma lover, who relies not so much on feelings as on logic. The pragma lover views love as a useful relationship, one that makes the rest of life easier. So the pragma lover asks such questions of a potential mate as "Will this person earn a good living?" "Can this person cook?" "Will this person help me advance in my career?" Pragma lovers' relationships rarely deteriorate. This is partly because pragma lovers choose their mates carefully and emphasize similarities. Another reason is that they have realistic romantic expectations.

Mania: Elation and Depression

9   Mania is characterized by extreme highs and extreme lows. The manic lover loves intensely and at the same time intensely worries about the loss of the love. This fear often prevents the manic lover from deriving as much pleasure as possible from the relationship. With little provocation, the manic lover may experience extreme jealousy. Manic love is obsessive; the manic lover has to possess the beloved completely. In return, the manic lover wishes to be possessed, to be loved intensely. The manic lover's poor self-image seems capable of being improved only by love; self-worth comes from being loved rather than from any sense of inner satisfaction. Because love is so important, danger signs in a relationship are often ignored; the manic lover believes that if there is love, then nothing else matters.

Agape: Compassionate and Selfless

10   Agape is a compassionate, egoless, self-giving love. The agapic lover loves even people with whom he or she has no close ties. This lover loves the stranger on the road even though they will probably never meet again. Agape is a spiritual love, offered without concern for personal reward or gain. This lover loves without expecting that the love will be reciprocate d. Jesus, Buddha, and Gandhi practiced and preached this unqualified love, agape (Lee 1976). In one sense, agape is more a philosophical kind of love than a love that most people have the strength to achieve.

Love Styles and Personality

11   In reading about the love styles, you may have felt that certain personality types are likely to favor one type of love over another. Here are personality traits that research finds people assign to each love style. Try identifying which personality traits

people think go with each of the six love styles: eros, ludus, storge, pragma, mania, and agape.

_____ 1. inconsiderate, secretive, dishonest, selfish, and dangerous

_____ 2. honest, loyal, mature, caring, loving, and understanding

_____ 3. jealous, possessive, obsessed, emotional, and dependent

_____ 4. sexual, exciting, loving, happy, and optimistic

_____ 5. committed, giving, caring, self-sacrificing, and loving

_____ 6. family-oriented, planning, careful, hard-working, and concerned

12 Very likely you perceived these personality factors in the same way as did the participants in research from which these traits were drawn (Taraban and Hendrick 1995): 1 = ludus, 2 = storge, 3 = mania, 4 = eros, 5 = agape, and 6 = pragma. Do note, of course, that these results do not imply that ludus lovers are inconsiderate, secretive, and dishonest. They merely mean that people think of ludus lovers as inconsiderate, secretive, and dishonest.

Love Styles in Combination

13 Each of these varieties of love can combine with others to form new and different patterns (for example, manic and ludic or storge and pragma). These six, however, identify the major types of love and illustrate the complexity of any love relationship. The six styles should also make it clear that different people want different things, that each person seeks satisfaction in a unique way. The love that may seem lifeless or crazy or boring to you may be ideal for someone else. At the same time, another person may see these very same negative qualities in the love you're seeking.

14 Love changes. A relationship that began as pragma may develop into ludus or eros. A relationship that began as erotic may develop into mania or storge. One approach sees this as a developmental process having three major stages (Duck 1986):

- First stage   Initial attraction; eros, mania, and ludus
- Second stage   Storge (as the relationship develops)
- Third stage   Pragma (as relationship bonds develop)

> ### A. UNDERSTANDING THE THESIS AND OTHER MAIN IDEAS

Select the best answer.

__b__ 1. The author's primary purpose is to

     a. compare a variety of theories on love.

     b. describe the theory that there are six types of love.

     c. disprove the theory that there are six types of love.

     d. identify the types of lovers who should change.

_____c_____ 2. According to the research program described in the photograph's caption, complete or consummate love consists of equal parts of

    a. intimacy, communication, and romance.

    b. sharing, mutual support, and romance.

    c. intimacy, passion, and commitment.

    d. infatuation, sharing, and physical attraction.

_____c_____ 3. According to the selection, all of the following reasons explain why pragma lovers' relationships rarely deteriorate *except*

    a. they choose their mates carefully.

    b. they emphasize similarities.

    c. their love is offered without concern for personal reward or gain.

    d. their romantic expectations are realistic.

_____d_____ 4. The topic of paragraph 11 is

    a. types of love.

    b. combinations of love styles.

    c. research on love.

    d. personality traits.

_____a_____ 5. The main idea of paragraph 13 is that

    a. each love relationship is unique and complex.

    b. only certain types of love can be combined successfully.

    c. the major types of love are too different to be combined at all.

    d. some people will not be able to find satisfaction with any of the major types of love.

_____d_____ 6. The main idea in paragraph 14 is that

    a. most relationships begin as erotic relationships.

    b. ludus and eros relationships often change.

    c. relationships that begin as pragma often change.

    d. relationships change and develop.

➤ **B.   IDENTIFYING DETAILS**

Read each of the following characteristics and determine which kind of love it describes. Indicate your answer by using the first letter of the name of each type of love on the list on the next page. The first one has been done for you.

E = Eros

L = Ludus

S = Storge

P = Pragma

M = Mania

A = Agape

___S___ 1. Love lacks passion and intensity; this kind of lover wants a companionable relationship consisting of shared interests and activities.

___L___ 2. Love is experienced as a fun game and sexual fidelity is unimportant; this kind of lover is self-controlled and wants to manage love.

___E___ 3. This kind of lover values beauty and physical attractiveness above other qualities and is sensitive to the physical imperfections of loved ones.

___A___ 4. Love is compassionate, self-giving, and spiritual; this kind of lover does not expect reciprocation.

___M___ 5. Intense love characterized by extreme highs and lows, obsessive behavior, and jealousy; this kind of lover gains self-worth only from being loved.

___P___ 6. Realistic, practical love; this kind of lover carefully and logically chooses a compatible mate for a relationship that satisfies important needs and desires.

➤ C.   RECOGNIZING METHODS OF ORGANIZATION AND TRANSITIONS

Complete the following statements by filling in the blanks.

___b___ 1. The primary organizational pattern of "Lovers" is _____ because it lists and describes the six types of love.

   a. time sequence

   b. classification

   c. cause and effect

   d. problem and solution

___c___ 2. The author also uses the _____ organizational pattern to explain each type of love.

   a. cause and effect

   b. time sequence

   c. definition

   d. problem and solution

> **D.   REVIEWING AND ORGANIZING IDEAS: MAPPING**

Complete the following maps of paragraphs 6 and 7 by filling in the missing words.

Paragraph 6 Map

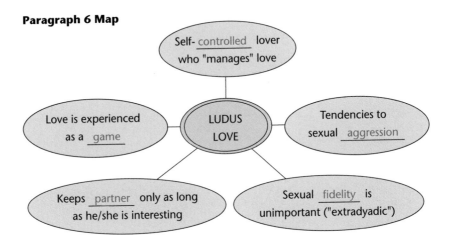

Paragraph 7 Map

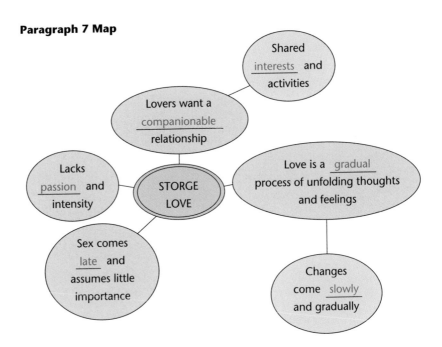

➤ E.   FIGURING OUT INFERRED MEANINGS

Indicate whether each statement is true (T) or false (F).

__T__ 1. The descriptions of each type of love may not always be accurate when applied to a specific individual.

__T__ 2. It can be inferred that not all interpersonal researchers subscribe to the theory that there are six types of love.

__F__ 3. It can be inferred that most happily married people have a strong ludus component to their love style.

__F__ 4. Storgic lovers probably believe in love at first sight.

➤ F.   THINKING CRITICALLY

Select the best answer.

__d__ 1. The central thesis of "Lovers" is supported primarily by
   a. personal experience.
   b. statistics.
   c. analogies.
   d. research evidence.

__b__ 2. The tone of the selection can best be described as
   a. concerned.
   b. objective.
   c. amused.
   d. disgusted.

__c__ 3. The selection "Lovers" would most likely be of most interest to
   a. elderly couples.
   b. dating service directors.
   c. people establishing new relationships.
   d. employers.

__b__ 4. The author begins with a quote by Disraeli (paragraph 1) in order to
   a. indicate that research on love goes back to the time of Disraeli.
   b. introduce the topic and demonstrate its importance.
   c. imply that Disraeli was an authority on the subject.
   d. compare American views on love with British views.

_d_ 5. The self-test is included primarily to

    a. entertain readers.

    b. help readers identify the undesirable aspects of their love styles so they can change.

    c. make readers realize that some types of love may be unhealthy.

    d. illustrate the characteristics of different types of love in a personal way.

➤ G. BUILDING VOCABULARY

➤ Context

Using context and a dictionary, if necessary, determine the meaning of each word as it is used in the selection.

_b_ 1. preface (paragraph 2)

    a. title   c. explanation

    b. introduction   d. list

_c_ 2. consummate (photo caption)

    a. strong   c. complete

    b. doubtful   d. equal

_b_ 3. idealized (paragraph 5)

    a. thoughtful   c. creative

    b. impractical   d. improved

_a_ 4. deteriorate (paragraph 8)

    a. fall apart   c. become better

    b. grow   d. continue

_c_ 5. manic (paragraph 9)

    a. depressed   c. frenzied/agitated

    b. harmless   d. uncertain

_a_ 6. provocation (paragraph 9)

    a. reason   c. suspicion

    b. hesitation   d. interruption

➤ **Word Parts**

A REVIEW OF PREFIXES
EXTRA- means *out of, outside*
IM- means *not*
INTER- means *between*
UN- means *not*

Using your knowledge of word parts and the review of prefixes and suffixes above, fill in the blanks in the following sentences.

1. An *interpersonal* relationship (paragraph 1) is a relationship that occurs _____between_____ two or more people.

2. The word *attain* means reach, so if an image of beauty is unattainable in reality (paragraph 5), that particular image is _____not_____ reachable or realistic.

3. If a person is sensitive to *imperfections* (paragraph 5) in a loved one, he or she notices the ways in which the loved one is not _____perfect_____.

4. The word *dyadic* means of or relating to a pair or couple, so *extradyadic* (paragraph 6) activities are those that take place _____outside_____ a couple's relationship.

➤ **H.   SELECTING A LEARNING/STUDY STRATEGY**

This selection describes six types of love. One way to remember the names of each type is by using a mnemonic device. Try making up a word using the first letter of each type of love, such as SPAMEL (sounds like "camel"), or use a real word, such as SAMPLE, to trigger your memory and help you to recall each type of love.

➤ **I.   EXPLORING IDEAS THROUGH DISCUSSION AND WRITING**

1. Did the mnemonic device suggested in the reading tips help you remember the types of love? Describe some other mnemonic devices that could be used with this selection. (For example, a nonsensical sentence using the type of love and a defining characteristic: "My friend Eros thinks he's beautiful and sexy.")

2. Did the self-test confirm or contradict your beliefs about your own love style? Did the characteristics of the love styles accurately describe people you know? Did the personality traits correspond with your own beliefs about the different love styles?

➤ **J. BEYOND THE CLASSROOM TO THE WEB**

Visit one of the pages at the Cyrano Server at **http://www.passionup.com/letters/index2.htm**.

Select "Love Letters." Fill in the love letter template at PassionUp.com and then submit it (you'll be able to cancel it). Does the resulting letter seem to be an example of one of the six types of love discussed in the reading selection? If so, which one, and why?

✔ **Tracking Your Progress**

Selection 6

Section	Number Correct		Score
A. Thesis and Main Idea (6 items)	_____	x 4	_____
B. Details (6 items)	_____	x 3	_____
C. Organization and Transitions (2 items)	_____	x 3	_____
E. Inferred Meanings (4 items)	_____	x 3	_____
F. Thinking Critically (5 items)	_____	x 4	_____
G. Vocabulary			
1. Context (6 items)	_____	x 2	_____
2. Word Parts (4 items)	_____	x 2	_____
	TOTAL SCORE	_____ %	

CHECKING YOUR READING RATE

Words in Selection 6: 1,680

	(hour)	(minutes)	(seconds)
Finishing Time:	_____	_____	_____
Starting Time:	_____	_____	_____
Total Reading Time:		_____	_____
		(minutes)	(seconds)

Words Per Minute Score (page 735) _____ WPM

13 | Anthropology

Anthropology is the study of humankind. It has five branches: cultural or social, linguistic, physical (or biological), archaeological, and applied. Anthropology attempts to understand all aspects that influence human thought and behavior. Anthropology stresses the importance of understanding the world from the perspective of different cultures, races, and ethnic groups. Studying anthropology will help you understand the world you live in and how people interact. You will study human relationships and their variations in different cultures. You will see that many modern-day traditions, problems, and issues are studied by anthropologists. In "To Love and to Cherish" you will examine the tradition of a marriage ceremony in a variety of religious groups. "Stand Off Begins to Protect Sacred Site" focuses on the issue of preservation of Native American burial sites. The reading "Apes and Language" deals with the biological question of whether apes can acquire a uniquely human trait—language.

TIPS FOR READING IN ANTHROPOLOGY

- **Pay attention to terminology.** Like other social sciences, anthropology uses precise terminology to describe its subject matter. Also learn the names of important researchers and theorists. As you read, highlight new terms. You can transfer them later to index cards or a vocabulary log for the course.

- **Focus on patterns of behavior.** People in separate cultures often differ not only in how they behave, but also in how they think. They may differ in food gathering methods, social activities, or what they value as art, for example. Try to identify patterns of behavior. As you read about apes learning human language, try to identify patterns of their behavior.

- **Make comparisons between and among groups and cultures.** Try to see relationships and make comparisons. Draw charts or maps that compare different practices, beliefs, or family structures. In "To Love and to Cherish" you could construct a chart comparing various marriage rituals.

- **Make practical applications.** As you read, consider how the information is useful to you in real-life situations. Make marginal notes of situations that illustrate what you are reading about. For example, as you read "Stand Off Begins to Protect Sacred Site," think of instances of the destruction or alteration of valued cultural sites or sites of ethnic or historical importance in your community.

228

SELECTION 7

To Love and to Cherish
Michele Kearns

From a four-part series published in *The Buffalo News* on religious ceremonies, this reading explores the wedding ceremonies. Read it to discover the traditions that various cultures include in marriage ceremonies.

> ## PREVIEWING THE READING

Using the steps listed on page 5, preview the reading selection. When you have finished, complete the following items.

1. What is the topic of this selection? ___religious wedding ceremonies___

2. List at least four religious groups whose wedding customs are described:

    a. ___Sikh___

    b. ___Catholic___

    c. ___African Methodist Episcopal___

    d. ___Hellenic Orthodox, Judaism, Islam___

MAKING CONNECTIONS

Think back to weddings that you have participated in or attended. How were they similar? How did they differ? What underlying theme(s) do they share?

➤ READING TIP

As you read, record the religious organizations mentioned, along with the traditions associated with each.

CHECKING YOUR READING RATE

If you plan to compute your reading rate, be sure to record your starting time in the box at the end of the exercises before you begin reading.

To Love and to Cherish

Sikh
a follower of Sikhism—a branch of Hinduism marked by monotheism (having one god) founded in India in the 16th century

1   By government standards Beatrice Pardeep Singh-Arnone was married on a Tuesday by a judge in the town hall. "It still wasn't real for me," she said. Days later in the rose garden at Delaware Park [in Buffalo, NY], it was. She wore a dress in red, the color of happiness. For her Sikh ceremony, parents exchanged carnation garlands to symbolize the new bond between the bride and groom's families. And Singh-Arnone and her husband made four trips around the holy book that is the foundation of the religion, which began in India. Each time, the couple walked to a different prayer reading about the physical, mental, soul-uniting and Godly aspects of their marriage. When they were done, friends and family showered them with flower petals, a kind of blessing.

Second Vatican Council
a meeting held by the Pope to address questions and issues in the Catholic Church; many new policies and practices resulted from "Vatican II"

2   Wedding rituals vary from religion to religion—from circling a holy book, as Sikhs do, to marrying under a canopy or chupah to show the beginning of a home together, as Jews do. Still, there is usually something universal among them: Religious rituals try to fortify couples in their lives together by showing support from God and the family, said Trevor Watt, a Protestant theologian at the Second Vatican Council convened by Pope John XXIII in the 1960s. "The most meaningful wedding ceremonies are the ones that name and articulate the values held by the couple getting married and hopefully by the family and their social community," said Watt. And, he said, the best rituals express an inner conviction. In some ceremonies love and its various forms—such as, romantic, friendship, physical and emotional—are described because they give the marriage strength "to get beyond the hurts and the anger that are inevitable," he said. "The reason that we seek a wedding ceremony is it's an acknowledgement of something that's ultimate," continued Watt, who is a religion professor at Canisius College and an ordained United Church of Christ minister at the Westminster Presbyterian Church in Buffalo. "In the Christian tradition it's called God's love," he said, "like light it can be refracted into many different forms."

sacrament
a formal Christian rite believed to be established by Jesus as a way to be with God

Christianity

3   For Catholics, the ceremony for the marriage sacrament gets part of its meaning from the bride and groom's work as ministers of their wedding service, said Father

Matthew Zirnheld, a priest at Our Lady of Victory in Lackawanna. To prepare for their day, the couple has already planned for marriage by taking church classes that include children and keeping religion in their lives. The modern service has changed some to reflect that a bride is no longer considered a possession of the family, as she once was, Zirnheld said. She can decide to have her father escort her to the altar to begin the service, or not. Instead, he said, Catholics now emphasize the importance of couples entering a marriage freely—so there is nothing to hold them back from keeping the union together. "It's not a contract. A contract can be broken. It's a covenant," he said. The couple demonstrates this by leading the wedding, which is their public commitment to each other. They choose the prayers, readings, music, said Zirnheld, who leads the exchange of vows. As modern evidence of the couple's leading role, it has become popular, within the last decade or so, to illustrate the new union with a "unity candle," that is lit with separate candles held by the bride and groom, Zirnheld said.

4   These candles are also popular at the African Methodist Episcopal Church in Buffalo, where couples include African traditions along with more traditional protestant steps, said Reverend Richard Stenhouse. After going to the alter for blessings and to exchange rings and vows, they may jump over a broom. This practice comes from times of slavery. Slaves were not allowed to marry, so couples used this tradition to "cross over from being separate to joined," said Stenhouse. A bride and groom may use another African ritual of pouring some water, the essence of life, on the ground. "It gives honor and recognition to those who've gone before," he said.

5   At the Hellenic Orthodox Church of the Annunciation in Buffalo—part of the Eastern Orthodox church led by **patriarchs** rather than the pope—the traditional Greek service is designed as preparation for heaven. Father James Doukas, the priest, places crowns of beaded circles on the bride and groom's heads to indicate that they're queen and king of their household and ready to begin a heaven-worthy life. Then the couple walks around the altar table three times in tribute to Jesus, the martyrs and the saints. The couple sips from a cup of wine to indicate they will drink the happiness of life together, as well as the sorrow.

patriarchs
church leaders or
bishops in the
Orthodox faith

Judaism

6   Jewish weddings can vary between temples and movements, such as reform, which is more liberal, and orthodox, which is more conservative. Yet there are rituals common among them. One is the signing of the ktuba, a marriage contract describing the obligations to behave in an ethical and moral way. During the wedding ceremony, as the couple stands beneath a chupah, a rabbi reads the ktuba and offers seven blessings to encourage the couple to live in unity and love. When the service is over, the couple breaks a wine glass as reminder of the destruction of the temple in Jerusalem.

7   This is a signal for some that there is lots of work ahead, explained Rabbi Benjamin Arnold, of Temple Sinai in Amherst. "The wedding is a symbol of redemption and fulfillment," he said. "This wedding can be our inspiration." The couple

sometimes retreats to a room with food, such as chocolate covered strawberries, so they can sit alone and break a pre-marriage fast. "It's a form of prayer, of asking God that he should be with this couple," said Rabbi Yirmiya Milevsky, of the Young Israel orthodox synagogue in Amherst.

Islam

8   Islam considers marriage a sacred duty, said Dawoud Adeyola, a leader of the Islamic Cultural Association of Western New York. "It's actually considered an act of worship," he said. Yet the ceremony itself is simple. First the couple must meet certain pre-conditions—they can't be closely related, the husband has to be able to support his wife—and have two Muslim witnesses. Adeyola will read a verse from the **Koran** about all of humankind being created from a single soul. The groom promises or gives a dowry chosen by the bride—a house, a car or a piece of jewelry. And the bride or the groom proposes marriage, the other accepts and the ceremony is complete after a prayer, said Adeyola.

9   He has conducted spare ceremonies in a room and more elaborate ones in the rose garden at Delaware Park. It is important to dress up so that the couple stands out in recognition of the importance of the occasion. African Americans sometimes incorporate African traditions, such as African-style robes or food, said Adeyola remembering the yams served at his own Muslim wedding in 1969.

Koran
the holy book of Islam, containing what followers believe to be revelations of Allah as told to Muhammad

Lasting power

10   In the nearly five years since Singh-Arnone was married, she has had two children and life struggles. Her 2-year-old son, who is now fine, was born prematurely, which provoked a worrying few weeks. In such times she thinks back to her wedding and the memories of it nurture her still. "That was one of the most moving days of my life besides the birth of my children," she said. "I did feel surrounded by the presence of God." It was, she said, beyond happiness. It was bliss.

▶ **A.   UNDERSTANDING THE THESIS AND OTHER MAIN IDEAS**

Select the best answer.

____d____ 1. The author's primary purpose in "To Love and To Cherish" is to

    a. present research findings on the strength of religion-based marriages.

    b. criticize couples who do not have a religious wedding ceremony.

    c. encourage couples to put religion into their weddings.

    d. describe various religious marriage traditions.

___c___ 2. In paragraph 2, the author

    a. introduces all the religions she will discuss further.

    b. provides general information on the Sikh religion.

    c. comments on the meaning and importance of rituals.

    d. quotes people who have recently been married.

___b___ 3. The topic of paragraph 3 is:

    a. the unity candle.

    b. the Catholic ceremony.

    c. Father Matthew Zirnheld.

    d. marriage as a covenant.

___c___ 4. All of the following are mentioned as reasons behind the rituals *except*:

    a. to honor one's ancestors.

    b. to worship.

    c. to prepare for a large family.

    d. to seek redemption and fulfillment.

___b___ 5. The main idea of paragraph 4 is

    a. candles are an important part of many ceremonies.

    b. couples may mix traditions from several cultures.

    c. an African tradition involves brooms.

    d. most rituals include recognition of people who have died.

➤ B.   IDENTIFYING DETAILS

Match the wedding ritual with the religious tradition as mentioned in the reading. The religions may be used more than once.

A. Sikhism	D. Hellenic Orthodox
B. Catholicism	E. Judaism
C. African Methodist Episcopal	F. Islam

___B___ 1. The bride and groom lead the wedding.

___D___ 2. A priest places crowns on the heads of the couple.

___E___ 3. A wine glass is smashed.

_A_   4. The couple walks around a holy book four times.

_C_   5. Water is poured onto the ground.

_D_   6. The bride and groom walk around the altar three times.

_F_   7. A verse from the Koran is read.

_B_   8. The couple takes pre-wedding classes.

_E_   9. A marriage contract is signed.

_B_   10. A unity candle is lit.

_D_   11. The marriage ceremony is preparation for heaven.

_F_   12. The bride chooses a dowry from the groom.

_A_   13. The couple is blessed with flower petals.

_A_   14. The parents exchange carnation garlands.

_C_   15. The bride and groom jump over a broom.

C.   RECOGNIZING METHODS OF ORGANIZATION AND TRANSITIONS

Complete the following statements by filling in the blanks.

1. The author lists religious traditions and wedding ceremony characteristics using the organizational pattern called _____enumeration_____.

2. The _____comparison and contrast_____ pattern is also used as the author examines similarities and differences among traditions.

D.   REVIEWING AND ORGANIZING IDEAS: OUTLINING

Complete the following outline of Beatrice Pardeep Singh-Arnone's experiences as described in the reading.

I. Civil Ceremony
   A. Conducted by a _____judge_____
   B. Held in _____town hall_____

II. Sikh ceremony
   A. Wore red dress—color of happiness
   B. Carnation garland exchange
      1. By parents
      2. Symbolizes _____the bond between bride's and groom's families_____
   C. Holy book
      1. Bride and groom walk _____around four times_____
      2. Foundation of _____the religion_____

3. Reading about aspects of the marriage

    a. _____physical_____

    b. _____mental_____

    c. soul-uniting

    d. Godly

D. Showered with flower petals as a blessing

E. FIGURING OUT INFERRED MEANINGS

Indicate whether each statement is true (T) or false (F).

__T__ 1. The Catholic couples are instructed on raising their children Catholic.

__F__ 2. Ministers won't allow African customs at religious wedding ceremonies.

__T__ 3. Some Jewish couples do not eat before their wedding.

__F__ 4. The Islamic couples view marriage in a civic way only.

__F__ 5. All Jewish wedding ceremonies contain the same rituals.

F. THINKING CRITICALLY

Indicate whether each quote from the selection is fact (F) or opinion (O).

__O__ 1. "It still wasn't real for me." (paragraph 1)

__F__ 2. Wedding rituals vary from religion to religion. (paragraph 2)

__O__ 3. "The most meaningful wedding ceremonies are the ones that name and articulate the values held by the couple getting married." (paragraph 2)

__F__ 4. "A contract can be broken." (paragraph 3)

__F__ 5. An African ritual uses water to give "honor and recognition to those who've gone before." (paragraph 4)

__O__ 6. "This wedding can be our inspiration." (paragraph 7)

G. BUILDING VOCABULARY

▶ Context
Using context and a dictionary, if necessary, determine the meaning of each word as it is used in the selection.

__a__ 1. fortify (paragraph 2)

    a. strengthen   c. control

    b. refresh   d. explain

___b___ 2. articulate (paragraph 2)

    a. speak eloquently

    b. put into words

    c. make significant

    d. identify

___a___ 3. inevitable (paragraph 2)

    a. certain to happen, unavoidable

    b. unthinkable, horrible

    c. painful, upsetting

    d. insurmountable, very difficult

___c___ 4. covenant (paragraph 3)

    a. a bargain

    b. a settlement

    c. a solemn promise, binding agreement

    d. a fair offer

___a___ 5. bliss (paragraph 10)

    a. complete happiness

    b. excitement

    c. sweet, nice

    d. pleasant

➤ **Word Parts**

A REVIEW OF PREFIXES
RE- means *back*
PRE- means *before*

Use the review of prefixes above to fill in the blanks in the following sentences.

1. When light is *refracted* (paragraph 2) off a surface, it is bent
   _____back_____ off its original path.

2. A baby that is born prematurely (paragraph 10) is born
   _____before_____ it is fully mature.

➤ **Unusual Words/Unusual Meanings**

Use the meanings given below to write a sentence using the underlined word or phrase.

1. The <u>ultimate</u> (paragraph 2) sacrifice is one that is final and the utmost and best you could do for someone.

   Your sentence: _____

2. Someone who is <u>spare</u> (paragraph 9) with money is frugal and refrains from spending unnecessarily.

   Your sentence: _____

➤ **H.   SELECTING A LEARNING/STUDY STRATEGY**

Suppose you had to study for an essay exam that asked you to summarize the wedding traditions of three religions. How would you prepare?

➤ **I.   EXPLORING IDEAS THROUGH DISCUSSION AND WRITING**

1. Write about a time that you witnessed or participated in a religious ceremony. What rituals were involved? Did the wedding guests seem to recognize their significance?

2. A wedding is just the official beginning of a marriage. Discuss what couples really need to know about being husband and wife.

3. Discuss the wedding industry in America. Has it gotten out of control in terms of cost and importance in the lives of the bride and groom?

➤ **J.   BEYOND THE CLASSROOM TO THE WEB**

Look at some sample nonreligious wedding ceremonies on the Web site at **http://www.nonreligiousweddings.com/samples.html**.
   How do these compare with what you know about religious weddings from this reading and your life?

✔ Tracking Your Progress

Selection 7

Section	Number Correct		Score
A. Thesis and Main Idea (5 items)	_____	x 5	_____
B. Details (15 items)	_____	x 1	_____
C. Organization and Transitions (2 items)	_____	x 2	_____
E. Inferred Meanings (5 items)	_____	x 4	_____
F. Thinking Critically (6 items)	_____	x 4	_____
G. Vocabulary			
1. Context (5 items)	_____	x 2	_____
2. Word Parts (2 items)	_____	x 1	_____

TOTAL SCORE _____ %

CHECKING YOUR READING RATE

Words in Selection 7: 1,250

Finishing Time:	_____	_____	_____
	(hour)	(minutes)	(seconds)
Starting Time:	_____	_____	_____
	(hour)	(minutes)	(seconds)
Total Reading Time:		_____	_____
		(minutes)	(seconds)

Words Per Minute Score (page 735) _____ WPM

SELECTION 8

Stand Off Begins
to Protect Sacred Site

David Melmer

Originally published in a volume of *Indian Country Today*, this article demonstrates how some Native Americans are still struggling for fair treatment from the U.S. government.

➤ PREVIEWING THE READING

Using the steps listed on page 5, preview the reading selection. When you have finished, complete the following items.

1. The topic of this selection is:

   Native American burial sites in South Dakota

2. List at least three questions you would expect to have answered by the reading.

   a. Where are the sites located?

   b. What caused the dispute?

   c. What other parties are involved in the dispute?

 ## MAKING CONNECTIONS

Have you ever participated in a march, demonstration, or protest? If so, what motivated you and how did you feel after it was over? If not, what would motivate you?

➤ READING TIP

This selection centers on a certain geographic region. Find a map of South Dakota using an atlas or other source, and locate the places mentioned.

CHECKING YOUR READING RATE

If you plan to compute your reading rate, be sure to record your starting time in the box at the end of the exercises before you begin reading.

Stand Off Begins to Protect Sacred Site

1   LAKE ANDES, S. D.—Alphonse Leroy said he would protect the sacred burial sites of his ancestors with his life. On a rainy afternoon along the Missouri River on the Yankton Reservation, Leroy said his people were pushed too much and a planned camping waste dump on an area where his ancestors were buried went too far and he was willing "to die" to protect that sacred site. He sat wrapped in a black plastic trash bag while a fire warmed the air inside the tipi to ward off the chill of the wind and rain. Leroy was serious and emotional when he said very simply he wanted people to stop. No construction was taking place because of the muddy conditions on April 30, but the area was pocked with little flags where surveyors mapped out the location of the waste deposit station. "I want to take care of the earth, the plants and ants, the water and air and over there are our relatives," he said as he gestured eastward toward an area known by Yankton elders to contain human remains.

2   Members of the Yankton Sioux Tribe had reached the end of their patience with the state of South Dakota Game Fish and Parks and the U.S. Army Corps of Engineers over the expansion of a recreation area located along the Missouri River on what the tribal elders assert is a sacred burial site. Recent meetings between the state, the Corps and tribal representatives brought about a temporary solution—return all remains to the original site and replace all dirt that was removed from that site. The dirt was removed to act as **back fill** for the construction areas. "After five meetings we worked through issues that were acceptable to all," said Larry Janis, cultural director for the U.S. Army Corps of Engineers.

back fill
in construction, material that is used to fill a hole that has been dug

3   Because the members of the Yankton Sioux Tribe were concerned that human remains were still in the dirt removed from the original site, the state Game Fish and Parks made the decision to return the dirt from both fill sites. "This is not required by the court order nor is there any evidence of human remains in (the area), but in an effort to work with the Yankton Sioux Tribe and accommodate their concerns, we are taking this action," stated Doug Hofer, director of the division of parks and recreation. But the encampment of tribal families will stay in place to protect the sacred site of their ancestors, tribal officials said.

funerary objects
items that are buried along with the deceased

buffer zone
an area set aside to separate two other areas

4   In March excavation overturned human remains and **funerary objects**, and a court order stopped the construction for a time, but U.S. District Court Judge Lawrence Piersol ruled the state could move forward on part of the construction, but had to secure the area from where the remains were removed. Two locations where dirt was placed were to be used by campers. One was found to have some funerary objects and particles of human remains, the other not. But Yankton members said the site was not properly tested. "Once the fill material is removed construction will begin and there will be a **buffer zone** of 100 feet surrounding the (original) site," Janis said. He said ceremonies will take place after the remains and artifacts are returned.

Alphonse Leroy, left; Aggie Drapeau, center; and Linsy Nelson, right, members of the Yankton Sioux Tribe warm themselves in a tipi used as a guard station while they protect a sacred site from construction during the beginning of the standoff between the tribe and the state of South Dakota.

5   The area, North Point, on the north side of Fort Randall Dam, is referred to as East White Swan by the Yankton tribal members. White Swan was a community that was flooded with the completion of Fort Randall Dam and is under Lake Francis Case. Two years ago low water levels on the Missouri River and on the lake uncovered grave sites at White Swan. Many of the graves were moved, and court action was required to stop filling the lake until the graves were moved. At the time elders told the Corps of Engineers and the state that North Point also was used as a burial site and many locations up and down the river will reveal the remains of many American Indians of various tribes, they said.

6   Linsy Nelson, a tribal member at the stand-off site said the state can legally continue construction, but he agreed that a higher moral and spiritual law prevailed. "This didn't start with this dig right now. It started in 1947 when human remains were pushed into the face of this dam. There has been one thing bad after another, the whites have to understand. "We did everything we were asked to do and they took the land away and gave it to the state. Our ancestors are in this land. I'm not one to break the law; I'm just making a statement. We are tired of being oppressed," Nelson said. He made the point that in the Act that began the creation of the hydro power dams along the Missouri River in 1947, it was made clear that when the Corps of Engineers no longer needed the land above the flood line it would be returned to the tribes along the river.

Just Compensation money that the government is legally bound to pay for land that it takes for various reasons such as construction of roads, bridges, or dams

7   Legislation that would pay for the land taken from the tribes by the flooding came in the form of **Just Compensation** payments to the tribes. The Yankton Sioux Tribe is the last of the Missouri River Tribes to receive that payment, which is held in a trust account and the tribe can use the interest. "They try to give us money for the taken land. The money is here today and gone tomorrow. The land will be here forever. We are selling rights to the river when we take the money. That is not the solution, the solution is to give us access to the river and the land," Nelson said. Nelson said he understood the need to have waste dump station for RVs and campers and for a fish

cleaning facility, but he questioned why it had to be located at an area that contained human remains. "This land and dirt came from a burial site," he said. And those camped at the site say they will be there as long as it takes. Most are ready to be arrested when they try to stop equipment from further construction.

8   Six families will take over duties of guarding the sacred area, with a different family each day. Tribes from throughout the region have been contacted and many are willing to send people to help. Historically, there could be members of many tribes buried in or near the site.

Evidence for more sacred sites

9   More sacred sites are likely to be located in the area because that part of the river was shallow and allowed people, wildlife and bison to cross. Pawnee, Kiowa, Arickara, Ponca, Lakota and other tribes have moved through and lived in this area. Faith Spotted Eagle, tribal member, said that when people died their bodies were dried on scaffolds on high ground and then buried at that spot. Many of the bluffs along the river contain the remains of many people.

10   For many tribal members it is difficult to trust the state and Corps of Engineers Archaeologists. When the first remains were found, the state claimed bones and artifacts were removed because it was not clear if the remains were American Indian or non-Indian. Claims that **pipestone** fragments from a pipe were discovered were later to be found untrue. Ellsworth Chytka, leader of the negotiating team for the tribe, said he and others saw a full pipe and full remains at the state's archaeological laboratory. The remains were removed and that is against the Native American Graves Protection and Repatriation Act, Chytka said.

pipestone
a particular red rock used by Native Americans to carve certain objects, such as sacred pipes

11   Spotted Eagle said that by claiming not to know which culture the remains belonged to gave the state an out for removing them. The site that was uncovered contained leg bones and many artifacts that are said to be funerary objects. Dirt moved to the location of the waste dump site also contained some remains, and at another site no fragments were found. Tribal attorneys in court claimed the search for fragments was inadequate.

12   Based on that testimony Judge Piersol allowed the construction to continue, but ordered the dirt placed at one site to be returned to the original burial site. "I have a grandmother and a grandfather buried underwater, just over that hill," Nelson said.

Learn to respect

13   "On CNN, President Bush said the United States honors all their commitments and treaties—I can't believe he would say something like that. But then our Senators and Congressmen . . . it all goes back onto the state offices, they hear all this and they act like that. They say, 'well that's okay—we don't have to honor this or honor that.' But then when we do something like make a stand, then they look at us . . . what are those Indians doing now, what are they up to again, what's bothering them, just like we are doing something just to be doing something. They have no respect. They have no understanding how hurt we feel when they dig up our ancestors' remains. It just doesn't register," Sharon Drappeau, member of the Tribe Repatriation Committee, said.

14   In contrast the soldiers' cemetery across the river from North Point is well mani-cured with a white picket fence and white grave markers. Spotted Eagle said, how-ever, that she was told by historic preservation officials that the remains of the soldiers were exhumed and reburied in Washington. "Of course they have no stock in oral history. So when we've told them time and again that certain places are burial sites, they don't listen, otherwise they wouldn't have done it here," Spotted Eagle said. "And yet they are aghast when somebody steals flowers off their cemetery graves or vandalizes their cemetery," Drappeau said.

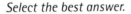

A. UNDERSTANDING THE THESIS AND OTHER MAIN IDEAS

Select the best answer.

  __c__ 1. The author's primary purpose in this article is to

      a. describe why Native Americans value burial sites.

      b. criticize the U.S. government for their treatment of Native American tribes.

      c. describe government interference with and destruction of sacred burial sites.

      d. propose a solution for the dispute.

  __d__ 2. The main topic of the first paragraph is:

      a. the Yankton Sioux Tribe's grievances.

      b. the status of construction at the site.

      c. the location of the burial sites.

      d. Alphonse Leroy's role in the standoff.

  __a__ 3. The purpose of paragraphs 2, 3, and 4 is to

      a. review the basics of the dispute.

      b. give a brief history of the region.

      c. provide a detailed time line of recent events.

      d. describe the laws that pertain to the dispute.

  __b__ 4. The main idea of paragraph 6 is that:

      a. Linsy Nelson feels oppressed.

      b. the Yankton Sioux Tribe has had continual problems with the government over land and river issues.

      c. the river does not belong to the Native Americans.

      d. the U.S. Army Corps of Engineers did not keep its promises.

_c_ 5. Which of the following questions in *not* answered in paragraph 7?

    a. How was the Yankton Sioux Tribe compensated for the taken land?

    b. What is Nelson's solution to the ongoing disputes?

    c. Why can't the dump station be located somewhere else?

    d. How dedicated are the protesters?

➤ B. IDENTIFYING DETAILS

Select the best answer.

_b_ 1. All of the following are tribal members named in the selection *except*:

    a. Linsy Nelson   c. Alphonse Leroy

    b. White Swan   d. Spotted Eagle

_d_ 2. Which group is *not* involved in the dispute as mentioned in the reading?

    a. South Dakota Game Fish and Parks

    b. a tribal negotiation team

    c. U.S. Army Corps of Engineers

    d. National Park Service

_d_ 3. According to Doug Hofer, the Game Fish and Parks Department

    a. did more than what was required by the court order.

    b. returned all the sacred dirt.

    c. desires to cooperate with the tribe.

    d. all of the above

_c_ 4. Human remains were recently revealed in White Swan when

    a. the land was flooded.

    b. Fort Randall Dam was built.

    c. water levels on the Missouri River were low.

    d. a court ordered excavation was performed.

_a_ 5. According to the selection, other tribes are interested in helping the Yankton Sioux with the protest because

    a. their ancestors might also be buried along the river.

    b. they are required by a tribal treaty to help other tribes.

c. the government has had disputes in the past with these other tribes as well.

d. they will receive more compensation if the land is determined to be sacred.

_b_ 6. The tribal members distrust the government, the state, and the Corps of Engineers archeologist because

a. a state lab was used to analyze the remains instead of an independent lab.

b. the government mishandled the investigation of the burial site.

c. their lawyers were ignored in court.

d. the archaeologists are not experienced in Native American funerary practices.

_b_ 7. The soldiers' cemetery

a. has never been vandalized.

b. does not contain bodies.

c. is located in North Point.

d. is visited frequently by Native Americans.

➤ **C.   RECOGNIZING METHODS OF ORGANIZATION AND TRANSITIONS**

Select the best answer.

_c_ 1. A primary organizational pattern used throughout the reading is

a. comparison and contrast.

b. order of importance.

c. cause and effect.

d. enumeration.

_c_ 2. In paragraph 5 which of the following transitions suggests the time sequence pattern?

a. north side

b. referred to

c. two years ago

d. also

➤ D.   REVIEWING AND ORGANIZING IDEAS: MAPPING

Complete the following time line of events in the selection. Put the events in the correct order on the time line by writing in the number from the time line that corresponds to the event.

```
   ❑      ❑      ❑      ❑      ❑      ❑      ❑      ❑
   1      2      3      4      5      6      7      8
```

___5___ Human remains and artifacts were analyzed.

___6___ A court order stated that the area where the remains were found must be secured.

___2___ White Swan sites revealed due to low water levels.

___7___ The disputed back fill was returned to the burial sites.

___1___ Human remains became part of the Fort Randall Dam in 1947.

___3___ A court ordered that revealed graves should be moved.

___8___ Members of the Yankton Sioux Tribe set up an encampment to protect burial sites.

___4___ Human remains and funerary objects were found in March.

➤ E.   FIGURING OUT INFERRED MEANINGS

Indicate whether each statement is true (T) or false (F).

___T___ 1. It can be inferred that Alphonse Leroy believes that there is a chance he could be killed during the protest.

___F___ 2. The U.S. Army Corps of Engineers does not care about Native American sacred sites.

___T___ 3. Campers need more room and facilities in the recreation area mentioned in the selection.

___T___ 4. The Missouri River water levels are not constant.

___T___ 5. There were no hydropower dams on the Missouri River in South Dakota before 1947.

___F___ 6. It can be inferred that the state of South Dakota archaeologists do not know how to analyze dirt from burial sites.

➤ F.   THINKING CRITICALLY

Indicate whether each quote from the selection is fact (F) or opinion (O).

___O___ 1. "After five meetings we worked through issues that were acceptable to all." (paragraph 2)

__F__ 2. "This is not required by the court order." (paragraph 3)

__O__ 3. "We are tired of being oppressed." (paragraph 6)

__F__ 4. "I have a grandmother and a grandfather buried underwater, just over that hill." (paragraph 12)

__O__ 5. "They have no respect." (paragraph 13)

__O__ 6. "Of course they have no stock in oral history." (paragraph 14)

➤ G. BUILDING VOCABULARY

➤ Context

Using context and a dictionary, if necessary, determine the meaning of each word as it is used in the selection.

__a__ 1. pocked (paragraph 1)
- a. marked, spotted
- b. marked by holes
- c. made totally full
- d. planned

__b__ 2. assert (paragraph 2)
- a. argue
- b. state with confidence
- c. confirm
- d. lie about

__d__ 3. oppressed (paragraph 6)
- a. blamed unfairly
- b. burdened
- c. depressed, sad
- d. harshly controlled

__b__ 4. aghast (paragraph 14)
- a. frightened
- b. shocked
- c. relieved
- d. sorry

➤ Word Parts

> ### A REVIEW OF PREFIXES AND SUFFIXES
> **EX-** means *out*
> **-IST** means *one who*

Use the review of prefixes and suffixes above to fill in the blanks in the following sentences.

1. If archaeology is the study of ancient cultures, then an archaeologist (paragraph 10) is a _____ person _____ who studies ancient cultures.

2. When a grave is *exhumed* (paragraph 14) the remains are brought _____ out _____ of the ground .

➤ **Unusual Words/Unusual Meanings**

Use the meanings given below to write a sentence using the underlined word or phrase.

1. To <u>secure</u> (paragraph 4) a building is to close it up and perhaps guard it so that no one has access to it.

   Your sentence: _____

2. When you <u>give someone an out</u> (paragraph 11) during a situation, you allow him or her to withdraw from that situation possibly by finding a loophole to slip through or excuse to use.

   Your sentence: _____

3. If you have <u>no stock</u> (paragraph 14) in an article's claims, then you have no confidence in what that article is proposing.

   Your sentence: _____

➤ **H. SELECTING A LEARNING/STUDY STRATEGY**

Select the best answer.

___d___   Assume you are preparing for an essay exam and your instructor has hinted that you should review this article, in addition to five other assigned readings. What is the best way to prepare for this exam?

a. Organize the information in a chart.

b. Write a list of the tribes involved.

c. Create a time line of events that occurred.

d. Summarize the issues surrounding the debate.

➤ **I. EXPLORING IDEAS THROUGH DISCUSSION AND WRITING**

1. Imagine you are part of the Yankton Sioux Tribe. Write a letter to the editor of a local newspaper explaining the issue.

2. Discuss the idea of nonviolent resistance. How useful is this tactic? Are there times when violence *must* be used?

3. Consider the field of archaeology. Is it useful only for historical information or does it somehow help us in today's world?

4. Discuss the possible solution to the dispute described in the reading.

> **J. BEYOND THE CLASSROOM TO THE WEB**

Visit the Army Corps of Engineers home page for the Fort Randall Dam at **http://www.nwo.usace.army.mil/html/Lake_Proj/fortrandall/welcome.html.** *Read through the main page and the history page. How does the information here compare with what you know from the reading?*

✔ **Tracking Your Progress**

Selection 8

Section	Number Correct	Score
A. Thesis and Main Idea (5 items)	_____ x 4	_____
B. Details (7 items)	_____ x 4	_____
C. Organization and Transitions (2 items)	_____ x 2	_____
E. Inferred Meanings (6 items)	_____ x 3	_____
F. Thinking Critically (6 items)	_____ x 4	_____
G. Vocabulary		
1. Context (4 items)	_____ x 1	_____
2. Word Parts (2 items)	_____ x 1	_____
	TOTAL SCORE	_____%

CHECKING YOUR READING RATE

Words in Selection 8: 1,623

Finishing Time:	_____ (hour)	_____ (minutes)	_____ (seconds)
Starting Time:	_____ (hour)	_____ (minutes)	_____ (seconds)
Total Reading Time:		_____ (minutes)	_____ (seconds)

Words Per Minute Score (page 735) _____ WPM

SELECTION 9

Apes and Language

Marvin Harris and Orna Johnson

From a textbook titled *Cultural Anthropology,* this reading selection looks at what researchers have found out about the communication abilities of apes.

➤ PREVIEWING THE READING

Using the steps listed on page 5, preview the reading selection. When you have finished, complete the following items.

1. What is the selection about? _____Teaching apes to communicate_____

2. List at least two questions you would expect to have answered by the reading.

a. What communication skills can apes learn? or

How do scientists teach apes?

b. Who are the animals and researchers highlighted in the reading? or

How successful have apes been in learning language?

 ## MAKING CONNECTIONS

Think about pets that you have or young children that you know. What types of things do they try to communicate? How do they get their messages across?

➤ READING TIP

As you read, highlight the major findings or conclusion of each study that is cited.

 ## CHECKING YOUR READING RATE

If you plan to compute your reading rate, be sure to record your starting time in the box at the end of the exercises before you begin reading.

Apes and Language

1   In recent years, a revolutionary series of studies has revealed that the gap between human and ape language capacities is not as great as had previously been supposed. Yet these same experiments have shown that innate species-specific factors prevent this gap from being closed.

Many futile attempts had been made to teach chimpanzees to speak in human fashion before it was found that the vocal tract of apes cannot make the sounds necessary for human speech.

2   Attention has shifted toward trying to teach apes to use sign languages and to read and write. Chimpanzees and gorillas trained in laboratory settings have acquired communication skills that far exceed those of animals in the wild. Experiments with a chimpanzee named Washoe soon demonstrated that apes could learn to communicate in Ameslan (American Sign Language). Washoe used sign language productively; that is, she combined the signs in novel ways to send many different messages. For example, she first learned how to sign the request "open" with a particular closed door and later spontaneously extended its use beyond the initial training context to all closed doors, then to closed containers such as the refrigerator, cupboards, drawers, briefcases, boxes, and jars. When Susan, a research assistant, stepped on Washoe's doll, Washoe had many ways to tell her what was on her mind: "Up Susan; Susan up; mine please up; gimme baby; please shoe; more mine; up please; please up; more up; baby down; shoe up; baby up; please move up" (Gardner and Gardner 1971, 1975).

3   Koko, a female gorilla trained by Francine Patterson, has acquired a vocabulary of 300 Ameslan words. Koko signed "finger bracelet" for ring, "white tiger" for zebra, and "eye hat" for mask. Koka also learned to talk about her inner feelings, signaling happiness, sadness, fear, and shame (Hill 1978:98–99).

4   A remarkable achievement of more recent studies is the demonstration that signing chimpanzees can pass on their signing skills as a cultural tradition to nonsigning chimpanzees without human mediation. Loulis, a 10-month-old chimp whose mother had been incapacitated by a medical experiment, was presented to Washoe, whose baby had died. Washoe adopted the infant and promptly began to sign to

Koko, shown here with Dr. Francine Patterson, has learned sign language and can talk about inner feelings. As of 2003, Koko knows about 1,000 English words.

Kanzi learned 150 words by merely listening to conversations since infancy.

him. By 36 months, Loulis was using twenty-eight signs that he had learned from Washoe. After about 5 years of learning to sign from Washoe and two other signing chimps, but not from humans, Loulis had acquired the use of fifty-five signs. Washoe, Loulis, and other signing chimps regularly used their sign language to communicate with each other even when humans were not present. These "conversations," as recorded on remote videotape, occurred from 118 to 659 times a month (Fouts and Fouts 1985, 1989:301).

pygmy 5
chimpanzee
also called a
bonobo—a small
chimpanzee of
Zaire in Africa

But it is Kanzi, the **pygmy chimpanzee** genius who has learned to make stone tools who has captured everybody's attention. Without training, Kanzi has developed a true comprehension of 150 spoken English words. Like a human child, Kanzi acquired his comprehension of spoken words merely by listening to the conversations that surrounded him from infancy on (Savage-Rumbaugh and Levin 1994:247ff.). With the help of a keyboard and voice synthesizer, Kanzi can carry on extensive conversations in English. Every precaution has been taken in testing Kanzi's comprehension of symbols to make sure that no unconscious prompting or scoring bias has been introduced by his guardian teachers. A vast gap still remains between the language performances of humans and apes.

semantic
universality
being able to
express anything
through language, 6
even a concept
that seems
understandable
only in another
language

Despite all the effort being expended on teaching apes to communicate, none has acquired the linguistic skills we take for granted in 3-year-old children. Still, what all these experiments have shown is that natural selection could easily have given rise to the human capacity for **semantic universality** by selecting for intellectual skills already present in rudimentary form among our apelike hominid ancestors (Lieberman 1991; Parker 1985:622; Savage-Rumbaugh 1987; Snowdon 1990).

►A. UNDERSTANDING THE THESIS AND OTHER MAIN IDEAS

Select the best answer.

_____^c 1. The author's primary purpose in "Apes and Language" is to

   a. evaluate the techniques used to teach chimpanzees sign language.

   b. promote the idea of natural selection.

    c. describe laboratory experiments in which chimps were taught to communicate.

    d. examine the purpose behind teaching chimps sign language.

___b___ 2. All of the following questions are answered in paragraph 2 *except*

    a. How do the skills of laboratory chimps compare to those of animals in the wild?

    b. Are chimps the only animals that can be taught sign language?

    c. Can chimpanzees transfer their knowledge to different situations?

    d. What types of things can chimpanzees learn how to "say"?

___b___ 3. The main idea of paragraph 4 is that

    a. humans have to be present for chimps to communicate with each other.

    b. chimpanzees can teach each other sign language.

    c. the recent research on apes and language is more important than the older studies.

    d. a female chimpanzee will "adopt" the baby of another female if necessary.

___a___ 4. The main topic of paragraph 5 is best expressed by sentence number

    a. two.

    b. three.

    c. four.

    d. five.

▶ B. IDENTIFYING DETAILS

Match the skill with the ape who has learned it. You may use a name more than once.

A. Washoe   C. Loulis

B. Koko   D. Kanzi

___D___ 1. Uses a keyboard and voice synthesizer.

___A___ 2. Could use signs in combination to send different messages.

___B___ 3. "Talks" about her inner feelings.

___D___ 4. Learned to communicate by listening to the conversations of humans.

___C___ 5. Learned signs from an ape that adopted him.

___A___ 6. Told her teacher to get her foot off her doll.

___B___ 7. Knows 300 Ameslan words.

___D___ 8. Has a true comprehension of 150 spoken English words.

___A___ 9. Taught Loulis 28 signs in three years.

___C___ 10. Acquired the use of 55 signs in five years.

C.   RECOGNIZING METHODS OF ORGANIZATION AND TRANSITIONS

Select the best answer.

___b___ 1. The author lists the chimpanzee studies

a. from most to least important

b. from less to more recent

c. alphabetically

d. by quantity of information

___d___ 2. What organizational pattern in used in paragraph 2?

a. comparison and contrast

b. cause and effect

c. spatial order

d. generalization and example

D.   REVIEWING AND ORGANIZING IDEAS: SUMMARIZING

Complete the following summary of the selection by filling in the blanks using words from the list.

intervention	keyboard	chimpanzee	Ameslan	gap	listening
language	Studies	synthesizer	human	spoken	Washoe
Loulis	Kanzi	Koko	combine	limit	

Apes and humans do not have the same ____language____ capabilities. ____Studies____ show that a ____chimpanzee____ cannot learn more than what a three-year-old ____human____ knows. However, several apes have been taught American Sign Language ____(Ameslan)____ over the past thirty-five years. Two of these, ____Washoe____ and ____Koko____, learned many signs and even figured out how to ____combine____ signs and use signs in new ways. One of these chimps even went on to teach her adopted baby, ____Loulis____, fifty-five signs in five years. Researchers were amazed that the chimps could teach each other without human____intervention____. The most amazing chimp, though, is

__Kanzi__, who can actually understand and communicate in __spoken__ English using a __keyboard__ and voice __synthesizer__. This ape learned by __listening__ to the conversations of humans from the time of his infancy. Although apes can learn to communicate, there is a __limit__ to their ability. Natural selection dictates that the __gap__ between us and them will never completely close.

➤ E.   FIGURING OUT INFERRED MEANINGS

Indicate whether each statement is true (T) or false (F).

__T__ 1. Washoe was not specifically taught how to tell Susan to get off the doll.

__F__ 2. It can be inferred that Francine Patterson trained other apes besides Koko.

__T__ 3. Humans can teach chimps more signs that chimps can teach each other.

__T__ 4. Kanzi was not trained in Ameslan.

__F__ 5. Researchers teach only deaf chimps sign language.

__F__ 6. The author believes that apes will progress beyond their current level of communication.

__T__ 7. It can be inferred that the author read all or part of numerous research studies to write this selection.

➤ F.   THINKING CRITICALLY

Select the best answer.

__b__ 1. The author supports the central thesis primarily with
   a. his own personal experiences.
   b. scientific research.
   c. newspaper articles.
   d. statistical data.

__d__ 2. The overall tone is
   a. excited.
   b. persuasive.
   c. comic.
   d. informative.

___a___ 3. The author mentions Susan by name in paragraph 2 because

    a. Washoe uses Susan's name.

    b. she was integral to the research project.

    c. Washoe taught her some sign language.

    d. Susan did not understand Washoe.

___b___ 4. People are amazed by Kanzi because he

    a. has gone beyond the three-year-old human level.

    b. can carry on conversations.

    c. learned so much at a young age.

    d. made stone tools.

➤ G. BUILDING VOCABULARY

➤ Context

Using context and a dictionary, if necessary, determine the meaning of each word as it is used in the selection.

___d___ 1. capacities (paragraph 1)

    a. duties   c. power supplies

    b. intellectual stimulation   d. skills, capabilities

___b___ 2. mediation (paragraph 4)

    a. approval   c. emotional support

    b. involvement   d. awareness

___a___ 3. incapacitated (paragraph 4)

    a. disabled   c. delayed

    b. killed   d. abused

___a___ 4. rudimentary (paragraph 6)

    a. basic   c. advanced

    b. earthly   d. important

➤ Word Parts

> **A REVIEW OF PREFIXES**
> **UN-** means *not*
> **-ARY** means *referring to*

Use the review of prefixes and roots on page 256 to fill in the blanks in the following sentences.

1. Revolutionary studies (paragraph 1) are those that pertain to a major change, or _____revolution_____.

2. Unconscious prompting (paragraph 5) means clues to answers that a researcher may _____not_____ be aware he or she is giving.

➤ Unusual Words/Unusual Meanings

Use the meaning given below to write a sentence using the underlined word or phrase.

To have a <u>novel</u> (paragraph 2) idea is to have an idea that is new, original, and perhaps fresh or unusual.

Your sentence: _____ .

➤ H. SELECTING A LEARNING/STUDY STRATEGY

Discuss whether case studies make learning about research easier.

➤ I. EXPLORING IDEAS THROUGH DISCUSSION AND WRITING

1. Does the capacity to learn language separate apes from other animals and make them more humanlike? If so, should they be treated differently than other animals?

2. Zoos keep apes, as well as other animals, in captivity. Discuss whether zoos are fair to animals.

3. Do you think animals other than apes communicate nonverbally, using expressions and movements, with humans? Cite examples from your own experience.

➤ J. BEYOND THE CLASSROOM TO THE WEB

Visit the Web site of the Chimpanzee and Human Communication Institute to see a picture of Washoe and read her biography (you can find a link to info about Loulis too) at **http://www.cwu.edu/~cwuchci/bios/washoe_bio.htm**. *Also see Koko at* **http://www.koko.org/world/**.

How does it feel to see pictures of these animals? Do they seem less like laboratory subjects now that you have seen them and read about their lives?

✔ **Tracking Your Progress**

Selection 9

Section	Number Correct		Score
A. Thesis and Main Idea (4 items)	_____	x 5	_____
B. Details (10 items)	_____	x 2	_____
C. Organization and Transitions (2 items)	_____	x 2	_____
E. Inferred Meanings (7 items)	_____	x 4	_____
F. Thinking Critically (4 items)	_____	x 4	_____
G. Vocabulary			
1. Context (4 items)	_____	x 2	_____
2. Word Parts (2 items)	_____	x 2	_____

TOTAL SCORE _____%

CHECKING YOUR READING RATE

Words in Selection 9: 634

Finishing Time:	_____	_____	_____
	(hour)	(minutes)	(seconds)
Starting Time:	_____	_____	_____
	(hour)	(minutes)	(seconds)
Total Reading Time:		_____	_____
		(minutes)	(seconds)

Words Per Minute Score (page 735) _____ WPM

14 Education

Introductory education courses provide an overview of the function and process of education. More advanced education courses, often restricted to majors, train potential teachers, counselors, administrators, and other professional staff.

Introductory education courses are useful because you will be involved with education most of your life either as a student, as a parent, or as a member of the workforce. Education in the workplace, in particular, is an ongoing process. Many companies encourage their employees to take courses to update their skills and remain current in their field. In addition to providing information, education is important because it transmits values and behaviors. It helps children understand right and wrong and what is acceptable behavior and what is not. Education, in a sense, is also a screening device. One function of schools is to award grades, certificates, and diplomas that are necessary for entry into many careers.

The readings in this chapter, too, emphasize the importance and value of education. In the pair of readings, "Should Students Attend School Year Round?" you will see one of many debates that focus on the educational process. The article "From the Beginning . . . There Needs to Be Light" considers the importance of preschool education for Hispanic children. Use the following tips for reading within the field of education:

TIPS FOR READING IN EDUCATION	■ **Pay attention to issues.** Education is a field that often involves controversy. Current issues include school vouchers, security within schools, and teacher and student competence. One current issue is year-round schooling, which is the topic of the pair of readings "Should Students Attend School Year Round?"

■ **Realize that measurement and assessment are important.** There is growing political and parental pressure to evaluate students' performance. Statewide competency tests are becoming commonplace, for example. You will see that performance is a factor in the debate on year-round schooling, discussed in the pair of readings in this chapter.

■ **Look for trends and innovations.** Educational reform is an ongoing process, and education is in a constant state of flux. The reading "From the Beginning . . . There Needs to Be Light" identifies preschool education as an important trend and emphasizes its benefits.

■ **Pay attention to multicultural aspects of education.** As Hispanic and other ethnic populations grow in the United States, cultural diversity and bilingual education will become increasingly important. "From the Beginning . . . There Needs to Be Light" considers the need for preschool education for Hispanic children.

259

SELECTION 10

Should Students Attend School Year Round? Yes

Daniel A. Domenech

This article and the one following it (Selection 11) appeared as a pair in *Spectrum: The Journal of State Government* in 1998. Read it to discover the arguments in favor of year-round schooling.

MAKING CONNECTIONS

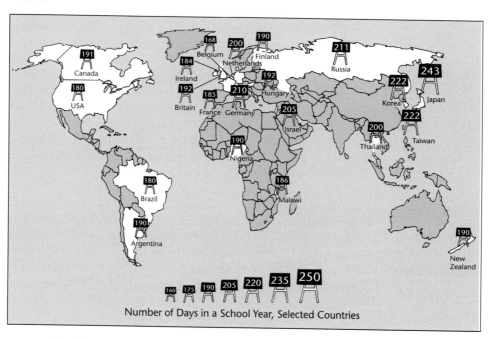

Number of Days in a School Year, Selected Countries

As this map shows, the number of days each year that high-school students are required to attend school varies quite a bit from country to country. Do you think the school year in the United States should be lengthened? Why or why not?

> **PREVIEWING THE READING**

Using the steps listed on page 5, preview the reading selection. When you have finished, complete the following items.

1. The issue that this selection addresses is _____year-round schooling_____.

2. List at least three questions you should be able to answer after reading the article.

   a. __What is the tradition of the ten-month year?__

   b. __What are the keys to year-round success?__

   c. __Is it time for a new tradition?/What would be the new tradition?__

> **READING TIP**

This selection proposes that students attend school year round and offers support for that proposal. Be sure to note the evidence the author uses to support his ideas.

CHECKING YOUR READING RATE

If you plan to compute your reading rate, be sure to record your starting time in the box at the end of the exercises before you begin reading.

Should Students Attend School Year Round? Yes

1   Education is one of the more traditional institutions in our society, and its traditions are valuable. At the same time, schools already are facing changes triggered by technology, **demographics**, economics, lifestyles and other forces that affect society.

demographics
characteristics
of human
population,
such as growth,
density, and
relocation

2   Making changes that can be controlled—rather than resisting or reacting piecemeal to imposed changes—will help schools adapt to the future and retain the most valuable traditions. Most important, controlled change will be best for students because it will ensure the quality of their education.

3   Many types of changes have been proposed for education, but one of those that makes sense is that schools remain open year-round rather than closing for two months in the summer.

The Tradition of the 10-Month Year

4   The 10-month school year was established in an agricultural society, when children were needed to work on the land during the summer. This schedule has become "traditional," and many practices have evolved around it. "Summer vacation" seems to be a fact of nature rather than an **historical artifact**. Day-care schedules assume that children are in school from September to June.

historical artifact
outcome of history

5   Summer camps and other businesses depend on children having summers off. In Virginia, where I am currently a superintendent of schools, the Legislature has, for several years, forbidden school boards from opening before Labor Day because the state's "hospitality industry" claims to need both student workers and family vacationers through Labor Day weekend.

6   Once something becomes as "traditional" as the 10-month school year, arguing against it is particularly difficult. The burden of proving the merits of change rest on those suggesting it. However, the question everyone should ask is not, "Why have year-round school," but, "Why not have year-round school?"

7   Our society no longer operates on an agricultural calendar; almost all institutions (public and private) operate year-round. School facilities that are not being used in the summer are inefficient. And most important, the children attending school are not being as effectively educated as they could be in year-round schools.

8   Year-round school offers two important benefits. The most important is continuity of instruction that currently is split by a two-month summer break. Everyone who has attended school, and certainly everyone who has taught school, recognizes that much is forgotten over the summer and that tedious review in the fall wastes time.

9   Not surprisingly, a great deal of research substantiates this observation. Research also shows that the vast majority of the more than 2,700 year-round schools show improved academic success. Keeping school open most of the year, with shorter breaks, obviates most of the forgetfulness and review, making instruction more effective without requiring students to attend more than the (traditional) 180 days of schooling per year.

10   The other important benefits are frequently recurring opportunities for "catching up," for extending and enriching learning in the basic instructional program, and for pursuing individual interests. For instance, in a school year that runs from August to June, one can provide optional "intersessions" in October and April. Students who need extra work or want to learn more science or even Web-page design can pursue those interests then. Unlike in summer-school courses, knowledge gained in a short intersession comes when the student needs it and has an immediate impact.

The Keys to 'Year-Round' Success

11   Like any change, year-round school is likely to fail if not done right. This is especially true because the change would violate long-standing tradition. For it to be successful, most parents of children who attend year-round schools need to believe the change will help their children.

12   Convincing parents is easier now that both parents in most families work, and parents recognize that only the well educated will be successful in the future. Businessmen in particular recognize that year-round schooling makes more efficient use of time and facilities. Lower-income parents understand that the change will benefit their children. Middle-income parents recognize that children forget over the summer.

13   Teachers also need to be convinced that year-round school is the right thing to do. There is an old saying among teachers that "the best two things about teaching are July and August." Nevertheless, because it violates perceived tradition, most people need to be convinced.

14   They also recognize that many of their July/August activities (studying, reading, traveling) could be accomplished within year-round schedules as such schedules become more widespread. The institutions that currently offer summer programs (e.g., universities, museums) will adjust to new realities, and new "traditions" will emerge.

15   The year-round program also needs to be well designed and implemented—both the overall calendar (which days school will be in session) and the substance of the intersession programs. Teachers and others need to think about how the new calendar can best be used to help all students.

16   How do you identify students who may be falling behind, for instance, and provide the necessary remediation during intersessions? How can public and private agencies be helped to reconfigure their day-care options for students in year-round schools?

Time for a New Tradition?

17   In Fairfax County, where I am superintendent, one elementary school will become a year-round facility this Aug. 3. The impetus for the program came from the school's teachers and parents. Over a two-year period, the community debated the idea, and the principal and faculty, with the assistance of specialists from outside it, developed the plan.

18   There has been some opposition, but the overwhelming percentage of parents in the community and all the school's teachers support the program. In Fairfax County, and in many other school systems, educators are breaking with the 10-month school year and other "traditions" in education, showing that controlled change—well-considered change based on solid research—can improve instruction and cost-effectiveness.

19   Most observers of American public education—especially the critics—recognize the need for change. The students in our schools and the society in which students and schools exist today are substantially different from the students and society of 25 years ago. I know. I was there.

20   Institutions all around us are changing to meet new circumstances, and we—the schools—need to change as well. This change needs to be thoughtful and careful, but it needs to happen. Ask yourselves not, "Why?" but "Why not?"

A.   UNDERSTANDING THE THESIS AND OTHER MAIN IDEAS

Select the best answer.

___c___ 1. The central thesis of the selection is that

   a. education is a traditional institution in our society.

   b. the quality of the educational system in the United States has declined dramatically in the last 50 years.

   c. schools should be kept open year round.

   d. school systems need to address alternative methods of instruction to improve the quality of education.

___a___ 2. The author's primary purpose is to

    a. argue that students should attend school year round.

    b. compare year-round schools with traditional schools.

    c. criticize opponents of the year-round school plan.

    d. present arguments for and against keeping schools open year round.

___d___ 3. The main idea of paragraph 10 is that the 10-month school year would provide opportunities for

    a. learning Web-page design.

    b. studying science.

    c. review of important material.

    d. catch-up and enrichment programs.

___b___ 4. The benefits that the author offers in favor of year-round schools include all of the following *except*

    a. continuity of instruction.

    b. keeping students in school for more than 180 days.

    c. improved academic success.

    d. frequent opportunities for learning enrichment.

___d___ 5. The topic of paragraph 12 is

    a. working parents.

    b. lower-income parents.

    c. middle-income parents.

    d. convincing parents.

___b___ 6. According to the selection, the author is

    a. a parent in favor of year-round schools.

    b. a school superintendent.

    c. a teacher.

    d. the principal of an elementary school.

➤ **B.   IDENTIFYING DETAILS**

Indicate whether each statement is true (T) or false (F).

___T___ 1. The Virginia Legislature has forbidden schools to open before Labor Day.

___F___ 2. Almost all public and private institutions still operate on an agricultural calendar.

___T___ 3. According to the selection, there are currently more than 2,700 year-round schools.

___F___ 4. The "intersessions" proposed by the author would be mandatory.

___F___ 5. All of the schools in Fairfax County, Virginia, are year-round schools.

➤ **C.   RECOGNIZING METHODS OF ORGANIZATION AND TRANSITIONS**

Select the best answer.

___b___ 1. The author offers reasons why year-round school would be beneficial. The overall organizational pattern used throughout the selection is

    a. comparison and contrast.   c. enumeration.

    b. cause and effect.   d. illustration.

___a___ 2. The phrase that indicates that the author is using the enumeration pattern in paragraphs 8–10 is

    a. two important benefits.   c. per year.

    b. a two-month summer break.   d. for instance.

___c___ 3. The author uses the comparison–contrast organizational pattern in paragraph 10 to contrast

    a. opportunities for learning enrichment with opportunities for pursuing individual interests.

    b. a traditional school year with a year-round school schedule.

    c. optional intersessions with summer-school courses.

    d. students who need extra work with students who want to learn more science.

➤ **D.   REVIEWING AND ORGANIZING IDEAS: MAPPING**

Complete the following comparison-contrast map of the selection by filling in the missing words.

TRADITIONAL SCHOOL YEAR	YEAR-ROUND SCHOOL YEAR
Based on an __agricultural__ society	Most __institutions__ now operate year round
School facilities used for __ten months__ per year	More __cost-effective__ to keep facilities open all year
Two-month __summer__ vacation	Shorter breaks mean less __forgetfulness__ and review
__180__ days of schooling per year	Would not require __students__ to attend more days
Summer school	Two optional __intersessions__ provide immediate impact
__Teachers'__ July/August activities	Activities can be done throughout the year

➤ E.   FIGURING OUT INFERRED MEANINGS

Indicate whether each statement is true (T) or false (F).

__T__ 1. It can be inferred that the number of farms in the United States has declined.

__F__ 2. The hospitality industry in Virginia supports the idea of year-round schools.

__F__ 3. Students attending year-round schools would not have any vacations.

__T__ 4. The author believes that parental support is essential to the success of year-round schools.

__F__ 5. The teachers in the elementary school that recently became a year-round facility were against the idea at first.

➤ F.   THINKING CRITICALLY

Select the best answer.

__d__ 1. The central thesis of the selection is supported by

    a. facts.   c. reasons.

    b. research.   d. all of the above.

__b__ 2. The tone of the selection can best be described as

    a. anxious.   c. cautionary.

    b. reasonable.   d. defiant.

___c___ 3. The author's qualifications to write this article can best be described as

    a. questionable.   c. credible.

    b. unlikely.   d. objective.

___d___ 4. Another title for this selection would be

    a. "Exploring Alternatives to Traditional Schooling."

    b. "The Pros and Cons of Public Education in America."

    c. "Tracing the History of American Institutions."

    d. "Say Yes to Year-Round Schools."

___c___ 5. Of the following statements from the selection, the only one that is a *fact* is

    a. "Education is one of the more traditional institutions in our society, and its traditions are valuable." (paragraph 1)

    b. "Most important, controlled change will be best for students because it will ensure the quality of their education." (paragraph 2)

    c. "The ten-month school year was established in an agricultural society." (paragraph 4)

    d. "Once something becomes as 'traditional' as the ten-month school year, arguing against it is particularly difficult." (paragraph 6)

___a___ 6. Of the following statements from the selection, the only one that is an *opinion* is

    a. "'Summer vacation' seems to be a fact of nature rather than an historical artifact." (paragraph 4)

    b. "In Virginia, the Legislature has, for several years, forbidden school boards from opening before Labor Day." (paragraph 5)

    c. "Our society no longer operates on an agricultural calendar." (paragraph 7)

    d. "In Fairfax County, one elementary school will become a year-round facility this August 3." (paragraph 17)

___b___ 7. As quoted in paragraph 13, the saying that "the best two things about teaching are July and August" means

    a. teachers like to use those months to plan their lessons for the coming school year.

    b. having two months off for study, research, and travel is one of the best things about being a teacher.

    c. those are the months that teachers really miss their students.

    d. teachers look forward to teaching summer school during those months.

___b___ 8. The author ends the selection with

    a. a quote from advocates of year-round schools.

    b. an appeal for change in public schools.

    c. a look back at the way schools used to be.

    d. a request for suggestions about how schools should change.

➤ G. BUILDING VOCABULARY

➤ Context

Directions: Using context and a dictionary, if necessary, determine the meaning of each word as it is used in the selection.

___c___ 1. continuity (paragraph 8)

    a. community   c. being uninterrupted

    b. intensity   d. tradition

___a___ 2. tedious (paragraph 8)

    a. tiresome   c. unnecessary

    b. detailed   d. challenging

___c___ 3. substantiates (paragraph 9)

    a. observes   c. supports

    b. breaks   d. suggests

___b___ 4. obviates (paragraph 9)

    a. proves   c. requires change

    b. makes unnecessary   d. causes

___a___ 5. implemented (paragraph 15)

    a. carried out   c. forced

    b. removed   d. counted

___d___ 6. impetus (paragraph 17)

    a. requirement   c. complaint

    b. opposition   d. motivation

➤ **Word Parts**

> ### A REVIEW OF PREFIXES
> **INTER-** means *between*
> **RE-** means *again*

Using your knowledge of word parts and the review of prefixes above, fill in the blanks in the following sentences.

1. The _____intersessions_____ (paragraph 10) described in the selection are intended to be sessions or classes that take place _____between_____ the regular school terms.

2. If day-care agencies needed to _____reconfigure_____ (paragraph 16) their options for year-round students, those options would have to be arranged or designed _____again_____ so they fit the new schedule.

➤ **Unusual Words/Unusual Meanings**
Use the meaning given below to write a sentence using the underlined word or phrase.

To react <u>piecemeal</u> (paragraph 2) to an idea or a change is to react in stages, or by a small amount at a time rather than all at once.

Your sentence: _____ .

➤ **H.   SELECTING A LEARNING/STUDY STRATEGY**

Discuss whether writing a list of pros and cons or outlining the article would be more helpful in learning the material. Is it possible that a particular strategy may work better for some students than for others?

➤ **I.   EXPLORING IDEAS THROUGH DISCUSSION AND WRITING**

1. Did the author convince you that schools should be open year round? Put into your own words what you consider to be his strongest argument in favor of year-round schools. What arguments would you use against year-round schools?

2. Discuss the author's tone. Does his language reveal his attitude toward the subject?

➤ J.   BEYOND THE CLASSROOM TO THE WEB

Visit the Perry McCleur High School Web site at http://www.buena-vista
.k12.va.us/yrschool.htm.

The Buena Vista City Public Schools has been operating this high school as a
year-round school since 1974. After reading the introduction, visit the page that
provides the program evaluation for the year-round school: http://www.buena-
vista.k12.va.us/evaluation.html.

Does the evaluation indicate that the benefits mentioned in the reading selection have been seen at Perry McCleur High School? If so, which ones? If not, what
other benefits does it discuss?

✔ **Tracking Your Progress**

Selection 10

Section	Number Correct		Score
A. Thesis and Main Idea (6 items)	_____	x 4	_____
B. Details (5 items)	_____	x 3	_____
C. Organization and Transitions (3 items)	_____	x 2	_____
E. Inferred Meanings (5 items)	_____	x 3	_____
F. Thinking Critically (8 items)	_____	x 3	_____
G. Vocabulary			
1. Context (6 items)	_____	x 2	_____
2. Word Parts (2 items)	_____	x 2	_____

TOTAL SCORE _____ %

CHECKING YOUR READING RATE

Words in Selection 10: 1,028

Finishing Time: _____ _____ _____
                     (hour)   (minutes)   (seconds)

Starting Time: _____ _____ _____
                   (hour)   (minutes)   (seconds)

Total Reading Time: _____ _____
                             (minutes)   (seconds)

Words Per Minute Score (page 735) _____ WPM

SELECTION 11

Should Students Attend School Year Round? No

Dorothy Rubin

This article and the one preceding it (Selection 10) appeared as a pair in *Spectrum: The Journal of State Government* in 1998. Read it to discover the arguments opposing year-round school.

▶ PREVIEWING THE READING

Using the steps listed on page 5, preview the reading selection. When you have finished, complete the following items.

1. Does the author believe students should attend school year round? ___No___.

2. List at least two questions you should be able to answer after reading the article.

   a. What questions should parents and taxpayers ask about year-round

   schools?

   b. How will summer heat affect year-round schools?

 ### MAKING CONNECTIONS

We are a nation of summer-vacationers, in part because of the traditional two-month break in the public school schedule. Which aspects of our usual way of life as a nation might not have developed without the traditional summer vacation?

▶ READING TIP

This selection proposes that year-round schools are not the answer to problems with education. Be sure to note the evidence the author uses to support her ideas, and be aware of emotional language.

CHECKING YOUR READING RATE

If you plan to compute your reading rate, be sure to record your starting time in the box at the end of the exercises before you begin reading.

Should Students Attend School Year Round? No.

1   Year-round schools have been huckstered as a way to raise students' achievement and a cure-all for what ails education. The year-round school proposal, however, does not get to the heart of our educational difficulties. It just relieves some school officials from attacking the real problems that plague their school systems.

self-aggrandizing 2   I am fed up with fads and with all **self-aggrandizing** individuals who, like vul-
exaggerating one's   tures, have targeted the rich educational terrain looking to pick its bones at the ex-
own importance   pense of our students, parents and all taxpayers. The school system should not be used as a political smoke screen to buy time for those school officials who need to show taxpayers that they are doing "something."

3   Parents, including all taxpayers, have a right and responsibility to ask questions when school officials recommend year-round schools. And because plans vary from one school system to another, here is a good first question: What does the phrase "year-round school" mean?

Parents and Taxpayers: Demand Answers

4   Would it mean that students would go to school the traditional 180 days but on a
staggered   **staggered** basis throughout the year or that students would go more days but for
alternating   shorter hours? Would the change to year-round schools include a schedule of more than 180 days? If a staggered system were used, how many students would be in session at once?

5   How long would each session last, and how many breaks would there be during the school year? (In some schools, students have classes for 90 days and are off for 30; others have classes for 45 days and are off for 15; and so forth.)

6   If those questions are answered sufficiently, there are plenty more to ask. Start with these: What other kinds of changes would occur besides those in the school calendar, and would there be better instruction? Would the calendar change make all children come to school ready to learn? Would it stem the dropout rate?

7   What about parents who have more than one child in the school system? Would their children who are in different schools attend during the same sessions? What would the extra cost be, and where would the money come from? When would necessary repairs to buildings occur?

8   Would exceptions in scheduling be made for students who rely on summer jobs? Would students who are in the band or on extracurricular sports teams have to do without those activities or would they have to attend school year round? What distractions would come from those students not in session?

9   And here is a most important question for summer schooling: What about air conditioning? Many overcrowded school systems have jumped on the year-round school bandwagon as a cost-saving device to avoid making capital investments in

new school buildings. But numerous schools in the United States are old and not air-conditioned.

10   How would year-round schools keep students cool who are attending during the dog days of summer? Imagine the cost of putting insulation and new electrical wiring into poorly insulated school buildings, including gyms and auditoriums, and then paying to air-condition them.

The Long, Hot Summer

11   Interestingly, numerous year-round school supporters claim they are child advocates. But how many of them would like to try to learn in unbearably hot classrooms? Most year-round school proponents probably make their pronouncements for year-round schools while in air-conditioned offices.

12   "It's Hot, Boring, Slow and Necessary. It's Summer School," read one *New York Times* headline for an article on going to school in the summer. The writer did an excellent job of describing the effect the heat has on children in buildings that are not air-conditioned. And one picture of the faces of young children in summer school to prepare for first grade because their first language is not English said it all: A stifling hot room is not conducive to learning.

13   Some school districts already have their schools open longer during the school day and have tutoring and recreational programs available year round. These are worthwhile programs; however, they are costly and often the first to go in a budget crunch. Also, unless the summer schools are air-conditioned, it is hard to compete with cooler alternatives.

14   A major advantage often cited for year-round schools is that more frequent and shorter breaks would enhance students' retention of what they have learned and require less review time than after a summer break. Some researchers, however, refute this claim and suggest that the more frequent breaks in year-round schools would cause more forgetfulness and require more review. Effective teachers, regardless of school organizational patterns, can reduce forgetfulness anyway—by using teaching strategies based on good learning theory.

15   A key question is whether the calendar change would improve students' education. If schools have poor instructors, poor administrators, low standards, poor **curricula**, poor parental involvement, poor school attendance, poorly motivated students and many students who cannot read, how will a change in the calendar help them?

curricula
the courses of study offered by a school or educational institution

16   Obviously, it is the quality of students' education that must change for improvement to occur. Good teaching helps increase students' retention of material and decreases the amount of review time teachers must spend on a topic after a break. If school districts want to upgrade their school systems, they should try to enhance their present school programs and raise all their students' standards.

17   The public also should be leery of pilot-program results for year-round schools in air-conditioned buildings if the majority of the district's schools are not air-conditioned and if many children do not live in air-conditioned homes. For the studies to have any merit, they must include randomly selected groups of students and be conducted in environments that are more typical of school districts.

rhetoric
persuasive speech
or writing

red herring
something
introduced in order
to divert attention
or mislead

panacea
cure-all

Going Beyond the 'Year-Round' Rhetoric

18   Usually, overcrowded school districts that are delaying new construction are likely to opt for year-round schools. The year-round school may work in the short run merely because something different is being done or because someone is paying attention to the program.

19   Year-round schools, however, are merely Band-Aid solutions that just delay the inevitable for these school districts. And for other districts that toy with this supposed cure-all, the year-round school may act as a **red herring** to distract attention from the real problems school systems face. If year-round schools are such a **panacea**, why, in 1993, did 540 mostly affluent school districts in California revert back to the traditional school year as soon as they could legally do so?

20   Education is too important for just a handful of individuals to be responsible for calling the shots. Let's not be bamboozled by slick talk and glossy brochures about year-round schools. Let's ask questions.

➤ A. UNDERSTANDING THE THESIS AND OTHER MAIN IDEAS

Select the best answer.

___c___ 1. The central thesis of the selection is that

    a. school officials blame year-round schools for the real problems with education.

    b. taxpayers should be concerned when school officials recommend year-round schools.

    c. year-round schools are not the solution to the current problems with public education.

    d. school systems use year-round schools to avoid having to make capital investments in new school buildings.

___a___ 2. The author's primary purpose is to

    a. raise questions about the use of year-round schools.

    b. persuade school systems to invest money in new school buildings.

    c. criticize supporters of the year-round school plan.

    d. report the advantages and disadvantages of year-round schools.

___a___ 3. The first question the author wants answered is

    a. What does the phrase "year-round school" mean?

    b. How much will year-round schools cost taxpayers?

c. Would the calendar changes result in better instruction?

d. How would year-round schools affect the dropout rate?

___a___ 4. The main idea of paragraph 6 is expressed in the

a. first sentence.

b. second sentence.

c. third sentence.

d. fourth sentence.

___d___ 5. The main idea of paragraph 12 is that

a. the *New York Times* article gave an accurate description of summer school.

b. summer school is necessary.

c. children who speak English as a second language must go to summer school to prepare for first grade.

d. children have difficulty learning in summer school if the buildings are not air-conditioned.

___d___ 6. Instead of adopting year-round schools, the author recommends that school districts

a. require all students to attend summer school.

b. make summer vacation shorter and add other breaks during the year.

c. leave schools open longer during the school day.

d. enhance existing school programs and raise the standards for all students.

➤ **B. IDENTIFYING DETAILS**

Indicate whether each statement is true (T) or false (F).

___F___ 1. All school systems use the same year-round school plan.

___T___ 2. The traditional school year is 180 days long.

___F___ 3. The children described in the *New York Times* article were in summer school because they had failed first grade.

___T___ 4. According to the author, some school districts already have tutoring and recreational programs available year round.

___T___ 5. In 1993, 540 school districts in California chose to revert from year-round schooling to a traditional school year.

C.   RECOGNIZING METHODS OF ORGANIZATION AND TRANSITIONS

Select the best answer.

_b_ 1. The organizational pattern the author uses in paragraphs 3–10 to list the many questions parents and taxpayers should ask about year-round schools is called

a. time sequence.

b. enumeration.

c. comparison and contrast.

d. problem–solution.

_b_ 2. In paragraph 12, the word that indicates that the author is supplying additional information about the *New York Times* article is

a. however.   c. often.

b. and.   d. unless.

_b_ 3. In paragraph 14, the word that indicates that the author is making a contrast between an advantage cited by year-round school supporters and research that refutes their claim is

a. major.   c. regardless.

b. however.   d. anyway.

D.   REVIEWING AND ORGANIZING IDEAS: PARAPHRASING

Complete the following paraphrases of paragraphs 13 and 16 by filling in the missing words or phrases.

Paragraph 13: In some ____school districts____, schools are kept open longer during the school day, and ____tutoring____ and recreational programs are available year round. Although these ____programs____ are valuable, they are also expensive and may be eliminated first if the ____budget____ is tight. Additionally, if the summer schools are not ____air-conditioned____, students may choose other options that are not as hot.

Paragraph 16: The quality of ____education____ for students must change for there to be ____improvement____. When instruction is good, students retain material better and need less ____review time____ after a ____break____. In order to improve school systems, school districts should work on improving the ____school programs____ that are already in place as well as raising the ____standards____ for their students.

➤ E.   FIGURING OUT INFERRED MEANINGS

For each of the following statements from the selection, write Y (for yes) if it reveals the author's bias against year-round schools and N (for no) if it does not.

___Y___ 1. "Year-round schools have been huckstered as a way to raise students' achievement and a cure-all for what ails education." (paragraph 1)

___Y___ 2. "I am fed up with fads and with all self-aggrandizing individuals who, like vultures, have targeted the rich educational terrain looking to pick its bones." (paragraph 2)

___N___ 3. "Parents have a right and responsibility to ask questions when school officials recommend year-round schools." (paragraph 3)

___N___ 4. "A major advantage often cited for year-round schools is that more frequent and shorter breaks would enhance students' retention of what they have learned." (paragraph 14)

___N___ 5. "Effective teachers, regardless of school organizational patterns, can reduce forgetfulness by using teaching strategies based on good learning theory." (paragraph 14)

___N___ 6. "Usually, overcrowded school districts that are delaying new construction are likely to opt for year-round schools." (paragraph 18)

___Y___ 7. "Year-round schools are merely Band-Aid solutions that just delay the inevitable for these school districts." (paragraph 19)

___Y___ 8. "Let's not be bamboozled by slick talk and glossy brochures about year-round schools." (paragraph 20)

➤ F.   THINKING CRITICALLY

Select the best answer.

___b___ 1. The tone of the selection can best be described as

    a. objective.   c. optimistic.

    b. persuasive.   d. humorous.

___c___ 2. Another title for this selection could be

    a. "The Trouble with Education Today."

    b. "The Pros and Cons of Year-Round Schools."

    c. "Asking Questions About Year-Round Schools."

    d. "Long-Term Solutions for Schools."

_d_ 3. Of the following statements from the selection, the only one that is an opinion is

a. "In some schools, students have classes for 90 days and are off for 30." (paragraph 5)

b. "Numerous schools in the United States are not air-conditioned." (paragraph 9)

c. "Some school districts already have their schools open longer during the school day." (paragraph 13)

d. "The year-round school may work in the short run merely because something different is being done." (paragraph 18)

_a_ 4. Of the following statements, the only one that is a *fact* is

a. "Others have classes for 45 days and are off for 15." (paragraph 5)

b. "These are worthwhile programs." (paragraph 13)

c. "The public should be leery of pilot-program results." (paragraph 17)

d. "Let's not be bamboozled by slick talk." (paragraph 20)

_b_ 5. The author suggests that many supporters of year-round schools who "claim they are child advocates" (paragraph 11)

a. do not have any formal training in child advocacy.

b. are not really child advocates if they would put children in non-air-conditioned classrooms.

c. promote year-round schools because they believe the program is best for children.

d. are actually just parents hoping to improve their children's education.

➤ G.   BUILDING VOCABULARY

➤ Context

Using context and a dictionary, if necessary, determine the meaning of each word as it is used in the selection.

_c_ 1. huckstered (paragraph 1)

a. discussed   c. promoted

b. designed   d. planned

____a____ 2. plague (paragraph 1)

    a. trouble

    b. precede

    c. disguise

    d. define

____c____ 3. self-aggrandizing (paragraph 2)

    a. highly observant

    b. supportive of others

    c. exaggerating one's own importance

    d. political

____b____ 4. terrain (paragraph 2)

    a. building

    b. territory

    c. limit

    d. history

____b____ 5. proponents (paragraph 11)

    a. principals

    b. supporters

    c. relatives

    d. critics

____d____ 6. conducive (paragraph 12)

    a. forceful

    b. imaginative

    c. distracting

    d. helpful

____b____ 7. retention (paragraph 14)

    a. confusion

    b. memory

    c. understanding

    d. examination

_c_ 8. refute (paragraph 14)

  a. criticize

  b. agree

  c. disprove

  d. support

_a_ 9. leery (paragraph 17)

  a. suspicious

  b. afraid

  c. hopeful

  d. flexible

_b_ 10. bamboozled (paragraph 20)

  a. convinced

  b. fooled

  c. threatened

  d. pressured

➤ **Word Parts**

A REVIEW OF PREFIXES AND SUFFIXES

EXTRA- means *beyond* or *outside of*
OVER- means *more than, beyond*
SELF- means *of, by, for,* or *in itself*
UN- means *not*
-AL means *relating to* or *characterized by*
-NESS means *state, quality,* or *condition*

Match each word in Column A with its meaning in Column B. Write your answers in the spaces provided.

Column A

_e_ 1. parental

_a_ 2. overcrowded

_c_ 3. extracurricular

_d_ 4. forgetfulness

_b_ 5. unbearably

_f_ 6. self-aggrandizing

Column B

a. filled beyond capacity

b. intolerably

c. outside of the traditional course of study

d. state of being absent-minded

e. relating to parents

f. pursuing one's own importance

➤ **Unusual Words/Unusual Meanings**
Use the meanings given below to write a sentence using the underlined phrase.

1. To put up a <u>smoke screen</u> (paragraph 2) is to do or say something in order to hide your true plans or intentions.

   Your sentence: _____ .

2. If you <u>jump on the bandwagon</u> (paragraph 9), you have joined a trend along with a lot of other people who like the same idea.

   Your sentence: _____ .

3. The <u>dog days of summer</u> (paragraph 10) are the hottest, most uncomfortable days in the summertime, from July to early September.

   Your sentence: _____ .

4. If you are responsible for <u>calling the shots</u> (paragraph 20), you are in charge of giving directions or telling people what they should be doing.

   Your sentence: _____ .

➤ H. SELECTING A LEARNING/STUDY STRATEGY

Select the best answer.

____b____   The best way to organize and study the information in this selection is to

a. reread it.

b. write a list of questions and answers given in the selection.

c. use vocabulary cards.

d. visualize year-round schools.

➤ I. EXPLORING IDEAS THROUGH DISCUSSION AND WRITING

1. Did the author convince you that students should not attend school year round? Put into your own words what you consider to be her strongest argument against year-round schools.

2. In paragraph 19, what does the author mean when she says year-round schools merely "delay the inevitable" for certain school districts?

➤ J. BEYOND THE CLASSROOM TO THE WEB

Visit Education World to read an article about the pros and cons of year-round schooling at **http://www.education-world.com/a_admin/admin137.shtml.**
  Make a list of the pros and cons of year-round schooling, according to this article. Which of these ideas seems the most important? Why?

✔ Tracking Your Progress

Selection 11

Section	Number Correct		Score
A. Thesis and Main Idea (6 items)	_____	x 4	_____
B. Details (5 items)	_____	x 3	_____
C. Organization and Transitions (3 items)	_____	x 2	_____
E. Inferred Meanings (8 items)	_____	x 3	_____
F. Thinking Critically (5 items)	_____	x 3	_____
G. Vocabulary			
1. Context (10 items)	_____	x 1	
2. Word Parts (6 items)	_____	x 1	_____

TOTAL SCORE _____ %

CHECKING YOUR READING RATE

Words in Selection 11: 1,101

Finishing Time:	_____	_____	_____
	(hour)	(minutes)	(seconds)
Starting Time:	_____	_____	_____
	(hour)	(minutes)	(seconds)
Total Reading Time:		_____	_____
		(minutes)	(seconds)

Words Per Minute Score (page 735) _____ WPM

➤ INTEGRATING THE READINGS (SELECTIONS 10 AND 11)

1. Which argument did you find more convincing? Why?

2. Evaluate the types of evidence each author provided. What additional evidence might have strengthened each article?

3. Discuss how the tone differs in the two articles.

4. Which author seemed more emotional? Which seemed more authoritative?

5. Which article did you find easier to read? Why?

SELECTION 12

From the Beginning . . . There Needs to Be Light!

Mayra Rodriguez Valladares

This reading from HispanicMagazine.com (Jan./Feb. 2003) explores the reasons that one important group of children—those of Latino descent—are missing out on the preschool educational opportunities that some other children experience as a normal part of early childhood.

> ### PREVIEWING THE READING

Using the steps listed on page 5, preview the reading selection. When you have finished, complete the following items.

1. The topic of this selection is ___Preschool attendance by Latino children___ .

2. List at least three questions you should be able to answer after reading the selection.

   a. _Why are Latino children not attending preschool?_

   b. _What happens to Latino children when they eventually do start school?_

   c. _What attempts are being made to get more Latino children into preschool?_

MAKING CONNECTIONS

What was your personal experience with early childhood education, if any? What can you recall about your earliest educational experiences?

> ### READING TIP

As you read, locate and highlight the advantages preschool attendance gives children.

CHECKING YOUR READING RATE

If you plan to compute your reading rate, be sure to record your starting time in the box at the end of the exercises before you begin reading.

From the Beginning . . . There Needs to Be Light

1   Aurora Valladares, a south Texas mother of six, remembers trying to raise her kids in the late '60s and '70s. "Pre-school?" she asks, her dark eyes widening, "I did not know English. I spent all day cooking and cleaning. Where would I find the time to find out about early education programs? How could we afford it?"

2   The experience of this petite and energetic Mexican immigrant is not one that has improved with time. It repeats itself today among other Latino immigrant parents, in Texas and all across the nation. Lack of knowledge or money prevents thousands of Latino children from ever attending early education programs.

3   Statistics are staggering. Almost one in five children under the age of 5 in the United States is Latino. And one in three of those Latinos lives under the **poverty line**. Teachers, experts and community leaders agree that it is almost impossible for Latino children to break the **cycle of poverty** unless their education starts at a very early age. If it does not, they are already at risk of dropping out of school and destined for a life of low-paying menial jobs. While efforts exist to provide children with early education through programs such as **Head Start**, the majority of Latino children often do not enter schools until kindergarten or even first grade. By then, they are behind their peers; more so, if they do not speak English.

Economics cannot be ignored

4   According to research by Bowling Green State University's professors Jenny van Hook and Kelly Stamper Balistreri, Hispanics in California present a clear example of what happens to Latino children all across the country. Because "they are the largest immigrant group and tend to be poor and to be residentially segregated . . . it is nearly impossible for school districts in Hispanic areas not to be mostly poor, mostly minority, and mostly non-English-speaking." They add that these problems have led scholars in the field of education of immigrants to argue that schools in these poor and residentially segregated neighborhoods "produce inequality rather than equalize opportunity." This is particularly grave for small children. The authors found that California children who attend "low-status, high-minority schools learn less than children who attend integrated schools," particularly in schools where the concentration of minority students is prevalent.

Education has to begin early

5   "At pre-school age is when children can learn the most. They are like sponges!" explains Sugatha Alladi, an experienced teacher of children from the ages of 2 to 6 at a Montessori school in Somerset, New Jersey.

6   Ynez Cruz, who taught kindergarten-to-eighth-grade students for 34 years in Dade County in Florida, contends that in kindergarten it was immediately evident who had been to pre-school or not. "Children who went to pre-school had an advantage," recalls Cruz. "They came with English, had the ability to manage pencils and paper, and were already adapted to a school environment."

7   She found that the children who had not been in pre-school programs took a long time to adjust to being in kindergarten. "The difference was still noticeable in

poverty line
an income level set by the government under which people are considered to be impoverished. According to the U.S. Census Bureau, in 2001, the poverty line for a four-person family was $18,104.

cycle of poverty
the concept that poor people will remain poor because they do not have access to the education, opportunities, and resources they need to break out of poverty

Head Start
an educational program operated by the U.S. Department of Health and Human Services aimed at children up to the age of five and their families based on income guidelines

IQ

Intelligence Quotient; a number that expresses the result of certain standardized tests intended to measure "intelligence"

the first grade. If a child had a high IQ and had a rich learning environment at home, then they could catch up. Most of the time, however, this does not take place. About 75 percent of the children who had not attended pre-school carried that disadvantage for a long time."

8   According to Early Child Initiative Foundation's Chief Operating Officer Ana Sejeck, "if a kid has a good caregiver who is dedicated to taking them to all sorts of things, like libraries, music programs, and settings for children to interact with each other, then the child will probably succeed as well as his/her peers who have been to a pre-school program. Unfortunately, the reality is that most parents have to work and hence cannot give children structured education and stimulus." Consequently, "a child with no early education is already at a disadvantage in the first grade. Parents need to understand that children have to be read to, that they have to play with other children, be fed properly, and have health care."

Parents' education and financial status are critical

9   The reasons why Latino children do not attend early education programs are numerous. "Pre-school (in Florida) is usually not free," Cruz says. "In Dade County, some of these programs can cost $65–$100 a week. For some families, especially if they have more than one child of pre-school age, those fees are unaffordable." When it comes to private school pre-school education, the cost can be prohibitive. In New York, Alicia Meléndez, a Puerto Rican mother, paid over $8,000 a year, or $211 a week, for her son Paulo to attend a private school for a 38-week, four-hours-a-day program. "Had I wanted to send him more hours," explains Meléndez, "it would have been even costlier."

10   Significant lack of knowledge about early education also exists. Parents often confuse day-care centers for pre-school. "Child care is not necessarily pre-school, and even some pre-schools are not teaching children anything," says Alladi. "A good pre-school is one with a solid curriculum." Sejeck agrees. "Often child-care centers are not accredited. In Dade County, there are 1,400 licensed day-care centers, but only 106 are accredited." Sejeck explained. "I did not know when I was putting my kids in day care, that there is a big difference (between programs). Now I say to parents, 'Do not just warehouse your children in a center.' "

11   Cultural issues also affect parental attitudes about such programs. Dr. Linda Espinosa, co-director of the National Institute for Early Education Research (NIEER) in New Brunswick, New Jersey, contends that early education programs "need to make a concerted effort to make families comfortable; otherwise, families feel alienated." Word-of-mouth reputation is what sells or destroys a program. "We made our program family friendly." The program now has a long waiting list.

12   According to Espinosa, Latino families have a very difficult time "letting go of their 3-year-olds to strangers who often speak another language and come from a different culture. Anglo middle-class families, on the other hand, accept that kids need to go to pre-school to get socialized." There is much to be done to convince the parents of Hispanic children of the benefits of pre-school programs and of the adverse consequences of a late start in school.

Head Start makes a good effort, but the majority of Latinos are not covered

13   Head Start, a national program created in 1965, provides early education to children under 5. Dr. Wade Horn, Director of the Administration for Children and Families at the U.S. Department of Health and Human Services, explains that each of his department's programs "help provide services to the most vulnerable children. Clearly economic disadvantage causes vulnerability. Disproportionately, Hispanic children are poor, so as a matter of course we provide services to them." He also stated that "in some areas we have specific outreach (programs) for Hispanic children. In others, we cover them through our regular programs that target lower-income families and children."

14   Head Start also runs a program for migrants, which covers 37,000. Many, if not most of them, are Latino. Providing for migrants is a "unique challenge because families are moving according to agricultural cycles." Head Start has made an effort to model some programs to try to serve these children. "One is a program that moves with families as they move for agricultural opportunities. The other model is one where centers (are placed) in areas where migrant families might live."

agricultural cycles farming patterns of planting and harvesting. Farm workers may move according to what is being planted or picked in certain areas.

15   The Administration for Families and Children recognizes the need to carry out specific outreach for Hispanics. Horn states that the Administration is involved "in public education and invariably in English and Spanish public service announcements." The Administration has also had Hispanic forums about child support issues and has tried to reach out to Hispanic media. He admits, however, that despite the Administration's best intentions, more effort needs to focus on reaching Latino families and children.

16   While the Latinos served by Head Start constitute 30 percent of all the children in the program, they only represent 19 percent of the 1.2 million poor Latino children who need to be covered. This means that 80 percent of Latino children who also cannot afford any other kind of early education programs are not going to school until they are 5 or 6 years old, by which time their peers have had exposure to the English language, engaging in educational activities, and interacting with children outside their families.

► A.   UNDERSTANDING THE THESIS AND OTHER MAIN IDEAS

Select the best answer.

   __c__ 1. The central thesis of the selection is that

      a. Head Start programs are vital to our country's educational system.

      b. Hispanic parents need to find the time to research early childhood education programs.

      c. Latino children are not exposed to the preschool experiences that they need to succeed in elementary school and beyond.

      d. Kindergarten teachers do not have the time to provide extra help to children who have not attended preschool.

_b_ 2. The author's primary purpose is to

    a. criticize those who create educational policy in our country.

    b. describe the problem of lack of preschool attendance by Latino children.

    c. explain why some Latino parents are reluctant to enroll their children in preschool.

    d. urge Latino parents to enroll their children in preschool programs.

_a_ 3. The main idea of paragraph 3 is that

    a. education for Latinos must start at an early age.

    b. many Latino children live in poverty.

    c. Head Start programs do not attract many Latino children.

    d. the cycle of poverty affects a child's entire life.

_c_ 4. The topic of paragraph 9 is

    a. benefits of private schools.

    b. family income.

    c. preschool costs.

    d. affordable programs.

_c_ 5. The main idea of paragraph 15 is that

    a. the Administration for Families and Children has done all it can to communicate with Hispanic families.

    b. Hispanic families are just not responsive to outreach programs.

    c. the Administration for Families and Children is trying to reach Hispanics but needs to do more.

    d. a very small percentage of eligible Latino preschoolers attends Head Start programs.

_c_ 6. All of the following are reasons given for the low numbers of Latino children in preschool _except_:

    a. the costs of preschool.

    b. lack of knowledge.

    c. safety concerns.

    d. misunderstandings about the importance of early childhood education.

➤ **B.   IDENTIFYING DETAILS**

Complete each of the following statements by filling in the blanks.

1. Paragraph 3

   Among U.S. children under the age of _____five_____, almost
   _____one_____ in five is Latino. One-third of these children lives in
   _____poverty_____.

2. Paragraphs 6–8

   Children who attend preschools enter kindergarten knowing
   _____English_____, and how to use _____pencils_____ and paper.
   However, young children can still be prepared for school if they have a quality _____caregiver_____ who takes them to the library, involves them in
   _____music_____ programs, and gets them around other
   _____children_____.

3. Paragraph 10

   Many parents do not understand the difference between preschool and
   _____day care_____. Quality preschools have a strong _____curriculum_____
   and are accredited. Early education programs need to make an effort to inform parents about what they offer.

➤ **C.   RECOGNIZING METHODS OF ORGANIZATION AND TRANSITIONS**

Select the best answer.

___a___ 1. Which organization pattern does the author use throughout the
   reading?

   a. cause and effect to present the factors that prevent Latino
      children from attending preschool and the consequences of lack
      of attendance.

   b. process to show how children learn.

   c. classification to divide Latino students into groups.

   d. comparison to focus on similarities between Latino and white
      children.

___d___ 2. A transitional word that suggests the organizational pattern used in
   paragraph 4 is

   a. according to research.

   b. clear example.

   c. this is.

   d. because.

___c___ 3. A transitional word or phrase that suggests the organizational pattern used in paragraph 8 is

    a. according to.

    b. unfortunately.

    c. consequently.

    d. like.

___a___ 4. The organizational pattern of paragraph 10 is

    a. comparison and contrast.

    b. time sequence.

    d. classification.

    e. summary.

➤ D.   REVIEWING AND ORGANIZING IDEAS: OUTLINING

Complete the following outline of paragraphs 5–8 by filling in the missing words or phrases.

  I. Child Development

    A. Preschool age children are learning a great deal.

    B. Sugatha Alladi; ____"they are like sponges"____ .

  II. Kindergarten Readiness

    A. Ynez Cruz

      1. ____Preschool children have an advantage in kindergarten____

        a. English skills

        b. ____can manage paper and pencils____

        c. used to school setting

      2. A difference still exists in first grade

        a High IQ + ____enriched learning environment at home____ can help students catch up

        b. ____75 percent____ of children who did not attend preschool were at a disadvantage

    B. Ana Sejeck

      1. A child can succeed without preschool if his caregiver exposes the child to enriching programs and ____other children____

2. Parents must make sure that their children receive basic early child-hood experiences

   a. being read to

   b. _playing with other children_

   c. eating healthy food regularly

   d. _____ health care _____

➤ E.   FIGURING OUT INFERRED MEANINGS

Indicate whether each statement is true (T) or false (F).

___T___ 1. It can be inferred that Aurora Valladares' children did not go to preschool.

___F___ 2. The professors in paragraph 4 do not think the Hispanics should live in their own neighborhoods.

___T___ 3. Ynez Cruz has had teaching experience with a wide variety of students.

___T___ 4. Ana Sejeck believes that regularly attending library story times will help a child succeed in school.

___T___ 5. According to paragraph 9, having one child in preschool in New York could cost as much as having two children in preschool in Dade County.

___F___ 6. Preschool programs and day-care centers provide the same level of educational experiences for young children.

___T___ 7. Hispanic families that rely on picking or planting crops could be relocating several times a year.

___T___ 8. Hispanic families do not have enough opportunities to learn about Head Start programs.

➤ F.   THINKING CRITICALLY

Select the best answer.

___d___ 1. The central thesis of the selection is supported by

   a. personal experiences of parents.

   b. statistics.

   c. expert opinion.

   d. all of the above

___c___ 2. The tone of the selection can best be described as

    a. frustrated.

    b. angry.

    c. concerned.

    d. persuasive.

___a___ 3. The author mentions the cycle of poverty in paragraph 3 in order to

    a. emphasize the role education plays in affecting a person's quality of life.

    b. shock the readers into action.

    c. gain sympathy for Hispanic families.

    d. explain how Head Start programs work.

___b___ 4. Of the following statements from the reading, which one is an opinion?

    a. "The majority of Latino children often do not enter schools until kindergarten or even first grade." (paragraph 3)

    b. "They are like sponges!" (paragraph 5)

    c. "Often child-care centers are not accredited." (paragraph 10)

    d. "The Administration has also had Hispanic forums about child support issues." (paragraph 15)

___b___ 5. The author includes the research of the Bowling Green State University professors in order to:

    a. present statistics on the number of Latino children living in poverty.

    b. emphasize that schools with a high minority enrollment do not provide quality education.

    c. support the idea that being poor is related to the quality of education a child receives.

    d. review recent studies on this issue.

___c___ 6. The phrase "Parents' education" in the heading before paragraph 9 refers to:

    a. the number of years a child's parent spent in school.

    b. whether a Latino child's parent attended preschool or not.

    c. how much parents know about preschools, child-care centers, and the importance of early childhood education.

    d. how well Hispanic parents did in school.

➤ **G. BUILDING VOCABULARY**

➤ **Context**

Using context and a dictionary, if necessary, determine the meaning of each word as it is used in the selection.

___c___ 1. menial (paragraph 3)

    a. challenging

    b. requiring physical strength

    c. unskilled

    d. hopeless, with no promise of a future

___b___ 2. equalize (paragraph 4)

    a. imbalance

    b. distribute evenly

    c. make symmetrical

    d. bring out of proportion

___a___ 3. grave (paragraph 4)

    a. very serious

    b. causing death

    c. dark, black

    d. sincere, in earnest

___a___ 4. prevalent (paragraph 4)

    a. widespread, dominant   c. unexpected

    b. unimportant   d. primary

___d___ 5. Stimulus (paragraph 8)

    a. emotional support

    b. a lesson

    c. a substance that causes wakefulness

    d. something that causes a response or action

___a___ 6. accredited (paragraph 10)

    a. given official recognition for maintaining certain standards

    b. recognized as outstanding by experts

    c. being credited with success

    d. appreciated by many

_c_ 7. warehouse (paragraph 10)

    a. shelter, protect

    b. act without making an informed decision

    c. store or put away like merchandise

    d. put into a big empty space

_a_ 8. alienated (paragraph 11)

    a. isolated   c. different

    b. welcome   d. confused

_c_ 9. disproportionately (paragraph 13)

    a. truly, without a doubt

    b. without reason

    c. unequal in degree or amount

    d. unfairly, unjustly

_d_ 10. forums (paragraph 15)

    a. safe places to talk

    b. court-ordered public complaint sessions

    c. heated arguments

    d. public meetings

➤ Word Parts

> ### A REVIEW OF PREFIXES AND SUFFIXES
> **IN-** means *not*
> **INTER-** means *between*
> **-ABLY** refers to a *state* or *condition*
> **-ANT-** means *one who*

Use the review of prefixes and suffixes above to fill in the blanks in the following sentences.

1. If children *interact*, there is communication _____between_____ them.

2. When your professor *invariably* gives your tests back the next day, it means she does _____not_____ vary from this routine.

3. If *migrate* means to move from place to place, then migrant children belong to migrant parents who _____move_____ to find work.

➤ **Unusual Words/Unusual Meanings**

Use the meanings given below to write a sentence using the underlined word or phrase.

1. When someone is <u>at risk</u> (paragraph 3) for a certain behavior, it means he or she starts out with certain characteristics or comes from certain circumstances that make exhibiting the behavior more likely.

   Your sentence: _____ .

2. To live in a manner that is <u>residentially segregated</u> (paragraph 4) is to be in a neighborhood made up primarily of one group of people.

   Your sentence: _____ .

3. News of something good (or bad) is spread by <u>word of mouth</u> (paragraph 11) when people tell one another about it.

   Your sentence: _____ .

➤ **H.   SELECTING A LEARNING/STUDY STRATEGY**

What study aid would you prepare if you knew you had to answer the following essay question? Describe the factors that contribute to the low numbers of Latino children in preschool. Explain how the lack of early childhood education affects a child's life.

➤ **I.   EXPLORING IDEAS THROUGH DISCUSSION AND WRITING**

1. Discuss the way our government tries to help poor Americans. What programs are in place and how effective are they?

2. Describe the importance of education in your family's life.

3. Has your opinion of preschool changed after reading this article? Why or why not?

➤ **J.   BEYOND THE CLASSROOM TO THE WEB**

Visit the home page for Head Start at (http://www2.acf.dhhs.gov/programs/hsb/. How easy is it to find information on programs in your area? What if you did not speak English—could you use this resource to find a preschool for your child? Recommend improvements to the site.

✔ Tracking Your Progress

Selection 12

Section	Number Correct		Score
A. Thesis and Main Idea (6 items)	_____	x 4	_____
B. Details (10 items)	_____	x 2	_____
C. Organization and Transitions (4 items)	_____	x 3	_____
E. Inferred Meanings (8 items)	_____	x 2	_____
F. Thinking Critically (6 items)	_____	x 2	_____
G. Vocabulary			
1. Context (10 items)	_____	x 1	_____
2. Word Parts (3 items)	_____	x 2	_____
	TOTAL SCORE	_____ %	

CHECKING YOUR READING RATE

Words in Selection 12: 1,420

Finishing Time:	_____	_____	_____
	(hour)	(minutes)	(seconds)
Starting Time:	_____	_____	_____
	(hour)	(minutes)	(seconds)
Total Reading Time:		_____	_____
		(minutes)	(seconds)

Words Per Minute Score (page 735) _____ WPM

15

Arts/Humanities/Literature

The humanities and arts are areas of knowledge concerned with human thoughts and ideas and their creative expression in written, visual, or auditory form. They deal with large, global issues such as "What is worthwhile in life?," "What is beautiful?," and "What is the meaning of human existence?" Works of art and literature are creative records of the thoughts, feelings, emotions, or experiences of other people. By studying art and reading literature you can learn about yourself and understand both joyful and painful experiences without going through them yourself. "Shaping Her People's Heritage Nampeyo (1852–1942)" focuses on the preservation of a Native American art form, pottery, among the Hopi. In the short story "Gregory," you can experience the moral dilemma of whether a soldier should follow orders to execute a prisoner who has become a friend. In the poem "The Truth Is," you share the conflicts of a woman who is part Native American, part white.

Use the following tips when reading and studying in the arts, humanities, and literature.

TIPS FOR READING IN THE ARTS/ HUMANITIES/ LITERATURE	■ **Focus on values.** Ask yourself why the work or piece is valuable and important. In "Shaping Her People's Heritage . . ." you will discover why pottery was nearly a lost art and how Nampeyo revived it.
	■ **Pay attention to the medium.** Words, sound, music, canvas, and clay are all means through which artistic expression occurs. Readings in this chapter are concerned with words and clay. Three different vehicles are used in this chapter to express meaning through words: a textbook excerpt, a short story, and a poem.
	■ **Look for a message or an interpretation.** Works of art and literature express meaning or create a feeling or impression. "Gregory" examines important moral dilemmas that surround wartime. As you read "The Truth Is," try to discover Hogan's feelings about being biracial.
	■ **Read literature slowly and carefully.** Rereading may be necessary. Pay attention to the writer's choice of words, descriptions, comparisons, and arrangement of ideas. You should definitely read poetry several times.

SELECTION 13

Shaping Her People's Heritage: Nampeyo (1852–1942)

Duane Preble, Sarah Preble, and Patrick Frank

Taken from an art textbook, *Artforms: An Introduction to the Visual Arts*, published in 1999, this reading describes the preservation of a Native American artform through one woman's efforts.

 PREVIEWING THE READING

Using the steps listed on page 5, preview the reading selection. When you have finished, answer the following questions.

1. What ethnic group does Nampeyo belong to? _____Native American_____

2. What kind of art is the selection about? _____pottery_____

3. What time period is the selection concerned with? _late 1800s/early 1900s_

 **MAKING CONNECTIONS**

View the photos of pottery at the Arizona State Museum Web site's "A Nampeyo Showcase": http://www.statemuseum.arizona.edu/nampeyo/sikyatki.html. *These photos show pottery upon which Nampeyo's work was based. Compare these pots with Nampeyo's pots, pictured in the next pages. What similarities and differences do you see?*

READING TIP

As you read, pay attention to dates and the sequence of events, since this reading describes Nampeyo's work from childhood to the present.

 CHECKING YOUR READING RATE

If you plan to compute your reading rate, be sure to record your starting time in the box at the end of the exercises before you begin reading.

Shaping Her People's Heritage: Nampeyo (1852–1942)

Hopi
a Native American
people of northeast
Arizona, known
especially for their
dry-farming
techniques, fine
craftsmanship,
and rich
ceremonial life

Pueblo
any of some 25
Native American
peoples descended
from the cliff-
dwelling Anasazi
people, living now
in northern and
western New
Mexico and
northeast Arizona;
they are known
for their skill in
pottery, basketry,
weaving, and
metalworking

ceramics
the art of making
pottery

curator
a person who
manages or
oversees a
museum
collection

1   Traditional Native American ceramic arts had fallen into decline when Nampeyo first learned the trade from her grandmother. Most Indians in the **Hopi** region of Arizona, and even the **Pueblo** peoples of New Mexico, made very little pottery. The encroachment of mass produced goods, coupled with the severe poverty of both regions, led most Native families in the late nineteenth century to buy low-priced dishes and cooking utensils from white traders rather than pursue the ancient and time-consuming art of **ceramics**. Nampeyo's fusion of artistic talent and interest in the past sparked a pottery revival that spread throughout the Southwest and continues to this day.

2   The date of her birth is uncertain, since no one kept close records of such things in the village of Hano, on land that the Hopis called First Mesa. She was born into the Snake Clan, and was given the name Nampeyo, which means "Snake That Does Not Bite." There were no paved roads leading to the village, and the nearest city—Winslow, Arizona—was three days' journey away. In that isolated environment Nampeyo grew up. Her family responded to her early artistic interests by sending her to a neighboring village to learn pottery making from her grandmother, one of the few who still made pots. Her grandmother's large water jars were rather simply decorated, with only one or two designs on the face of each one.

3   Sometime in the middle 1890s, Nampeyo began picking up broken shards of pottery from the nearby site of an ancient Hopi village called Sikyatki. This village had been abandoned well before the Spanish Conquest. The ancient pottery fragments were more ornate and abstract than the basic symbols that Nampeyo had been painting; she was fascinated by the ancient designs and began to incorporate them into her own pots.

4   In 1895, the anthropologist Jesse Walter Fewkes arrived to dig and study the ruins of Sikyatki, and his presence transformed Nampeyo's work. Her husband was one of several assistants to Fewkes; he helped with the digging and told the anthropologists what he knew about the ancestral customs of the Hopi peoples. Fewkes and his assistants and students unearthed hundreds of burials, finding many more examples of ancient Hopi pottery in excellent condition. It was traditional to bury the dead with a seed jar, a low container with a narrow opening at the top, as a symbol of spiritual rebirth. These jars had abstract designs in brown or black over a rich yellow body. Her husband brought pieces home for Nampeyo, and soon she met Fewkes and accompanied him on digs.

5   Nampeyo invigorated her pottery by her sustained exposure to the work of her ancestors. She copied, studied, and practiced the ancient symbols. She mastered the shape of the traditional seed jar. Because the clay in the ancient pots was of finer quality than she was used to making, she sought new places to dig better clay from the earth. Fewkes, keenly interested in this revival of ancient techniques, took Nampeyo to Chicago so that she could demonstrate her knowledge to the **curators** of the Field Museum of Natural History. She also demonstrated her skills to tourists and archaeologists at the Grand Canyon.

6   Once she learned the vocabulary of symbols, she found that she could freely adapt and combine them, rather than merely copy ancient models. She told an an-

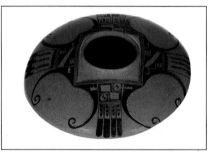

Top left: Nampeyo decorating pottery. 1901. Displaying pottery: ollas, dippers, bowls, vases, Hopi Tewa. Courtesy of the Southwest Museum, Los Angeles.

Top right: Nampeyo, "Canteen," c. 1880. Polacca Polychrome Style c. Arizona State Museum, University of Arizona, Miller Collection, ASM Cat. #4099.

Bottom right: Nampeyo. Seed Jar, c. 1915–1916. Hopi. Museum of Indian Arts & Culture/Laboratory of Anthropology Collections, Museum of New Mexico. Photographer, Doug Kahn. 18838/12.

thropologist, "When I first began to paint, I used to go to the ancient village and pick up pieces of pottery and copy the designs. That is how I learned to paint. But now I just close my eyes and see designs and I paint them." Fewkes referred to her as "a thorough artist."

7   Probably Nampeyo's biggest surprise was that non-Native Americans were interested in buying her pots. She discovered that there was a ready market for pottery with the ancient designs. In this effort she was a pioneer. The relatively rare ancient pottery had always found buyers among a few select collectors; however, when Nampeyo began making pots in that style, to her delight she found that she could easily sell her entire production. She used the new income to support her entire extended family and alleviate some of the poverty on First Mesa.

8   Nampeyo's success became a pattern that other Indian artists would follow. In the Pueblo of San Ildefonso, María Martínez and her husband, in collaboration with anthropologist Edgar Hewitt, soon reintroduced ancient black pottery from that Pueblo. Lucy Lewis of Acoma was similarly inspired by ancient designs. The revival of Pueblo and Hopi pottery contributed to the creation, in 1932, of the Native American Arts and Crafts Board, the first government attempt to encourage Native creators to practice their traditional art forms.

9   Nampeyo continued to produce work herself until she began to lose her eyesight in the 1920s. Her husband painted some of her designs until his death in 1932. Today, her great-granddaughters continue the tradition.

➤ **A.   UNDERSTANDING THE THESIS AND OTHER MAIN IDEAS**

Select the best answer.

___b___ 1. The author's primary purpose is to

    a. trace the history of ceramics among Native American peoples.

    b. describe the life and work of the Native American artist Nampeyo.

    c. compare Nampeyo's work with the work of other ceramists of the era.

    d. describe the discovery of ancient artifacts from the Hopi culture.

___d___ 2. The central thesis of the selection is best expressed in which statement from the first paragraph?

    a. "Traditional Native American ceramic arts had fallen into decline when Nampeyo first learned the trade from her grandmother."

    b. "Most Indians in the Hopi region of Arizona made very little pottery."

    c. "Most Native families in the late nineteenth century [bought] low-priced dishes and cooking utensils from white traders rather than [pursuing] the ancient and time-consuming art of ceramics."

    d. "Nampeyo's fusion of artistic talent and interest in the past sparked a pottery revival that spread throughout the Southwest and continues to this day."

___a___ 3. The topic of paragraph 4 is

    a. Jesse Walter Fewkes.   c. burials.

    b. anthropology.   d. Nampeyo's husband.

___a___ 4. The main idea of paragraph 5 is expressed in the

    a. first sentence.   c. third sentence.

    b. second sentence.   d. last sentence.

___d___ 5. The main idea of paragraph 8 is that

    a. ancient black pottery from the Pueblos of San Ildefonso was reintroduced by María Martínez.

    b. Lucy Lewis of Acoma was, like Nampeyo, inspired by ancient designs.

    c. the Native American Arts and Crafts Board was established in 1932.

    d. Nampeyo's work was an inspiration to other Indian artists.

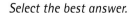

B. IDENTIFYING DETAILS

Select the best answer.

___b___ 1. The name "Nampeyo" means

    a. First Mesa.

    b. Snake That Does Not Bite.

    c. One Who Shapes Pots.

    d. Spiritual Rebirth.

___d___ 2. Nampeyo's family responded to her early interest in art by

    a. ignoring her interest and hoping she would forget about it.

    b. discouraging her from pursuing art by teaching her another trade.

    c. enrolling her in art courses in the nearest city.

    d. sending her to a nearby village to learn how to make pottery from her grandmother.

___b___ 3. The connection between Nampeyo and the anthropologist Jesse Walter Fewkes began when

    a. he saw her work at a local market and admired it.

    b. her husband went to work as an assistant to Fewkes at the ruins of Sikyatki.

    c. she wrote him for advice about ancient designs on pottery.

    d. he saw her demonstrating her skills for tourists at the Grand Canyon.

___b___ 4. According to the selection, Nampeyo's biggest surprise regarding her work was that

    a. so many Native Americans wanted to copy her work.

    b. Native Americans objected to her use of spiritually significant designs.

    c. non-Native Americans wanted to buy her pots.

    d. no one was interested in pottery with ancient designs.

___d___ 5. Nampeyo used the income from her pottery to

    a. establish the Native American Arts and Crafts Board.

    b. fund an archaeological dig near her village of Hano.

    c. arrange for mass production of her designs.

    d. support her entire extended family and alleviate some of the poverty in the area.

➤ **C.   RECOGNIZING METHODS OF ORGANIZATION AND TRANSITIONS**

Select the best answer.

___b___ 1. The author gives the history of Nampeyo and her work using the organizational pattern called

a. enumeration.

b. time sequence.

c. comparison and contrast.

d. definition.

___c___ 2. The author indicates this organizational pattern by

a. including dates.

b. using transitional phrases such as *soon* and *today*.

c. both a and b

d. neither a nor b

➤ **D.   REVIEWING AND ORGANIZING IDEAS: MAPPING**

Complete the following time line of the selection by filling in the blanks.

1852?	Early life	Mid-1890s	1895	1920s	1932	1942	Today
Nampeyo is born in Hano	N. learns how to make pottery	N. finds & uses ancient designs in Sikyatki	Fewkes arrives; N. masters ancient Hopi techniques	N. begins to lose her eyesight	N.'s husband dies; Native Arts & Crafts Board created	N. dies	N.'s great-grand-daughters continue her work

➤ E.   FIGURING OUT INFERRED MEANINGS

Indicate whether each statement is true (T) or false (F).

__F__ 1. It can be inferred that white traders in the late nineteenth century encouraged Native Americans to make their own ceramic goods.

__T__ 2. Nampeyo's family encouraged her to develop her artistic ability.

__F__ 3. The Spanish Conquest occurred in the early 1890s.

__F__ 4. Nampeyo probably had been to Chicago many times before she went there with Fewkes.

__T__ 5. The Native American Arts and Crafts Board might not have been created had it not been for Nampeyo and her work.

➤ F.   THINKING CRITICALLY

Select the best answer.

__b__ 1. The central thesis is supported primarily by

    a. research evidence.

    b. facts and descriptions.

    c. cause and effect relationships.

    d. statistics.

__b__ 2. The tone of the reading can best be described as

    a. hopeful.

    b. informative.

    c. anxious.

    d. humorous.

__a__ 3. According to the selection, the creation of the Native American Arts and Crafts Board in 1932 was significant because it was the

    a. government's first attempt to encourage Native Americans to practice their traditional art forms.

    b. first time Native Americans had been allowed to serve on a national board.

    c. Native Americans' first expression of interest in their cultural history.

    d. first time the various Native American nations had been able to put aside their differences for a common goal.

___c___ 4. The title "Shaping Her People's Heritage" refers to

    a. Nampeyo's skill at shaping pottery.

    b. Nampeyo's impact on Native American art.

    c. both a and b

    d. neither a nor b

___b___ 5. The statement that "Nampeyo invigorated her pottery" (paragraph 5) means that

    a. it took a lot of strength to do her work.

    b. her own work was revitalized by her exposure to ancient techniques.

    c. her work gave her energy.

    d. she made the clay more supple and easier to work with.

___a___ 6. The "vocabulary of symbols" (paragraph 6) refers to the

    a. meaning of the Hopi symbols on the ancient pottery.

    b. English words that Nampeyo had to learn in order to communicate with Fewkes.

    c. language used by potters to describe different techniques.

    d. names of the different types of ceramic.

___c___ 7. Fewkes' description of Nampeyo as "a thorough artist" (paragraph 6) meant that she

    a. needed more training.

    b. always finished her work.

    c. was utterly and completely an artist.

    d. worked very carefully.

➤ G. BUILDING VOCABULARY

➤ Context

Using context and a dictionary, if necessary, determine the meaning of each word as it is used in the selection.

___b___ 1. encroachment (paragraph 1)

    a. need   c. affordability

    b. advancement   d. attraction

___c___ 2. fusion (paragraph 1)

    a. ability   c. combination

    b. adoption   d. blessing

_a_ 3. shards (paragraph 3)

    a. pieces

    b. plates

    c. bowls

    d. fossils

_d_ 4. ornate (paragraph 3)

    a. unpleasant

    b. sturdy

    c. repetitive

    d. elaborate

_a_ 5. unearthed (paragraph 4)

    a. found

    b. surprised

    c. buried

    d. lost

_b_ 6. sustained (paragraph 5)

    a. interrupted

    b. steady

    c. temporary

    d. important

_c_ 7. alleviate (paragraph 7)

    a. separate

    b. aggravate

    c. lessen

    d. understand

_d_ 8. collaboration (paragraph 8)

    a. assistance

    b. imitation

    c. preparation

    d. cooperation

➤ **Word Parts**

> **A REVIEW OF ROOTS AND SUFFIXES**
> **ANTHROPO** means *human being*
> **ARCHAEO** means *ancient* or *past*
> **-AL** means *characteristic of*
> **-IST** means *a person who*

Using your knowledge of word parts and the review above, fill in the blanks in the following sentences.

1. An *anthropologist* (paragraph 4) is a person who studies the origin, behavior, and development of _____human beings_____.

2. The *ancestral* customs (paragraph 4) of a certain people are customs that are _____characteristic of_____ the ancestors of those people.

3. An *archaeologist* (paragraph 5) is _____a person who_____ systematically recovers and studies material evidence, such as pottery, of _____ancient or past_____ human life and culture.

H.   SELECTING A LEARNING/STUDY STRATEGY

Prepare an outline or rough draft answer to the following essay question: Discuss the impact of Nampeyo's work on the continuation and preservation of Native American art.

I.   EXPLORING IDEAS THROUGH DISCUSSION AND WRITING

1. Why do you think a seed jar was used as a symbol of spiritual rebirth? Describe any other symbols of rebirth that you know about.

2. Explain what Nampeyo meant by the statement, "But now I just close my eyes and see designs and I paint them."

3. Do you consider it a loss or progress when a culture gives up its traditions in favor of modern ways? Discuss the reasons that Native Americans gave up their traditional art of ceramics in the late nineteenth century. Are the people in that culture the only ones affected by this kind of progress?

J.   BEYOND THE CLASSROOM TO THE WEB

Visit "Hopi-Tewa Vessels" at the Getty Arts Ed Net at **http://www.getty.edu/ artsednet/resources/Maps/hopi.html**.

Read the time line, noting Nampeyo's birth and death dates. How would you describe the cultural and political changes that happened during Nampeyo's lifetime?

✔ **Tracking Your Progress**

Selection 13

Section	Number Correct		Score
A. Thesis and Main Idea (5 items)	_____	x 4	_____
B. Details (5 items)	_____	x 3	_____
C. Organization and Transitions (2 items)	_____	x 1	_____
E. Inferred Meanings (5 items)	_____	x 3	_____
F. Thinking Critically (7 items)	_____	x 3	_____
G. Vocabulary			
1. Context (8 items)	_____	x 3	_____
2. Word Parts (3 items)	_____	x 1	_____
		TOTAL SCORE	_____ %

CHECKING YOUR READING RATE

Words in Selection 13: 825

Finishing Time:	_____	_____	_____
	(hour)	(minutes)	(seconds)
Starting Time:	_____	_____	_____
	(hour)	(minutes)	(seconds)
Total Reading Time:		_____	_____
		(minutes)	(seconds)

Words Per Minute Score (page 735) _____ WPM

SELECTION 14

Gregory

Panos Ioannides

This short story by Panos Ioannides, a writer born in Cyprus, gives an account of an executioner's final thoughts before killing his prisoner. The story is based on a true incident that occurred in the 1950s during a liberation struggle between Cyprus and Great Britain. The story describes the conflict a soldier experiences when he is ordered to shoot a prisoner who has saved his life and become his friend.

> ## PREVIEWING THE READING

Short stories are not previewed in the same way as textbooks. For that reason, the headnote above gives you an overview of the plot. Based on the information in the headnote, write at least three questions you expect to be answered in the story.

a. Answers will vary, but may include Why was the prisoner ordered

   to be shot?

b. Did the soldier shoot the prisoner?

c. How did the prisoner save the soldier's life?

 ## MAKING CONNECTIONS

Think about some difficult decisions you have had to make. Have you ever had to choose between duty and friendship? What did you do?

> ## READING TIP

As you read, create a time line of the major events in the story.

 ## CHECKING YOUR READING RATE

If you plan to compute your reading rate, be sure to record your starting time in the box at the end of the exercises before you begin reading.

Gregory

1   My hand was sweating as I held the pistol. The curve of the trigger was biting against my finger.

2   Facing me, Gregory trembled.

3   His whole being was beseeching me, "Don't!"

4   Only his mouth did not make a sound. His lips were squeezed tight. If it had been me, I would have screamed, shouted, cursed.

5   The soldiers were watching. . . .

6   The day before, during a brief meeting, they had each given their opinions: "It's tough luck, but it has to be done. We've got no choice."

7   The order from Headquarters was clear: "As soon as Lieutenant Rafel's execution is announced, the hostage Gregory is to be shot and his body must be hanged from a telegraph pole in the main street as an exemplary punishment."

8   It was not the first time that I had to execute a hostage in this war. I had acquired experience, thanks to Headquarters which had kept entrusting me with these delicate assignments. Gregory's case was precisely the sixth.

9   The first time, I remember, I vomited. The second time I got sick and had a headache for days. The third time I drank a bottle of rum. The fourth, just two glasses of beer. The fifth time I joked about it, "This little guy, with the big pop-eyes, won't be much of a ghost!"

10   But why, dammit, when the day came did I have to start thinking that I'm not so tough, after all? The thought had come at exactly the wrong time and spoiled all my disposition to do my duty.

11   You see, this Gregory was such a miserable little creature, such a puny thing, such a nobody, damn him.

12   That very morning, although he had heard over the loudspeakers that Rafel had been executed, he believed that we would spare his life because we had been eating together so long.

mess tins
sets of eating utensils and dishes that fit together into compact units used by soldiers

13   "Those who eat from the same **mess tins** and drink from the same **water canteen**," he said, "remain good friends no matter what."

14   And a lot more of the same sort of nonsense.

15   He was a silly fool—we had smelled that out the very first day Headquarters gave him to us. The sentry guarding him had got dead drunk and had dozed off. The rest of us with **exit permits** had gone from the barracks. When we came back, there was Gregory sitting by the sleeping sentry and thumbing through a magazine.

water canteen
a flask for carrying water

16   "Why didn't you run away, Gregory?" we asked, laughing at him, several days later.

17   And he answered, "Where would I go in this freezing weather? I'm O.K. here."

18   So we started teasing him.

exit permits
passes that allow soldiers to leave their camps or bases

19   "You're dead right. The accommodations here are splendid. . . ."

20   "It's not so bad here," he replied. "The barracks where I used to be are like a sieve. The wind blows in from every side. . . ."

21   We asked him about his girl. He smiled.

22   "Maria is a wonderful person," he told us. "Before I met her she was engaged to a no-good fellow, a pig. He gave her up for another girl. Then nobody in the village

wanted to marry Maria. I didn't miss my chance. So what if she is second-hand. Nonsense. Peasant ideas, my friend. She's beautiful and good-hearted. What more could I want? And didn't she load me with watermelons and cucumbers every time I passed by her vegetable garden? Well, one day I stole some cucumbers and melons and watermelons and I took them to her. 'Maria,' I said, 'from now on I'm going to take care of you.' She started crying and then me, too. But ever since that day she has given me lots of trouble—jealousy. She wouldn't let me go even to my mother's. Until the day I was recruited, she wouldn't let me go far from her apron strings. But that was just what I wanted. . . ."

23   He used to tell this story over and over, always with the same words, the same commonplace gestures. At the end he would have a good laugh and start gulping from his water jug.

24   His tongue was always wagging! When he started talking, nothing could stop him. We used to listen and nod our heads, not saying a word. But sometimes, as he was telling us about his mother and family problems, we couldn't help wondering, "Eh, well, these people have the same headaches in their country as we've got."

25   Strange, isn't it!

26   Except for his talking too much, Gregory wasn't a bad fellow. He was a marvelous cook. Once he made us some apple tarts, so delicious we licked the platter clean. And he could sew, too. He used to sew on all our buttons, patch our clothes, darn our socks, iron our ties, wash our clothes. . . .

27   How the devil could you kill such a friend?

28   Even though his name was Gregory and some people on his side had killed one of ours, even though we had left wives and children to go to war against him and his kind—but how can I explain? He was our friend. He actually liked us! A few days before, hadn't he killed with his own bare hands a scorpion that was climbing up my leg? He could have let it send me to hell!

29   "Thanks, Gregory!" I said then, "Thank God who made you. . . ."

30   When the order came, it was like a thunderbolt. Gregory was to be shot, it said, and hanged from a telegraph pole as an exemplary punishment.

31   We got together inside the barracks. We sent Gregory to wash some underwear for us.

32   "It ain't right."

33   "What is right?"

34   "Our duty!"

35   "Shit!"

court-martial   36   "If you dare, don't do it! They'll drag you to **court-martial** and then bang-bang...."
a special court   37   Well, of course. The right thing is to save your skin. That's only logical. It's either
for trying your skin or his. His, of course, even if it was Gregory, the fellow you've been sharing
members of the the same plate with, eating with your fingers, and who was washing your clothes
armed forces that very minute.

38   What could I do? That's war. We had seen worse things.

39   So we set the hour.

40   We didn't tell him anything when he cam back from the washing. He slept peacefully. He snored for the last time. In the morning, he heard the news over the loudspeaker and he saw that we looked gloomy and he began to suspect that something was up. He tried talking to us, but he got no answers and then he stopped talking.

41   He just stood there and looked at us, stunned and lost. . . .

Now, I'll squeeze the trigger. A tiny bullet will rip through his chest. Maybe I'll lose my sleep tonight but in the morning I'll wake up alive.

Gregory seems to guess my thoughts. He puts out his hand and asks, "You're kidding, friend! Aren't you kidding?"

What a jackass! Doesn't he deserve to be cut to pieces? What a thing to ask at such a time. Your heart is about to burst and he's asking if you're kidding. How can a body be kidding about such a thing? Idiot! This is no time for jokes. And you, if you're such a fine friend, why don't you make things easier for us? Help us kill you with fewer qualms? If you would get angry—curse our **Virgin**, our God— if you'd try to escape it would be much easier for us and for you.

So it is *now*.

Now, Mr. Gregory, you are going to pay for your stupidities wholesale. Because you didn't escape the day the sentry fell asleep; because you didn't escape yester-day when we sent you all alone to the laundry—we did it on purpose, you idiot! Why didn't you let me die form the sting of the scorpion?

So now don't complain. It's all your fault, nitwit.

Eh? What's happening to him now?

Gregory is crying. Tears flood his eyes and trickle down over his cleanshaven cheeks. He is turning his face and pressing his forehead against the wall. His back is shaking as he sobs. His hands cling, rigid and helpless, to the wall.

Now is my best chance, now that he knows there is no other solution and turns his face form us.

I squeeze the trigger.

Gregory jerks. His back stops shaking up and down.

I think I've finished him! How easy it is. . . . But suddenly he starts crying out loud, his hands claw at the wall and try to pull it down. He screams, "No, no. . . ."

I turn to the others. I expect them to nod, "That's enough."

They nod, "What are you waiting for?"

I squeeze the trigger again.

The bullet smashed into his neck. A thick spray of blood spurts out.

Gregory turns. His eyes are all red. He lunges at me and starts punching me with his fists.

"I hate you, hate you . . .," he screams.

I emptied the barrel. He fell and grabbed my leg as if he wanted to hold on.

42   He died with a terrible spasm. His mouth was full of blood and so were my boots and socks.

43   We stood quietly, looking at him.

44   When we came to, we stooped and picked him up. His hands were frozen and wouldn't let my legs go.

45   I still have their imprints, red and deep, as if made by a hot knife.

46   "We will hang him tonight," the men said.

47   "Tonight or now?" they said.

48   I turned and looked at them one by one.

49   "Is that what you all want?" I asked.

50   They gave me no answer.

virgin
the Virgin Mary,
mother of Jesus

51   "Dig a grave," I said.

52   Headquarters did not ask for a report the next day or the day after. The top brass were sure that we had obeyed them and had left him swinging from a pole.

53   They didn't care to know what happened to that Gregory, alive or dead.

➤ A. UNDERSTANDING THE THESIS AND OTHER MAIN IDEAS

Select the best answer.

__d__ 1. The central theme of "Gregory" is that

   a. friendship is more important than following orders.

   b. humans have a natural tendency to be violent.

   c. killing during wartime is justified.

   d. duty can cause people to perform acts they feel are wrong.

__c__ 2. The author's primary purpose is to

   a. express support for soldiers who do their duty.

   b. criticize soldiers who do not follow orders.

   c. comment on the personal and moral conflicts that arise during war.

   d. recount a war story to show that war is wrong.

➤ B. IDENTIFYING DETAILS

Select the best answer.

__b__ 1. Officially, Gregory was killed

   a. because he was a prisoner of war.

   b. in retaliation for Lieutenant Rafel's execution.

   c. for being "puny" and a "nobody."

   d. when he tried to escape.

__a__ 2. The narrator was chosen to perform the execution because he

   a. was experienced in killing hostages.

   b. hated Gregory.

   c. never disobeyed an order.

   d. was a close friend of Lieutenant Rafel.

__a__ 3. Gregory believed the soldiers would not kill him since he

   a. was their friend.

   b. had told them stories about his life.

c. washed their underwear.

d. begged them not to kill him.

___d___ 4. When did Gregory have the chance to escape?

a. the first day he was there.

b. while he was off washing underwear

c. when the guard fell asleep while the other soldiers were away.

d. all of the above.

___c___ 5. All of the following are mentioned as tasks done by Gregory for the soldiers *except*

a. cooking tarts.

b. ironing.

c. emptying garbage cans.

d. sewing on buttons.

___a___ 6. On the day he died, Gregory

a. was stunned that his friends would kill him.

b. wrote a letter to his family.

c. told the soldiers to do their duty.

d. asked the soldiers to contact Maria.

► C. RECOGNIZING METHODS OF ORGANIZATION AND TRANSITIONS

Select the best answer.

___b___ 1. What organizational pattern is used throughout this story?

a. comparison and contrast

b. chronological order

c. classification

d. cause and effect

List one transitional word or phrase that is used in each of the following paragraphs.

2. Paragraph 6: ___the day before, during___.

3. Paragraph 9: ___first time, second time, etc.___.

4. Paragraph 12: ___that very morning___.

5. Paragraph 15: ___very first day___.

➤ D.   REVIEWING AND ORGANIZING IDEAS: SUMMARIZING

Use the following list of words and phrases to complete the paraphrase of paragraph 22.

left	Gregory	happy	beautiful	together
jealous	Maria	second-hand	garden	

_____Gregory_____ told the soldiers about his girlfriend, _____Maria_____. She had been engaged, but her fiancé _____left_____ her for another girl. Maria was then considered _____second-hand_____ goods by the villagers, but Gregory saw her as _____beautiful_____ and good-natured. She always gave him food from her _____garden_____. Finally Gregory stole some food, gave it to her, and proclaimed that they would be _____together_____ from then on. She turned out to be a _____jealous_____ woman, wanting Gregory to always be with her, but Gregory was actually _____happy_____ with that.

➤ E.   FIGURING OUT INFERRED MEANINGS

Indicate whether each statement is true (T) or false (F).

__T__ 1. The soldiers liked Gregory.

__T__ 2. Gregory liked the soldiers.

__F__ 3. The war is almost over.

__F__ 4. The sentry was punished for falling asleep.

__T__ 5. The soldiers liked Gregory's cooking.

__T__ 6. The narrator could have died from the scorpion's bite.

__T__ 7. Gregory was not hung from the telephone pole.

__T__ 8. The soldiers' superiors expected the soldiers to follow orders without question.

➤ F.   THINKING CRITICALLY

Select the best answer.

__a__ 1. The narrator's dilemma is mostly presented through

   a. personal experience.

   b. historical documentation.

   c. analogies.

   d. expert opinion.

__b__ 2. The tone of the selection can best be described as
  a. bitter.   c. light.
  b. conflicted.   d. worried.

__d__ 3. The author tells the story through the use of flashbacks in order to
  a. mislead the reader.
  b. describe how time stood still for Gregory during the last few minutes of his life.
  c. comment on the importance of memory in our decision-making process.
  d. show what went through the mind of the narrator when he was forced to make an important decision.

__c__ 4. The story about Maria is included for all the following reasons *except:*
  a. as an example of how Gregory talked so much.
  b. to show yet another side of Gregory's personality.
  c. as an example of something stupid that Gregory had done.
  d. to reveal how well the soldiers had come to know Gregory.

➤ **G. BUILDING VOCABULARY**

➤ **Context**
Using context and a dictionary, if necessary, determine the meaning of each word as it is used in the selection.

__a__ 1. beseeching (paragraph 3)
  a. begging   c. nagging
  b. suggesting to   d. opposing

__d__ 2. delicate (paragraph 8)
  a. pleasant   c. classified, secret
  b. easily messed up   d. requiring special skill or tact

__d__ 3. disposition (paragraph 10)
  a. fear   c. nervousness
  b. distress   d. tendency

__a__ 4. imprints (paragraph 45)
  a. pressed-in shapes   c. wounds
  b. colorful drawings   d. displays

➤ **Word Parts**

> **A REVIEW OF ROOTS, PREFIXES, AND SUFFIXES**
> **GRAPH** means *write*
> **TELE-** means *far, at a distance*
> **-ARY** means *pertaining to*

Use the review of prefixes, suffixes, and roots above to fill in the blanks in the following sentences.

1. An exemplary punishment (paragraph 7) is intended to set an ___example___ .

2. A message sent by *telegraph* (paragraph 30), is a message that travels ___a long distance___ through wires.

➤ **Unusual Words/Unusual Meanings**
Use the meanings given below to write a sentence using the underlined word or phrase.

1. Being <u>dead right</u> (paragraph 19), means that you are absolutely certain or correct.

    Your sentence: _____ .

2. A man is said to be tied to his mother's <u>apron strings</u> (paragraph 22) when she has total control over him even during his adult life.

    Your sentence: _____ .

3. When someone <u>saves their skin</u> (paragraph 37), they do whatever it takes to prevent themselves from getting into trouble or danger.

    Your sentence: _____ .

➤ **H.   SELECTING A LEARNING/STUDY STRATEGY**

In preparation for a class discussion in a literature class, make a list of the issues or moral questions raised by this story.

➤ **I.   EXPLORING IDEAS THROUGH DISCUSSION AND WRITING**

1. Discuss Gregory's motivation for helping the soldiers. Was he just trying to get on their good side or was he just a good guy?
2. Write an alternate ending to the story in which Gregory is not killed.
3. How do the last two paragraphs affect your feelings about Gregory and the narrator? What if the story had ended with paragraph 51?
4. Write an accompanying story from Gregory's point of view. Discuss how point of view affects a story's message.

➤ **J.   BEYOND THE CLASSROOM TO THE WEB**

Explore the Web site for an online exhibit about Japanese-American internment during World War II at **http://www.lib.washington.edu/exhibits/harmony/ Exhibit/default.htm**.
    You will find many points of view expressed in letters and official documents. How do these resources help you understand what life was really like in the camp?

✔ **Tracking Your Progress**

Selection 14

Section	Number Correct		Score
A. Thesis and Main Idea (2 items)	_____	x 4	_____
B. Details (6 items)	_____	x 4	_____
C. Organization and Transitions (5 items)	_____	x 2	_____
E. Inferred Meanings (8 items)	_____	x 4	_____
F. Thinking Critically (4 items)	_____	x 4	_____
G. Vocabulary			
1. Context (4 items)	_____	x 2	_____
2. Word Parts (2 items)	_____	x 1	_____
		TOTAL SCORE	_____ %

CHECKING YOUR READING RATE

Words in Selection 14: 1,660

Finishing Time:	_____ (hour)	_____ (minutes)	_____ (seconds)
Starting Time:	_____ (hour)	_____ (minutes)	_____ (seconds)
Total Reading Time:		_____ (minutes)	_____ (seconds)

Words Per Minute Score (page 737) _____ WPM

SELECTION 15

The Truth Is

Linda Hogan

Linda Hogan is an award-winning author of poetry, fiction, essays, and plays who writes about humankind, politics, and the environment. Her father was a member of the Chickasaw tribe and her mother was non-native. She was born in 1947.

➤ PREVIEWING THE READING

Previewing, as described on p. 5, does not work well for poetry. Instead of previewing the poem, read the it through once to determine the literal content—who is doing what, when, and where. When you have finished, complete the following item.

1. List at least three facts mentioned in the poem.

   a. <u>She has one Chickasaw hand and one white hand.</u>

   b. <u>She sleeps in a twin bed.</u>

   c. <u>She pockets are empty.</u>

MAKING CONNECTIONS

Write a list of words describing yourself. Do this again tomorrow. What has changed? What remains the same?

➤ READING TIP

As you read and reread the poem, make annotations about the meanings of certain words, phrases, lines, and stanzas.

CHECKING YOUR READING RATE

Reading rate cannot be meaningfully computed when reading poetry since numerous rereadings are necessary to uncover various levels of meaning.

The Truth Is

Chickasaw 1	In my left pocket a **Chickasaw** hand
a Native American 2	rests on the bone of the pelvis.
tribe that 3	In my right pocket
originated in 4	a white hand. Don't worry. It's mine
Mississippi and 5	and not some thief's.
spread to 6	It belongs to a woman who sleeps in a twin bed
Alabama and 7	even though she falls in love too easily,
Oklahoma 8	and walks along with hands
amnesty 9	in her own empty pockets
pardon; 10	even though she has put them in others
prosecution-free 11	for love not money.
period during	
which crimes 12	About the hands, I'd like to say
committed can 13	I am a tree, grafted branches
be admitted 14	Bearing two kinds of fruit,
without 15	Apricots maybe and pit cherries.
prosecution 16	It's not that way. The truth is
17	We are crowded together
civilian 18	And knock against each other at night.
conservation 19	We want **amnesty**.
corps	
in operation	
from 1933–1942, 20	Linda, girl, I keep telling you
one of the 21	this is nonsense
programs of the 22	about who loved who
New Deal during 23	and who killed who.
the Great	
Depression in 24	Here I am, taped together
which 25	like some old **civilian conservation corps**
participants, 26	passed by from the great depression
among other 27	and my pockets are empty.
things, planted 28	It's just as well since they are masks
millions of trees 29	for the soul, and since coins and keys
throughout the 30	both have the sharp teeth of property.
country	

> **A. UNDERSTANDING THE THESIS AND OTHER MAIN IDEAS**

Select the best answer.

___c___ 1. The poem is primarily concerned with

a. outward appearances.

b. racial hatred.

c. self-identify.

d. fear.

____a____ 2. In the first stanza, the poet

    a. describes herself.

    b. examines her feelings about money.

    c. criticizes her appearance.

    d. reveals a secret.

____b____ 3. The second stanza emphasizes the author's

    a. love of fruit.

    b. dual heritage.

    c. trouble sleeping.

    d. love life.

____c____ 4. In stanza 3, the poet addresses

    a. a little girl.

    b. a friend.

    c. herself.

    d. no one.

____a____ 5. In the final stanza the author comments on

    a. personal possessions.

    b. the value of pockets.

    c. Native American tribal masks.

    e. civilian attitudes.

B. IDENTIFYING DETAILS

Select the best answer.

____c____ 1. In the poet's right pocket there is a

    a. thief's hand.   c. white hand.

    b. lover's hand.   d. Chickasaw hand.

____a____ 2. The author would like to think of herself as a

    a. tree.   c. thief.

    b. piece of property.   d. little girl.

____d____ 3. Which of the following is *not* mentioned as something to go into pockets?

    a. keys   c. coins

    b. hands   d. food

___a___ 4. In stanza 2 the author compares

    a. what she would like to be with what she is.

    b. two kinds of truth.

    c. two types of fruit trees.

    d. what she would like to do versus what she has accomplished.

➤ C. RECOGNIZING METHODS OF ORGANIZATION AND TRANSITIONS

Select the best answer.

___a___ 1. Which of the following patterns does the poet use in stanza 1?

    a. spatial   c. cause and effect

    b. time sequence   d. enumeration

___d___ 2. Which of the following patterns does the poet use in stanza 2?

    a. time sequence   c. cause and effect

    b. process   d. comparison and contrast

➤ D. REVIEWING AND ORGANIZING IDEAS: MAPPING

Complete the following map with ideas that you have about the meanings and themes in the poem.

Possible AIE Answers: is concerned about her identity, has been in love, wants amnesty, half-white, feels conflict, does not value material goods

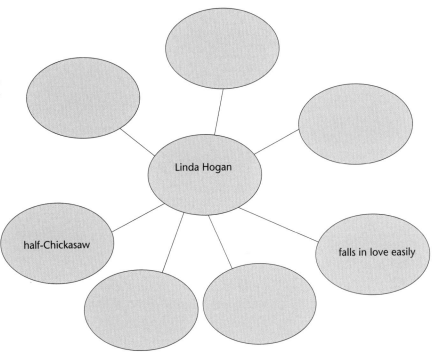

➤ **E.   FIGURING OUT INFERRED MEANINGS**

Indicate whether each statement is true (T) or false (F).

It can be inferred that the poet

___F___ 1. has never stolen anything.

___F___ 2. loves apricots and pit cherries.

___T___ 3. wears clothing with pockets.

___F___ 4. lived during the Great Depression.

___T___ 5. does not care to have a lot of money.

➤ **F.   THINKING CRITICALLY**

Select the best answer.

___c___ 1. The fact that the poet walks along with her hands in her own empty pockets may suggest

    a. frustration or concern.

    b. uncertainty or fear.

    c. independence or loneliness.

    d. depression or regret.

___b___ 2. The tone of the poem can best be described as

    a. angry.

    b. concerned.

    c. ironic.

    d. absurd.

___b___ 3. When the poet says she has put her hands in the pockets of others she means she has

    a. stolen personal property.

    b. been involved with other people.

    c. felt lonely.

    d. tried to live like other people.

___a___ 4. Line 5 contains

    a. a comparison.

    b. a contrast.

    c. an opinion of another person.

    d. data and evidence.

_a_ 5. In the second stanza, the poet says she would like to be a tree of grafted branches because she

    a. is biracial.

    b. feels grounded, but also feels like going off in different directions.

    c. cannot decide who she is.

    d. has two children.

_d_ 6. In stanza 3, the poet

    a. introduces a completely unrelated topic.

    b. searches for acceptance.

    c. consoles herself.

    d. tries to settle an old argument with herself.

_d_ 7. Overall, the author

    a. releases her feelings in the poem.

    b. attempts to convey a message to the reader.

    c. examines parts of her life.

    d. all of the above.

_d_ 8. The fact that the tree branches knock against each other suggests

    a. harmony.

    b. distance.

    c. fear.

    d. conflict.

_a_ 9. Lines 22–23 most likely refer to

    a. earlier conflicts between whites and Native Americans.

    b. the poet's parents.

    c. the poet's children.

    d. the civilian conservation corps.

➤ **G.   SELECTING A LEARNING/STUDY STRATEGY**

How would you prepare for a class discussion of this poem?

Reread, annotate, write a statement of its theme.

H.   EXPLORING IDEAS THROUGH DISCUSSION AND WRITING

1. Discuss who you think the "we" are in lines 17–19.

2. Write a paragraph about lines 28–30. What is the poet trying to say?

3. Discuss how you feel about the writing and study of poetry. How relevant is it to your life?

I.   BEYOND THE CLASSROOM TO THE WEB

Read about Linda Hogan at the Voices from the Gaps web site at **http://voices .cla.umn.edu/newsite/authors/HOGANlinda.htm.** *Does this information change your interpretation of the poem "The Truth Is"?*

✔ Tracking Your Progress

Selection 15

Section	Number Correct		Score
A. Thesis and Main Idea (5 items)	_____	x 5	_____
B. Details (4 items)	_____	x 5	_____
C. Organization and Transitions (2 items)	_____	x 4	_____
E. Inferred Meanings (5 items)	_____	x 4	_____
F. Thinking Critically (9 items)	_____	x 3	_____
	TOTAL SCORE		_____%

CHECKING YOUR READING RATE

Words in Selection 15

Computing reading rate for poetry is not meaningful or useful.

16 Public Policy/ Contemporary Issues

The field of public policy is concerned with the study of topics that affect the good of society. It includes laws, traditions, conventions, and procedures that affect society as a whole. Contemporary issues is a field that focuses on current topics of importance and interest. These fields give you an opportunity to discuss issues that affect and involve all of us in our daily lives. You might consider such questions as: "Does society have the right to take someone's life (the death penalty)?" or "Is human cloning moral?" In this chapter you will read a pair of readings that examine the right-to-die issue. Both "What to Do About Terri" and "When Living Is a Fate Worse Than Death" deal with the question of when to end the life of a critically ill person. "Seoul Searching" concerns another contemporary issue—adoption.

Use the following suggestions when reading in the fields of public policy and contemporary issues.

TIPS FOR READING IN PUBLIC POLICY/ CONTEMPORARY ISSUES

- **Read critically.** Some material in these fields, especially that that deals with controversial issues, is opinion, not fact. You have the right to ask questions and disagree. For example, after reading "Seoul Searching," you may agree or disagree that a child has the right to search for his or her birth mother.
- **Look for reasons that support a position.** When an author takes a stance on an issue, examine the reasons the author offers that indicate the position is reasonable or justifiable. When reading "When Living Is a Fate Worse Than Death," look for the reasons the author offers allowing a child to die peacefully.
- **Consider opposing viewpoints.** When an author takes a stand on an issue, always look at the other side of the issue. Although the author of "When Living Is a Fate Worse Than Death" argues for allowing a child to die without taking extreme measures to keep her alive, consider the opposing viewpoint as well. Why shouldn't doctors do everything they can to prevent death?

325

SELECTION 16

What to Do About Terri

Richard Jerome, with Lori Rozsa and Don Sider

This article first appeared in *People Weekly* in February 2000. Read it to discover differing viewpoints on the right-to-die issue.

▶ PREVIEWING THE READING

Using the steps listed on page 5, preview the reading selection. When you have finished, complete the following items.

1. The subject of this selection is a woman named _____Terri_____ and the battle between her _____parents_____ and her _____husband_____ .

2. List two questions you should be able to answer after reading the article.

   a. What happened to Terri? _____

   b. Why is her family battling over her? _____

 MAKING CONNECTIONS

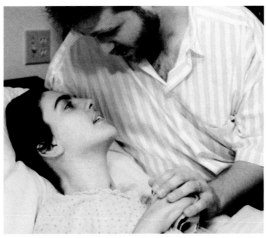

Terry Schiavo, the subject of this article, is shown here with her husband, Michael. Since she had a heart attack at age 26 in 1990, Terri has been brain-damaged. Her husband wants permission to end her life, but Terri's parents disagree. Who should have the right to decide when a patient ought to be allowed to die?

> **READING TIP**

Terri's husband and parents hold different viewpoints; be sure to highlight each.

CHECKING YOUR READING RATE

If you plan to compute your reading rate, be sure to record your starting time in the box at the end of the exercises before you begin reading.

What to Do About Terri: A Florida Woman's Husband and Parents Battle over Her Right to Live—Or to Die

1   Ten years ago, Michael and Terri Schiavo were just beginning their young lives to-gether. Raised in the Philadelphia suburbs, they'd left four years before for St. Petersburg, Fla., where Terri's parents planned to retire. They worked long hours, Michael as a restaurant manager, Terri as a Prudential secretary who spent much of her free time at the beach. "She was a sun goddess," says Schiavo, 36. A fan of singer George Michael, she also "liked action movies," he says, "adventures, ro-mance and mysteries. She loved to read books."

2   But that life was suddenly undone. On Feb. 25, 1990, Schiavo awoke to use the bathroom and heard a thud. "I saw Terri on the floor, facedown," he recalls. "I was shaking her. I heard a rush of air come out of her mouth." Her heart had stopped. After a rescue squad performed **CPR** and rushed Terri, then 26, to a hospital, her heartbeat was stabilized. "I thought, 'Good,'" Schiavo recalls. "'I can take her home now.'"

CPR
cardiopulmonary resuscitation, an emergency procedure used to maintain the circulation of oxygenated blood to the brain

3   But he could not, for Terri's still-unexplained heart attack had robbed her brain of oxygen for five critical minutes and left her in what is described by doctors as a per-sistent vegetative state—neither comatose nor brain-dead, yet so badly brain-dam-aged that she seems unaware of the small, unchanging world she inhabits. At 36, Terri now lives in the Palm Gardens nursing home in Largo, Fla., the unwitting center of a moral and legal storm over the **parameters** of human life. Convinced by doc-tors that she will never recover, her husband has, since 1994, sought to let Terri die rather than linger in her twilight. At a January bench trial before Pinellas County cir-cuit court Judge George Greer, he petitioned to remove her feeding tube. (She breathes on her own.) But Terri's parents, Robert and Mary Schindler, are fiercely op-posed. "I stroke her cheek, I kiss her face, and I can hear her laugh or moan," says Mary, 58. "If I move around the room, her eyes follow me. There is a life there." In fact the Schindlers would like Schiavo, as Terri's legal guardian, to continue to pursue experimental therapy intended to stimulate her brain with electrodes. "She deserves a chance," says Robert Schindler, 62. Adds Terri's sister Suzanne Carr, 31: "She's only 36 now. What if they find something to help in a few years? In 10? In 20?"

parameters
boundaries or limiting factors

4   Doctors have said that Terri's prognosis appears hopeless. But what of the laughs and moans that the family videotaped and played at the hearing? James Barnhill, a neu-rologist who examined Terri, characterizes them as mere reflexes. "I can't get inside her head," he says, "but by every test you can do, there was no discernible response."

living will
a document that specifies a person's wishes not to be kept alive by artificial life support systems in case of a terminal illness

5   With a ruling expected by mid-February, the case hinges largely on the intent of the patient. Terri left no **living will** ordering that her life be ended should she be

hearsay
evidence based on
the reports of
others, usually
not admissible in
court

6   reduced to a vegetative state. But Schiavo insists she did express that intention after watching a documentary about people on life support. "She said, 'Don't ever let me live like that,'" he says. Her parents counter that while discussing the landmark 1976 Karen Ann Quinlan case, Terri said it was wrong for the family to have taken her off a respirator. Robert Jarvis, a professor at Nova Southeastern University Law Center near Fort Lauderdale, suggests that such conflicting **hearsay** weighs against Schiavo. "You have no way of knowing what the patient wanted," he says. "If nobody can know, there's nothing to be done."

6   Casting a cloud over the medical issues at play is the specter of money. In 1993 the Schiavos won a $1 million-plus malpractice settlement against a gynecologist who had failed to administer a blood test when Terri complained of menstrual problems. Had the doctor done the test, it was alleged, he might have found that her potassium levels were low, a possible cause of her heart attack. Schiavo received $300,000; the rest was awarded to Terri and placed in an account administered by a bank for her care. Should she die, Schiavo, now a respiratory therapist who has been dating a woman for five years, would inherit that money. But Schiavo has said he would donate it to charity if the Schindlers allow him to end what he feels is Terri's needless suffering—an offer they have refused. Should Schiavo divorce Terri, her parents would be granted guardianship and control of her estate, which they say they would use to find Terri new treatments. If she were to die, the Schindlers would inherit the money.

7   Now bitterly divided, the two sides were once united. Michael and his in-laws used to take turns dressing Terri, changing her diapers and taking her to specialists. Now they make sure to visit on different days. The Schindlers bring tapes of George Michael and other pop stars. Schiavo buys Terri clothes, jewelry and perfume. Whatever their differences, the parents and husband share an intense devotion to the stricken woman, who now has so little to offer in return. Declares Mary: "She has a feeding tube; other than that, she's perfect." Says Schiavo: "I love Terri deeply. It's my job to see this through."

➤ A.   UNDERSTANDING THE THESIS AND OTHER MAIN IDEAS

Select the best answer.

__b__ 1. The author's primary purpose is to

   a. explain the purpose of living wills.

   b. describe the battle between a woman's husband and her family about whether to continue her life support.

   c. criticize the woman's husband for wanting to discontinue her life support.

   d. criticize the woman's parents for keeping her on life support.

__d__ 2. The main idea of paragraph 3 is that

   a. Terri cannot survive without life support.

   b. Terri seems to be unaware of what is happening around her.

      c. doctors have convinced Terri's husband that she will never recover.

      d. Terri's husband wants to remove her from life support and her parents oppose him.

_a_ 3. The main idea of paragraph 5 is expressed in the

      a. first sentence.

      b. second sentence.

      c. third sentence.

      d. last sentence.

_b_ 4. The topic of paragraph 6 is

      a. the mistake made by Terri's gynecologist.

      b. the malpractice settlement money.

      c. Terri's guardianship.

      d. Terri's estate.

_c_ 5. According to doctors, Terri's "persistent vegetative state" means that she is

      a. comatose.

      b. brain-dead.

      c. badly brain-damaged.

      d. unable to accept food.

➤ B. IDENTIFYING DETAILS

Indicate whether each statement is true (T) or false (F).

_F_ 1. Terri's brain damage resulted from a car accident.

_T_ 2. According to a neurologist, Terri does not respond to any tests.

_F_ 3. Terri cannot breathe on her own.

_F_ 4. If Terri dies now, her parents will inherit the money from the malpractice settlement.

_T_ 5. Terri's guardian is her husband, Michael.

➤ C. RECOGNIZING METHODS OF ORGANIZATION AND TRANSITIONS

In "What to Do About Terri," the author uses the time sequence pattern to describe the events in the order in which they occurred. For each of the following transitional words or phrases from paragraphs 1–4, write Y (yes) if it indicates the time sequence pattern, or N (no) if it does not. An example has been done for you.
Example: Y ten years ago

___Y___ 1. four years before

___N___ 2. But

___Y___ 3. On Feb. 25, 1990

___Y___ 4. then 26

___N___ 5. yet

___Y___ 6. At 36

___Y___ 7. since 1994

___Y___ 8. At a January bench trial

___N___ 9. In fact

___N___ 10. but

▶ D. REVIEWING AND ORGANIZING IDEAS: SUMMARIZING

Complete the following summary of paragraphs 1–5 by filling in the missing words or phrases.

Paragraphs 1–5: Michael and Terri _____Schiavo_____ moved to Florida from _____Philadelphia_____ in 1986. In _____1990_____, Terri had a _____heart attack_____ which left her brain-_____damaged_____. She is now _____36_____ years old and lives in a _____nursing home_____. She can _____breathe_____ on her own but she is fed through a _____tube_____. Her _____husband_____ wants Terri to be _____taken off_____ life support but her _____parents_____ are against it. Since Terri did not have a _____living will_____, the case will be decided by a _____judge_____. A ruling is expected in _____mid-February_____.

▶ E. FIGURING OUT INFERRED MEANINGS

Indicate whether each statement is true (T) or false (F).

___T___ 1. It can be inferred that Terri's parents do not believe doctors who say she will never recover.

___T___ 2. It can be inferred that the experimental therapy that has already been pursued has not improved Terri's condition.

___T___ 3. Because Terri's husband was a restaurant manager before her heart attack but is now a respiratory therapist, he probably changed careers as a result of her condition.

___F___ 4. Terri's husband wants to take her off life support so he can inherit the settlement money.

___T___ 5. It can be inferred that low levels of potassium can cause heart attacks.

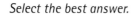

F.   THINKING CRITICALLY

Select the best answer.

___c___ 1. The authors support the central thesis of "What to Do About Terri" with

    a. personal experience.

    b. statistics.

    c. facts and descriptions.

    d. analogies.

___c___ 2. The authors use the first paragraph to

    a. gain sympathy for Terri's parents.

    b. describe Terri's relationship with her family.

    c. provide background information about Terri and her husband.

    d. imply that Terri and her husband were young and irresponsible.

___b___ 3. The author's description of Terri's "twilight" (paragraph 3) refers to

    a. her inability to see light and dark.

    b. her current existence between life and death.

    c. the fact that she is approaching middle age.

    d. her declining health.

___a___ 4. The authors include the quote from Terri's parents that "There is a life there" (paragraph 3) in order to

    a. indicate that Terri's parents believe that she responds to them.

    b. prove that the doctors are mistaken about Terri's condition.

    c. argue that the taking of any life is wrong.

    d. show that Terri will someday resume her old life.

___c___ 5. In paragraph 5, the conflicting versions of Terri's intentions in a life support situation are included in order to

    a. imply that Terri's parents and her husband are making up statements to support their own side of the debate.

    b. reveal that Terri had not made up her mind about her intentions.

    c. indicate that, without a living will, there is no way of knowing what Terri would have wanted.

    d. show that there are two sides to the argument.

➤ G.   BUILDING VOCABULARY

➤ Context

Using context and a dictionary, if necessary, determine the meaning of each word as it is used in the selection.

__b__ 1. unwitting (paragraph 3)

    a. emotional   c. private

    b. unaware   d. reluctant

__a__ 2. petitioned (paragraph 3)

    a. requested   c. permitted

    b. promoted   d. agreed

__c__ 3. prognosis (paragraph 4)

    a. current condition

    b. identification of a disease

    c. likelihood of recovery

    d. lack of ability

__b__ 4. discernable (paragraph 4)

    a. accountable   c. encouraging

    b. apparent   d. hidden

__d__ 5. hinges (paragraph 5)

    a. replaces   c. returns

    b. advances   d. depends

__a__ 6. specter (paragraph 6)

    a. prospect   c. effect

    b. absence   d. influence

__b__ 7. stricken (paragraph 7)

    a. upset   c. concerned

    b. afflicted   d. careless

➤ Word Parts

> **A REVIEW OF ROOTS, PREFIXES, AND SUFFIXES**
>
> **GYNECO** means *woman*
> **MAL-** means *bad* or *wrong*
> **-IST** means *a person who*

Using your knowledge of word parts and the review on page 332, fill in the blanks in the following sentences.

1. A *gynecologist* (paragraph 6) is _____ a person who _____ specializes in the health care of _____ women _____.

2. The term *malpractice settlement* (paragraph 6) refers to a settlement against a medical caregiver because of _____ bad _____ or improper medical treatment that results in harm to a patient.

➤ **H.   SELECTING A LEARNING/STUDY STRATEGY**

Select the best answer.

____b____   To prepare for a class discussion on this selection for a philosophy class, it would be most helpful to

a. mark key vocabulary.

b. summarize the differing viewpoints expressed.

c. highlight key events in Terri's life.

d. draw a time line.

➤ **I.   EXPLORING IDEAS THROUGH DISCUSSION AND WRITING**

1. The situation described in "What to Do About Terri" is an emotional one. Do you think the authors reveal their feelings about the case? Discuss language and tone.

2. Compare the situations in both selections. Do you have strong feelings about whether one or the other is more clear-cut as far as what the outcome should be?

3. How did the degree of objectivity shown by the authors of each selection affect the selection's credibility?

➤ **J.   BEYOND THE CLASSROOM TO THE WEB**

Visit LegalDocs Living Wills at **http://www.legaldocs.com/htmdocs/livin_st.htm**.
Click on the listing for your home state. Complete the information form (with real or fictitious information), and print the living will document. Does the language used in the document accurately reflect your concerns and expectations? Why or why not?

✔ Tracking Your Progress

Selection 16

Section	Number Correct		Score
A. Thesis and Main Idea (5 items)	_____	x 5	_____
B. Details (5 items)	_____	x 3	_____
C. Organization and Transitions (10 items)	_____	x 1	_____
E. Inferred Meanings (5 items)	_____	x 3	_____
F. Thinking Critically (5 items)	_____	x 3	_____
G. Vocabulary			
1. Context (7 items)	_____	x 2	_____
2. Word Parts (3 items)	_____	x 2	_____

TOTAL SCORE _____ %

CHECKING YOUR READING RATE

Words in Selection 16: 883

Finishing Time:	_____	_____	_____
	(hour)	(minutes)	(seconds)
Starting Time:	_____	_____	_____
	(hour)	(minutes)	(seconds)
Total Reading Time:		_____	_____
		(minutes)	(seconds)

Words Per Minute Score (page 737) _____ WPM

SELECTION 17

When Living Is a Fate Worse Than Death

Christine Mitchell

This reading first appeared in *Newsweek,* a weekly news magazine, in 2000. The author, a medical ethicist, describes a dilemma faced by hospital staff in treating a young child.

► PREVIEWING THE READING

Using the steps listed on page 5, preview the reading selection. When you have fin-ished, complete the following statements.

1. The title indicates that the selection is about a situation in which living is worse than _____ dying _____.

2. Most of the action in the selection takes place in a _____ hospital _____.

MAKING CONNECTIONS

Imagine that you are responsible for deciding whether to withhold further treat-ment from someone who is terminally ill. What factors will you consider in your decision?

► READING TIP

As you read, highlight reasons that support the child's right to die.

CHECKING YOUR READING RATE

If you plan to compute your reading rate, be sure to record your starting time in the box at the end of the exercises before you begin reading.

When Living Is a Fate Worse Than Death

1   The baby died last winter. It was pretty terrible. Little Charlotte (not her real name) lay on a high white bed, surrounded by nurses and doctors pushing drugs into her veins, tubes into her **trachea** and needles into her heart, trying as hard as they could to take over for her failing body and brain. She was being **coded,** as they say in the **ICU.** It had happened several times before, but this time it would fail. Her parents, who were working, weren't there.

trachea
the windpipe that carries air from the larynx to the lungs

coded
the action taken by medical professionals to restart a person's heart after it has stopped beating

ICU
the intensive care unit of a hospital

ER
the emergency room of a hospital

ethicist
a specialist in ethics, the rules or standards guiding the conduct and decisions of members of a profession

2   Charlotte was born with too few brain cells to do much more than breathe and pull away from pain. Most of her malformed brain was wrapped in a sac that grew outside her skull and had to be surgically removed to prevent immediate death.

3   Her parents were a young, unmarried couple from Haiti. They loved Charlotte and wanted her to live. The nurses and doctors thought she should be allowed to die peacefully. They recommended that a Do Not Resuscitate order be placed in Charlotte's chart. The new parents disagreed. Surely, they thought, medical care in the United States could save their baby. They bought their daughter a doll.

4   For 16 months Charlotte bounced back and forth—between hospital, home, the ER and pediatric nursing homes. Wherever she was, every time her body tried to die, nurses and doctors staved off death. Each time, Charlotte got weaker.

5   Charlotte's medical team at the hospital asked to talk with the Ethics Advisory Committee and, as the hospital's ethicist, I got involved. Is it right to keep doing painful things just to keep Charlotte alive a little longer, her doctors and nurses asked us. To whom are we most obligated: the patient or the family? The committee advised that in this case the parents' rights superseded the caregivers' beliefs about what was right. Painful procedures should be avoided, the panel believed, but the care that Charlotte's parents wanted for her should be provided unless there was a medical consensus that it would not prolong her life. Such a consensus was elusive. There's almost always another procedure that can be tried to eke out a little more time until the patient dies despite everything—as Charlotte did.

6   A week after Charlotte's death, I met with the doctors, nurses and therapists who had done everything they could for her and yet felt terrible about having done too much. We talked for almost two hours about how Charlotte had died.

7   "It was horrible," said a doctor. "We tried to resuscitate her for over an hour. It's the worst thing I've ever done. I actually felt sick." A nurse talked about the holes that were drilled in Charlotte's bones to insert lines they couldn't get in anywhere else.

8   Why didn't Charlotte's parents spare Charlotte—and us—the awfulness of her death? Because they were too young? Too hopeful? Because they were distrustful of white nurses and doctors who they thought might really be saying that their black baby wasn't worth saving? Or because they believed that a "good" death is one in which everything possible has been tried?

9   Why didn't the hospital staff, including the ethics committee, save Charlotte from that kind of death? Maybe we feared that her parents would take us to court, like the mother in Virginia who got a judge to order the hospital to provide lifesaving treatment for her anencephalic baby, who was born without most of her brain. Maybe we were afraid of seeing ourselves in the news—as the staff of a Pennsylvania hospital did when they withdrew life support, against the parents' wishes, from a comatose 3-year-old with fatal brain cancer. Maybe we were thinking about what was best for the parents, not just the child. Maybe we were wrong.

10   The nurse sitting next to me at the meeting had driven two hours from the nursing home where she used to care for Charlotte. She had attended the wake. She said the parents had sobbed; that Dad said he felt terrible because he wasn't there when his little girl died, that Mom still couldn't believe that she was dead.

11   It could have been different. They could have been there holding her. That's the way it happens most of the time in ICUs today. Family and staff make the decision together, machines are removed and death comes gently.

12   As a hospital ethicist, a large part of my job is helping staff and families distinguish between sustaining life and prolonging death. Sometimes I join the staff, as I did that night, in second-guessing decisions and drawing distinctions between the dignified death of a child held by parents who accept their child's dying, and the death that occurs amid technologically desperate measures and professional strangers.

13   Sooner or later, every person will die. I wish, and the hospital staff I work with wishes, almost beyond telling, that people could know what they are asking when they ask that "everything" be done.

➤ A. UNDERSTANDING THE THESIS AND OTHER MAIN IDEAS

Select the best answer.

__d__ 1. The author's primary purpose is to

   a. describe the current technology used in hospitals to prolong life.

   b. explain that hospital personnel grieve along with a patient's family when the patient dies.

   c. contrast the rights of a patient's family with the beliefs of caregivers.

   d. argue that prolonging life is sometimes worse than letting the patient die peacefully.

__b__ 2. The main idea of paragraph 3 is that

   a. Charlotte's parents were young and from another country.

   b. Charlotte's parents disagreed with the hospital staff about what was best for her.

   c. a Do Not Resuscitate order should have been placed in Charlotte's chart.

   d. Charlotte's parents believed that U.S. medical care should have been able to save her.

__c__ 3. The Ethics Advisory Board ruled that

   a. the Ethics Advisory Committee made the wrong recommendation.

   b. there are many possible procedures that can be done to prolong life.

   c. the hospital staff would have to provide the care that Charlotte's parents wanted for her.

   d. it was difficult to reach a medical consensus about Charlotte's care.

___d___ 4. The question that the author is asking in paragraph 9 is

    a. Would Charlotte's parents have taken the hospital staff to court?

    b. Would the hospital staff have been on the news because of their treatment of Charlotte?

    c. Was the staff thinking about what was best for the parents or for Charlotte?

    d. Why didn't the hospital staff do something to change the way that Charlotte died?

___a___ 5. The main idea of paragraph 11 is expressed in the

    a. first sentence.

    b. second sentence.

    c. third sentence.

    d. fourth sentence.

➤ B. IDENTIFYING DETAILS

Indicate whether each statement is true (T) or false (F).

___T___ 1. Charlotte's parents were from Haiti.

___F___ 2. Charlotte was in the hospital because she had developed brain cancer.

___F___ 3. Charlotte lived her entire life in the hospital.

___T___ 4. The hospital's Ethics Advisory Committee believed the staff should avoid painful procedures for Charlotte.

___F___ 5. After Charlotte died, the hospital staff wished that they had tried more techniques to save her.

___F___ 6. The nurse who attended the wake said the parents were angry at the hospital.

___T___ 7. Charlotte's parents were not at the hospital with Charlotte when she died.

➤ C. RECOGNIZING METHODS OF ORGANIZATION AND TRANSITIONS

Select the best answer.

___a___ 1. The organizational pattern that the author uses to describe events in the order in which they occurred during Charlotte's brief life is

    a. time sequence.   c. enumeration.

    b. definition.   d. comparison and contrast.

___b___ 2. Throughout the reading, the author uses the comparison and contrast organizational pattern to contrast the opinions of

  a. Charlotte's medical team and the Ethics Advisory Committee.

  b. Charlotte's parents and the hospital staff.

  c. Charlotte's parents and the Ethics Advisory Committee.

  d. the hospital ethicist and Charlotte's medical team.

➤ D.   REVIEWING AND ORGANIZING IDEAS: PARAPHRASING

Complete the following paraphrases of paragraphs 4 and 11 by filling in the missing words or phrases.

Paragraph 4: Charlotte was moved between the ___hospital___, her ___home___, the hospital's ___emergency room___, and pediatric ___nursing homes___ for ___16___ months. Whenever she came close to ___death___, nurses and ___doctors___ were able to hold it off, but she grew ___weaker___ each time it happened.

Paragraph 11: Charlotte's ___death___ could have been different if her ___parents___ had been there holding her. It usually happens like that now in ___ICUs___. Together, the patient's ___family___ and the hospital ___staff___ decide to remove the ___machines___ and let ___death___ come peacefully.

➤ E.   FIGURING OUT INFERRED MEANINGS

Indicate whether each statement is true (T) or false (F).

___T___ 1. Charlotte's parents believed that the medical care in the United States was better than the medical care in Haiti.

___T___ 2. Because of her condition at birth, Charlotte always would have been dependent on medical care even if she had survived longer.

___F___ 3. It can be inferred that the white hospital staff was prejudiced against the black couple and their baby.

___T___ 4. A hospital ethicist helps make decisions about removing life support for terminally ill patients.

___F___ 5. The hospital Ethics Advisory Committee thought that Charlotte would eventually get better.

➤ **F. THINKING CRITICALLY**

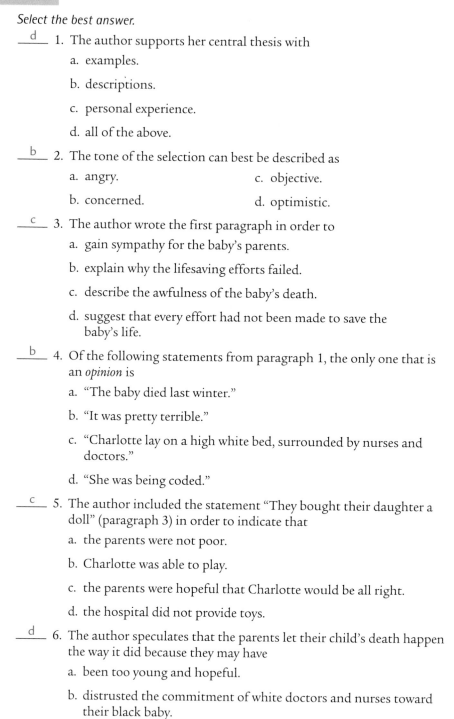

Select the best answer.

___d___ 1. The author supports her central thesis with

  a. examples.

  b. descriptions.

  c. personal experience.

  d. all of the above.

___b___ 2. The tone of the selection can best be described as

  a. angry.   c. objective.

  b. concerned.   d. optimistic.

___c___ 3. The author wrote the first paragraph in order to

  a. gain sympathy for the baby's parents.

  b. explain why the lifesaving efforts failed.

  c. describe the awfulness of the baby's death.

  d. suggest that every effort had not been made to save the baby's life.

___b___ 4. Of the following statements from paragraph 1, the only one that is an *opinion* is

  a. "The baby died last winter."

  b. "It was pretty terrible."

  c. "Charlotte lay on a high white bed, surrounded by nurses and doctors."

  d. "She was being coded."

___c___ 5. The author included the statement "They bought their daughter a doll" (paragraph 3) in order to indicate that

  a. the parents were not poor.

  b. Charlotte was able to play.

  c. the parents were hopeful that Charlotte would be all right.

  d. the hospital did not provide toys.

___d___ 6. The author speculates that the parents let their child's death happen the way it did because they may have

  a. been too young and hopeful.

  b. distrusted the commitment of white doctors and nurses toward their black baby.

    c. believed that death should come only after every possible procedure had been tried.

    d. all of the above.

_d_ 7. In paragraph 12, the author considers the decisions that were made in this case by comparing

    a. her responsibilities as an ethicist with those of the medical caregivers.

    b. her beliefs with those of the parents.

    c. the ICUs of today with the traditional ICUs of the past.

    d. a peaceful, dignified death with the kind that occurs only after desperate medical efforts have failed.

➤ **G. BUILDING VOCABULARY**

➤ **Context**

Using context and a dictionary, if necessary, determine the meaning of each word as it is used in the selection.

_b_ 1. resuscitate (paragraph 3)

    a. disturb   c. allow

    b. revive   d. review

_b_ 2. elusive (paragraph 5)

    a. difficult to reach   c. permanent

    b. temporary   d. unlucky

_c_ 3. eke (paragraph 5)

    a. harm   c. draw out

    b. leave out   d. hide

_b_ 4. comatose (paragraph 9)

    a. diagnosed   c. terminally ill

    b. unconscious   d. recovering

➤ **Word Parts**

> **A REVIEW OF PREFIXES AND SUFFIXES**
>
> **MAL-** means *poorly* or *wrongly*
> **SUPER-** means *above*
> **-IST** means *one who*

Fill in the blanks using your knowledge of word parts.

1. The word *malformed* (paragraph 2) means ___abnormally or wrongly formed___.

2. The word *superseded* (paragraph 5) means to have been put ___above___ in importance.

3. A person who provides therapy is called a ___therapist___ (paragraph 6).

➤ **H.   SELECTING A LEARNING/STUDY STRATEGY**

Select the best answer.

___a___   If you were using this article as a source for a paper on the right-to-die issue, which of the following techniques would be most helpful?

   a. highlighting useful information and quotations

   b. drawing a time line

   c. rereading the article

   d. summarizing the parents' opinions

➤ **I.   EXPLORING IDEAS THROUGH DISCUSSION AND WRITING**

1. What do you consider a "good" death?

2. Do you agree more with the author or with those who would do everything possible to prevent, or delay, death?

3. What did the author mean by the phrase "almost beyond telling" (paragraph 13)?

➤ **J.   BEYOND THE CLASSROOM TO THE WEB**

Read the policy statement of the American Academy of Pediatrics about "Infants with Anencephaly as Organ Sources: Ethical Considerations" at **http:// www.aap .org/policy/04790.html**.

Anencephaly is the condition of being born with most or all of the brain missing. This article discusses the ethical considerations of using babies born in this condition as organ donors. Which of the ethical considerations mentioned in this article and in "When Living Is a Fate Worse Than Death" do you find most compelling? Why?

✔ **Tracking Your Progress**

Selection 17

Section	Number Correct		Score
A. Thesis and Main Idea (5 items)	_____	x 5	_____
B. Details (7 items)	_____	x 3	_____
C. Organization and Transitions (2 items)	_____	x 2	_____
E. Inferred Meanings (5 items)	_____	x 3	_____
F. Thinking Critically (7 items)	_____	x 3	_____
G. Vocabulary			
1. Context (4 items)	_____	x 2	_____
2. Word Parts (3 items)	_____	x 2	_____
	TOTAL SCORE	_____ %	

CHECKING YOUR READING RATE

Words in Selection 17: 830

Finishing Time:	_____	_____	_____
	(hour)	(minutes)	(seconds)
Starting Time:	_____	_____	_____
	(hour)	(minutes)	(seconds)
Total Reading Time:		_____	_____
		(minutes)	(seconds)

Words Per Minute Score (page 737) _____ WPM

▶ **INTEGRATING THE READINGS (SELECTIONS 16 AND 17)**

1. Which argument did you find more convincing? Why?

2. Evaluate the types of evidence each author provided. What additional evidence might have strengthened each article?

3. Discuss how the tone differs in the two articles.

4. Which article did you find easier to read? Why?

SELECTION 18

Seoul Searching

Rick Reilly

This article appeared in *Time* magazine in August 2000. The author, a professional writer, describes a search for his adopted daughter's birth mother in Korea.

▶ PREVIEWING THE READING

Using the steps listed on page 5, preview the reading selection. When you have finished, answer the following questions.

1. What is the article about? <u>the search for the birth mother of the author's</u>

   <u>adopted daughter</u>

2. Where does most of the action take place? <u>Seoul, Korea</u>

 ## MAKING CONNECTIONS

Do you know anyone who was adopted? If so, has that person searched for his or her birth mother? Why?

▶ READING TIP

As you read, highlight words, phrases, and dialogue that reveal the feelings of the birth mother, of Rae, and of her adoptive parents.

 ## CHECKING YOUR READING RATE

If you plan to compute your reading rate, be sure to record your starting time in the box at the end of the exercises before you begin reading.

Seoul Searching

1   After 11 years and 6,000 miles, we still hadn't met our daughter's mother. We had come only this close: staked out in a van across from a tiny Seoul coffee shop, the mother inside with a Korean interpreter, afraid to come out, afraid of being discovered, afraid to meet her own flesh.

2   Inside the van, Rae, our 11-year-old Korean adopted daughter, was trying to make sense of it. How could we have flown the entire family 6,000 miles from

Denver to meet a woman who was afraid to walk 20 yards across the street to meet us? Why had we come this far if she was only going to reject Rae again?

3   We were told we had an hour. There were 40 minutes left. The cell phone rang. "Drive the van to the alley behind the coffee shop," said the interpreter. "And wait."

4   When a four-month-old Rae was hand-delivered to us at Gate B-7 at Denver's Stapleton Airport, we knew someday we would be in Korea trying to find her **birth mother**. We just never dreamed it would be this soon. Then again, since Rae was a toddler, we've told her she was adopted, and she has constantly asked about her birth mother. "Do you think my birth mother plays the piano like I do?" "Do you think my birth mother is pretty?" And then, at 10, after a day of too many stares: a teary "I just want to meet someone I'm related to."

5   "When they start asking that," the adoption therapist said, "you can start looking."

6   We started looking. We asked the agency that had arranged the adoption, Friends of Children of Various Nations, to begin a search. Within six months our **caseworker**, Kim Matsunaga, told us they had found the birth mother but she was highly reluctant to meet us. She had never told anyone about Rae. In Korea, the shame of unwed pregnancy is huge. The mother is disowned, the baby rootless. Kim guessed she had told her parents she was moving to the city to work and had gone to a home for unwed mothers.

7   Kim told us the agency was taking a group of Colorado and New Mexico families to Korea in the summer to meet birth relatives. She said if we went, Rae's would probably show up. "The birth mothers almost always show up," she said. Almost.

8   We were unsure. And then we talked to a family who had gone the year before. They said it would be wonderful. At the very least, Rae would meet her **foster mother**, who had cared for her those four months. She would meet the doctor who delivered her. Hell, I had never met the doctor who delivered me. But meeting the birth mother was said to be the sweetest. A 16-year-old Korean-American girl told Rae, "I don't know, it just kinda fills a hole in your heart."

9   We risked it. Five plane tickets to Seoul for our two redheaded birth boys—Kellen, 15, and Jake, 13—Rae, me and my wife Linda. We steeled Rae for the chance that her birth mother wouldn't show up. Come to think of it, we steeled ourselves.

10   At first it was wonderful. We met Rae's foster mother, who swooped in and rushed for Rae as if she were her long-lost daughter, which she almost was. She bear-hugged her. She stroked her hair. She touched every little nick and scar on her tan arms and legs. "What's this from?" she asked in Korean. She had fostered 31 babies, but it was as if she'd known only Rae. Rae was half grossed out, half purring. Somebody had just rushed in with the missing four months of her life. The foster mother wept. We wept.

11   All of us, all six American families, sat in one room at a home for unwed mothers outside Seoul across from 25 unwed mothers, some who had just given up their babies, some soon to. They looked into their unmet children's futures. We looked into our unmet birth mothers' pasts. A 17-year-old Korean-American girl—roughly the same age as the distraught girls in front of her—rose and choked out, "I know it's hard for you now, but I want you to know I love my American family."

12   Another 17-year-old adoptee met not only her birth father but also her four older birth sisters. They were still a family —had always been one—but they had given her up as one mouth too many to feed. Then they told her that her birth mother had

birth mother
the biological
mother of a child

caseworker
the social worker
from the adoption
agency who is
handling the details
of the search

foster mother
a woman providing
care for a child
who is unrelated to
her by blood or
legal ties

died of an aneurysm two weeks earlier. So how was she supposed to feel now? Joy at finding her father and her sisters? Grief at 7 years without them? Anger at being given up? Gratitude for her American parents? Horror at coming so close to and then missing her birth mother? We heard her story that night on the tour bus, went to our hotel room and wept some more.

13   All these kids—even the three who never found their birth relatives—were piecing together the puzzle of their life at whiplash speed. This is where you were born. This is the woman who held you. This was the city, the food, the smells. For them, it was two parts home ("It's so nice," Rae said amid a throng of Koreans on a street. "For once, people are staring at Kel and Jake instead of me") and three parts I'm-never-coming-here-again (a teenage boy ate dinner at his foster parents' home only to discover in mid-bite that they raise dogs for meat).

14   When the day came for our visit with Rae's birth mother, we were told "It has to be handled very, very carefully." She had three children by a husband she had never told about Rae, and she was terribly afraid someone would see her. And that's how we found ourselves hiding in that van like **Joe Friday**, waiting for the woman of a lifetime to show up. It is a very odd feeling to be staring holes in every Korean woman walking down a Korean street, thinking that your daughter may have sprung from her womb. All we knew about her was that she 1) might have her newborn girl with her, 2) was tiny—the birth certificate said she was 4 ft. 10 in.—and 3) would look slightly more nervous than a cat burglar.

Joe Friday
a detective on the 1950s television show *Dragnet*

15   First came a youngish, chic woman pushing a stroller. "That might be her!" yelled Rae—until she strolled by. Then a short, fat woman with a baby tied at her stomach. "There she is!" yelled Rae—until she got on a bus. Then a pretty, petite woman in yellow with an infant in a baby carrier. "I know that's her!" yelled Rae—and lo and behold the woman quick-stepped into the coffee shop across the street.

16   The only problem was, she didn't come out. She stayed in that coffee shop, talking to the interpreter for what seemed like six hours but was probably only 20 minutes. We stared at the dark windows of the shop. We stared at the cell phone. We stared at one another. What was this, **Panmunjom**? Finally, the interpreter called Kim: Drive down the alley and wait. We drove down the alley and waited. Nothing.

Panmunjom
the village in South Korea where truce negotiations for the Korean War were held

17   By this time, I could have been the centerfold for *Psychology Today*. Rae was still calm. I told her, "If she's not out here in five minutes, I want you to walk right in and introduce yourself." Rae swallowed. Suddenly, at the van window . . . and now opening the van door the woman in yellow with the baby. And just as suddenly, inside . . . sitting next to her daughter. Our daughter—all of ours. She was nervous. She wouldn't look at us, only at her baby and the interpreter. "We'll go somewhere," said the interpreter.

18   Where do you go with your deepest, darkest secret? We went to a park. Old Korean men looked up from their chess games in astonishment to see a gaggle of whites and redheads and Koreans sit down at the table next to them with cameras, gifts and notebooks. Rae presented her birth mother with a book she had made about her life—full of childhood pictures and purple-penned poems—but the woman showed no emotion as she looked at it. Rae presented her with a silver locket—a picture of herself inside but again, no eye contact, no hugs, no touches. The woman was either guarding her heart now the way she'd done 11 years ago, or she simply didn't care anymore, maybe had never cared.

19   Months before, Rae had drawn up a list of 20 questions she wanted to ask at the big moment. Now, unruffled, she pulled it out of her little purse. Some of us forgot to breathe. "Why did you give me up?" Rae asked simply. All heads turned to the woman. The interpreted answer: Too young, only 19 then, no money, great shame. "Where is my birth dad?" The answer: No idea. Only knew him for two dates. Long gone. Still no emotion. I ached for Rae. How would she handle such iciness from the woman she had dreamed of, fantasized about, held on to? Finally, this one: "When I was born, did you get to hold me?" The woman's lips parted in a small gasp. She swallowed and stared at the grass. "No," she said slowly, "they took you from me." And that's when our caseworker, Kim, said, "Well, now you can."

20   That did it. That broke her. She lurched, tears running down her cheeks, reached for Rae and pulled her close, holding her as if they might take her again. "I told myself I wouldn't cry," she said. The interpreter wept. Linda wept. I wept. Right then, right at that minute, the heavens opened up, and it poured a **monsoon** starter kit on us, just an **all-out Noah**. Yeah, even the sky wept.

monsoon
the heavy rainfall that accompanies a seasonal wind system in southern Asia

21   Any sane group of people would have run for the van, but none of us wanted the moment to end. We had finally got her, and we would float to **Pusan** before we would give her up. We were all crying and laughing and trying to fit all of us under the birth mother's tiny pink umbrella. But the rain was so loud you couldn't talk. We ran for the van and sat in there, Rae holding her half sister and her birth mother holding the daughter she must have thought she would never see.

an all-out Noah
a reference to the biblical story of Noah's ark, built during a flood

22   Time was so short. Little sentences contained whole lifetimes. She thanked us for raising her baby. "You are a very good family," she said, eyeing the giants around her. "Very strong and good." And how do you thank someone for giving you her daughter? Linda said, "Thank you for the gift you gave us." The birth mother smiled bittersweetly. She held Rae with one arm and the book and the locket tight with the other.

Pusan
a city in southeast South Korea on Korea Strait southeast of Seoul

23   Then it was over. She said she had to get back. She asked the driver to pull over so she could get out. We started pleading for more time. Meet us for dinner? No. Breakfast tomorrow? No. Send you pictures? Please, no. The van stopped at a red light. Somebody opened the door. She kissed Rae on the head, stroked her hair one last time, stepped out, finally let go of her hand and closed the door. The light turned green. We drove off and watched her shrink away from us, dropped off on the corner of Nowhere and Forever.

24   I think I was still crying when I looked at Rae. She was beaming, of course, which must be how you feel when a hole in your heart finally gets filled.

A.   UNDERSTANDING THE THESIS AND OTHER MAIN IDEAS

Select the best answer.

 a   1. The author's primary purpose in "Seoul Searching" is to

   a. describe his family's search for his adopted daughter's birth mother in Korea.

   b. encourage people to consider international adoption.

c. criticize his daughter's birth mother for giving up her baby.

d. compare the cultures of Korea and America.

___d___ 2. The birth mother gave her child up for adoption for all of the following reasons *except*

a. she was ashamed of being unmarried and pregnant.

b. she had kept her pregnancy a secret from her parents.

c. she felt she was too young and had no money.

d. she and her husband had too many children already.

___a___ 3. The main idea of paragraph 8 is that

a. the author and his wife were unsure about going to Korea.

b. another family had made the same trip a year earlier.

c. the author never met the doctor who had delivered him.

d. the author's daughter would at least get to meet her foster mother.

___b___ 4. The topic of paragraph 10 is

a. the wonderful trip.

b. Rae's foster mother.

c. the language barrier between Rae's family and her Korean foster mother.

d. the missing four months of Rae's life.

___a___ 5. The main point of paragraph 13 is expressed in the

a. first sentence.   c. third sentence.

b. second sentence.   d. last sentence.

___c___ 6. When the author and his family were waiting to meet Rae's birth mother, they were expecting all of the following about her *except* that

a. she was petite.

b. her newborn baby might be with her.

c. her husband would be with her.

d. she would be quite nervous.

___d___ 7. The main idea of paragraph 19 is that

a. Rae's birth mother refused to answer any questions.

b. Rae forgot her list of questions.

c. the author was angry at the birth mother's responses.

d. Rae's birth mother at first appeared unemotional.

➤ **B. IDENTIFYING DETAILS**

Indicate whether each statement is true (T) or false (F).

___T___ 1. Denver is 6,000 miles from Seoul.

___F___ 2. The adoption agency refused to assist in the search for Rae's birth mother.

___F___ 3. Only the author and his daughter traveled to Korea to find her birth mother.

___F___ 4. Rae's birth mother had died of an aneurysm two weeks before they arrived.

___F___ 5. After their meeting, Rae's birth mother promised to keep in touch.

➤ **C. RECOGNIZING METHODS OF ORGANIZATION AND TRANSITIONS**

Select the best answer.

___b___ 1. Throughout the reading, the author describes the events that took place in the search for his daughter's birth mother. When he describes these events in the order in which they occurred, he is using the organizational pattern called

    a. enumeration.

    b. time sequence.

    c. cause and effect.

    d. comparison and contrast.

___d___ 2. Which of the following transitional words or phrases does not suggest a direction or sequence in time?

    a. After

    b. And then

    c. At first

    d. However

➤ D.   REVIEWING AND ORGANIZING IDEAS: MAPPING

Complete the following time line of the events described in "Seoul Searching." Put the events in the correct order on the time line by writing in the number from the time line that corresponds to the event.

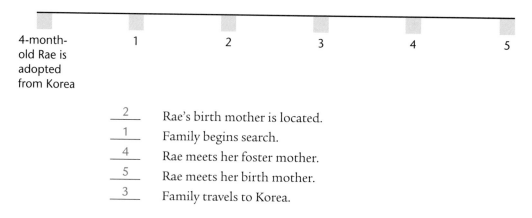

4-month-old Rae is adopted from Korea   1   2   3   4   5

2	Rae's birth mother is located.
1	Family begins search.
4	Rae meets her foster mother.
5	Rae meets her birth mother.
3	Family travels to Korea.

➤ E.   FIGURING OUT INFERRED MEANINGS

Indicate whether each statement is true (T) or false (F).

__F__ 1. The author never planned to try to find his daughter's birth mother.

__F__ 2. The author and his wife did not want Rae to know she was adopted.

__T__ 3. Rae's foster mother was thrilled to meet her.

__T__ 4. Rae's birth mother had to be persuaded to meet her.

__F__ 5. Rae planned to search for her birth father while she was in Korea.

➤ F.   THINKING CRITICALLY

Select the best answer.

__d__ 1. The title "Seoul Searching" refers to

    a. the author's difficult decision to begin the search for his daughter's birth mother.

    b. an American family's struggle to adopt a Korean baby.

    c. the physically stressful search for Rae's birth mother.

    d. both the physical search in Seoul for Rae's birth mother and Rae's emotional search for a missing part of her heart.

_____c_____ 2. The author supports his thesis primarily with

    a. facts and statistics.

    b. cause and effect relationships.

    c. personal experience.

    d. research evidence.

_____c_____ 3. Of the following statements, the only one that expresses an *opinion* is

    a. "After 11 years and 6,000 miles, we still hadn't met our daughter's mother." (paragraph 1)

    b. "We were told we had an hour." (paragraph 3)

    c. "But meeting the birth mother is said to be the sweetest." (paragraph 8)

    d. "The foster mother wept." (paragraph 10)

_____a_____ 4. Of the following statements, the only one that is a *fact* is

    a. "All of us, all six American families, sat in one room at a home for unwed mothers outside Seoul across from 25 unwed mothers, some who had just given up their babies, some soon to." (paragraph 11)

    b. "She had three children by a husband she had never told about Rae, and she was terribly afraid someone would see her." (paragraph 14)

    c. "First came a youngish, chic woman pushing a stroller." (paragraph 15)

    d. "By this time I could have been the centerfold for *Psychology Today*." (paragraph 17)

_____d_____ 5. The most important aspect of paragraph 20 is that

    a. a monsoon had just begun.

    b. the interpreter was upset.

    c. the author and his wife were afraid they would lose their daughter.

    d. the birth mother finally allowed her emotions to show.

_____b_____ 6. The statement "Little sentences contained whole lifetimes" (paragraph 22) means that

    a. the birth mother only knew a little English.

    b. Rae's parents and her birth mother expressed a wealth of meaning in very few words.

    c. the interpreter had trouble translating their conversation.

    d. Rae's birth mother described her life after Rae's birth in short sentences.

_c_ 7. The best description of the author's tone throughout the reading would be

    a. lighthearted and humorous.   c. sympathetic and anxious.

    b. sad and unforgiving.   d. bitter and angry.

➤ G.   BUILDING VOCABULARY

➤ Context

Using context and a dictionary, if necessary, determine the meaning of each word as it is used in the selection.

_b_ 1. reject (paragraph 2)

    a. take back

    b. turn away

    c. agree

    d. dislike

_c_ 2. steeled (paragraph 9)

    a. deceived

    b. talked into

    c. strengthened/made strong/prepared

    d. looked forward to

_d_ 3. distraught (paragraph 11)

    a. childish

    b. immature

    c. distracted

    d. emotionally upset

_b_ 4. throng (paragraph 13)

    a. few

    b. crowd

    c. confusion

    d. family

_a_ 5. gaggle (paragraph 18)

    a. disorderly group

    b. serious mistake

    c. class

    d. annoying tourists

➤ Word Parts

> ### A REVIEW OF PREFIXES AND SUFFIXES
>
> **DIS-** means *not* (disagree)
> **UN-** means *not* (unhappy)
> **-EE** means *one who* (employee)
> **-ER** means *one who* (employer)
> **-ISH** refers to *a quality* (girlish)
> **-IST** means *one who* (typist)
> **-LESS** refers to *a state* (hopeless)

Match each word in Column A with its meaning in Column B. Write your answers in the spaces provided.

Column A		Column B
_e_ 1. interpreter (paragraph 1)		a. one who handles casework
_d_ 2. therapist (paragraph 5)		b. without a home or "roots"
_a_ 3. caseworker (paragraph 6)		c. not acknowledged or "owned"
_f_ 4. unwed (paragraph 6)		d. one who provides therapy
_c_ 5. disowned (paragraph 6)		e. one who interprets
_b_ 6. rootless (paragraph 6)		f. not married
_i_ 7. unmet (paragraph 11)		g. not flustered
_j_ 8. adoptee (paragraph 12)		h. youthful quality
_h_ 9. youngish (paragraph 15)		i. not acquainted
_g_ 10. unruffled (paragraph 19)		j. one who is adopted

➤ Unusual Words/Unusual Meanings

Select the best answer.

_d_ 1. When the author states that "Rae was half grossed out, half purring" upon meeting her foster mother (paragraph 10), he means that Rae

    a. was sick from the long flight to Korea.

    b. felt like a cat being stroked by her foster mother.

    c. wanted to get away from her foster mother.

    d. felt both pleased and repulsed by the way her foster mother treated her.

_b_ 2. The phrase "staring holes" in someone (paragraph 14) means

    a. giving someone angry looks.

    b. looking hard at someone.

    c. judging someone by his or her clothing.

    d. frightening someone away.

___a___ 3. The author describes the "iciness" that Rae's birth mother showed toward her (paragraph 19) as a way of saying that she was

    a. emotionally cold to Rae.

    b. chilled by the weather.

    c. uncomfortable on the icy road.

    d. as sweet as icing on a cake.

➤ H.   SELECTING A LEARNING/STUDY STRATEGY

Suppose you read this article in preparation for a class discussion on the pros and cons of international adoption. What techniques would you use to study the article?

➤ I.   EXPLORING IDEAS THROUGH DISCUSSION AND WRITING

1. What does the girl mean when she says finding your birth mother "fills a hole in your heart" (paragraph 8)? Why did the author repeat the phrase at the end of the story?

2. An especially poignant part of the story is described in paragraph 11: "They looked into their unmet children's futures. We looked into our unmet birth mothers' pasts." Explain the meaning of this statement.

3. How does the author illustrate the cultural differences between the visiting Americans and the Koreans?

4. Evaluate the questions Rae asked her birth mother. Would you have asked similar questions? What additional questions would you ask?

➤ J.   BEYOND THE CLASSROOM TO THE WEB

Visit the Rainbow Kids Personal Adoption Stories Web site at **http://www .rainbowkids.com/stories/**.

    Read the stories posted there. How do the experiences seem similar to those of women in "Seoul Searching?"?

✔ Tracking Your Progress

Selection 18

Section	Number Correct		Score
A. Thesis and Main Idea (7 items)	_____	x 4	_____
B. Details (5 items)	_____	x 3	_____
C. Organization and Transitions (2 items)	_____	x 3	_____
E. Inferred Meanings (5 items)	_____	x 3	_____
F. Thinking Critically (7 items)	_____	x 3	_____
G. Vocabulary			
1. Context (5 items)	_____	x 1	_____
2. Word Parts (10 items)	_____	x 1	_____

TOTAL SCORE _____ %

CHECKING YOUR READING RATE

Words in Selection 18: 1,965

Finishing Time:	_____ (hour)	_____ (minutes)	_____ (seconds)
Starting Time:	_____ (hour)	_____ (minutes)	_____ (seconds)
Total Reading Time:		_____ (minutes)	_____ (seconds)

Words Per Minute Score (page 737) _____ WPM

17 Political Science/Government/ History

We live in a political world shaped by history and current events. The economy, the job market, and even television sitcoms are influenced by national and international events. To study political science, government, and history is to understand factors that influence your daily life. Readings in this chapter demonstrate the relevance of these disciplines. In "The Beautiful Laughing Sisters—An Arrival Story" you will read the plight of twenty-first-century refugees arriving in America from countries with oppressive regimes. "Profile of a Terrorist" addresses an important question that has arisen since the September 11 terrorist attacks: How can we identify and cope with terrorists? "American Communities: Los Alamos, New Mexico" provides an historical picture of a community of scientists sequestered during the 1940s.

Use the following suggestions when reading in the fields of political science, government, and history.

TIPS FOR READING IN POLITICAL SCIENCE/ GOVERNMENT/ HISTORY	■ **Focus on the significance of events, both current and historical.** What immediate and long-range effects will or did a particular event, situation, or action have? As you read "Profile of a Terrorist," consider the impact of terrorism on American life.

- **Focus on the significance of events, both current and historical.** What immediate and long-range effects will or did a particular event, situation, or action have? As you read "Profile of a Terrorist," consider the impact of terrorism on American life.

- **Analyze motivations.** What causes people and groups to take political action? What political beliefs do people hold? As you read "American Communities: Los Alamos, New Mexico," consider how the threat of an atomic bomb forced the government isolate scientists in a remote community.

- **Consider political organizations.** How and why do people organize themselves into political groups and parties? Observe how political power is distributed and who makes important political decisions. As you read "The Beautiful Laughing Sisters," you will see how political oppression affected and controlled a family's life.

- **Be alert for bias and partisanship** (support of a viewpoint or position because it is held by one's political party). "Profile of a Terrorist" presents only the viewpoint of the victims of terrorism; it does not present the viewpoint of those who commit terrorism.

- **Sort facts from opinions.** Opinions and historical interpretation are worthwhile but need to be evaluated. What is fact and what is opinion in the description of the lives of the Kurdish refugees?

SELECTION 19

The Beautiful Laughing Sisters— An Arrival Story

Mary Pipher

This reading is taken from Mary Pipher's book *The Middle of Everywhere* which examines the plight of refugees who have fled to America from countries where they have been mistreated and abused. This selection tells the story of a courageous Kurdish family.

➤ PREVIEWING THE READING

Using the steps listed on page 5, preview the reading selection. When you have finished, complete the following items.

1. This selection is about <u>The journey of sisters from Iraq to America.</u>

2. List at least four questions you should be able to answer after reading the selection:

   a. <u>Why did the family leave Iraq?</u>

   b. <u>Where did their journey take them?</u>

   c. <u>Where did they end up living in the United States?</u>

   d. <u>How are they adjusting to life in America?</u>

 ## MAKING CONNECTIONS

The sisters in the story arrive in a new place that is foreign to them. Think about a time when you visited a new place for the first time (perhaps your college campus). How did you feel? What problems or difficulties did you face?

➤ READING TIP

As you read, look at a map of the Middle East, and locate the places that are mentioned.

CHECKING YOUR READING RATE

If you plan to compute your reading rate, be sure to record your starting time in the box at the end of the exercises before you begin reading.

The Beautiful Laughing Sisters–An Arrival Story

1   One of the best ways to understand the refugee experience is to befriend a family of new arrivals and observe their experiences in our country for the first year. That first year is the hardest. Everything is new and strange, and obstacles appear like the stars appear at dusk, in an uncountable array. This story is about a family I met during their first month in our country. I became their friend and **cultural broker** and in the process learned a great deal about the refugee experience, and about us Americans.

cultural broker someone who helps people from other countries learn the customs of the new country

2   On a fall day I met Shireen and Meena, who had come to this country from Pakistan. The Kurdish sisters were slender young women with alert expressions. They wore blue jeans and clunky high-heeled shoes. Shireen was taller and bolder, Meena was smaller and more soft-spoken. Their English was limited and heavily accented. (I later learned it was their sixth language after Kurdish, Arabic, Farsi, Urdu, and Hindi.)* They communicated with each other via small quick gestures and eye movements. Although they laughed easily, they watched to see that the other was okay at all times.

3   Shireen was the youngest and the only one of the six sisters who was eligible for high school. Meena, who was twenty-one, had walked the ten blocks from their apartment to meet Shireen at school on a bitterly cold day. Shireen told the family story. Meena occasionally interrupted her answers with a reminder, an amendment, or laughter.

4   Shireen was born in Baghdad in 1979, the last of ten children. Their mother, Zeenat, had been a village girl who entered an arranged marriage at fourteen. Although their father had been well educated, Zeenat couldn't read or write in any language. The family was prosperous and "Europeanized," as Shireen put it. She said, "Before our father was in trouble, we lived just like you. Baghdad was a big city. In our group of friends, men and women were treated as equals. Our older sisters went to movies and read foreign newspapers. Our father went to cocktail parties at the embassies."

5   However, their father had opposed Saddam Hussein, and from the time of Shireen's birth, his life was in danger. After Hussein came to power, terrible things happened to families like theirs. One family of eleven was taken to jail by his security forces and tortured to death. Prisoners were often fed rice mixed with glass so that they would quietly bleed to death in their cells. Girls were raped and impregnated by the security police. Afterward, they were murdered or killed themselves.

---

* These languages, in addition to many others, are spoken in the Middle Eastern countries of Iran, Iraq, India, and Palestine.

6   It was a hideous time. Schoolteachers tried to get children to betray their parents. One night the police broke into the family's house. They tore up the beds, bookcases, and the kitchen, and they took their Western clothes and tapes. After that night, all of the family except for one married sister made a daring escape into Iran.

7   Meena said, "It was a long time ago but I can see everything today." There was no legal way to go north, so they walked through Kurdistan at night and slept under bushes in the day. They found a guide who made his living escorting **Kurds** over the mountains. Twice they crossed rivers near flood stage. Entire families had been swept away by the waters and one of the sisters almost drowned when she fell off her horse. The trails were steep and narrow and another sister fell and broke her leg. Meena was in a bag slung over the guide's horse for three days. She remembered how stiff she felt in the bag, and Shireen remembered screaming, "I want my mama."

Kurds
a people of the Middle East whose homeland is in the mountainous regions of Iraq, Iran, and Turkey

8   This was in the 1980s. While this was happening I was a psychologist building my private practice and a young mother taking my kids to *Sesame Street Live* and **Vacation Village on Lake Okoboji**. I was dancing to the music of my husband's band, Sour Mash, listening to Van Morrison and Jackson Browne and reading P. D. James and Anne Tyler. Could my life have been happening on the same planet?

Vacation Village on Lake Okoboji
a family resort in northwestern Iowa

9   The family made it to a refugee camp in Iran. It was a miserable place with smelly tents and almost no supplies. Shireen said this was rough on her older siblings who had led lives of luxury. She and Meena adjusted more quickly. The sisters studied in an Iranian school for refugees.

10   They endured this makeshift camp for one very bad year. The Iranians insisted that all the women in the camp wear heavy scarves and robes and conform to strict rules. The soldiers in the camp shouted at them if they wore even a little lipstick. Shireen once saw a young girl wearing makeup stopped by a guard who rubbed it off her face. He had put ground glass in the tissue so that her cheeks bled afterward.

11   They decided to get out of Iran and traveled the only direction they could, east into Pakistan. They walked all the way with nothing to drink except salty water that made them even thirstier. I asked how long the trip took and Shireen said three days. Meena quickly corrected her: "Ten years."

12   Once in Pakistan they were settled by a relief agency in a border town called Quetta, where strangers were not welcome. The family lived in a small house with electricity that worked only sporadically. The stress of all the moves broke the family apart. The men left the women and the family has never reunited.

13   Single women in Quetta couldn't leave home unescorted and the sisters had no men to escort them. Only their mother, Zeenat, dared go out to look for food. As Meena put it, "She took good care of us and now we will take care of her."

14   The sisters almost never left the hut, but when they did, they wore robes as thick and heavy as black carpets. Meena demonstrated how hard it was to walk in these clothes and how she often fell down. Even properly dressed, they were chased by local men. When they rode the bus to buy vegetables, they were harassed.

15   Without their heroic mother, they couldn't have survived. For weeks at a time, the family was trapped inside the hut. At night the locals would break their windows with stones and taunt the sisters with threats of rape. Meena interrupted to say that every house in the village but theirs had weapons. Shireen said incredulously, "There were no laws in that place. Guns were laws."

16   One night some men broke into their hut and took what little money and jewelry they had left. They had been sleeping and woke to see guns flashing around them. The next day they reported the break-in to the police. Shireen said, "The police told us to get our own guns." Meena said, "We were nothing to them. The police slapped and pushed us. We were afraid to provoke them."

17   During the time they were there, the Pakistanis tested a nuclear bomb nearby and they all got sick. An older sister had seizures from the stress of their lives. Shireen said defiantly, "It was hard, but we got used to hard."

18   Still, the young women laughed as they told me about the black robes and the mens with guns. Their laughter was a complicated mixture of anxiety, embarrassment, and relief that it was over. It was perhaps also an attempt to distance themselves from that time and place.

19   They'd studied English in the hut and made plans for their future in America or Europe. Shireen said, "I always knew that we would escape that place."

20   In Quetta the family waited ten years for papers that would allow them to immigrate. Shireen looked at me and said, "I lost my teenage years there—all my teenage years."

21   Finally, in frustration, the family went on a hunger strike. They told the relief workers they would not eat until they were allowed to leave Quetta. After a few days, the agency paperwork was delivered and the family was permitted to board a train for Islamabad.

22   In Islamabad they lived in a small apartment with no air conditioning. Every morning they would soak their curtains in water to try to cool their rooms. It was dusty and polluted and they got typhoid fever and heat sickness. They had a year of interviews and waiting before papers arrived that allowed them to leave for America. Still, it was a year of hope. Zeenat picked up cans along the roads to make money. One sister ran a beauty parlor from their home. They all watched American television, studied English, and dreamed of a good future.

23   Finally they flew to America—Islamabad to Karachi to Amsterdam to New York to St. Louis to Lincoln. Shireen said, "We came in at night. There were lights spread out over the dark land. Lincoln looked beautiful."

24   We talked about their adjustment to Lincoln. Five of the sisters had found work. They didn't have enough money though, and they didn't like the cold. Meena needed three root canals and Zeenat had many missing teeth and needed bridgework, false teeth, everything really. Still, they were enjoying the sense of possibilities unfolding. Shireen put it this way, "In America, we have rights." She pronounced "rights" as if it were a sacred word.

25   Meena mentioned that traffic here was more orderly and less dangerous than in Pakistan. The girls loved American clothes and makeup. Two of their sisters wanted to design clothes. Another was already learning to do American hairstyles so that she could work in a beauty shop. Meena wanted to be a nurse and Shireen a model or flight attendant. She said, "I have traveled so much against my will. Now I would like to see the world in a good way."

26   Shireen said that it was scary to go to the high school. Fortunately, her study of English in Pakistan made it easy for her to learn Nebraska English. She liked her teachers but said the American students mostly ignored her, especially when they heard her thick accent.

27   I was struck by the resilience of these sisters. In all the awful places they had been, they'd found ways to survive and even joke about their troubles. These young women used their intelligence to survive. Had they lived different lives, they would probably have been doctors and astrophysicists. Since they'd been in Lincoln, they'd been happy. Shireen said, "Of course we have problems, but they are easy problems."

28   I gave the sisters a ride home in my old Honda. They invited me in for tea, but I didn't have time. Instead I wrote out my phone number and told them to call if I could help them in any way.

29   When I said good-bye, I had no idea how soon and how intensely I would become involved in the lives of this family. Two weeks later Shireen called to ask about an art course advertised on a book of matches. It promised a college degree for thirty-five dollars. I said, "Don't do it." A couple of weeks later she called again. This time she had seen an ad for models. She wondered if she should pay and enter the modeling contest. Again I advised, "Don't do it." I was embarrassed to tell her that we Americans lie to people to make money. Before I hung up, we chatted for a while.

30   I wanted to make sure they learned about the good things in our city. Advertisers would direct them to the bars, the malls, and anything that cost money. I told them about what I loved: the parks and prairies, the lakes and sunsets, the sculpture garden, and the free concerts. I lent them books with Georgia O'Keeffe paintings and pictures of our national parks.

31   For a while I was so involved with the lives of the sisters that Zeenat told me that her daughters were now my daughters. I was touched that she was willing to give her daughters away so that they could advance. I tactfully suggested we could share her daughters, but that she would always be the real mother.

➤ A.   UNDERSTANDING THE THESIS AND OTHER MAIN IDEAS

Select the best answer.

___d___ 1. The author's primary purpose in "The Beautiful Laughing Sisters" is to

    a. examine the official channels people must go through to immigrate.

    b. comment on the racism that exists worldwide.

    c. encourage people to make friends with refugees.

    d. describe the experience of a refugee family.

___b___ 2. In paragraphs 2–4, the author

    a. introduces all six sisters.

    b. provides background information on the family and their early life in Iraq.

    c. describes the mother's childhood.

    d. sets out a plan for the rest of the article.

___a___ 3. The topic of paragraphs 5 and 6 is the

    a. conditions in Iraq under Saddam Hussein.

    b. treatment of prisoners in Iraq.

    c. tactics of the security police.

    d. night the sisters' house was broken into.

___d___ 4. Paragraphs 9 and 10 focus on

    a. the clothing the women were forced to wear.

    b. education at the camp.

    c. the journey to Iran.

    d. the conditions in the Iranian refugee camp.

___b___ 5. Which of the following questions is *not* answered in the paragraphs about the family's time in Quetta (paragraphs 12–16)?

    a. How did the local people treat refugees?

    b. What happened to the men of the family after they left?

    c. Which member of the family kept them going during this time?

    d. Why were these women so vulnerable?

___d___ 6. Paragraph 24 is primarily concerned with

    a. monetary problems.

    b. social life.

    c. sacred beliefs.

    d. adjustment to American life.

___a___ 7. The final three paragraphs (29–31) are included in order to

    a. describe the author's involvement in the family's life.

    b. criticize certain American businesses.

    c. draw conclusions about the girls' relationship with their mother.

    d. encourage the reader to learn more about the plight of refugees.

➤ B. IDENTIFYING DETAILS

Select the best answer.

___c___ 1. How many languages do Shireen and Meena know?

    a. 2   c. 6

    b. 5   d. 7

_a_ 2. The girls' parents
   a. had an arranged marriage.
   b. were both from villages.
   c. had been well educated.
   d. were very young when they got married.

_c_ 3. What finally made the family decide to escape from Iraq?
   a. the father's opposition to Hussein
   b. families being taken off to jail
   c. their own home being broken into
   d. the tactics of school teachers

_d_ 4. On the way through Kurdistan, people
   a. had to cross mountains.
   b. could get badly injured.
   c. might be swept away by flooding rivers.
   d. all of the above

_b_ 5. According to the reading, the author
   a. plays in a band.
   b. is a psychologist.
   c. does not like to read.
   d. none of the above

_a_ 6. In the town of Quetta,
   a. the women had to wear heavy robes.
   b. the family finally had regular access to electricity.
   c. the sisters spent the day searching for food.
   d. the family bought guns to protect themselves.

_d_ 7. After Quetta, the family went to
   a. America.   c. Iran.
   b. Lincoln.   d. Islamabad.

_c_ 8. In Lincoln, all the sisters except Shireen
   a. had no problems.
   b. went to school.
   c. found jobs.
   d. became clothes designers.

<u> a </u> 9. In the end, the author

    a. helped the family adjust to America.

    b. hardly ever saw the sisters.

    c. adopted the sisters.

    d. bid farewell as the family moved to another state.

➤ C. RECOGNIZING METHODS OF ORGANIZATION AND TRANSITIONS

Select the best answer.

<u> b </u> 1. The overall organizational pattern that the author uses to describe the events in the reading is

    a. classification.   c. cause and effect.

    b. time sequence   d. enumeration.

2. For the pattern you chose in #1 above, list transitions that suggest this pattern.

    a. Paragraph 4 <u>Shireen was born in 1979.</u>

    b. Paragraph 5 <u>After Hussein came to power</u>

    c. Paragraph 6 <u>After that night</u>

    d. Paragraph 16 <u>One night</u>

    e. Paragraph 21 <u>Finally</u>

➤ D. REVIEWING AND ORGANIZING IDEAS: SUMMARIZING

Use the following list of words and phrases to complete the summary of paragraphs 24–26.

futures	students	Lincoln	high school	clothes
teachers	opportunities	makeup	rights	jobs

After the sisters arrived in <u>Lincoln</u>, five of them found <u>jobs</u> while the youngest, Shireen, attended <u>high school</u>, where she had good experiences with the <u>teachers</u>, but not much interaction with the <u>students</u>. Despite this and money problems, they realized that <u>opportunities</u> had once again opened up to them and they planned for bright <u>futures</u>. American <u>clothes</u> and <u>makeup</u> appealed to the sisters, but mostly they were happy to have <u>rights</u>.

➤ E. FIGURING OUT INFERRED MEANINGS

Indicate whether each statement is true (T) or false (F).

___T___ 1. The author is an American.

___F___ 2. The sisters have relatives in Lincoln.

___T___ 3. The hunger strike worked for the family.

___F___ 4. Shireen made lots of new friends at her Nebraska school.

___F___ 5. The author regretted offering to help the family.

➤ F. THINKING CRITICALLY

Select the best answer.

___c___ 1. The author presents information about the refugee experience primarily through

    a. figurative language.

    b. historical facts.

    c. the family's personal experience.

    d. expert opinion.

___d___ 2. The author's tone can best be described as

    a. persuasive.   c. grim.

    b. worried.   d. sympathetic.

___a___ 3. In the first paragraph the phrase, "obstacles appear like the stars appear at dusk" is an example of a(n)

    a. comparison.

    b. unimportant detail.

    c. cause and effect relationship

    d. contrast.

___a___ 4. Which of the following statements from the selection expresses an opinion?

    a. "The Kurdish sisters were slender young women with alert expressions." (paragraph 2)

    b. "Prisoners were often fed rice mixed with glass." (paragraph 5)

    c. "Even properly dressed, they were chased by local men." (paragraph 14)

    d. "They had a year of interviews and waiting." (paragraph 22) _a_ 5. When the author asks in paragraph 8, "Could my life have been happening on the same planet?" she means that

    a. it's hard to believe that there is such a big difference in lifestyles throughout the world.

    b. Americans do not understand the motives of refugees.

    c. everyone on Earth is unique.

    d. she was not paying attention to the current events of the time.

_c_ 6. According to the reading, who was responsible for the sisters' survival?

    a. their father

    b. the sisters themselves

    c. their mother

    d. their brothers

_c_ 7. What underlying feeling helped the family make it through their journey?

    a. love

    b. anger

    c. hope

    d. religious faith

_d_ 8. In paragraph 24 the author states that Shireen said the word "'rights' as if it were a sacred word." Shireen felt this way because she

    a. had been without rights for so long.

    b. had been so focused on and worked so hard to come to America to attain her rights.

    c. believes that rights are so very important.

    d. all of the above

_d_ 9. The author was concerned that the sisters were

    a. were too interested in clothes and makeup.

    b. spent too much money at the mall.

    c. were ignoring their mother.

    d. would be taken advantage of by other Americans.

➤ **G.   BUILDING VOCABULARY**

➤**Context**

Using context and a dictionary, if necessary, determine the meaning of each word as it is used in the selection.

___c___ 1. amendment (paragraph 3)

    a. correction   c. additional comment

    b. question   d. formal statement

___c___ 2. makeshift (paragraph 10)

    a. dirty and dangerous   c. temporary and rough

    b. well-built and permanent   d. a place for refugees

___d___ 3. sporadically (paragraph 12)

    a. seldom

    b. unfailingly, reliably

    c. regularly over time

    d. at infrequent and irregular intervals

___c___ 4. defiantly (paragraph 17)

    a. casually

    b. quickly

    c. boldly, with an attitude of resistance

    d. superficially

___b___ 5. resilience (paragraph 27)

    a. the way a person copes with stress

    b. the ability to recover or adjust quickly and easily from a bad experience

    c. someone's attitude toward hard times

    d. courage, bravery

➤**Word Parts**

A REVIEW OF ROOTS, PREFIXES, AND SUFFIXES

CRED means *believe*

IN- means *not*

UN- means *not*

-ABLE refers to a *state, condition,* or *quality*

Using your knowledge of word parts and the review on the previous page, fill in the blanks in the following sentences.

1. If the display of stars is uncountable (paragraph 1) it is not able to be _____counted_____ or measured.

2. If someone is incredulous (paragraph 15) it means that he or she does not or is unwilling to _____believe_____ .

Unusual Words/Unusual Meanings

Use the meanings given below to write a sentence using the underlined word or phrase.

1. If a salesperson is <u>building</u> (paragraph 8) a clientele, she is increasing her base of customers and professional reputation.

   Your sentence: _____.

2. Groups that provide <u>relief</u> (paragraph 12) to victims of a natural disaster make sure those people receive the food, clothing, shelter, and other help that are necessary for them to get their lives back in order.

   Your sentence: _____.

➤ H.   SELECTING A LEARNING/STUDY STRATEGY

Suppose you were preparing to participate in a class discussion on the refugee experience in America. How could you use this reading to prepare for the discussion?

Make notes on the reading, paying particular attention to the problems this family experienced.

➤ I.   EXPLORING IDEAS THROUGH DISCUSSION AND WRITING

1. Discuss the issue of immigration. Who should be allowed to enter our country? Should our laws be stricter or more lenient?

2. What are the main immigrant groups in your community? What services are available to help them adjust? What sort of contact, if any, do you have with new people in our country?

3. Brainstorm a list of aspects of American life or culture that may have been unfamiliar to the sisters. (Pipher provides such a list later in the book, p. 90, and includes such things as what vitamins are, how to write a check, what elections are, and how to play cards.)

4. Discuss whether it would be beneficial for international students on your campus to have other students serve as culture brokers.

➤ **J.   BEYOND THE CLASSROOM TO THE WEB**

Take a virtual tour of a refugee camp at the Web site of the organization Doctors Without Borders at http://www.doctorswithoutborders.org/index.shtml.
Also visit Refugee Camp Tour at http://www.refugeecamp.org/.
How do these conditions compare with those described in the selection?

✔ **Tracking Your Progress**

Selection 19

Section	Number Correct		Score
A. Thesis and Main Idea (7 items)	_____	x 4	_____
B. Details (9 items)	_____	x 2	_____
C. Organization and Transitions (2 items)	_____	x 2	_____
E. Inferred Meanings (5 items)	_____	x 4	_____
F. Thinking Critically (9 items)	_____	x 2	_____
G. Vocabulary			
1. Context (5 items)	_____	x 2	_____
2. Word Parts (2 items)	_____	x 1	_____
	TOTAL SCORE		_____ %

CHECKING YOUR READING RATE

Words in Selection 19: 2,031

Finishing Time:	_____	_____	_____
	(hour)	(minutes)	(seconds)
Starting Time:	_____	_____	_____
	(hour)	(minutes)	(seconds)
Total Reading Time:		_____	_____
		(minutes)	(seconds)

Words Per Minute Score (page 737) _____ WPM

SELECTION 20

Profile of a Terrorist

Cindy C. Combs

This reading was taken from the book *Terrorism in the Twenty-First Century* by Cindy C. Combs, and offers information about the individuals behind terrorist attacks. Read it to find out what motivates different types of terrorists.

➤ PREVIEWING THE READING

Using the steps listed on page 5, preview the reading selection. When you have finished, complete the following items.

1. What is the topic of this selection? _____terrorists_____

2. List at least three questions you should be able to answer after reading this selection:

   a. What types of terrorists are there? _____

   b. What are the characteristics of terrorists? _____

   c. Why is it important to know about the different types of terrorists? _____

MAKING CONNECTIONS

How has terrorism affected your life? How did the events of September 11, 2001, change your perceptions of terrorism?

➤ READING TIP

As you read, highlight the types of terrorists and their characteristics.

CHECKING YOUR READING RATE

If you plan to compute your reading rate, be sure to record your starting time in the box at the end of the exercises before you begin reading.

Profile of a Terrorist

Nothing is easier than to denounce the evil doer; nothing is more difficult than to understand him.

Fyodor Dostoyevsky

ideologues
people who blindly follow a certain set of theories

1   Why do people become terrorists? Are they crazy? Are they thrill seekers? Are they religious fanatics? Are they **ideologues**? Is there any way to tell who is likely to become a terrorist?

2   This final question provides a clue as to why political scientists and government officials are particularly interested in the psychological factors relating to terrorism. If one could identify the traits most closely related to a willingness to use terrorist tactics, then one would be in a better position to predict, and prevent, the emergence of terrorist groups.

Three Types of Terrorists

3   Unfortunately, identifying such traits is not easy. Just as not all violence is terrorism, and not all revolutionaries are terrorists, not all persons who commit acts of terrorism are alike. Frederick Hacker suggested three categories of persons who commit terrorism: *crazies, criminals,* and *crusaders.* He notes that an individual carrying out a terrorist act is seldom "purely" one type or the other but that each type offers some insights into why an individual will resort to terrorism.

4   Understanding the individual who commits terrorism is vital, not only for humanitarian reasons, but also to decide how best to deal with those individuals *while they are engaged in terrorist acts.* From a law enforcement perspective, for example, it is important to appreciate the difference between a criminal and a crusading terrorist involved in a hostage-taking situation. Successful resolution of such a situation often hinges on understanding the mind of the individual perpetrating the crime.

5   Let us consider the three categories of terrorists suggested by Hacker: crazies, criminals, and crusaders. For the purposes of this study, we need to establish loose descriptions of these three types. Hacker offers some useful ideas on what is subsumed under each label. **Crazies,** he suggests, are *emotionally disturbed individuals who are driven to commit terrorism "by reasons of their own that often do not make sense to anybody else."*

6   **Criminals,** on the other hand, *perform terrorist acts for more easily understood reasons: personal gain.* Such individuals transgress the laws of society knowingly and, one assumes, in full possession of their faculties. Both their motives and their goals are usually clear, if still deplorable, to most of humanity.

7   This is not the case with the crusaders. These individuals commit terrorism for reasons that are often unclear both to themselves and to those witnessing the acts. Their ultimate goals are frequently even less understandable. Although such individuals are usually idealistically inspired, their idealism tends to be a rather mixed bag of half-understood philosophies. **Crusaders,** according to Hacker, *seek not personal gain, but prestige and power for a collective cause.* They commit terrorist acts in the belief "that they are serving a higher cause," in Hacker's assessment.

8   The distinction between criminals and crusaders with respect to terrorism needs some clarification. Clearly, when anyone breaks the law, as in the commission of a terrorist act, he or she becomes a criminal, regardless of the reason for the transgression. The distinction between criminal and crusader, though, is useful in understanding the differences in the motives and goals moving the person to commit the act.

A Trend Toward Crusaders

9   The majority of the individuals and groups carrying out terrorist acts in the world in the last decade of the twentieth and the beginning of the twenty-first century have been crusaders. This does not mean that there are not occasional instances in which individuals who, reacting to some real or perceived injury, decide to take a machine gun to the target of their anger or kidnap or destroy anyone in sight. Nor does it mean that there are not individual criminals and criminal organizations that engage in terrorist activities.

10   Nonetheless, the majority of individuals who commit modern terrorism are, or perceive themselves to be, crusaders. According to Hacker, the typical crusading terrorist appears to be normal, no matter how crazy his or her cause or how criminal the means he or she uses for this cause may seem. He or she is neither an idiot nor a fool, neither a coward nor a weakling. Instead, the crusading terrorist is frequently a professional, well trained, well prepared, and well disciplined in the habit of blind obedience to a cause.

Negotiating with Terrorists

sublime
lofty, highly
regarded

11   Table A indicates a few dramatic differences between the types of terrorists Hacker profiles. One is that crusaders are the least likely to negotiate a resolution to a crisis, both because such action can be viewed as a betrayal of a **sublime** cause and because there is little that the negotiator can offer, because neither personal gain nor safe passage out of the situation are particularly desired by true crusaders. Belief in the cause makes death not a penalty, but a path to reward and glory; therefore, the threat of death and destruction can have little punitive value. What can a police or military negotiator offer to a crusader to induce the release of hostages or the defusing of a bomb?

12   In terms of security devices and training, the profiles become even more vital. The events of September 11, 2001, illustrate dramatically the consequences of training and equipping for the wrong type of perpetrators. The pilots of airlines in the United States had been trained to respond to attempts to take over flights as hostage situations and thus were engaged in trying to keep the situation calm and to "talk down" the plane, to initiate a hostage release without violence. But the individuals engaged in the takeover were crusaders, not criminals or crazies, who did not plan to live through the incidents. Only the passengers on the flight that crashed in Pennsylvania were able to offer substantial resistance—perhaps in part because they had not been trained to assume that a peaceful resolution could be negotiated with hostage takers.

13   This does not suggest that the pilots and crew were not vigilant and did not make every effort to save the lives of the passengers. But because the profile they had been trained to respond to did not match that with which they were confronted, they were unable to respond successfully to the demands of the situation. Thus, inaccu-

TABLE A   Hacker's Typology of Terrorists

Type of Terrorist	Motive/Goal	Willing to Negotiate?	Expectation of Survival
Crazy	Clear only to perpetrator	Possible, but only if negotiator can understand motive and offer hope/alternatives	Strong, but not based on reality
Criminal	Personal gain/ profit	Usually, in return for profit and/or safe passage	Strong
Crusader	"Higher cause" (usually a blend of religious and political)	Seldom, because to do so could be seen as a betrayal of the cause	Minimal, because death offers reward in an afterlife

rate profiling in pilot training was a serious contributing factor to the sequence of events on that day.

14   To political scientists, as well as to military, police, and other security and intelligence units assigned the task of coping with terrorism, an understanding of the type of person likely to commit acts of terrorism is invaluable. As our understanding of a phenomenon increases, our ability to predict its behavior with some accuracy also increases. Thus, as we try to understand who terrorists are and what they are like, we should increase our ability to anticipate their behavior patterns, thereby increasing our ability to respond effectively and to prevent more often the launching of successful terrorist attacks.

► A. UNDERSTANDING THE THESIS AND OTHER MAIN IDEAS

Select the best answer.

___b___ 1. The central thesis of the selection is that

    a. governments need to provide better training for terrorist situations.

    b. understanding terrorists can help prevent terrorism.

    c. all terrorists fit into one of three categories.

    d. nothing can prevent terrorism.

___a___ 2. The author's primary purpose is to

    a. provide insight into what motivates terrorists and how terrorists act.

    b. criticize the government for not knowing enough about terrorism.

    c. compare our current understanding of terrorists with what we knew prior to September 11, 2001.

    d. evaluate current terrorist profile training.

___d___ 3. The focus of paragraph 3 is to

    a. describe in detail the three types of terrorists.

    b. explain why it is important to understand terrorists.

    c. comment on Hacker's typology.

    d. introduce Frederick Hacker's three categories.

___b___ 4. In paragraphs 5, 6, and 7, the author

    a. compares and contrasts the types of terrorists.

    b. gives Hacker's definitions of crazies, criminals, and crusaders.

    c. describes how to handle each type of terrorist.

    d. explains what law enforcement personnel know about each type of terrorist.

___c___ 5. The main idea of paragraph 11 is to

    a. summarize the contents of table A.

    b. use table A to support an idea.

    c. discuss in detail one of the elements of table A.

    d. explain all the information in table A.

___a___ 6. Which question is *not* answered in paragraph 12?

    a. What kind of terrorist training are pilots currently receiving?

    b. What type of terrorists were the pilots trained to respond to?

    c. What is the relationship between terrorist profiling and the September 11, 2001, attacks?

    d. What type of terrorists were involved in the September 11, 2001, attacks?

➤ B. IDENTIFYING DETAILS

Select the best answer.

___c___ 1. Which of the following in *not* a type of terrorist as described by Hacker?

    a. crusader

    b. crazy

    c. professional

    d. criminal

_a_ 2. According to the reading, it is important to understand the types of terrorists in order to

a. deal with them effectively.

b. write articles about them.

c. identify children who might grow up to be terrorists.

d. keep government files on them.

_c_ 3. All of the following are characteristics of Hacker's crusader type of terrorists *except*

a. They are acting on behalf of a "higher cause."

b. Death as a penalty is not feared.

c. They are always religiously motivated.

d. Negotiation is seen as a betrayal to the cause.

_a_ 4. The motive of the crazy type of terrorist

a. may only be understood by the terrorist himself/herself.

b. is clearly defined.

c. is not important to the negotiation process.

d. almost always has a political basis.

_b_ 5. According to the reading, the passengers on the flight that crashed in Pennsylvania

a. understood that they had crusader terrorists aboard their flight.

b. did not try to reach a peaceful resolution with the terrorists.

c. understood the terrorists' motives.

d. knew more about handling terrorists than the pilots.

► C. RECOGNIZING METHODS OF ORGANIZATION AND TRANSITIONS

Fill in the blanks.

1. The author uses one primary organizational pattern. ___Classification___ is used to divide terrorists into categories. Transitional words or phrases used for this pattern are

Paragraph 3: Frederick Hacker suggested three categories

Paragraph 5: Let us consider the three categories of terrorists

2. The author also uses ___comparison and contrast___ to show the similarities and differences among the types of terrorists. Transitional words or phrases used for this type of pattern are

Paragraph 6: on the other hand

Paragraph 8: the distinction between

➤ D.   REVIEWING AND ORGANIZING IDEAS: MAPPING

Complete the following map by filling in the missing words.

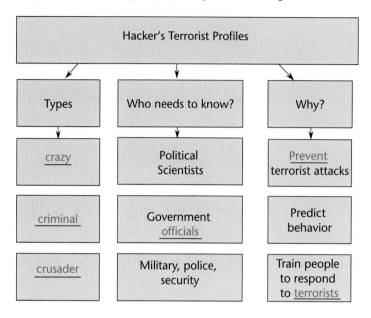

Hacker's Terrorist Profiles		
Types	**Who needs to know?**	**Why?**
crazy	Political Scientists	Prevent terrorist attacks
criminal	Government officials	Predict behavior
crusader	Military, police, security	Train people to respond to terrorists

➤ E.   FIGURING OUT INFERRED MEANINGS

Indicate whether each statement is true (T) or false (F).

__F__ 1. Terrorists are born, not made.

__T__ 2. Frederick Hacker is an expert on terrorist types.

__T__ 3. The "crazies" type of terrorists are mentally ill.

__F__ 4. It can be inferred that terrorism is the problem the U.S. government faces this century.

__T__ 5. Some terrorists are not afraid to die.

➤ F.   THINKING CRITICALLY

Select the best answer.

__c__ 1. The author supports the central thesis of "Profile of a Terrorist" primarily by

   a. citing statistics.

   b. describing a personal experience.

   c. giving expert theory.

   d. offering reasons.

_a___ 2. The tone of the selection can best be described as

    a. informative and hopeful.

    b. factual and cynical.

    c. serious and outraged.

    d. tragic and depressing.

_d___ 3. The author begins the reading with a series of questions in order to

    a. get the reader thinking about what makes a terrorist.

    b. briefly mention the basic terrorist types.

    c. provide an interesting and engaging start.

    d. all of the above

_d___ 4. In paragraph 10, the author suggests that crusader terrorists

    a. are less common than other types.

    b. are the only type of terrorist we should worry about.

    c. do not think they are committing a crime.

    d. may not look or act like terrorists.

_b___ 5. Table A is included primarily in order to

    a. add a great deal of new information to the reading.

    b. compare and contrast the terrorist types in a simple, clear way.

    c. have the reader refer to it several times throughout the reading.

    d. stimulate further discussion.

_d___ 6. The events of September 11, 2001, are mentioned in order to

    a. offer praise for the passengers who showed resistance.

    b. evaluate the training of the pilots.

    c. remind the readers of a tragic event involving terrorists.

    d. give an example of a time when proper terrorist profile training would have been useful.

➤ **G. BUILDING VOCABULARY**

➤ **Context**

Using context and a dictionary, if necessary, determine the meaning of each word as it is used in the selection.

_d___ 1. vital (paragraph 4)

    a. prerequisite   c. inherent

    b. logical   d. essential

___a___ 2. perpetrating (paragraph 4)

      a. committing

      b. entrusting

      c. perpetuating

      d. delivering

___b___ 3. faculties (paragraph 6)

      a. teachers

      b. mental abilities

      c. physical skills

      d. qualifications

___c___ 4. deplorable (paragraph 6)

      a. weird

      b. overwhelming

      c. hateful

      d. beneficial

___c___ 5. resolution (paragraph 11)

      a. cause

      b. distinction

      c. solution

      d. motive

___c___ 6. punitive (paragraph 11)

      a. correcting

      b. causing fame

      c. involving a punishment

      d. frightening

___a___ 7. vigilant (paragraph 13)

      a. very alert, watching for danger

      b. awake and lively

      c. brave, courageous

      d. intelligent and fast-thinking

➤ Word Parts

> **A REVIEW OF PREFIXES**
> **DE-** means *away, from*
> **TRANS-** means *across, over*

Use the review of prefixes above to fill in the blanks in the following sentences.

1. If you *transgress* (paragraph 6) a law, you go _____across_____ established legal boundaries and commit a crime.

2. To *defuse* (paragraph 11) a bomb, you take _____away_____ its harmfulness by removing its detonating device.

➤ Unusual Words/Unusual Meanings

Use the context of each sentence to discover the meaning of the underlined word or phrase and to write your own sentence.

1. When a job applicant possess a <u>mixed bag</u> (paragraph 7) of qualifications, she can do an assortment of tasks that may not be related to each other.

   Your sentence: _____.

2. People who follow a leader with <u>blind obedience</u> (paragraph 10) will unquestioningly do and believe what the leader tells them.

   Your sentence: _____.

➤ H. SELECTING A LEARNING/STUDY STRATEGY

Select the best answer.

    ___d___ 1. What part of the reading could best be expanded and used as a study aid?

        a. paragraph 1

        b. paragraph 4

        c. paragraph 12

        d. Table A

➤ I. EXPLORING IDEAS THROUGH DISCUSSION AND WRITING

1. Evaluate the government's role in protecting us against terrorism. What should our leaders be doing? Are they doing enough? How far should they go in areas such as airport security and immigration?

2. Write a few paragraphs describing your day on September 11, 2001. Be sure to include factual information as well as your emotional responses to the events.

3. Discuss Hacker's categories of terrorists. How useful do you think they are?

➤ J. BEYOND THE CLASSROOM TO THE WEB

Visit the Patterns of Global Terrorism 2002 report on the Web site of the U.S. Department of State at **http://www.state.gov/s/ct/rls/pgtrpt/2002/html/**. *Explore sections of the report. Does the number of terrorist groups surprise you? How do you think Hacker's typology fits in with the information contained in this report?*

✔ Tracking Your Progress

Selection 20

Section	Number Correct		Score
A. Thesis and Main Idea (6 items)	_____	x 4	_____
B. Details (5 items)	_____	x 3	_____
C. Organization and Transitions (6 items)	_____	x 1	_____
E. Inferred Meanings (5 items)	_____	x 3	_____
F. Thinking Critically (6 items)	_____	x 4	_____
G. Vocabulary			
1. Context (7 items)	_____	x 2	_____
2. Word Parts (2 items)	_____	x 1	_____
	TOTAL SCORE	_____	%

CHECKING YOUR READING RATE

Words in Selection 20: 1,238

Finishing Time:	_____	_____	_____
	(hour)	(minutes)	(seconds)
Starting Time:	_____	_____	_____
	(hour)	(minutes)	(seconds)
Total Reading Time:		_____	_____
		(minutes)	(seconds)

Words Per Minute Score (page 737) _____ WPM

SELECTION 21

American Communities: Los Alamos, New Mexico

John Mack Faragher et al.

This reading was taken from the book titled *Out of Many: A History of the American People*. It is part of a chapter on World War II (1941–1945) and describes the formation of a war-related community.

> ### PREVIEWING THE READING

Using the steps listed on page 5, preview the reading selection. When you have finished, answer the following questions.

1. What is the topic of this selection? <u>the scientific community at Los Alamos</u>

2. What do you already know about the Los Alamos community as described in the selection?

   a. <u>It is situated in a remote area in New Mexico.</u>

   b. <u>There is conflict between the scientists and the army.</u>

   c. <u>Secrecy was important.</u>

   d. <u>The community included scientists as well as their families.</u>

MAKING CONNECTIONS

What communities are you a part of? What unites these communities? What divides them?

> ### READING TIP

As you read, make notes in three categories—scientists, government, nation—to keep track of the characteristics, trends, and actions of each of these groups.

CHECKING YOUR READING RATE

If you plan to compute your reading rate, be sure to record your starting time in the box at the end of the exercises before you begin reading.

American Communities: Los Alamos, New Mexico

Mountain War Time
same as Daylight Saving Time— started during World War I to conserve fuel by taking advantage of extended daylight hours; President Roosevelt invoked MWT again during World War II

1   On Monday, July 16, 1945, at 5:29:45 A.M., **Mountain War Time**, the first atomic bomb exploded in a brilliant flash visible in three states. Within just seven minutes, a huge, multicolored, bell-shaped cloud soared 38,000 feet into the atmosphere and threw back a blanket of smoke and soot to the earth below. The heat generated by the blast was four times the temperature at the center of the sun,* and the light produced rivaled that of nearly twenty suns. Within a second, the giant fireball hit the ground, ripping out a crater a half-mile wide and fusing the surrounding sand into glass. The shock wave blew out windows in houses more than 200 miles away. Within a mile of the blast, every living creature was killed—squirrels, rabbits, snakes, plants, and insects—and the smells of death persisted for nearly a month.

2   Very early that morning, Ruby Wilkening had driven to a nearby mountain ridge, where she joined several other women waiting for the blast. Wilkening worried about her husband, a physicist, who was already at the test site. No one knew exactly what to expect, not even the scientists who developed the bomb.

3   The Wilkenings were part of a unique community of scientists who had been marshaled for war. President Franklin D. Roosevelt, convinced by Albert Einstein and other physicists that the Nazis might successfully develop an atomic bomb, had inaugurated a small nuclear research program. Shortly after the United States entered World War II the scientists reported that, with sufficient support, they could produce an atomic weapon in time to affect the course of the conflict. The program, known as the Manhattan Project, was directed by the Army Corps of Engineers. By December 1942 a team headed by italian-born Nobel Prize–winner Enrico Fermi had produced the first chain reaction in uranium under the University of Chicago's football stadium. Now the mission was to build a new, formidable weapon of war, the atomic bomb.

4   The government moved the key researchers and their families to Los Alamos in the remote and sparsely populated Sangre de Cristo Mountains of New Mexico, a region of soaring peaks, ancient Indian ruins, modern **Pueblos**, and villages occupied by the descendants of the earliest Spanish settlers. The scientists and their families arrived in March 1943. They occupied a former boys' preparatory school until new houses could be built. Some families doubled up in rugged log cabins or nearby ranches. Telephone service to the outside world was poor, and the mountain roads were so rough that changing flat tires became a tiresome but familiar routine. Construction of new quarters proceeded slowly, causing nasty disputes between the "long-hairs" (scientists) and the "plumbers" (army engineers) in charge of the grounds. Despite the chaos, outstanding American and European scientists eagerly signed up. Most were young, with an average age of twenty-seven, and quite a few were recently married. Many couples began their families at Los Alamos, producing a total of nearly a thousand babies between 1943 and 1949.

Pueblos
Native American villages of the southwestern United States

5   The scientists and their families formed an exceptionally close-knit community united by secrecy as well as antagonism toward the army. Most annoying was the

---

* Temperature at the core of the sun is about 28,000,000 °F.

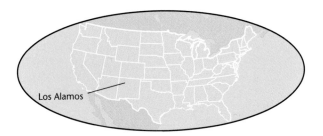

military atmosphere. Homes and laboratories were cordoned off by barbed wire and guarded by military police. Everything, from linens to food packaging, was stamped with the words *Government Issue.* Security personnel followed the scientists whenever they left Los Alamos. The scientists' homes were wired for sound, and several scientists were reprimanded for discussing their work with their wives. All outgoing mail was censored. Well-known scientists commonly worked under aliases—Fermi became "Eugene Farmer"—and code names were used for such terms as atom, bomb, and uranium fission. Children registered without surnames at nearby public schools. Only a group thoroughly committed to the war effort could accept such restrictions on their personal liberty.

6   A profound feeling of urgency motivated the research team, which included refugees from Nazi Germany and Fascist Italy and a large proportion of Jews. The leadership of California physicist J. Robert Oppenheimer created a scientific élan that offset the military style of commanding general Leslie Groves. Just thirty-eight, slightly built, and deeply emotional, "Oppie" personified the idealism that helped the community of scientists overcome whatever moral reservations they held about placing such an ominous weapon in the hands of the government.

7   Once a week Oppenheimer called together the heads of the various technical divisions to discuss their work in round-table conferences. From May to November 1944 the key issue was testing the bomb. Many scientists feared that the test might fail, and, with the precious plutonium scattered and lost, the entire project might be discredited. But as plutonium production increased, the Los Alamos team agreed to test "the gadget" on a site 160 miles away.

8   The unprecedented scientific mobilization at Los Alamos mirrored changes occurring throughout American society as the nation rallied behind the war effort. In addition to the 16 million men and women who left home for military service, nearly as many moved to take advantage of wartime jobs. Several states in the South and Southwest experienced huge surges in population. California alone grew by 2 million people, a large proportion from Mexico. Many broad social changes—such as the massive economic expansion in the West, the erosion of farm tenancy among black people in the South and white people in Appalachia, and the increased employment of married women—accelerated during the war. Although reluctant to enter the war, the United States emerged from under the weight of the Great Depression and became the leading superpower. The events of World War II, eroding old communities and creating new ones such as Los Alamos, transformed nearly all aspects of American society.

élan
enthusiasm, vigor

farm tenancy
renting out farm land for money, labor, or a portion of the crops grown on the land

Appalachia
the area of the Appalachian Mountains, a range in eastern North America from southern Quebec to central Alabama

Great Depression
A period of difficult economic times in the U.S. from 1929 to 1939

> ### A.   UNDERSTANDING THE THESIS AND OTHER MAIN IDEAS

Select the best answer.

___a___ 1. The central thesis of the selection is that

    a. World War II caused a great deal of change in the social fabric of America, including the development of new communities.

    b. the atomic bomb was created by dedicated, intelligent individuals.

    c. our government regularly keeps secrets from the public.

    d. close-knit communities such as Los Alamos are rare.

___b___ 2. The author's primary purpose is to

    a. explain how the atom bomb was built.

    b. describe the development of the Los Alamos scientific community.

    c. comment on the government's relationship with scientists.

    d. prove that planned communities can be successful.

___c___ 3. The main topic of paragraph 1 is the

    a. speed of the explosion.

    b. amount of destruction the atom bomb caused.

    c. explosion of the first atom bomb.

    d. temperature of the sun.

___a___ 4. The main idea of paragraph 3 is best expressed in

    a. the first sentence.   c. the third sentence.

    b. the second sentence.   d. the fourth sentence.

___a___ 5. The focus of paragraph 4 is the

    a. living conditions at Los Alamos.

    b. history of the area.

    c. construction schedule.

    d. conflict between the scientists and army engineers.

___a___ 6. Overall, the creation of Los Alamos

    a. is an example of changes in American society brought about by World War II.

    b. unified the scientific community against the government.

    c. has gone pretty much unnoticed in history.

    d. brought about changes in the way the government deals with researchers.

➤ **B.   IDENTIFYING DETAILS**

Select the best answer.

___c___ 1. The test bomb killed everything
   a. within 200 miles.

   b. outside a half-mile-wide crater.

   c. within one mile.

   d. in three states.

___b___ 2. Ruby Wilkening
   a. was a physicist.

   b. was worried about her husband.

   c. opposed the test.

   d. became ill from exposure.

___d___ 3. Who first feared that the Nazis may have developed an atomic
          bomb?
   a. Enrico Fermi

   b. the Army Corps of Engineers

   c. President Franklin D. Roosevelt

   d. Albert Einstein and other scientists

___b___ 4. In general the scientists who went to Los Alamos were
   a. antiwar activists.

   b. young.

   c. Pulitzer Prize winners.

   d. from other countries.

___b___ 5. The military subjected the families to all of the following *except*
   a. censorship of mail.   c. wire-tapping of homes.

   b. surprise home searches.   d. secrecy.

___a___ 6. Which of the following was *not* part of the effort to keep the project
          a secret?
   a. not allowing refugee scientists from enemy countries to
      participate

   b. calling it the Manhattan Project

   c. picking a remote spot for the researchers to live and work

   d. using code names and aliases

_b_ 7. How did Oppenheimer regularly communicate with the project managers?

    a. e-mail

    b. weekly meetings

    c. by written messages delivered by military personnel

    d. through spy cameras and tape recorders

_d_ 8. Which of the following social trends was *not* mentioned in the reading?

    a. more women in the workforce

    b. population surges

    c. people relocating to find work

    d. increasing divorce rates

C.   RECOGNIZING METHODS OF ORGANIZATION AND TRANSITIONS

Select the best answer.

_c_ 1. What is the organizational pattern used to show the relationship between World War II and community building and changes in society?

    a. classification

    b. addition

    c. cause and effect

    d. comparison and contrast

_d_ 2. What pattern is used to organize information in paragraphs 1 and 3?

    a. listing

    b. comparison and contrast

    c. classification

    d. chronological order

D.   REVIEWING AND ORGANIZING IDEAS: SUMMARIZING

Complete the following time line of the events described in the selection.

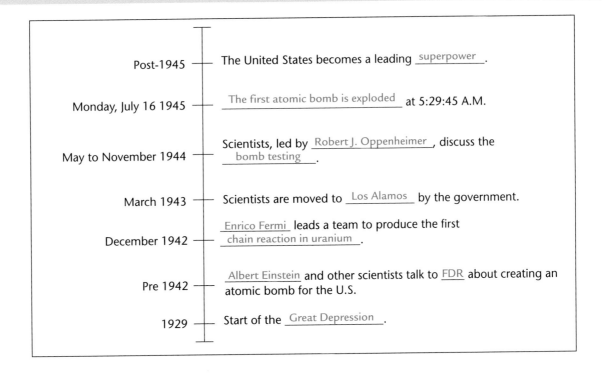

Post-1945 — The United States becomes a leading _superpower_ .

Monday, July 16 1945 — _The first atomic bomb is exploded_ at 5:29:45 A.M.

May to November 1944 — Scientists, led by _Robert J. Oppenheimer_ , discuss the _bomb testing_ .

March 1943 — Scientists are moved to _Los Alamos_ by the government.

December 1942 — _Enrico Fermi_ leads a team to produce the first _chain reaction in uranium_ .

Pre 1942 — _Albert Einstein_ and other scientists talk to _FDR_ about creating an atomic bomb for the U.S.

1929 — Start of the _Great Depression_ .

➤ **E. FIGURING OUT INFERRED MEANINGS**

Indicate whether each statement is true (T) or false (F).

_F_ 1. The atomic bomb exploded in 1945 was less powerful than the nuclear weapons the U.S. now possesses.

_T_ 2. The researchers and their families were isolated from the outside world.

_T_ 3. The women watching the blast (paragraph 2) were more than a mile away from the test site.

_F_ 4. Oppenheimer mediated between the scientists and the army engineers.

_T_ 5. World War II was a turning point in the history of American foreign policy.

➤ **F. THINKING CRITICALLY**

Select the best answer.

_a_ 1. The author supports the central thesis of "American Communities" primarily by

    a. reporting facts.   c. making comparisons.

    b. citing personal experience.   d. quoting statistics.

___c___ 2. The tone of the selection can best be described as

    a. bitter.

    b. excited.

    c. informative .

    d. sympathetic.

___c___ 3. Of the following statements from the reading, which is an opinion?

    a. "The Wilkenings were part of a unique community of scientists who had been marshaled for war." (paragraph 3)

    b. "Most were young, with an average age of twenty-seven, and quite a few were recently married." (paragraph 4)

    c. "Only a group thoroughly committed to the war effort could accept such restrictions on their personal liberty." (paragraph 5)

    d. "Oppenheimer called together heads of the various technical divisions . . ." (paragraph 7)

___b___ 4. The author included Ruby Wilkenings in the reading in order to

    a. recognize her contribution to the project.

    b. provide a personal story to make the reading seem real and interesting.

    c. comment on the attitudes toward the researchers' families.

    d. give background information.

___a___ 5. The author describes the difficult living and working conditions at Los Alamos in order to

    a. emphasize the researchers' commitment.

    b. criticize the government.

    c. sympathize with the wives and children.

    d. examine the factors that led to the creation of the bomb.

___d___ 6. In the final paragraph, the author

    a. explains how the war caused widespread social changes.

    b. shows how the experience at Los Alamos was like the experiences of many other areas of the country.

    c. lists the experiences of other groups of Americans.

    d. all of the above

➤ **G.   BUILDING VOCABULARY**

➤ **Context**

Using context and a dictionary, if necessary, determine the meaning of each word as it is used in the selection.

__a__ 1. marshaled (paragraph 3)

    a. gathered together   c. commanded

    b. escorted   d. approached

__a__ 2. inaugurated (paragraph 3)

    a. brought about the start of   c. discovered

    b. fabricated   d. imagined

__a__ 3. formidable (paragraph 3)

    a. causing fear or dread   c. surprising

    b. amazing   d. unequaled

__d__ 4. antagonism (paragraph 5)

    a. indifference, lack of concern c. annoyance

    b. fearfulness   d. opposition, hostility

__c__ 5. reprimanded (paragraph 5)

    a. warned   c. officially scolded

    b. punished   d. blamed

__c__ 6. ominous (paragraph 6)

    a. fated   c. menacing, threatening

    b. important   d. destructive

➤ **Word Parts**

A REVIEW OF PREFIXES AND SUFFIXES

PRE- means *before*

UN- means *not*

-EE means *one who*

Use the review of prefixes and suffixes above to fill in the blanks in the following sentences.

1. If you attend a college *preparatory* (paragraph 4) school, you are attending an educational institution whose mission is to prepare you for college ___before___ you get there.

2. A *refugee* (paragraph 6) is ___one who___ seeks refuge from oppression.

3. An *unprecedented* (paragraph 8) event is one that has not happened ___before___.

➤ **Unusual Words/Unusual Meanings**

Use the meanings given below to write a sentence using the underlined word or phrase.

1. A <u>close-knit</u> (paragraph 5) family is one that is tied together by strong relationships.

   Your sentence: _____.

2. If a protest at your school <u>mirrored</u> (paragraph 8) the attitudes of college students across the country, then it reflected what other students were thinking.

   Your sentence: _____.

➤ **H.   SELECTING A LEARNING/STUDY STRATEGY**

Select the best answer.

___b___   This reading contains many facts about life in Los Alamos during WWII. What would be the best way to learn these facts?

   a. visualize Los Alamos

   b. put the facts into outline form

   c. read the facts over and over

   d. summarize the reading

➤ **I.   EXPLORING IDEAS THROUGH DISCUSSION AND WRITING**

1. The author begins the selection with a description of the test explosion. Discuss the effect this technique has on the reader. What if this information had been left out?

2. Do you think some of the scientists had "moral reservations" about the Manhattan Project? Do you think scientists today have similar reservations about working on nuclear weapons projects?

3. Write an essay about governmental invasion of privacy. Under what circumstances, if any, should the government be allowed to wiretap citizens' homes, track their whereabouts, and so forth?

➤ **J.   BEYOND THE CLASSROOM TO THE WEB**

Visit the home page of the Los Alamos National Laboratory at **http://www.lanl.gov/worldview/**. *What projects are being worked on these days?*

Find the information on life at the laboratory. How do the living and working conditions appear to be today?

Also, visit this online paper about the Manhattan Project. The appendix at **http://www.me.utexas.edu/~uer/manhattan/people.html** *gives brief biographical information about "Key Figures" in the project. Can you find the people mentioned in the reading? What additional information did you learn?*

✔ Tracking Your Progress

Selection 21

Section	Number Correct		Score
A. Thesis and Main Idea (6 items)	_____	x 4	_____
B. Details (8 items)	_____	x 3	_____
C. Organization and Transitions (2 items)	_____	x 2	_____
E. Inferred Meanings (5 items)	_____	x 3	_____
F. Thinking Critically (6 items)	_____	x 3	_____
G. Vocabulary			
1. Context (6 items)	_____	x 2	_____
2. Word Parts (3 items)	_____	x 1	_____
	TOTAL SCORE	_____ %	

CHECKING YOUR READING RATE

Words in Selection 21: 968

Finishing Time:	_____	_____	_____
	(hour)	(minutes)	(seconds)
Starting Time:	_____	_____	_____
	(hour)	(minutes)	(seconds)
Total Reading Time:		_____	_____
		(minutes)	(seconds)

Words Per Minute Score (page 737) _____ WPM

18 Business/Advertising/Economics

Business is a diverse field that includes business management, marketing, finance, statistics, retailing, information systems, and organizational behavior. In general, business is concerned with the production and sale of economic goods and services. All of us are in contact with businesses on a daily basis. When you stop for gas, buy a sandwich, or pick up the telephone, you are involved in a business transaction. In "Four Simple Words That Guarantee the Job of Your Dreams," you will learn how to pursue a career that will bring satisfaction as well as a paycheck. Studying business can also make you a savvy, better-informed consumer. When you read "McDonald's Makes a Lot of People Angry for a Lot of Different Reasons," you will learn how McDonald's, a popular fast food chain, has not acted as a responsible business leader in the opinion of the authors. Business courses can help you make career decisions and discover a wide range of employment opportunities. Business courses also examine the issue of ethnic and cultural diversity since today's workforce consists of individuals from a variety of cultural and ethnic groups. As you read "Hispanic Americans: A Growing Market Segment," you will discover how advertisers and media corporations are targeting the growing Hispanic population in the United States.

Use the following techniques for reading in business.

TIPS FOR READING IN BUSINESS/ ADVERTISING/ ECONOMICS

- **Focus on process.** Many courses in business examine how things work and how things get done. In "Hispanic Americans: A Growing Market Segment" you will see how advertisers have analyzed Hispanic cultural values and adjusted their advertising accordingly. In "Four Simple Words That Guarantee the Job of Your Dreams," you will discover how to find a rewarding job.

- **Focus on the theme of globalization.** Growing numbers of U.S. businesses are doing business with firms in other countries and are competing in foreign markets. In "McDonald's Makes a Lot of People Angry for a Lot of Different Reasons," you will see that McDonald's has become a global corporation.

- **Consider ethical decision-making and social responsibility.** The application of moral standards to business activities and operations is of increasing importance in the field of business. Issues of honesty, fairness, environmental safety, and public health are often discussed in business courses. In "McDonald's Makes a Lot of People Angry for a Lot of Different Reasons," the authors suggest that McDonald's has acted irresponsibly in a number of different areas.

SELECTION 22

Four Simple Words That Guarantee the Job of Your Dreams

Martha I. Finney

This article first appeared in *Career Magazine* in 1999. Read it to discover how to find the ideal job.

➤ **PREVIEWING THE READING**

Using the steps listed on page 5, preview the reading selection. When you have finished, answer the following questions.

1. What are the "four simple words" from the title? ___right time/right place___

2. The topic of the reading is _____jobs_____.

 MAKING CONNECTIONS

With a classmate, discuss what you know about how to find a good job.

➤ **READING TIP**

As you read, highlight tips that will help you find the ideal job.

 CHECKING YOUR READING RATE

If you plan to compute your reading rate, be sure to record your starting time in the box at the end of the exercises before you begin reading.

Four Simple Words That Guarantee the Job of Your Dreams

1   Actually, these are also the most exasperating words. Say you meet up with a friend who just landed the all-time best job: the responsibilities suit your friend perfectly; the hours are right; the company is congenial; and there's a future in the position, complete with raises and promotions. So, you ask, how did you get that job? The answer, always delivered in an infuriatingly cagey, off-hand sort of way:

2   I dunno, right time/right place, I guess.

3   Right time/right place. That magic formula is about as elusive as true love.

4   I had a right time/right place experience once. Although I wouldn't recommend that anyone else duplicate this particular incident. Especially these days. I interviewed

Cousteau Society
an organization
devoted to
continuing the
work begun by
underwater pioneer
Jacques Cousteau

for my first real adult job in my underwear. And I landed a job as a writer for the **Cousteau Society**.

5   Let me explain: I was working as a lowly, underpaid, over-abused receptionist for a nasty public relations firm in Manhattan. About the only perk that came with the job is that sometimes the owners would receive boxes of designer clothes . . . samples, they were. And we could buy them cheap. So now and then I would take a bundle into the ladies room and try them on. But to get to the ladies room, I'd always pass the closed door of our neighboring office, the Cousteau Society. And I would sigh. Saving whales seemed much more up my alley than promoting fiction about fashion. And I bet the people inside were nice, too.

6   One day I was in the ladies' room, in my scivvies, about to try on some ridiculous new fashion idea. And in walked the woman who would become my future boss. Just like in **Ally McBeal**. By the sinks, in between the flushes, we got an interview done. And I got the job as member correspondent. It was a cool job, complete with a desk on the 32nd floor right by a gigantic window overlooking the East River, with a view of the 59th Street Bridge.

Ally McBeal
a popular
contemporary
television program
about the life of
a young female
lawyer named
Ally McBeal

7   That was about the coolest way I ever got a job, except for the time I made my interviewer cry by telling him the storyline of the **Twilight Zone** episode that aired the night before. But that's a different story.

8   So how do you get to right time/right place (besides standing around in your underwear)? There must be a secret. Yes, there is. And here it is, another four words: Do what you love.

Twilight Zone
a popular
television
program from the
1960s featuring
a new mystery/
science fiction
plot each week

9   That's it, it's that simple. So, if it's that simple, why doesn't everyone do it? I have my theories. But it boils down to our tendencies to put our marketable skills ahead of what poet William Blake called our divine spark—that passion, that interest, that cause that ignites our eyes.

10   Somewhere along the line we were trained that marketable skills and divine spark were mutually exclusive. Don't mix work with pleasure, and all that rot. Well, we find ourselves at the right place at the right time when we combine our skills with our love of life. It's in the fun where we discover the part of ourselves that has wings. And wouldn't it be nice to be able to take our wings to work?

11   Unrealistic, you say? Just about every activity that brings us joy has an industry that supports it. Snowboarding, eating chocolate, going to the movies, even sex. Whatever you love to do, there's a job description with your name on it.

12   Take sailing, for instance. (Indulge me here. I live in one of the most beautiful sailing grounds on the planet. But I'm 1,000 miles away and I'm homesick at the moment.) Say you loved to sail while you were a kid. But you gave it up in favor of investing time to learn a profession. And now you're as far away from that old life as you could possibly be. And there's a hollow in your heart that used to be filled by days under the mainsail.

cartographer
mapmaker

meteorologist
one who studies
and reports on
the weather

13   Okay, what professions support sailing? Racing, yes. Sailboat delivery, yes. Sailing instructor, yes. Okay, let's stretch our imaginations just a little bit. How about: chef, physician, economist, computer programmer, chemist, **cartographer, meteorologist,** club manager, construction worker, secretary, writer, advertising executive, physical therapist, statistician.

14   See what I mean? All these professionals can find a lucrative career in the sailing world if they don't lose sight of the fact they love the sailing world. So they hang out. And they make friends. And one day they're in the right place at the right time.

15   Here's how indulging your passions makes you happy and gets you at the right place at the right time:

- You spend time and work in an environment that fascinates you.
- You spend time with kindred spirits who share your values and mission. They're your playmates and they like you. How mentally healthy is that?
- You become a learning sponge. And you never obsolete yourself. You would never pass up the chance to learn something new if it had something to do with your passion.
- Your network of contacts will be gigantic and it will cross all the hierarchical barriers that you typically find in a strictly corporate relationship.
- Your reputation will precede you everywhere you go.
- You'll know who the up-and-comers are . . . the ones behind you, the ones you will help bring up through the ranks.

16   Even if your next job is found through the classifieds or computer listings, the depth of experience you get by indulging your loves will make you stand out from among the other, more generic, candidates. Say you're a chemist with a passion for sailboat racing. And Gore-Tex announces an opening for a chemist to develop formulas for high-performance sailcloth. Who do you think they're going to pick?

17   Four words to guarantee you the job of your dreams: Right place/right time.

18   Four more words to unlock that marvelous coincidence: Do what you love.

➤ A.   UNDERSTANDING THE THESIS AND OTHER MAIN IDEAS

Select the best answer.

___d___ 1. The central thesis of "Four Simple Words" is that

   a. most jobs are not meant to be fun.

   b. the "perfect" job is impossible to find.

   c. the demands of most jobs leave no time for the pursuit of hobbies.

   d. it is important and possible to find a job that you love.

___c___ 2. The author's primary purpose in "Four Simple Words" is to

   a. describe her job search.

   b. report employment trends.

   c. urge readers to find work that they love.

   d. persuade employers to make jobs more interesting.

___a___ 3. The main idea of paragraph 5 is that the

    a. author was unhappy in her job as a receptionist.

    b. author enjoyed all the perks that came with her job.

    c. author wanted to save whales.

    d. owners of the public relations firm received clothing samples.

___b___ 4. The topic of paragraph 12 is

    a. the best sailing locations.   c. sailing as a child.

    b. a passion for sailing.   d. learning a profession.

___d___ 5. According to the author, indulging your passions allows you to

    a. spend time in an interesting environment with people you like.

    b. be happy while improving your chances of getting a job you love.

    c. widen your network of contacts outside a corporate setting.

    d. do all of the above.

B.   IDENTIFYING DETAILS

Indicate whether each statement is true (T) or false (F).

___F___ 1. The author currently works as a receptionist in a public relations firm.

___T___ 2. The author was interviewed in a restroom for her job at the Cousteau Society.

___F___ 3. The author believes that you shouldn't mix work with pleasure.

___T___ 4. When she wrote this article, the author was 1,000 miles away from home.

___T___ 5. The author's office at the Cousteau Society had a view of the East River.

C.   RECOGNIZING METHODS OF ORGANIZATION AND TRANSITIONS

➤ Methods of Organization

Select the answer that best completes the following statements.

___d___ 1. In paragraph 13, the author describes many professions that support a love of sailing. The type of organizational pattern used in this paragraph is ___enumeration___ because the author ___lists___ the information.

    a. cause and effect . . . relates

    b. definition . . . defines

    c. time sequence . . . dates

    d. enumeration . . . lists

_____a_____ 2. In paragraphs 5 and 6, the author describes her interview for the Cousteau Society. The type of organizational pattern used in these paragraphs is

    a. time sequence.

    b. comparison and contrast.

    c. definition.

    d. cause and effect.

➤ **Transitional Words and Phrases**
Complete the following statements by filling in the blanks.

3. In paragraph 5, the phrase ____Let me explain____ indicates that an explanation is to follow.

4. In paragraph 12, the phrase ____for instance____ indicates that the paragraph contains an example.

➤ **D.   REVIEWING AND ORGANIZING IDEAS: PARAPHRASING**

Complete the following paraphrase of paragraphs 1–2 by filling in the missing words and phrases.

Paragraphs 1–2: These ____four____ words are simple but ____exasperating____. Assume you run into a ____friend____ who has just gotten the ____best job____, with ____responsibilities____ that perfectly ____suit____ him. The job features excellent ____hours____ at a ____congenial____ company, and the job has a ____future____ that includes raises and ____promotions____. When you ask ____how____ your friend got the ____job____, the ____reply____, which is given in an irritatingly casual way, is that your friend doesn't know but ____guesses____ he was in the ____right place____ at the ____right time____.

➤ **E.   FIGURING OUT INFERRED MEANINGS**

Each of the following underlined words has a strong positive or negative connotation (shade of meaning). Make inferences by indicating whether the word creates a positive (P) or negative (N) image for the reader.

____P____ 1. "...the Job of Your <u>Dreams</u>" (title)

____N____ 2. "I was working as a <u>lowly</u> ... receptionist" (paragraph 5)

____N____ 3. "... about to try on some <u>ridiculous</u> new fashion idea" (paragraph 6)

____P____ 4. "That was about the <u>coolest</u> way I ever got a job ..." (paragraph 7)

__P__ 5. "... it's that <u>simple</u>." (paragraph 9)

__N__ 6. "... and all that <u>rot</u>." (paragraph 10)

__P__ 7. "... the part of ourselves that has <u>wings</u>." (paragraph 10)

__N__ 8. "And there's a <u>hollow</u> in your heart ..." (paragraph 12)

__P__ 9. "They're your <u>playmates</u> ..." (paragraph 15)

➤ **F. THINKING CRITICALLY**

Select the best answer.

__a__ 1. One way the author supports her ideas is by
   a. describing her personal experience.

   b. reporting statistics.

   c. quoting authorities.

   d. defining terms.

__b__ 2. The author's tone throughout the article can best be described as
   a. sharp and sarcastic.

   b. informal and friendly.

   c. cold and impersonal.

   d. dull and serious.

__d__ 3. Of the following statements from paragraph 6, the only one that is
   an *opinion* is
   a. "One day I was in the ladies' room."

   b. "And in walked the woman who would become my future boss."

   c. "And I got the job as member correspondent."

   d. "It was a cool job."

__c__ 4. When the author asks, "How mentally healthy is that?" (paragraph
   15), she means that
   a. it is not actually healthy.

   b. she doesn't know if it is healthy.

   c. it is actually very healthy.

   d. she doubts whether it is mentally or physically healthy.

➤ **G. BUILDING VOCABULARY**

➤ **Context**

Using context and a dictionary, if necessary, determine the meaning of each word as it is used in the selection.

___b___ 1. congenial (paragraph 1)

    a. sharp   c. unlike

    b. pleasant   d. complex

___a___ 2. elusive (paragraph 3)

    a. difficult to grasp   c. within reach

    b. easy to see   d. under control

___a___ 3. tendencies (paragraph 9)

    a. inclinations   c. reluctance

    b. attitudes   d. abilities

___d___ 4. lucrative (paragraph 14)

    a. lucky   c. rewarding

    b. fancy   d. challenging

___c___ 5. hierarchical (paragraph 15)

    a. educational   c. having levels of authority

    b. displaying social skills   d. physical

___b___ 6. generic (paragraph 16)

    a. distinctive   c. minor

    b. common   d. untrained

➤ **Word Parts**

> **A REVIEW OF PREFIXES AND SUFFIXES**
>
> **-UN** means *not*
>
> **-IAN** means *one who*

Complete each of the following sentences.

1. Statistics refers to numerical data. A ___statistician___ is a person who collects and interprets numerical data.

2. Realistic ideas are practical; ___unrealistic___ ideas are ___not practical, impractical___.

➤ **Unusual Words/Unusual Meanings**
Use context to match each word or phrase in Column A with its meaning in Column B. Write your answers in the spaces provided. Note that there is one extra meaning.

Column A	Column B
_f_ 1. cagey (paragraph 1)	a. underwear
_d_ 2. up my alley (paragraph 5)	b. people who are moving up professionally
_a_ 3. scivvies (paragraph 6)	c. someone who feels trapped in his or her job
_e_ 4. kindred spirits (paragraph 15)	d. to my liking
_b_ 5. up-and-comers (paragraph 15)	e. people who have the same interests
	f. sly or secretive

➤ **H.   SELECTING A LEARNING/STUDY STRATEGY**

Discuss the best way to record useful information from this reading.

➤ **I.   EXPLORING IDEAS THROUGH DISCUSSION AND WRITING**

1. Have you ever been in the right place at the right time? If so, describe the experience and explain its outcomes.

2. Do you agree or disagree with Finney's method of finding an ideal job?

3. Write a list of ten things you love that might help you find an ideal job.

➤ **J.   BEYOND THE CLASSROOM TO THE WEB**

Visit the University Career Services office at the University of Virginia at http://www.virginia.edu/~career/.

In the search box, type the word "handouts." Read one of the handouts posted at the career services center. Does the general view of how a person gets a good job seem similar to or different from the idea that one just has to be in the "right place at the right time"? Why?

✔ **Tracking Your Progress**

Selection 22

Section	Number Correct		Score
A. Thesis and Main Idea (5 items)	_____	x 5	_____
B. Details (5 items)	_____	x 4	_____
C. Organization and Transitions (4 items)	_____	x 2	_____
E. Inferred Meanings (9 items)	_____	x 3	_____
F. Thinking Critically (4 items)	_____	x 3	_____
G. Vocabulary			
1. Context (6 items)	_____	x 1	_____
2. Word Parts (2 items)	_____	x 1	_____

TOTAL SCORE _____%

CHECKING YOUR READING RATE

Words in Selection 22: 1,001

Finishing Time:	_____ (hour)	_____ (minutes)	_____ (seconds)
Starting Time:	_____ (hour)	_____ (minutes)	_____ (seconds)
Total Reading Time:		_____ (minutes)	_____ (seconds)

Words Per Minute Score (page 737) _____ WPM

SELECTION 23

McDonald's Makes a Lot of People Angry for a Lot of Different Reasons

This article appears on the McSpotlight Web site, a site sponsored by McInformation Network, a volunteer organization dedicated to collecting information and encouraging debate about the workings, policies, and practices of the McDonald's Corporation.

▶ PREVIEWING THE READING

Using the steps listed on page 5, preview the reading selection. When you have finished, complete the following items.

1. What question do you expect the reading to answer?

   How or why does McDonald's make people angry?

2. List at least four issues addressed in the reading.

   a. nutrition, environment

   b. advertising, employment

   c. animals, expansion

   c. free speech, capitalism

 MAKING CONNECTIONS

Do the customers look satisfied?

> **READING TIP**

This reading uses emotional language to present information. Be sure to note whether the authors' statements are based on facts or opinions.

CHECKING YOUR READING RATE

If you plan to compute your reading rate, be sure to record your starting time in the box at the end of the exercises before you begin reading.

McDonald's Makes a Lot of People Angry for a Lot of Different Reasons

1   McDonald's makes a lot of people angry for a lot of different reasons.

Nutrition

nutritionists
experts in the
field of nutrition

2   **Nutritionists,** for example, argue that the type of high fat, low fiber diet promoted by McDonald's is linked to serious diseases such as cancer, heart disease, obesity, and diabetes—the sort of diseases that is now responsible for nearly three-quarters of premature deaths in the western world. McDonald's responds that the scientific evidence is not conclusive and that its food can be a valuable part of a balanced diet.

3   Some people say McDonald's is entitled to sell junk food in exactly the same way that chocolate or cream cake manufacturers do: if people want to buy it that's their decision. But should McDonald's be allowed to advertise its products as nutritious? Why does it sponsor sports events when it sells unhealthy products? And what on earth is McDonald's doing opening restaurants in hospitals?

Environment

conservationists
people who
advocate the
conservation of
natural resources

4   **Conservationists** have often focused on McDonald's as an industry leader promoting business practices detrimental to the environment. And yet the company spends a fortune promoting itself as environmentally friendly. What's the story?

5   One of the most well-known and sensitive questions about McDonald's is: is McDonald's responsible for the destruction of tropical forests to make way for cattle ranching? McDonald's says no. Many people say yes. So McDonald's sues them. Not so many people say yes anymore, but does this mean McDonald's isn't responsible?

6   McDonald's annually produces over a million tons of packaging, used for just a few minutes before being discarded. What environmental effect does the production and disposal of all this have? Is its record on recycling and recycled products as green as it makes out? Is McDonald's responsible for litter on the streets, or is that the fault of the customer who drops it? Can any multinational company operating on McDonald's scale *not* contribute to global warming, ozone destruction, depletion of mineral resources and the destruction of natural habitats?

Advertising

7   McDonald's spends over two billion dollars each year on advertising: the Golden Arches are now more recognized than the Christian cross. Using collectible toys,

television ads, promotional schemes in schools, and figures such as Ronald McDonald, the company bombards its main target group: children. Many parents object strongly to the influence this has over their own children.

8   McDonald's argues that its advertising is no worse than anyone else's and that it adheres to all the advertising codes in each country. But others argue it still amounts to cynical exploitation of children—some consumer organizations are calling for a ban on advertising to children. Why does McDonald's sponsor so many school events and learning programs? Is its Children's Charities genuine **philanthropy** or is there a more explicit publicity and profit motive?

philanthropy
an activity or institution intended for the good of humankind

Employment

9   The Corporation has pioneered a global, highly standardized and fast production-line system, geared to maximum turnover of products and profits. McDonald's now employs more than a million mostly young people around the world. Some say a million people might otherwise be out of work; others, however, consider that McDonald's is in fact a net destroyer of jobs by using low wages and the huge size of its business to undercut local food outlets and thereby force them out of business. Is McDonald's a great job opportunity or is it taking advantage of high unemployment to exploit the most vulnerable people in society, working them very hard for very little money? Complaints from employees range from discrimination and lack of rights, to understaffing, few breaks and illegal hours, to poor safety conditions and kitchens flooded with sewage, to the sale of food that has been dropped on the floor. This type of low-paid work has even been termed "McJobs."

trade unionists
members of a labor union, especially those in the same trade

10   **Trade unionists** don't like McDonald's either. The company is notorious for the vehemence with which it tries to crush any unionization attempt. McDonald's argues that all its workers are happy and that any problems can be worked out directly without the need for interference from a third party, but is McDonald's in fact just desperate to prevent any efforts by the workers to improve wages and conditions?

Animals

vegetarians
people who maintain a meat-free diet

11   **Vegetarians** and animal welfare campaigners aren't too keen on McDonald's—for obvious reasons. As the world's largest user of beef McDonald's is responsible for the slaughter of hundreds of thousands of cows per year. In Europe alone McDonald's uses half a million chickens every week, all from windowless factory farms. All such animals suffer great cruelty during their unnatural, painful and short lives, many being kept inside with no access to fresh air and sunshine, and no freedom of movement—how can such cruelty be measured? Is it acceptable for the food industry to exploit animals at all? Again, McDonald's argues that it sticks to the letter of the law and if there are any problems it is a matter for government. McDonald's also claims to be concerned with animal welfare.

Expansion

12   In 1996 McDonald's opened in India for the first time: a country where the majority of the population is vegetarian and the cow is sacred. This is just one example of the inexorable spread of western multinationals into every corner of the globe, a

spread which is creating a globalized system in which wealth is drained out of local economies into the hands of a very few, very rich elite. Can people challenge the undermining of long-lived and stable cultures and regional diversity? Self-sufficient and sustainable farming is replaced by cash crops and agribusiness under control of multinationals—but how are people fighting back?

Free Speech

capitalism
an economic system in which the means of production and distribution are privately or corporately owned

13   So, it seems as though lots of people are opposed to the way McDonald's goes about its business. So there is a big global debate going on about them, right? Wrong. McDonald's knows full well how important its public image is and how damaging it would be if any of the allegations started becoming well-known among its customers. So McDonald's uses its financial clout to influence the media and legal powers to intimidate people into not speaking out, directly threatening free speech. The list of media organizations who have been sued in the past is daunting, and the number of publications suppressed or pulped is frightening. But what are the lessons of the successful and ever-growing anti-McDonald's campaign for those also determined to challenge those institutions which currently dominate society?

socialism
a social system in which the means of producing and distributing goods are owned collectively and political power is exercised by the whole community

Capitalism

anarchism
the theory or doctrine that all forms of government are oppressive and undesirable and should be abolished

14   Nobody is arguing that the huge and growing global environmental and social crisis is entirely the fault of one high-profile burger chain, or even just the whole food industry. McDonald's is, of course, simply a particularly arrogant, shiny and self-important example of a system that values profits at the expense of anything else. Even if McDonald's were to close down tomorrow, someone else would simply slip straight into its position. There is a much more fundamental problem than Big Macs and French fries: capitalism. But what about anti-capitalist beliefs like **socialism** and **anarchism**? Is it possible to create a world run by ordinary people themselves, without multinationals and governments—a world based on sharing, freedom and respect for all life?

► A.   UNDERSTANDING THE THESIS AND OTHER MAIN IDEAS

Select the best answer.

_d_ 1. The central thesis of "McDonald's Makes a Lot of People Angry for a Lot of Different Reasons" is that

a. many customers are unhappy with the service they get at McDonald's.

b. competitors, such as Burger King and Hardee's, resent the success of McDonald's.

c. McDonald's restaurants have been a target for robbery, vandalism, and other serious crimes.

d. many different groups of people are disturbed by the global effects of McDonald's and other multinational corporations.

__c__ 2. The authors' primary purpose in the article is to

    a. describe their efforts to bring about reform.

    b. compare McDonald's with more environmentally sensitive corporations.

    c. describe the harmful effects of McDonald's.

    d. persuade consumers to boycott McDonald's and other fast-food restaurants.

__a__ 3. The topic of paragraph 6 is

    a. McDonald's environmental effects.

    b. consumers who litter.

    c. recycling.

    d. global warming.

__d__ 4. The topic of paragraph 8 is

    a. children's charities.

    b. consumer organizations.

    c. philanthropy.

    d. advertising.

__a__ 5. The main idea of paragraph 11 is expressed in the

    a. first sentence.   c. third sentence.

    b. second sentence.   d. last sentence.

__b__ 6. The main idea of paragraph 13 is that

    a. there is currently a global debate about McDonald's practices.

    b. McDonald's uses its power to silence critics, thus threatening free speech.

    c. a lot of people are opposed to the way McDonald's conducts business.

    d. the anti-McDonald's campaign is successful and ever-growing.

__c__ 7. The statement that best expresses the main idea of paragraph 14 is

    a. "Nobody is arguing that the huge and growing global environmental and social crisis is entirely the fault of one high-profile burger chain . . ."

    b. "Even if McDonald's were to close down tomorrow, someone else would simply slip straight into its position."

c. "There is a much more fundamental problem than Big Macs and French fries: capitalism."

d. "McDonald's is, of course, simply a particularly arrogant . . . example . . ."

➤ B.   IDENTIFYING DETAILS

Indicate whether each statement is true (T) or false (F).

___T___ 1. The term "McJobs" has been used to describe a type of low-paid work.

___F___ 2. McDonald's is not permitted to open restaurants in hospitals.

___T___ 3. According to the authors, McDonald's annually spends more than two billion dollars on advertising.

___T___ 4. McDonald's opened in India for the first time in 1996.

___F___ 5. McDonald's employs more than a million people in America.

➤ C.   RECOGNIZING METHODS OF ORGANIZATION AND TRANSITIONS

Fill in the blanks to complete the following statements.

1. In paragraph 2, the authors report that nutritionists believe McDonald's food can be linked to serious diseases and that McDonald's disagrees. This organizational pattern is __comparison and contrast__, because the authors present both points of view.

2. In paragraph 9, the authors use __comparison and contrast__ to present opposing points of view about McDonald's employment.

3. The transitional phrase in paragraph 9 that indicates a contrast between two ideas is ___however___.

➤ D.   REVIEWING AND ORGANIZING IDEAS: OUTLINING

Complete the following outline of the "Employment" section (paragraphs 9–10) by filling in the missing words.

I. McDonald's system

   A. Global _____ market _____

   B. Highly _____ standardized _____

   C. Fast _____ production line _____

   D. Geared to _____ maximum turnover _____ of products and _____ profits _____

II. Employees

   A. More than _____ 1 million _____ employees worldwide

     1. Great job opportunity for people who would otherwise be _____ unemployed _____

     2. Net _____ destroyer _____ of jobs

       a. Uses _____ low _____ wages

       b. Huge size forces _____ local food outlets _____ out of business

       c. Exploiting most _____ vulnerable _____ people in society?

     3. _____ Employee complaints _____

       a. Discrimination

       b. Lack of _____ rights _____

       c. _____ Understaffing _____

       d. Few _____ breaks _____

       e. _____ Illegal _____ hours

       f. Poor _____ safety _____ conditions

       g. Kitchens flooded with _____ sewage _____

       h. Sale of food that has been _____ dropped on the floor _____

     4. Low-paid work called _____ "McJobs" _____

III. _____ Trade unionists _____

   A. Don't like McDonald's

   B. McDonald's prevents _____ unionization attempts _____

     1. Argues that employees are _____ happy _____

     2. _____ Problems _____ can be worked out without the need for _____ third-party _____ interference

     3. Desperate to prevent _____ workers _____ from improving _____ wages and conditions _____

► **E.   FIGURING OUT INFERRED MEANINGS**

Make inferences by indicating whether each of the following underlined words creates a positive (P) or negative (N) image for the reader.

____P____ 1. "... part of a <u>balanced</u> diet." (paragraph 2)

____P____ 2. "... environmentally <u>friendly</u>." (paragraph 4)

____N____ 3. "... the company <u>bombards</u> its main target group ..." (paragraph 7)

____N____ 4. "... is McDonald's in fact just <u>desperate</u> ..." (paragraph 10)

____N____ 5. "... wealth is <u>drained</u> out of local economies ..." (paragraph 12)

► **F.   THINKING CRITICALLY**

Select the best answer.

____a____ 1. The authors' tone throughout the article can best be described as

    a. critical and concerned.

    b. sympathetic.

    c. realistic and honest.

    d. objective and unbiased.

____c____ 2. When the authors ask questions throughout the reading, they are primarily trying to

    a. add humor to the article.

    b. emphasize how curious they are.

    c. provoke thought about the issues.

    d. show that they don't know the answers.

____b____ 3. The authors refer to all of the following groups to support their thesis *except*

    a. nutritionists.

    b. politicians.

    c. conservationists.

    d. animal welfare campaigners.

____c____ 4. According to the authors, McDonald's has responded to critics in environmental groups and the media by

    a. ignoring them.

    b. bribing them.

    c. suing them.

    d. amending its operations.

➤ **G.   BUILDING VOCABULARY**

➤ **Context**

Using context and a dictionary, if necessary, determine the meaning of each word as it is used in the selection.

___c___ 1. detrimental (paragraph 4)

    a. advantageous   c. harmful

    b. minor   d. intense

___b___ 2. depletion (paragraph 6)

    a. discussion   c. replacement

    b. reduction   d. contribution

___a___ 3. adhere (paragraph 8)

    a. abide by   c. separate

    b. explain   d. market

___b___ 4. notorious (paragraph 10)

    a. having a common trait

    b. famous for something undesirable

    c. well respected

    d. strong and forceful

___a___ 5. vehemence (paragraph 10)

    a. forcefulness   c. sympathy

    b. professionalism   d. calmness

___c___ 6. diversity (paragraph 12)

    a. agreement   c. variety

    b. similarity   d. divisions

___d___ 7. daunting (paragraph 13)

    a. lengthening   c. harmful

    b. diminishing   d. intimidating

➤ **Word Parts**

> **A REVIEW OF PREFIXES**
>
> **ANTI-** means *against*
> **IN-** means *not*
> **MULTI-** means *many*
> **PRE-** means *before*
> **UN-** means *not*

Match each word in Column A with its meaning in Column B. Write your answers in the spaces provided.

Column A	Column B
_c_ 1. anticapitalist	a. lack of work
_d_ 2. multinational	b. before the normal time
_e_ 3. inexorable	c. against capitalism
_b_ 4. premature	d. having operations or investments in more than two countries
_a_ 5. unemployment	e. not preventable, relentless

▶ **Unusual Words/Unusual Meanings**
Select the best answer.

_b_ 1. When the authors ask if McDonald's has a record on recycling that is as "green" as it claims (paragraph 6), the word "green" refers to

    a. the color green.   c. money.

    b. the environment.   d. a lack of experience.

_c_ 2. The word "pulped" (paragraph 13) means

    a. inflated.   c. crushed.

    b. reduced.   d. turned to paper.

▶ **H.   SELECTING A LEARNING/STUDY STRATEGY**

Suppose you have been asked to evaluate the evidence the authors provide to support their accusations against McDonald's. For each accusation, highlight the specific evidence the authors provide. For each statement you highlight, decide whether there is sufficient or insufficient evidence to support the claim.

▶ **I.   EXPLORING IDEAS THROUGH DISCUSSION AND WRITING**

1. The authors are biased against McDonald's. In what ways is this bias revealed?

2. What ethical or moral issues does this selection raise?

3. What is the opposing viewpoint not presented in this article? That is, in what ways does McDonald's benefit society?

➤ **J. BEYOND THE CLASSROOM TO THE WEB**

Visit the McSpotlight Web site at **http://www.mcspotlight.org/campaigns/current/mckids.html**.

The selection you have just read was posted on the McSpotlight Web site. Another selection from that site is "What's Wrong with Ronald McDonald?" This selection includes much of the same basic information as the article you just read, but presents the information in a very different way. How do the two readings differ and why?

✔ **Tracking Your Progress**

Selection 23

Section	Number Correct		Score
A. Thesis and Main Idea (7 items)	_____	x 4	_____
B. Details (5 items)	_____	x 3	_____
C. Organization and Transitions (3 items)	_____	x 2	_____
E. Inferred Meanings (5 items)	_____	x 3	_____
F. Thinking Critically (4 items)	_____	x 3	_____
G. Vocabulary			
1. Context (7 items)	_____	x 2	_____
2. Word Parts (5 items)	_____	x 2	_____
	TOTAL SCORE		_____%

CHECKING YOUR READING RATE

Words in Selection 23: 1,179

Finishing Time: _____ _____ _____
(hour) (minutes) (seconds)

Starting Time: _____ _____ _____
(hour) (minutes) (seconds)

Total Reading Time: _____ _____
(minutes) (seconds)

Words Per Minute Score (page 737) _____ WPM

SELECTION 24

Hispanic Americans: A Growing Market Segment

Michael R. Solomon

This excerpt was taken from *Consumer Behavior,* a business textbook published in 1999. It is part of a chapter titled "Ethnic, Racial, and Religious Subcultures."

➤ PREVIEWING THE READING

Using the steps listed on page 5, preview the reading selection. When you have finished, complete the following items.

1. What ethnic group is the selection about? ___Hispanic Americans___

2. List four questions you should be able to answer after reading this selection.

    a. ___What is the allure of the Hispanic market?___

    b. ___What are Hispanic subcultures?___

    c. ___What are some blunders that have been made in marketing to Hispanics?___

    d. ___What is the Hispanic identity?___

➤ READING TIP

This selection contains many Spanish words and phrases. If you do not know Spanish, pay attention to the synonyms and definitions the author has included.

CHECKING YOUR READING RATE

If you plan to compute your reading rate, be sure to record your starting time in the box at the end of the exercises before you begin reading.

MAKING CONNECTIONS

PERCENT OF THE U.S. POPULATION BY RACE
AND HISPANIC ORIGIN—2000, 2025, AND 2050

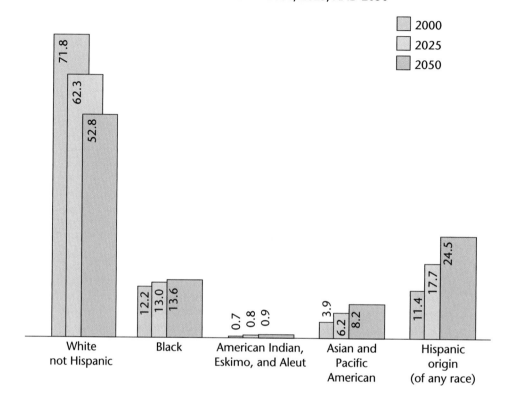

What does this graph indicate is the probable reason for marketers to be interested in the Hispanic market?

prime time
the time period
from 7:00 P.M.
until 11:00 P.M.
when the largest
television audience
is available

Dominican
Republic
a country in the
West Indies on the
eastern part of the
island of Hispaniola

Hispanic Americans: A Growing Market Segment

1   The Hispanic subculture is a sleeping giant, a segment that was until recently largely ignored by many marketers. The growth and increasing affluence of this group has now made it impossible to overlook, and Hispanic consumers are now diligently courted by many major corporations. Nike made history in 1993 by running the first Spanish-language commercial ever broadcast in **prime time** on a major American network. The spot, which ran during the All-Star baseball game, featured boys in tattered clothes playing ball in the **Dominican Republic**, or *La Tierra de Mediocampistas* (the Land of Shortstops). This title refers to the fact that over 70 Dominicans have played for major league ball clubs, many of whom started at the shortstop position. This ground-breaking spot also laid bare some of the issues involved in marketing to Hispanics: Many found the commercial condescending (espe-

cially the ragged look of the actors), and felt that it promoted the idea that Hispanics don't really want to assimilate into mainstream Anglo culture.

Anglo
short for Anglo-
American, an
English-speaking,
white resident of
the United States

2   If nothing else, though, this commercial by a large corporation highlights the indisputable fact that the Hispanic American market is now being taken seriously by major marketers. Some are rushing to sign Hispanic celebrities, such as Daisy Fuentes and Rita Moreno, to endorse their products. Others are developing separate Spanish-language campaigns, often with entirely different emphases calculated to appeal to the unique characteristics of this market. For example, the California Milk Processor Board discovered that its hugely successful "got milk?" campaign was not well received by Hispanics, because biting, sarcastic humor is not part of the Hispanic culture. In addition, the notion of milk deprivation is not funny to the Hispanic homemaker, because running out of milk means she has failed her family. An alternative targeted to Hispanics features a grandmother who teaches her granddaughter how to drink milk. As she explains to her granddaughter that "*cocinado con amor y con leche*" (she cooks with love and milk), this execution reinforces cultural beliefs that old people are to be revered, a grandmother is sweet, knowledgeable and strong, and the kitchen is a magical place where food is turned into love.

The Allure of the Hispanic Market

demographically
using the
characteristics of
a particular
population to
identify consumer
markets

3   **Demographically,** two important characteristics of the Hispanic market are worth noting: First, it is a young market. The median age of Hispanic Americans is 23.6, compared with the U.S. average of 32. That helps to explain why General Mills developed a breakfast cereal called Buñuelitos specifically for this market. The brand name is an adaptation of *buñuelos*, a traditional Mexican pastry served on holidays.

4   Second, the Hispanic family is much larger than the rest of the population's. The average Hispanic household contains 3.5 people, compared to only 2.7 for other U.S. households. These differences obviously affect the overall allocation of income to various product categories. For example, Hispanic households spend 15 to 20 percent more of their disposable income than the national average on groceries. There are now over 19 million Hispanic consumers in the United States, and a number of factors make this market segment extremely attractive:

- Hispanics tend to be brand loyal, especially to brands from their country of origin. In one study, about 45 percent reported that they always buy their usual brand, whereas only one in five said they frequently switch brands. Another found that Hispanics who strongly identify with their ethnic origin are more likely to seek Hispanic vendors, to be loyal to brands used by family and friends, and to be influenced by Hispanic media.
- Hispanics are highly concentrated geographically by country of origin, which makes them relatively easy to reach. Over 50 percent of all Hispanics live in the Los Angeles, New York, Miami, San Antonio, San Francisco, and Chicago metropolitan areas.
- Education levels are increasing dramatically. In the period between 1984 and 1988, the number of Hispanics with four years of college increased by 51 percent. Although the absolute numbers are still low compared to the general population, the number of Hispanic men in managerial and professional jobs

increased by 42 percent, and the corresponding increase of 61 percent for Hispanic women during this period was even more encouraging.

Appealing to Hispanic Subcultures

5   The behavior profile of the Hispanic consumer includes a need for status and a strong sense of pride. A high value is placed on self-expression and familial devotion. Some campaigns have played to Hispanics' fear of rejection and apprehension about loss of control and embarrassment in social situations. Conventional wisdom recommends creating action-oriented advertising and emphasizing a problem-solving atmosphere. Assertive role models who are cast in nonthreatening situations appear to be effective.

6   As with other large subcultural groups, marketers are now beginning to discover that the Hispanic market is not homogenous. Subcultural identity is not as much with being Hispanic as it is with the particular country of origin. Mexican Americans, who make up about 62 percent of all Hispanic Americans, are also the fastest-growing subsegment; their population has grown by 40 percent since 1980. Cuban Americans are by far the wealthiest subsegment, but they also are the smallest Hispanic ethnic group. Many Cuban American families with high educational levels fled **Fidel Castro's** communist regime in the late 1950s and early 1960s, worked hard for many years to establish themselves, and are now firmly entrenched in the Miami political and economic establishment. Because of this affluence, businesses in South Florida now make an effort to target "YUCAs" (young, upwardly mobile Cuban Americans), especially since the *majority* of Miami residents are Hispanic American!

Fidel Castro
Cuban leader who established a socialist state in Cuba in 1959

Marketing Blunders

7   Many initial efforts by Americans to market to Hispanics were, to say the least, counterproductive. Companies bumbled in their efforts to translate advertising adequately or to compose copy that could capture desired nuances. These mistakes do not occur so much anymore as marketers become more sophisticated in dealing with this market and as Hispanics themselves become involved in advertising production. The following are some translation mishaps that have slipped through in the past:

- The Perdue slogan, "It takes a tough man to make a tender chicken," was translated as "It takes a sexually excited man to make a chick affectionate."
- Budweiser was promoted as the "queen of beers."
- A burrito was mistakenly called a *burrada,* which means "big mistake."
- Braniff, promoting its comfortable leather seats, used the headline, *Sentado en cuero,* which was interpreted as "Sit naked."
- Coors beer's slogan to "get loose with Coors" appeared in Spanish as "get the runs with Coors."

Understanding Hispanic Identity

8   Native language and culture are important components of Hispanic identity and self-esteem (about three-quarters of Hispanics still speak Spanish at home), and these consumers are very sympathetic to marketing efforts that acknowledge and empha-

size the Hispanic cultural heritage. More than 40 percent of Hispanic consumers say they deliberately attempt to buy products that show an interest in the Hispanic consumer, and this number jumps to over two-thirds for Cuban Americans.

9   Many Hispanic Americans are avid consumers of soap operas, called *telenovelas*. Ethnic soap operas, shown on American television, are becoming big business. Univision, the biggest Spanish-language network, airs 10 different ones each day. These shows are produced by Latin American networks, but some viewers have complained that they do not address problems of Hispanic Americans such as illegal immigration, getting a job, or speaking the language.

10   Since the beginning of the 1990s, Hispanic radio stations have been blossoming—there are now over 390 stations in the United States. This growth is partly due to the increasing size and economic clout of Hispanic consumers. It is also attributable to stations' efforts to attract younger listeners by playing more contemporary musical styles, such as *tejano, banda, ranchera,* and *nortena*. A movie about the shooting death of Selena, a popular young *tejano* singer, has fueled this interest. These new formats feature bilingual disk jockeys, who are developing a patter that some have called "Spanglish."

Level of Acculturation

11   One important way to distinguish among members of a subculture is to consider the extent to which they retain a sense of identification with their country of origin. Acculturation refers to the process of movement and adaptation to one country's cultural environment by a person from another country.

12   This factor is especially important when considering the Hispanic market, because the degree to which these consumers are integrated into the American way of life varies widely. For instance, about 38 percent of all Hispanics live in *barrios,* or predominantly Hispanic neighborhoods, which tend to be somewhat insulated from mainstream society.

13   The acculturation of Hispanic consumers may be understood in terms of the **progressive learning model**. This perspective assumes that people gradually learn a new culture as they increasingly come in contact with it. Thus, we would expect the consumer behavior of Hispanic Americans to be a mixture of practices taken from their original culture and those of the new or *host culture.*

14   Research has generally obtained results that support this pattern when factors such as shopping orientation, the importance placed on various product attributes, media preference, and brand loyalty are examined. When the intensity of ethnic identification is taken into account, consumers who retained a strong ethnic identification differed from their more assimilated counterparts in the following ways:

- They had a more negative attitude toward business in general (probably caused by frustration due to relatively low income levels).
- They were higher users of Spanish-language media.
- They were more brand loyal.
- They were more likely to prefer brands with prestige labels.
- They were more likely to buy brands specifically advertised to their ethnic group.

15   Overall, the Hispanic subculture has become an important marketing segment that advertisers and media corporations cannot afford to ignore.

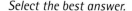

A.   UNDERSTANDING THE THESIS AND OTHER MAIN IDEAS

Select the best answer.

___b___ 1. The central thesis of "Hispanic Americans" is that

    a. Hispanic Americans are concentrated geographically in large metropolitan areas.

    b. marketers are becoming aware of Hispanic Americans as an important consumer group in America.

    c. American companies have had little success in their marketing efforts to Hispanic American consumers.

    d. Hispanic Americans have become an essential part of America.

___c___ 2. The author's primary purpose in "Hispanic Americans" is to

    a. compare Hispanic Americans with other major ethnic groups in America.

    b. criticize marketers for their depictions of Hispanic Americans in commercials.

    c. describe the characteristics of the Hispanic American market segment.

    d. persuade marketers to use more Hispanic Americans in their advertising campaigns.

___a___ 3. The main idea of paragraph 2 is that

    a. marketers are attempting to appeal to the unique Hispanic American market.

    b. Hispanic celebrities are benefiting from the growth of the Hispanic American market.

    c. marketers should translate commercials into Spanish to appeal to more Hispanic Americans.

    d. the California Milk Processor Board had to revise its campaign for Hispanics.

___d___ 4. The topic of paragraph 5 is

    a. Hispanic subcultures.

    b. action-oriented advertising.

    c. Hispanic role models.

    d. a profile of the Hispanic consumer.

___a___ 5. The main idea of paragraph 6 is expressed in the

    a. first sentence.   c. third sentence.

    b. second sentence.   d. last sentence.

___d___ 6. The main idea of paragraph 7 is that

    a. it is impossible to translate advertising from English to Spanish.

    b. Hispanics need to become more involved in advertising production.

    c. companies such as Perdue and Budweiser are unable to reach the Hispanic market.

    d. American companies made mistakes in their early attempts to market to Hispanics.

➤ B. IDENTIFYING DETAILS

Select the best answer.

___a___ 1. The first Spanish-language commercial ever broadcast in prime time on a major American network was made by

    a. Nike.   c. Budweiser.

    b. Perdue.   d. Braniff.

___c___ 2. The Dominican Republic is called the "Land of Shortstops" because

    a. most airlines only make a brief stopover in that country before going on to other destinations in the West Indies.

    b. Columbus made a short stop there when he discovered the island of Hispaniola in 1492 and claimed it for Spain.

    c. more than 70 Dominicans have played for major league baseball, often starting in the shortstop position.

    d. the country's major export is baseball equipment for shortstops.

___b___ 3. The California Milk Processor Board's "got milk?" advertising campaign was not successful with Hispanics because

    a. the campaign made mistakes in its translation of some of the words from English to Spanish.

    b. sarcastic humor is not part of the Hispanic culture and milk deprivation is not funny to Hispanic homemakers.

    c. most Hispanics don't drink milk.

    d. many Hispanics found the commercial condescending.

_d_ 4. The alternative ad produced by the Milk Board reinforced all of the following Hispanic cultural beliefs *except*

   a. old people are to be treated with reverence.

   b. grandmothers are sweet, wise, and strong.

   c. kitchens are magical places where food becomes love.

   d. milk is an essential part of Hispanic diets.

_b_ 5. According to the author, one factor that makes Hispanic consumers an extremely attractive market segment is the

   a. tendency of most Hispanics to switch brands frequently.

   b. dramatic increase in Hispanics' education levels.

   c. comparatively small size of the Hispanic family.

   d. desire of Hispanics to assimilate into mainstream America.

_d_ 6. The largest percentage of Hispanic Americans is from Mexico, and the wealthiest subsegment is from

   a. the Dominican Republic.

   b. Miami.

   c. South Florida.

   d. Cuba.

_b_ 7. The term "YUCAs" refers to

   a. the Spanish word for residents of South Florida.

   b. young, upwardly mobile Cuban Americans.

   c. Cuban Americans who fled Castro's regime in the 1950s and 1960s.

   d. a contemporary musical style.

_a_ 8. According to the article, Hispanic consumers of ethnic soap operas have complained that the shows

   a. do not address important problems of Hispanic Americans.

   b. do not feature Hispanic American actors.

   c. are not produced by Latin American networks.

   d. are not translated into Spanish.

C. RECOGNIZING METHODS OF ORGANIZATION AND TRANSITIONS

Complete the following statements by filling in the blanks.

A combination of organizational patterns is used in paragraphs 3–4. When the two demographic characteristics of the Hispanic market are listed, the pattern is called ____enumeration____. The two transitional words in these paragraphs that indicate this pattern are ____First____ and ____Second____. When differences are noted between the characteristics of Hispanics and the U.S. average, the pattern being used is called ____comparison and contrast____.

D. REVIEWING AND ORGANIZING IDEAS: MAPPING

Complete the following map of paragraph 5 by filling in the missing information.

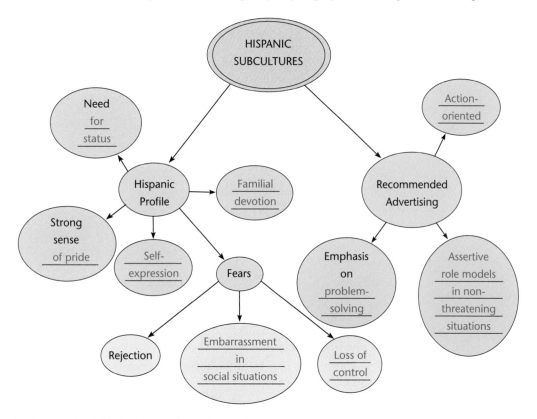

E. FIGURING OUT INFERRED MEANINGS

Indicate whether each statement is true (T) or false (F).

__T__ 1. It can be inferred that Nike's marketers believe that many Hispanics are baseball fans.

__T__ 2. The cereal developed by General Mills was intended to appeal to young Hispanics.

___F___ 3. It can be inferred that Hispanics spend more than the national average on groceries because they buy more expensive food.

___F___ 4. Cuban Americans are not important to the economy of Miami.

___T___ 5. It can be inferred that Hispanics were not involved in the production of the commercials that contained translation mistakes.

___T___ 6. The word "Spanglish" is a combination of the words Spanish and English.

➤ **F. THINKING CRITICALLY**

Select the best answer.

___b___ 1. The central thesis of "Hispanic Americans" is supported by all of the following kinds of evidence *except*

    a. facts.   c. statistics.

    b. personal experience.   d. examples.

___c___ 2. Another title for this reading might be

    a. "Amusing Marketing Mishaps."

    b. "Hispanics on the Move Across America."

    c. "Marketers Discover Hispanic Americans."

    d. "The Miami-Cuba Connection."

___a___ 3. The tone of the reading can best be described as

    a. objective.   c. forceful.

    b. concerned.   d. optimistic.

___d___ 4. Of the following statements from paragraph 4 of the reading, the only one that is an *opinion* is

    a. "There are now over 19 million Hispanic consumers in the United States."

    b. "Hispanics are highly concentrated geographically by country of origin."

    c. "In the period between 1984 and 1988, the number of Hispanics with four years of college increased by 51 percent."

    d. "The corresponding increase of 61 percent for Hispanic women during this period was even more encouraging."

_c_ 5. The list of translation mistakes is included in the reading primarily to

    a. change the tone of the reading to make it less serious.

    b. point out the differences between Hispanic humor and Anglo humor.

    c. illustrate the humorous and absurd nature of the mistakes.

    d. make fun of the companies that made the mistakes.

➤ G. BUILDING VOCABULARY

➤ Context

Using context and a dictionary, if necessary, determine the meaning of each word as it is used in the selection.

_b_ 1. affluence (paragraph 1)

    a. control

    b. wealth

    c. power

    d. influence

_c_ 2. assimilate (paragraph 1)

    a. originate

    b. stand out

    c. become absorbed

    d. invest in

_c_ 3. allocation (paragraph 4)

    a. cost

    b. salary

    c. distribution

    d. earning

_c_ 4. regime (paragraph 6)

    a. education

    b. society

    c. government

    d. routine

_b_ 5. entrenched (paragraph 6)

    a. returned

    b. established

    c. departed

    d. disagreed

___a___ 6. bumbled (paragraph 7)

    a. made a mistake

    b. hurried

    c. made an effort

    d. became angry

___b___ 7. nuances (paragraph 7)

    a. types of business

    b. shades of meaning

    c. obvious points

    d. sources of income

___d___ 8. avid (paragraph 9)

    a. irregular

    b. unwilling

    c. new

    d. enthusiastic

___c___ 9. patter (paragraph 10)

    a. tapping or other forms of noise

    b. program intended to amuse

    c. language specific to a group

    d. design or plan

➤ Word Parts

┌───┐

A REVIEW OF PREFIXES

BI- means *two*

COUNTER- means *against* or *opposite*

HOMO- means *same*

IN- means *not*

MIS- means *wrong* or *bad*

NON- means *not*

RE- means *again*

SUB- means *under* or *below*

└───┘

Match each word in Column A with its meaning in Column B. Write your answers in the spaces provided.

Column A	Column B
___c___ 1. homogenous	a. not questionable
___e___ 2. subculture	b. makes stronger
___a___ 3. indisputable	c. the same throughout
___b___ 4. reinforces	d. unfortunate accidents

_d_ 5. mishaps

_g_ 6. nonthreatening

_h_ 7. bilingual

_f_ 8. counterproductive

e. a distinct culture within a larger culture

f. working against one's purpose

g. not dangerous or risky

h. speaking two languages

➤ Unusual Words/Unusual Meanings

Write a sentence using the underlined word or phrase.

1. The phrase "The Hispanic subculture is a <u>sleeping giant</u>" (paragraph 1) means a large group of people with a lot of potential but unrealized buying power.

   Your sentence: _____.

2. The phrase <u>diligently courted</u> (paragraph 1) means actively being paid attention to.

   Your sentence: _____.

➤ H.   SELECTING A LEARNING/STUDY STRATEGY

Select the best answer.

_b_   Suppose you are preparing for an essay exam in your business marketing class. The chapter from which this excerpt was taken will be included on the exam. Which of the following would be the best way to prepare for the exam?

a. visualize the Hispanic market

b. predict questions and practice answering them

c. highlight key statistics

d. define important terminology

➤ I.   EXPLORING IDEAS THROUGH DISCUSSION AND WRITING

1. If you read the selection "McDonald's Makes a Lot of People Angry for a Lot of Different Reasons," compare the tone of that reading to this one. Which selection had more emotion?

2. Why do you think the Hispanic subcultures identify more with their country of origin than simply with being Hispanic?

3. Have you observed an increased awareness of the Hispanic market in advertising or the media? If so, give several examples.

➤ **J.   BEYOND THE CLASSROOM TO THE WEB**

Visit the Hispanic Marketing Call Center at **http://www.hispaniccallcenter.com/**.
In the article *"Hispanic Marketing Affluence,"* what additional kinds of information can you find about (a) how much money Hispanics in the United States have to spend and (b) what they spend it on?

✔ **Tracking Your Progress**

Selection 24

Section	Number Correct		Score
A. Thesis and Main Idea (6 items)	_____	x 4	_____
B. Details (8 items)	_____	x 3	_____
C. Organization and Transitions (4 items)	_____	x 2	_____
E. Inferred Meanings (6 items)	_____	x 2	_____
F. Thinking Critically (5 items)	_____	x 3	_____
G. Vocabulary			
1. Context (9 items)	_____	x 1	_____
2. Word Parts (8 items)	_____	x 1	_____
	TOTAL SCORE _____%		

CHECKING YOUR READING RATE

Words in Selection 24: 1,616

Finishing Time:	_____	_____	_____
	(hour)	(minutes)	(seconds)
Starting Time:	_____	_____	_____
	(hour)	(minutes)	(seconds)
Total Reading Time:		_____	_____
		(minutes)	(seconds)

Words Per Minute Score (page 737) _____ WPM

19 Technology/Computers

Technology has become an important part of our daily lives. In some cases, technology directly controls our lives. For example, if your car does not start or the bus breaks down, you may miss class. People's lives have been saved by medical technology: for example, when a person's heart has stopped and been restarted by a machine. In other situations, technology influences the quality of our lives. Without technology we would lack many conveniences that we take for granted. For example, we would not have computers, elevators, automated teller machines, or microwave ovens. Technology affects our communication through radio, television, and the Internet; our comfort through furnaces, air conditioners, and plumbing systems; our health through vaccines, drugs, and medical research; and our jobs through computers, copiers, and fax machines. In fact, it is difficult to think of any aspect of our daily lives untouched by technology.

In this chapter you will explore the effects of technology and read about upcoming innovations. In "Senses on the Net" you will discover how it may be possible in the future to smell, taste, and touch using computers. "A Mania for Messaging" explores a current and very popular computer technology—instant messaging. As you read "House Arrest and Electronic Monitoring," you will learn about an alternative to imprisonment based on electronic technology.

Use the following suggestions when reading technical material.

TIPS FOR READING IN TECHNOLOGY/ COMPUTERS

- **Read slowly.** Technical material tends to be factually dense and requires careful, slow reading.
- **Pay attention to technical vocabulary.** "A Mania for Messaging," for example, includes numerous technical terms and abbreviations related to computers.
- **Focus on process.** Much technical writing focuses on how things work. "Senses on the Net" explains how taste, smell, and touch can be transmitted over the Internet.
- **Use visualization.** Visualization is a process of creating mental pictures or images. As you read, try to picture in your mind the process or procedure that is being described. Visualization makes reading these descriptions easier and will improve your ability to recall details. As you read "House Arrest and Electronic Monitoring," try visualizing how electronic monitoring works.

SELECTION 25

Senses on the Net

Anick Jesdanun

This article appeared in the *Buffalo News* and other newspapers in January of 2001. Read it to learn about the computer technology of the future.

> ## PREVIEWING THE READING

Using the steps listed on page 5, preview the reading selection. When you have finished, complete the following items.

1. The two subjects of this selection are _____senses_____ and the _____Internet_____.

2. One question you should be able to answer after reading the article is

   How can technology let users taste recipes and sniff fragrances?

MAKING CONNECTIONS

Do you use the Internet? If so, have you ever used it to listen to an audio recording or watch a video? What did you think about the experience?

> ## READING TIP

As you read, highlight examples of new ways the senses are used in computer technology of the future.

CHECKING YOUR READING RATE

If you plan to compute your reading rate, be sure to record your starting time in the box at the end of the exercises before you begin reading.

Web site
a location on the
World Wide Web
that provides
information about
a particular subject

Senses on the Net

1   Palo Alto, Calif.—Wouldn't you like to sample a chicken entree before making dinner reservations, simply by visiting a restaurant's **Web site**? Or how about stroking the cashmere sweater you're thinking of purchasing online?

2   People are pretty much limited to seeing and hearing things over the Internet these days. But efforts are under way to make the Internet more sensory—by adding smell, taste and touch.

3   It's no joke, but skepticism is understandable.

4   After all, it wasn't too long ago that computers could display little more than text. At the time, researchers had difficulty explaining that the machines would evolve to eventually show movies and play music.

5   "Our largest challenge is trying to convince people that this is indeed possible," said Bruce M. Schena, chief technical officer for Immersion Corp. "It seems like a lot of science fiction to a lot of people."

6   Some of the rudimentary capabilities are available today. Others are expected in the next year or two—and beyond.

computer mice
the hand-manipulated, button-activated devices connected to a computer that allow the user to select functions on the computer screen

7   Late last year, Logitech began selling iFeel **computer mice**, using touch technology from San Jose–based Immersion.

8   The devices produce bumps as you run across icons on the desktop, and Web sites can program them to vibrate with the contours of a photographed sweater.

9   Immersion is also working with researchers at Stanford University in Palo Alto and the University of Wisconsin at LaCrosse to develop surgical simulation for medical students.

virtual forceps
a computer simulation of a surgical instrument

10   Using scissor-like handles attached to **virtual forceps**, you can feel tension as you pull computer-generated skin, a hard knock as you hit bone.

11   The technology could help students learn and practice advanced procedures with top-rated surgeons from far away. Doctors could also prepare for complicated procedures by first simulating them using a real patient's attributes.

computer peripheral
an accessory that works in conjunction with a computer

12   Meanwhile, Trisenx Inc. of Savannah, Ga., is developing a device to "print" flavors on a potato wafer. The **computer peripheral**, due out by early next year, would allow you to sample a chocolate cake you see at a Web site by spraying chemicals that mimic the cake's smell and taste.

13   AromaJet.com of Plano, Texas, has an Internet-based kiosk for perfume stores in the works, while DigiScents of Oakland, Calif., is developing smell attachments for computers.

14   The DigiScents units could blow pleasant scents like fruit—along with foul ones like burning rubber. Those attributes have earned the speaker-like iSmell units the nickname "reeker."

15   How do they work?

16   The smell and taste devices come with basic chemicals that are combined in various proportions, using "recipes" from a Web site. It's similar to how computers combine the primary colors of red, blue and yellow to represent varying hues.

haptic devices
computer accessories related to the sense of touch

17   For touch, sites tell **haptic devices** like the iFeel mice when and how to vibrate.

18   Bringing these senses to the Internet permits new forms of communications—for the blind, as well as the sighted.

19   Novint Technologies in Albuquerque, N.M., is developing a three-dimensional Web browser to navigate touch-sensitive environments.

20   "You can walk into a (virtual) store and actually push around a shopping cart," said Tom Anderson. Novint's chief executive. "With things like jewelry, if you just see a picture, you don't know if you want to buy it. With this, I could turn it around and see it sparkle and feel its weight."

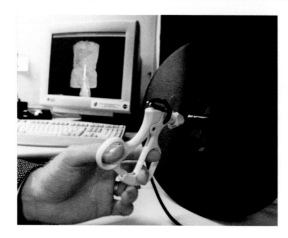

Researchers at Stanford University in Palo Alto are developing surgical simulations for medical students. Using scissor-like handles attached to virtual forceps, the students can feel the difference between skin and bone.

21   One could use a smell device to add rose scents to an online card for Valentine's Day, or help schoolchildren smell a foreign land during a geography lesson.

22   Game developers, meanwhile, are looking to add touch and smell to action and fantasy games, while online adult companies have developed suits and devices to simulate sexual pleasures.

23   Beyond the Internet and computers, how about scent-enabled movies?

24   "We use musical scores to create mood, to manipulate your emotion," said Joel Lloyd Bellenson, co-founder and chief executive of DigiScents. "Scent will have the real thing. You can feel anticipation, exhilaration and arousal."

25   Or what about television? With a new round of "Survivor" about to debut on CBS, notes Trisenx marketing director Kathey Porter, "wouldn't it be great if you could smell the Australian Outback?"

26   Years from now, scent "cameras" may even complement personal Webcams or video recorders. Devices that can analyze and reproduce the chemical composition of smells are costly, cumbersome and limited to scientists now. But DigiScents is trying to develop a consumer version.

27   For now, online "touching" is akin to touching an object with a pen or a stick. Reproducing the sensation felt by fingertips is still years away.

28   "Generally speaking," noted Ralph Hollis, a principal research scientist at Carnegie Mellon University in Pittsburgh, "people are not completely fooled yet."

29   Then there's delay, the fraction of a second it takes light—your data—to travel through the Net. For truly interactive applications, such as virtual surgery, those milliseconds can be crucial. It's those first few milliseconds that tell your brain what you are hitting, and even the shortest delay can be deadly.

30   The smell devices, meanwhile, are limited to the chemicals that come with them. You may be able to reproduce a pepperoni pizza, but not the one from Pizza Hut. You may get a basic rose scent, but not the traces of other fragrances that accompany roses in nature.

receptors
nerve endings that respond to sensory stimuli

31   Plus, scientists do not know all the basic ingredients of scent. The human body has hundreds of smell **receptors**, and some may work in combination to recognize thousands of odors.

32   Pam Dalton, a research scientist at the nonprofit Monell Chemical Senses Center in Philadelphia, believes that once those odors are cataloged and reproduced, "the potential is limitless."

33   But even then, will computer users really want to eat something from a printer-like device, or inhale artificial fragrances?

34   Or in the case of a glove that might one day reproduce the sensation of fingers, will people want to share the device with a sweaty co-worker?

35   And will people even want computers to invade their lives—by manipulating sensations—in yet another way?

36   Proponents believe so and expect the devices to be as common as audio speakers once they overcome the social hurdles.

37   "It's not different from when sound was first added to the computer," said Porter of Trisenx. "People said, 'We don't need to hear our computers talking all day. It's just some additional chatter and noise.'"

38   Soon, she said, people will wonder how they got by with only sight and sound. "They will feel like the Internet experience is not complete unless they have this."

➤ **A.   UNDERSTANDING THE THESIS AND OTHER MAIN IDEAS**

Select the best answer.

___b___ 1. The central thesis of the selection is best expressed in the statement

a. "People are pretty much limited to seeing and hearing things over the Internet these days." (paragraph 2)

b. "Efforts are under way to make the Internet more sensory—by adding smell, taste and touch." (paragraph 2)

c. "It wasn't too long ago that computers could display little more than text." (paragraph 4)

d. "Researchers had difficulty explaining that the machines would evolve to eventually show movies and play music." (paragraph 4)

___a___ 2. The author's primary purpose is to

a. report on a developing technology.

b. compare the Internet today with the Internet of the future.

c. promote the development of surgical simulation techniques.

d. cast doubt on the possibility of a more sensory Internet.

___c___ 3. The topic of paragraph 11 is

a. medical students.

b. top surgeons.

c. surgical simulation.

d. real patients.

___c___ 4. The answer to the question "How does the technology for smell and taste work?" can be found in paragraph

    a. 13.

    b. 14.

    c. 16.

    d. 17.

___a___ 5. The main idea of paragraph 20 is that

    a. sensory technology can help customers decide whether they want to buy a product.

    b. jewelry stores can use sensory technology to reduce theft.

    c. shopping carts are unnecessary when shopping on the Internet.

    d. customers will not have to leave their homes to go shopping.

___b___ 6. According to the selection, a current drawback to the sensory technology of smell is that

    a. analyzing and reproducing the chemical composition of smells is too time-consuming.

    b. scientists do not know all of the basic ingredients of smell.

    c. smell devices are restricted by federal law.

    d. all of the above

▶ B.   IDENTIFYING DETAILS

Select the best answer.

___b___ 1. The company that is developing a device that would put flavors on a potato wafer is

    a. Logitech.

    b. Trisenx Inc.

    c. Immersion Corp.

    d. AromaJet.com.

___a___ 2. According to the selection, surgical simulation is being developed to enable all of the following kinds of experiences *except* for

    a. medical students practicing on real patients.

    b. medical students feeling the difference between skin and bone.

c. medical students practicing advanced procedures with top surgeons from far away.

d. doctors preparing for complicated procedures by first simulating them using the attributes of a real patient.

___c___ 3. Novint Technologies is developing a

a. speaker-like smell attachment for computers.

b. scent camera that complements video recorders.

c. three-dimensional Web browser to navigate touch-sensitive environments.

d. device that produces bumps as the user runs across icons on the computer desktop.

___c___ 4. According to the selection, smell technology could be used to do all of the following *except*

a. help schoolchildren smell a foreign land during a geography lesson.

b. create moods and manipulate emotions during movies.

c. help consumers recognize the smell of carbon monoxide in their homes.

d. add the scent of flowers to an online Valentine's Day card.

> **C. RECOGNIZING METHODS OF ORGANIZATION AND TRANSITIONS**

Select the best answer.

___a___ 1. In paragraph 8, the organizational pattern used is

a. process.

b. definition.

c. enumeration.

d. statement and clarification.

___b___ 2. In paragraph 7, a transitional phrase that suggests a sequence in time is

a. it seems like.

b. late last year.

c. after all.

d. some of.

➤ D.   REVIEWING AND ORGANIZING IDEAS: MAPPING

Complete the following map of the sensory technology described in the selection by filling in the missing words.

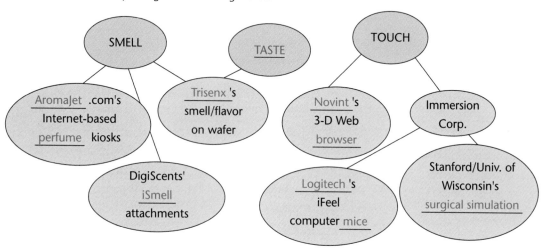

➤ E.   FIGURING OUT INFERRED MEANINGS

Indicate whether each statement is true (T) or false (F).

__T__ 1. The surgical simulation technology would be most valuable to medical schools and hospitals.

__T__ 2. The taste and smell technology may take years to perfect.

__T__ 3. Sensory technology could be especially valuable to blind people or those with limited vision.

__F__ 4. The time delay in data transmission would not matter to patients undergoing virtual surgery.

__F__ 5. The companies developing smell technology are only interested in reproducing pleasant smells.

__T__ 6. Online (virtual) stores would benefit from the technology described in this article.

➤ F.   THINKING CRITICALLY

Select the best answer.

__c__ 1. The author's tone can best be described as

a. critical.

b. skeptical.

c. informative.

d. formal.

_a___ 2. The statement, "It seems like a lot of science fiction to a lot of people" (paragraph 5) means that

 a. many people believe that sensory technology sounds like something from a futuristic story.

 b. the idea for sensory technology was stolen from a science fiction book.

 c. people who do not understand how the Internet works will not be able to use this technology.

 d. the most popular use for sensory technology will be in conjunction with science fiction movies.

_b___ 3. The iSmell units are nicknamed "reeker" (paragraph 14) because

 a. the word rhymes with leaker and the units resemble reeks.

 b. the units can produce strong odors, or odors that reek.

 c. both a and b

 d. neither a nor b

_d___ 4. The statement, "Generally speaking, people are not completely fooled yet" (paragraph 28) means that

 a. most people are not foolish enough to believe in sensory technology.

 b. most people don't want sensory devices for their computers.

 c. people will have to be fooled into buying sensory devices for their computers.

 d. sensory technology for touch is not yet a believable or realistic sensation for most people.

➤ G.   BUILDING VOCABULARY

➤ Context

Using context and a dictionary, if necessary, determine the meaning of each word as it is used in the selection.

_b___ 1. skepticism (paragraph 3)

 a. intelligence

 b. disbelief

 c. criticism

 d. support

_c_ 2. evolve (paragraph 4)

    a. return   c. develop

    b. target   d. promote

_a_ 3. rudimentary (paragraph 6)

    a. basic   c. stable

    b. complex   d. advanced

_b_ 4. simulation (paragraph 9)

    a. test   c. picture

    b. imitation   d. proposal

_a_ 5. navigate (paragraph 19)

    a. work within   c. understand

    b. leave   d. apply

_b_ 6. manipulate (paragraph 24)

    a. handle   c. regard

    b. influence   d. use

_b_ 7. cumbersome (paragraph 26)

    a. unattractive   c. expensive

    b. awkward   d. complicated

_c_ 8. akin (paragraph 27)

    a. painful   c. similar

    b. unrelated   d. separate

_d_ 9. proponents (paragraph 36)

    a. experts   c. critics

    b. advisors   d. supporters

▶ Word Parts

Read each of the statements from the selection again, and then use the hints to fill in the meaning of the underlined word or phrase.

1. "Years from now, scent 'cameras' may even complement personal <u>Webcams</u> or video recorders." (paragraph 26)

    Hints: The word *cam* is short for *camera.*

                 The word *Web* refers to the World Wide Web.

Therefore, a Webcam is a _____camera_____ that projects images from a person using the __World Wide Web__.

2. "For truly <u>interactive</u> applications, such as virtual surgery, those <u>milliseconds</u> can be crucial." (paragraph 29)

Hints: The prefix *inter-* means *among* or *between.*

The prefix *milli-* means *one-thousandth.*

Therefore, interactive applications such as virtual surgery take place __between or among__ two systems with direct and continual responses, and milliseconds are _____thousandths_____ of seconds.

➤ H.   SELECTING A LEARNING/STUDY STRATEGY

Assume you were reading this article for a sociology class in which you are studying the influence of technology on society. Write a list of ways you think our lives might be affected by sense technology.

➤ I.   EXPLORING IDEAS THROUGH DISCUSSION AND WRITING

1. Does sensory technology seem like science fiction to you?

2. Can you think of any other applications for this kind of technology?

3. Do you think technology like this will be common in the near future, as its proponents believe? Would you want such technology for your computer?

➤ J.   BEYOND THE CLASSROOM TO THE WEB

Visit the "Company" page of AromaJet's Web site at **http://AromaJet.com/comp.htm.**
Read the press release announcing the first fragrance transmission over the Internet. According to the press release, what benefits will come from the ability to send fragrance this way?

✔ **Tracking Your Progress**

Selection 25

Section	Number Correct		Score
A. Thesis and Main Idea (6 items)	_____	x 4	_____
B. Details (4 items)	_____	x 3	_____
C. Organization and Transitions (2 items)	_____	x 2	_____
E. Inferred Meanings (6 items)	_____	x 3	_____
F. Thinking Critically (4 items)	_____	x 4	_____
G. Vocabulary			
1. Context (9 items)	_____	x 2	_____
2. Word Parts (4 items)	_____	x 2	_____

TOTAL SCORE _____ %

CHECKING YOUR READING RATE

Words in Selection 25: 1,202

Finishing Time:	_____	_____	_____
	(hour)	(minutes)	(seconds)
Starting Time:	_____	_____	_____
	(hour)	(minutes)	(seconds)
Total Reading Time:		_____	_____
		(minutes)	(seconds)

Words Per Minute Score (page 737) _____ WPM

SELECTION 26

A Mania for Messaging
Chris Wood

This article was first published in a magazine called *Maclean's Toronto* in 2000. Read it to discover one of the newest trends in computer technology.

> ### PREVIEWING THE READING

Using the steps listed on page 5, preview the reading selection. When you have finished, complete the following items.

1. The subject of this article is ___instant messaging___.

2. List several types of computer technology you expect this reading to discuss:

   a. ___e-mail___

   b. ___instant messaging___

   c. ___PCs___

 ### MAKING CONNECTIONS

If you use instant messaging, have you used or read any of the following instances of message-speak? Did you understand what was meant?

MESSAGE-SPEAK
Instant messengers have spread and intensified the quick-typing, rarely capitalized vocabulary of online chat rooms. Translated samples:

sup?	Whassup? (Similar to howzigoin)
nm	Nothing much (or spelled out, nutin)
a/s/l	Age/sex/location? (Meaning, who r u?)
stats	Answered by: brown hair, 115 lb. . . .
oic	I get it
kewl	Rhymes with, but does not describe, skool
rox	It rox, they rawk
brb	Be right back
wth	What the, er, heck. Sometimes wtf
cu	See you . . .
l8r	. . . Later

> **READING TIP**

As you read, highlight the advantages and disadvantages of instant messaging.

CHECKING YOUR READING RATE

If you plan to compute your reading rate, be sure to record your starting time in the box at the end of the exercises before you begin reading.

PC
the abbreviation for personal computer

Internet
a system comprising millions of computers interconnected worldwide through telephone lines, digital cables, optical fiber, and satellite links

Net
the abbreviation for Internet

e-mail
electronic mail, or typed messages sent over the Internet

Web
the World Wide Web, the combined 3.5 million Web page servers that make their Web pages available to anyone with a Web browser and Internet access

A Mania for Messaging

1   Stuffed animals fill the bookshelf behind Mira Barnett's desk, threatening to overrun the trophies she won for public speaking. A blue cordless telephone matches her bedroom's color scheme. But these days, the Vancouver Grade 8 student is more likely to gab with friends over her **PC** than on her phone. Using one of half a dozen instant messaging programs available free from the **Internet**, Barnett converses by exchanging short text messages with friends down the block or as far away as Mexico. Opening duplicate windows on her computer screen, Barnett shows how she keeps several "chats" going at once. Most are with schoolmates. But she also stays in touch with a Los Angeles friend and practices her Hebrew with a 75-year-old woman in Israel whom she met on the **Net**. Among the advantages, the 12-year-old says, "you can make conversations with a whole bunch of people at once, and talk to your friends all over and not pay long distance."

2   Mira's experience isn't likely to surprise anyone under the age of 20 with access to a computer—or their parents. Among Netliterate teenagers, instant messaging—which combines the immediacy of the phone with the brevity of **e-mail** text—has become the hottest social advance since the mall. Talky teenage girls seem particularly smitten by the technology, helping propel female users of the Internet to more than half of total users for the first time. But the young are not alone. As the growing popularity of instant messaging (IM) outstrips that of either regular e-mail or conventional **Web**-browsing, adults and businesses are waking up to its potential. Much of that is to the good, saving time and boosting productivity. But not all: experts worry that IM exposes already overloaded workers to yet another powerful distraction. "It is one of the major concerns of our clients," says John West, president of Priority Management Inc., a Vancouver company that trains executives in 16 countries. "They're leaving important projects undone and getting less important e-mail attended to."

3   Nonetheless, IM's rise has made the sector a rare hot spot of Web commerce, and driven the topic to center stage in the debate over America Online's proposed $205-billion takeover of Time Warner Inc. AOL's two IM services—ICQ (for "I seek you") and AIM (AOL Instant Messenger)—account for an estimated 80 to 90 percent of the world's 140 million or so registered instant-message users. Rivals, including giant Microsoft with its MSN Messenger program (number 2 in popularity in Canada after ICQ, according to research firm Media Metrix Canada), want regulators to loosen AOL's hold on those customers before approving the mega-merger.

Barnett: conversations with 'a whole bunch of people at once'

icon
a picture on a computer screen that represents a specific function or command

software
the programs, routines, and symbolic languages that direct the operation of a computer's hardware

logging on
the process of beginning an Internet session on the computer

4   At its heart, IM gives anyone with an Internet connection access to the same type of real-time chat that users of large corporate, academic or government networks have long enjoyed. Unlike conventional Internet e-mail, which can sometimes take hours or even days to reach its destination, IM systems deliver the message just as the name suggests—instantly. A flashing on-screen **icon** or sound alerts recipients. Moreover, while e-mail is open to all, IM networks are closed: users can only message others who subscribe to the same service.

5   That is half the trick. The other half is something IM users know by the name "buddy lists," but engineers call "presence awareness." This is the **software** that makes it possible for people **logging on** to know who else among their list of friends is online at the same time. Alli Aziz, for instance, has about 20 names on her buddy list—all belonging to friends from her London, Ont., elementary school. Like Mica Barnett, 12-year-old Aziz usually pursues more than one chat thread at a time, with different individuals or groups. "The most I've ever had going at once," she says, "was five."

6   Alli's mom understands the appeal. She doesn't use instant messaging at home, but her employer's e-mail system operates much like an IM service, showing an alert whenever a new communication arrives. "I do find it's compulsive," Kathy Glasgow says. "I'm probably a little obsessed about checking it and getting back to people right away." But as director of records services at London's St. Joseph's Health Care Centre, Glasgow also keenly appreciates the swiftness with which a well-timed message exchange can resolve an issue. "The benefits outweigh the distraction," she concludes.

7   Millions agree. Forrester Research, which gathers Net statistics, estimates that more than a third of Web-connected North Americans use IM at least weekly. Within 18 months, an industry group expects the number of regular users to more than triple. That growth rate is one reason AOL's rivals are pushing so hard to loosen the Dulles, Va.-based Internet giant's hold on IM. The bigger one is the future profits corporate strategists believe IM will unlock. Because users access IM services frequently, and often keep their windows open on-screen for long periods, those windows make appealing delivery vehicles for e-commerce advertising. IM is also being launched for

cell phones and personal digital assistants like the Palm. Many analysts believe instant messaging is emerging as the "killer app" of wireless.

8   For it to reach its fullest potential, however, existing barriers between different IM networks must fall, allowing open communication among users of all services—just as conventional e-mail does. So far, AOL has refused to open AIM and ICQ to such inter-operability, citing unspecified security concerns. Its rivals, including Microsoft, Yahoo! and AT&T, are working on a protocol to get the services working together. They have asked regulators not to approve AOL's acquisition of Time Warner until the issue is resolved.

9   Other companies, meanwhile, are looking for their own share of messaging profits. Several have developed programs that let IM users communicate directly by voice using microphones and speakers built into their computers—in effect turning their PCs into telephones. Both MSN Messenger and AIM now offer free calls from computers directly to phone numbers across North America. Last month, Eyeball.com of Vancouver launched a video-chat service that lets IM users equipped with PC video cameras see each other.

PDA
the abbreviation for personal digital assistant, a small, handheld device that has features such as a date book, address book, calculator, etc.

10   Down the road, believes Toronto market analyst Charley Whaley, "IM could become the glue that finally makes the Holy Grail of 'unified messaging' possible." Presence-awareness software will deliver incoming messages from any source to whatever digital device you happen to be using—PC, cell phone, pager or **PDA**—translating text to voice (or vice versa) as necessary. Many older Canadians may feel information overload has reached a bewildering new level. Chances are Alli Aziz and Mira Barnett will feel right at home.

► A.   UNDERSTANDING THE THESIS AND OTHER MAIN IDEAS

Select the best answer.

___c___ 1. The central thesis of the selection is that

   a. teenage girls are becoming interested in the Internet because of instant messaging (IM) technology.

   b. IM technology is more popular than e-mail and conventional Web-browsing.

   c. IM technology is a high-growth industry that appeals to teenagers, adults, and businesses.

   d. businesses are beginning to recognize the potential profits linked to IM technology.

___b___ 2. The author's primary purpose is to

   a. promote the use of IM technology.

   b. describe IM technology, its users, and the issues that will affect its success.

   c. compare the different providers of IM technology.

   d. express disapproval of Internet-based socializing.

_b_ 3. The topic of paragraph 4 is

   a. the Internet.

   b. advantages of IM.

   c. disadvantages of IM.

   d. e-mail.

_d_ 4. The main idea of paragraph 7 is that

   a. the number of regular users of IM is expected to triple in less than two years.

   b. America Online (AOL) currently has a monopoly on IM technology.

   c. AOL's rivals are pushing for deregulation of IM.

   d. the growing popularity of IM represents potential profits to Internet businesses.

_a_ 5. The main idea of paragraph 9 is expressed in the

   a. first sentence.   c. third sentence.

   b. second sentence.   d. last sentence.

➤ **B. IDENTIFYING DETAILS**

Select the best answer.

_b_ 1. Mira Barnett can best be described as

   a. the author of the selection.

   b. a 12-year-old Canadian girl who uses IM.

   c. a 75-year-old Hebrew woman in Israel.

   d. the president of an executive training company in Canada.

_c_ 2. The name of Microsoft's IM program is

   a. ICQ.   c. MSN Messenger.

   b. AIM.   d. Media Matrix.

_a_ 3. The term "presence awareness" refers to

   a. the software that makes it possible for people to know who else is online at the same time.

   b. online address books that automatically record frequent e-mail destinations.

   c. the barriers that currently exist between different IM networks.

   d. the efforts of online businesses to tap into the IM market.

_c_ 4. According to Internet statistics gathered by Forrester Research, more than a third of Web-connected North Americans use IM at least

   a. once a day.

   b. twice a day.

   c. weekly.

   d. once a month.

_a_ 5. According to the selection, Eyeball.com has introduced a service that lets IM users

   a. see each other using PC video cameras.

   b. communicate directly by voice using microphones and speakers built into their PCs.

   c. make free calls from computers directly to telephone numbers across North America.

   d. send messages to users who subscribe to different IM services.

➤ C. RECOGNIZING METHODS OF ORGANIZATION AND TRANSITIONS

Complete the following statements by filling in the blanks.

1. In paragraph 4, the author uses the comparison and contrast organizational pattern to show the differences between conventional Internet e-mail and IM systems. The transitional word that indicates this pattern is _____unlike_____.

2. The transitional phrase in paragraph 5 that indicates that the author is going to illustrate his or her ideas is _____for instance_____.

➤ D. REVIEWING AND ORGANIZING IDEAS: PARAPHRASING

Complete the following paraphrase of paragraph 6 by filling in the missing words or phrases.

Paragraph 6: Kathy _____Glasgow_____ knows why her daughter _____Alli_____ likes _____IM_____. Although Glasgow _____doesn't use_____ IM at _____home_____, the _____e-mail system_____ where she works is similar to an _____IM service_____ in that it signals the arrival of each _____new communication_____. Glasgow, who is the _____director of_____

<u>records services</u> at St. Joseph's Health Care Center in <u>London</u>, admits that she is somewhat obsessive about <u>checking</u> her messages and responding immediately. However, she does appreciate how <u>IM</u> allows <u>issues</u> to be resolved quickly through the timely exchange of <u>messages</u>. She has decided that the <u>benefits</u> of <u>IM</u> are greater than its <u>distractions</u>.

➤ E.   FIGURING OUT INFERRED MEANINGS

Some of the words used in "A Mania for Messaging" create an informal, youthful tone. Make inferences by deciding whether the underlined word or phrase in each of the following sentences is intended to create that tone. Write Y for yes or N for no.

__Y__ 1. "But these days, the Vancouver Grade 8 student is more likely to <u>gab</u> with friends over her PC than on her phone." (paragraph 1)

__Y__ 2. "Barnett shows how she keeps several '<u>chats</u>' going at once." (paragraph 1)

__Y__ 3. "Among Netliterate teenagers, instant messaging has become the <u>hottest</u> social advance since the mall." (paragraph 2)

__Y__ 4. "<u>Talky</u> teenage girls seem particularly smitten by the technology." (paragraph 2)

__N__ 5. "Experts worry that IM exposes already <u>overloaded workers</u> to yet another powerful distraction." (paragraph 2)

__Y__ 6. "Many analysts believe instant messaging is emerging as the '<u>killer app</u>' of wireless." (paragraph 7)

__N__ 7. "Many older Canadians may feel <u>information overload</u> has reached a bewildering new level." (paragraph 10)

➤ F.   THINKING CRITICALLY

Select the best answer.

__c__ 1. The author begins the selection by telling about Mira Barnett in order to

a. generate controversy about the use of IM by preteens.

b. compare Mira's generation with an older generation that is uncomfortable with IM technology.

c. illustrate the type of IM user who has propelled the popularity of IM.

d. encourage other 12-year-olds to begin using IM.

_d_ 2. The phrase "chat thread" (paragraph 5) means

   a. the IM software.

   b. e-mail.

   c. an Internet connection.

   d. an online conversation.

_a_ 3. The statement that "those windows make appealing delivery vehicles" (paragraph 7) means that

   a. advertisers are interested in promoting products to IM users while they are online.

   b. advertisers want to get IM users to promote products to the people on their buddy lists.

   c. IM technology allows users to order certain products for delivery.

   d. advertisers can access buying information about IM users through their IM accounts.

_b_ 4. The statement that "Chances are Alli Aziz and Mira Barnett will feel right at home" (paragraph 10) means that the two girls will

   a. be using IM at home rather than in school or in the workplace.

   b. feel comfortable with future technological advances because Internet technology is already part of their lives.

   c. be part of the information overload.

   d. be asked to explain the new technology to older generations.

➤ G.   BUILDING VOCABULARY

➤ Context

Using context and a dictionary, if necessary, determine the meaning of each word as it is used in the selection.

_b_ 1. converses (paragraph 1)

   a. consumes   c. repeats

   b. talks   d. types

_a_ 2. smitten (paragraph 2)

   a. affected   c. confused

   b. tricked   d. uncertain

_c_ 3. propel (paragraph 2)

   a. replace   c. push

   b. hide   d. support

_b_ 4. rivals (paragraph 3)

    a. friends   c. peers

    b. competitors   d. supporters

_a_ 5. launched (paragraph 7)

    a. introduced   c. considered

    b. ditched   d. eliminated

_c_ 6. protocol (paragraph 8)

    a. permission   c. procedure

    b. agreement   d. regulation

▶ **Word Parts**

Read each of the statements from the selection again, then use the hints to fill in the meaning of the underlined word or phrase.

1. "Among <u>Netliterate</u> teenagers, instant messaging has become the hottest social advance since the mall." (paragraph 2)

    Hints: The word *Net* refers to the Internet.

             The word *literate* means *knowledgeable in a particular field.*

    Therefore, if the teenagers are Netliterate, they are __knowledgeable__ about using the Internet.

2. "Rivals want regulators to loosen AOL's hold on those customers before approving the <u>mega-merger</u>." (paragraph 3)

    Hints: The prefix *mega-* means *large.*

             To *merge* is to *combine* or *unite.*

    Therefore, the mega-merger between AOL and Time-Warner would be considered a __large combination or union__ of the two companies.

3. "So far, AOL has refused to open AIM and ICQ to such <u>inter-operability</u>." (paragraph 8)

    Hints: The prefix *inter-* means *between* or *among.*

             The root of the word *operability* is *operate.*

             The suffix *able* means *capable of performing an action.*

    Therefore, AOL is refusing to open its IM systems to a capability to __operate between or among__ the other companies' systems.

➤ **H.   SELECTING A LEARNING/STUDY STRATEGY**

Select the best answer.

___d___   If you were writing a research paper on instant messaging and were using this article as one of your sources, the most useful strategy would be to

a. record details about Mira Barnett.

b. outline the selection.

c. draw a map.

d. paraphrase useful information.

➤ **I.   EXPLORING IDEAS THROUGH DISCUSSION AND WRITING**

1. What do you think are the biggest advantages of IM, especially as compared to e-mail? Do you think IM is an idea that will go away, or do you agree with analysts that its popularity will continue to grow?

2. What impact do you think IM will have on global communication?

3. Why should or shouldn't AOL be forced to "loosen its hold" on its IM customers? Support your viewpoint.

➤ **J.   BEYOND THE CLASSROOM TO THE WEB**

Type the search term "instant message" into a search engine such as AltaVista or Lycos. Judging from the summary information under the first twenty listings or so, what are some of the uses of instant messaging?

✔ **Tracking Your Progress**

Selection 26

Section	Number Correct		Score
A. Thesis and Main Idea (5 items)	_____	x 5	_____
B. Details (5 items)	_____	x 4	_____
C. Organization and Transitions (2 items)	_____	x 2	_____
E. Inferred Meanings (7 items)	_____	x 3	_____
F. Thinking Critically (4 items)	_____	x 3	_____
G. Vocabulary			
1. Context (6 items)	_____	x 2	_____
2. Word Parts (3 items)	_____	x 2	_____

TOTAL SCORE _____ %

CHECKING YOUR READING RATE

Words in Selection 26: 1,089

Finishing Time:	_____	_____	_____
	(hour)	(minutes)	(seconds)
Starting Time:	_____	_____	_____
	(hour)	(minutes)	(seconds)
Total Reading Time:		_____	_____
		(minutes)	(seconds)

Words Per Minute Score (page 737) _____ WPM

SELECTION
27

House Arrest and Electronic Monitoring

Hugh D. Barlow

This selection is taken from a criminal justice textbook, *Criminal Justice in America*, by Hugh D. Barlow, published in 2000. It appeared in a chapter titled "Community-Based Corrections."

➤ PREVIEWING THE READING

Using the steps listed on page 5, preview the reading selection. When you have finished, answer the following questions.

1. The subject of this selection is <u>house arrest (or) electronic monitoring</u>.

2. List four questions you expect to be able to answer after reading the article.

   a. <u>How does electronic monitoring work?</u>

   _____

   b. <u>Is there support for electronic monitoring of offenders?; What are</u>

   <u>the benefits of electronic monitoring for offenders?</u>

   c. <u>What are the attitudes of offenders toward electronic monitoring?</u>

   _____

   d. <u>How successful is home confinement with electronic monitoring?</u>

   _____

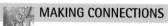

MAKING CONNECTIONS

For what kinds of crimes should people be able to be restrained at home instead of having to go to prison? Why?

> ➤ READING TIP

As you read, highlight information about how electronic monitoring works and its effectiveness.

CHECKING YOUR READING RATE

If you plan to compute your reading rate, be sure to record your starting time in the box at the end of the exercises before you begin reading.

House Arrest and Electronic Monitoring

surveillance
close observation of a person under suspicion

probation officer
the official who supervises a convict who is either serving a suspended sentence or on probation

jurisdictions
areas of authority

transmitter
an electronic device that sends signals from an antenna to a central receiver

1   Electronic monitoring is part of a "new age of **surveillance**," according to one criminologist (Lilly, 1990). It is a means by which criminal justice personnel can monitor the movements of offenders who have been released into the community with severe restrictions—the most restrictive being *house arrest,* also called *home confinement.* Offenders under house arrest are confined to their homes when they are not working or engaged in activities pre-approved by their **probation officer**. Their movements are monitored through electronic devices described in the following section.

2   The rules of confinement vary, but in some **jurisdictions** every adult in the offender's house is expected to abide by them. "No alcohol, no parties, and no weapons" is one such rule in Cook County, Illinois (Turnbaugh, 1995a:7).

How Electronic Monitoring Works

3   The origins of electronic monitoring are traced back to the 1960s, when researchers at Harvard University constructed a belt-worn **transmitter** and a series of repeater stations in the Boston area that were linked to a central monitoring station (Renzema, 1992). Signals from the transmitter allowed the wearer to be tracked over several blocks.

4   The most widespread application today consists of a number of computer terminals, or monitoring towers, linked via phone lines to a receiver that resembles a cable TV box in the offender's home. The offender wears a nonremovable ankle band holding a transmitter that sends a signal to the receiver. Beyond a certain range, from 100 to as much as 750 feet, the signal fades and the receiver triggers a violation report, which is printed out at the monitoring station. In the Cook County program mentioned earlier, the monitoring towers are manned by six technicians who constantly check the activity of 180 to 200 individuals under house arrest.

5   Early experiments with electronic monitoring equipment in the field uncovered various problems, from equipment failures to radio interference and weather-related difficulties. It was found that signals could be masked by simple household products such as aluminum foil. But the idea had caught on by the 1980s and the prospect of growing profits attracted the resources and ingenuity of the private sector. Continued refinements by manufacturers and vendors have resulted in all sorts of innovations: Whereas early electronic monitoring required a phone line to the

House arrest with electronic monitoring is an intermediate sanction that combines control and restraint with freedoms that promote responsibility and enable offenders to make a living or improve their skills. It is growing in popularity as a low-cost alternative to imprisonment but its overall impact on recidivism and public safety is uncertain.

offender's home, cellular technology has replaced lines and allows for continuous and random checks by probation officers. Today, numerous companies compete for this growing business (Klein, 1997:288).

6   One company, called Sentencing Alternatives, markets both single-offender and multiple-offender systems—which are capable of monitoring up to 40 offenders with one telephone line and one receiver. They offer "full services" such as free officer safety devices, free expert court witnesses, and 24-hour monitoring done on a sophisticated, powerful **mainframe computer system**, not a PC. The company claims that "only you will know when or where the offender will be subject to being checked, and at the same time the officer never has to leave the comfort and safety of the automobile" (Sentencing Alternatives, 1997, http://www.sentalt.com/).

mainframe computer system
a system in which a large, powerful computer serves numerous connected terminals

Support for Electronic Monitoring of Offenders

7   In 1986, there were only 95 offenders on electronic monitoring in the entire country (Renzema, 1992:41). By 1995 there were an estimated 70,000 people under some kind of electronic monitoring (Lilly, 1995). In Florida alone, more than 13,000 offenders were on house arrest in 1993 (Blomberg, Bales, and Reed, 1993).

8   Home confinement with electronic monitoring is appealing because it promises so much. Its supporters usually cite four distinct benefits: (1) it protects society; (2) it punishes offenders; (3) it allows offenders to work and to improve their future prospects through counseling and education; and (4) it reduces prison overcrowding and correctional costs. A 1994 national survey of criminal justice professionals found widespread support for electronic monitoring (McEwen, 1995:51–52). One of the few studies of public attitudes toward electronic house arrest found strong yet conditional support for the practice (Brown and Elrod, 1995). Most respondents felt that house arrest was appropriate for low-risk, nondangerous offenders. However, some officials have expressed concern over the criteria for selecting offenders for monitoring. Individual jurisdictions have largely followed a trial-and-error process, with mixed results.

9   In Mississippi, for example, electronic monitoring was restricted at first to a "very select group" of nonviolent offenders (Gowen, 1995). As time passed, several high-

risk offenders with backgrounds of violence, mental illness, or severe drug abuse slipped by the screening yet successfully completed the program. This encouraged officials to widen the class of offenders placed in the program. However, that decision meant an increase in the need for supervision and greater risks to probation officers. The officers adapted by using two-way mobile radios, cellular pages, and bulletproof vests—and many began carrying firearms as well.

Attitudes of Offenders

10   The attitudes toward electronic house arrest among offenders are mixed. Not surprisingly, offenders like being close to their families and loved ones, and those who work or attend school appreciate the rehabilitative possibilities of this community-based sanction. But some have reacted negatively to the constant surveillance. In an English study, a relative of someone under house arrest emphasized the humiliation associated with wearing the device: "[S]he would not use tagging [a British term for electronic monitoring] on a dog as it was so demeaning" (Mair and Mortimer, 1996:20). In contrast, however, when offenders under electronic surveillance in Indianapolis were asked if they would recommend electronic monitoring to "somebody in your situation," nearly 75 percent said they would (Baumer and Mendelsohn, 1989).

How Successful Is Home Confinement with Electronic Monitoring?

11   Electronic monitoring is still a new practice, and there have been few comprehensive studies of its use. In the earlier days, technological problems compromised its use, and while there is more confidence in the technology today, defects still surface from time to time. Some have come to light as a result of lawsuits filed by citizens who have been robbed, raped, or assaulted by offenders under electronic surveillance (Christianson, 1995).

12   In a 1994 case, a Chicago firefighter had been murdered by a gang whose members included a convicted armed robber who had escaped from his electronic confinement. The suit alleged that the equipment had failed because it was poorly maintained and improperly used; it was revealed that over a seven-year period, 120 other offenders had cut off their monitors and had not been recaptured. The jury awarded $3 million in damages to the firefighter's estate.

13   The Cook County sheriff maintained that the incident represented an isolated case, and this appears to be justified. Nevertheless, if only one potentially violent offender escapes from home confinement, questions are raised about public safety. Perhaps the best answer to public safety is to make the selection process an informed and rigorous one. This is also the recommendation of the American Bar Association, in its 1994 Model Adult Community Corrections Act.

14   Concerning the two other promised benefits of electronic monitoring—reduction of correctional costs and offender recidivism—most case studies show considerable cost savings over imprisonment, even with the increased probation costs associated with electronic monitoring (Gowdy, n.d.). Evidence on recidivism is more mixed. Not surprisingly, the few studies that have been conducted show more success with low-risk offenders, particularly those convicted of drunk driving. However, some experts remain skeptical of the incapacitative benefits of house arrest (Tonry,

recidivism
the tendency of convicted offenders to return to criminal behavior after being released from confinement

1996:120). Electronic monitoring does not prevent offenders from committing domestic crimes, and motivated offenders can steal from the workplace or commit crimes by enlisting the help of others. More research will reveal the benefits and limitations of electronic house arrest. As things stand today, it remains a popular alternative to traditional imprisonment for nonviolent offenders.

➤ A. UNDERSTANDING THE THESIS AND OTHER MAIN IDEAS

Select the best answer.

__d__ 1. The central thesis of the selection is that

    a. electronic monitoring companies are part of a growing industry that offer alternatives to imprisonment.

    b. the electronic monitoring system is a humiliating alternative to traditional probation.

    c. the system that is used to select offenders for electronic monitoring is seriously flawed.

    d. electronic monitoring provides a low-cost alternative to traditional imprisonment for nonviolent offenders.

__a__ 2. The author's primary purpose is to

    a. describe electronic monitoring as it is used with house arrest.

    b. argue against electronic monitoring as an alternative to imprisonment.

    c. compare different alternatives to traditional imprisonment.

    d. criticize the criminal justice system in America.

__c__ 3. The question that is answered in paragraph 4 is

    a. What is electronic monitoring?

    b. Who is eligible for electronic monitoring?

    c. How does electronic monitoring work?

    d. Why is electronic monitoring a popular alternative to imprisonment?

__c__ 4. In paragraph 6, the "full services" offered by Sentencing Alternatives include all of the following *except*

    a. free officer safety devices.

    b. free expert court witnesses.

    c. portable PCs for officers' cars.

    d. 24-hour monitoring on a mainframe computer system.

__b__ 5. The topic of paragraph 8 is
   a. home confinement.
   b. benefits of electronic monitoring.
   c. criminal justice professionals.
   d. selection criteria.

__a__ 6. The main idea of paragraph 10 is expressed in the
   a. first sentence.   c. third sentence.
   b. second sentence.   d. last sentence.

__c__ 7. According to the selection, the best way to address questions about public safety is to
   a. widen the class of offenders eligible for home confinement.
   b. eliminate home confinement as an option for repeat offenders.
   c. make the selection process an informed and rigorous one.
   d. eliminate home confinement as an option for those convicted of drunk driving.

__d__ 8. The topic of paragraph 14 is
   a. correctional costs.
   b. offender recidivism.
   c. low-risk offenders.
   d. benefits and limitations of electronic monitoring.

▶ B. IDENTIFYING DETAILS

Indicate whether each statement is true (T) or false (F).

__T__ 1. Unless they are working or engaged in preapproved activities, offenders under house arrest are confined to their homes.

__F__ 2. The rules of confinement for house arrest are the same in every jurisdiction in America.

__F__ 3. The transmitter worn by the offender under house arrest sends signals through the offender's cable TV box.

__T__ 4. If an offender under house arrest goes outside the signal range, the receiver triggers a violation report, which is printed out at the monitoring station.

__F__ 5. The number of offenders on electronic monitoring in the United States has declined since 1986.

➤ C.   RECOGNIZING METHODS OF ORGANIZATION AND TRANSITIONS

Select the best answer.

___b___ 1. In paragraph 1, the organizational pattern the author uses to explain the terms "house arrest" and "electronic monitoring" is

a. time sequence.

b. definition.

c. enumeration.

d. comparison and contrast.

___c___ 2. The author uses the comparison and contrast organizational pattern in paragraph 5 to contrast

a. early equipment failures with radio interference.

b. weather-related difficulties with technological difficulties.

c. early electronic monitoring systems with current technology.

d. early equipment failures with current failures.

___a___ 3. In paragraph 8, the organizational pattern the author uses to present the benefits of home confinement with electronic monitoring is

a. enumeration.

b. definition.

c. time sequence.

d. comparison and contrast.

___d___ 4. The phrase in paragraph 10 that indicates that the author is using the comparison and contrast organizational pattern is

a. not surprisingly.

b. in an English study.

c. associated with.

d. in contrast.

➤ D.   REVIEWING AND ORGANIZING IDEAS: OUTLINING

Complete the following outline of paragraph 8 by filling in the missing words and phrases.

Support for Electronic Monitoring of Offenders

I.   Four benefits cited by supporters

    A. It protects _____society_____

    B. It _____punishes_____ offenders

    C. It allows offenders to _____work_____ and to improve
        their _____future prospects_____

       1. Counseling

       2. _____Education_____

    D. It reduces _____prison overcrowding_____ and _____correctional costs_____

II. _____Criminal justice_____ professionals

    A. Widespread support in 1994 _____national survey_____

III. Public attitudes

    A. Strong but _____conditional_____ support

       1. Appropriate for _____low-risk, nondangerous_____ offenders

IV. Officials

    A. Concern over the _____criteria_____ for selecting
        _____offenders_____

    B. _____Trial-and-error_____ process has mixed results

➤ E.   FIGURING OUT INFERRED MEANINGS

Indicate whether each statement is true (T) or false (F).

__T__ 1. It can be inferred that the nonremovable ankle band worn by an
offender under house arrest is removed once the offender's sentence
has been served.

__T__ 2. The involvement of private manufacturers and vendors has
improved the electronic monitoring process.

__F__ 3. Probation officers let offenders under house arrest know the exact
times when their activity will be checked.

__F__ 4. Many probation officers in Mississippi began carrying two-way
mobile radios so they could stay in close contact with their high-risk
offenders.

___T___ 5. Although relatives of offenders under electronic surveillance may find it demeaning, most offenders consider it better than prison.

___T___ 6. Electronic monitoring works well for offenders convicted of drunk driving because it keeps them from driving.

➤ **F.   THINKING CRITICALLY**

Select the best answer.

___d___ 1. The central thesis of "House Arrest and Electronic Monitoring" is supported by

    a. facts.

    b. statistics.

    c. research evidence.

    d. all of the above.

___b___ 2. The tone of the selection can best be described as

    a. critical.

    b. objective.

    c. warning.

    d. protective.

___c___ 3. The author includes the quote, "No alcohol, no parties, and no weapons" (paragraph 2) in order to

    a. gain sympathy for offenders under house arrest.

    b. add humor to a grim situation.

    c. offer an example of a rule of confinement.

    d. explain why so many offenders eventually fall back into criminal habits.

___b___ 4. In paragraph 6, the author describes Sentencing Alternatives, the electronic monitoring company, in order to

    a. promote the services of that particular company.

    b. illustrate how electronic monitoring companies market their services.

    c. compare the services offered by that company with those of other electronic monitoring companies.

    d. challenge the marketing claims made by that company.

_d_ 5. The author included the 1994 case about the murdered Chicago firefighter as

    a. a call to action against unreliable electronic monitoring companies.

    b. an argument against electronic monitoring as an alternative to imprisonment.

    c. a warning to electronic monitoring companies about the legal and financial consequences of faulty equipment.

    d. an example of the potentially tragic consequences of defects in the electronic confinement system.

➤ G. BUILDING VOCABULARY

➤ Context

Using context and a dictionary, if necessary, determine the meaning of each word as it is used in the selection.

_b_ 1. ingenuity (paragraph 5)

    a. emotion

    b. cleverness

    c. finances

    d. attention

_c_ 2. sector (paragraph 5)

    a. neighborhood

    b. business

    c. part

    d. tradition

_a_ 3. sanction (paragraph 10)

    a. penalty

    b. promotion

    c. permission

    d. license

_c_ 4. demeaning (paragraph 10)

    a. harmless

    b. uncertain

    c. humiliating

    d. hilarious

___d___ 5. rigorous (paragraph 13)

    a. accountable

    b. strict

    c. respectful

    d. generous

➤ Word Parts

Read each of the statements from the selection again, then use the hints to fill in the meaning of the underlined word or phrase.

1. "Electronic monitoring is part of a 'new age of surveillance,' according to one <u>criminologist</u>." (paragraph 1)

    Hints: The root of *criminologist* is *crime.*

                The root *–logy* means *study.*

                The suffix *–ist* means *a person who.*

    Therefore, a criminologist is ___a person who studies crime___.

2. "Continued refinements by manufacturers and vendors have resulted in all sorts of <u>innovations</u>." (paragraph 5)

    Hints: To *refine* means to *improve upon.*

                To *innovate* means to *introduce a new feature or idea.*

    Therefore, the manufacturers and vendors have made improvements that have resulted in ___the introduction of new features or ideas___ about electronic monitoring.

3. "[Offenders] who work or attend school appreciate the <u>rehabilitative</u> possibilities of this community-based sanction." (paragraph 10)

    Hint: To *rehabilitate* is to *restore to a useful life.*

    Therefore, these offenders are glad for the chance to ___restore themselves to a useful life___, especially in contrast to a prison-based sanction where rehabilitative opportunities are more limited.

➤ Unusual Words/ Unusual Meanings

Use the meanings given below to write a sentence using the underlined word or phrase.

1. A <u>trial-and-error process</u> (paragraph 8) means a way of finding the right solution by trying out various methods and eliminating the ones that don't work.

    Your sentence: _____.

2. When something <u>comes to light</u> (paragraph 11), it has been revealed or made known to the public.

Your sentence: _____.

➤ **H.   SELECTING A LEARNING/STUDY STRATEGY**

Select the best answer.

    <u>c</u>   If you were preparing for an essay exam that included this material, which of the following items would you predict might be on the exam?

    a. Explain why early experiments with electronic monitoring did not work.

    b. Describe the services Sentencing Alternatives offers.

    c. Define electronic monitoring and explain its advantages and disadvantages.

    d. Summarize the findings of the 1994 national survey of criminal justice professionals.

➤ **I.   EXPLORING IDEAS THROUGH DISCUSSION AND WRITING**

1. What kind of offenders do you think should be able to qualify for electronic monitoring?

2. Do you think the potential humiliation of living under house arrest outweighs the advantages?

3. Explain how the public nature of this "community-based sanction" might contribute in a positive or negative way to the offender's experience while under house arrest.

➤ **J.   BEYOND THE CLASSROOM TO THE WEB**

Visit the University of Florida News Desk at **http://www.napa.ufl.edu/99news/ homecell.htm.**

Read the article "UF Study Shows House Arrest Is No Easy Out for Criminal Offenders." Why does the article have this particular title? What specific information does the article give to support the title?

✔ **Tracking Your Progress**

Selection 27

Section	Number Correct		Score
A. Thesis and Main Idea (8 items)	_____	x 4	_____
B. Details (5 items)	_____	x 3	_____
C. Organization and Transitions (4 items)	_____	x 1	_____
E. Inferred Meanings (6 items)	_____	x 3	_____
F. Thinking Critically (5 items)	_____	x 3	_____
G. Vocabulary			
1. Context (5 items)	_____	x 2	_____
2. Word Parts (3 items)	_____	x 2	_____

TOTAL SCORE _____ %

CHECKING YOUR READING RATE

Words in Selection 27: 1,261

	(hour)	(minutes)	(seconds)
Finishing Time:	_____	_____	_____
Starting Time:	_____	_____	_____
	(hour)	(minutes)	(seconds)
Total Reading Time:		_____	_____
		(minutes)	(seconds)

Words Per Minute Score (page 739) _____ WPM

20 Health-Related Fields

"Nothing can be more important than your health." This is an overused saying, but it remains meaningful. As the medical field and health-care systems become more complex and as medical knowledge expands, it is becoming necessary for you to assume greater responsibility in your health-care management. Doctors expect you to be able to report your symptoms and many assume you to have some basic knowledge of the functioning of the human body. Certainly keeping yourself healthy on a day-to-day basis by eating properly and getting adequate exercise is your responsibility. In "Use It and Lose It" you will read about a woman who decided to take charge of her body through an exercise program. Making sure you get the right prescription and that your medications do not interact is also important. As you will learn in "Make No Mistake: Medical Errors Can Be Deadly Serious," medical errors do occur, and patient awareness is a primary means of prevention. Use and misuse of drugs is also an individual responsibility. "Athletes Looking Good and Doing Better with Anabolic Steroids?" describes the use of anabolic steroids by athletes to improve their strength and endurance.

Use the following tips when reading in health-related fields.

TIPS FOR READING IN HEALTH-RELATED FIELDS	■ **Learn necessary terminology.** Each of the articles in this chapter uses some technical and specialized terms. Reading in the field and speaking with health care professionals will be much easier if you have a mastery of basic terminology.

■ **Learn about basic human body systems.** You have to know how your body works in order to take care of it and to understand readings in the field. For example, in reading "Athletes Looking Good and Doing Better with Anabolic Steroids?" you need to know about hormonal and muscular systems of the body.

■ **Read critically.** There are many different viewpoints, different proposed cures, numerous lose-20-pounds-in-a-week diets, and many "miracle" exercise programs. Read critically, ask questions, and look for supporting evidence. As you read "Use It and Lose It," for example, you will read about one woman's fitness program. Can you be sure that what worked for her will work for you? Ask yourself, "On what principles of diet and exercise was her fitness program based?"

463

SELECTION 28

Use It and Lose It

Bonnie Schiedel

This reading was taken from the July 2000 issue of a women's magazine, *Chatelaine*. Read it to learn how one woman became healthier and more physically fit.

➤ **PREVIEWING THE READING**

Using the steps listed on page 5, preview the reading selection. When you have finished, complete the following items.

1. The woman featured in the article is named _____Marilee Arthur_____.

2. List at least three questions you expect to be able to answer after reading "Use It and Lose It."

   a. How do you squelch starch in your diet? _____

   b. What does timing have to do with meals? _____

   c. How do you get out of a workout rut? _____

MAKING CONNECTIONS

One component of maintaining a fit body is eating the right amounts of different kinds of food. This Food Guide Pyramid, published by the U.S. Department of Agriculture in 1998, recommends a certain number of servings per day for each food group. Think about your own eating habits. Do they lead to a healthy body? What other behaviors lead to good health?

> **READING TIP**

As you read, highlight advice the author offers that would help someone become more physically fit.

 CHECKING YOUR READING RATE

If you plan to compute your reading rate, be sure to record your starting time in the box at the end of the exercises before you begin reading.

Use It and Lose It

1   Five dress sizes and 100 pounds later, fitness instructor Marilee Arthur is trimmer and more vibrant than ever, thanks to smart and sensible new habits that turn fat to muscle. Read on to learn her secrets.

2   Marilee Arthur knows about breaking the rules. She's been doing it all her life, as a plus-size fitness instructor who won aerobics competitions, taught exercise classes and ran 25 kilometers a week. Baffled doctors and trainers told her that she had the **cardiovascular** system of a high-level athlete and the body fat of a high-level couch potato. She was fat—and fit.

3   When Marilee, now 37, was profiled in the June 1997 issue of *Chatelaine,* she told us she wanted to lose weight. "But," she added, "I think this is the body I have to live with." Then a little over two years ago, going through a split with her husband and frustrated with her inability to lose weight no matter how active she was, the Plattsville, Ont., resident decided she was fed up with being the exception to the rule. "I wanted to attain some semblance of normalcy."

4   She consulted an exercise physiologist, and together they worked out a customized plan to reduce her overall body fat and gain muscle. "I decided the numbers on the scale were no longer significant. I wanted a healthy body that was strong and well defined with a good distribution of lean body mass to body fat."

5   There was no magic formula that melted the excess body fat. "I tried new things, constantly tweaked my routine, consulted so many different people and books. I refused to give up." And her determination has paid off. Now in the third year of her program, she's gone from a high of 267 pounds down to about 175 pounds (she doesn't know her exact weight because she doesn't look at a scale), trimmed 70 inches from all over her five-foot-seven frame (including nearly 12 from her abdomen and six and a half from each thigh) and dropped five dress sizes, from 24 to 16. Most important, she's reduced her body fat percentage from an obese 38 to a healthy 24 and is well on her way to her goal of 20 percent.

cardiovascular involving the heart and the blood vessels

6   "I have a fairly large bone structure and I put on muscle easily, so I realized early on I'd never be one of those 120-pound women," says the mother of two children. "But I love being strong and active and not having to carry all that extra weight around anymore."

7   Here are the secrets to her success—with tips on how to make them work for you.

The Menu: Squelching Starch

8   Like many athletes looking to fuel their activities, Marilee used to load up on starchy carbohydrates such as pasta, rice, potatoes and bagels. "I didn't dump anything fattening on these carbs, but they were the mainstay of my diet. I didn't give much thought to getting enough protein."

9   Carbohydrates are not the enemy—our bodies need them for energy. "If your body doesn't get enough carbohydrates, it will start using fat and protein to provide energy instead. Then that protein isn't being used to build muscle. It's an inefficient system," explains Pam Lynch, a professional dietitian and sports nutritionist in Halifax. The problem is the quantity of carbs you reach for the most—pasta, rice and bread. You can easily eat too much of them at one meal, sometimes taking seconds. Your body uses carbohydrates (or any food) first for immediate energy, then stores the excess as glycogen in your muscles and liver. Whatever the liver and muscles don't use is converted to fat.

glycogen
a compound stored in the liver and muscles that is converted to glucose when the body needs energy

10   Now Marilee enjoys rye bread, baked potatoes and brown rice in moderation—two servings a day—and gets the majority of her carbs from other sources such as fruit and vegetables. They are packed with vitamins and minerals as well as fiber, which fills you up faster, cleanses your system and keeps you regular. She also eats several daily servings of good-quality lean protein such as turkey, fish and beans. Fish, olive oil, a daily flaxseed-oil capsule and almonds supply the monounsaturated "good" fat her body needs. "I'm actually eating a greater volume of food now. And I really enjoy what I eat. I don't feel like I'm depriving myself." She's disciplined but not fanatical. "I don't work out on Sunday and if I feel like having a small amount of ice cream or a couple cookies, that's the day I do it."

The Meals: Timing Is Everything

11   Marilee eats regular healthful meals to keep her blood sugar level on an even keel. Our bodies strive to keep blood sugar within a certain range. If you reach for a sugary treat when you're starving, your blood sugar will go up, then crash down, leaving you cranky, headachy and hungry again.

12   Dinner is her smallest meal of the day, and she tries to eat by 6 p.m.—advice many personal trainers swear by. "If you're loading up on calories at the end of the day when you're relaxing, you're not burning them off," says Susan Cantwell, a Fredericton personal trainer.

13   If you simply must have a starchy carb such as bread, Marilee advises eating it shortly following exercise, when your body is looking to replenish energy. "There's a 15-minute window immediately after exercise," says Lynch. "Your body is more receptive to replacing the glycogen in the muscles and liver, rather than converting it to fat."

The Workout: Busting a Rut

14   Marilee was a fitness nut, but she hadn't changed her aerobics-and-running routine much for years. "I see a lot of fitness instructors who get stuck in a rut and get frustrated because they aren't seeing results anymore," says Cantwell. "You should change your routine every six to eight weeks. Otherwise your body adapts and the exercise isn't as effective." Marilee added interval training to her thrice-weekly runs (see Kick It Up a Notch, on page 468). Cantwell approves. "This is an excellent way to burn more calories because you're increasing your intensity without having to increase the duration. It shakes up your routine and can be applied to most forms of exercise."

Tae Bo
a type of aerobic exercise that combines a modified form of martial arts with boxing

15   Marilee also began to develop a **Tae-Bo**-like routine with her business partner, Terry Yanke. They drew on her aerobics background and his martial arts knowledge and created Ty-Jitsu, a kicking-punching-hee-yaw aerobic-martial arts workout that's easier on the joints than Tae-Bo. "My body changed—my hips, thighs and abdomen got more toned and defined. I was using new muscles in new ways," she says. Her experience doesn't surprise Heather Long, owner of Adventure Fitness, a Winnipeg fitness-consultation business. "Your body likes change and responds to it. You tap into a pool of underused muscles and see a more visible improvement."

The Routine: Early Birds Catch the Burn

16   Conventional wisdom says you should exercise whenever you can fit it into your day. The new thinking is that exercising first thing in the morning burns stored fat, whereas exercising later tends to burn calories that you consumed over the course of the day. Long tells her clients to set their alarms earlier than usual. "If you can't manage a full-length workout in the morning, divide it and have a short workout in the morning and a short one in the evening," she says. "Morning workouts increase your heart rate and keep it at a higher level during the day, which keeps your metabolism revved up."

17   Marilee's running routine consists of a 30-minute high-intensity or interval run at 5:30 a.m. three days a week. She exercises on an empty stomach. For those people who would otherwise end up light-headed or with an acidic stomach after exercising on an empty stomach, Long suggests eating an apple or banana or drinking a glass of juice 15 to 20 minutes before the workout.

Weights: The Secret Weapon

18   Marilee also added more weight training (using both free weights and weight machines) to her exercise mix three times a week. Smart move: a muscular body burns more calories than a fat body, even at rest. Why? Muscle tissue requires more oxygen than fatty tissue does, and you use more calories to get this oxygen. The result: a pound of muscle burns between 20 and 50 calories a day, while a pound of fat burns less than 10. "Weight training has been called the 'missing link' for weight loss," explains Cantwell. "Not only does muscle burn calories at rest, but after you lift weights, your muscles use energy to repair themselves for up to three hours. That burns calories too."

19   The key to building muscle is to progressively overload it. As she works out, Marilee increases the amount of weight she lifts and decreases the number of repetitions. She was already a strong woman, so she's able to heft some heavy weights: **bicep** easy **curls**, for instance, consist of 12 **reps** of 27 pounds, 10 reps of 35 pounds, eight reps of 44 pounds and six reps of 50 pounds. Between each set there is a one-minute rest. Beginners, of course, would start at about two-pound weights and work up from there.

bicep
the muscle at the front of the upper arm that flexes the forearm, and also the muscle at the back of the thigh that flexes the knee joint

20   It's important to do each lift up and back down smoothly and slowly, resisting both ways. Those bicep curls should take about eight seconds—four to lift and four to lower.

21   "It's important to work your muscles to fatigue, otherwise you're just increasing endurance, not strength," says Cantwell. "The last two or three reps should be really challenging. This tears the muscle fibers microscopically, and then your body expends energy to repair them."

curls
a weightlifting exercise using a barbell

Kick It Up a Notch

reps
short for repetitions

22   Whether you're running, biking or swimming you can maximize your workout benefit by varying the intensity of your routine in specific time segments. By doing so, you increase the amount of calories burned without increasing the duration of your workout. Here's what Marilee does over a 30-minute interval run with her running partners and a stopwatch:

- **Warm-up:** Walk or jog for five minutes
- **Intensify pace minute by minute:** Total of five minutes
- **Decrease pace minute by minute:** Total of five minutes until she reaches her original pace. Repeat increasing/decreasing cycle.
- **All-out sprint:** One minute
- **Walking cool-down:** Three to five minutes

Fat and Fit Revisited

mortality
the rate of death associated with a certain cause, such as cardiovascular disease

23   *Chatelaine's* first article on Marilee Arthur ("*Fat and Fit*" by Kim Pittaway, June 1997) discussed new research, most notably a 1995 study by the Cooper Institute for Aerobics Research in Dallas, that indicated overweight but fit men lived longer than unfit men. A subsequent study by the Cooper Institute, published in the International Journal of Obesity in 1998, followed more than 20,000 men aged 30 to 83 over eight years. They found, not surprisingly, that fit men of normal weight had the lowest rate of cardiovascular disease **mortality**, while unfit and overweight men experienced the highest cardiovascular disease mortality. Bottom line: being obese (BMI 30-plus) is never a good idea because you put yourself at high risk for disease.

➤ A.   UNDERSTANDING THE THESIS AND OTHER MAIN IDEAS

Select the best answer.

___b___   1. The author's primary purpose in "Use It and Lose It" is to

a. promote weight loss programs offered by local health clubs.

b. describe ways to successfully build muscle while reducing body fat.

    c. compare traditional methods of losing weight to new theories of weight loss.

    d. inform readers about the health risks associated with obesity.

___c___ 2. Marilee Arthur is

    a. the author of "Use It and Lose It."

    b. an exercise physiologist.

    c. a fitness instructor who wanted to lose weight.

    d. a professional dietician.

___d___ 3. The main idea of paragraph 3 is that Marilee

    a. was resigned to being overweight.

    b. had not lost weight since her original interview several years earlier.

    c. was frustrated by her inability to lose weight.

    d. made the decision to lose weight.

___a___ 4. The topic of paragraph 9 is

    a. carbohydrates.   c. protein.

    b. energy.   d. fat.

___b___ 5. The statement that best expresses the main idea of paragraph 14 is

    a. "Marilee was a fitness nut but she hadn't changed her aerobics-and-running routine much for years."

    b. "You should change your routine every six to eight weeks."

    c. "Marilee added interval training to her thrice-weekly runs."

    d. "It shakes up your routine and can be applied to most forms of exercise."

___c___ 6. The main idea of paragraph 22 is that

    a. you can maximize your workout by running, biking, and swimming.

    b. Marilee's workout is about 30 minutes long, including warming up, sprinting, and cooling down.

    c. you can get the most out of your workout by varying the intensity of your routine in specific intervals.

    d. it is impossible to increase the amount of calories burned without increasing the duration of your workout.

___d___ 7. The main idea of paragraph 23 is expressed in the

    a. first sentence.   c. third sentence.

    b. second sentence.   d. last sentence.

➤ B.   IDENTIFYING DETAILS

Select the best answer.

__d__ 1. According to the author, the most important result of
Marilee's weight loss is that she has

   a. lost almost 100 pounds.

   b. taken a total of 70 inches off her frame.

   c. gone down five dress sizes.

   d. reduced her body fat to a healthy percentage.

__a__ 2. Marilee adjusted her diet in all of the following
ways *except*

   a. eliminating monounsaturated fats from her diet.

   b. reducing the amount of starch she consumes.

   c. eating regular meals.

   d. making dinner her smallest meal of the day.

__d__ 3. Fruits and vegetables provide Marilee with all of the
following *except*

   a. vitamins and minerals.

   b. fiber.

   c. carbohydrates.

   d. protein.

__a__ 4. The key to building muscle is to

   a. progressively overload it.

   b. avoid working your muscles to fatigue.

   c. focus on increasing endurance rather than
strength.

   d. use light weights than can be lifted quickly.

__a__ 5. According to the selection, it is best to exercise

   a. early in the day, because you will be burning
stored fat.

   b. late in the day, because you will be burning calories that
you consumed during the day.

   c. whenever you can fit it in during the day.

   d. late in the day, and only on a full stomach.

➤ **C. RECOGNIZING METHODS OF ORGANIZATION AND TRANSITIONS**

Select the best answer.

___a___ 1. In paragraph 9, the author uses the cause and effect organizational pattern. In this paragraph, the cause is

    a. too many carbohydrates and the effect is fat.

    b. protein and the effect is energy.

    c. energy and the effect is glycogen.

    d. too much fiber and the effect is low blood sugar.

___b___ 2. In paragraph 16, the author makes a comparison between exercising early in the day and exercising later. The transitional word she uses to indicate the comparison is

    a. whenever.   c. earlier.

    b. whereas.   d. If.

➤ **D. REVIEWING AND ORGANIZING IDEAS: MAPPING**

Fill in the blanks to complete the following process diagram based on paragraph 9.

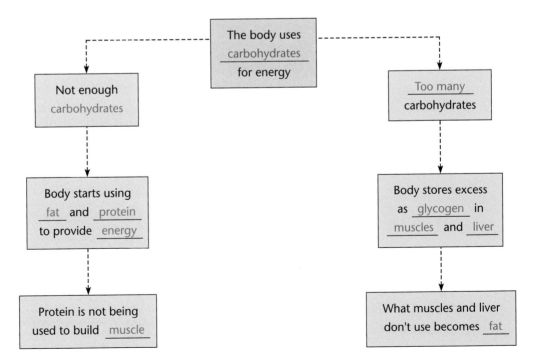

➤ **E.   FIGURING OUT INFERRED MEANINGS**

Indicate whether each statement is true (T) or false (F).

_T_ 1. It can be inferred that a "plus-size" person is one who wears large sizes in clothing.

_F_ 2. Doctors and trainers were baffled by Marilee Arthur because she was very strong even though she never exercised.

_T_ 3. Marilee considered herself to be abnormally overweight.

_F_ 4. Marilee doesn't look at a scale because she's afraid to know how much she weighs now.

_T_ 5. Personal trainers encourage their clients to eat dinner by 6 P.M.

➤ **F.   THINKING CRITICALLY**

Select the best answer.

_d_ 1. The author supports her thesis with all of the following types of evidence *except*

   a. giving examples.

   b. quoting authorities.

   c. citing facts.

   d. describing her own personal experience.

_b_ 2. Of the following excerpts from the selection, the only one that is a *fact* is

   a. "Fitness instructor Marilee Arthur is trimmer and more vibrant than ever." (paragraph 1)

   b. "She consulted an exercise physiologist and together they worked out a customized plan." (paragraph 4)

   c. "She's disciplined but not fanatical." (paragraph 10)

   d. "Marilee was a fitness nut . . ." (paragraph 14)

_c_ 3. Of the following excerpts from the selection, the only one that is an *opinion* is

   a. "Our bodies strive to keep blood sugar within a certain range." (paragraph 11)

   b. "There's a 15-minute window immediately after exercise." (paragraph 13)

   c. "Marilee was a fitness nut . . ." (paragraph 14)

   d. "Morning workouts increase your heart rate and keep it at a higher level during the day." (paragraph 16) _d_ 4. The author includes references to weight training as the "missing link" and the "secret weapon" in order to

    a. explain that weight training incorporates elements of the martial arts.

    b. inject a note of humor into the discussion about workout programs.

    c. emphasize that weight lifting is more important than diet in any weight loss program.

    d. imply that many people are unaware of the benefits of weight training as part of a weight loss program.

➤ G.   BUILDING VOCABULARY

➤ Context

Using context and a dictionary, if necessary, determine the meaning of each word as it is used in the selection.

_b_ 1. vibrant (paragraph 1)

    a. calm

    b. lively

    c. nervous

    d. colorful

_b_ 2. attain (paragraph 3)

    a. eliminate

    b. achieve

    c. let go

    d. replace

_c_ 3. obese (paragraph 5)

    a. average

    b. unhealthy

    c. overweight

    d. underweight

_a_ 4. mainstay (paragraph 8)

    a. chief support

    b. downfall

    c. minor aspect

    d. reward

_d_ 5. replenish (paragraph 13)

    a. overlook

    b. eliminate

    c. use up

    d. restore

_c_ 6. receptive (paragraph 13)

    a. dishonest

    b. obvious

    c. open to

    d. unavailable

_d_ 7. heft (paragraph 19)

    a. weight

    b. push

    c. build

    d. lift

_b_ 8. fatigue (paragraph 21)

    a. strength

    b. exhaustion

    c. illness

    d. exercise

➤ Word Parts

A REVIEW OF PREFIXES AND SUFFIXES

EX- means *out*

IN- means *out*

-AL means *characteristic of*

-ANCE means *the quality of*

-IST means *a person who*

Using your knowledge of word parts and the review of prefixes and suffixes above, fill in the blanks in the following sentences.

1. A <u>physiologist</u> (paragraph 4) is ___a person who___ studies physiology, or the functions of living organisms and their parts.

2. A system that is <u>inefficient</u> (paragraph 9) is ___not___ efficient; it does not work well.

3. Someone who is <u>fanatical</u> (paragraph 10) behaves in a way that is ___characteristic of___ a fanatic, or a person who is extreme in his or her enthusiasm for a subject.

4. When your body <u>expends</u> (paragraph 21) energy to repair torn muscle fibers, it puts _____out_____, or spends, energy.

5. When you are trying to increase your <u>endurance</u> (paragraph 21), you are trying to improve ___the quality of___ your ability to endure something.

➤ **Unusual Words/Unusual Meanings**

Use the meanings given below to write a sentence using the underlined word or phrase.

1. The term <u>couch potato</u> (paragraph 2) refers to a person who spends a lot of time sitting or lying down, usually watching television, rather than engaging in physical activity.

   Your sentence: _____.

2. The word <u>tweak</u> (paragraph 5) means to adjust or fine-tune something.

   Your sentence: _____.

3. The author uses the word <u>fuel</u> (paragraph 8) as a verb, meaning to stimulate or sustain an activity.

   Your sentence: _____.

4. The word <u>nut</u> (paragraph 14) is used in the selection to mean a person who is very enthusiastic about something; in this case, fitness.

   Your sentence: _____.

5. To be <u>stuck in a rut</u> (paragraph 14) is to remain in the same, boring routine.

   Your sentence: _____.

➤ **H.   SELECTING A LEARNING/STUDY STRATEGY**

Suppose you were taking a health and fitness class to meet your physical education requirements. Discuss what method(s) you would use to learn this material in preparation for a multiple-choice test.

➤ **I.   EXPLORING IDEAS THROUGH DISCUSSION AND WRITING**

1. Why is the information about mortality and cardiovascular disease included at the end of the selection? How do you think Marilee Arthur has lessened her chances of developing cardiovascular disease?

2. Did you find any parts of this information useful? If so, which ones?

3. Discuss whether Americans are overly concerned with body image.

➤ J.   BEYOND THE CLASSROOM TO THE WEB

Visit Karate Tournament Central at **http://www.karatetournaments.com/taebo.htm.**
Read this interview with Master Billy Blanks, the person who invented Tae-Bo.
What three areas of physical conditioning did he draw on to create Tae-Bo?

✔ Tracking Your Progress

Selection 28

Section	Number Correct		Score
A. Thesis and Main Idea (7 items)	_____	x 4	_____
B. Details (5 items)	_____	x 3	_____
C. Organization and Transitions (2 items)	_____	x 2	_____
E. Inferred Meanings (5 items)	_____	x 3	_____
F. Thinking Critically (4 items)	_____	x 3	_____
G. Vocabulary			
1. Context (8 items)	_____	x 2	_____
2. Word Parts (5 items)	_____	x 2	_____

TOTAL SCORE _____ %

CHECKING YOUR READING RATE

Words in Selection 28: 1,830

Finishing Time: _____   _____   _____
                                    (hour)   (minutes)   (seconds)

Starting Time: _____   _____   _____
                                    (hour)   (minutes)   (seconds)

Total Reading Time: _____   _____
                                              (minutes)   (seconds)

Words Per Minute Score (page 739) _____ WPM

SELECTION 29

Make No Mistake: Medical Errors Can Be Deadly Serious

Tamar Nordenberg

This article appeared on the Federal Drug Administration (FDA) consumer magazine Web site in October 2000. Read it to learn why you must be a wary consumer, even in a hospital.

➤ **PREVIEWING THE READING**

Using the steps listed on page 5, preview the reading selection. When you have finished, complete the following items.

1. The topic of this selection is <u>serious medical mistakes</u>.

2. Based on the subheadings, list three questions you expect to be able to answer after reading the selection:

   a. <u>What kinds of mistakes are made in medication?</u>

   _____

   b. <u>How do human limitations cause errors? (or) How can human</u>

   <u>limitations in the medical field be minimized?</u>

   c. <u>How can humans improve in preventing medical errors?</u>

   _____

➤ **READING TIP**

As you read, highlight the types of medical errors that can occur.

CHECKING YOUR READING RATE

 If you plan to compute your reading rate, be sure to record your starting time in the box at the end of the exercises before you begin reading.

MAKING CONNECTIONS

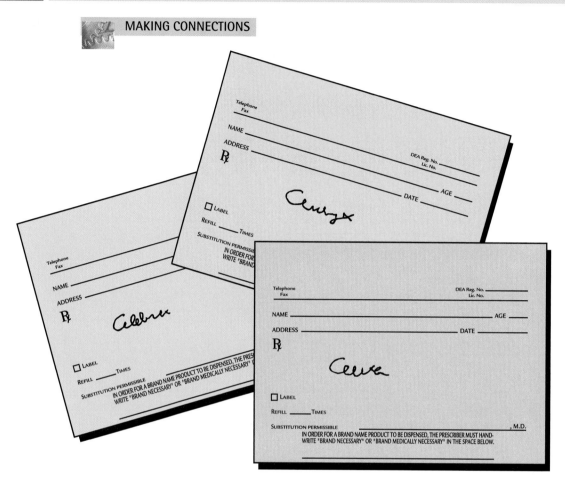

What is one type of medical mistake that can cause problems for patients, as suggested by this image? What others can you think of?

double bypass heart operation
a surgical procedure to create alternative passages for diverting blood around obstructions in coronary arteries

artery
the vessels that carry oxygenated blood from the heart to the rest of the body

Make No Mistake: Medical Errors Can Be Deadly Serious

1   Two months after a **double bypass heart operation** that was supposed to save his life, comedian and former *Saturday Night Live* cast member Dana Carvey got some disheartening news: the cardiac surgeon had bypassed the wrong **artery**. It took another emergency operation to clear the blockage that was threatening to kill the 45-year-old funnyman and father of two young kids. Responding to a $7.5 million lawsuit Carvey brought against him, the surgeon said he'd made an honest mistake because Carvey's artery was unusually situated in his heart. But Carvey didn't see it that way. "It's like removing the wrong kidney. It's that big a mistake," the entertainer told *People* magazine.

2   Based on a recent report on medical mistakes from the National Academy of Sciences' Institute of Medicine, Carvey might fairly be characterized as one of the lucky survivors. In its report, "To Err Is Human: Building a Safer Health System," the

IOM estimates that 44,000 to 98,000 Americans die each year not from the medical conditions they checked in with, but from preventable medical errors. A medical error, under the report's definition, could mean a health-care provider chose an inappropriate method of care, such as giving a patient a certain asthma drug without knowing that he or she was allergic to it. Or it could mean the health provider chose the right course of care but carried it out incorrectly, such as intending to infuse a patient with diluted potassium chloride—a potassium supplement—but inadvertently giving the patient a concentrated, lethal overdose.

3   The Institute of Medicine (IOM) estimates that fully half of adverse reactions to medicines are the result of medical errors. Other adverse reactions—those that are unexpected and not preventable—are not considered errors. (See "When Is a Medical Product Too Risky?" in the September–October 1999 FDA Consumer.) The statistics in the IOM report, which were based on two large studies, suggest that medical errors are the eighth leading cause of death among Americans, with error-caused deaths each year in hospitals alone exceeding those from motor vehicle accidents (43,458), breast cancer (42,297), or AIDS (16,516).

4   But the numbers in the report don't tell the whole story, its authors acknowledge. People in the hospital are just a small proportion of those at risk. Doctors' offices, clinics, and outpatient surgical centers treat thousands of patients each day; retail pharmacies fill countless prescriptions; and nursing homes and other institutional settings serve vulnerable patient populations.

5   Despite the recent focus on the IOM statistics, experts assure that the health system in the United States is safe. But its safety record is a far cry from the enviable record of the similarly complex aviation industry, which is being held up as an example for the medical world. A person would have to fly nonstop for 438 years before expecting to be involved in a deadly airplane crash, based on recent airline accident statistics. That, IOM says, places health-care at least a decade behind aviation in safeguarding consumers' lives and health.

6   The report is a self-described "call to action" for the health-care system. "Whether a person is sick or just trying to stay healthy, he or she should not have to worry about being harmed by the health system itself," its authors say.

Medication Mistakes

7   Even the seemingly simple process of giving a patient medicine—the right drug, in the right dose, to the right patient, at the right time—is, in reality, teeming with opportunities for error. The IOM estimates that preventable medication errors result in more than 7,000 deaths each year in hospitals alone, and tens of thousands more in outpatient facilities.

8   Name confusion is among the most common causes of drug-related errors, says Peter Honig, M.D., an FDA expert on drug risk-assessment. A recent example: the sound-alike names for the antiepileptic drug Lamictal and the antifungal drug Lamisil. The volume of dispensing errors involving these two drugs prompted the manufacturer of Lamictal, Glaxo Wellcome Inc., of Research Triangle Park, N.C., to launch a campaign warning pharmacists of the potential confusion. The possible consequences of prescribing the wrong drug are grave: Epileptic patients receiving the anti-fungal drug Lamisil by mistake could experience continuous seizures.

Patients erroneously receiving the antiepileptic drug Lamictal might experience a serious rash, blood pressure changes, or other side effects.

9   Under FDA's authority to regulate drug labeling, the agency's new Office of Postmarketing Drug Risk Assessment evaluates medicines' brand names in an attempt to avoid sound-alike and look-alike names. If FDA considers the name of a new medical product to be potentially confusing to health professionals, the agency works with the drug company to change the product's name. FDA is developing new standards to prevent such name mix-ups, as well as to prevent confusion between similar-looking drug packaging. Also, the agency is developing new label standards to highlight common interactions between drugs so that doctors are less likely to mistakenly prescribe dangerous combinations. And even after a drug is approved, FDA monitors its use to see if unexpected adverse events occur and whether any labeling changes are required to help avoid medication mishaps.

10   So where does FDA's responsibility end and the health professionals' judgment take over? "FDA must do everything within its authority to maximize the likelihood that approved products will be used correctly in the real world," says Honig. But, he notes, "We don't regulate the practice of medicine, such as the sloppy handwriting when prescribing a drug." The real-world practice of medicine occurs within an intricate system, says Woodcock. "It's that complexity," she says, "coupled with the limitations of humans, that makes avoiding mistakes a consuming task."

Human Limitations

11   As its title—To Err Is Human—suggests, the IOM report supports moving away from the traditional culture of "naming, shaming, and blaming" individual health providers who make mistakes. Instead, the institute believes that preventing future errors is best achieved by designing a safer overall system.

12   Some medical centers have begun using computer programs and other system supports to curtail medical mishaps by double-checking the care decisions doctors and nurses make. Even simple computer systems that use electronic prescriptions in place of handwritten ones have in some cases already paid off with substantial error reductions.

13   But systems, too, can fail, cautions Raymond L. Woosley, M.D., a professor and chairman of **pharmacology** at Georgetown University Medical Center. Woosley's example: "It's true that if you have a prescription drug with an electronic bar code on it—the right code—it can help prevent errors. But if the wrong code is on there, you may have even more errors. There will always be mistakes, though they will be different mistakes as the systems change. You've got to be ready to handle them."

pharmacology
the study of drugs, including their compositions, uses, and effects

14   Despite technological advances, preventing mistakes will always depend on the vigilance of health professionals, Woosley says. Otherwise, human carelessness can render useless the very systems designed to avert mistakes. Even among pharmacies with a computer program to highlight dangerous drug interactions, according to a study published in the *Journal of the American Medical Association,* one-third of pharmacists nevertheless continued to fill prescriptions for a known killer combination: the prescription antihistamine Seldane (terfenadine) with the antibiotic erythromycin. (Seldane has since been removed from the market.) "The pharmacists would get the computer warnings and zip right on by them," Woosley says. "Or they would turn off

the program entirely." Why turn off the computer program? Because, Woosley explains, it was slowing down the pharmacists when they wanted to print labels.

15 Health professionals "are trained to memorize everything and are rewarded for it," says the pharmacology professor. "The medical student who says, 'I don't know; I've got to look it up,' is likely to fail an exam, yet that's the one who is less likely to make an error." Woosley hopes medical students will be taught to accept their limitations and admit their mistakes. Under the current system, however, some people call that goal pie-in-the-sky.

To Improve Is Human

16 Woodcock (head of the FDA's Center for Drug Evaluation and Research) encourages consumers to help prevent errors by being vigilant about their health care—understanding their treatment, keeping organized records of what doctors they see and what medications they take, and asking questions when things don't seem right. For example, "If your pills look different than they have in the past, they might be the right medication, and they might not. But raise the issue."

17 Honig calls consumer education the "secret weapon" in the war against medical errors. "It's unfortunate that people research buying a car better than they research health-care decisions. They're willing to tolerate more uncertainty with their health care than their mode of transportation." He encourages patients to feel comfortable asking more questions about their medical care.

18 With everyone from pharmaceutical manufacturers to consumers playing a role in improving the safety of the health system, Woodcock believes that the already "very safe" medical system in the United States will become even safer. "There are fixes," she says. "We know that from other industries." The spotlight on the health system's problems might be just what the system needs to transform itself, says Woodcock. After all, as the IOM report notes, "It may be part of human nature to err, but it is also part of human nature to create solutions, find better alternatives, and meet the challenges ahead."

► **A.   UNDERSTANDING THE THESIS AND OTHER MAIN IDEAS**

Select the best answer.

_c_ 1. The central thesis of "Make No Mistake" is that
   a. thousands of dollars are lost every year because of billing errors in America's health system.
   b. physicians and pharmacists should be held accountable for the medical errors they make.
   c. preventable medical errors cause thousands of deaths in America each year.
   d. the Food and Drug Administration (FDA) must set standards for evaluating new medical products.

_b_ 2. The author's primary purpose is to

    a. compare America's health-care system with that of other countries.

    b. report on the types and causes of medical mistakes as well as efforts to address those mistakes.

    c. assign blame to the medical professionals who are most at fault.

    d. urge people to sue medical professionals who have misdiagnosed or mistreated patients.

_d_ 3. The topic of paragraph 4 is

    a. the Institute of Medicine (IOM) report.

    b. hospital patients.

    c. outpatients.

    d. at-risk patients.

_a_ 4. The main idea of paragraph 8 is expressed in the

    a. first sentence.   c. third sentence.

    b. second sentence.   d. last sentence.

_a_ 5. The statement that best expresses the main idea of paragraph 14 is

    a. "Despite technological advances, preventing mistakes will always depend on the vigilance of health professionals."

    b. "Otherwise, human carelessness can render useless the very systems designed to avert mistakes."

    c. "Even among pharmacies with a computer program to highlight dangerous drug interactions, one-third of pharmacists nevertheless continued to fill prescriptions for a known killer combination."

    d. "It was slowing down the pharmacists when they wanted to print labels."

_b_ 6. The main idea of paragraph 15 is that health professionals

    a. are trained to memorize everything.

    b. should learn to accept their limitations.

    c. are rewarded for their memorization skills.

    d. will never admit their mistakes.

_c_ 7. The topic of paragraph 18 is

    a. pharmaceutical manufacturers.

    b. consumers.

    c. the U.S. health system.

    d. the IOM report.

➤ **B.   IDENTIFYING DETAILS**

Select the best answer.

__c__ 1. Under the definition given in the IOM's report, all of the following would be considered medical errors *except*

a. an inappropriate method of care chosen by a health-care provider.

b. a method of care incorrectly carried out by a health-care provider.

c. unexpected and unpreventable adverse reactions to medicines.

d. dispensing the wrong medication because of name confusion.

__b__ 2. Of the following causes of death, the greatest number of deaths resulted from

a. car accidents.

b. medical errors.

c. breast cancer.

d. AIDS.

__b__ 3. In the example describing prescription errors for the sound-alike drugs Lamictal and Lamisil, the drug manufacturer decided to

a. take both drugs off the market.

b. launch a campaign warning pharmacists of the potential confusion.

c. rename one of the drugs.

d. disclaim all responsibility for any mistakes.

__c__ 4. The Food and Drug Administration (FDA) and its Office of Postmarketing Drug Risk Assessment address the problem of medical mistakes in all of the following ways *except*

a. monitoring the use of approved drugs to see whether labeling changes are necessary.

b. working with drug companies to change potentially confusing product names and packaging.

c. reprimanding individual health-care providers who make prescription mistakes or write difficult-to-read prescriptions.

d. developing new label standards that highlight common interactions between drugs.

_d__ 5. According to FDA expert Peter Honig, the secret weapon in the war against medical errors is

  a. medical lawsuits.

  b. electronic prescription-writing.

  c. the FDA's new label standards.

  d. consumer education.

► C. RECOGNIZING METHODS OF ORGANIZATION AND TRANSITIONS

Fill in the blanks in the following statements.

1. In paragraph 2, the author describes what constitutes a medical error according to the IOM report. The organizational pattern in this paragraph is __definition__ .

2. In paragraph 5, the author uses the __comparison and contrast__ organizational pattern to contrast the safety record of America's health system with the safety record of the aviation industry.

3. In paragraph 8, the author uses cause and effect to describe one type of medical mistake. In this paragraph, the cause is __name confusion__ and the effects are the serious physical reactions of patients who receive the wrong drug.

4. In paragraph 16, the phrase that indicates that Janet Woodcock's point about consumer vigilance will be illustrated is __for example__ .

► D. REVIEWING AND ORGANIZING IDEAS: PARAPHRASING

Complete the paraphrase of paragraph 1 by filling in the missing words and phrases.

Paragraph 1: Comedian and former __Saturday Night Live__ cast member Dana Carvey had to have a __double bypass heart operation__ to save his life. Two __months__ later, the 45-year-old __father__ of two young __children__ found out that the __surgeon__ had bypassed the wrong __artery__; Carvey would have to have an emergency __operation__ to clear the life-threatening blockage. When Carvey __sued__ the surgeon for $7.5 million, the __surgeon__ said that the unusual placement of Carvey's __artery__ in his __heart__ caused the mistake. Carvey disagreed, telling __People magazine__ that it was as major a __mistake__ as removing the wrong __kidney__ would be.

➤ E. FIGURING OUT INFERRED MEANINGS

Indicate whether each statement is true (T) or false (F).

___T___ 1. It can be inferred that many more deaths from medical mistakes probably occur outside hospital settings.

___F___ 2. A person has a much greater chance of being in an airplane crash than being the victim of a serious medical mistake.

___F___ 3. The health-care industry requested that the IOM conduct research into medical mistakes.

___T___ 4. The volume of dispensing errors for the two similarly named drugs (Lamictal and Lamisil) was significant.

___T___ 5. The IOM believes that the traditional culture of punishing health-care providers who made mistakes was not effective in preventing future mistakes.

➤ F. THINKING CRITICALLY

Select the best answer.

___c___ 1. Most of the evidence supporting the central thesis is based on

    a. interviews with health-care providers.

    b. interviews with victims of medical mistakes.

    c. a report by the National Academy of Sciences' Institute of Medicine.

    d. the personal experiences of the author.

___a___ 2. The tone of the reading can best be described as

    a. cautionary.

    b. bitter.

    c. angry.

    d. humorous.

___b___ 3. When this selection first appeared, its intended audience most likely was

    a. health-care providers.

    b. health-care consumers.

    c. lawyers.

    d. medical students.

_d_ 4. The author captures the reader's attention by beginning the article with

    a. a funny story about medical mistakes.

    b. several quotations from health-care providers.

    c. shocking statistics about medical mistakes.

    d. the serious account of a medical mishap affecting a popular entertainer.

_a_ 5. By calling their IOM report a "call to action," the report's authors mean that the report is intended to

    a. put pressure on the health-care system to improve its safety.

    b. challenge health-care providers to dispute the IOM findings.

    c. encourage consumers to pursue legal action against their health-care providers.

    d. prompt the government to become less involved in regulating the safety of the health-care system.

➤ **G.   BUILDING VOCABULARY**

➤ **Context**

Using context and a dictionary, if necessary, determine the meaning of each word as it is used in the selection.

_c_ 1. infuse (paragraph 2)

    a. connect   c. inject

    b. recover   d. diagnose

_b_ 2. lethal (paragraph 2)

    a. effective

    b. deadly

    c. illegal

    d. unfortunate

_d_ 3. adverse (paragraph 3)

    a. likely

    b. common

    c. expected

    d. harmful

_a_ 4. teeming (paragraph 7)

   a. filled with

   b. searching

   c. leaving

   d. forming

_d_ 5. erroneously (paragraph 8)

   a. occasionally

   b. purposely

   c. repeatedly

   d. mistakenly

_d_ 6. intricate (paragraph 10)

   a. expensive

   b. old-fashioned

   c. dangerous

   d. complicated

_b_ 7. curtail (paragraph 12)

   a. encourage

   b. limit

   c. hide

   d. find

▶ **Word Parts**

> **A REVIEW OF PREFIXES**
> **ANTI-** means *against*
> **DIS-** means *not*
> **IN-** means *not*

Match each word in Column A with its meaning in Column B. Write your answers in the spaces provided.

Column A	Column B
_b_ 1. inappropriate	a. not encouraging
_d_ 2. antifungal	b. not proper
_a_ 3. disheartening	c. not on purpose
_e_ 4. antibiotic	d. destroying fungi
_c_ 5. inadvertently	e. destroying harmful bacteria

➤ **Unusual Words/Unusual Meanings**
Use the meanings given below to write a sentence using the underlined phrase.

1. The phrase <u>tell the whole story</u> (paragraph 4) means to give a complete account of the facts of the situation.

    Your sentence: _____.

2. The phrase <u>pie-in-the-sky</u> (paragraph 15) describes an unrealistic wish or an empty promise.

    Your sentence: _____.

➤ **H.   SELECTING A LEARNING/STUDY STRATEGY**

Select the best answer.

____b____   If you were preparing for an essay exam in a health class and the material in this selection was to be covered on the exam, which of the following strategies would be most useful?

a. making a list of specific medical errors described in the article

b. preparing a chart listing types of medical errors and means of prevention

c. making a list of IOM report findings

d. writing a list of quotations by medical experts cited in the article.

➤ **I.   EXPLORING IDEAS THROUGH DISCUSSION AND WRITING**

1. How will this reading change the way you view your health care? Do you think the author presented an unbiased account of medical mistakes?

2. Do you agree with the health-care experts who say the American health-care system is safe?

3. Explain what is meant by a "culture of 'naming, shaming, and blaming.'" What do you think happened to the health-care providers who made mistakes in that environment?

4. Explain why the medical student who has to look up the answers is more likely to fail the exam but less likely to make a mistake. Why do you think some people believe it is unrealistic to expect medical students to learn to accept their limitations?

➤ J.   BEYOND THE CLASSROOM TO THE WEB

Visit FDA Consumer *magazine, published by the U.S. Food and Drug Administration at* **http://www.fda.gov/fdac/features/1999/599_med.html.**

Read the article on this page, "When Is a Medical Product Too Risky?" (This article was referred to in paragraph 3 of "Make No Mistake.") What are two reasons FDA Commissioner Jane Henney gives for the risks associated with a drug not being completely known before the medication becomes available for sale?

✔ **Tracking Your Progress**

Selection 29

Section	Number Correct		Score
A. Thesis and Main Idea (7 items)	_____	x 4	_____
B. Details (5 items)	_____	x 3	_____
C. Organization and Transitions (4 items)	_____	x 2	_____
E. Inferred Meanings (5 items)	_____	x 3	_____
F. Thinking Critically (5 items)	_____	x 3	_____
G. Vocabulary			
1. Context (7 items)	_____	x 2	_____
2. Word Parts (5 items)	_____	x 1	_____

TOTAL SCORE _____ %

CHECKING YOUR READING RATE

Words in Selection 29: 1,557

Finishing Time: _____   _____   _____
                  (hour)   (minutes)   (seconds)

Starting Time: _____   _____   _____
                 (hour)   (minutes)   (seconds)

Total Reading Time: _____   _____
                      (minutes)   (seconds)

Words Per Minute Score (page 739) _____ WPM

Athletes Looking Good and Doing Better with Anabolic Steroids?

Elaine Marieb

This reading was taken from a biology book titled *Human Anatomy and Physiology,* published in 2001. It appears as a boxed insert in the chapter titled "Muscles and Muscle Tissue."

➤ **PREVIEWING THE READING**

Using the steps listed on page 5, preview the reading selection. When you have finished, complete the following items.

1. The topic of this selection is ___anabolic steroids___ .

2. List three questions you expect to be able to answer after reading the article.

   a. ___What are anabolic steroids?___

   b. ___Why do athletes use anabolic steroids?___

   c. ___What are the risks of anabolic steroid use?___

 MAKING CONNECTIONS

What would you be willing to do in order to win an athletic competition—a weight-lifting contest, a race, a football game? Would you be willing to take drugs? Why or why not?

> ➤ **READING TIP**

This selection contains many examples of the effects of steroid use, both positive and negative. Create two columns in your notes, one labeled "Benefits" and the other labeled "Risks," so you can keep track of both types of effects as you read.

 CHECKING YOUR READING RATE

If you plan to compute your reading rate, be sure to record your starting time in the box at the end of the exercises before you begin reading.

Athletes Looking Good and Doing Better with Anabolic Steroids?

anabolic steroids
synthetic hormones
that promote
protein storage
and tissue growth

testosterone
the male hormone
that causes
increased muscle
and bone mass
and other physical
changes during
male puberty and
maintains
masculine traits
throughout life

anemia
condition in which
an abnormally low
amount of
hemoglobin or a
low number of red
blood cells results
in the body's cells
not receiving
enough oxygen

muscle atrophy
the deterioration
of a muscle due to
disease, injury, or
lack of use

1   Society loves a winner and top athletes reap large social and monetary rewards. Thus, it is not surprising that some will grasp at anything that will increase their performance—including **anabolic steroids**. Anabolic steroids, variants of the male sex hormone **testosterone** engineered by pharmaceutical companies, were introduced in the 1950s to treat victims of **anemia** and certain muscle-wasting diseases and to prevent **muscle atrophy** in patients immobilized after surgery. Testosterone is responsible for the increase in muscle and bone mass and other physical changes that occur during puberty and convert boys into men. Convinced that megadoses of the steroids could produce enhanced masculinizing effects in grown men, many athletes and bodybuilders were using the steroids by the early 1960s, and the practice is still going strong today. Indeed, it has been estimated that nearly one in every ten young men has tried steroids, so use is no longer confined to athletes looking for the edge.

2   It has been difficult to determine the incidence of anabolic steroid use among athletes because the use of drugs has been banned by most international competitions, and users (and prescribing physicians or drug dealers) are naturally reluctant to talk about it. Nonetheless, there is little question that many professional bodybuilders and athletes competing in events that require muscle strength (e.g., **shot put**, discus throwing, and weight lifting) are heavy users. Sports figures such as football players have also admitted to using steroids as an adjunct to training, diet, and psychological preparation for games. Advantages of anabolic steroids cited by athletes include enhanced muscle mass and strength, increased oxygen-carrying capability owing to greater red blood cell volume, and an increase in aggressive behavior.

3   Typically, bodybuilders who use steroids combine high doses (up to 200 mg/day) with heavy resistance training. Intermittent use begins several months before an event, and commonly entails the use of many anabolic steroid supplements (a method called stacking). Injected or transdermal (taken via a skin patch) steroid doses are increased gradually as the competition nears.

4   But do the drugs do all that is claimed for them? Research studies have reported increases in **isometric** strength and a rise in body weight in steroid users. While these are results weight lifters dream about, there is a hot dispute over whether this also translates into athletic performance requiring the fine muscle coordination and endurance needed by runners, etc. The "jury is still out" on this question, but if you ask users, the answer will most likely be a resounding yes.

shot put 5
athletic event
involving
throwing a heavy
metal ball

isometric
a form of exercise
in which muscles
are pushed
against something 6
or against other
muscles to
strengthen them

androstenedione
an oral supplement
that temporarily
raises testos-
terone levels by 7
converting to
testosterone in
the body

Do the proclaimed advantages conferred by steroid use outweigh the risks? Absolutely not. Physicians say they cause bloated faces (Cushingoid sign of steroid excess); shriveled testes and infertility; damage to the liver that promotes liver cancer; and changes in blood cholesterol levels (which may predispose long-term users to coronary heart disease). The psychiatric hazards of anabolic steroid use may be equally threatening: Recent studies have indicated that one-third of users have serious mental problems. Manic behavior in which the users undergo Jekyll-Hyde personality swings and become extremely violent (termed the 'roid rage) is common, as are depression and delusions.

A recent arrival on the scene, sold over the counter and touted as a "nutritional performance-enhancer," is **androstenedione**, which is converted to testosterone in the body. Though it is taken orally (and much of it is destroyed by the liver soon after ingestion), the few milligrams that survive temporarily boost testosterone levels. Reports of its use by baseball great Mark McGwire in the summer of '98, and of athletic wannabes from the fifth grade up recently sweeping the supplement off the drugstore shelves are troubling, particularly since it is not regulated by the FDA and its long-term effects are unpredictable and untested.

The question of why some athletes use these drugs is easy to answer. Some admit to a willingness to do almost anything to win, short of killing themselves. Are they unwittingly doing this as well?

➤ A.   UNDERSTANDING THE THESIS AND OTHER MAIN IDEAS

Select the best answer.

___b___ 1. The central thesis of the selection is that

    a. steroid use is common among professional athletes.

    b. the risks of anabolic steroid use are much greater than the benefits.

    c. synthetic steroids such as androstenedione should be regulated by the FDA.

    d. most international athletic competitions ban the use of steroids.

___c___ 2. The author's primary purpose is to

    a. describe the history of anabolic steroids.

    b. reassure readers that the effects of anabolic steroids are not as serious as some people think.

    c. inform readers about the benefits and risks of anabolic steroid use.

    d. criticize the professional athletes who have popularized the use of anabolic steroids.

Match each question in Column A with the paragraph in the selection that primarily answers that question in Column B.

Column A

_____ e _____ 3. What are the risks/hazards of anabolic steroid use?

_____ a _____ 4. What are anabolic steroids?

_____ b _____ 5. Who uses anabolic steroids?

_____ c _____ 6. How and when do athletes use anabolic steroids?

_____ d _____ 7. Why do athletes use anabolic steroids?

Column B

a. paragraph 1

b. paragraph 2

c. paragraph 3

d. paragraphs 2 and 4

e. paragraph 5

> **B.   IDENTIFYING DETAILS**

Complete the following statement by filling in the blanks.

1. Anabolic steroids were first introduced in the _____1950s_____.

2. Anabolic steroids were originally intended to treat victims of _____anemia_____ and certain muscle-wasting diseases and to prevent _____muscle atrophy_____ in patients immobilized after surgery.

3. It has been estimated that nearly one out of every_____ten_____ young men has tried steroids.

4. The use of many anabolic steroid supplements is called _____stacking_____.

5. A high dose of steroids is up to _____200 mg/day_____.

6. The steroid androstenedione is converted to _____testosterone_____ in the body.

7. The long-term effects of androstenedione are _____unpredictable_____ and untested.

> **C.   RECOGNIZING METHODS OF ORGANIZATION AND TRANSITIONS**

Select the best answer.

_____ b _____ 1. In paragraph 2, the organizational pattern the author uses to present the advantages of anabolic steroids cited by athletes is

    a. time sequence.   c. cause and effect.

    b. enumeration.   d. problem–solution.

_c_ 2. The author uses the cause and effect organizational pattern in paragraph 5. The cause in this paragraph is

   a. steroid use and the effects are increased strength and weight.

   b. athletic competition and the effects are steroid use.

   c. steroid use and the effects are physical and psychiatric hazards.

   d. athletes and the effects are improved performance.

➤ D.   REVIEWING AND ORGANIZING IDEAS: OUTLINING

Complete the following outline of paragraphs 4 and 5 by filling in the missing words and phrases.

Results of Anabolic Steroid Use

   I.   Benefits

       A. For weight lifters

           1. Increase in _____isometric_____ strength

           2. Rise in _____body weight_____

       B. For _____runners_____ and other athletes

           1. Uncertain effects

   II.   Hazards/Risks

       A. Physical

           1. Bloated _____faces_____

               a. Cushingoid sign of _____steroid excess_____

           2. Shriveled testes and _____infertility_____

           3. Damage to _____liver_____

               a. Promotes liver _____cancer_____

           4. Changes in _____blood cholesterol_____ levels

               a. May predispose _____long-term users_____ to _____coronary heart disease_____

B. _____Psychiatric/Mental_____

  1. One-third of users have serious _____mental problems_____

  2. _____Manic_____ behavior

   a. Jekyll-Hyde _____personality_____ swings

   b. Extreme _____violence_____ or 'roid rage

  3. Depression

  4. _____Delusions_____

➤ **E. FIGURING OUT INFERRED MEANINGS**

Indicate whether each statement is true (T) or false (F).

__F__ 1. Most athletes are proud of their steroid use.

__T__ 2. Increased isometric strength and body weight are goals of weight lifters.

__F__ 3. Steroid users believe runners and other athletes whose performance depends on fine muscle coordination and endurance do not benefit from steroids.

__T__ 4. Many young athletes do not know about the risks of steroid use.

➤ **F. THINKING CRITICALLY**

Select the best answer.

__d__ 1. The thesis is supported primarily by
   a. personal experience.   c. analogies.
   b. statistics.   d. facts and examples.

__b__ 2. The tone of the selection can best be described as
   a. pessimistic.   c. admiring.
   b. serious.   d. disgusted.

__c__ 3. The author opens with the words "Society loves a winner" in order to
   a. add humor to the subject of steroid use.
   b. defend steroid use by athletes.
   c. offer a possible motivation for steroid use.
   d. ridicule steroid users.

___b___ 4. In paragraph 2, the statement that "users are naturally reluctant to talk about it" means that

    a. these athletes don't want to give away the secrets of their success.

    b. athletes who use steroids are breaking the rules of most international competitions.

    c. these athletes would be arrested if they talked about their steroid use.

    d. athletes who do not use steroids would criticize the ones who do.

___d___ 5. Of the following statements based on paragraph 6, the only one that is an *opinion* is

    a. Androstenedione is sold over the counter as a nutritional supplement.

    b. Although androstenedione is taken orally, the liver destroys much of it soon after ingestion.

    c. Androstenedione is not regulated by the FDA.

    d. Reports of its use by baseball great Mark McGwire are troubling.

___a___ 6. The author ends the selection with a question primarily to

    a. prompt readers and possibly athletes to think about the effects of steroid use.

    b. reveal why some athletes use steroids.

    c. demonstrate sympathy for athletes who use steroids.

    d. present another side of the issue.

➤ G. BUILDING VOCABULARY

➤ Context

Using context and a dictionary, if necessary, determine the meaning of each word as it is used in the selection.

___b___ 1. monetary (paragraph 1)

    a. emotional   c. social

    b. related to money   d. related to status

___c___ 2. masculinizing (paragraph 1)

    a. strengthening   c. giving a masculine appearance

    b. hormone-altering   d. taking away masculinity

___b___ 3. adjunct (paragraph 2)

    a. replacement

    b. supplement

    c. alternative

    d. advantage

___a___ 4. intermittent (paragraph 3)

    a. periodic

    b. constant

    c. intensive

    d. careful

___c___ 5. entails (paragraph 3)

    a. realizes

    b. eliminates

    c. involves

    d. relaxes

___a___ 6. resounding (paragraph 4)

    a. strong and forceful

    b. slow and hesitant

    c. suspicious or doubtful

    d. restricted and limited

___b___ 7. touted (paragraph 6)

    a. counted

    b. promoted

    c. respected

    d. performed

➤ Word Parts

A REVIEW OF PREFIXES

IM- means *not*

IN- means *in, into*

MEGA- means *large*

PRE- means *before, in advance*

TRANS- means *across, over, through*

UN- means *not*

Match each word in Column A with its meaning in Column B. Write your answers in the spaces provided.

Column A	Column B
_d_ 1. transdermal	a. taking into the body by the mouth
_e_ 2. unwittingly	b. exceptionally large quantities
_f_ 3. predispose	c. not able to move
_a_ 4. ingestion	d. through the skin
_c_ 5. immobilized	e. not knowingly or not intentionally
_b_ 6. megadoses	f. make someone susceptible in advance

► Unusual Words/Unusual Meanings

Read each of the statements from the selection again, and then use the hints to fill in the meaning of the underlined word or phrase.

1. "[Anabolic steroid] use is no longer confined to athletes <u>looking for the edge</u>." (paragraph 1)

   Hint: An *edge* means an advantage or a margin of superiority over someone or something.

   Therefore, athletes who are looking for the edge are hoping to find ___an advantage over their competitors___.

2. "The '<u>jury is still out</u>' on this question." (paragraph 4)

   Hint: The expression refers to a situation in which the jury for a case presented in court has not yet agreed upon its decision.

   Therefore, there has not yet been ___a decision or agreement___ about this particular question.

3. "Reports of . . . athletic <u>wannabes</u> from the fifth grade up recently sweeping the supplement off the drugstore shelves are troubling." (paragraph 6)

   Hint: The term *wannabe* is a shortened version of the phrase "want to be."

   Therefore, athletic *wannabes* are young people who ___want to be athletes___.

► H.   SELECTING A LEARNING/STUDY STRATEGY

Evaluate the two-column list you created on page 491 as a study aid. For what types of exams would it be most and least useful?

► I.   EXPLORING IDEAS THROUGH DISCUSSION AND WRITING

1. Why do you think so many young men have tried steroids? Does society do more to promote steroid use or discourage it?

2. How can you tell that the author disapproves of steroid use? Give an example.

3. Do you think the advantages of steroid use outweigh the disadvantages? Defend your opinion.

➤ **J. BEYOND THE CLASSROOM TO THE WEB**

Visit Anabolic Steroid Abuse, published by the National Institute on Drug Abuse at **http://steroidabuse.org/**.

According to the home page of this organization's Web site, what are at least five risks for women who take anabolic steroids?

✔ **Tracking Your Progress**

Selection 30

Section	Number Correct		Score
A. Thesis and Main Idea (7 items)	_____	x 4	_____
B. Details (7 items)	_____	x 3	_____
C. Organization and Transitions (2 items)	_____	x 1	_____
E. Inferred Meanings (4 items)	_____	x 3	_____
F. Thinking Critically (6 items)	_____	x 3	_____
G. Vocabulary			
1. Context (7 items)	_____	x 1	_____
2. Word Parts (6 items)	_____	x 2	_____
		TOTAL SCORE	_____ %

CHECKING YOUR READING RATE

Words in Selection 30: 659

Finishing Time:	_____	_____	_____
	(hour)	(minutes)	(seconds)
Starting Time:	_____	_____	_____
	(hour)	(minutes)	(seconds)
Total Reading Time:		_____	_____
		(minutes)	(seconds)

Words Per Minute Score (page 739) _____ WPM

21 Life Sciences

The sciences investigate the physical world around us. The life sciences are concerned with living organisms—how they grow, develop, and function. The life sciences explore many important questions that affect our daily lives and are essential to our well-being. The study of science is fun and rewarding because you come to understand more about yourself and how you interact with other living things around you. "Baby, Oh, Baby" explores the changing world of human reproduction. "Bugs in Your Pillow," in addition to encouraging you to go pillow shopping, examines the unseen world of micro-organisms. "The Biodiversity Crisis" decries the dramatic loss of species and examines the causes.

Use the following suggestions for reading in the life sciences.

TIPS FOR READING IN LIFE SCIENCES

- **Adopt a scientific mind-set.** To read successfully in the sciences, get in the habit of asking questions and seeking answers, analyzing problems, and looking for solutions or explanations. For example, when reading "The Biodiversity Crisis" ask what can be done to slow species loss.

- **Learn new terminology.** To read in the sciences, you have to learn the language of science. Science is exact and precise, and scientists use specific terminology to make communication as error-free as possible. In "Bugs in Your Pillow," for example, you will encounter biological terms used to name particular species of bugs.

- **Focus on cause and effect and process.** Since science is concerned with how and why things happen, cause and effect and process are most always important. In "Bugs in Your Pillow," for example, you will learn how tiny bugs inhabit your pillows.

SELECTION 31

Baby, Oh, Baby
Jonathan Dube

This article first appeared on the ABCNEWS Web site in October 1999. Read it to learn about how recent technological advances may affect human reproduction and what changes in human reproduction you can expect to occur during the twenty-first century.

➤ PREVIEWING THE READING

Using the steps listed on page 5, preview the reading selection. When you have finished, complete the following items.

1. What time period is this reading concerned with?

   the twenty-first century

2. Name at least one technological advance in reproduction that you think is discussed in this reading.

   gene therapy, reproductive health techniques,

   early diagnosis of diseases

 MAKING CONNECTIONS

If you were going to have a (or another) baby, which of his or her traits would you like to be able to choose if you could? Why?

➤ READING TIP

As you read, look for and highlight each technological advance that is mentioned. Using a different color highlighter, mark the effects of each technological advance.

 CHECKING YOUR READING RATE

If you plan to compute your reading rate, be sure to record your starting time in the box at the end of the exercises before you begin reading.

Baby, Oh, Baby

1   Every parent wants the perfect child.

2   In the next millennium, every parent may get that chance.

3   Of all the changes sure to come in the 21st century and beyond, reproductive advances, with their potential to alter fundamentally who we are, could be the most significant and profound.

gene therapy procedures that correct genetic disorders or abnormalities

4   **Gene therapy** may eliminate hereditary diseases. Improved infant nutrition could curb later-life health problems. Ever-tinier premature babies will survive and thrive. Contraception may be perfected to the point that we'll eliminate the need for abortions.

5   And, most significantly, we'll probably be able to order up designer babies with whatever features we desire. Or, if we prefer, simply clone ourselves.

bioethics the study of the moral implications of new biological discoveries and advances

6   "I do believe we'll go there," says Arthur Caplan, director of the University of Pennsylvania's Center of **Bioethics**. "And it'll create a whole new array of ethical problems."

Brave New Babies

7   In the next 25 years, between 131 million and 136 million infants will be born each year worldwide—mostly in sub-Saharan Africa and southern Asia. More than 90 percent of these brave new babies will be born in the least developed nations, pushing the world's population to as high as 8.9 billion in 50 years, according to the U.S. Census Bureau.

8   "People will die less frequently at young ages and live longer," forecasts Peter Way, chief of the U.S. Census Bureau's International Programs Center.

9   Reproductive health care will get better around the world, but at a much slower pace in less developed regions. Eventually, though, widespread contraceptive use and safer childbirth techniques could help lower infant mortality and prevent sexually transmitted diseases in poorer nations. How long that takes depends on when—and if—the more developed countries pony up the billions of dollars necessary to improve pre- and postnatal care.

10   "Unless the political will develops to dedicate the necessary resources, that gap will continue to widen," says William Ryan, a spokesman for the United Nations Population Fund.

Techno Tots

11   Closing that gap could become even more important in the next millennium, Ryan says, as new reproductive health techniques develop.

neonatologists those who study the care and diseases of newborn infants

12   Babies born prematurely will survive outside the womb at earlier stages, **neonatologists** say, thanks to technology that will simulate life inside the womb. Preemies as young as 19 or 20 weeks who would have died because of underdeveloped lungs will survive on oxygen-rich "liquid air." Nutritional boosters and ever more sophisticated ventilators and respirators will decrease the likelihood that these microbabies will suffer complications such as brain damage.

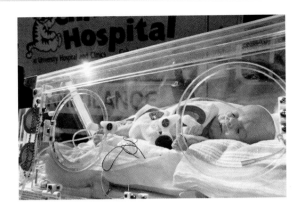

In the next century, it won't be so unusual for infants like Tanner Durham, born 12 weeks premature in 1996 and weighing only 1 pound, to undergo complicated heart surgery in utero or shortly after birth. (L. G. Patterson/AP Photo)

13   "It continues to be a moving target to see how small a baby can be and still survive," says Dr. James Lemons, director of neonatology at the University of Indiana School of Medicine and the chair of the American Academy of Pediatrics Committee on Fetus and Newborn.

14   Even breast-feeding will become part of the high-tech approach, Lemons says. By feeding pregnant and nursing mothers certain foods, we'll "program" infants to be healthier later in life. For example, we may be able to improve a child's ability to **metabolize** cholesterol or enhance brain and nerve development by using specific fatty acids.

metabolize
to break down a substance to yield energy to support life

Womb with a View

15   By 2003 the Human Genome Project should be complete, providing a road map to human **DNA**. Eventually, doctors will be able to diagnose diseases such as cystic fibrosis and muscular dystrophy in fetuses, giving parents prenatal options they've never had before.

DNA
a nucleic acid that carries genetic information in the cell

16   While abortion may be the first such option that comes to mind, it's likely to shrink in importance as in-utero surgery continues to advance. Many in the medical world confidently predict that in the early 21st century, doctors will be able to perform nearly every surgery on a fetus that they now do on adults. In-utero gene therapy is the next great frontier. It would enable doctors to tinker with fetal DNA and cure congenital conditions before birth.

17   When **genetic engineering** becomes a reality—within 50 years, some predict—we'll even be able to program babies to be disease-free, eliminating the need for gene therapy.

genetic engineering
the scientific alteration of genetic material in a living organism

18   By midcentury, innovations in test-tube fertility, genetics and preemie care may lead to the use of artificial wombs, where babies could be conceived and brought to term in a simulated uterine environment carefully monitored to eliminate complications.

19   "Absolutely, somewhere in the next millennium, making babies sexually will be rare," Caplan speculates.

20   Cloning will be possible, but Caplan expects it'll be little more than a novelty, as most people won't be interested in virtually duplicating themselves.

Parlez-vous Y2K?

21   But many parents will leap at the chance to make their children smarter, fitter and prettier. Ethical concerns will be overtaken, says Caplan, by the realization that technology simply makes for better children.

22   "In a competitive market society, people are going to want to give their kids an edge," says the bioethicist. "They'll slowly get used to the idea that a genetic edge is not greatly different from an environmental edge."

eugenic
relating to the
study of
hereditary
improvement of
the human race
by controlled
selective
breeding

23   At first, such **eugenic** science will most probably be available only to the wealthy, but once people realize the social benefits—lower health-care costs, for one—Caplan says he thinks the technology will become widely available. In fact, he says, it will be so beneficial that governments may *require* children to be engineered genetically to prevent development of new socioeconomic gaps.

24   By the time these "smart" babies are born, they could be taught via direct transmission of electrical impulses into chips implanted in their brains.

25   "You might download French into the 3-year-old's brain directly," Caplan says.

26   Who knows? Maybe all this technology will make humans so smart they'll be able to predict the future.

➤ A.   UNDERSTANDING THE THESIS AND OTHER MAIN IDEAS

Select the best answer.

__b__ 1. The central thesis of the article is that in the twenty-first century
    a. cloning may become more than a novelty.

    b. technological advances may affect human reproduction.

    c. many diseases may be eliminated.

    d. abortion may soon become unnecessary.

__a__ 2. The author's primary purpose is to
    a. describe changes that may occur.

    b. report technological research.

    c. suggest that some reproductive changes may be unethical.

    d. urge readers to pay more attention to less developed countries.

__b__ 3. According to the reading, infants may be programmed to be healthier later in life by
    a. reducing cholesterol intake.

    b. feeding pregnant women and nursing mothers specific foods.

c. enhancing brain development.

d. feeding infants fatty acids.

___c___ 4. In the future, genetic engineering may be used to eliminate

a. contraception.

b. hunger.

c. hereditary diseases.

d. infertility.

___d___ 5. The main idea of paragraph 9 is that

a. safer childbirth practices are needed in less developed countries.

b. developed nations are reluctant to offer aid to underdeveloped nations.

c. contraception should be more widely used in less developed nations.

d. poorer nations will experience fewer and slower changes in reproductive health care than will wealthier nations.

___b___ 6. The main idea of paragraph 12 is that

a. premature babies under 20 weeks seldom survive.

b. due to advanced technology, more premature babies will be able to survive.

c. more ventilators will need to be manufactured.

d. premature babies have underdeveloped lungs.

___d___ 7. The topic of paragraph 16 is

a. DNA.

b. abortion.

c. congenital diseases.

d. in-utero surgery.

___a___ 8. The main idea of paragraph 16 is expressed in the

a. first sentence.

b. second sentence.

c. third sentence.

d. fourth sentence.

➤ **B.   IDENTIFYING DETAILS**

Indicate whether each statement is true (T) or false (F).

___T___ 1. In the twenty-first century, the largest number of babies will be born in the least developed nations.

___F___ 2. How rapidly pre- and postnatal care in less developed nations improves depends on the willingness of the countries' scientists to participate.

___T___ 3. Technology may be developed that simulates life inside the womb.

___T___ 4. It may be possible to improve infants' health later in life by feeding their mothers certain foods.

___F___ 5. Doctors predict that in-utero surgery will become unpopular.

➤ **C.   RECOGNIZING METHODS OF ORGANIZATION AND TRANSITIONS**

Complete the following statements by filling in the blanks.

1. This selection is concerned with changes and events that may occur in the future. For each technological advance, the writer explains what may happen as a result of that advance. The organizational pattern used in this reading is ____cause and effect____.

2. Identify one transitional word or phrase that suggests a direction or sequence in time. (Example: In paragraph 1 the phrase *in the next millennium* suggests a time sequence.) _in the next 25 years, eventually, By 2003,_

   in the early twenty-first century

3. Locate a phrase in paragraph 14 that indicates that the author will illustrate his ideas. ____For example____

4. Locate a phrase in paragraph 23 that indicates that further information or explanation is to follow. _____in fact_____

D. REVIEWING AND ORGANIZING IDEAS: MAPPING

The following map is a useful way to organize causes and effects. Complete the following cause and effect map of the reading by filling in the empty boxes.

BABY, OH BABY: CAUSE AND EFFECT MAP

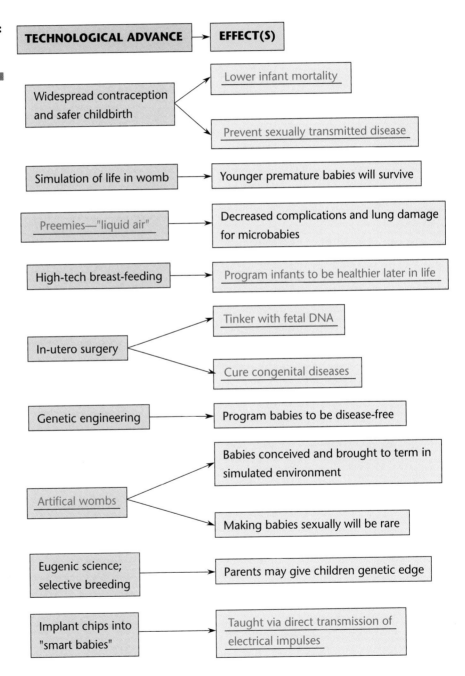

TECHNOLOGICAL ADVANCE → EFFECT(S)

Widespread contraception and safer childbirth →
- Lower infant mortality
- Prevent sexually transmitted disease

Simulation of life in womb → Younger premature babies will survive

Preemies—"liquid air" → Decreased complications and lung damage for microbabies

High-tech breast-feeding → Program infants to be healthier later in life

In-utero surgery →
- Tinker with fetal DNA
- Cure congenital diseases

Genetic engineering → Program babies to be disease-free

Artifical wombs →
- Babies conceived and brought to term in simulated environment
- Making babies sexually will be rare

Eugenic science; selective breeding → Parents may give children genetic edge

Implant chips into "smart babies" → Taught via direct transmission of electrical impulses

➤ E. FIGURING OUT INFERRED MEANINGS

Select the best answer.

___c___ 1. If the technological advances that are forecast in the selection occur, it can be inferred that

    a. political problems will increase.

    b. sexually transmitted diseases will increase.

    c. the world population will increase.

    d. the need for doctors will decrease.

___d___ 2. According to the article, it is reasonable to infer that in less developed countries

    a. abortion is widespread.

    b. abortion is not available.

    c. people are religiously opposed to contraception.

    d. contraception is not widely used.

___b___ 3. With increased technology to perform in-utero surgery, it is possible that doctors may be able to eliminate

    a. abortion.   c. heart disease.

    b. birth defects.   d. aging.

➤ F. THINKING CRITICALLY

Select the best answer.

___a___ 1. The author supports his ideas primarily by

    a. quoting authorities.

    b. making comparisons.

    c. describing events.

    d. offering analogies.

___d___ 2. Of the following statements, the only one that is a *fact* is

    a. Contraception may eliminate the need for abortions.

    b. In the next 25 years, between 131 million and 136 million infants will be born each year.

    c. Every parent would like to have the perfect child.

    d. Some premature babies die because their lungs are underdeveloped.

_c_ 3. By stating that "You might download French into the 3-year-old's brain directly" (paragraph 25), Caplan is suggesting that

a. technological advances may have long-term physiological effects.

b. technology will have far-reaching international effects.

c. new technology may affect how humans learn.

d. technological advances may alter patterns of human behavior.

_d_ 4. The concluding paragraph (26) of the article adds a humorous touch because

a. no one can predict the future.

b. humans are already smart.

c. technology can never be predicted.

d. the article itself predicts the future.

➤ G. BUILDING VOCABULARY

➤ Context

Using context and a dictionary, if necessary, determine the meaning of each word as it is used in the selection.

_a_ 1. array (paragraph 6)

a. collection

b. gallery

c. limitation

d. comparison

_d_ 2. enhance (paragraph 14)

a. destroy

b. control

c. restrict

d. improve

_d_ 3. in-utero (paragraph 16)

a. outside the uterus

b. a substitute for the uterus

c. similar to the uterus

d. within the uterus

_b_ 4. congenital (paragraph 16)

    a. determined by research

    b. existing at birth

    c. caused by birth trauma

    d. developed after birth

_a_ 5. simulated (paragraph 18)

    a. imitated

    b. observed

    c. initiated

    d. monitored

▶ **Word Parts**

A REVIEW OF PREFIXES

CONTRA- means *against* (contradict, contraband)
MILLI- means *thousand* (millisecond, millimeter)
MORT- means *death* (mortician, mortally wounded)
POST- means *after* (postwar, postoperative care)
PRE- means *before* (prewar, premarital agreement)

Match each word in Column A with its meaning in Column B. Write your answers in the spaces provided.

Column A	**Column B**
_c_ 1. contraception	a. care after delivery
_a_ 2. postnatal care	b. death rate of infants
_e_ 3. millennium	c. preventing conception
_b_ 4. infant mortality	d. infants born too early
_d_ 5. premature babies	e. one thousand years

▶ **Unusual Words/Unusual Meanings**
Complete the following items.

1. The expression <u>pony up</u> as used in paragraph 9 is an idiom—an expression that cannot be understood by studying the individual meanings of the words contained in it. It has nothing to do with horses or ponies. Instead, the phrase has a unique meaning in English. It means *to come up with a sum of money.* Write a sentence using this phrase.

    Your sentence: _____.

2. <u>Designer babies</u> are mentioned in paragraph 5. The word "designer" is a reference to people who design or manufacture specialized lines of clothing or furnishings. Usually designer items attempt to be unique and individual. Explain the meaning of the term *designer babies*.

Your sentence: _____.

➤ H.   SELECTING A LEARNING/STUDY STRATEGY

1. Assume this reading will be tested on an upcoming exam. Evaluate the usefulness of the cause and effect map you completed on page 507 as a study tool. How would you use it to study?

2. What methods could you use to learn all the new terminology introduced in this reading? Make a list of possible strategies.

➤ I.   EXPLORING IDEAS THROUGH DISCUSSION AND WRITING

1. What reservations, if any, would you have about using the technology described in this reading to conceive and bring a baby to term?

2. If test tube babies become common, how do you think the practice might alter the parent-child bond that now exists?

3. What moral or ethical problems can you foresee as the technologies discussed in this section develop?

➤ J.   BEYOND THE CLASSROOM TO THE WEB

Visit the ABCNEWS *Web site at* **http://more.abcnews.go.com/ABC2000/living/ babies2000.html.**

Explore the other Web pages related to this article by selecting some of the links that appear on the first page.

✔ Tracking Your Progress

Selection 31

Section	Number Correct	Score
A. Thesis and Main Idea (8 items)	_____ x 4	_____
B. Details (5 items)	_____ x 3	_____
C. Organization and Transitions (4 items)	_____ x 3	_____
E. Inferred Meanings (3 items)	_____ x 3	_____
F. Thinking Critically (4 items)	_____ x 3	_____
G. Vocabulary		
1. Context (5 items)	_____ x 2	_____
2. Word Parts (5 items)	_____ x 2	_____
TOTAL SCORE		_____ %

CHECKING YOUR READING RATE

Words in Selection 31: 920

	(hour)	(minutes)	(seconds)
Finishing Time:	_____	_____	_____
Starting Time:	_____	_____	_____
	(hour)	(minutes)	(seconds)
Total Reading Time:		_____	_____
		(minutes)	(seconds)

Words Per Minute Score (page 739) _____ WPM

SELECTION 32

Bugs in Your Pillow

David Bodanis

This reading is taken from a book titled *The Secret Family,* published in 1997. The book follows a typical family for a twenty-four hour period, exposing real-life science behind our everyday routines and surroundings.

▶ PREVIEWING THE READING

Using the steps listed on page 5, preview the reading selection. When you have finished, complete the following items.

1. The topic of this selection is ___bugs/pillow mites___.

2. List three questions you expect to be able to answer after reading the article.

   a. Where are the bugs found? _____

   b. What kind of bugs are they? _____

   c. What can be done about them? _____

MAKING CONNECTIONS

Have you ever encountered a "bug" infestation in your home or in a place you have stayed overnight? What was your response?

▶ READING TIP

As you read, highlight startling or unusual facts about the contents of pillows.

CHECKING YOUR READING RATE

If you plan to compute your reading rate, be sure to record your starting time in the box at the end of the exercises before you begin reading.

Bugs in Your Pillow

1   There's an entire neo-dinosaur landscape of lumbering creatures deep inside the pillows, even in the cleanest of homes. We nourish our pillows with hours of moisture-rich exhaled air each night—a drenching half pint per night is typical—and that, combined with the skin oils and surface skin flakes we can't help but scrape loose, is enough to keep their population at levels immensely greater than the hair-follicle dwelling demodex we saw at breakfast. The demodex existed by the mere hundreds; here, on the pillow, the human family is cozily surrounded by a world—mercifully invisible to the naked eye—with hundreds of thousands of busy inhabitants.

2   These are *Dermatophagoides pteronyssinus*—the flesh-eating pillow mites. Unlike the cuddly rounded demodex, a microscope reveals the *Dermatophagoides* as hulking armored beasts, with eight legs and massive rhinolike necks. They're also superbly equipped for life inside the pillow—their feet even have flaring pads, like a *Star Wars* desert planet beast, to keep them from suddenly sinking in the soft filling— and despite the forbidding name and appearance, they are actually quite mild.

3   As it's difficult to see well in the dim light reaching their depths, they signal romantic availability not by crude bellowing calls, but by the polite release of a floating vapor. The targeted one swivels its huge neck to get a directional fix, and then, as gracefully and balletically as an armored monster is able, trundles shyly forward for the hopeful tryst that awaits.

4   It seems to be a near perfect life, with several generations of these bulky creatures—from gnarled grandparents to thin-walled frisky juveniles—resting, strolling, romancing, or, greatest of pleasures and definitely greatest use of time, tilting their heads up to grab the gently swirling skin flakes tumbling down. But paradise is not for our planet, and there's also one other sort of creature in the pillow: the dreaded, jaw-slobbering *Cheyletus*—a relative giant in this subvisible domain, that lives by tracking down the ordinary peaceable mites in our pillows, and eating them. Let a *Dermatophagoides* adult release a mate-luring **pheromone** cloud, and this *Cheyletus* will hurry along faster than the intended, to wait, jaws ready, there in the dark, till one of the hopeful suitors lumbers into reach. If the *Cheyletus* can't find suitably nutritious adults it'll simply pick off bite-size morsels of baby *Dermatophagoides*.

5   If this were all that happened, it wouldn't matter much that this odd world is so busily active beneath us. But the mother plumps up the pillow for her and her baby son. Any such plumping, or even any twists and turns we take on the clutched pillow at night, forces windstorm velocity air gusts into that hidden world. The air then whooshes back up, forming great arcing **parabolas** that rise a full three inches or even more above the pillowcase, loaded with thousands of the discreetly named "anal pellets" each *Cheyletus* has produced. They explode apart in our open air and then float. Since they were recently inside the digestive system of an enzyme-secreting arthropod, they're not especially healthy to have floating around, especially as they're exactly the right size to get breathed in.

6   Adults are fairly well protected by their developed immune systems, but kids, and especially babies, can suffer, as the gut enzymes slip loose from the floating pellets or land on insufficiently blinking eyes. The baby's cells that will later be powerful **histamine** producers can become oversensitized when enough pellets touch and

pheromone
a chemical secreted by an animal, especially an insect, that influences the behavior of other members of its species

parabolas
curves

histamine
a chemical released from cells in the immune system as part of an allergic reaction

Pillow mite. Too small to see, colonies of 40,000 or more pillow mites inhabit the warmth of even the cleanest household pillows. Most are harmless scavengers, living on our scraped-loose skin, though a small number of microcarnivores—hunting these skin-eaters—rampage through their midst under our resting heads each night.

epidemiological related to the branch of medicine that studies the causes, distribution, and control of disease in populations

will stay that way for years. The effect is greater than that of anything else the baby encountered in the hallway: a large **epidemiological** study in Britain, tracing several hundred Southampton families over the years, found that one of the best predictors of getting asthma as an adolescent was living in a home with large numbers of pillow mites as a baby. It's not just a problem in the bedroom, for the haze of broken pellets floats to all the rooms, settling on baby-exposed carpets everywhere in the house. Regularly allowing the dog or cat to sleep on the bed during the day provides further supplies of warmth and nutrient breath vapor when the animals rest their heads on the pillows, thus incubating even greater numbers of pillow mites. A teenager who spends hours leaning on her pillow during her life-sustaining phone calls—her body thereby acting as a radiant heating coil for the life underneath her—will be guaranteed supremely high numbers in her room.

flamethrowers weapons that project a stream of burning liquid

7   The results of these studies make people inquire about the price of **flamethrowers**. The populations are impressive, for the pillow mites have been found in virtually 100 percent of the homes studied, be it in Germany, America, or Britain. There are usually at least 10,000 mites per pillow in the most hygienic of traditional homes. If it is a house where busy professional parents only change the pillow*cases,* but somehow have forgotten to ever rinse, soak, boil, or in the faintest way wash the pillow *itself*—thereby letting the sheltered inhabitants be discreetly fruitful and multiply for weeks, months, or years on end—then the pillows they're using, and considerately providing for the rest of the family, will be home to 400,000 or more creatures. In the distressing estimate of Britain's leading pillow-mite specialist, an unwashed pillow can end up being stuffed with up to 10 percent living or deceased *Dermatophagoides* by weight over the years. Along with cleaning one's pillows, at least occasionally, it's also good to keep the windows open sometimes. Double-glazed windows and central heating encourage the warm, moist conditions the mites like, and wherever that's kept down, their numbers fall too. Arizona and the Alps work as resorts, partly because their dry air helps kill off the **asthma**-production machines of such pillows.

asthma a chronic respiratory disease often resulting from allergies

8   The wife hears a call from downstairs, glances at her bedside clock to confirm the late time, and quickly gets up, one soothed baby son happy in her arms. A number of the mites come along too, clinging tightly to wife and baby alike. Habitat destruction

is a continual threat. In a pillow not used for five or six months, the entire population of mites will starve. A proportion of the population valiantly travels with us all the time as a safeguard against such disasters. Most die before they're ever brought to another pillow for recolonization. But a number will survive, for the species is photophobic (averse to light) and so without quite knowing why, they do try to hunker down, tiny feet working their way down from any sun or artificial light, to clamp around our clothing fibers—wool and brushed cotton do best—till they're at least partially protected.

9   We accordingly are the vehicles that transport these city-state populations around from room to room in our homes, as well as carrying them to offices, schools, and one of the most fruitful switching stations: hotel rooms, with their nice, constantly reinvigorated, traveler-awaiting pillows. Here in this house representatives of the several different pillow colonies are being carried on the human family as they begin to assemble downstairs; adults and babies and juveniles and even some of the awful *Cheyletus* predators, though humbled now, and cowering away from the light as much as the others. All the movement is just a vague blur to the diverse *Dermatophagoides* holding on, as the humans collect money and jackets and candy bars and shopping lists; as the baby's bag is rechecked for extra diapers, and the dad tries not to be too impatient, holding the car keys, as the daughter comes down. Even she's been willing to hurry up, for the sake of what's coming next. The traveling mites are going to get a treat today.

10   This family is going to the mall.

A.   UNDERSTANDING THE THESIS AND OTHER MAIN IDEAS

Select the best answer.

__b__ 1. The author's primary purpose is to
   a. entertain readers with a story about tiny mites.
   b. describe pillow mites and their effect on human health.
   c. urge readers to have their homes inspected for pests.
   d. compare two types of microscopic insects that live in most homes.

__a__ 2. The topic of paragraph 2 is
   a. the *Dermatophagoides pteronyssinus* (pillow mites).
   b. the demodex.
   c. a *Star Wars* character.
   d. flesh-eaters.

__c__ 3. The main idea of paragraph 4 is that *Dermatophagoides*
   a. lives harmlessly in pillows.
   b. lures mates by releasing pheromones.

c. has a natural predator in *Cheyletus.*

d. typically lives with several generations of other *Dermatophagoides.*

___a___ 4. The main idea of paragraph 6 is expressed in the

a. first sentence.

b. second sentence.

c. third sentence.

d. last sentence.

___d___ 5. The question that is answered in paragraph 7 is

a. What do pillow mites look like?

b. Who is most at risk from the effects of pillow mites?

c. How do pillow mites form new colonies?

d. What can be done about pillow mites?

___b___ 6. The topic of paragraph 9 is the

a. pillows in hotel rooms.

b. transportation of pillow mites.

c. photophobia of pillow mites.

d. human family.

➤ B. IDENTIFYING DETAILS

Indicate whether each statement is true (T) or false (F).

___T___ 1. Pillow mites exist even in households that are kept very clean.

___T___ 2. Pillow mites are microscopic creatures.

___F___ 3. Pillow mites attract other mites by bellowing crudely.

___F___ 4. Pillow mites are called flesh-eaters because they bite humans while we are sleeping.

___F___ 5. The *Cheyletus* only eats adult *Dermatophagoides.*

___T___ 6. According to a British study, one of the best predictors of getting asthma as an adolescent was living in a home with large populations of pillow mites as a baby.

___F___ 7. The anal pellets produced by *Cheyletus* are typically only a problem in the bedroom.

___T___ 8. Pillow mites have been found in practically 100 percent of the homes studied.

___T___ 9. The number of mites per pillow ranges from at least 10,000 to 400,000 or more.

> ## C.   RECOGNIZING METHODS OF ORGANIZATION AND TRANSITIONS

Select the best answer.

___d___ 1. In paragraph 2, the author describes the *Dermatophagoides pteronyssinus* using the organizational pattern known as

    a. time sequence.

    b. enumeration.

    c. cause and effect.

    d. definition.

___a___ 2. In paragraphs 5–6, the author describes what happens when a pillow is plumped. The author is using the organization pattern known as

    a. cause and effect.

    b. problem and solution.

    c. definition.

    d. enumeration.

> ## D.   REVIEWING AND ORGANIZING IDEAS: PARAPHRASING

Complete the following paraphrases of paragraphs 2–3 and paragraph 6 by filling in the missing words.

Paragraphs 2–3: The ___Dermatophagoides___ *pteronyssinus,* or flesh-eating ___pillow mite___, appears under a ___microscope___ to have a protective covering, eight ___legs___, and a thick ___neck___. It also has ___pads___ on its ___feet___ that flare to prevent it from going down into the pillow's ___filling___. Although it may seem to be dangerous, it is really harmless.

Paragraph 6: When a ___pillow___ is fluffed up, air rushes into it and forces out thousands of ___anal pellets___ produced by ___Cheyletus___. The pellets break apart in the air and drift around, where they can be ___breathed___ in by humans and cause health problems.

> ## E.   FIGURING OUT INFERRED MEANINGS

Indicate whether each phrase from the selection is meant to be taken literally (L) or figuratively (F). Literal statements are facts. Figurative expressions are imaginative comparisons (see Section 6g).

___F___ 1. "We nourish our pillows . . ." (paragraph 1)

___F___ 2. "They signal romantic availability . . ." (paragraph 3)

___F___ 3. "...as gracefully and balletically as an armored monster is able, [it] trundles shyly forward..." (paragraph 3)

___L___ 4. "They're exactly the right size to get breathed in." (paragraph 5)

___L___ 5. "The baby's cells that will later be powerful histamine producers can become oversensitized when enough pellets touch." (paragraph 6)

___F___ 6. "The traveling mites are going to get a treat today." (paragraph 9)

➤ F. THINKING CRITICALLY

Select the best answer.

___c___ 1. The author supports the thesis of "Bugs in Your Pillow" by
- a. making comparisons.
- b. quoting authorities.
- c. including descriptions.
- d. all of the above.

___d___ 2. The author writes the selection in a way that appeals to the reader's sense of
- a. humor.
- b. imagination.
- c. horror.
- d. all of the above

___c___ 3. The author uses the phrase "mercifully invisible" (paragraph 1) in order to imply that
- a. people would kill the mites without mercy if they could see them.
- b. it is fortunate that microscopes can show us what the mites look like.
- c. people would rather not be able to see these mites.
- d. the mites would be even more unhealthy if they were large enough to see.

___b___ 4. The phrase "But paradise is not for our planet" (paragraph 4) is the author's way of saying with
- a. sincere regret that people are not meant to be completely happy on Earth.
- b. humor that the pillow mite's life would be almost perfect if not for its predator *Cheyletus*.
- c. disgust that our planet would be perfect without insects like pillow mites.
- d. sympathy that there is no way we can completely eliminate pillow mites in our homes.

___c___ 5. The statement "The results of these studies make people inquire about the price of flamethrowers" (paragraph 7) means that people

    a. are referring to pest control companies as flamethrowers.

    b. believe the money spent on the pillow mite studies was wasted.

    c. are so disgusted with the results that they want to take immediate and drastic action to destroy the mites.

    d. are asking seriously for information on how to set fire to their pillows.

___b___ 6. In paragraphs 7–8, one word that indicates the author's true feelings about pillow mites is

    a. impressive.

    b. distressing.

    c. fruitful.

    d. valiantly.

___d___ 7. The author ends the selection (paragraphs 8–9) with an image of pillow mites as

    a. allergy-producing agents.

    b. microscopic household pests.

    c. filthy and dangerous parasites.

    d. brave and civilized members of a colony of creatures.

➤ G. BUILDING VOCABULARY

➤ Context

Using context and a dictionary, if necessary, determine the meaning of each word as it is used in the selection.

___b___ 1. lumbering (paragraph 1)

    a. sleeping   c. snoring

    b. moving clumsily   d. reproducing

___c___ 2. vapor (paragraph 3)

    a. signal   c. mist

    b. flash   d. color

___b___ 3. balletically (paragraph 3)

    a. noisily   c. hopefully

    b. gracefully   d. anxiously

__a__ 4. trundles (paragraph 3)

    a. moves slowly and heavily   c. avoids carefully

    b. crunches loudly and forcefully   d. changes quickly

__c__ 5. tryst (paragraph 3)

    a. victory   c. meeting

    b. effort   d. reward

__a__ 6. velocity (paragraph 5)

    a. speed   c. shadow

    b. dustiness   d. damage

__b__ 7. incubating (paragraph 6)

    a. counting   c. destroying

    b. heating   d. introducing

__c__ 8. predators (paragraph 9)

    a. victims   c. hunters

    b. pests   d. insects

▶ Word Parts

> **A REVIEW OF PREFIXES**
>
> **ARTHRO-** means *jointed*
> **MICRO-** means *tiny*
> **NEO-** means *new, recent*
> **PHOTO-** means *light*
> **RE-** means *again*
> **SUB-** means *under, beneath*

Match each word in Column A with its meaning in Column B. Write your answers in the spaces provided.

Column A	Column B
__d__ 1. recolonization	a. beneath our normal vision
__c__ 2. arthropod	b. new kind of dinosaur
__b__ 3. neodinosaur	c. creature with jointed legs
__a__ 4. subvisible	d. establishment of a new colony
__f__ 5. photophobic	e. added strength or vitality
__g__ 6. microcarnivores	f. fearing light
__e__ 7. reinvigorated	g. tiny flesh-eaters

➤ H.   SELECTING A LEARNING/STUDY STRATEGY

1. You probably had little or no difficulty concentrating while reading this selection. Why?

2. The author provides a photo and a description of a pillow mite. Which was more memorable and meaningful? What does this suggest about your learning style (how you learn)?

➤ I.   EXPLORING IDEAS THROUGH DISCUSSION AND WRITING

1. How does the author's tone affect how you feel about the information in the selection? Does the descriptive language affect the author's credibility, or simply make the selection more entertaining?

2. Did this information make you wonder about other "creatures" that may be living in your house? Describe your reaction to some of the statistics quoted in the selection.

➤ J.   BEYOND THE CLASSROOM TO THE WEB

Visit the Excite search engine at **http://www.excite.com**.

Dust mite feces is only one of many proposed causes of asthma. Search on Excite for Web sites related to "asthma+cause" (include the quotation marks and the plus sign in your search phrase). How many proposed causes for asthma can you list from the first ten search results shown?

✔ **Tracking Your Progress**

Selection 32

Section	Number Correct		Score
A. Thesis and Main Idea (6 items)	_____	x 4	_____
B. Details (9 items)	_____	x 2	_____
C. Organization and Transitions (2 items)	_____	x 2	_____
E. Inferred Meanings (6 items)	_____	x 3	_____
F. Thinking Critically (7 items)	_____	x 3	_____
G. Vocabulary			
1. Context (8 items)	_____	x 1	_____
2. Word Parts (7 items)	_____	x 1	_____
	TOTAL SCORE	_____ %	

CHECKING YOUR READING RATE

Words in Selection 32: 1,291

Finishing Time: _____   _____   _____
                    (hour)   (minutes)   (seconds)

Starting Time: _____   _____   _____
                    (hour)   (minutes)   (seconds)

Total Reading Time: _____   _____
                               (minutes)   (seconds)

Words Per Minute Score (page 739) _____ WPM

SELECTION 33

The Biodiversity Crisis

Neil A. Campbell and Jane B. Reece

This selection was taken from a biology textbook, *Essential Biology*, published in 2001. It appears in a chapter titled "Ecosystems and Conservation Biology."

▶ PREVIEWING THE READING

Using the steps listed on page 5, preview the reading selection. When you have finished, complete the following items.

1. The selection is about the loss of <u>species</u>   .

2. List two questions you should be able to answer after reading the article.

   a. <u>What are the three main causes of the biodiversity crisis?</u>

   b. <u>Why does biodiversity matter?</u>

 ### MAKING CONNECTIONS

What species in your area are in danger of becoming extinct? If you don't know, discuss how you could find out.

▶ READING TIP

As you read, highlight sections that define the biodiversity problem, reveal its causes, and explain why the issue is an important one.

 ### CHECKING YOUR READING RATE

If you plan to compute your reading rate, be sure to record your starting time in the box at the end of the exercises before you begin reading.

The Biodiversity Crisis

1   As a result of our numbers and technology and incessant intrusions in the world's **ecosystems**, we are now presiding over an alarming **biodiversity** crisis, a precipitous decline in Earth's great variety of life.

ecosystem
a system made up
of a community
of animals, plants,
and bacteria
interrelated
together with its
physical and
chemical
environment

biodiversity
short for
"biological
diversity," refers to
the range and
variety of organisms
existing in a given
place. It is
measured by the
numbers and types
of different species
or variations within
a species.

Cretaceous
the third and last
geologic time
period of the
Mesozoic Era,
ending 65 million
years ago and
characterized by
the development
of flowering
plants and the
disappearance
of dinosaurs

biosphere
the global
ecosystem; the
part of Earth that
is alive and capable
of sustaining life

radiated
spread into new
habitats and
thereby diversified

The Loss of Species

2 The seventh mass extinction in the history of life is well under way. Previous episodes, including the **Cretaceous** crunch that claimed the dinosaurs and many other groups, pale by comparison. The current mass extinction is both broader and faster, extinguishing species at a rate at least 50 times faster than just a few centuries ago. And unlike past poundings of biodiversity, which were triggered mainly by physical processes, such as climate change caused by volcanism or asteroid crashes, this latest mass extinction is due to the evolution of a single species—a big-brained, manually dexterous, environment-manipulating toolmaker that has named itself *Homo sapiens.*

3 We do not know the full scale of the biodiversity crisis in terms of a species "body count," for we are undoubtedly losing species that we didn't even know existed; the 1.5 million species that have been identified probably represent less than 10 percent of the true number of species. However, there are already enough signs to know that the **biosphere** is in deep trouble:

- About 11 percent of the 9040 known bird species in the world are endangered. In the past 40 years, population densities of migratory songbirds in the mid-Atlantic United States dropped 50 percent.

- Of the approximately 20,000 known plant species in the United States, over 600 are very close to extinction.

- Throughout the world, 970 tree species have been classified as critically endangered. At least 5 of those species are down to fewer than a half dozen surviving individuals.

- About 20 percent of the known freshwater fishes in the world have either become extinct during historical times or are seriously threatened. The toll on amphibians and reptiles has been almost as great.

- Harvard biologist Edward O. Wilson, a renowned scholar of biodiversity, has compiled what he grimly calls the Hundred Heartbeat Club. The species that belong are those animals that number fewer than 100 individuals and so are only that many heartbeats away from extinction.

- Several researchers estimate that at the current rate of destruction, over half of all plant and animal species will be gone by the end of this new century.

4 The modern mass extinction is different from earlier biodiversity shakeouts in still another important way. The prehistoric crashes were all followed by rebounds in diversity as the survivors **radiated** and adapted to ecological niches left vacant by the extinctions. But as long as we humans are around to destroy habitats and degrade biodiversity at the ecosystem level, there can be no rebound in the evolutionary diversification of life. In fact, the trend is toward increased geographic range and prevalence of "disaster species," those life-forms such as house mice, kudzu and other weeds, cockroaches, and fire ants that seem to thrive in environments disrupted by human activities. Unless we can reverse the current trend of increasing loss of biodiversity, we will leave our children and grandchildren a biosphere that is much less interesting and much more biologically impoverished.

The three main causes of the biodiversity crisis.
Habitat destruction. This is an all-too-common scene in the tropics: the clearing of a rain forest for lumber, agriculture, housing projects, or, in this case, a road.

The Three Main Causes of the Biodiversity Crisis

Habitat Destruction

5   Human alteration of habitats poses the single greatest threat to biodiversity throughout the biosphere. Assaults on diversity at the ecosystem level result from the expansion of agriculture to feed the burgeoning human population, urban development, forestry, mining, and environmental pollution. The amount of human-altered land surface is approaching 50 percent, and we use over half of all accessible surface fresh water. Some of the most productive aquatic habitats in **estuaries** and intertidal wetlands are also prime locations for commercial and residential developments. The loss of marine habitats is also severe, especially in coastal areas and coral reefs.

estuaries
areas where
fresh water
merges with sea
water

Introduced Species

6   Ranking second behind habitat loss as a cause of the biodiversity crisis is human introduction of exotic (non-native) species that eliminate native species through predation or competition. For example, if your campus is in an urban setting, there is a good chance that the birds you see most often as you walk between classes are starlings, rock doves (often called "pigeons"), and house sparrows—all introduced species that have replaced native birds in many areas of North America. One of the largest rapid-extinction events yet recorded is the loss of freshwater fishes in Lake Victoria in East Africa. About 200 of the 300 species of native fishes, found nowhere else but in this lake, have become extinct since Europeans introduced a non-native predator, the Nile perch, in the 1960s.

Introduced species. One of the largest freshwater fishes (up to 2 meters long and weighing up to 450 kilograms), the Nile perch was introduced to Lake Victoria in East Africa to provide high-protein food for the growing human population. Unfortunately, the perch's main effect has been to wipe out about 200 smaller native species, reducing its own food supply to a critical level.

Overexploitation. Until the past few decades, the North Atlantic bluefin tuna was considered a sport fish of little commercial value—just a few cents per pound as cat food. Then, beginning in the 1980s, wholesalers began airfreighting fresh, iced bluefin to Japan for sushi and sashimi. In that market, the fish now brings up to $100 per pound! With that kind of demand, the results are predictable. It took just ten years to reduce the North Atlantic bluefin population to less than 20 percent of its 1980 size. In spite of quotas, the high price that bluefin tuna brings probably dooms the species to extinction.

Overexploitation

7   As a third major threat to biodiversity, overexploitation of wildlife often compounds problems of shrinking habitat and introduced species. Animal species whose numbers have been drastically reduced by excessive commercial harvest or sport hunting include whales, the American bison, Galapagos tortoises, and numerous fishes. Many fish stocks in the ocean have been overfished to levels that cannot sustain further human exploitation. In addition to the commercially important species, members of many other species are often killed by harvesting methods; for example, dolphins, marine turtles, and seabirds are caught in fishing nets, and countless numbers of invertebrates are killed by marine trawls (big nets). An expanding, often illegal world trade in wildlife products, including rhinocerous horns, elephant tusks, and grizzly bear gallbladders, also threatens many species.

Why Biodiversity Matters

8   Why should we care about the loss of biodiversity? First of all, we depend on many other species for food, clothing, shelter, oxygen, soil fertility—the list goes on and on. In the United States, 25 percent of all prescriptions dispensed from pharmacies contain substances derived from plants. For instance, two drugs effective against Hodgkin's disease and certain other forms of cancer come from the rosy periwinkle, a flowering plant native to the island of Madagascar. Madagascar alone harbors some 8000 species of flowering plants, 80 percent of which occur only there. Among these unique plants are several species of wild coffee trees, some of which yield beans lacking caffeine (naturally "decaffeinated"). With an estimated 200,000 species of plants and animals, Madagascar is among the top five most biologically diverse countries in the world. Unfortunately, most of Madagascar's species are in serious trouble. People have lived on the island for only about 2000 years, but in that time, Madagascar has lost 80 percent of its forests and about 50 percent of its native species. Madagascar's dilemma represents that of much of the developing world. The island is home to over 10 million people, most of whom are desperately poor and hardly in a position to be concerned with environmental conservation. Yet the people of Madagascar as well as others around the globe could derive vital benefits from the biodiversity that is being destroyed.

9   Another reason to be concerned about the changes that underlie the biodiversity crisis is that the human population itself is threatened by large scale alterations in the

biosphere. Like all other species, we evolved in Earth's ecosystems, and we are dependent on the living and nonliving components of these systems. By allowing the extinction of species and the degradation of habitats to continue, we are taking a risk with our own species' survival.

► A.   UNDERSTANDING THE THESIS AND OTHER MAIN IDEAS

Select the best answer.

__b__ 1. The central thesis of the selection is that the biodiversity of species on Earth

   a. has increased so rapidly since the Cretaceous period that it presents a threat to humankind.

   b. is seriously threatened by the continuing impact of humans on the world's ecosystems.

   c. came about through the efforts of humans to provide food for a growing world population.

   d. can be traced to many species that originated on the island of Madagascar.

__c__ 2. The author's primary purpose is to

   a. compare earlier mass extinctions with the one currently taking place.

   b. argue that the modern mass extinction is not as critical as some people think.

   c. describe the causes and effects of the current biodiversity crisis.

   d. suggest possible solutions for the current biodiversity crisis.

__d__ 3. The main idea of paragraph 3 is that

   a. only a small percentage of the true number of species on Earth have been identified.

   b. both plant and animal species currently face endangerment and extinction.

   c. many species of fish, amphibians, and reptiles have been dramatically reduced during historical times.

   d. the full extent of the biodiversity crisis is unknown but signs indicate that the biosphere is in danger.

__d__ 4. According to the selection, the single greatest threat to biodiversity throughout the biosphere is posed by

   a. the increasing prevalence of disaster species.

   b. physical processes such as climate changes.

c. asteroids that may crash into Earth as in prehistoric times.

d. the alteration of habitats by humans.

___c___ 5. The main idea of paragraph 8 is that biodiversity is important because

a. the people of Madagascar live on the income they get from species unique to the island.

b. many prescription drugs contain substances derived from plants.

c. people around the world are dependent on many other species.

d. once a species becomes extinct, it is gone forever.

➤ **B.   IDENTIFYING DETAILS**

Select the best answer.

___b___ 1. Biologist Edward O. Wilson compiled the Hundred Heartbeat Club to describe the

a. 100 people who have done the most to reverse the effects of the biodiversity crisis.

b. species of animals that include fewer than 100 individuals remaining on Earth.

c. top 100 companies who have the largest impact on the world's ecosystems.

d. species of animals and plants that have become extinct in the last 100 years.

___c___ 2. The "disaster species" referred to in the selection include all of the following life-forms *except*

a. house mice.

b. cockroaches.

c. marine turtles.

d. kudzu and other weeds.

___d___ 3. According to the selection, the amount of human-altered land surface is approaching

a. 10 percent.

b. 20 percent.

c. 25 percent.

d. 50 percent.

_c_ 4. All of the following birds are given as examples of introduced species *except*

   a. starlings.

   b. house sparrows.

   c. migratory songbirds.

   d. rock doves or pigeons.

_d_ 5. During the 2,000 years that people have lived on Madagascar, the island has lost about

   a. 25 percent of its forests and about 80 percent of its flowering plants.

   b. 50 percent of its accessible surface fresh water and 80 percent of its marine habitats.

   c. 200 of the 300 species of native fishes.

   d. 50 percent of its native species and 80 percent of its forests.

▶ C.   RECOGNIZING METHODS OF ORGANIZATION AND TRANSITIONS

Select the best answer.

_b_ 1. In paragraph 2, the author uses the comparison and contrast organizational pattern to contrast the

   a. Cretaceous period and the modern period.

   b. current biodiversity crisis and previous episodes of mass extinction.

   c. extinction of plant species and animal species.

   d. beneficial and harmful aspects of human evolution.

_c_ 2. In paragraph 3, the author presents six specific signs that indicate that the biosphere is in danger, using the organizational pattern called

   a. definition.   c. enumeration.

   b. time sequence.   d. problem and solution.

_a_ 3. The primary organizational pattern in paragraphs 5–7 is

   a. cause and effect.   c. time sequence.

   b. problem and solution.   d. definition.

_b_ 4. The transitional word or phrase in paragraph 6 that indicates that the author is going to illustrate introduced species is

a. second.

b. for example.

c. one of.

d. but.

➤ D. REVIEWING AND ORGANIZING IDEAS: OUTLINING

Complete the following outline of paragraphs 5–7 by filling in the missing words or phrases.

The Three Main Causes of the Biodiversity Crisis

I. Habitat Destruction

    A. Expansion of ___agriculture___ to feed a growing human population

    B. Urban development

    C. ___Forestry___

    D. Mining

    E. ___Environmental pollution___

II. ___Introduced Species___

    A. Exotic (non-native) species eliminate ___native species___

        1. Through predation

        2. Through ___competition___

III. Overexploitation of ___Wildlife___

    A. Excessive ___commercial___ harvest

    B. Sport hunting

    C. ___Harvesting___ methods

    D. Expanding, often illegal world trade in ___wildlife products___

➤ **E.   FIGURING OUT INFERRED MEANINGS**

Read each of the excerpts from the selection again and decide whether it reveals the author's attitude toward the subject. Write Y (yes) if it does or N (no) if it does not.

___Y___ 1. "We are now presiding over an alarming biodiversity crisis." (paragraph 1)

___N___ 2. "Past poundings of biodiversity, which were triggered mainly by physical processes . . ." (paragraph 2)

___Y___ 3. "This latest mass extinction is due to . . . a big-brained, manually dexterous, environment-manipulating toolmaker." (paragraph 2)

___Y___ 4. "Harvard biologist Edward O. Wilson . . . has compiled what he grimly calls . . ." (paragraph 3)

___Y___ 5. "But as long as we humans are around to destroy habitats . . ." (paragraph 4)

___N___ 6. "We depend on many other species for food." (paragraph 8)

___Y___ 7. "We are taking a risk with our own species' survival." (paragraph 9)

➤ **F.   THINKING CRITICALLY**

Select the best answer.

___b___ 1. The central thesis of "The Biodiversity Crisis" is supported primarily by

   a. the opinions of experts.

   b. facts and statistics.

   c. personal experience.

   d. all of the above

___a___ 2. The first sentence in paragraph 2 is intended to

   a. capture the reader's attention with a shocking statement.

   b. indicate that the crisis is not critical.

   c. both a and b

   d. neither a nor b

___c___ 3. The author ends the selection with

   a. a sympathetic description of Madagascar's dilemma.

   b. a suggestion for how we can reverse the current trend.

   c. a warning about the effect of the biodiversity crisis on our own survival.

   d. an alarming statistic about the biodiversity crisis.

The first word in each of the following analogies is from the selection. Complete each analogy by filling in the missing word from the list below.

leave   famous   varied   disappear

4. Evolution is to develop as extinction is to _____disappear_____.

5. Migratory is to _____leave_____ as stationary is to remain.

6. Renowned is to _____famous_____ as obscure is to unknown.

7. Diversification is to _____varied_____ as homogeneity is to same.

➤ G.   BUILDING VOCABULARY

➤ **Context**
Using context and a dictionary, if necessary, determine the meaning of each word as it is used in the selection.

___b___ 1. presiding (paragraph 1)

  a. judging

  b. watching

  c. leaving

  d. avoiding

___c___ 2. precipitous (paragraph 1)

  a. weak

  b. expected

  c. dramatic

  d. gradual

___a___ 3. rebounds (paragraph 4)

  a. recoveries

  b. declines

  c. interruptions

  d. replacements

___c___ 4. niches (paragraph 4)

  a. trends

  b. preferences

  c. areas

  d. groups

_a_ 5. prevalence (paragraph 4)

    a. commonness

    b. lack of

    c. decline

    d. unusualness

_c_ 6. compounds (paragraph 7)

    a. improves

    b. allows

    c. worsens

    d. changes

_b_ 7. dilemma (paragraph 8)

    a. development

    b. problem

    c. location

    d. task

➤ Word Parts

> **A REVIEW OF PREFIXES**
> **IN-** means *not*
> **DE-** means *reduce*
> **EN-** means *to put into* or *cause to be*
> **INTER-** means *between, among*
> **PRE-** means *before*

Match each word in Column A with its meaning in Column B. Write your answers in the spaces provided

Column A	Column B
_d_ 1. endangered	a. animals that do not have a backbone
_f_ 2. intertidal	b. belonging to the era before recorded history
_a_ 3. invertebrates	c. continuing without interruption
_c_ 4. incessant	d. caused to be at risk of becoming extinct
_b_ 5. prehistoric	e. reduce the quality of
_e_ 6. degrade	f. the region between the high and low tide marks

➤ Unusual Words/Unusual Meanings

Use the context of each sentence to discover the meaning of the underlined word or phrase and to write your own sentence.

1. To say that previous episodes of extinction <u>pale by comparison</u> (paragraph 2) means that those episodes seem relatively minor compared to what is happening now.

   Your sentence: _____.

2. In the business world, the term <u>shakeouts</u> (paragraph 4) means the elimination of competing businesses or products in a particular field; in the biological world, the author means the elimination of species.

   Your sentence: _____.

➤ H. SELECTING A LEARNING/STUDY STRATEGY

Select the best answer.

    _c_   If you were preparing for an essay exam that included this selection, which of the following items would you predict would be on the exam?

    a. Name all species that are endangered.

    b. Name three exotic species that were introduced and discuss the dangers they present.

    c. Define the diversity crisis and identify its causes.

    d. Explain what the Hundred Heartbeat Club is.

➤ I. EXPLORING IDEAS THROUGH DISCUSSION AND WRITING

1. Did you feel alarmed by the statistics quoted in the selection? Why or why not?

2. Where could you look to find out how to address the problems described in the selection?

3. To what extent do you feel you have personally contributed to the biodiversity crisis?

➤ J. BEYOND THE CLASSROOM TO THE WEB

Visit Rainforests Net at **http://www.ovearth.net/worldcounters.htm.**
Click on "Rainforest Acres Cut in 2003." Does the article you just read ("The Biodiversity Crisis") or this visual aid more effectively increase your concern regarding the issue? Why?

✔ **Tracking Your Progress**

Selection 33

Section	Number Correct		Score
A. Thesis and Main Idea (5 items)	_____	x 4	_____
B. Details (5 items)	_____	x 3	_____
C. Organization and Transitions (4 items)	_____	x 1	_____
E. Inferred Meanings (7 items)	_____	x 3	_____
F. Thinking Critically (7 items)	_____	x 3	_____
G. Vocabulary			
1. Context (7 items)	_____	x 1	_____
2. Word Parts (6 items)	_____	x 2	_____
	TOTAL SCORE		_____ %

CHECKING YOUR READING RATE

Words in Selection 33: 1,206

	Finishing Time:	_____	_____	_____
		(hour)	(minutes)	(seconds)
	Starting Time:	_____	_____	_____
		(hour)	(minutes)	(seconds)
	Total Reading Time:		_____	_____
			(minutes)	(seconds)

Words Per Minute Score (page 739) _____ WPM

22 Physical Sciences/Mathematics

The physical sciences are concerned with the properties, functions, structure, and composition of matter, substances, and energy. They include physics, chemistry, astronomy, physical geography, and geology. Mathematics is the study of relationships among numbers, quantities, and shapes using signs, symbols, and proofs (logical solutions of problems). Often mathematics and physical science work together to address interesting questions important to our life and well-being. "Are Lotteries Fair?" uses mathematics to examine a popular American pastime—playing the lottery. "Effects of Radiation on Humans" takes another daily occurrence—exposure to radiation—and examines its effects. "Moon Trips and Asteroid Mining Might Be Coming" shows how advances in astronomy and physics have brought us to the point of considering the business and economic issues of outer space travel and exploration.

Use the following suggestions for reading in the physical sciences.

TIPS FOR READING IN PHYSICAL SCIENCES/ MATHEMATICS

- **Read slowly and reread if necessary.** Both mathematics and the physical sciences are technical and detailed. Do not expect to understand everything on your first reading. When reading "Are Lotteries Fair?" you might read it once to grasp the overall issue—fairness of lotteries—and then reread, concentrating on the role mathematics plays in examining the issue.

- **Focus on new terminology.** To read mathematics and the physical sciences, you have to learn the language of science. Mathematics and physical science are exact and precise, using terminology to make communication as error-free as possible. In "Effects of Radiation," for example, you will encounter technical terms describing global combustion, radioactivity, and radiation exposure.

- **Use writing to learn.** Reading alone is often not sufficient for learning mathematics and physical sciences. While highlighting and annotating a text work well for many subjects, they do not for math and science textbooks where everything seems important. Try writing; express ideas in your own words. This method will test your understanding, too. If you cannot explain an idea in your own words, you probably do not understand it. After reading "Moon Trips and Asteroid Mining Might Be Coming," try explaining in your own words the economic value of asteroids.

SELECTION 34

Are Lotteries Fair?

Jeffrey O. Bennett, William L. Briggs, and Mario F. Triola

Taken from the college mathematics textbook, *Statistical Reasoning for Everyday Life*, this reading looks at lotteries from a statistical perspective.

> ## PREVIEWING THE READING

Using the steps listed on page 5, preview the reading selection. When you have finished, complete the following items.

1. The title of this selection suggests that the author will be discussing
   <u>the fairness of lotteries</u> .

2. List at least three questions that you should be able to answer after reading the selection:

   a. <u>Who plays the lottery?</u>

   b. <u>In what ways is the lottery unfair?</u>

   c. <u>What is the evidence for lotteries being unfair?</u>

MAKING CONNECTIONS

Have you ever played the lottery or some type of game of chance? If so, did you feel you had a good chance of winning? If not, why not? If you did not win, how did you react?

> ## READING TIP

Be sure to refer to the charts mentioned in the reading; they will help you grasp the concepts presented in the reading.

CHECKING YOUR READING RATE

If you plan to compute your reading rate, be sure to record your starting time in the box at the end of the exercises before you begin reading.

Are Lotteries Fair?

1   Lotteries have become part of the American way of life. Most states now have legal lotteries, including multi-state lotteries such as Powerball and the Big Game. National statistics show that per capita (average per person) lottery spending is approaching $200 per year. Since many people do not play lotteries at all, this means that active players tend to spend much more than $200 per year.

2   The mathematics of lottery odds involves counting the various combinations of numbers that are winners. While these calculations can become complex, the essential conclusion is always the same: The probability of winning a big prize is infinitesimally small. Advertisements may make lotteries sound like a good deal, but the expected value associated with a lottery is always negative. On average, those who play regularly can expect to lose about half of what they spend.

representative cross-section
a particular part that displays the characteristics of and typifies the whole

3   Lottery proponents point to several positive aspects. For example, lotteries produce billions of dollars of revenue that states use for education, recreation, and environmental initiatives. This revenue allows states to keep tax rates lower than they would be otherwise. Proponents also point out that lottery participation is voluntary and enjoyed by a **representative cross-section** of society. Indeed, a recent Gallup poll shows that three-fourths of Americans approve of state lotteries (two-thirds approve of legal gambling in general).

histogram
a bar graph used for large sets of data to show relationships and frequencies

4   This favorable picture is part of the marketing and public relations of state lotteries. For example, Colorado state lottery officials offer statistics on the age, income, and education of lottery players compared to the general population (Figure A). Within a few percentage points, the age of lottery players parallels that of the population as a whole. Similarly, the **histogram** of the income of lottery players gives the impression

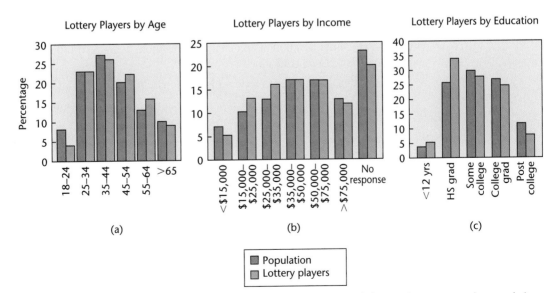

Figure A   Three figures showing (a) age, (b) income, and (c) education of colorado lottery players compared to population.

that lottery players as a whole are typical citizens—with the exception of the bars for incomes of $15,000-$25,000 and $25,000-$35,000, which show that the poor tend to play more than we would expect for their proportion of the population.

5   Despite the apparent benefits of lotteries, critics have long argued that lotteries are merely an unfair form of taxation. Some support for this view comes from a recent report by the National Gambling Impact Study Commission and a *New York Times* study of lotteries in New Jersey. Both of these studies focus on the *amount* of money spent on lotteries by individuals.

6   The *New York Times* study was based on data from 48,875 people who had won at least $600 in New Jersey lottery games. (In an ingenious bit of sampling, these winners were to be a random sample of all lottery players; after all, lottery winners are determined randomly. However, the sample is not really representative of all lottery players because winners tend to buy more than an average number of tickets.) By identifying the home zip codes of the lottery players, researchers were able to determine whether players came from areas with high or low income, high or low average education, and various demographic characteristics. The overwhelming conclusion of the *New York Times* study is that lottery spending has a much greater impact in *relative terms* on those players with lower incomes and lower educational background. For example, the following were among the specific findings:

- People in the state's lowest income areas spend five times as much of their income on lotteries as those in the state's highest income areas. Spending in the lowest income areas on one particular lottery game was $29 per $10,000 of annual income, compared to less than $5 per $10,000 of annual income in the highest income areas.

- The number of lottery sales outlets (where lottery tickets can be purchased) is nearly twice as high per 10,000 people in low-income areas as in high-income areas.

- People in areas with the lowest percentage of college education spent over five times as much per $10,000 of annual income as those in areas with the highest percentage of college education.

- Advertising and promotion of lotteries is focused in low-income areas.

7   Some of the results of the *New York Times* study are summarized in Figure B suggests that while New Jersey has a progressive tax system (higher-income people pay a greater percentage of their income in taxes), the "lottery tax" is **regressive**. Moreover, the study also found that the areas that generate the largest percentage of lottery revenues do not receive a proportional share of state funding.

8   Similar studies reveal the same patterns in other states. The overall conclusions are inescapable: While lotteries provide many benefits to state governments, the revenue they produce comes disproportionately from poorer and less educated individuals. Indeed, a report by the National Gambling Impact Study Commission concluded that lotteries are "the most widespread form of gambling in the United States" and that state governments have "irresponsibly intruded gambling into society on a massive scale . . . through such measures as incessant advertising and the ubiquitous placement of lottery machines in neighborhood stores."

regressive
describing a tax in which the tax rate goes down as the amount of income being taxed increases

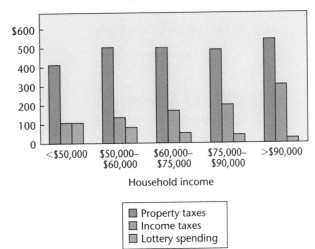

Taxes and Lottery Spending (per $10,000 of income)

Household income

Property taxes
Income taxes
Lottery spending

> ### A. UNDERSTANDING THE THESIS AND OTHER MAIN IDEAS

Select the best answer.

___b___ 1. The central thesis of "Are Lotteries Fair"? is that

   a. the chances of winning the lottery are very slim.

   b. it is poor, undereducated people who play the lottery but do not receive its benefits.

   c. lotteries are an acceptable form of gambling.

   d. advertising for lotteries is too aggressive.

___c___ 2. The author's primary purpose is to

   a. stop people from playing the lottery.

   b. criticize the government's promotion of the lottery.

   c. report on research that finds lotteries to be unfair.

   d. urge readers to write to their state leaders about this issue.

___a___ 3. The Colorado state lottery statistics are used in the reading to

   a. compare lottery players with the general public.

   b. prove that lottery players are unfairly taxed.

   c. suggest that most people in Colorado are well educated.

   d. identify groups that are at risk of developing gambling problems.

___b___ 4. The topic of paragraph 6 is

    a. the gambling problem of lottery players.

    b. *The New York Times* study.

    c. the tax structure in New Jersey.

    d. sampling.

___a___ 5. In the final paragraph, the author

    a. refers to other studies and reports.

    b. restates the first paragraph.

    c. recommends ways to make the lottery more fair.

    d. suggests a plan for abolishing the lottery.

➤ B.   IDENTIFYING DETAILS

Match each statement with the study to which it refers.

a. Colorado statistics

b. The *New York Times* study

c. The National Gambling Impact Study Commission Report

___c___ 1. stated that lotteries are "the most widespread form of gambling in the United States."

___a___ 2. indicates that "the age of lottery players parallels that of the population as a whole."

___c___ 3. suggests that lottery advertising is never-ending.

___b___ 4. determined that lottery revenues do not go to the areas that need them most.

___a___ 5. compared lottery players with the general population.

___b___ 6. looked at demographic factors of lottery winners.

___b___ 7. found that lottery advertising is aimed at poor people.

➤ C.   RECOGNIZING METHODS OF ORGANIZATION AND TRANSITIONS

1. The author makes use of the generalization and example organizational pattern to make statements and then gives specific instances of the idea expressed in the statement. Place an "X" next to the number of each paragraph that illustrates this pattern.

___ 1	___ 5
___ 2	_X_ 6
_X_ 3	___ 7
_X_ 4	___ 8

2. The author also uses _the cause and effect pattern_ to describe factors that lead to lottery playing and show what happens as a result of playing the lottery.

➤ D.   REVIEWING AND ORGANIZING IDEAS: PARAPHRASING

Complete the following paraphrase of paragraphs 1–2 from the selection by filling in the blanks.

_____Lotteries_____ are very _____popular_____ in our _____country_____. There are legal state lotteries and multistate lotteries such as _____Powerball_____ and _____The Big Game_____. Regular _____players_____ spend well over $200 per _____year_____. The odds of winning are computed by _____counting_____ how many combinations of numbers are possible to produce a winner. The odds of _____winning_____ a large payout are extremely slim. People still play, though, partially due to _____advertisements_____ that _____portray_____ the lottery as a good _____deal_____. These regular players end up losing _____half_____ of what they _____spend_____.

➤ E.   FIGURING OUT INFERRED MEANINGS

Indicate whether each statement is true (T) or false (F).

_F_ 1. Rich people do not play the lottery.

_T_ 2. In Colorado, no one under 18 plays the lottery.

_F_ 3. It can be inferred that the property tax rate in New Jersey is high.

_T_ 4. The reading suggests that state governments are not forthcoming in their ads about the real chances of winning the lottery.

_F_ 5. Going to college will teach you not to buy lottery tickets.

➤ F.   THINKING CRITICALLY

Select the best answer.

_a_ 1. The author of "Are Lotteries Fair?" supports the thesis primarily with

a. research evidence.

b. personal experience.

c. historical information.

d. expert opinion.

_c_ 2. The tone of the selection can best be described as

    a. apathetic.

    b. frustrated.

    c. serious.

    d. indirect.

_d_ 3. Of the following statements from the reading, which is an opinion?

    a. "The mathematics of lottery odds involves counting the various combinations of numbers that are winners." (paragraph 2)

    b. "Advertising and promotion of lotteries is focused in low-income areas." (paragraph 6)

    c. "Similar studies reveal the same patterns in other states." (paragraph 8)

    d. "State governments 'have irresponsibly intruded gambling into our society on a massive scale.' " (paragraph 8)

_a_ 4. The author

    a. presents strong data as evidence that lotteries are unfair.

    b. does not offer any information from the proponents of lotteries.

    c. is biased against state government.

    d. twists the findings of the studies to fit his opinion.

_b_ 5. The final quotations from the National Gambling Impact Study Commission are intended to

    a. shock the reader.

    b. reinforce the central thesis with a powerful conclusion.

    c. provide more statistical data.

    d. contradict the main argument of the reading.

➤ G.   BUILDING VOCABULARY

➤ Context

Using context and a dictionary, if necessary, determine the meaning of each word as it is used in the selection.

_b_ 1. infinitesimally (paragraph 2)

    a. definitely

    b. in a tiny, minuscule amount

    c. very unlikely

    d. amazingly

    __a__   2. ingenious (paragraph 6)

        a. clever

        b. mean-spirited

        c. dishonest

        d. suitable

    __d__   3. disproportionately (paragraph 8)

        a. unresponsively

        b. conveniently

        c. logically

        d. unequally in amount

    __d__   4. ubiquitous (paragraph 8)

        a. careful

        b. underhanded

        c. skillful

        d. widespread, prevalent

➤ Word Parts

> ### A REVIEW OF ROOTS AND PREFIXES
> **POS, PON** mean *place, put*
> **PRO-** means *forth, in front of*
> **IN-** means *not*

Use the review of roots and prefixes above to fill in the blanks in the following sentences.

1. If you are a *proponent* (paragraph 3) of a new subway system in your city, you __put__ yourself __forth__ in favor of the cause.

2. The *incessant* (paragraph 8) barking of your neighbor's dog does __not__ ever stop!

➤ Unusual Words/Unusual Meanings
Use the meanings given below to write a sentence using the underlined word or phrase.

1. An <u>essential</u> (paragraph 2) text in a field of study is one that is fundamental to the basic understanding of that field.

    Your sentence: _____.

2. When something is <u>intruded</u> (paragraph 8) it is put where it does not belong or where it would be wrong or rude for it to be.

    Your sentence: _____.

➤ H. SELECTING A LEARNING/STUDY STRATEGY

Select the best answer.

    _c_   This reading appears in a college mathematics textbook in a chapter on probability. As a class activity you can most likely expect your mathematics professor to ask you to

a. read the National Impact Study Commission report.

b. buy a lottery ticket and report on your process of choosing numbers.

c. solve a word problem that asks you to calculate the odds of wining a certain lottery.

d. research systems lottery players use to attempt to enhance their winnings.

➤ I. EXPLORING IDEAS THROUGH DISCUSSION AND WRITING

1. Some billboards that advertise the lottery show outrageous items that a person could buy with the winnings. Design a billboard that shows alternative uses for the money.

2. Write a list of other types of "gambling" that we engage in (for example, church bingo).

3. Discuss what factors motivate people to gamble, despite the poor odds of winning.

➤ J. BEYOND THE CLASSROOM TO THE WEB

Visit the home page of the New York State Lottery at **http://www.nylottery.org/ index.php.**

    How easy is it to find information on where the money raised by the lottery goes? Is there any information about the dangers of gambling? What information is missing from this site?

✔ Tracking Your Progress

Selection 34

Section	Number Correct		Score
A. Thesis and Main Idea (5 items)	_____	x 5	_____
B. Details (7 items)	_____	x 3	_____
C. Organization and Transitions (2 items)	_____	x 2	_____
E. Inferred Meanings (5 items)	_____	x 4	_____
F. Thinking Critically (5 items)	_____	x 4	_____
G. Vocabulary			
1. Context (4 items)	_____	x 2	_____
2. Word Parts (2 items)	_____	x 1	_____
		TOTAL SCORE	_____ %

CHECKING YOUR READING RATE

Words in Selection 34: 822

Finishing Time:	_____	_____	_____
	(hour)	(minutes)	(seconds)
Starting Time:	_____	_____	_____
	(hour)	(minutes)	(seconds)
Total Reading Time:		_____	_____
		(minutes)	(seconds)

Words Per Minute Score (page 739) _____ WPM

SELECTION 35

Moon Trips and Asteroid Mining Might Be Coming

Doug McPherson

Originally appearing in the *Sacramento Business Journal,* this article discusses the economic and business potential of outer space travel and exploration.

➤ PREVIEWING THE READING

Using the steps listed on page 5, preview the reading selection. When you have finished, complete the following items.

1. This selection is about _____space travel and colonization_____.

2. List at least three questions you should be able to answer after reading the selection:

   a. What are the business opportunities in outer space? _____

   b. Who is interested in the potential of outer space? _____

   c. What plans are in the works for space travel? _____

MAKING CONNECTIONS

Would you be among the first to sign up for a trip to outer space if cost were not an issue? What adventurous or dangerous things have you done in your life?

➤ READING TIP

As you read keep track of the companies and people and what they are planning.

CHECKING YOUR READING RATE

If you plan to compute your reading rate, be sure to record your starting time in the box at the end of the exercises before you begin reading.

Moon Trips and Asteroid Mining Might Be Coming

1   About 140 years ago, folks from all over the nation came to Colorado to mine for gold.* In November, scientists from all over the world came to Colorado to talk about mining space. Space experts attending the Space Resources Round Table at the Colorado School of Mines were talking seriously about building hotels in space, mining asteroids for precious metals, and creating markets in space. A strong blend of capitalism and science would crank out products such as solar cells, fiber-optic cable, construction materials, rocket fuel and oxygen, along with services such as cheap lunar transportation and real estate.

2   Before you dismiss all this talk as pie-in-the-sky nonsense, experts say trends point to commercial development of space:

lunar ice
water ice
crystals found in
craters on the
north and south
poles of the
moon

- The recent discovery of the possibility of **lunar ice** has renewed interest in the moon.
- Interest is growing in power sources, such as beaming solar power from space to Earth.
- Knowledge of space resources is growing tremendously.
- The cost of spacecraft missions is dropping.

Moon Flight Now boarding

3   While the cost of missions is going down, scientists say it hasn't gone down enough, and transportation is one of the first hurdles to clear for business to work in space. "Currently, space is a transportation frontier. It is similar in many respects to historic ocean-crossing or transcontinental transportation frontiers," said Dale Gray of Frontier Historical Consultants in Grand View, Idaho. "To my knowledge, no frontier transportation system has ever come on line, on budget and on time." Before now, Gray said, bureaucracies directed rocket design with little incentive to lower launch costs. "With a direct link to profits, there is now economic pressure," he said, "and as launch costs are reduced, many space-based enterprises become possible." Launches today cost $10 million to $800 million each. To spur exploration and lower those costs, a group called the X-Prize Foundation in St. Louis has created a competition for scientists to create an affordable launch vehicle to carry passengers into space. The winning team gets $10 million. So far, 18 teams around the world have signed up.

publicly traded
describes a
company whose
shares are
bought and sold
on the stock
market

Boeing Co.
a major aircraft
and spacecraft
manufacturer

4   Experts predict that space planes likely will routinely rocket back and forth between Earth and the moon. But paying customers are needed. To date, some 500 people have traveled into space. Surveys show there's a large and eager public ready to follow and pay cash for a ticket. One company is already preparing to take that cash, from citizens and from companies. SpaceDev, formed in 1997, is the world's first **publicly traded** commercial space exploration and development company. Based near San Diego, it offers low-cost commercial space missions and spacecraft. SpaceDev last year announced a partnership with **Boeing Co.** to "investigate opportunities of mutual interest in the commercial deep-space arena."

---

*Colorado experienced a gold rush starting in 1858.

5   "We are (building) the foundation for a new type of commercial space enterprise, one that is focused on smaller, lower-cost mission solutions for a wide variety of space applications," said Jim Benson, chief executive officer of SpaceDev. Scientists say that once habitats exist in space, the market for life-support products, radiation shielding and artificial gravity will naturally follow.

Around the Water Cooler

6   Of course, business in space will need water coolers so that workers can discuss the latest lunar lunacy going on around the office. But more important than the gossip, they'll need the water that goes in the cooler. Conference participants agreed that water, which could yield both rocket fuel and oxygen, would be a resource bonanza, and ideal for supporting future moon bases and other space exploration goals.

7   A 1998 mission saw fields of hydrogen on the moon, and some scientists infer that means water is there. But others say it's just deposits of hydrogen from blasts of solar wind across the moon's face. Alan Binder, director of the Lunar Research Institute in Tucson, Ariz., the keynote speaker at the conference, estimates that 300 million metric tons of water may be available on the moon. But he admits more knowledge is needed about exactly where it is and how much is there.

Rich Rubble

8   Another item that holds economic promise is the asteroid. Scientists believe this roaming rubble has nearly all the raw materials needed to build a self-sufficient space colony, and at least half of the material in asteroids could also be put to human use. Most asteroids are made from iron, nickel and cobalt—elements for pure stainless steel, researchers say. Approximately 500,000 football field–sized asteroids come close to Earth's orbit, and scientists say it's easier to reach them and return a payload to Earth than it is to return the same payload from the moon.

9   One asteroid that orbits close to Earth is called Amun, a mile-wide chunk unusually rich in metals. Scientist John Lewis from the University of Arizona says Amun is worth about $20 quadrillion at market prices. In January 2002, Japan plans to explore the 4660 Nereus asteroid. If all goes well, the first samples of an asteroid will be brought back to Earth. "Ultimately, there is no way to predict what will pull our civilization off the face of the Earth and into orbit," said Gray. "When the English established colonies, they hoped to recoup their investments harvesting something called silk grass that was used as a padding material in shipping. They had no concept of tobacco, nor could they imagine the boom it would create."

> ### A.   UNDERSTANDING THE THESIS AND OTHER MAIN IDEAS

Select the best answer.

  __a__ 1. The central thesis of the selection is that
  a. scientists and businesspeople are interested in exploring and developing outer space.
  b. space travel and mining will never be cost-effective enough to attract customers.

c. asteroids could supply us with valuable materials.

d. not enough is known about the resources available in outer space.

__b__ 2. The author's primary purpose is to

a. persuade readers to invest in one of the companies mentioned in the reading.

b. report that outer space exploration is a new business trend.

c. speculate on the likelihood of commercial development in space.

d. describe the business plans of several companies.

__d__ 3. The topic of paragraph 3 is

a. frontier transportation.

b. a launch vehicle competition.

c. rocket design.

d. cost of space missions.

__c__ 4. Which of the following questions is not answered in paragraph 4?

a. What are companies doing to get started on space development projects?

b. Is anyone really interested in taking a space vacation?

c. When will regularly scheduled space trips begin to fly?

d. What do experts think about the future of space travel?

__c__ 5. The main ideas of paragraphs 6 and 7 is that

a. no one knows how much water is on the moon.

b. hydrogen is important to the success of space exploration.

c. water is a key to space development plans.

d. experts do not agree on what the hydrogen fields on the moon indicate.

__a__ 6. The final paragraph

a. invites readers to think about the future by looking back at the past.

b. concludes that we have no choice but to develop space.

c. expresses concern that Japan might surpass the U.S. in space development.

d. warns readers about an asteroid close to the Earth.

➤ **B.   IDENTIFYING DETAILS**

Match each item in Column A with its contribution or significance in Column B. Items may be used more than once.

Column A

a. Space Resources Round Table

b. the moon

c. Frontier Historical Consultants

d. X-Prize Foundation

e. SpaceDev

f. Alan Bender, Lunar Research Institute

g. Amum

h. 4660 Nereus

Column B

___e___   1. is the first publically traded space exploration company

___b___   2. may have 300 million metric tons of water

___a___   3. discussed business development of outer space

___g___   4. is worth 20 quadrillion dollars

___b___   5. is home to hydrogen fields

___e___   6. has created a competition for scientists to create an affordable launch vehicle

___f___   7. estimates the amount of water on the moon

___h___   8. is under exploration by Japan

___c___   9. reports parallels to other historical transportation frontiers

_g or h_   10. contains iron, nickel, and cobalt

➤ **C.   RECOGNIZING METHODS OF ORGANIZATION AND TRANSITIONS**

Select the best answer.

___d___ 1. The overall general organizational pattern that the author uses to list the aspects of the space exploration issue is

   a. classification.   c. cause and effect.

   b. time sequence.   d. enumeration.

___c___ 2. An example of a transition for this overall pattern is

   a. "Launches today cost . . ." (paragraph 3)

   b. "Conference participants agreed . . ."(paragraph 6)

c. "Another item that holds economic promise . . ." (paragraph 8)

d. "If all goes well . . ." (paragraph 9)

➤ D. REVIEWING AND ORGANIZING IDEAS: MAPPING

Complete the following map of the main issues and details in the reading.

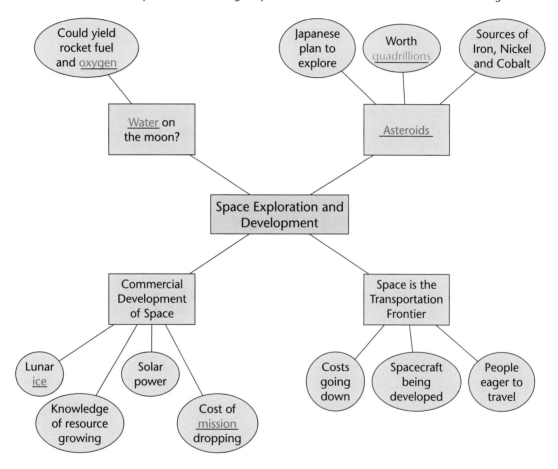

➤ E. FIGURING OUT INFERRED MEANINGS

Indicate whether each statement is true (T) or false (F).

__F__ 1. Scientists will be unwilling to work with commercial developers in space.

__F__ 2. It can be inferred that buying shares in SpaceDev would be a good investment.

_T_ 3. The author assumes that readers might be skeptical about the possibilities in space.

_F_ 4. It can be inferred that the 500 people mentioned in paragraph 4 paid large sums to travel in space.

_T_ 5. Solar winds do not deposit water.

_F_ 6. It can be inferred that Japan made stainless steel from what it found on 4660 Nereus.

➤ F. THINKING CRITICALLY

Indicate whether each statement from the article is fact (F) or opinion (O).

_O_ 1. "Knowledge of space resources is growing tremendously." (paragraph 2)

_O_ 2. "To my knowledge, no frontier transportation system has ever come on line, on budget and on time." (paragraph 3)

_F_ 3. "One company is already preparing to take that cash, from citizens and from companies." (paragraph 4)

_F_ 4. "We are (building) the foundation for a new type of commercial space enterprise." (paragraph 5)

_O_ 5. "Of course, business in space will need water coolers so that workers can discuss the latest lunar lunacy going on around the office." (paragraph 6)

_O_ 6. "Ultimately, there is no way to predict what will pull our civilization off the face of the Earth and into orbit." (paragraph 9)

➤ G. BUILDING VOCABULARY

➤ Context
Using context and a dictionary, if necessary, determine the meaning of each word as it is used in the selection.

_d_ 1. bureaucracies (par. 3)

    a. business executives   c. labor leaders

    b. private enterprise   d. governmental systems

_a_ 2. spur (paragraph 3)

    a. stimulate, urge   c. introduce

    b. suddenly go ahead quickly   d. challenge

_d_ 3. payload (paragraph 8)

  a. burden

  b. delivery, load

  c. the profit-making cargo on a vehicle

  d. passengers and equipment needed for a flight

_c_ 4. recoup (paragraph 9)

  a. profit from

  b. discover, find

  c. make up for, get back

  d. surpass

➤ Word Parts

> **A REVIEW OF PREFIXES AND SUFFIXES**
> **TRANS-** means *across*
> **-ANT** means *one who*

Use the review of prefixes and suffixes above to fill in the blanks in the following sentences.

1. Transcontinental transportation frontiers (paragraph 3) refers to travel
   _____across_____ continents.

2. A conference participant (paragraph 6) is _____someone who_____ takes part
   in a conference.

➤ Unusual Words/Unusual Meanings

Use the meanings given below to write a sentence using the underlined word or phrase.

1. If you have a <u>pie-in-the-sky</u> (paragraph 2) idea to get rich quickly, you have
   an unrealistic dream for becoming wealthy fast.

   Your sentence: _____.

2. A <u>bonanza</u> (paragraph 6) day at the races is one on which you win a large
   amount of money.

   Your sentence: _____.

H. SELECTING A LEARNING/STUDY STRATEGY

Select the best answer.

___c___ The best way to study for an essay exam on this selection would be to

a. list all the facts.

b. visualize what outer space would look like in the future after space development.

c. write a summary of the main issues discussed in the reading.

d. reread the selection.

I. EXPLORING IDEAS THROUGH DISCUSSION AND WRITING

1. Discuss the ethical issues surrounding space development. For example, to whom do space resources really belong?

2. Write an advertisement for a space travel agency.

3. Space missions are not only costly, but also dangerous. Discuss whether people should risk their lives for the purpose of furthering scientific knowledge.

J. BEYOND THE CLASSROOM TO THE WEB

Look at the Web sites for the companies mentioned in the article.

SpaceDev: **http://www.spacedev.com/newsite/templates/homepage.php?pid=2**

Frontier Historical Consultants: **http://www.frontierstatus.com/**

X-Prize Foundation: **http://www.xprize.org/**

Lunar Research Institute: **http://www.lunar-exploration.net/**

How much work have they done to achieve their space development goals?

Read about and discuss the fate of the 4660 Nereus project at **http://www.space. com/scienceastronomy/solarsystem/muses-c_cancelled_ 001103.html**

✔ **Tracking Your Progress**

Selection 35

Section	Number Correct		Score
A. Thesis and Main Idea (6 items)	_____	x 5	_____
B. Details (10 items)	_____	x 2	_____
C. Organization and Transitions (2 items)	_____	x 2	_____
E. Inferred Meanings (6 items)	_____	x 3	_____
F. Thinking Critically (6 items)	_____	x 3	_____
G. Vocabulary			
1. Context (4 items)	_____	x 2	_____
2. Word Parts (2 items)	_____	x 1	_____

TOTAL SCORE _____ %

CHECKING YOUR READING RATE

Words in Selection 35: 898

Finishing Time:	_____	_____	_____
	(hour)	(minutes)	(seconds)
Starting Time:	_____	_____	_____
	(hour)	(minutes)	(seconds)
Total Reading Time:		_____	_____
		(minutes)	(seconds)

Words Per Minute Score (page 739) _____ WPM

SELECTION 36

Effects of Radiation on Humans

Paul G. Hewitt

This selection was taken from a college physics textbook titled *Conceptual Physics* by Paul G. Hewitt. Read it to learn about the radiation in our daily lives.

➤ PREVIEWING THE READING

Using the steps listed on page 5, preview the reading selection. When you have finished, complete the following items.

1. This selection is about _____Radiation exposure_____

2. List at least three questions you should be able to answer after reading the selection:

   a. ___How much radiation are we exposed to on a regular basis?___

   b. ___What are the sources of radiation in our lives?___

   c. ___What does radiation do to us?___

 MAKING CONNECTIONS

Fill in the following chart about your exposure to potentially harmful substances in your daily life (for example, pesticides and bleach).

Substance	Pesticides	Household Cleaners	Air Pollution
Frequency of Exposure	Every time I eat fruit and vegetables—several times daily	Once a week	Many workdays when I travel into the city
How Can I Limit My Exposure	Buy organically grown produce	Use natural cleaners	Find a job in the country where the air is cleaner
Possible Adverse Effects of Exposure	Depends on the pesticide; some could cause cancer or nerve damage	Depends on the cleaner; some could cause cancer or asthma	Asthma, lung cancer

> ## READING TIP

As you read, highlight the topic sentence of each paragraph.

CHECKING YOUR READING RATE

If you plan to compute your reading rate, be sure to record your starting time in the box at the end of the exercises before you begin reading.

Effects of Radiation on Humans

1   A common misconception is that radioactivity is something new in the environment. But radioactivity has been around far longer than the human race. It is as much a part of our environment as the sun and the rain. It is what warms the interior of the Earth and makes it molten. In fact, radioactive decay inside the Earth is what heats the water that spurts from a geyser or what wells up from a natural hot spring. Even the helium in a child's balloon is the offspring of radioactivity. Its **nuclei** are nothing more than the alpha particles that were once shot out of radioactive nuclei.

nuclei
the plural form
of nucleus,
which is the
center

2   As Figure A shows, nearly half of our annual exposure to radiation comes from non-natural sources—primarily medical X rays and radiotherapy. Television sets, fallout from nuclear testing, and the coal and nuclear power industries are also contributors. Amazingly, the coal industry far outranks the nuclear power industry as a source of radiation. The global combustion of coal annually releases about 9000 tons of radioactive thorium and about 4000 tons of radioactive uranium into the atmosphere. Worldwide, the nuclear power industries generate about 10,000 tons of radioactive waste each year. Almost all of this waste, however, is contained and *not* released into the environment.

3   Most of the radiation we encounter originates in the natural surroundings. It is in the ground we stand on and in the bricks and stones of surrounding buildings. Every ton of ordinary granite contains some 20 grams of thorium and 9 grams of uranium on average. Because of the traces of radioactive elements in most rocks, people who

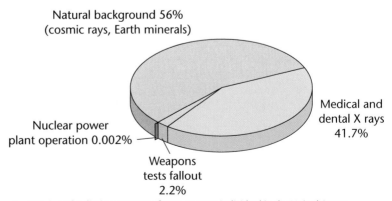

Natural background 56%
(cosmic rays, Earth minerals)

Medical and
dental X rays
41.7%

Nuclear power
plant operation 0.002%

Weapons
tests fallout
2.2%

Figure A   Origins of radiation exposure for an average individual in the United States.

Figure B   A commercially available radon test kit for the home

live in brick, concrete, or stone buildings are exposed to greater amounts of radiation than people who live in wooden buildings. This natural background radiation was present before humans emerged in the world. If our bodies couldn't tolerate it, we wouldn't be here. Apart from radioactivity, we are bombarded by cosmic rays. At sea level the protective blanket of the atmosphere reduces cosmic-ray intensity, while at higher altitudes radiation is more intense. In Denver,* the "mile-high city," a person receives more than twice as much radiation from cosmic rays as at sea level. A couple of round-trip flights between distant places such as New York and San Francisco exposes us to as much radiation as we receive in a normal chest X ray. (This extra radiation is a factor in limiting the air time of airline personnel.)

4   Even the human body is a source of natural radiation, primarily from the potassium we ingest. Our bodies contain about 200 grams of potassium. Of this quantity, about 20 milligrams is the radioactive isotope potassium-40. Between every heartbeat, about 5,000 potassium-40 atoms undergo spontaneous radioactive decay. Added to this is some 3,000 beta particles per second emitted by carbon-14 in your body. We and all living creatures are to some degree radioactive.

inert describes the gases that are very stable and slow to react

5   The leading source of naturally occurring external radiation is radon-222, an **inert** gas arising from uranium deposits. Radon is a heavy gas that tends to accumulate in basements after it seeps up through cracks in the floor. Levels of radon vary from region to region depending upon local geology. You can check the radon level in your home with a radon detector kit. If levels are abnormally high, corrective measures such as sealing the basement foundation and maintaining adequate ventilation are recommended.

6   Exposure to radiation greater than normal background should be avoided because of the damage it can do.† The cells of living tissue are composed of intricately structured molecules in a watery, ion-rich brine. when X radiation or nuclear radiation encounters this highly ordered soup, it produces chaos on the atomic scale. A

---

*According to the U.S. Geological survey, the elevation of Denver is 5,260 ft. One mile = 5,280 ft.
†For some cancer patients, a high level of radiation, carefully directed, can be beneficial by selectively killing cancer cells. This is the province of radiation oncology.

beta particle, for example, passing through living matter collides with a small percentage of the molecules and leaves a randomly dotted trail of altered or broken molecules along with newly formed, chemically active ions and free radicals. Free radicals are unbonded, electrically neutral, very chemically active atoms or molecular fragments. The ions and free radicals may break even more molecular bonds or they may quickly form strong new bonds, creating molecules that may be useless or harmful to the cell. Gamma radiation produces a similar effect. As a high-energy gamma-ray photon moves through matter, it may rebound from an electron and give the electron a high kinetic energy. The electron then may career through the tissue, creating havoc in the ways described above. All types of high-energy radiation break or alter the structure of some molecules and create conditions in which other molecules will be formed that may be harmful to life processes.

7   Cells are able to repair most kinds of molecular damage if the radiation is not too intense. A cell can survive an otherwise lethal dose of radiation if the dose is spread over a long period of time to allow intervals for healing. When radiation is sufficient to kill cells, the dead cells can be replaced by new ones. An important exception to this is most nerve cells, which are irreplaceable. Sometimes a radiated cell will survive with a damaged DNA molecule. Defective genetic information will be transmitted to offspring cells when the damaged cell reproduces, and a cell *mutation* will occur. Mutations are usually insignificant, but if significant they will probably result in cells that do not function as well as undamaged ones. In rare cases a mutation will be an improvement. A genetic change of this type could also be part of the cause of a cancer that will develop later.

trajectory
the path
something takes
as it moves
along

8   The concentration of disorder produced along the **trajectory** of a particle depends upon its energy, charge, and mass. Gamma-ray photons and very energetic beta particles spread their damage out over a long track. They penetrate deeply with widely separated interactions, like a very fast BB fired through a hailstorm. Slow, massive, highly charged particles such as low-energy alpha particles do their damage in the shortest distance. They have collisions that are close together, more like a bull charging through a flock of sleepy sheep. They do not penetrate deeply because their energy is absorbed by many closely spaced collisions. Particles that produce especially concentrated damage are the assorted nuclei (called *heavy primaries*) flung outward by the sun in solar flares and contained in small percentage in the cosmic radiation. These include all the elements found on Earth. Some of them are captured in the Earth's magnetic field and some are stopped by collisions in the atmosphere, so practically none reaches the Earth's surface. We are shielded from most o these dangerous particles by the very property that makes them a threat—their tendency to have many collisions close together.

9   Astronauts do not have this protection, and they absorb large doses of radiation during the time they spend in space. Every few decades there is an exceptionally powerful solar flare that would almost certainly kill any conventionally protected astronaut who is unprotected by the Earth's atmosphere and magnetic field.

10   We are bombarded most by what harms us least—neutrinos. Neutrinos are the most weakly interacting particles. They have near-zero mass, no charge, and are produced frequently in radioactive decays. They are the most common high-speed particles known, zapping the universe, and passing unhindered through our bodies by

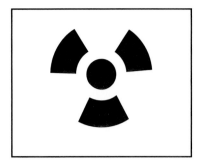

Figure C   The internationally used symbol to indicate an area where radioactive material is being handled or produced.

many millions every second. They pass completely through the Earth with only occasional encounters. It would take a "piece" of lead 6 light years in thickness to absorb half the neutrinos incident upon it. Only about once per year on the average, a neutrino triggers a nuclear reaction in your body. We don't hear much about neutrinos because they ignore us.

11   Of the radiations we have focused upon in this chapter, gamma radiation is the most penetrating and therefore the hardest to shield against. This, combined with its ability to interact with the matter in our bodies, makes it potentially the most dangerous radiation. It emanates from radioactive materials and makes up a substantial part of the normal background radiation. Exposure to it should be minimized.

➤ A. UNDERSTANDING THE THESIS AND OTHER MAIN IDEAS

Select the best answer.

___b___ 1. The central thesis of the selection is that

    a. people should avoid overexposure to natural source radiation.

    b. radiation is all around us, but we can and should minimize our exposure.

    c. radiation damages human cells.

    d. most radiation is not harmful.

___c___ 2. The author's primary purpose is to

    a. frighten readers into being tested for radiation damage.

    b. examine the latest research findings concerning radiation exposure.

    c. identify and describe the types of radiation and what effect they have on us.

    d. recommend lifestyle changes that reduce radiation exposure.

_____c_____ 3. The topic of paragraph 3 is

    a. trace amounts of radiation.

    b. cosmic rays.

    c. natural sources of radiation.

    d. our tolerance for radiation.

_____b_____ 4. Which of the following questions is *not* answered in paragraph 6?

    a. How do beta particles affect cells?

    b. Who first identified radioactive particles?

    c. How does gamma radiation harm living tissue?

    d. Why should radiation be avoided?

_____d_____ 5. What is the main idea of paragraph 7?

    a. Strong doses of radiation are used to treat cancer.

    b. Nerve cells are irreplaceable.

    c. Radiation causes mutation.

    d. Some damage by certain kinds of radiation can be repaired.

_____a_____ 6. The purpose of paragraph 8 is to

    a. describe the types of damage caused by each type of radiation.

    b. explain why the particles are so damaging.

    c. recommend ways to limit radiation damage.

    d. compare earth-based radiation with cosmic rays.

_____a_____ 7. The topic of paragraph 10 is

    a. neutrinos.

    b. radioactive decay.

    c. less common high-speed particles.

    d. nuclear reactions in the body.

➤ **B. IDENTIFYING DETAILS**

Select the best answer.

_____d_____ 1. Most of the radiation that we are exposed to comes from

    a. nuclear and coal power plants.   c. natural sources.

    b. x-rays and radiotherapy.   d. radioactive waste.

_b_ 2. All of the following are natural sources of radiation mentioned in the reading *except*

 a. granite.

 b. sea water.

 c. radon.

 d. cosmic rays.

_d_ 3. What is the primary source of radiation in the human body?

 a. radioactive decay.

 b. beta particles.

 c. carbon-14.

 d. potassium.

_d_ 4. What do all kinds of high-energy radiation have in common?

 a. They can break apart molecules.

 b. They cause chaos within cells.

 c. They may cause new, harmful molecules to be formed.

 d. all of the above

_c_ 5. According to the reading, astronauts in space

 a. absorb the same amount of radiation as people on an airplane.

 b. can see cosmic rays.

 c. could be killed by radiation from a solar flare.

 d. are exposed to less radiation than the residents of Denver.

_c_ 6. The most dangerous radiation is

 a. alpha.   c. gamma.

 b. beta.   d. neutrinos.

C. RECOGNIZING METHODS OF ORGANIZATION AND TRANSITIONS

Select the best answer.

_c_ 1. Because the reading discusses the different types of radiation, one organizational pattern used in this reading is

 a. time sequence.

 b. comparison and contrast.

 c. classification.

 d. generalization and example.

___c___ 2. The pattern used to describe how the radioactive particles act (paragraph 6) uses

    a. comparison and contrast.

    b. enumeration.

    c. process.

    d. statement and clarification.

➤ D. REVIEWING AND ORGANIZING IDEAS: OUTLINING

Fill in this outline about natural radiation (paragraph 1).

  I. Sources

    A. Rocks

      1. granite

      2. ____bricks____

      3. ____concrete____

    B. Cosmic Rays

    C. Human body

      1. potassium-40

      2. ____carbon-14____

    D. ____Radon-222____

      1. inert gas

      2. seeps into basements

➤ E. FIGURING OUT INFERRED MEANINGS

Indicate whether each statement is true (T) or false (F).

___F___ 1. Non-natural sources of radiation do not hurt us.

___F___ 2. Living in a wood frame house increases your cancer risk.

___T___ 3. Airplanes do not protect the people inside from cosmic rays.

___T___ 4. People should check for radon before buying a house.

___F___ 5. Free radicals are harmless.

➤ F.   THINKING CRITICALLY

Select the best answer.

__a__ 1. The author supports the central thesis with
   a. facts and descriptions.
   b. analogies.
   c. expert opinion.
   d. research citations.

__d__ 2. The tone of the selection is
   a. worried.
   b. persuasive.
   c. uncomfortable.
   d. informative.

__b__ 3. Which of the following statements from the reading is an opinion?
   a. The global combustion of coal annually releases about 9000 tons of radioactive thorium. (paragraph 2)
   b. If our bodies couldn't tolerate it, we wouldn't be here. (paragraph 3)
   c. Even the human body is a source of natural radiation. (paragraph 4)
   d. Neutrinos are the most weakly interacting particles. (paragraph 10)

__a__ 4. In paragraph 8, the author explains his ideas by
   a. making comparisons.
   b. giving statistics.
   c. repeating information.
   d. making inferences.

__d__ 5. In the last paragraph, the author
   a. summarizes the entire reading.
   b. rephrases the first paragraph.
   c. gives suggestions on how to avoid radiation exposure.
   d. identifies the most dangerous type of radiation and urges that exposure be minimized.

➤ **G.   BUILDING VOCABULARY**

➤ **Context**

Using context and a dictionary, if necessary, determine the meaning of each word as it is used in the selection.

__a__ 1. combustion (paragraph 2)

    a. burning

    b. mixing

    c. polluting

    d. disposing

__a__ 2. careen (paragraph 6)

    a. to weave through at high speed

    b fall off the edge of

    c. split in half

    d. blast apart

__b__ 3. conventionally (paragraph 9)

    a. simply

    b. traditionally, regularly

    c. poorly, badly

    d. natural

__c__ 4. emanates (paragraph 11)

    a. is caused by

    b. skips

    c. comes out from

    d. resembles

➤ **Word Parts**

A REVIEW OF ROOTS AND PREFIXES

GEO means *earth*

IR- means *not*

Use the review of roots and prefixes above to fill in the blanks in the following sentences.

1. If -ology means *the study of,* then geology (paragraph 5) is the study of the __earth__ .

2. Nerve cells are irreplaceable (paragraph 7); other cells __cannot__ be substituted.

➤ **Unusual Words/Unusual Meanings**

Use the meanings given below to write a sentence using the underlined word or phrase.

1. When tears <u>well up</u> (paragraph 1) in your eyes, they come to the surface of your eyes, ready to stream out.

   Your sentence: _____.

2. Something can be called a <u>soup or soupy</u> (paragraph 6) if it has the consistency of the soup or if it is foggy or chaotic.

   Your sentence: _____.

➤ **H.   SELECTING A LEARNING/STUDY STRATEGY**

Select the best answer.

___a___   What would be the best way to clarify the meanings of all the technical terms used in the reading, such as *radioactive isotope?*

   a. Look them up in a physics dictionary or other science reference book.

   b. Ask your classmate who is majoring in chemistry.

   c. Do an Internet search for each term.

   d. Look them up in a general encyclopedia.

➤ **I.   EXPLORING IDEAS THROUGH DISCUSSION AND WRITING**

1. Discuss what you think are the most serious health hazards in America.

2. Write a list of ways you could live a more healthy life.

3. Look around you. What potential health hazards exist in your community or on campus? Discuss ways to eliminate or avoid these hazards.

➤ **J.   BEYOND THE CLASSROOM TO THE WEB**

*Read about the government's efforts to compensate people who have been exposed to radiation at **http://www.usdoj.gov/civil/torts/const/reca/about.htm**.*

   Be sure to click on the link "Awards to Date" to see the percentage of claims being settled and the amount of money being paid out. What does this indicate about the government's attitude toward radiation exposure?

✔ **Tracking Your Progress**

Selection 36

Section	Number Correct		Score
A. Thesis and Main Idea (7 items)	_____	x 4	_____
B. Details (6 items)	_____	x 3	_____
C. Organization and Transitions (2 items)	_____	x 2	_____
E. Inferred Meanings (5 items)	_____	x 4	_____
F. Thinking Critically (5 items)	_____	x 4	_____
G. Vocabulary			
1. Context (4 items)	_____	x 2	_____
2. Word Parts (2 items)	_____	x 1	_____

TOTAL SCORE _____%

CHECKING YOUR READING RATE

Words in Selection 36: 1,335

Finishing Time:	_____	_____	_____
	(hour)	(minutes)	(seconds)
Starting Time:	_____	_____	_____
	(hour)	(minutes)	(seconds)
Total Reading Time:		_____	_____
		(minutes)	(seconds)

Words Per Minute Score (page 739) _____ WPM

23 Workplace/Career Fields

Work is a complex, important part of our lives and serves a number of different functions. It provides essential income to purchase life's necessities. It also offers an outlet for creative expression, helps us learn new skills, and allows us to explore new interests and talents. Jobs can be a source of personal satisfaction, a means of demonstrating that we are competent, self-sufficient individuals. Work can also make leisure time valuable and meaningful. Finally, work can lead to new friends, new relationships, new experiences, and new realizations.

The readings in this chapter provide several different perspectives on work and the workplace. The article "Building Toward a Career" offers partial suggestions to help you prepare for the career of your choice while you are attending college. In "Rx for Anger at Work" you will learn causes of anger on the job and discover ways to cope with anger. "The Sandman Is Dead—Long Live the Sleep Deprived Walking Zombie" addresses a serious problem many of us with hectic lives face—sleep deprivation.

Use the following tips when reading about the workplace.

TIPS FOR READING IN WORKPLACE/ CAREER FIELDS

- **Focus on practical information.** As you read the selections in this chapter, try to find techniques and strategies that you can use on the job or to find a better job. You may find some practical suggestions for coping with anger and frustrations on the job in "Rx for Anger at Work."

- **Pay attention to trends and projections.** The workplace is constantly changing and evolving. The job you have today may not exist in 20 years. Read to find out how to make yourself marketable and competitive.

- **Apply what you learn.** The information in the readings on sleep deprivation and anger management can be put to immediate use, both in the workplace and in the college environment.

SELECTION 37

Building Toward a Career

Courtland L. Bovee, John V. Thill, and Barbara E. Shatzman

This article originally appeared in a business textbook titled *Business Communication Today,* published in 2003. Read it to discover what you can do now to discover the right career choice and prepare for that career upon graduation.

➤ **PREVIEWING THE READING**

Using the steps listed on page 5, preview the reading selection. When you have finished, answer the following questions.

1. This selection is primarily about ___Finding a job you are suited for___.

2. List at least three questions you should be able to answer after reading the selection:

   a. ___How can you find out what you have to offer employers?___

   b. ___How can you discover what you want to do?___

   c. ___How can you make yourself valuable to employers?___

 MAKING CONNECTIONS

Fill in the following chart with what you have done and what you plan to do toward obtaining several jobs that interest you.

Potential careers Categories of experience	School Music Teacher	Performer	Music Therapist
COURSES	Classes toward BA in music; certification	Opera workshop Musical theater	Psychology
INTERNSHIPS			County Psychiatric Hospital (last summer)
EMPLOYMENT PORTFOLIO	Tutoring children at a supervised homework session	Singing at church Playing piano hospital charity auction	Playing piano for nursing home sing-alongs
JOBS	Camp Counselor—three summers—taught guitar and led sing-alongs	Auditioning for summer shows (this summer)	

➤ **READING TIP**

As you read, highlight specific actions you can take to choose a career that is best suited to your interests and prepare for a job in that career field.

 CHECKING YOUR READING RATE

If you plan to compute your reading rate, be sure to record your starting time in the box at the end of the exercises before you begin reading.

Building Toward a Career

1   Getting the job that is right for you takes more than sending out a few resumes and application letters. Before entering the workplace, you need to learn as much as you can about your capabilities and the job marketplace.

Adapting to the Changing Workplace

2   Do you have what employers are looking for? Before you limit your employment search to a particular industry or job, it's a good idea to analyze what you have to offer and what you hope to get from your work. This advance preparation allows you to identify employers who are likely to want you and vice versa.

What Do You Have to Offer?

3   Get started by jotting down 10 achievements you're proud of, such as learning to ski, taking a prize-winning photo, tutoring a child, or editing your school paper. Think carefully about what specific skills these achievements demanded. For example, leadership skills, speaking ability, and artistic talent may have helped you coordinate a winning presentation to your school's administration. As you analyze your achievements, you'll begin to recognize a pattern of skills. Which of them might be valuable to potential employers?

4   Next, look at your educational preparation, work experience, and extracurricular activities. What do your knowledge and experience qualify you to do? What have you learned from volunteer work or class projects that could benefit you on the job? Have you held any offices, won any awards or scholarships, mastered a second language?

5   Take stock of your personal characteristics. Are you aggressive, a born leader? Or would you rather follow? Are you outgoing, articulate, great with people? Or do you prefer working alone? Make a list of what you believe are your four or five most important qualities. Ask a relative or friend to rate your traits as well.

6   If you're having difficulty figuring out your interests, characteristics, or capabilities, consult your college placement office. Many campuses administer a variety of tests to help you identify interests, aptitudes, and personality traits. These tests won't reveal your "perfect" job, but they'll help you focus on the types of work best suited to your personality.

What Do You Want to Do?

7   Knowing what you can do is one thing. Knowing what you want to do is another. Don't lose sight of your own values. Discover the things that will bring you satisfaction and happiness on the job.

- What would you like to do every day? Talk to people in various occupations about their typical workday. You might consult relatives, local businesses, or former graduates (through your school's alumni relations office). Read about various occupations. Start with your college library or placement office.

- How would you like to work? Consider how much independence you want on the job, how much variety you like, and whether you prefer to work with products, machines, people, ideas, figures, or some combination thereof. Do you like physical work, mental work, or a mix? Constant change or a predictable role?

- What specific compensation do you expect? What do you hope to earn in your first year? What kind of pay increase do you expect each year? What's your ultimate earnings goal? Would you be comfortable getting paid on commission, or do you prefer a steady paycheck? Are you willing to settle for less money in order to do something you really love?

- Can you establish some general career goals? Consider where you'd like to start, where you'd like to go from there, and the ultimate position you'd like to attain. How soon after joining the company would you like to receive your first promotion? Your next one? What additional training or preparation will you need to achieve them?

- What size company would you prefer? Do you like the idea of working for a small, entrepreneurial operation? Or would you prefer a large corporation?

- What type of operation is appealing to you? Would you prefer to work for a profit-making company or a nonprofit organization? Are you attracted to service businesses or manufacturing operations? Do you want regular, predictable hours, or do you thrive on flexible, varied hours? Would you enjoy a seasonally varied job such as education (which may give you summers off) or retailing (with its selling cycles)?

- What location would you like? Would you like to work in a city, a suburb, a small town, an industrial area, or an uptown setting? Do you favor a particular part of the country? A country abroad? Do you like working indoors or outdoors?

- What facilities do you envision? Is it important to you to work in an attractive place, or will simple, functional quarters suffice? Do you need a quiet office to work effectively, or can you concentrate in a noisy, open setting? Is access to public transportation or freeways important?

- What sort of corporate culture are you most comfortable with? Would you be happy in a formal hierarchy with clear reporting relationships? Or do you prefer less structure? Are you looking for a paternalistic firm or one that fosters individualism? Do you like a competitive environment? One that rewards teamwork? What qualities do you want in a boss?

How Can You Make Yourself More Valuable to Employers?

8   While you're figuring out what you can offer an employer and what you want from a job, you can take positive steps toward building your career. There is a lot you can do before you graduate from college and while you are seeking employment. The following suggestions will help potential employers recognize the value of hiring you:

9   Keep an employment portfolio. Get a three-ring notebook and a package of plastic sleeves that open at the top. Collect anything that shows your ability to perform (classroom or work evaluations, certificates, awards, papers you've written). Your portfolio is a great resource for writing your resume, and it gives employers tangible evidence of your professionalism.

10   Take interim assignments. As you search for a permanent job, consider temporary or freelance work. Also gain a competitive edge by participating in an internship program. These temporary assignments not only help you gain valuable experience and relevant contacts but also provide you with important references and with items for your portfolio.

11   Work on polishing and updating your skills. Whenever possible, join networks of professional colleagues and friends who can help you keep up with your occupation and industry. While waiting for responses to your resume, take a computer course or seek out other educational or life experiences that would be hard to get while working full-time,

12   Even after an employer hires you, continue improving your skills to distinguish yourself from your peers and to make yourself more valuable to current and potential employers. Becoming a lifelong learner will help you reach your personal goals in the workplace.

➤ A.   UNDERSTANDING THE THESIS AND OTHER MAIN IDEAS

Select the best answer.

___b___ 1. The central thesis of the selection is that

    a. recruiters are looking for well-rounded candidates, not those with specific skills.

    b. students should analyze their skills and values and take steps toward preparing for a career while in college.

    c. you should plan to update your skills regularly.

    d. an employment portfolio is an employee's strongest asset.

___c___ 2. The author's primary purpose is to

    a. discourage students from focusing only on salary.

    b. explain how to polish your skills.

    c. encourage students to plan ahead when pursing a career.

    d. advise job seekers on the fundamentals of networking and business etiquette.

___c___ 3. What topic does the author address in paragraph 5?

    a. aggression.

    b. leadership.

    c. personal traits.

    d. work preferences.

___d___ 4. The main idea of paragraph 7 is

    a. start your job search at your college's placement office

    b. you should set a salary goal before you go job hunting

c. you should consider whether you prefer mental or physical tasks

d. you should identify things that bring you happiness and job satisfaction.

_d_ 5. The main idea of paragraph 8 is

a. temporary jobs often lead to permanent ones.

b. if students find careers they love, the money will follow.

c. an employment portfolio demonstrates your professionalism.

d. students should take steps while in college that will enable them to demonstrate their value to employers.

➤ B. IDENTIFYING DETAILS

Indicate whether each statement is true (T) or false (F).

_T_ 1. Listing achievements you are proud of will help you discover skills you have to offer employers.

_F_ 2. Tests offered by the college placement office may identify the perfect job for you.

_T_ 3. It is helpful to develop a career plan that includes long term goals.

_F_ 4. An employment portfolio should contain testimonials from friends and family who are familiar with your personal traits.

_T_ 5. Part time or temporary jobs provide important contacts and useful references.

➤ C. RECOGNIZING METHODS OF ORGANIZATION AND TRANSITIONS

Select the best answer.

_c_ 1. The overall general organizational pattern that the author uses to explain what students need to do to build toward a career is

a. classification.

b. order of importance.

c. process.

d. comparison and contrast.

_d_ 2. An example of a transition for this overall pattern in paragraphs 3–6 is

a. As you analyze

b. for example

c. If you're having difficulty

d. next

➤ **D.   REVIEWING AND ORGANIZING IDEAS: SUMMARIZING**

Complete the following summary of paragraphs 29-32 by filling in the missing words or phrases.

Paragraph 8: Before you graduate from _____college_____ and while you are looking for a _____job_____, there are _____three_____ steps you can take to help _____employers_____ recognize your value. First, prepare an employment _____portfolio_____. It is a collection of documents that demonstrate your ability to _____perform_____. Second, when looking for a permanent job, accept _____temporary_____ jobs or internships. Third, polish and update your _____skills_____.

➤ **E.   FIGURING OUT INFERRED MEANINGS**

Indicate whether each statement is probably true (T) or probably false (F) based on information contained in the reading.

___T___ 1. Friends or relatives are capable of assessing your personal characteristics.

___F___ 2. Tests offered by the college placement office are unfair and often misused.

___T___ 3. A student who prefers physical tasks probably would not be happy as a stock market analyst.

___T___ 4. Volunteer work can help you learn what is involved in a particular job.

___F___ 5. Speaking a second language is probably not a career asset.

___F___ 6. If you are proud that you learned to drive a race car, then you should include awards that you have won in your employment portfolio in preparation for a job in accounting.

___T___ 7. While searching for a full time job, you should consider taking a part time job.

___T___ 8. If a student likes regular, predictable hours, he or she might be happy with a career in nursing.

➤ **F.   THINKING CRITICALLY**

___a___ 1. The tone of the reading can best be described as

a. encouraging

b. anxious

c. biased

d. eager

___b___ 2. Of the following statements based on the reading, the only one that is a fact is

a. your values are your most important asset.

b. making a list of achievements is one way to discover your values and skills.

c. advance job preparation is always a good idea for everyone.

d. job location is more important than the job itself.

___d___ 3. Another accurate and descriptive title for the entire reading would be

a. The Workplace: A Changing Scene

b. Getting Back to Basics

c. Analyzing Your Talents

d. Advance Preparation for the Job Market

___c___ 4. The author ends the selection with a(an)

a. summary statement

b. example of a student who followed his advice.

c. look ahead to after you get your first career position.

d. warning to be cautious in the workplace.

___a___ 5. The author asks numerous questions throughout the reading primarily to

a. encourage readers to analyze their skills and values.

b. give himself an opportunity to provide answers.

c. help readers stay focused on the subject.

d. avoid sounding too authoritative.

➤ G. BUILDING VOCABULARY

➤ **Context**
Using context and a dictionary, if necessary, determine the meaning of each word as it is used in the selection.

___b___ 1. alumni (paragraph 7)

a. organization of professors

b. graduates or former students

c. students' rights group

d. group of high achieving students

___a___ 2. suffice (paragraph 7)

    a. be enough

    b. be expensive

    c. be beneficial

    d. be productive

___a___ 3. hierarchy (paragraph 7)

    a. group ranked by authority

    b. group with equal power

    c. group without a mission

    d. group to replace another group

___d___ 4. tangible (paragraph 8)

    a. replaceable

    b. reachable

    c. portable

    d. touchable

___c___ 5. interim (paragraph 8)

    a. convenient

    b. important

    c. temporary

    d. instructive

➤ **Word Parts**

> **A REVIEW OF PREFIXES AND ROOTS**
> **EXTRA-** means *out of*
> **VIS** means *see*

Use the review of prefixes, suffixes and roots above to fill in the blanks in the following sentences.

1. Extracurricular activities (paragraph 4) occur ___outside of___ the regular school curriculum.

2. If you can *envision* (paragraph 7) the office you would like to work in, you can see or form a mental ___picture___ of it.

➤ **Unusual Words/Unusual Meanings**

Use the meanings given below to write a sentence using the underlined word or phrase.

1. <u>Vice versa</u> (paragraph 2) means the other way around.

   Your sentence: _____.

2. A <u>born leader</u> (paragraph 5) is someone who naturally possesses many of the qualities of an effective leader.

   Your sentence: _____.

➤ **H.   SELECTING A LEARNING/STUDY STRATEGY**

Select the best answer.

___b___   What would be the best way to remember all the tips described in this selection?

   a. Visualize each piece of advice.

   b. remember the individual pieces by grouping them into more general, broader categories

   c. make a chart listing ideas you agree and disagree with.

   d. Write an essay summarizing what you have already decided about your career.

➤ **I.   EXPLORING IDEAS THROUGH DISCUSSION AND WRITING**

1. Discuss whether any of the ideas in this article were new or surprised you.

2. Explain the ways in which you have already worked toward attaining your career goals.

3. Evaluate how useful this advice is as you work toward your career.

➤ **J.   BEYOND THE CLASSROOM TO THE WEB**

Explore a career of interest to you on the Web. You can start by selecting the "Careers" section of a browser or search engine or by typing in a keyword search. Visit several sites that explain how to prepare for or what to expect in a particular career. Then write a paragraph that describes what you learned.

✔ **Tracking Your Progress**

Selection 37

Section	Number Correct	Score
A. Thesis and Main Idea (5 items)	_____ x 4	_____
B. Details (5 items)	_____ x 4	_____
C. Organization and Transitions (2 items)	_____ x 2	_____
E. Inferred Meanings (8 items)	_____ x 3	_____
F. Thinking Critically (5 items)	_____ x 3	_____
G. Vocabulary		
1. Context (5 items)	_____ x 3	_____
2. Word Parts (2 items)	_____ x 1	_____
	TOTAL SCORE _____ %	

CHECKING YOUR READING RATE

Words in Selection 37: 1,128

Finishing Time: _____   _____   _____
                  (hour)   (minutes)   (seconds)

Starting Time: _____   _____   _____
                  (hour)   (minutes)   (seconds)

Total Reading Time: _____   _____
                     (minutes)   (seconds)

Words Per Minute Score (page 739) _____ WPM

SELECTION 38

Rx for Anger at Work

Kathy Simmons

This reading appears on *Career Magazine*'s Web site. Read it to discover how anger works and how to control it.

➤ PREVIEWING THE READING

Using the steps listed on page 5, preview the reading selection. When you have finished, complete the following items.

1. The selection is about <u>anger at work</u>.

2. List three questions you should be able to answer after reading the article:

   a. <u>What makes us angry at work?</u>

   b. <u>Is there such a thing as bad anger?</u>

   c. <u>How can you avoid feeling out of control when angry?</u>

MAKING CONNECTIONS

Have you ever gotten angry at work? Who or what provoked your anger? How did you express your anger?

➤ READING TIP

This selection includes the work of several experts on the subject of anger. Keep track of who said what, and in what context (for example, three books are mentioned, and all three have a slightly different focus).

CHECKING YOUR READING RATE

If you plan to compute your reading rate, be sure to record your starting time in the box at the end of the exercises before you begin reading.

Rx
the abbreviation
for prescription

pink slip
a notice of
termination of
employment

martyr
one who
endures great
suffering for the
sake of a belief
or principle, or
one who makes
a show of
suffering in
order to gain
sympathy

Rx for Anger at Work

1   A fable is told about a young lion and a cougar. The animals arrived at their usual water hole at the same time. They were both very thirsty, and immediately began to argue about who should take the first drink. The argument escalated rapidly. As they stubbornly clung to their anger, it quickly turned to rage. Their vicious attacks on each other were suddenly interrupted when they both looked up. Circling overhead was a flock of vultures waiting for the loser to fall. Quietly, the two beasts turned and walked away. The thought of being devoured was all they needed to end their quarrel.

2   Have you ever lost your cool at work? Warning: Seeing red too often might lead to seeing pink: the pink slip, that is. The workplace can be a regular breeding ground for anger, considering the amount of time we are around people of different value systems, deadlines, competitive co-workers, gossip and misunderstandings. The ugly consequences of mishandled anger include such "vultures" as lost credibility, damaged relationships, and stress.

3   A solid understanding of anger is a giant leap toward mastering this "most misunderstood emotion." You can strengthen your anger IQ with the following information.

What Makes Us Angry at Work?

4   According to Dr. Hendrie Weisinger, author of *The Anger Work-Out Book,* there are five work situations that provoke anger.

5   **Being left out.** Not being accepted by your peers provokes anger for two reasons: 1) It severely limits how effective you can be on the job, and 2) It shakes your fundamental need for acceptance and a sense of belonging.

6   **The critical boss.** Nit-picking bosses are infuriating. To add insult to injury, you are severely restricted in how much anger you can express toward him or her. Weisinger comments, "We tend to get back at our boss by taking a passive-aggressive stance. We do everything the job dictates, but not one iota more." This often makes the boss even more critical, and the vicious cycle continues.

7   **Not getting the promotion you deserve.** You bust your butt and it's not acknowledged. Who wouldn't feel cheated? Most people handle this perceived injustice poorly by becoming negative—and angry—martyrs.

8   **Being maligned by co-workers.** Dr. Weisinger points out that "being victimized by false rumors is a consistent anger arouser. It is abusive and unjust. And the rumors frequently cause irrevocable damage."

9   **Dealing with an incompetent boss.** Everyone has an innate need to admire their leader and follow their direction confidently and cheerfully. An incompetent boss can stifle your enthusiasm, and bring down the effectiveness of your organization.

Is There Such a Thing as Bad Anger?

10   Dr. Paul Meier, M.D., author of *Don't Let Jerks Get the Best of You,* offers three main causes of illegitimate anger: selfishness, perfectionism, and paranoia.

11   Selfishness carries the unrealistic expectation that people should never disagree with you, get to go first, or receive more recognition than you. You expect too much, and inevitably end up angry.

12   Perfectionists also have a difficult time with anger. According to Meier, "Some of the angriest people I know are perfectionists." When perfectionism rules your life, the person you are hardest on is yourself. Expecting flawless results causes continual anger, which accelerates as the same unrealistic demands are imposed on those with whom you work.

13   Paranoid people misinterpret situations—a glance from the boss or a co-worker passing by without saying hello, for instance. Too much energy is spent on insignificant and meaningless trivia, which can lead to a high anger level.

How Can You Avoid Feeling Out of Control When Angry?

Accept the Anger

14   Susanna McMahon, Ph.D., author of *The Portable Therapist,* points to the importance of acknowledging angry feelings. "Give yourself permission to feel angry. You do not always know when and why and how you will feel angry. Sometimes you may feel angry without knowing why. And sometimes, when you would expect to feel angry, you do not."

15   McMahon explains that anger lives inside of you along with your other feelings. Accepting anger does not mean you express it. You can control what you choose to do when you are angry. The reality is that most of us are afraid of what we might do when we are angry. As a result, we deny rage until it finally explodes into destructive behavior. You can be sure this will affect your career success.

16   A study by the Center of Creative Leadership indicates the primary reason executives were fired or forced to retire was their inability to handle anger—especially under pressure. Accepting the angry feeling as it occurs means that we do not accumulate the feelings until they become rage.

Acknowledge Your Choices

17   Don't repeat helpless statements like "I can't do anything about it." *The Anger Work-Out Book* encourages readers to keep one fact in mind: When angry, you must acknowledge that you want to keep your job. However **cathartic** it might be to "tell someone off," the more rational choice is to avoid doing permanent damage to your career.

cathartic
producing
emotional
release

18   Weisinger explains, "This allows you to get angry and yet keep things in perspective as coming with the territory. 'I don't like it, but I will learn to deal with it' is much more productive than 'Nothing I can do about it, it's not that bad.' The latter statement denies the anger where the former is task oriented. You can then move on to workable solutions, in other words considering the fact I am angry, but I also want to keep my job, what is the best way to handle the situation?"

19   Your focus should be on keeping your job, *and* refusing to let unconstructive anger derail your career success. In the words of Roman philosopher Seneca, "The greatest cure of anger is delay."

Cool Your Anger with Humor

20   Steven Sultanoff, Ph.D., licensed psychologist and president of The American Association for Therapeutic Humor explains, "Anger and the experience of humor cannot occupy the same psychological space." Can you recall a situation when you were really angry with someone, and they spontaneously did something to make

you laugh? In that moment you probably had a split second of disappointment—you wanted to be angry!

21   Sultanoff explains, "When we experience humor, distressing emotions like anger disappear. When we are angry, if we can look to our funny bone we will experience some relief." The root cause of anger at work is a belief that everything should be fair. Laughing at the "unfairness" will help you gain perspective and dissipate your anger.

Practice Forgiveness

22   When you are mistreated at work, the last thing you want to do is practice forgiveness. While it may be absolutely true that the offender does not deserve your kindness, remember this: *You do!*

23   By forgiving abusive jerks, you are actually giving yourself a break.

24   It has been said that recovering from wounds makes us extremely powerful. With this in mind, can you look at others' assaults against you that way? Rather than wallowing in despair and focusing on the inequity of the situation, can you view those painful wounds as growth opportunities?

25   Anger is a natural part of being human, but success-minded people have a healthy respect for—and control of—this emotion. By raising your awareness of what provokes your anger, and determining ways to handle it well, you can see clearly—even when you see red!

Ways to Deal with Your Anger

26   1. *Physically.* Get a tennis racquet and hit a pillow. Work out. Break something. I once broke all the dishes in my cabinet. It was a mess, but I felt good.

27   2. *Mentally.* Talk out your anger, with a confidante or with yourself. Ask yourself, "How is holding on to this anger serving me? Do I want to stay in this state?"

28   3. *Emotionally.* Underneath anger is pain, and underneath pain are tears. Have a good cry.

29   4. *Spiritually.* Seek guidance from a higher power. If you believe in God, pray for help. Ask that your anger be lifted, or imagine that your anger is like a lump of dough that you heave out into space. See your anger as something outside of you. Ask God to take it from you. (From: *Since Strangling Isn't An Option* by Sandra A. Crowe, M.A.)

> ### A.   UNDERSTANDING THE THESIS AND OTHER MAIN IDEAS

Select the best answer.

__d__ 1. The central thesis of the selection is that

a. employees who lose their temper at work often end up being fired.

b. certain work situations can provoke anger that is justified.

c. most anger in the workplace is based on misunderstandings that are easily resolved with proper communication.

d. mishandled anger in the workplace can have serious consequences and workers can learn to manage their anger.

<u>a</u>   2. The author's primary purpose is to

    a. describe anger in the workplace and how to cope with it.

    b. compare various strategies for coping with disappointment at work.

    c. report on the best types of therapy for anger management.

    d. urge people who feel mistreated at work to express their emotions.

<u>c</u>   3. The topic of paragraph 12 is

    a. Paul Meier.

    b. illegitimate anger.

    c. perfectionism.

    d. paranoia.

<u>a</u>   4. The main idea of paragraph 15 is that

    a. angry feelings do not have to be expressed.

    b. most people are afraid of their anger.

    c. destructive behavior can ruin your career.

    d. denying rage is better than expressing it.

<u>c</u>   5. The method promoted by Steven Sultanoff in paragraphs 20–21 to deal with anger is

    a. delay.

    b. denial.

    c. humor.

    d. acceptance.

➤ B. IDENTIFYING DETAILS

Indicate whether each statement is true (T) or false (F).

<u>F</u>   1. Kathy Simmons wrote *The Anger Work-Out Book*.

<u>T</u>   2. According to Dr. Hendrie Weisinger, not being accepted by peers at work severely limits a person's effectiveness.

<u>F</u>   3. The two main causes of illegitimate anger identified by Dr. Paul Meier are false rumors and an incompetent boss.

<u>T</u>   4. The author of *The Portable Therapist* emphasizes the importance of acknowledging angry feelings.

<u>F</u>   5. A study by the Center of Creative Leadership indicated that the primary reason executives were fired was their inability to adapt to the stress of new technology.

➤ C.   RECOGNIZING METHODS OF ORGANIZATION AND TRANSITIONS

Select the best answer.

__b__ 1. In paragraph 2, the organizational pattern the author uses to describe the consequences of mishandled anger at work is

a. time sequence.

b. cause and effect.

c. problem and solution.

d. definition.

__c__ 2. In paragraph 4, the organizational pattern the author uses to describe the five anger-provoking work situations identified by Dr. Weisinger is

a. time sequence.

b. definition.

c. enumeration.

d. comparison and contrast.

➤ D.   REVIEWING AND ORGANIZING IDEAS: OUTLINING

Complete the following outline of the selection by filling in the missing words and phrases.

I.   What Makes Us Angry at Work?

A. Hendrie Weisinger—*The Anger Work-Out Book*

B. _____ Work situations that provoke anger _____

1. Being left out by your peers

2. _____ The critical boss _____

3. Not getting the ____promotion____ you deserve

4. _____ Being maligned by coworkers _____

5. Dealing with the __incompetent boss__

II. Is There Such a Thing as Bad Anger?

A. _____Paul Meier_____—*Don't Let Jerks Get the Best of You*

B. Main causes of __illegitimate anger__

   1. Selfishness

   2. ____Perfectionism____

   3. Paranoia

III. How Can You Avoid Feeling Out of Control When Angry?

A. Accept the anger

   1. Susanna McMahon—*The Portable Therapist*

B. Acknowledge your choices

   1. *The Anger Work-Out Book*

C. _____Cool your anger with humor_____

   1. Steven Sultanoff—The American Association for Therapeutic Humor

D. Practice forgiveness

➤ **E.   FIGURING OUT INFERRED MEANINGS**

Indicate whether each statement is true (T) or false (F).

__T__ 1. When the author refers to "your anger IQ," she means your understanding of what anger is.

__F__ 2. It can be inferred that *The Anger Work-Out Book* is primarily a book about exercising and working out.

__F__ 3. Taking a passive-aggressive stance is an effective way to express anger toward one's coworkers.

__T__ 4. A lack of respect for one's boss can affect the success of the entire organization.

__T__ 5. Perfectionists set impossible standards for themselves and others.

__T__ 6. Humor can help people deal with other distressing emotions in addition to anger.

➤ **F.   THINKING CRITICALLY**

Select the best answer.

___d___ 1. The central thesis of "Rx for Anger at Work" is supported primarily by

 a. the personal experience of the author.

 b. statistics from the Center of Creative Leadership.

 c. interviews with employees.

 d. evidence from authorities on anger.

___b___ 2. The author begins with a fable in order to

 a. show that many work situations can be described in fable form.

 b. illustrate her point about the consequences of anger at work.

 c. introduce the idea that coworkers can be like vultures.

 d. appeal to very young readers.

___b___ 3. The tone of the selection can best be described as

 a. humorous.

 b. encouraging.

 c. anxious.

 d. angry.

___c___ 4. The author chose the title in order to

 a. advocate the use of prescription medication to cope with anger at work.

 b. imply that the "ingredients" for anger are in the workplace.

 c. indicate that the selection offers remedies or treatments for anger at work.

 d. suggest that society's reliance on prescription medication is one of the causes of anger in the workplace.

___b___ 5. The quote by Seneca (paragraph 19) means that

 a. anger becomes even more intense with the passage of time.

 b. letting time pass is the best way to get over anger.

 c. the best way to make someone angry is to make them wait.

 d. it is impossible to hold someone back from expressing their anger.

➤ **G.   BUILDING VOCABULARY**

➤ **Context**

Using context and a dictionary, if necessary, determine the meaning of each word as it is used in the selection.

___b___ 1. escalated (paragraph 1)

    a. provoked

    b. intensified

    c. avoided

    d. improved

___a___ 2. fundamental (paragraph 5)

    a. basic

    b. hidden

    c. creative

    d. purposeful

___c___ 3. infuriating (paragraph 6)

    a. harmful

    b. uncertain

    c. maddening

    d. humorous

___b___ 4. accelerates (paragraph 12)

    a. improves

    b. increases

    c. threatens

    d. deflates

___d___ 5. derail (paragraph 19)

    a. promote

    b. speed up

    c. cause questions

    d. go off course

___a___ 6. dissipate (paragraph 21)

    a. dissolve

    b. spread

    c. encourage

    d. replace

_b_ 7. wallowing (paragraph 24)

    a. wondering

    b. indulging

    c. recovering

    d. planning

➤ Word Parts

A REVIEW OF PREFIXES THAT MEAN *NOT*
IL-
IN-
IR-
UN-

For each word in Column A, write the correct prefix (il-, in-, ir-, or un-) in the blank before the word. Then select the new word's meaning from Column B and write the letter in the space to the left of the number. The first one has been done for you as an example.

Column A	**Column B**
_d_ 1. _in_ justice	a. not according to rules or laws
_c_ 2. _ir_ revocable	b. not qualified or effective
_b_ 3. _in_ competent	c. impossible to undo or take back
_a_ 4. _il_ legitimate	d. lack of fair treatment
_g_ 5. _un_ realistic	e. not important or meaningful
_h_ 6. _in_ evitable	f. lack of fairness
_e_ 7. _in_ significant	g. not reasonable or practical
_f_ 8. _in_ equity	h. impossible to avoid or prevent

➤ Unusual Words/Unusual Meanings
Use the meanings below to write a sentence using the underlined word or phrase.

1. To <u>lose your cool</u> (paragraph 2) is to lose your composure or self-control; in other words, to become angry.

    Your sentence: _____.

2. Red is a color associated with rage, so when someone is <u>seeing red</u> (paragraph 2), that person has become angry.

    Your sentence: _____.

3. A <u>nit-picking</u> person (paragraph 6) doesn't literally pick nits, which are the tiny eggs of lice; the person figuratively "picks nits" by focusing on minor or trivial details, usually in order to criticize.

Your sentence: _____.

4. When you <u>bust your butt</u> (paragraph 7) for someone or something, you put forth a lot of effort, or work very hard.

Your sentence: _____.

5. The <u>funny bone</u> (paragraph 21) in this case is not an actual bone, but an expression that means a sense of humor.

Your sentence: _____.

➤ H.   SELECTING A LEARNING/STUDY STRATEGY

Discuss methods of studying the outline shown on pages 586–587 in preparation for an exam that covers this reading.

➤ I.   EXPLORING IDEAS THROUGH DISCUSSION AND WRITING

1. Anger management is a timely topic in today's world, especially in light of the number of crimes committed in recent years by enraged employees at the workplace. Describe a situation in which you have observed anger expressed at work.

2. Discuss the author's tone. Does the author's language reveal her attitude toward the subject?

3. What does the author mean when she says, "By forgiving abusive jerks, you are actually giving yourself a break" (paragraph 23)?

➤ J.   BEYOND THE CLASSROOM TO THE WEB

Visit ITWorld.com at **http://www.itworld.com/Career/3708/ITW0305joch/.**
    Read the article "Defuse Workplace Anger." What factors does this article list as being the most likely causes of workplace anger?

✔ **Tracking Your Progress**

Selection 38

Section	Number Correct		Score
A. Thesis and Main Idea (5 items)	_____	x 4	_____
B. Details (5 items)	_____	x 3	_____
C. Organization and Transitions (2 items)	_____	x 1	_____
E. Inferred Meanings (6 items)	_____	x 3	_____
F. Thinking Critically (5 items)	_____	x 3	_____
G. Vocabulary			
1. Context (7 items)	_____	x 2	_____
2. Word Parts (8 items)	_____	x 2	_____

TOTAL SCORE _____ %

CHECKING YOUR READING RATE

Words in Selection 38: 1,374

Finishing Time:	_____	_____	_____
	(hour)	(minutes)	(seconds)
Starting Time:	_____	_____	_____
	(hour)	(minutes)	(seconds)
Total Reading Time:		_____	_____
		(minutes)	(seconds)

Words Per Minute Score (page 739) _____ WPM

SELECTION 39

The Sandman Is Dead—Long Live the Sleep Deprived Walking Zombie

Dorrit T. Walsh

This reading appears on HR Plaza, a Web site for professionals in the human resources (recruiting and managing employees) field. Read it to find out if you are getting enough sleep and the effects of sleep deprivation.

➤ PREVIEWING THE READING

Using the steps listed on page 5, preview the reading selection. When you have finished, complete the following items.

1. The topic of this selection is <u>sleep or sleep deprivation</u>.

2. List four questions you should be able to answer after reading the selection:

   a. <u>Why is sleep important?</u>

   b. <u>How much sleep do we need?</u>

   c. <u>How much sleep are we getting?</u>

   d. <u>What are the effects of sleeplessness?</u>

MAKING CONNECTIONS

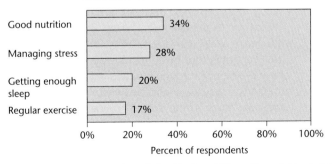

MOST IMPORTANT FACTORS IN MAINTAINING HEALTH

Good nutrition	34%
Managing stress	28%
Getting enough sleep	20%
Regular exercise	17%

Percent of respondents

This graph is part of the results of the National Sleep Foundation's 2000 survey of Americans and sleep. It shows what factors U.S. adults consider most important in maintaining good health. How would you rank these four factors?

> READING TIP

This selection contains a lot of information about the effects of sleeplessness on individuals and on businesses. Highlight or write a list of these effects as you read.

 CHECKING YOUR READING RATE

If you plan to compute your reading rate, be sure to record your starting time in the box at the end of the exercises before you begin reading.

The Sandman Is Dead—Long Live the Sleep Deprived Walking Zombie

1   Back in 1954, the Chordettes had a number one hit singing the praises of "Mr. Sandman," but today he's dead. It was a slow death; gradually, over a few decades, Americans killed him. Farewell sweet dreams and golden slumbers—we've entered into the age of waking up tired. Don't assume it's not you, either. Here's a quick quiz: do you get less than eight hours of sleep a night? Fall asleep almost as soon as your head hits the pillow? Need an alarm clock to wake up? And sometimes that doesn't even work? A "yes" to any of those questions means you're probably one of the chronically sleep deprived.

2   Before I continue, let me clarify why an article on lack of sleep is on a business Website. After all, not getting enough sleep is a personal problem, right? Wrong. While it is up to the individual to control his or her sleeping habits, unfortunately, for various reasons that I'll discuss in this article, today more than 100 million Americans are sleep deprived. And this lack of sleep has a direct and substantial effect on American businesses. In 1990 the National Commission on Sleep Disorders put the direct costs of sleep loss at $15.9 billion, and the indirect costs, such as higher stress and diminished productivity, clocked in at $150 billion. One hundred and fifty billion dollars is way more than a "personal problem."

The Basics: Why Sleep Is Important

3   Before going into the facts about why Americans aren't getting enough sleep, or the problems sleep deprivation causes, the first logical step is a brief explanation of exactly why sleep is so important to humans.

4   Contrary to popular belief, sleep isn't just a wasteful state of inertness. In fact, your brain when it's "sleeping" is often more active than when you're awake— **neural** activity drops by about only 10 percent when we're asleep. Sleeping consists of five cycles, one through four and REM sleep, so depending on how long you sleep at night you may experience anywhere from three to five cycles. The most significant stages are Stage 4, the deepest phase of sleep, and REM or Rapid Eye Movement Sleep. Stage 4 plays a major part in maintenance of our general health, including our natural **immune system**. REM sleep is when we dream, but more importantly, it's the key player in maintaining the various aspects of memory. It also has a lot to do with how we're able to learn new things and general mental performance.

5   Sleep restores and rejuvenates us, and affects everything from our creativity and communication skills to reaction times and energy levels.

neural
related to the body's nervous system

immune system
the system of organs, tissues, cells, and cell products that works as the body's defense against infections and disease

How Much Sleep Do We Need? How Much Are We Getting?

6   The simple answer to this question is: more than we're getting. According to Dr. James b. Maas, Cornell University professor and author of the book *Power Sleep,* the optimal amount of sleep we should be getting nightly is ten hours. Although ten hours of sleep per night may seem high by today's standards, it actually used to be the standard in this country. Before the invention of the electric light in 1879, most people slept ten hours per night. In fact, Einstein said that he could only function well if he had a full ten hours of sleep every night.

7   Since the late 1800s we've gradually cut back the time we sleep each night by a full 20 percent, to eight hours. However, even with a "standard" at two hours less than optimal, according to the National Sleep Foundation's "1998 Omnibus Sleep in America" poll, most Americans now average seven hours (actually only six hours and fifty-seven minutes) of sleep per night during the work week, or 30 percent less than the ideal. Nearly 32 percent only get six hours of sleep during the work week.

8   As far as why we're getting less sleep, there's no one single answer. Part of it's due to increased workloads (since 1977 Americans have added 158 hours annually to our working/commuting time), and then there's the stress that comes from the increased workloads. Or the fact that many people today, especially a number of "motivational speakers," downplay the need for sleep, so we don't want to be perceived as lazy. Or it could be what's on TV, or the book we just "have" to read, or the kids, or whatever.

Effects of Sleeplessness

9   Because many adults have never gotten sufficient sleep, or have gotten so used to getting by on less sleep than they need, many of the effects often go unnoticed. They don't realize that if they got more sleep, they could be in a better mood, be more productive, more creative, and think more clearly.

10   However, there are far reaching, quantifiable consequences that result from not getting enough sleep. Some of the most significant are:

- Thirty-one percent of all drivers say they've fallen asleep at the wheel at least once.
- Accidents resulting from falling asleep at the wheel cost Americans more than $30 billion each year.
- The National Transportation Safety Board cited fatigue as the number one factor detrimentally affecting airline pilots.
- Shiftworkers are particularly affected by lack of sleep. Fifty-six percent of them say they fall asleep on the job at least once a week.
- According to the *Wall Street Journal,* $70 billion is lost annually in productivity, health costs and accidents, a direct result of shiftworkers' not being able to adjust to late-night schedules.
- Forty percent of adults say that they're so sleepy during the day that it interferes with their daily activities, including work (remember, these are only the people who acknowledge or realize that their productivity is lessened).
- Research done at Leicestershire, England's Sleep Research Center found that not getting enough sleep has noticeable negative effects on our ability to understand situations that change rapidly. They found sleep deprivation also made us more likely to be distracted, makes us think less flexibly, and hampers our ability to solve problems innovatively.

- Studies at Loughborough University have shown a direct connection between our abilities to remember and concentrate, and sleep deprivation.
- The U.S. National Highway Traffic Safety Administration has proven that there's a direct connection between hand-eye coordination (a necessity when you're driving) and lack of sleep.

11   And according to the National Sleep Foundation survey, an incredible one-third of American adults tested reached levels of sleepiness that are known to be dangerous.

What To Do?

12   Again, there's no one simple answer to this question. Obviously people need more sleep. And one of the problems is that many people simply don't realize how important sleep is to us, or how serious the effects of sleep deprivation are. The National Sleep Foundation's "1998 Omnibus Sleep in America Poll" rated the sleep knowledge of 1,027 Americans, and it showed that Americans are generally ignorant when it comes to sleep and many sleep myths (e.g., that you need more sleep as you get older—you don't; sleep needs remain the same throughout adulthood).

13   Along with self education, employers could help both by providing the facts about sleep to employees and stressing how important an adequate amount of sleep is to everyday performance. Don't equate sleepiness with laziness; they're two totally different issues. Sleepy workers are more likely to cause accidents, make mistakes, and are more susceptible to heart attacks. Lazy workers, for whatever reason, just don't do their jobs.

14   One thing employers can do is give the okay to napping at work. This doesn't have to be the old kindergarten version with blankets on the floor; just closing the door and sitting in your chair with your eyes closed and trying to sleep for fifteen minutes will help to restore your energy. That's all you need, 15–30 minutes. Besides relieving stress, naps increase your ability to make important decisions and pay sufficient attention to details.

15   If you employ shift workers, realize that shift work simply isn't natural and humans cannot simply adapt to just any work cycle. Also, get more information on recommendations (the National Sleep Foundation Web site and/or the book *Power Sleep* are good places to start) on how to help arrange shift working schedules to help your employees stay alert and healthy.

16   It's time that Americans, both as individuals and businesses, start to acknowledge the vital importance sleep plays in our everyday lives and in our society. Although he wrote in the 1600s, Miguel de Cervantes may have described the importance of sleep best in *Don Quixote de la Mancha*:

17   "Now blessings light on him that first invented this same

sleep! It covers a man all over, thoughts and all, like a cloak;

'tis meat for the hungry, drink for the thirsty, heat for the cold,

and cold for the hot . . . and the balance that sets the kind and

the shepherd, the fool and the wise man even."*

---

*From *Bartlett's Familiar Quotations*. Little, Brown and Company.

➤ **A.   UNDERSTANDING THE THESIS AND OTHER MAIN IDEAS**

Select the best answer.

___c___ 1. The central thesis of "The Sandman Is Dead" is that

      a. sleep loss costs American businesses millions of dollars a year.

      b. most people don't realize the importance of sleep.

      c. Americans are not getting enough sleep.

      d. sleep is essential to human health.

___b___ 2. The author's primary purpose is to

      a. compare sleep statistics in America with statistics in other countries.

      b. educate people about the importance of sleep and the effects of sleeplessness.

      c. entertain readers with humorous anecdotes about sleeplessness.

      d. encourage employers to stress the importance of sleep to their employees.

Match each question in Column A with the paragraph listed in Column B that answers that question.

Column A	Column B
___d___ 3. How much sleep do Americans average per night?	a. paragraph 4
___c___ 4. What is the optimal amount of sleep per night?	b. paragraphs 4–5
___e___ 5. What are the consequences of insufficient sleep?	c. paragraph 6
___b___ 6. Why is sleep important to humans?	d. paragraph 7
___a___ 7. What are the stages of sleep?	e. paragraph 10

➤ **B.   IDENTIFYING DETAILS**

Select the best answer.

___d___ 1. According to the National Commission on Sleep Disorders, the *indirect* costs of sleep loss to American businesses in 1990 equaled

      a. $15.9 billion.   c. $70 billion.

      b. $30 billion.   d. $150 billion.

___d___ 2. The most significant stages of sleep are

    a. Stages 1 and 2.

    b. Stages 2 and 3.

    c. Stages 3 and 4.

    d. Stage 4 and REM sleep.

___b___ 3. The selection links all of the following aspects of health to REM sleep *except*

    a. memory.

    b. immune system.

    c. learning.

    d. general mental performance.

___b___ 4. According to the selection, the U.S. National Highway Traffic Safety Administration has proven that there is a direct connection between a lack of sleep and our

    a. ability to understand situations that change rapidly.

    b. hand-eye coordination.

    c. ability to solve problems innovatively.

    d. productivity at work.

___c___ 5. According to the selection, employers could help reduce the effects of sleeplessness in all of the following ways *except*

    a. allowing 15–30 minute naps at work.

    b. emphasizing how important an adequate night's sleep is to everyday performance.

    c. informing employees that they need more sleep as they get older.

    d. arranging shift working schedules to help employees stay alert and healthy.

▶ C.   RECOGNIZING METHODS OF ORGANIZATION AND TRANSITIONS

Select the best answer.

___b___ 1. The overall organizational pattern used throughout this selection is

    a. comparison and contrast.   c. definition.

    b. cause and effect.   d. time sequence.

<u>d</u>   2. In paragraphs 12–16, the organizational pattern the author uses to offer suggestions of what to do about sleep deprivation is

    a. time sequence.   c. comparison and contrast.

    b. definition.   d. enumeration.

➤ D.   REVIEWING AND ORGANIZING IDEAS: MAPPING

Fill in the blanks to complete the map of the quantifiable effects of sleeplessness described in paragraph 10 of the reading.

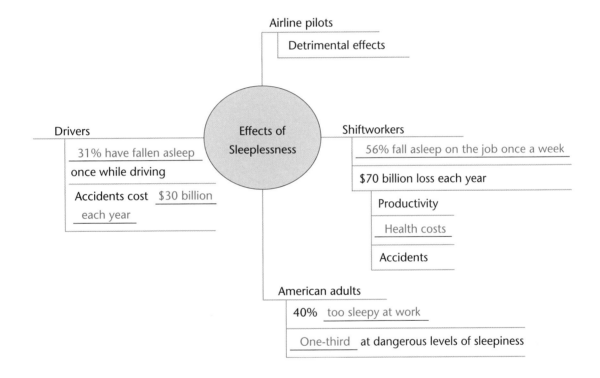

➤ E.   FIGURING OUT INFERRED MEANINGS

Indicate whether each statement is true (T) or false (F).

  <u>T</u>   1. It can be inferred that people who are sleep deprived have a more difficult time fighting infection.

  <u>F</u>   2. The percentage of adults whose sleepiness interferes with their daily activities is probably much smaller than the number reported.

___T___ 3. It can be inferred that sleep-deprived students have difficulty studying and learning.

___F___ 4. It can be inferred that sleep needs for children are the same as those for adults.

> F. **THINKING CRITICALLY**

Select the best answer.

___c___ 1. The title of the selection is intended to

   a. project a sense of horror about chronic sleeplessness in America.

   b. establish a tone of dread about the serious consequences of sleep deprivation.

   c. capture the reader's attention with a humorous reference to an old song and a horror movie.

   d. introduce the subject of myths.

___d___ 2. The thesis of the selection is supported by

   a. statistics.

   b. appeals to authority.

   c. research evidence.

   d. all of the above

___c___ 3. The tone of the selection can best be described as

   a. informal but concerned.

   b. critical but objective.

   c. optimistic and humorous.

   d. alarmed and distressed.

___d___ 4. Of the following statements from paragraphs 1–2, the only one that is an *opinion* is

   a. "In 1954, the Chordettes had a number one hit [called] 'Mr. Sandman.'"

   b. "It is up to the individual to control his or her sleeping habits."

   c. "One hundred and fifty billion dollars is way more than a 'personal problem.'"

   d. "Today more than 100 million Americans are sleep deprived."

_d_   5. The author puts quotation marks around the phrase "motivational speakers" (paragraph 8) in order to

    a. show respect for the title.

    b. indicate that motivational speakers are popular in today's culture.

    c. signify that this is one of many names for public speakers.

    d. point out that any speaker who discourages the need for sleep is not truly being motivational.

_b_   6. The statement that an "incredible one-third of American adults" have reached dangerous levels of sleepiness (paragraph 11) means that

    a. these adults are amazing because they are still able to work.

    b. this number represents a startlingly large fraction of the population.

    c. this number represents a reassuringly small fraction of the population.

    d. the survey did not include the other two-thirds of the population.

_a_   7. The author includes the quote by Miguel de Cervantes in order to

    a. end the selection with a thoughtful and historical perspective on the importance of sleep.

    b. point out that sleep is really a more light-hearted topic than the statistics seem to indicate.

    c. prove that sleep was much more important to people in the 1600s.

    d. appeal to Cervantes' authority as a writer.

G.   BUILDING VOCABULARY

Context

Using context and a dictionary, if necessary, determine the meaning of each word as it is used in the selection.

_c_   1. chronically (paragraph 1)

    a. temporarily   c. continually

    b. undiagnosed   d. suddenly

_d_   2. diminished (paragraph 2)

    a. insulted   c. expected

    b. improved   d. lessened

___c___ 3. inertness (paragraph 4)

    a. animation   c. inactivity

    b. similarity   d. productivity

___a___ 4. rejuvenates (paragraph 5)

    a. refreshes   c. pleases

    b. calms   d. entertains

___d___ 5. optimal (paragraph 6)

    a. occasional   c. standard

    b. likely   d. ideal

___c___ 6. detrimentally (paragraph 10)

    a. purposefully   c. harmfully

    b. actively   d. helpfully

___a___ 7. susceptible (paragraph 13)

    a. vulnerable   c. careless

    b. ignorant   d. unhealthy

➤ Word Parts

> **A REVIEW OF SUFFIXES**
>
> **-ABLE** means *capable of*
> **-ANCE** means *state* or *condition*
> **-ITY** means *state* or *quality*

Using your knowledge of word parts and the review above, complete the following sentences by filling in the blanks.

1. Creativity is the state of being _____creative_____.

2. An automobile maintenance agreement specifies the __state or condition__ in which the car is maintained.

3. If a heap of junk from the attic is quantifiable, then you are ___able to___ count the items and assign a value.

➤ Unusual Words/Unusual Meanings

Use the meanings given below to write a sentence using the underlined phrase.

1. The phrase <u>clocked in at</u> (paragraph 2) usually refers to the finish time of a race. (For example, "In the 50-yard dash, Jamal clocked in at 5:30 seconds.") In this case, it is used to show what the costs of sleep loss *amounted* to.

    Your sentence: _____.

2. The phrase <u>key player</u> (paragraph 4) can mean a person in a game who played an important role ("Gus was the key player in our baseball game last night"), or one who had an important role in a certain situation ("Maria was the key player in the real estate deal"). In this case, it is used to describe REM sleep as the most important *element* in the maintenance of memory.

Your sentence: _____.

> ## H.   SELECTING A LEARNING/STUDY STRATEGY

Select the best answer.

   d   This reading contains numerous statistics about sleeplessness. The best way to learn these statistics for an upcoming multiple-choice exam would be to

a. map the entire reading.

b. reread the selection.

c. summarize the reading.

d. prepare a study sheet.

> ## I.   EXPLORING IDEAS THROUGH DISCUSSION AND WRITING

1. How did you do on the quiz in the first paragraph of the selection? Was the quiz successful in capturing your attention?

2. Have you ever experienced the effects of sleep deprivation? How do you think it affected your judgment? Your ability to learn? Your memory?

> ## J.   BEYOND THE CLASSROOM TO THE WEB

Visit the 2000 Omnibus Sleep in America Poll results at **http://www.sleep foundation.org/publications/2000poll.html#6.**

Study the tables in the Work and Sleep section of this survey report. What problems do workers report that stem from not getting enough sleep? Which of these problems are most widespread?

✔ Tracking Your Progress

Selection 39

Section	Number Correct		Score
A. Thesis and Main Idea (7 items)	_____	x 4	_____
B. Details (5 items)	_____	x 3	_____
C. Organization and Transitions (2 items)	_____	x 2	_____
E. Inferred Meanings (4 items)	_____	x 3	_____
F. Thinking Critically (7 items)	_____	x 3	_____
G. Vocabulary			
1. Context (7 items)	_____	x 2	_____
2. Word Parts (3 items)	_____	x 2	_____

TOTAL SCORE _____ %

CHECKING YOUR READING RATE

Words in Selection 39; 1,499

Finishing Time:	_____	_____	_____
	(hour)	(minutes)	(seconds)
Starting Time:	_____	_____	_____
	(hour)	(minutes)	(seconds)
Total Reading Time:		_____	_____
		(minutes)	(seconds)

Words Per Minute Score (page 739) _____ WPM

PART THREE

Textbook Chapter Readings

This part of the book contains two complete textbook chapters. Questions are included for each major section of each chapter, but these sets of questions appear at the end of the entire chapter, not after each section.

To work through the psychology chapter, for example, first turn to Psychology 1 and note which pages in the chapter it covers. Then read Previewing the Section, Making Connections, and the Reading Tip. After you complete these exercises, turn to the appropriate section of the psychology chapter and read the material. After you have finished reading, go to the After Reading exercises, begin with Understanding Main Ideas, and work through the remainder of the questions.

Please note that the page numbers mentioned in the exercises refer to the page numbering of the textbook chapter itself, not to the pages of this book.

Chapter 9

Behavior in Social
and Cultural Context

From
INVITATION TO PSYCHOLOGY

Carole Wade
Carol Tavris

9

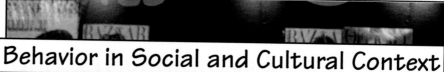

Behavior in Social and Cultural Context

PSYCHOLOGY IN THE NEWS

Homeowner Fatally Shoots Exchange Student in Cultural Misunderstanding

Slain exchange student Yoshihiro Hattori posed with his new American friends after arriving in the United States.

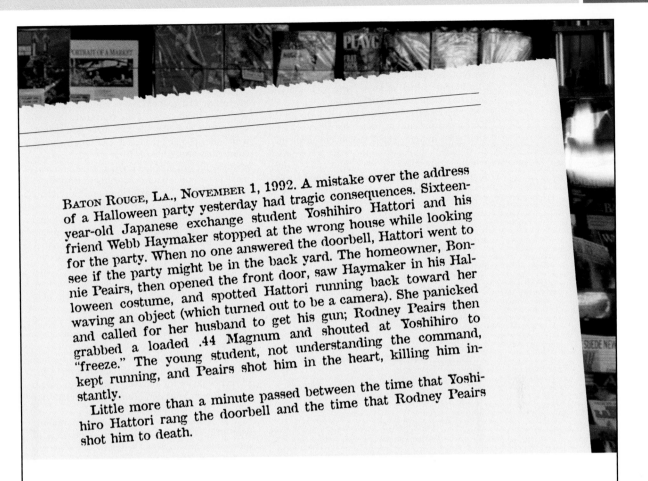

BATON ROUGE, LA., NOVEMBER 1, 1992. A mistake over the address of a Halloween party yesterday had tragic consequences. Sixteen-year-old Japanese exchange student Yoshihiro Hattori and his friend Webb Haymaker stopped at the wrong house while looking for the party. When no one answered the doorbell, Hattori went to see if the party might be in the back yard. The homeowner, Bonnie Peairs, then opened the front door, saw Haymaker in his Halloween costume, and spotted Hattori running back toward her waving an object (which turned out to be a camera). She panicked and called for her husband to get his gun; Rodney Peairs then grabbed a loaded .44 Magnum and shouted at Yoshihiro to "freeze." The young student, not understanding the command, kept running, and Peairs shot him in the heart, killing him instantly.

Little more than a minute passed between the time that Yoshihiro Hattori rang the doorbell and the time that Rodney Peairs shot him to death.

How would you explain the actions taken by Bonnie and Rodney Peairs? A learning theorist might seek an explanation in their individual histories, in the role models of violence that all Americans see in the media, and in the ways that handguns literally trigger aggressive behavior. Similarly, researchers in the fields of *social psychology* and *cultural psychology* address the many puzzles of human behavior by emphasizing the external environment rather than internal personality dynamics or individual pathology. But social and cultural psychologists broaden our vision by examining the entire sociocultural context in which an individual lives. *Social* psychologists study how social roles, attitudes, relationships, and groups influence people to do things they would not necessarily do on their own—act bravely, mindlessly, aggressively, or even cruelly. *Cultural* psychologists study the origins of roles, attitudes, and group norms in people's larger cultural worlds—their ethnic, regional, and national communities.

Together, social and cultural psychology cover a lot of territory, from first impressions on meeting a stranger to international diplomacy. In this book, we have already reported on sociocultural influences on child-rearing practices, moral development, and intelligence test scores. In later chapters we will discuss other

298   PART FOUR   Your Environment

areas of sociocultural research, including love and attachment, social processes in psychotherapy, and the communication of emotion.

In this chapter, however, we will focus on the basic social and cultural forces that affect behavior and make human beings less independent than they might think. As you read, ask yourself whether *you* would ever "shoot now and ask questions later," as Rodney Peairs did. Could a social situation or cultural attitude ever induce you to behave in a way that violates your code of ethics? Would you vote to convict Rodney Peairs or acquit him, and how does your culture affect your answer?

When Bonnie Peairs took the witness stand, she wept. "There was no thinking involved," she said. "I wish I could have thought. If I could have just thought." An awareness of social and cultural influences might help us all to act more mindfully and think more critically.

<hr>

What's Ahead

- *How do social rules guide behavior—and what is likely to happen when you violate them?*

- *Do you have to be mean or disturbed to inflict pain on someone just because an authority tells you to?*

- *How can ordinary college students be transformed into sadistic prison guards?*

- *How can people be "entrapped" into violating their moral principles?*

ROLES AND RULES

"We are all fragile creatures entwined in a cobweb of social constraints," social psychologist Stanley Milgram once said. The cobweb he referred to consists of social **norms,** rules about how we are supposed to act, enforced by threats of punishment if we violate them and promises of reward if we follow them (Kerr, 1995). Norms are the conventions of everyday life that make interactions with other people predictable and orderly. Every culture has norms, passed from one generation to another, for just about everything in the human-made environment: for conducting courtships, for raising children, for making decisions, for behavior in public places. Some norms are matters of law, such as, "A person may not beat up another person, except in self-defense." Some are unspoken cultural understandings, such as, "A man may beat up another man who insults his masculinity." And some are tiny, invisible regulations that people learn to follow unconsciously, such as, "You may not sing at the top of your lungs on a public bus."

Within any society, people fill a variety of social **roles,** positions that are regulated by norms about how people in those positions should behave. Gender roles define the proper behavior for a man and a woman. Occupational roles determine the correct behavior for a manager and an employee, a professor and a student. Family roles set tasks for parent and child, husband and wife.

Most people follow their culture's prescriptions without being conscious of them. When one of these prescriptions is violated, however, a person is likely to feel extremely uncomfortable. Other people may respond, whether intentionally or not, by making the violator feel guilty or inadequate. For instance, in your family, whose job is it to buy gifts for parents, send greeting cards to friends, organize parties, prepare the food, remember an aunt's birthday, and call friends to see how they're doing? Chances are you are thinking of a woman. These duties are considered part of the woman's role in most cultures, and women are usually blamed if they are not carried out (di Leonardo, 1987; Lott & Maluso, 1993). Similarly,

norms (social)
Social conventions that regulate human life, including explicit laws and implicit cultural standards.

role
A given social position that is governed by a set of norms for proper behavior.

Get Involved

Either alone or with a friend, try a mild form of "norm violation"—nothing alarming, obscene, dangerous, or offensive. For example, stand backward in line at the grocery store or cafeteria; sit right next to a stranger in the library or at a movie, even when other seats are available; sing or hum loudly for a couple of minutes in a public place; face the back wall of an elevator instead of the doors. Notice the reactions of onlookers, as well as your own feelings, while you violate this norm. (If you do this exercise with someone else, one of you can be the "violator" and the other can note the responses of onlookers; then switch places.) Was it easy to do this exercise? Why or why not?

Many roles in modern life require us to give up individuality, as conveyed by this dazzling image of white-suited referees at the Seoul Olympics. If each referee behaved out of role, the games could not continue. When is it appropriate to suppress your personal desires for the sake of the role, and when not?

what is likely to happen to a man who reveals his fears and worries although his culture's male gender role condemns such revelations as signs of weakness? Men who deviate from the masculine role by disclosing their emotions and fears are frequently regarded by both sexes as being "too feminine" and "poorly adjusted" (Peplau & Gordon, 1985; Taffel, 1990).

Naturally, people bring their own personalities and interests to the roles they play. Although two actresses who play the role of Cleopatra must follow the same script, you can bet that Kate Winslet and Whitney Houston will have different interpretations. In the same way, you will impose your own interpretation on the role of friend, parent, student, or employer. Nonetheless, the requirements of a social role affect nearly everyone who fills it, and they may even cause you to behave in ways that shatter your fundamental sense of who you are. We turn now to two classic and controversial studies that illuminate the power of social roles in our lives.

The Obedience Study

In the early 1960s, Stanley Milgram (1963, 1974) designed a study that was to become one of the most famous in all of psychology. Milgram wanted to know how many people would obey an authority figure when directly ordered to violate their own ethical standards. Participants in the study thought they were taking part in an experiment on the effects of punishment on learning.

Each was assigned, apparently at random, to the role of "teacher." Another person, introduced as a fellow volunteer, played the role of "learner." Whenever the learner, seated in an adjoining room, made an error in reciting a list of word pairs he was supposed to have memorized, the teacher had to give him an electric shock by depressing a lever on a machine (see Figure 9.1). With each error, the voltage (marked from 0 to 450) was to be increased by another 15 volts. The shock levels on the machine were labeled from SLIGHT SHOCK to DANGER—SEVERE SHOCK and, finally, ominously, XXX. In reality, the learners were confederates of Milgram and did not receive any shocks, but none of the teachers ever realized this during the experiment. The actor–victims played their parts convincingly: As the study continued, they shouted in pain and pleaded to be released, all according to a prearranged script.

When Milgram first designed this study, he asked a number of psychiatrists, students, and middle-class adults how many people they thought would "go all the way" to XXX on orders from the experimenter. The psychiatrists predicted that most people would refuse to go beyond 150 volts, the point at which the learner first demanded to be freed, and that only one person in a thousand, someone who was emotionally disturbed and sadistic, would administer the highest voltage. The nonprofessionals agreed with this prediction, and all of them said that they personally would disobey early in the experiment.

That's not the way the results turned out, however. Every single subject administered some

300   PART FOUR   Your Environment

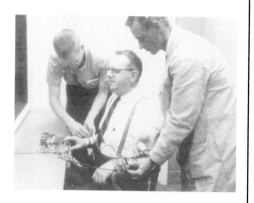

Figure 9.1

The Milgram Obedience Experiment

On the left is Milgram's original shock machine; in 1963, it looked pretty ominous. On the right, the "learner" is being strapped into his chair by the experimenter and the "teacher."

Copyright 1965 by Stanley Milgram. From the film OBEDIENCE, distributed by Penn State Media Sales.

shock to the learner, and about two-thirds of the participants, of all ages and from all walks of life, obeyed to the fullest extent. Many protested to the experimenter, but they backed down when he merely asserted, "The experiment requires that you continue." They obeyed no matter how much the victim shouted for them to stop and no matter how painful the shocks seemed to be. They obeyed even when they themselves were anguished about the pain they believed they were causing. They obeyed even as they wept and implored the experimenter to release them from further participation. As Milgram (1974) noted, participants would "sweat, tremble, stutter, bite their lips, groan, and dig their fingernails into their flesh"—but still they obeyed.

More than 1,000 participants at several American universities eventually went through the Milgram study. Most of them, men and women equally, inflicted what they thought were dangerous amounts of shock to another person (Blass, 1993). Researchers in at least eight other countries have also found high percentages of obedience, ranging to more than 90 percent in Spain and the Netherlands (Meeus & Raaijmakers, 1995; Smith & Bond, 1993/1994).

Milgram and his team subsequently set up several variations of the study to determine the circumstances under which people might disobey the experimenter. They found that virtually nothing the victim did or said changed the likelihood of the person's compliance—even when the victim said he had a heart condition, screamed in agony, or stopped responding entirely as if he had collapsed. However, people *were* more likely to disobey under the following conditions:

- *When the experimenter left the room.* Many people then subverted authority by giving low levels of

shock while reporting that they had followed orders.

- *When the victim was right there in the room,* and the teacher had to administer the shock directly to the victim's body.
- *When two experimenters issued conflicting demands* to continue the experiment or to stop at once. In this case, no one kept inflicting shock.
- *When the person issuing the orders was an ordinary man,* apparently another volunteer, instead of the authoritative experimenter.
- *When the subject worked with peers who refused to go further.* Seeing someone else rebel gave participants the courage to disobey.

Obedience, Milgram concluded, was more a function of the situation than of the particular personalities of the participants. "The key to [their] behavior," Milgram (1974) summarized, "lies not in pent-up anger or aggression but in the nature of their relationship to authority. They have given themselves to the authority; they see themselves as instruments for the execution of his wishes; once so defined, they are unable to break free."

The Milgram experiment has had its critics. Some consider it unethical because people were kept in the dark about what was really happening until the session was over (of course, telling them in advance would have invalidated the findings) and because many suffered emotional pain (Milgram countered that they wouldn't have felt pain if they had disobeyed instructions). Others question the conclusion that the situation often overrules personality; they note that some personality traits, such as hostility and authoritarianism, do predict obedience to authority in real life (Blass, 1993).

Some psychologists also object strenuously to the parallel Milgram drew between the behavior of his experimental volunteers and the brutality of Nazi doctors, concentration-camp executioners, and soldiers who massacre civilians. As John Darley (1995) noted, the people in Milgram's study obeyed only when the experimenter was hovering right there, and many of them felt enormous discomfort and conflict; in contrast, the defining characteristic of those who commit atrocities is that they do so without supervision by authorities, without external pressure, and without feelings of anguish.

Nevertheless, this experiment has had a tremendous influence on public awareness of the dangers of uncritical obedience. As Darley himself observed, "Milgram shows us the beginning of a path by means of which ordinary people, in the grip of social forces, become the origins of atrocities in the real world."

The Prison Study

Imagine that one day, as you are walking home from school, a police car pulls up. Two uniformed officers get out, arrest you, and take you to a prison cell. There you are stripped of your clothes, sprayed with delousing fluid, assigned a uniform, photographed with a prison number, and put behind bars. You feel a bit queasy, but you are not panicked because you have agreed to play the part of prisoner for two weeks and your arrest is merely part of the script. Your prison cell, while apparently authentic, is located in the basement of a university building.

So began an effort to discover what happens when ordinary college students take on the roles of prisoners and guards (Haney, Banks, & Zimbardo, 1973). The young men who volunteered for this study were paid a nice daily fee. They were randomly assigned to be prisoners or guards, but they were given no instructions about how to behave. The results were dramatic. Within a short time, the prisoners became distressed, helpless, and panicky. They developed emotional symptoms and physical ailments. Some became depressed and apathetic; others became rebellious and angry. After a few days, half of the prisoners begged to be let out. They were more than willing to forfeit their pay to gain an early release.

Within an equally short time, the guards adjusted to their new power. Some tried to be nice, helping the prisoners and doing little favors for them. Some were "tough but fair," holding strictly to "the rules." But about a third became tyrannical. Although they had complete freedom to use

any method to maintain order, they almost always chose to be abusive, even when the prisoners were not resisting in any way. One guard, unaware that he was being observed by the researchers, paced the corridor while the prisoners were sleeping, pounding his nightstick into his hand. Another put a prisoner in solitary confinement (a small closet) and tried to keep him there all night, concealing this information from the researchers, who, he thought, were "too soft" on the prisoners. Many guards were willing to work overtime without additional pay.

The researchers, who had not expected such a speedy and terrifying transformation of normal college students, ended this study after only six days. The prisoners were relieved by this decision, but most of the guards were disappointed. They had enjoyed their short-lived authority.

Critics of this research maintain that you can't learn much from such an artificial setup. They argue that the volunteers already knew, from movies, TV, and games, how they were supposed to behave. They acted their parts to the hilt, in order to have fun and not disappoint the researchers. Their behavior was no more surprising than if young men had been dressed in football gear and then had been found to be willing to bruise each other. For all its drama, say the critics, the study provided no new information (Festinger, 1980).

Philip Zimbardo, who designed the prison study, responds that this dramatization illustrated the power of roles in a way that no ordinary lab experiment could. After all, real prisoners and

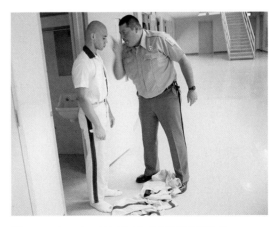

Prisoners and guards quickly learn their respective roles, as they have done at this correctional facility.

guards know their parts, too. Moreover, if the students were having so much fun, why did the prisoners beg for early release? Why did the guards lose sight of the "game" and behave as if it were a real job? Twenty-five years after the prison study was done, Zimbardo (1996) reflected on its contribution to psychology and to public awareness of how situations can outweigh personality in influencing behavior. The study showed, said Zimbardo, that roles can transform people as profoundly as the potion that transformed Dr. Jekyll into Mr. Hyde, especially when people cannot call upon past experience to guide their behavior and when their own habitual ways of behaving are not reinforced.

The Power of Roles

The two imaginative studies we have described vividly demonstrate the power of social roles and obligations to influence the behavior of individuals. The behavior of the prisoners and guards varied—some prisoners were more rebellious than others—some guards were more abusive than others—but ultimately, what the students did depended on the roles they were assigned. And whatever their personal traits, when people in the Milgram experiment believed they had to follow the legitimate orders of authority, most of them put their private values aside.

Obedience, of course, is not always harmful or bad. A certain amount of routine compliance with rules is necessary in any group, and obedience to authority can have constructive as well as destructive results (Darley, 1995). A nation could not operate if all its citizens ignored traffic signals, cheated on their taxes, dumped garbage wherever they chose, or assaulted each other. An organization could not function if its members came to work only when they felt like it. But obedience also has a darker aspect. Throughout history, the plea "I was only following orders" has been offered to excuse actions carried out on behalf of orders that were foolish, destructive, or illegal. The writer C. P. Snow once observed that "more hideous crimes have been committed in the name of obedience than in the name of rebellion."

Most people follow orders because of the obvious consequences of disobedience: They can be suspended from school, fired from their jobs, or arrested. They may also obey because they respect the authority who is giving the orders; because

they want to be liked; or because they hope to gain advantages. But what about all those obedient people in Milgram's experiment who felt they were doing wrong, who wished they were free, but who could not untangle themselves from the cobweb of social constraints? Why do people obey when it is not in their interests, or when obedience requires them to ignore their own values or even commit a crime?

Social psychologists Herbert Kelman and Lee Hamilton (1989) have studied "crimes of obedience," ranging from military massacres of civilians to bureaucratic crimes such as Watergate (in which Richard Nixon and his advisors tried to cover up the attempted theft of files from a Democratic headquarters) and the Iran–Contra scandal (in which Ronald Reagan's administration sold arms to Iran in order to unlawfully fund the Contra forces in Nicaragua). They and other researchers draw our attention to several factors that cause people to obey when they would rather not:

1. *Legitimization of the authority* allows people to absolve themselves of accountability for their actions. In Milgram's study, many of those who administered the highest levels of shock relinquished responsibility to the experimenter. A 37-year-old welder explained that the experimenter was responsible for any pain the victim might suffer "for the simple reason that I was paid for doing this. I had to follow orders." In contrast, individuals who refused to give high levels of shock took responsibility for their actions and refused to grant the authority legitimacy. "One of the things I think is very cowardly," said a 32-year-old engineer, "is to try to shove the responsibility onto someone else. See, if I now turned around and said, 'It's your fault . . . it's not mine,' I would call that cowardly" (Milgram, 1974).

2. *Routinization* is the process of defining an activity in terms of routine duties and roles so that your behavior becomes normalized, a job to be done, and there is little opportunity to raise doubts or ethical questions. In the Milgram study, some people became so fixated on the "learning task" that they shut out any moral concerns about the learner's demands to be let out. Routinization is typically the mechanism by which governments get citizens to aid and abet programs of genocide: German bureaucrats kept meticulous records of every Nazi victim, and in Cambodia, the Khmer Rouge recorded the names and histories of the millions of victims they tortured and

The routinization of horror enables people to commit or collaborate in atrocities. More than 16,000 political prisoners were tortured and killed at Tuol Sleng prison by members of Cambodia's Khmer Rouge, during the regime of Pol Pot. Prison authorities kept meticulous records and photos of each victim in order to make their barbarous activities seem mundane and normal. This man, Ing Pech, was one of only seven survivors, spared because he had skills useful to his captors. He now runs a memorial museum at the prison.

killed. "I am not a violent man," said Sous Thy, one of the clerks who recorded these names, to a reporter from the *New York Times*. "I was just making lists."

3. *The rules of good manners* smooth over the rough spots of social interaction, making relationships and civilization possible; but once people are caught in what they perceive to be legitimate roles and are obeying an authority, good manners ensnare them into further obedience. Most people don't like to rock the boat, challenge the experts, or appear to be rude because they know they will be disliked for doing so (Collins, 1993). And many lack the words to explain or justify disobedience. One woman in the Milgram study kept apologizing to the experimenter, trying not to offend him with her worries for the victim: "Do I go right to the end, sir? I hope there's nothing wrong with him there." (She did go right to the end.) A man repeatedly protested and questioned the experimenter, but he too obeyed, even when the victim had apparently collapsed in pain. "He thinks he is killing someone," Milgram (1974) commented, "yet he uses the language of the tea table."

4. *Entrapment* is a process in which individuals increase their commitment to a course of action in order to justify their investment in it (Brockner & Rubin, 1985). The first steps of entrapment pose no difficult choices, but one step leads to another, and before you realize it, you have become committed to a course of action that poses problems, and it is hard to free yourself. In Milgram's study, once participants had given a 15-volt shock, they had committed themselves to the experiment.

The next level was "only" 30 volts. Unless they resisted the authority soon afterward, they were likely to go on to administer what they believed were dangerously strong shocks. At that point, it was difficult to explain a sudden decision to quit (Modigliani & Rochat, 1995).

A chilling study of entrapment was conducted with 25 men who had served in the Greek military police during the authoritarian regime that ended in 1974 (Haritos-Fatouros, 1988). A psychologist who interviewed the men identified the steps used in training them to use torture when questioning prisoners. First the men were ordered to stand guard outside the interrogation cells. Then they stood guard in the detention rooms, where they observed the torture of prisoners. Then they "helped" beat up prisoners. Once they had obediently followed these orders and became actively involved, the torturers found their actions easier to carry out.

Many people expect solutions to moral problems to fall into two clear categories, with right on one side and wrong on the other. Yet in everyday life, as in the Milgram study, people often set out on a path that is morally ambiguous, only to find that they have traveled a long way toward violating their own principles. From Greece's cruel torturers to the Khmer Rouge's dutiful clerks to Milgram's "well-meaning" volunteers, people share the difficult task of drawing a line beyond which they will not go. Those who mindlessly succumb to the power of roles are less likely to hear the voice of conscience.

entrapment

A gradual process in which individuals escalate their commitment to a course of action to justify their investment of time, money, or effort.

???QUICK QUIZ

Step into your role as student to answer these questions.

1. About what percentage of the people in Milgram's obedience study administered the highest level of shock? (a) two-thirds, (b) one-half, (c) one-third, (d) one-tenth

2. Which of the following actions by the "learner" reduced the likelihood of being shocked by the "teacher" in Milgram's study? (a) protesting noisily, (b) screaming in pain, (c) complaining of having a heart ailment, (d) nothing he did made a difference

3. In the Milgram and Zimbardo studies, the participants' behavior was predicted most strongly by (a) their personality traits, (b) the dictates of conscience, (c) their assigned roles, (d) norms codified in law.

4. Suppose that a friend of yours, who is moving, asks you to bring over a few boxes. Since you are there anyway, he asks you to fill them with books, and before you know it, you have packed up his entire kitchen, living room, and bedroom. What social-psychological process is at work here?

5. Sam is having dinner with a group of fellow students when one of his friends tells a joke about how dumb women are. Sam is angry and disgusted but doesn't say anything. What social-psychological concept might help explain his silence?

Answers:
1. a 2. d 3. c 4. entrapment 5. the rules of good manners (and perhaps Sam also lacks the words to protest effectively)

What's Ahead

- *In what ways do people balance their ethnic identity and membership in the larger culture?*

- *What's one of the most common mistakes people make when explaining the behavior of others?*

- *What is the "Big Lie"—and why does it work so well?*

- *What's the difference between ordinary techniques of persuasion and the coercive techniques used by cults?*

social cognition

An area in social psychology concerned with social influences on thought, memory, perception, and other cognitive processes.

social identity

The part of a person's self-concept that is based on identification with a nation, culture, or ethnic group or with gender or other roles in society.

IDENTITY, ATTRIBUTIONS, AND ATTITUDES

Social psychologists are interested not only in what people do in social situations, but also in what goes on in their heads while they're doing it. Researchers in the area of **social cognition** examine how the social environment and relationships influence thoughts, beliefs, and memories; and how people's perceptions of themselves and one another affect their relationships (A. Fiske & Haslam, 1996). We will consider three important topics in this area: self-identity, attributions (explanations) about behavior, and the formation of attitudes.

Self-identity

Each of us, while growing up, develops a *personal identity*, a sense of who we are that is based on our own unique traits and history. In addition, we develop **social identities,** aspects of our self-concepts that are based on nationality, ethnicity, religion, and social roles (Brewer & Gardner, 1996; Hogg & Abrams, 1988). In Chapter 2, we saw that *collectivist cultures* and *individualist cultures* differ in how they balance the independence of the individual with social harmony within groups. But in all cultures, including individualist ones, social identities are an important part of people's self-concepts because they provide a feeling of place and position in the world. Without them, most of us would feel like loose marbles rolling around in an unconnected universe.

| Table 9.1 | Patterns of Ethnic Identity and Acculturation | | |

		Ethnic identity is	
		Strong	Weak
Acculturation is	Strong	Bicultural	Assimilated
	Weak	Separatist	Marginal

In multicultural societies such as the United States, different social identities sometimes collide. In particular, people often face the dilemma of balancing an **ethnic identity,** a close identification with a religious or ethnic group, with **acculturation,** an identification with the dominant culture (Cross, 1971; Phinney, 1996; Spencer & Dornbusch, 1990). As Table 9.1 shows, four outcomes are possible, depending on whether ethnic identity is strong or weak, and whether identification with the larger culture is strong or weak (Berry, 1994; Phinney, 1990).

People who are *bicultural* have strong ties both to their ethnicity and to the larger culture: They say, "I am proud of my ethnic heritage, but I identify just as much with my new country." They can alternate easily between their culture of origin and the majority culture, slipping into the customs and language of each, as circumstances dictate (LaFromboise, Coleman, & Gerton, 1993). People who choose *assimilation* have weak feelings of ethnicity but a strong sense of acculturation: Their attitude, for example, might be "I'm an American, period." *Ethnic separatists* have a strong sense of ethnic identity but weak feelings of acculturation: They may say, "My ethnicity comes first; if I join the mainstream, I'm betraying my origins." And some people feel *marginal,* connected to neither their ethnicity nor the dominant culture: They may say, "I'm an individual and don't identify with any group" or "I don't belong anywhere."

Some of the conflicts between cultural groups in North America stem from disagreements about how (or even whether) acculturation and ethnic identity should be balanced. These tensions are reflected in the touchy subject of what groups should be called. Because this issue is understandably emotional for many people, they fail to question their own assumptions—and fail to realize that even within ethnic groups, there are different views. For example, the label *Hispanic* is used by the U.S. government to include all Spanish-speaking groups, but many "Hispanics" dislike the term. Some prefer *Latino* and *Latina,* or, for Mexican-Americans, *Chicano* and *Chicana;* others prefer national-origin labels such as Cuban or Cuban-American, or just

Thinking Critically About Ethnic Labels

These children are observing the December festival of Kwanzaa, an African-American holiday that celebrates traditional African spiritual values. In a culturally diverse society, many people maintain a strong attachment to their ethnic heritage.

ethnic identity
A person's identification with a racial, religious, or ethnic group.

acculturation
The process by which members of minority groups come to identify with and feel part of the mainstream culture.

306   PART FOUR   Your Environment

The tension in America between ethnic identity and acculturation was apparent during the 1996 Hispanic March on Washington, when thousands of Hispanic Americans demanded rights for immigrants—while waving flags from their countries of origin. To the demonstrators, the flags symbolized pride in their heritage, but many other Americans regarded the flags as evidence of the demonstrators' lack of commitment to the United States. What would be your interpretation?

American (de la Garza et al., 1992). Similarly, although *African-American* is now widely accepted, some blacks reject the term because they feel no special kinship to Africa. For that matter, not all white Americans want to be called Anglos, which refers to a British heritage, or European-American, as if all European countries, from Greece to Norway, France to Poland, were the same. And the growing numbers of people of multiethnic backgrounds are exasperated by society's efforts to squeeze them into a single category—which is why the U.S. government has finally decided to include a multiethnic category in its census. Debates about ethnic labels, and about the proper balance between ethnicity and acculturation, are likely to continue, as ethnic groups struggle to define their place in a medley of cultures.

attribution theory
The theory that people are motivated to explain their own and other people's behavior by attributing causes of that behavior to a situation or a disposition.

fundamental attribution error
The tendency, in explaining other people's behavior, to overestimate personality factors and underestimate the influence of the situation.

Attributions

Detective stories are known as "whodunits," but real life is a "*why*dunit": Everyone wants to know *why* people do what they do. Is it something in people's genes, their upbringing, or their current circumstances? According to **attribution theory,**

the explanations we make of our own behavior and the behavior of others generally fall into two categories. When we make a *situational attribution,* we are identifying the cause of an action as something in the environment: "Joe stole the money because his family is starving." When we make a *dispositional attribution,* we are identifying the cause of an action as something in the person, such as a trait or a motive: "Joe stole the money because he is a born thief."

Social psychologists have discovered some of the conditions in which people prefer situational or dispositional attributions. For example, when people are trying to find reasons for someone else's behavior, one of the most common mistakes they make is to overestimate personality factors and underestimate the influence of the situation (Nisbett & Ross, 1980). This tendency has been called the **fundamental attribution error.** Were the hundreds of people who obeyed Milgram's experimenters sadistic by nature? Were the student guards in the prison study basically mean and the prisoners basically cowardly? Those who think so are committing the fundamental attribution error.

People are especially likely to overlook situational attributions when they are distracted or preoccupied and don't have time to ask themselves, for example, "Why, exactly, *is* Aurelia behaving like a dork today?" Instead, they leap to the easiest attribution, which is dispositional: Aurelia simply has a dorky personality.

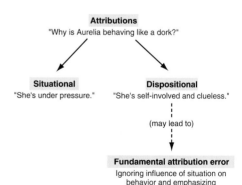

Attributions
"Why is Aurelia behaving like a dork?"

Situational
"She's under pressure."

Dispositional
"She's self-involved and clueless."

(may lead to)

Fundamental attribution error
Ignoring influence of situation on behavior and emphasizing personality traits alone

So powerful is this bias that people will often make a dispositional attribution even when they know that a person had no choice about how to act in a particular setting (Taylor, Peplau, & Sears, 1997).

The fundamental attribution error is especially prevalent in Western nations, where middle-class people tend to believe that individuals are responsible for their own actions. In countries such as India, where everyone is deeply embedded in caste and family networks, and in Japan, China, and Hong Kong, where people are more group oriented than in the West, people are more likely to recognize situational constraints on behavior (Lee, Hallahan, & Herzog, 1996; Morris & Peng, 1994). Thus if someone is behaving oddly, makes a mistake at work, or plays badly in a soccer match, an Indian or Chinese, unlike a Westerner, is more likely to make a situational attribution of the person's behavior ("He's under pressure") than a dispositional one ("He's incompetent").

Westerners do not always prefer dispositional attributions, however. When it comes to explaining their *own* behavior, they often have a **self-serving bias:** They tend to choose attributions that are favorable to them, taking credit for their good actions (a dispositional attribution) but letting the situation account for their bad ones. For instance, most Westerners, when angry, will say, "I am furious for good reason—this situation is intolerable." They are less likely to say, "I am furious because I am an ill-tempered grinch." On the other hand, if they do something admirable, such as donating money to charity, they are likely to attribute their motives to a personal disposition ("I'm so generous") instead of the situation ("That guy on the phone pressured me into it").

Like the fundamental attribution error, the self-serving bias is more common in some situations and cultures than in others. For example, in Japan, heads of companies are expected to take responsibility not only for their own failings, but also for the failings of their employees or products—and they do (Hamilton & Sanders, 1992; Markus & Kitayama, 1991). In the United States, in contrast, the common practice is for heads of corporations to get huge salaries and bonuses even when the company is doing poorly, and to blame the economy, government policies, or their employees if something goes wrong. (Of course, many Americans also deny responsibility for their mistakes because they fear lawsuits.)

People's attributions are also affected by the need to believe that the world is fair, that good people are rewarded and villains punished. According to the **just-world hypothesis** (Lerner, 1980), the belief in a just world helps people make sense out of senseless events and feel safe in the presence of threatening events. It often leads to a dispositional attribution called *blaming the victim.* If a friend loses his job, if a woman is raped, if a prisoner is tortured, it is reassuring to think that they all must have done something to deserve what happened, or at least to cause it. This kind of attribution was apparent in the Milgram study: Many of the "teachers" spoke harshly of the learner. "Such comments as, 'He was so stupid and stubborn he deserved to get shocked,' were common," wrote Milgram (1974).

Of course, most human actions are determined both by personality and by environment. Therefore, attributing someone else's behavior to a disposition, or explaining your own behavior in terms of noble motives, is not always an error. The point to keep is mind is that attributions, whether they are accurate or not, have important consequences for decisions, actions, emotions, and everyday relations. Happy couples, for example, tend to attribute their partners' occasional lapses to something in the situation ("Poor Harold is under a lot of stress at work"), whereas unhappy couples tend to make dispositional attributions ("Harold is a thoughtless, selfish skunk") (Fincham & Bradbury, 1993; Karney et al., 1994). As you can imagine, your attributions about your partner will make a big difference in how the two of you get along—and how long you'll put up with the person!

Attitudes

People hold attitudes about all sorts of things—politics, people, food, children, movies, sports heroes, you name it. An *attitude* is a relatively stable opinion containing a cognitive element (perceptions and beliefs about the topic) and an emotional element (feelings about the topic, which can range from negative and hostile to positive and loving).

Where Do Attitudes Come From?   Most people think their attitudes are based on reasoned conclusions about how things work. Sometimes, of course, that's true. But social psychologists have found that some attitudes are a result of not thinking at all. They are a result of conformity, habit, rationalization, economic self-interest, and many subtle social and environmental influences.

Some attitudes, for example, arise by virtue of the *cohort effect.* Each generation, or age cohort, has its own experiences and economic concerns, and therefore its own characteristic opinions about the world. The ages of 16 to 24 appear to be critical for the formation of these attitudes; a

self-serving bias

The tendency, in explaining one's own behavior, to take credit for one's good actions and rationalize one's mistakes.

just-world hypothesis

The notion that many people need to believe that the world is fair and that justice is served; that bad people are punished and good people rewarded.

survey of the American population found that the major political events and social changes that occur during these years make deeper impressions and exert a more lasting influence than those that happen later in a person's life (Schuman & Scott, 1989). Some of the key events that have affected American generational cohorts in this century include the Great Depression (1930s), World War II (1940s), the dropping of the atomic bomb on Hiroshima (1945), the rise of the civil rights movement (1950s–1960s), the assassination of John F. Kennedy (1963), the Vietnam War (1965–1973), the rebirth of the women's rights movement (1970s), and the legalization of abortion (1973). People who were between 16 and 24 when these events occurred regard them as "peak memories" that have shaped their political philosophy, values, and attitudes about life. (What do you think might be the critical generational events affecting the attitudes of your own cohort?)

Psychologists have argued for years about which comes first, attitudes or behavior. Of

cognitive dissonance

A state of tension that occurs when a person simultaneously holds two cognitions that are psychologically inconsistent, or when a person's belief is incongruent with his or her behavior.

validity effect

The tendency of people to believe that a statement is true or valid simply because it has been repeated many times.

Each age group has a generational identity that stems from shared experiences and values. What, if any, are the defining experiences of "Generation X," those who are in their twenties today, or of the as-yet-nameless generation of those who are now in their teens? The news media keep trying to find the answer!

course, attitudes often dispose people to behave in certain ways (Kraus, 1995); if you have a positive attitude toward martial-arts movies, you'll go to as many as you can, and if you hate them, you'll probably stay away from them. But it also works the other way around: Changing behavior can lead to a change in attitude because the new behavior alters a person's knowledge or experience. Suppose you dislike exercise and have always avoided it, but your friend persuades you to begin jogging with her. Once you get the hang of it, you may find that you enjoy it and that your attitude has completely changed.

A change in behavior may also lead to a change in attitudes because of **cognitive dissonance,** which we discussed in Chapter 6. Cognitive dissonance is the uncomfortable feeling that occurs when two attitudes, or an attitude and behavior, are in conflict (are dissonant). People are often motivated to resolve this dissonance by changing their attitudes. For example, if a politician or celebrity you admire does something immoral or illegal, you can reduce the dissonance by changing your attitude toward the person ("Guess he's not such a swell guy after all") or toward the person's behavior ("It's not so bad; everyone does it").

Friendly Persuasion.   All around you, every day, people are trying to get you to change your attitudes. One weapon they use is the drip, drip, drip of a repeated idea. Repeated exposure even to a nonsense syllable such as *zug* is enough to make a person feel more positive toward it (Zajonc, 1968). The effectiveness of familiarity has long been known to politicians and advertisers: Repeat something often enough, even the basest lie, and eventually the public will believe it. Indeed, the Nazis called this phenomenon the "Big Lie." Its formal name is the **validity effect.**

In a series of experiments, Hal Arkes and his associates demonstrated how the validity effect operates (Arkes, 1991; Arkes, Boehm, & Xu, 1991; Boehm, 1994). In a typical study, people read a list of statements, such as "Mercury has a higher boiling point than copper" or "Over 400 Hollywood films were produced in 1948." The participants had to rate each statement for its validity, where "1" meant that the rater thought the statement was definitely false and "7" that it was definitely true. A week or two later, they again rated the validity of some of these statements and also rated others they hadn't seen previously. The result: Mere repetition increased the perception that the familiar statements were true. The same effect also occurred for unverifiable opinions (e.g., "At least 75 percent of all politicians are basically dishonest"), opinions that people initially felt were true, and even opinions that they initially felt were false. "Note that no attempt has been made to persuade," wrote Arkes (1991). "No supporting arguments are offered. We just have subjects rate the statements. Mere repetition seems to increase rated validity. This is scary."

Another effective technique for getting people to change their minds is to have your arguments presented by someone who is admired or attractive—which is why advertisements are full of beautiful models, sports heroes, and "experts" (Cialdini, 1993). Persuaders may also try to link their message with a good feeling. In one classic study, students who were given peanuts and Pepsi while listening to a speaker's point of view were more likely to be convinced by it than were students who listened without the pleasant munchies and soft drinks (Janis, Kaye, & Kirschner, 1965). Perhaps this explains why so much business is conducted over lunch, and so many courtships over dinner!

In sum, here are 3 good ways to affect attitudes:

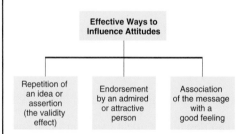

Effective Ways to Influence Attitudes

Repetition of an idea or assertion (the validity effect)	Endorsement by an admired or attractive person	Association of the message with a good feeling

In contrast, the emotion of fear can cause people to resist arguments that are in their own best interest (Pratkanis & Aronson, 1992). Fear tactics are often used to try to persuade people to quit smoking or abusing other drugs, drive only when sober, use condoms, check for signs of cancer, and prepare for earthquakes. However, fear works only if people become moderately anxious, not scared to death, *and* if the message also provides information about how to avoid the danger (Leventhal & Nerenz, 1982). When messages about a potential disaster are too terrifying and when people believe that they can do nothing to avoid it, they tend to deny the danger.

Coercive Persuasion.   Sometimes, efforts to change attitudes go beyond exposing people to a new idea and persuading them to accept it. The

FEELING NO PAIN

IF YOU DRINK, DON'T DRIVE.

R. Roy McMurtry
Attorney General

Would this ad keep you from drinking and driving? Ads that arouse fear often backfire. Successful campaigns to prevent drunk driving include increased penalties, efforts to change social norms by making drunk driving "uncool," promoting the use of designated drivers, and providing other transportation, such as free cab rides.

manipulator uses harsh tactics, not just hoping that people will change their minds, but attempting to force them to. These tactics are sometimes referred to as *brainwashing*, a term first used during the Korean War to describe techniques used on American prisoners of war to get them to collaborate with their Chinese Communist captors and to endorse anti-American propaganda. Most psychologists, however, prefer the phrase *coercive persuasion.* "Brainwashing," they argue, implies that a person has a sudden change of mind and is unaware of what is happening. **Thinking Critically About "Brainwashing"** It sounds mysterious and powerful. In fact, the methods involved are neither mysterious nor unusual. The difference between "persuasion" and "brainwashing" is often only a matter of degree and the observer's bias, just as a group that is a crazy cult to one person may be a group of devoutly religious people to another.

How, then, might we distinguish coercive persuasion from the usual techniques of persuasion that occur in daily life? Studies of religious, political, and other cults have identified some of the processes by which individuals can be coerced by these groups (Galanter, 1989; Mithers, 1994; Ofshe & Watters, 1994; Singer, Temerlin, & Langone, 1990; Zimbardo & Leippe, 1991):

1. *The person is put under physical or emotional distress.* The individual may not be allowed to eat, sleep, or exercise; may be isolated in a dark room with no stimulation or food; or may be induced into a trancelike state through repetitive chanting, hypnosis, or deep relaxation.

2. *The person's problems are defined simplistically, and simple answers are offered repeatedly.* There are as many of these answers as there are persuasive groups. Here are some actual examples: Are you afraid or unhappy? It all stems from the pain of being born. Are you worried about homeless earthquake victims? It's not your problem; victims are responsible for everything that happens to them. Are you struggling financially? It's your fault for not wanting to be rich fervently enough.

3. *The leader offers unconditional love, acceptance, and attention.* A new recruit may be given a "love

bath" from the group—constant praise, support, applause, and affection. Positive emotions of euphoria and well-being are generated. In exchange, the leader demands everyone's attachment, adoration, and idealization.

4. *A new identity based on the group is created.* The recruit is told that he or she is part of the chosen, the elite, the redeemed. To foster this new identity, many cults have their members wear identifying clothes or eat special diets, and they assign each member a new name. All members of the Philadelphia group MOVE were given the last name "Africa"; all members of the Church of Armageddon took the last name "Israel."

5. *The person is subjected to entrapment.* At first, the person agrees only to small things, but gradually the demands become greater: for example, to spend a weekend with the group, then take weekly seminars, then advanced courses. During the Korean War, the Chinese first got the American POWs to agree with mild remarks, such as "The United States is not perfect." Then the POWs had to add their own examples of the imperfections. At the end, they were signing their names to anti-American broadcasts (Schein, Schneier, & Barker, 1961).

6. *The person's access to information is severely controlled.* As soon as a person is a committed believer or follower, the group limits the person's choices, denigrates critical thinking, makes fun of doubts, and insists that any private distress is due to lack of belief in the group. The person may be isolated from the outside world and thus from antidotes to the leader's ideas. Members may be taught to hate certain "evil" enemies: parents, capitalists, blacks, whites, nonbelievers. Total conformity is demanded.

Even in groups that allow members to leave freely, you can see many of these strategies in operation. In the Heaven's Gate cult, for example, the leader, Marshall Applewhite, offered members a new identity (as extraterrestrials in human bodies) and a simplistic solution to their problems (suicide would free them to be whisked away to a spaceship hiding in the tail of the Hale-Bopp comet). He encouraged members to sever their relationships with friends and relatives, had them dress alike, and censored all dissenting opinions. By all accounts, his followers were pleasant, nice people, and many were well-educated. Most of them would probably not have considered killing themselves when they first joined the group. Yet eventually, 38 men and women, along with Applewhite, did just that.

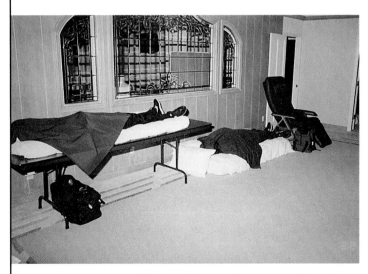

Cults persuade their members to suppress all signs of individual identity and yield to the will of the leader—even when the leader requires mass suicide, as he did in the Heaven's Gate cult. Police found 39 identically clad bodies laid out on beds or tables, all but 2 of them covered by purple cloths and each with a packed suitcase nearby. The members all had close-cropped hair, and despite their differences in age and sex, they looked so much alike that at first the police mistakenly thought they were all young men.

Research on persuasion, like the research on roles, shows us that you do not have to be evil to do evil things, stupid to do self-destructive things, or crazy to do irrational things. Some people may be more vulnerable than others to coercive tactics, but these techniques are powerful enough to overwhelm even strong, well-educated individuals.

???QUICK QUIZ

Now, how can we persuade you to take this quiz without using coercion?

1. Frank, an African-American student, finds himself caught between two philosophies on his campus. One holds that blacks should move toward full integration into mainstream culture. The other holds that blacks should immerse themselves in the history, values, and contributions of African culture. Frank is caught between his _____ and _____.

2. In each of the following cases, what kind of attribution is being made—situational or dispositional? (a) A man says, "My wife has sure become a grouchy person." (b) The same man says, "I'm grouchy because I've had a bad day at the office." (c) A woman reads about high unemployment in inner-city communities and says, "Well, if those people weren't so lazy, they would find work."

3. What principles of attribution theory are suggested by the items in the preceding question?

4. Candidate Carson spends $3 million to make sure his name is seen and heard frequently, and to repeat unverified charges that his opponent is a thief. What psychological phenomenon is he relying on to win?

5. Your best friend urges you to join a "life-renewal" group called "The Feeling Life." Your friend has been spending increasing amounts of time with her fellow Feelies, and you have some doubts about them. What questions would you want to have answered before joining up?

Answers: 1. ethnic identity and acculturation 2. a. dispositional b. situational c. dispositional 3. Item a illustrates the fundamental attribution error; b. the self-serving bias; and c. blaming the victim because of the just-world hypothesis. 4. the validity effect 5. A few things to consider: Is there an autocratic leader who tolerates no dissent or criticism, while rationalizing this practice as a benefit for members? ("Doubt and disbelief are signs that your feeling side is being repressed.") Have long-standing members given up their friends, families, interests, and ambitions for this group? Does the leader offer simple but unrealistic promises to repair your life and all that troubles you? Are members required to make extreme sacrifices by donating large amounts of time and money?

What's Ahead

- Why do people in groups often go along with the majority even when the majority is dead wrong?

- How can "groupthink" lead to bad—even catastrophic—decisions?

- Why is it common for a group of people to hear someone shout for help without one of them calling the police?

- What enables some people to dissent, take moral action, or blow the whistle on wrongdoers?

INDIVIDUALS IN GROUPS

Even when a group is not at all coercive, something happens to individuals when they join a bunch of other people. They act differently than they would on their own, regardless of whether the group has convened to solve problems and make decisions, has gathered to have fun, consists of anonymous bystanders, or is just a loose collection of individuals waiting around in a room. The decisions group members make and the actions they take may depend less on their own desires than on the structure and dynamics of the group itself.

Conformity

One thing people in groups do is conform, taking action or adopting attitudes as a result of real or imagined pressures.

Suppose that you are required to appear at a psychology laboratory for an experiment on perception. You join seven other students seated in a room. You are shown a 10-inch line and asked which of three other lines is identical to it:

Test line   A   B   C

The correct answer, line A, is obvious, so you are amused when the first person in the group chooses line B. "Bad eyesight," you say to yourself. "He's off by 2 whole inches!" The second person also chooses line B. "What a dope," you think. But by the time the fifth person has chosen line B, you are beginning to doubt yourself. The sixth and seventh students also choose line B, and now you are worried about *your* eyesight. The experimenter looks at you. "Your turn," he says. Do you follow the evidence of your own eyes or the collective judgment of the group?

This was the design for a series of famous studies of conformity conducted by Solomon Asch (1952, 1965). The seven "nearsighted" students were actually Asch's confederates. Asch wanted to know what people would do when a group unanimously contradicted an obvious fact. He found that when people made the line comparisons on their own, they were almost always accurate. But in the group, only 20 percent of the students remained completely independent on every trial, and often they were apologetic for not going along. One-third conformed to the group's incorrect decision more than half the time, and the rest conformed at least some of the time. Whether they conformed or not, the students often felt uncertain of their decision. As one participant later said, "I felt disturbed, puzzled, separated, like an outcast from the rest."

Asch's experiment has been replicated many times over the years, in the United States and in many other countries. A meta-analysis of 133 studies in 17 countries revealed three general findings (Bond & Smith, 1996). First, in America, conformity has declined since Asch's work in the 1950s, suggesting that conformity reflects prevailing social norms. Second, people in individualistic cultures, such as that of the United States, are less likely to conform than are people in group-oriented cultures, where social harmony is more highly valued than individual assertiveness. Third, regardless of culture, conformity increases as the stimulus becomes more ambiguous, as the number of accomplices giving the wrong answer increases, and as members of the group become more alike in age, ethnicity, gender, and so on.

Like obedience, conformity has both its positive and its negative sides. Society runs more smoothly

Sometimes people like to conform in order to feel part of the group . . .

. . . and sometimes they like to rebel a little in order to assert their individuality.

when people know how to behave in a given situation and when they go along with cultural rules of dress and manners. But conformity can also suppress critical thinking and creativity. In a group, many people will deny their private beliefs, agree with silly notions, and violate their own values (Aronson, 1995; Cialdini, 1993). Some do so because they identify with group members and want to be like them in dress, attitudes, or behavior. Some want to be liked and know that disagreeing with a group can make them unpopular. Some believe the group has knowledge or abilities that are superior to their own. And some go along out of pure self-interest—to keep their jobs, win promotions, or win votes.

Groupthink

Close, friendly groups usually work well together, but they also face the problem of how to get the best ideas and efforts of their members while reducing the risk of conformity. In particular, members of such groups must avoid a problem called **groupthink,** the tendency for all members to think alike and to suppress dissent. According to Irving Janis (1982, 1989), groupthink occurs when a group's need for total agreement overwhelms its need to make the wisest decision, and when the members' needs to be liked and accepted overwhelm their ability to disagree with a bad decision.

Throughout history, groupthink has resulted in disastrous military decisions, as two American examples illustrate. In 1961, President John F. Kennedy, after meeting with his advisers, approved a CIA plan to invade Cuba at the Bay of Pigs and overthrow the government of Fidel Castro; the invasion was a humiliating disaster. In the mid-1960s, President Lyndon Johnson and his cabinet escalated the war in Vietnam in spite of obvious signs that further bombing and increased troops were not bringing the war to an end. Janis (1982) examined the historical records pertaining to these two decisions and identified typical features of groups that are susceptible to groupthink: They are highly cohesive; they are isolated from other viewpoints; they feel under pressure from outside forces; and they have a strong, directive leader. Under these conditions, the following symptoms of groupthink tend to appear:

- *An illusion of invulnerability.* The group believes that it can do no wrong, that it is 100 percent correct in its decisions.

- *Self-censorship.* Dissenters decide to keep quiet in order not to rock the boat, offend their friends, or risk being ridiculed. For example, Arthur Schlesinger, a college professor who was one of Kennedy's advisers, decided not to express his doubts about the Bay of Pigs invasion because he feared others would regard him as presumptuous for disagreeing with high government officials.
- *Direct pressure on dissenters to conform,* either by the leader or other group members. For example, President Johnson, who favored increased bombing of North Vietnam, ridiculed his adviser Bill Moyers by greeting him with "Well, here comes Mr. Stop-the-Bombing."
- *An illusion of unanimity.* By discouraging dissent, leaders and group members create an illusion of consensus. Arthur Schlesinger did eventually voice his doubts to the secretary of state, who passed them along to Kennedy, who was not pleased. When it came time to vote on whether to invade, Kennedy asked each of his advisers to voice an opinion—except for Schlesinger.

Fortunately, groupthink can sometimes be counteracted by creating conditions that explicitly encourage and reward the expression of doubt and dissent—for example, by basing decisions on majority rule instead of unanimity (Kameda & Sugimori, 1993). President Kennedy apparently learned this lesson from the Bay of Pigs decision. In his next major foreign policy decision, during the 1962 crisis over missiles placed in Cuba by the Soviet Union, Kennedy brought in outside experts to advise his inner circle, often absented himself from the group so as not to influence their discussions, and encouraged free debate between the "hawks" and the "doves" (Aronson, Wilson, & Akert, 1997; May & Zelikow, 1997). The crisis, one of the most dangerous in post-World War II history, was resolved peacefully.

groupthink
In close-knit groups, the tendency for all members to think alike for the sake of harmony and to suppress dissent.

Of course, it is easy to see *after the fact* how conformity contributed to a bad decision or open debate led to a good one. If we want to predict whether a group will make good or bad decisions in the future, however, we need to know its history, the nature of the decision to be made, the characteristics of the leader, and many other things (Aldag & Fuller, 1993). Nevertheless, Janis put his finger on a phenomenon that many people have experienced: individual members of a group suppressing their real opinions and doubts so as to be good team players.

The Anonymous Crowd

Many years ago, in an incident that received much public attention, a woman named Kitty Genovese was stabbed repeatedly in front of her apartment building. She screamed for help for more than half an hour, but not one of the 38 neighbors who heard her, who came to their windows to watch, even called the police. Kitty Genovese was a victim of a process called the **diffusion of responsibility,** in which responsibility for an outcome is diffused, or spread, among many people, and individuals fail to take action because they believe that someone else will do so. The many reports of *bystander apathy* in the news—people watching as a woman is attacked, as a man struggles with a stalled car on a freeway, as a child is eventually beaten to death by disturbed parents—reflect the diffusion of responsibility on a large scale.

In work groups, the diffusion of responsibility sometimes takes the form of *social loafing:* Each member of a team slows down, letting others work harder (Karau & Williams, 1993; Latané,

Williams, & Harkins, 1979). This slowdown of effort and abdication of responsibility does not happen in all groups. It occurs primarily when individual group members are not accountable for the work they do; when people feel that working harder would only duplicate their colleagues' efforts; when workers feel exploited; or when the work itself is uninteresting (Shepperd, 1995). When the challenge of the job is increased or when each member of the group has a different, important job to do, the sense of individual responsibility rises, and loafing declines. Loafing also declines when people know their group's performance will be evaluated against that of another group, or if they are working on a group project that really matters to them (Harkins & Szymanski, 1989; Williams & Karau, 1991).

The most extreme instances of the diffusion of responsibility occur when members of a group lose all awareness of their individuality and sense of self, a state called **deindividuation** (Festinger, Pepitone, & Newcomb, 1952). Deindividuated people "forget themselves"; they are more likely to act mindlessly, and their behavior becomes disconnected from their values. They may do destructive things: break store windows, loot, get into fights, riot at a sports event, or commit rape. Or they may become more friendly; think of all the chatty people on buses and planes who reveal things to their seatmates they would never tell anyone they knew. Not surprisingly, deindividuation increases in situations that make people feel anonymous. It is more likely to occur when a person is in a large city rather than a small town; in a faceless mob rather than an intimate group; when signs of individuality are covered by uniforms or masks; or in a large and impersonal class of hundreds of students rather than a small class of only 15.

diffusion of responsibility

In organized or anonymous groups, the tendency of members to avoid taking responsibility for actions or decisions, assuming that others will do so.

deindividuation

In groups or crowds, the loss of awareness of one's own individuality and the abdication of mindful action.

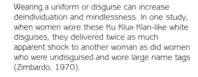

Wearing a uniform or disguise can increase deindividuation and mindlessness. In one study, when women wore these Ku Klux Klan-like white disguises, they delivered twice as much apparent shock to another woman as did women who were undisguised and wore large name tags (Zimbardo, 1970).

Get Involved

For this exercise in deindividuation, choose two situations: one in which you are one of many people, perhaps hundreds (as in a large classroom or a concert audience); and one in which you are one of a few (as in a small discussion group). In both situations, close your eyes and pretend to fall asleep. Is this easier to do in one context than in the other? Why? In each case, what is the reaction of other people around you?

Just as extreme deindividuation has its hazards, so does extreme *individuation*, which can cause people to become too self-aware and self-focused, and to forget their dependence on others. Cultures that emphasize the importance of individual action consider deindividuation a bad thing, but those that emphasize the importance of social cohesiveness see it differently. Asians are on the average less individuated than whites, blacks, and Latinos, reflecting the Asian cultural emphasis on social harmony (Maslach, Stapp, & Santee, 1985).

Courage and Nonconformity

We have seen how social roles and cultural norms can cause people to obey orders or conform to ideas that they believe are wrong. Sometimes, however, people have disobeyed such orders or have gone against prevailing beliefs, and their actions have changed the course of history. Many blacks and whites disobeyed the laws of segregation. Many individuals have stopped conforming to traditional gender roles. Many men and women have decided to "blow the whistle" on company or government practices they consider immoral or unfair, risking their jobs and friendships to do so (Glazer & Glazer, 1990).

Dissent and *altruism*, the willingness to take selfless or dangerous action on behalf of others, are in part a matter of personal convictions and conscience. The Quakers and other white abolitionists who risked their lives to help blacks escape their captors before the Civil War did so because they believed in the inherent evil of slavery. In the former Soviet Union, a KGB officer named Viktor Orekhov secretly informed political dissidents of planned KGB action against them, thereby saving hundreds of people from arrests and grueling interrogations. Orekhov was eventually caught and spent eight years in a Soviet jail. On his release, he explained why he felt he had to help the protest-

ers: "I was afraid that [unless I acted] my children would be ashamed of me" (Fogelman, 1994).

However, just as there are many external reasons for obedience and conformity, so there are many external influences on a person's decision to dissent, take moral action, or help a stranger in trouble. Instead of condemning bystanders and conformists for their laziness or cowardice, social psychologists have identified the social and situational factors that predict independent actions such as whistle-blowing, voicing a minority opinion, or helping others:

1. *The individual perceives the need for intervention or help.* It may seem obvious, but before people can take independent action, they must realize that such action is necessary. Unfortunately, sometimes people willfully blind themselves to this need in order to justify their own inaction. During World War II, the German citizens of Dachau didn't "see" the local concentration camp, although it was in plain view. Similarly, many employees choose not to see flagrant examples of bribery and other illegal actions. Blindness to the need for action also occurs when people have too many demands on their attention. Workers who must juggle many demands on their time cannot stop to correct every problem they notice. Likewise, residents of crowded, densely populated cities cannot stop to offer help to everyone who seems to need it (Levine et al., 1994). Crowding increases the sensory overload on people and makes them more deindividuated.

2. *The individual decides to take responsibility.* In a large crowd or a large organization, it is easy for people to avoid action because of the diffusion of responsibility. When people are alone and hear someone call for help, they usually do intervene (Latané & Darley, 1976). But the decision to take responsibility also depends on the degree of risk involved. For example, helping a stranger in trouble can sometimes be dangerous, even fatal. A Good Samaritan in San Francisco intervened in an

316   PART FOUR   Your Environment

Many people retain their individuality and courage even at great risk to themselves. On the left, Terri Barnett and Gregory Alan Williams are honored at Los Angeles City Hall for rescuing white people during the violence that followed the 1992 acquittal of four white police officers who beat black motorist Rodney King. On the right are Ria Solomon, Sylvia Robins, and Al Bray, three whistle-blowers from Rockwell International who tried to inform NASA that the space shuttle *Challenger* was unsafe.

angry dispute between two men in the street and was stabbed to death as a consequence; he had interrupted a quarrel between drug dealers. In cities where homeless persons number in the thousands, many people are feeling "compassion fatigue": How many can they help? What kind of help is best? It is easier to be a whistle-blower or to protest a company policy when you know it will be easy to find another job, but what if jobs in your field are scarce and you have a family to support?

3. *The individual decides that the costs of doing nothing outweigh the costs of getting involved.* The cost of helping or protesting might be embarrassment and wasted time or, more seriously, lost income, loss of friends, and even physical danger. The cost of not helping or remaining silent might be guilt, blame from others, loss of honor, or, in some tragic cases, responsibility for the injury or death of others. Although three courageous whistle-blowers from Rockwell International tried to inform NASA that the space shuttle *Challenger* was not safe, the NASA authorities remained silent. No one was prepared to take responsibility for the costly decision to postpone the launch. The price of their silence was an explosion that caused the deaths of the entire crew.

4. *The individual has an ally.* In Asch's conformity experiment, the presence of one other person who gave the correct answer was enough to overcome agreement with the majority. In Milgram's experiment, the presence of a peer who disobeyed the experimenter's order to shock the learner sharply increased the number of people who disobeyed. One dissenting member of a group may be viewed as a troublemaker, but two dissenters are a coalition. Having an ally reassures a person of the rightness of the protest. Allies also make minority members seem less deviant or rebellious and make their ideas seem more legitimate (Wood et al., 1994).

5. *The individual becomes entrapped.* Once having taken the initial step of getting involved, most people will increase their commitment to taking action. In one study, 8,587 federal employees were asked whether they had observed any wrongdoing at work, whether they had told anyone about it, and what happened if they had told. Nearly half of the sample had observed some serious cases of wrongdoing, such as someone stealing federal funds, accepting bribes, or creating a situation that was dangerous to public safety. Of that half, 72 percent had done nothing at all, but the other 28 percent reported the problem to their immediate supervisors. Once they had taken that step, nearly 60 percent of the whistle-blowers eventually took the matter to higher authorities (Graham, 1986).

As you can see, independent action is not just the spontaneous or selfless expression of a desire to do the right thing. Certain social conditions make altruism, whistle-blowing, and dissent more likely to occur, just as certain conditions suppress them. What anyone does in a given situation depends on a constellation of beliefs and perceptions, personality traits, and aspects of the situation itself. This is why a man may leap into a frozen river to rescue a child on Monday and keep silent on Tuesday when his employer orders him to ignore worker-safety precautions at a factory because they are too expensive.

How do you think you would behave if you were faced with a conflict between social pressure and conscience? Would you blow the whistle on a fellow student who cheated, call 911 if you saw someone being injured in a fight, or voice your true opinion in class even though everyone else disagreed? Would you act to rescue someone from persecution or discrimination? What aspects of the situation would influence your responses?

???QUICK QUIZ

No matter how your fellow students feel about quizzes, you should answer this one.

A. See whether you can name the social-psychological phenomenon represented by each of the following situations.

1. The president's closest advisers are afraid to disagree with his views on arms negotiations.

2. You are at a Halloween party wearing a silly gorilla suit. Although you usually don't play practical jokes, when you see a chance to play one on your host, you do it.

3. Walking down a busy street, you see that fire has broken out in a store window. "Someone must have called the fire department," you say, and walk on.

B. What five conditions tend to encourage independent action such as dissent, whistle-blowing, and altruism?

Answers:
A. 1. groupthink 2. deindividuation 3. diffusion of responsibility B. Seeing the need for action, deciding to take responsibility, deciding that the costs of inaction outweigh the costs of involvement, having an ally, and becoming entrapped

---

What's Ahead ■ ■ ■ ■ ■

- *How do stereotypes benefit us—and how do they distort reality?*

- *Why does prejudice increase in times of social and economic unrest?*

- *Why do well-intentioned people sometimes get caught up in a "cycle of distrust" with other ethnic groups?*

- *Why isn't mere contact between cultural groups enough to resolve their conflicts? What would work?*

CROSS-CULTURAL RELATIONS

By now, we hope you're persuaded that all of us are affected by the social roles we play in society and the cultural norms we are expected to follow. Most people rarely pause to question these roles and norms, assuming instead that their own culture's way of doing things is logical, normal, and right—and that other people's cultural rules and norms are irrational, peculiar, and wrong. **Ethnocentrism,** the belief that your own culture or ethnic group is superior to all others, is universal, probably because it aids survival by increasing people's attachment to their own group and willingness to work on its behalf. Ethnocentrism is even embedded in some languages: The Chinese word for China means "the center of the world" and the Navajo and the Inuit call themselves simply "The People."

Ethnocentrism rests on a fundamental social identity: Us. As soon as people have created a category called "us," however, they invariably perceive everybody else as "not-us." It almost does not matter what the "us" category is, as Henri Tajfel and his colleagues (1971) demonstrated in an experiment with British schoolboys. Tajfel showed the boys slides with varying numbers of dots on them and asked the boys to guess how many dots there were. The boys were then arbitrarily told that they were "overestimators" or

ethnocentrism
A person's belief that his or her own ethnic group, nation, or religion is superior to all others.

"underestimators." On a subsequent task, they had a chance to give points to other boys identified as overestimators or underestimators. The researchers had created in-group favoritism: Although each boy worked alone in his cubicle, almost every single one assigned far more points to boys he thought were like him, an overestimator or an underestimator. As the boys emerged from their rooms, they were asked, "Which were you?"—and the answer received a mix of cheers and boos from the others.

Because of ethnocentrism, the possibility of harmonious relations among ethnic groups and cultures often looks bleak. All over the world, cultural animosities perpetually erupt in bloody battles. And in multicultural societies, differences in customs, values, and beliefs can produce a clash between the laws of the majority and the practices of minorities. In California, a man from Laos killed a puppy—a sacrifice he believed would help his wife recover from illness but one that enraged his neighbors and violated the animal-cruelty laws. In Nebraska, two Iraqi men, ages 34 and 28, married 13-year-old Iraqi girls—a normal custom to them, but statutory rape under Nebraska law. Some immigrants from Africa, the Middle East, and Indonesia are determined to continue their tradition of female genital mutilation—cutting off a girl's clitoris and often the rest of the external genitals as well—a practice they believe ensures a girl's chastity before marriage and her fidelity after-

ward; the United States (and other Western nations) have outlawed the procedure.

Some people take a *relativist* position on these differences, arguing that cultures should be judged strictly on their own terms—that we should not pass judgment on the customs of others even when those customs cause suffering or death. Others take an *absolutist* position, maintaining that when cultures violate certain universal human rights, the correct response is moral indignation and censure. Cultural psychologists try to help us reconcile these two views (Adamopoulos & Lonner, 1994). It is important, most would say, to morally oppose customs that violate universal human rights (although not every culture will agree on what those are—for example, whether all children are entitled to an education, whether all women are entitled to sexual pleasure, or whether torture and genocide are reprehensible). But cultural psychologists also caution us to be wary of our own ethnocentrism, the impulse to judge other cultures' practices as immoral simply because they differ from our own. We need to understand that customs are not arbitrary; they are adaptations to specific kinds of kinship systems and economic arrangements. In countries that practice genital mutilation, for example, the tradition ensures women a secure place in society; most women who do not have the operation will remain unmarried and unprotected by their extended families. This is why efforts to eliminate

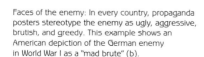

Faces of the enemy: In every country, propaganda posters stereotype the enemy as ugly, aggressive, brutish, and greedy. This example shows an American depiction of the German enemy in World War I as a "mad brute" (b).

(b)

female genital mutilation without also raising the status and economic security of women have failed (Dawit & Mekuria, 1993).

Social and cultural psychologists strive to understand not only the functions of cultural practices, but also the conditions that promote harmony or conflict between cultures. We turn now to their findings on stereotypes and prejudice, which so often fuel the flames of cultural misunderstanding and intolerance.

Stereotypes

A **stereotype** is a summary impression of a group of people in which all members of the group are viewed as sharing a common trait or traits. Stereotypes may be negative, positive, or neutral. There are stereotypes of people who drive Jeeps or BMWs, of men who wear earrings and of women who wear business suits, of engineering students and art students, of feminists and fraternities.

Stereotypes have a valid role to play in human thinking. They help us quickly process new information and retrieve memories. They allow us to organize experience, make sense of differences among individuals and groups, and predict how people will behave. They are, as some psychologists have called them, useful "tools in the mental toolbox"—energy-saving devices that allow us to make efficient decisions (Macrae, Milne, & Bodenhausen, 1994).

The problem is that stereotypes also distort reality in three ways (Judd et al., 1995). First, *they exaggerate differences between groups*, making the stereotyped group seem odd, unfamiliar, or dangerous. Second, *they produce selective perception;* people tend to see only what fits the stereotype and to reject any perceptions that do not fit. Third, *they underestimate differences within other groups.* People realize that their own groups are made up of all kinds of individuals, but stereotypes create the impression that all members of other groups (say, all Texans or all teenagers) are the same.

Many stereotypes have a grain of truth, capturing with some accuracy something about a group (Allport, 1954/1979). The difficulties occur when people assume that the grain of truth is the whole seashore. For example, many American whites have a stereotype about blacks that is based on the troubling statistics in the news, such as the number of young black men who are in prison. But recent decades have also seen an enormous expansion of blacks into the middle class and into

Which woman is the chemical engineer and which is the assistant? The Western stereotype holds that (a) women are not engineers in the first place, but (b) if they are, they are Western. Actually, the engineer at this refinery is the Kuwaiti woman on the left.

integrated occupations and communities, and many whites have not assimilated these positive changes into their racial stereotypes. For their part, many blacks hold negative stereotypes about whites, whom they often see as unvarying in their attributes and prejudices (Judd et al., 1995).

Stereotypes, both positive and negative, affect the way we react to the behavior of someone from the stereotyped group (Peabody, 1985). If you have a positive stereotype of Scots, for example, you might decide that a Scottish uncle of yours is "thrifty"; but if your stereotype is negative, you might think of him as "stingy." Likewise, depending on whether your stereotypes are positive or negative, you may see the behavior of others as "exuberant" or "noisy," "family-oriented" or "clannish" (Peabody, 1985).

Positive and negative stereotypes, in turn, depend on the values, cultural norms, and attributions of the observer. For example, students in Mexico and African-American students are significantly more accepting of heavy people and less concerned about their own weight than are white American students. Whites tend to have strongly negative stereotypes about fat people, which stem from a cultural ideology that individuals are responsible for what happens to them and for how they look (Crandall & Martinez, 1996).

Differences in ideology and values also affect how people from different cultures evaluate the same event (Taylor & Porter, 1994). Is coming late to class good, bad, or neutral? Is it good or bad to

stereotype
A cognitive schema or a summary impression of a group, in which a person believes that all members of the group share a common trait or traits (positive, negative, or neutral).

argue with your parents about grades? Chinese students in Hong Kong, where communalism and respect for one's elders are highly valued, and students in Australia, where individualism is highly valued, give entirely different interpretations of these two actions (Forgas & Bond, 1985). It is a small step from different interpretations to negative stereotypes: "Australians are selfish and disrespectful of adults"; "The Chinese are mindless slaves of authority." And it is a small step from negative stereotyping to prejudice.

Prejudice

A *prejudice* consists of a negative stereotype and a strong, unreasonable dislike or hatred of a group or a cultural practice. Feelings of prejudice violate the spirit of critical thinking because they resist rational argument and evidence. In his classic book *The Nature of Prejudice,* Gordon Allport (1954/1979) described the responses characteristic of a prejudiced person when confronted with evidence contradicting his or her beliefs:

MR. X: The trouble with Jews is that they only take care of their own group.

MR. Y: But the record of the Community Chest campaign shows that they give more generously, in proportion to their numbers, to the general charities of the community, than do non-Jews.

MR. X: That shows they are always trying to buy favor and intrude into Christian affairs. They think of nothing but money; that is why there are so many Jewish bankers.

MR. Y: But a recent study shows that the percentage of Jews in the banking business is negligible, far smaller than the percentage of non-Jews.

MR. X: That's just it; they don't go in for respectable business; they are only in the movie business or run night clubs.

Notice that Mr. X doesn't even try to respond to Mr. Y's evidence; he just moves along to another reason for his dislike of Jews. That is the nature of prejudice.

THE MANY FACES OF PREJUDICE

Prejudice has a long history in the United States. Hotels and job ads used to make it clear that "Gentiles only" were wanted, and anti-Semitism still exists today. In the 1920s and during World War II, anti-Japanese feelings ran high, . . .

The Origins of Prejudice.   One reason for the persistence of prejudice lies in its ability to ward off feelings of doubt and fear. Prejudiced persons often project their fears or feelings of insecurity onto the target group. For example, a person who has doubts or anxieties about his own sexuality may develop a hatred toward gay people. In uncertain times, prejudice allows people to reduce complex problems to one cause, using the target group as a scapegoat: "Those people are the source of all my troubles." Most important, as research on samples from many nations has repeatedly confirmed, prejudice is a tonic for low self-esteem: People puff up their own low feelings of self-worth by disliking or hating groups they see as inferior (Islam & Hewstone, 1993; Stephan et al., 1994; Tajfel & Turner, 1986).

Not all prejudices have deep-seated psychological roots, however. As social-learning theorists have shown, some people acquire prejudices from advertising, entertainment shows, and news reports that perpetuate derogatory images and stereotypes of groups such as old people and fat people. Some prejudices are acquired mindlessly in the process of socialization; parents may communicate subtle messages to their children that say, "We don't associate with people like that," sometimes without either generation having ever met the object of their dislike. Pressures to conform can make it difficult for people to break away from the prejudices of their friends, families, and associates.

Perhaps the most important reason for prejudice, in the sociocultural view, is that it brings economic benefits and justifies the majority group's dominance (Sidanius, Pratto, & Bobo, 1996). That is why prejudice always rises when groups are in direct competition for jobs. In the nineteenth century, when Chinese immigrants in the United States were working in the gold mines, local whites described them as depraved, vicious, and bloodthirsty. Just a decade later, when the Chinese began working on the transcontinental railroad—doing difficult and dangerous jobs that few white men wanted—prejudice against them declined. Whites described them as hard-working, industrious, and law-abiding. Then, after the railroad was finished and the Chinese had to compete with Civil War veterans for scarce jobs, white

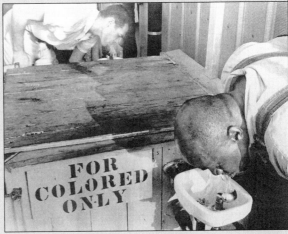

. . . and hostility returned during the economic recession of the early 1990s, when Iranians and other immigrants also became targets. Native Americans have been objects of hatred since Europeans first arrived on the continent. Segregated facilities for blacks were legal until the 1950s, and today many neighborhoods and schools remain separate and unequal. . . .

322   PART FOUR   Your Environment

attitudes changed again. Whites now considered the Chinese to be "criminal," "crafty," "conniving," and "stupid" (Aronson, 1995).

Years ago, a classic study confirmed the strong link between economic conditions and scapegoating in America. Data from 14 states showed a strong negative correlation between the number of black lynchings in the American South and the economic value of cotton: the poorer the economic conditions for whites, the greater the number of lynchings (Hepworth & West, 1988; Hovland & Sears, 1940). More recently, another project examined several measures of economic and social insecurity (including the unemployment rate, the rate of serious crimes, the number of work stoppages, and income levels) and of prejudice (including the number of anti-Semitic incidents, activities by the Ku Klux Klan, and attitudes toward other groups). Again, during times of high social and economic threat, prejudice increased significantly (Doty, Peterson, & Winter, 1991).

Varieties of Prejudice. Studies that define prejudice in terms of people's expressed attitudes

report that prejudice in the United States and Canada is declining. White attitudes toward integration have become steadily more favorable, and the belief that blacks are inferior to whites has become much less prevalent (Devine, 1995). Similarly, men's endorsement of gender equality has steadily increased. The number of men openly expressing prejudice toward women executives declined from 41 percent in 1965 to only 5 percent in 1985 (Tougas et al., 1995), and between 1970 and 1995 antiwoman attitudes in general dropped sharply (Twenge, 1996).

Thinking Critically About the Prevalence of Prejudice

However, some social scientists believe that these statistics are misleading. Overt attitudes, they say, are not an accurate measure of prejudice because people know they should not admit feeling prejudiced (Bell, 1992; Tougas et al., 1995). These observers maintain that racial animosity and sexism are undiminished. Prejudice toward blacks, they argue, lurks behind a mask of *symbolic racism*, in which whites focus not on dislike of black individuals but on issues such as "reverse

. . . Despite great gains by women, anti-female prejudice remains widespread, as does anger against gay men and lesbians. Why do new prejudices keep emerging and why do some old ones persist?

Get Involved

Are you prejudiced against a specific group of people? Is it a group defined by gender, ethnicity, sexual orientation, nationality, religion, physical appearance, or political views? Write down your deepest thoughts and feelings about this group. Take as long as you want, and do not censor yourself or say what you think you ought to say. Now reread what you have written. Which of the many reasons for prejudice discussed in the text might be supporting your views? Do you feel that your attitudes toward the group are legitimate, or are you uncomfortable about them?

discrimination," "hard-core criminals," or "welfare abuse." In this view, such issues have become code words for the continuing animosity that many whites have for blacks.

The way to measure racism, according to this argument, is by using unobtrusive measures rather than direct attitude questionnaires. You might observe how people behave when they are with a possible object of prejudice; do they sit farther away than they normally would? You might observe how quickly people come up with positive or negative associations to pictures of people from different races—a possible measure of unconscious prejudice (Fazio et al., 1995). You might observe how people who say they are unprejudiced behave when they are emotionally upset (Jones, 1991).

In one such experiment, students administered shock to confederates in an apparent study of biofeedback. White students initially showed *less* aggression toward blacks than toward whites. But as soon as the white students were angered by overhearing derogatory remarks about themselves, they showed *more* aggression toward blacks than toward whites (Rogers & Prentice-Dunn, 1981). This finding implies that whites may be willing to control their negative feelings toward blacks or other targets of prejudice under normal conditions. But as soon as they are angry, stressed, provoked, or suffer a blow to their self-esteem, their real prejudice reveals itself.

One complication in measuring prejudice is that not all people are prejudiced in the same way. Some people are unapologetically racist, sexist, or antigay. Others have a patronizing but unconscious sense of superiority over other groups. And some people hold remnants of prejudices that were acquired in childhood but feel guilty about having such feelings. Gordon Allport (1954/1979) observed that "defeated intellectually, prejudice lingers emotionally." That is, a person might realize that prejudice against a certain group is unwarranted, yet still feel uncomfortable with members of that group. Should we put this person in the same category as one who is an outspoken bigot or who actively discriminates against others because of their sex, culture, sexual orientation, weight, disability, or skin color? What if a person is ignorant of another culture or group and mindlessly blurts out a remark that reflects that ignorance? Does that count as prejudice or mere thoughtlessness?

Can Cultures Get Along?

Given the many sources and definitions of prejudice, no one method of reducing it is likely to work (Monteith, 1996). That is why social and cultural psychologists have designed different programs to try to reduce misunderstanding and prejudice, depending on the origins of a given conflict.

For example, according to Patricia Devine (1995), people who are actively trying to break their "prejudice habit" should not be lumped together with bigots. Their discomfort could reflect an honest effort to put old prejudices aside or simple unfamiliarity with another group's ways. When people are unfamiliar or uncomfortable with members of another group, a "cycle of distrust" and animosity can emerge even when individuals start off with the best intentions to get along. Some majority-group members, although highly motivated to work well with minorities, may be self-conscious and anxious about doing "the wrong thing." Their anxiety makes them behave awkwardly, for instance by blurting out dumb remarks and avoiding eye contact with minority-group members. The minority members, based on their own history of discrimination, may interpret the majority-group members' behavior as evidence of hostility and respond with withdrawal, aloofness, or anger. The majority members, not understanding that their own anxieties have been interpreted as evidence of prejudice,

Some doubts and insecurities felt by minority-group members.

regard the minority members' behavior as unreasonable or mysterious, so they reciprocate the hostility or withdraw. This behavior confirms the minority members' suspicions about the majority's true feelings and prejudices (Devine, Evett, & Vasquez-Suson, 1996).

By understanding this cycle, Devine argues, people of goodwill can learn to break it. Majority members can become aware of the discrepancy between their intentions and their actual behavior. They can learn to reduce their discomfort with people unlike themselves and acquire the skills that will lessen their anxiety. But breaking the cycle of distrust and hostility is not just the majority's problem. Minorities can become part of the solution too, for example, by recognizing their possible biases in seeing the majority members' behavior only in a negative light. Both sides, Devine (1995) emphasizes, should remember that reducing prejudice is a *process;* it does not happen overnight. It is important, she argues, to reward people who are making an effort to change their biases, instead of condemning them for not being perfect.

What happens, however, when two groups really do bear enormous animosity toward each other, for historical, economic, or emotional reasons? How then might their conflicts be reduced? Sociocultural research emphasizes the importance of changing people's circumstances, rather than waiting around for individuals to undergo a moral or psychological conversion.

One line of attack is to change the laws that make discrimination—the official endorsement of

prejudice against certain groups—acceptable. Integration of public facilities in the American South would never have occurred if civil-rights advocates had waited for segregationists to have a change of heart. Women would never have gotten the right to vote, attend college, or do "men's work" without persistent challenges to the laws that permitted discrimination. Laws, however, do not necessarily change attitudes if all they do is produce unequal contact between groups or if economic competition for jobs continues. Even with legal reforms, de facto segregation of schools and neighborhoods is still the rule in the United States and other countries, and racial prejudices are still deeply felt.

Another approach, based on the *contact hypothesis,* holds that the best way to end prejudice is to bring members of both sides together and let them get acquainted; in this way, they will discover their shared humanity. The contact hypothesis had a moment of glory during the 1950s and 1960s, when contact between blacks and whites did reduce hostility in some settings, such as newly integrated housing projects (Deutsch & Collins, 1951; Wilner, Walkley, & Cook, 1955). However, as is apparent at most big-city high schools today, desegregation and opportunities to socialize are often unsuccessful. Ethnic groups still form cliques and gangs, fighting other groups and defending their own ways.

A third approach is to go directly into desegregated schools and businesses and set up cooperative situations in which antagonistic groups have to work together for a common goal. The importance of cooperation was demonstrated years ago, when Muzafer Sherif and his colleagues conducted an experiment in a natural setting, a Boy Scout camp called Robbers Cave (Sherif, 1958; Sherif et al., 1961). Sherif randomly assigned 11- and 12-year-old boys to two groups: the Eagles and the Rattlers. To build team spirit, he had each group work on communal projects, such as making a rope bridge and building a diving board. Sherif then put the teams in competition for prizes. During fierce games of football, baseball, and tug-of-war, the boys developed a competitive fever that spilled off of the playing fields. They began to raid each other's cabins, call each other names, and start fistfights. No one dared to have a friend from the rival group. Before long, the Rattlers and the Eagles were as hostile toward each other as any two rival gangs fighting for turf, any two siblings fighting for a parent's attention, and any two nations fighting for dominance. Their hostility continued even when they were just sitting around together watching movies.

To undo the hostility he had created, Sherif set up a series of predicaments in which the Eagles and the Rattlers had to work together to reach a desired goal. The boys had to cooperate to get the water-supply system working. They had to pool their resources to get a movie they all wanted to see. When the staff truck broke down on a camping trip, they all had to join forces to pull the truck up a steep hill and get it started again. This policy of *interdependence in reaching mutual goals* was highly successful in reducing the boys' competitiveness and hostility. The boys eventually made friends with their former enemies.

Several years later, another team of researchers used a similar strategy, the "jigsaw method," to try to reduce ethnic conflict among white, Chicano, and black children in Texas elementary schools (Aronson et al., 1978). Classes were divided into groups of six students of mixed ethnicity, and every group worked together on a shared task that was broken up like a jigsaw puzzle. Each child needed the contributions of the others to put the assignment together; for instance, each child might be given one paragraph of a six-paragraph biography and be asked to learn the whole story. The cooperative students, in comparison to classmates in regular classes, had greater self-esteem, liked their classmates better, showed a decrease in prejudice, and improved their grades.

These findings, and studies of other versions of cooperative learning, have been replicated in many classrooms (Aronson, Wilson, & Akert, 1997; Johnson & Johnson, 1989). However, cooperation doesn't work when members of a group have unequal status, blame one another for loafing or "dropping the ball," or perceive that their teachers or employers are playing favorites.

Because the origins of tensions between groups in today's world are so complex, no single arrow is likely to hit the bull's-eye of prejudice. Each of the strategies we have described can be effective—making discrimination illegal, increasing contact and

In the first stage of the Robbers Cave study, a harmonious atmosphere was created by having campers cooperate and function as a team—for example, by having them work together carrying canoes to the lake (left). In the second stage, competitive games such as tug-of-war (right) fostered stereotyping and hostility between the Rattlers and the Eagles. Eventually, peace among the boys was again established when the two groups had to work together on problems such as the repair of the camp's water-supply system.

326   PART FOUR   Your Environment

Cultural and ethnic tensions tend to subside when people from different groups work together on a common goal. Here, volunteers from Habitat for Humanity, a group that constructs housing for low-income people, build a new home in the Watts area of Los Angeles.

cooperation between antagonistic groups—but for any of them to have its greatest impact, four conditions must be met (Amir, 1994; Fisher, 1994; Rubin, 1994; Staub, 1996; Stephan & Brigham, 1985):

1. *Both sides must have equal status and equal economic standing.* If one side has more power or greater economic opportunity, prejudice can continue. Thus, simply putting blacks and whites in the same situation won't necessarily reduce conflict if the whites have all the decision-making authority and economic resources.

2. *Both sides must cooperate, working together for a common goal,* an enterprise that reduces us–them thinking and creates an encompassing social identity ("We're all in this together"). If one side tries to bully and dominate the other, if one side passively capitulates or withdraws, or if both sides compete to see who will win, the conflict will continue (Rubin, 1994).

3. *Both sides must have the moral, legal, and economic support of authorities,* such as teachers, employers, the judicial system, government officials, and the police. In other words, the larger culture must support the goal of equality in its laws and in the actions of its officials.

4. *Both sides must have opportunities to work and socialize together, formally and informally.* Prejudice declines when people have the chance to get used to one another's food, music, customs, and attitudes (Fisher, 1994).

Perhaps one reason that cultural conflicts have been so persistent around the world is that these four conditions are rarely met all at the same time.

???QUICK QUIZ

Try to overcome your prejudice against quizzes by taking this one.

A. Which concept—ethnocentrism, stereotyping, or prejudice—is illustrated by each of the following statements?

   1. Juan believes that all Anglos are uptight and cold, and he won't listen to any evidence that contradicts his belief.

   2. John knows and likes the Mexican minority in his town, but he privately believes that Anglo culture is superior to all others.

   3. Jane believes that Honda owners are thrifty and practical. June believes that Honda owners are stingy and dull.

B. What strategy does the Robbers Cave study suggest for reducing hostility between groups?

 C. Surveys find that large percentages of African-Americans, Asian-Americans, and Latinos hold negative stereotypes of one another and resent other minorities almost as much as they resent whites. What are some of the reasons that people who have themselves been victims of stereotyping and prejudice would hold the same attitudes toward others?

Answers:
A. 1. prejudice 2. ethnocentrism 3. stereotypes   B. the fostering of interdependence in reaching mutual goals   C. socialization by parents and messages in the larger society; conformity with friends who share these prejudices; and economic competition for jobs and other resources

If ever an incident illustrated the power of social norms and cultural differences, the shooting of Yoshihiro Hattori is it. When Rodney Peairs's case came to trial, the jury acquitted him of manslaughter after only three hours of deliberation. The Japanese were appalled at this verdict. To them, it illustrated everything that is wrong with America. In their view, the United States is a nation rife with guns and violence—a "developing nation," as one news commentator put it, that is still growing out of its Wild-West past. Japanese television reporters, in amazement, showed their viewers American gun stores, restaurants that display guns on the walls, and racks of gun magazines. The Japanese cannot imagine a nation in which private individuals are allowed to keep guns, and the murder rate in Japan is a tiny percentage of what it is in America.

"I think for Japanese the most remarkable thing is that you could get a jury of Americans together, and they could conclude that shooting someone before you even talked to him was reasonable behavior," Masako Notoji, a professor of American cultural studies in Tokyo, told the *New York Times* (May 25, 1993). "We are more civilized. We rely on words." In contrast, the citizens of Baton Rouge were surprised that the case came to trial at all. What is more right and natural, they asked, than protecting yourself and your family from intruders? "A man's home is his castle," said one potential juror, expressing puzzlement that Peairs had even been arrested. A local man, joining the many sympathizers of Rodney Peairs, said, "It would be to me what a normal person would do under those circumstances."

But what is normal? As findings in cultural psychology have shown, what is normal in some cultures—emphasizing group harmony over individual rights, prohibiting individuals from owning guns or encouraging gun use, excising the genitals of women, killing a puppy for religious sacrifice—may be considered abnormal, immoral, or unnatural in other cultures.

Moreover, as findings in social psychology have shown, even within a culture, "normal" people can do some terribly disturbing things when norms and roles encourage or require them to do so—when the situation "takes over" and, like Bonnie Peairs, they don't stop to think critically and ask questions. Normal people may join self-destructive cults, harm others, and go along with the crowd, even when the crowd is performing brutal acts. They may then call upon self-serving attributions to rationalize their behavior; they may even blame the victims of their actions.

Philosopher Hannah Arendt (1963) used the phrase "the banality of evil" to describe how it was possible for "normal" people in Nazi Germany to commit the monstrous acts they did. (*Banal* means "commonplace" or "unoriginal.") The compelling evidence for the banality of evil is, perhaps, the hardest lesson in psychology. Most people want to believe that harm to others is done only by evil people who are bad down to their bones, or that wars are started only by evil cultures that don't have a single good custom to recommend them. It is reassuring to divide the world into those who are good or bad, kind or cruel, moral or immoral.

Of course, some people do stand out as particularly cruel or particularly kind. But from the standpoint of social and cultural psychology, all human beings, like all cultures, contain the potential for both good and bad. All of us, depending on circumstances, are susceptible to mindless obedience and conformity, bystander apathy, groupthink, deindividuation, ethnocentrism, stereotyping, and prejudice. All of us are subject to the same psychological, social, and economic forces that foster tolerance or animosity, conformity or dissent, courage or cowardice.

The findings from cultural and social psychology suggest that ethnocentrism and cultural conflict will always be with us, as long as economic, cultural, and status differences exist among groups. But this research can also help us formulate realistic goals for living in a diverse world. For example, because of cross-cultural findings, businesses are now hiring cultural advisers to help them make the best use of their employees' diversity and do better business with other countries. And research on bystander intervention is being used in the training of police officers in California, to encourage them to intervene when their colleagues use too much force. (The man hired to design the program is Ervin Staub, whose family was saved from the Nazis in 1944—by concerned bystanders.)

By recognizing that conflicts and misunderstandings will always occur, we can turn our attention to finding nonviolent ways of resolving them. By identifying the social conditions that have created the banality of evil, we can create others that foster the "banality of virtue"—everyday acts of kindness, selflessness, and generosity.

Taking Psychology with You

Travels Across the Cultural Divide

A French salesman worked for a company that was bought by Americans. When the new American manager ordered him to step up his sales within the next three months, the employee quit in a huff, taking his customers with him. Why? In France, it takes years to develop customers; in family-owned businesses, relationships with customers may span generations. The American wanted instant results, as Americans often do, but the French salesman knew this was impossible and quit. The American view was, "He wasn't up to the job; he's lazy and disloyal, so he stole my customers." The French view was, "There is no point in explaining anything to a person who is so stupid as to think you can acquire loyal customers in three months" (Hall & Hall, 1987).

Many corporations are beginning to realize that such cultural differences are not trivial and that success in a global economy depends on understanding such differences. You, too, can benefit from the psychological research on cultures, whether you plan to do business abroad, visit as a tourist, or just want to get along better in an increasingly diverse society.

• *Be sure you understand the other culture's rules*, not only of manners and customs but also of nonverbal gestures and methods of communication. If you find yourself getting angry over something a person from another culture is doing, try to find out whether your expectations and perceptions of that person's behavior are appropriate. For example, Koreans typically do not shake hands when greeting strangers, whereas most African-Americans and whites do. People who shake hands as a gesture of friendship and courtesy are likely to feel insulted if another person refuses

to do the same—unless they understand that what is going on is a cultural difference. Here's another example: Suppose you want to go shopping in Morocco or Mexico. If you are not used to bargaining, the experience may be exasperating. It will help to find a cultural "translator" who can show you the ropes. On the other hand, if you are from a culture where people bargain for everything, you will be just as exasperated in a place where everything is sold for a fixed price. "Where's the fun in this?" you'll say. "The whole human transaction of shopping is gone!"

• *When in Rome, do as the Romans do—as much as possible.* Most of the things you really need to know about a culture are not to be found in the guidebooks or travelogues. To learn the unspoken rules of a culture, keep your eyes open and your mouth shut: Look, listen, and observe. What is the pace of life like? Which is more valued in this culture, relationships or schedules? Do people regard brash individuality as admirable or embarrassing? When customers enter a shop, do they greet and chat with the shopkeeper or ignore the person as they browse?

Remember, though, that even when you know the rules, you may find it difficult to carry them out. For example, cultures differ in their tolerance for prolonged gazes (Keating, 1994). In the Middle East, two men will look directly at one another as they talk, but such direct gazes would be deeply uncomfortable to most Japanese or white Americans and a sign of insult to some African-Americans. Knowing this fact about gaze rules can help people accept the reality of different customs, but most of us will still feel uncomfortable trying to change our own ways.

• *Nevertheless, avoid stereotyping.* Try not to let your awareness of cultural differences cause you to overlook individual variations within cultures. During a dreary Boston winter, social psychologist Roger Brown (1986) went to the Bahamas for a vacation. To his surprise, he found the people he met unfriendly, rude, and sullen. He decided that the reason was that Bahamians had to deal with spoiled, critical foreigners, and he tried out this hypothesis on a cab driver. The cab driver looked at Brown in amazement, smiled cheerfully, and told him that Bahamians don't mind tourists—just *unsmiling* tourists.

And then Brown realized what had been going on. "Not tourists generally, but this tourist, myself, was the cause," he wrote. "Confronted with my unrelaxed wintry Boston face, they had assumed I had no interest in them and had responded non-committally, inexpressively. I had created the Bahamian national character. Everywhere I took my face it sprang into being. So I began smiling a lot, and the Bahamians changed their national character. In fact, they lost any national character and differentiated into individuals."

Wise travelers will use cultural findings to expand their understanding of other societies, while avoiding the trap of reducing all behavior to a matter of culture. Sociocultural research teaches us to appreciate the countless explicit and implicit rules that govern our behavior, values, and attitudes, and those of others. Yet we should not forget Roger Brown's lesson that every human being is an individual: one who not only reflects his or her culture, but who shares the common concerns of all humanity.

SUMMARY

1) Like learning theorists, social and cultural psychologists emphasize environmental influences on behavior, but they broaden their attention to include the entire sociocultural context. Social psychologists study the influence of *norms*, *roles*, and groups on behavior and cognition; cultural psychologists study the cultural origins of and variations in norms and roles.

Roles and Rules

2) Two classic studies illustrate the power of roles to affect individual actions. In Milgram's obedience study, most people in the role of "teacher" inflicted what they thought was extreme shock on another person because an authoritative experimenter told them to. In Zimbardo's prison study, college students quickly fell into the role of "prisoner" or "guard."

3) A certain amount of routine obedience to authority is necessary for the smooth running of any society, but obedience can also lead to actions that are deadly, foolish, or illegal. People follow orders because of the obvious consequences of disobedience, out of respect for authority, and to gain advantages. Even when they would rather not obey, they may do so because they believe the authority is *legitimate;* because their role is *routinized* into duties that are performed mindlessly; because they are embarrassed to violate the rules of good manners; or because they have been *entrapped.*

Identity, Attributions, and Attitudes

4) In addition to having their own individual identities, people develop *social identities,* aspects of self-identity that are based on nationality, ethnicity, and social roles. Social identities provide a feeling of place and connection in the world.

5) In culturally diverse societies, many people face the problem of balancing their *ethnic identity* with *acculturation* into the larger society. Depending on whether ethnic identity and acculturation are strong or weak, a person may become *bicultural;* choose *assimilation;* become an *ethnic separatist;* or feel *marginal.*

6) According to *attribution theory,* people are motivated to search for causes to which they can attribute their own and other people's behavior. These attributions may be *situational* or *dispositional.* The *fundamental attribution error* occurs when people overestimate personality traits as a cause of behavior and underestimate the influence of situation. A *self-serving bias* allows people to take credit for their good deeds and to excuse their own mistakes by blaming the situation. According to the *just-world hypothesis,* most people need to believe that the world is fair and that people get what they deserve; to preserve this belief, they may blame victims of abuse or injustice instead of the perpetrators.

7) People hold many *attitudes,* which are composed of cognitions and feelings about a subject. Some attitudes are a result of conformity, habit, rationalization, economic self-interest, and subtle social and environmental influences, including the *cohort effect.* Although attitudes influence behavior, a change in behavior can also lead to a change in attitudes, often as a result of *cognitive dissonance.*

8) One way to persuade others to change their attitudes is to take advantage of the *validity effect:* Simply repeating a statement over and over again makes it seem more believable. Other everyday techniques of attitude change include associating a product or message with someone who is famous, attractive, or expert, and linking the product with good feelings. Fear tactics, however, tend to backfire.

9) Some methods of attitude change are intentionally manipulative. Tactics of *coercive persuasion* include putting a person under stress; defining problems and their solutions simplistically; offering unconditional love and acceptance in exchange for unquestioning loyalty; creating a new identity for the person; using entrapment; and controlling access to outside information.

Individuals in Groups

10) In groups, individuals may conform to social pressure because they identify with the group, trust the group's judgment or knowledge, hope for personal gain, or wish to be liked. They may even conform mindlessly and self-destructively, violating their own preferences and values because "everyone else is doing it."

11) Cohesive, friendly groups are particularly vulnerable to *groupthink,* the tendency of group members to think alike, censor themselves, actively suppress disagreement, and feel that their decisions are invulnerable. Groupthink can produce faulty decisions because group members fail to seek disconfirming evidence for their ideas. However, groups can be structured to discourage groupthink.

12) *Diffusion of responsibility* in a group can lead to inaction on the part of individuals—to *bystander apathy* and, in work groups, *social loafing.* The most extreme instances of the diffusion of responsibility occur when people are in a state of *deindividuation,* losing awareness of their individuality. Deindividuation increases under conditions of anonymity.

13) Although the willingness to speak up for an unpopular opinion, blow the whistle, or help a stranger is in part a matter of personal belief and conscience, social and situational factors are also important. Dissent, moral action, and altruism increase when individuals are able to recognize a need for intervention or help; decide to take responsibility; conclude that the costs of inaction outweigh the costs of getting involved; have an ally; and become entrapped in a commitment.

Cross-cultural Relations

14) *Ethnocentrism*, the belief that your own ethnic group or culture is superior to all others, promotes "us–them" thinking. Because of ethnocentrism and genuine differences in values and beliefs, cultural animosities and conflicts are common throughout the world.

15) *Stereotypes* help people rapidly process new information and retrieve memories, but they also distort reality by exaggerating differences between groups; producing selective perception; and underestimating the differences within groups. Positive and negative stereotypes affect whether we see the behavior of another person in a positive or negative light—for example, as thrifty or stingy.

16) A *prejudice* is an unreasonable negative feeling toward a category of people or a cultural practice. Prejudice reduces anxiety by allowing people to feel superior; bolsters self-esteem when they feel threatened; and provides a simple explanation of complex problems. Some people acquire prejudices from media images or from their parents. Prejudice protects economic interests and justifies the majority group's dominance. During times of social and economic insecurity, prejudice rises significantly.

17) Overtly prejudiced and sexist attitudes are declining in the United States and Canada, but scientists disagree on the significance of this fact. Some argue that prejudice toward African-Americans lurks behind a mask of *symbolic racism*. In studies, expressed attitudes toward other groups are sometimes at odds with actual behavior. Debates over whether prejudice is declining are complicated by the fact that not all prejudiced people are prejudiced in the same way. Some people may feel guilty about their discomfort with members of other groups and may wish to overcome such feelings.

18) When prejudice arises from a "cycle of distrust," people can learn to break the cycle by recognizing their biases and learning to reduce their discomfort with members of the other group. But when two groups feel animosity toward each other for historical, economic, or emotional reasons, four conditions are necessary for prejudice to decline: The groups must have equal status and economic standing; they must cooperate for a common goal; they must have the legal, moral, and economic support of authorities; and, as the *contact hypothesis* would predict, they must have opportunities to work and socialize together.

19) Social and cultural psychology show that under certain conditions, good people can be induced to do bad things; normal sociocultural processes can lead to bystander apathy, groupthink, and conflict. But the sociocultural context can also be designed to encourage selflessness, group harmony, and constructive dissent.

KEY TERMS

social psychology 297	individualist versus collectivist cultures 304	attribution theory 306
cultural psychology 297	ethnic identity 305	situational attributions 306
norms (social) 298	acculturation 305	dispositional attributions 306
role 298	bicultural identity 305	fundamental attribution error 306
routinization 302	assimilation 305	
entrapment 303	ethnic separatism 305	self-serving bias 307
social cognition 304	marginal identity 305	just-world hypothesis 307
social identity 304		blaming the victim 307

attitude   307

cohort effect   307

cognitive dissonance   308

validity effect   308

coercive persuasion   309

groupthink   313

diffusion of responsibility   314

bystander apathy   314

social loafing   314

deindividuation   314

altruism   315

ethnocentrism   317

stereotype   319

prejudice   320

symbolic racism   322

contact hypothesis   324

LOOKING BACK

* *How do social rules guide behavior—and what is likely to happen when you violate them? (pp. 298–299)*

* *Do you have to be mean or disturbed to inflict pain on someone just because an authority tells you to? (pp. 299–300)*

* *How can ordinary college students be transformed into sadistic prison guards? (p. 301)*

* *How can people be "entrapped" into violating their moral principles? (p. 303)*

* *In what ways do people balance their ethnic identity and membership in the larger culture? (p. 305)*

* *What's one of the most common mistakes people make when explaining the behavior of others? (p. 306)*

* *What is the "Big Lie"—and why does it work so well? (pp. 308–309)*

* *What's the difference between ordinary techniques of persuasion and the coercive techniques used by cults? (p. 310)*

* *Why do people in groups often go along with the majority even when the majority is dead wrong? (p. 313)*

* *How can "groupthink" lead to bad—even catastrophic—decisions? (p. 313)*

* *Why is it common for a group of people to hear someone shout for help without one of them calling the police? (p. 314)*

* *What enables some people to dissent, take moral action, or blow the whistle on wrongdoers? (pp. 315–316)*

* *How do stereotypes benefit us—and how do they distort reality? (p. 319)*

* *Why does prejudice increase in times of social and economic unrest? (pp. 321–322)*

* *Why do well-intentioned people sometimes get caught in a "cycle of distrust" with members of other ethnic or cultural groups? (pp. 323–324)*

* *Why isn't mere contact between groups enough to resolve cultural conflict? What would work? (pp. 324, 326)*

PSYCHOLOGY SELECTION 1

Roles and Rules

(pages 296–304)

To locate a paragraph by number as referred to in an exercise, start counting with the first paragraph on the page, regardless of whether it is an incomplete paragraph continuing from a previous page or a new full paragraph. Please note that page numbers refer to the pages of the textbook chapter, not to the pages of this book.

1   BEFORE READING

> ### PREVIEWING THE SECTION

Using the steps listed on page 5, preview pages 296–304 of Invitation to Psychology. *When you have finished, complete the following items.*

1. What is the topic of this section of the chapter?_____roles and rules_____

2. List three questions you should be able to answer after reading this section of the chapter.

   a. ___What was the obedience study?___

   b. ___What was the prison study?___

   c. ___What power do roles have?___

 ### MAKING CONNECTIONS

Choose one of the questions in the "What's Ahead" box on page 298 to answer for yourself.

> ### READING TIP

As you read, highlight the findings of each of the studies described in this section.

> ### VOCABULARY

social psychologists (page 297) psychologists who study the influence of social roles, attitudes, relationships, and groups on behavior and cognition

cultural psychologists (page 297) psychologists who study the cultural origins of roles, attitudes, and group norms

confederates (page 299) people who are informed about the purpose of an experiment but agree to keep it a secret from other participants

atrocities (page 301) acts of appalling cruelty and violence inflicted on civilians or prisoners

genocide (page 302) the deliberate and systematic extermination of an entire national, racial, political, or ethnic group

1 AFTER READING

> ### A. UNDERSTANDING MAIN IDEAS

Select the best answer.

___d___ 1. The purpose of Stanley Milgram's obedience study was to find out
   a. how learning is affected by punishment or pain.
   b. why certain people respond positively to authoritative figures and others do not.
   c. what personality traits are associated with obedience and disobedience.
   d. how many people will obey an authority figure when directly ordered to violate their own ethical standards.

___c___ 2. The Milgram study indicated that subjects were more likely to disobey the experimenter under all of the following conditions *except* when the
   a. experimenter left the room.
   b. victim was in the same room and the shock had to be administered directly by the subject.
   c. victim stopped responding completely as if unconscious.
   d. subject worked with peers who refused to go further.

___d___ 3. In the prison study, the researchers decided to end the study early because
   a. all of the participants complained that they were not being paid enough.
   b. the participants were having too much fun and were not taking the experiment seriously enough.
   c. the prison was taken over when the "prisoners" rebelled against the "guards."
   d. the transformation of the participants into their respective roles was too speedy and terrifying.

➤ **B.   IDENTIFYING DETAILS**

Complete the following statements by underlining the correct answer in the parentheses.

1. The rules about how we are supposed to act, enforced by threats of punishment and promises of reward, are called social (<u>norms</u>/roles).

2. In the Milgram study, about (one-third/<u>two-thirds</u>) of the participants obeyed to the fullest extent.

3. Milgram's conclusion was that the subjects' behavior was more related to their (<u>situation</u>/personality).

4. In the prison study, participants (were/<u>were not</u>) given instructions about how to behave.

5. When the researchers ended the prison study early, most of the guards were (relieved/<u>disappointed</u>).

➤ **C.   RECOGNIZING METHODS OF ORGANIZATION AND TRANSITIONS**

Select the best answer.

_a_ 1. On pages 302–303, the authors list several factors that cause people to obey when they would rather not, using the organizational pattern known as

a. enumeration.

b. problem and solution.

c. time sequence.

d. comparison and contrast.

_b_ 2. Under the first factor listed on page 302, the transitional word or phrase that indicates that a comparison is being made is

a. in Milgram's study.

b. in contrast.

c. but.

d. at that point.

➤ D.   REVIEWING AND ORGANIZING IDEAS: MAPPING

Fill in the blanks to complete the following map based on the factors that cause people to obey when they would rather not (pp. 302–303).

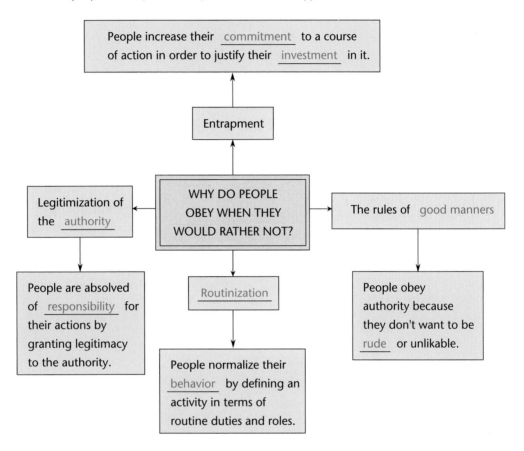

People increase their commitment to a course of action in order to justify their investment in it.

Entrapment

WHY DO PEOPLE OBEY WHEN THEY WOULD RATHER NOT?

Legitimization of the authority

The rules of good manners

People are absolved of responsibility for their actions by granting legitimacy to the authority.

Routinization

People obey authority because they don't want to be rude or unlikable.

People normalize their behavior by defining an activity in terms of routine duties and roles.

➤ E.   FIGURING OUT INFERRED MEANINGS

Indicate whether each statement is true (T) or false (F).

____T____ 1. Gender roles in America may be different from gender roles in other countries.

____F____ 2. The type of people who signed up for the Milgram study were those who enjoy inflicting pain on other people.

____F____ 3. The subjects in the Milgram study obeyed because they were afraid of the experimenter.

____F____ 4. In the prison study, the guard who put a prisoner in solitary confinement was only doing what he had been told to do.

____T____ 5. Some people obey because they don't know how to refuse to obey.

> ### F. THINKING CRITICALLY

Select the best answer.

___d___ 1. The authors capture the reader's attention at the beginning of the chapter by describing

    a. the results of a study exploring the effect of authority on obedience.

    b. an informal experiment in which participants violate common social norms.

    c. infamous episodes in history in which ordinary people committed atrocities because of pressure from authority figures.

    d. a shocking incident in which a cultural misunderstanding ended in tragedy.

___a___ 2. The authors support the main ideas in this section of the chapter primarily with

    a. research evidence.   c. statistics.

    b. personal experience.   d. analogies.

___d___ 3. In contrast to the subjects in the Milgram study, people who commit atrocities do so without

    a. supervision by authorities.

    b. external pressure.

    c. feelings of conflict or anguish.

    d. all of the above.

___b___ 4. The authors included the quote from Sous Thy, the clerk whose job was to record the names of victims of the Khmer Rouge (page 303), in order to

    a. defend the clerk's behavior.

    b. illustrate how governments get citizens to assist in genocide.

    c. show that some participants in genocide are completely innocent.

    d. criticize the clerk for not disobeying the Khmer Rouge.

___c___ 5. Milgram's comment that one of his subjects used "the language of the tea table" (page 303) was intended to illustrate that

    a. the subject was polite and apologetic to the person he was shocking.

    b. some of the subjects were not polite to the victims.

    c. most people don't want to be rude even when they are doing something apparently horrific.

    d. many of his subjects had educated backgrounds.

➤ G. BUILDING VOCABULARY

➤ Context

Using context and a dictionary, if necessary, determine the meaning of each word as it is used in the selection.

__b__ 1. revelations (page 299, paragraph 1)

    a. secrets   c. concerns

    b. confessions   d. predictions

__c__ 2. countered (page 300, paragraph 5)

    a. agreed   c. argued

    b. asked   d. competed

__b__ 3. strenuously (page 300, paragraph 6)

    a. doubtfully   c. repeatedly

    b. strongly   d. mildly

__c__ 4. queasy (page 301, paragraph 3)

    a. pleasant   c. nauseated

    b. curious   d. panicked

__c__ 5. compliance (page 302, paragraph 3)

    a. disregard   c. obedience

    b. ignorance   d. doubt

__a__ 6. relinquished (page 302, paragraph 6)

    a. yielded   c. expected

    b. defied   d. rewarded

__d__ 7. fixated (page 302, paragraph 7)

    a. overlooked   c. restored

    b. eliminated   d. focused

__c__ 8. interrogation (page 303, paragraph 4)

    a. invitation   c. questioning

    b. explanation   d. release

➤ Word Parts

> ### A REVIEW OF PREFIXES
> **AB-** means *away from*
> **DE-** means *to remove*
> **IN-** means *not*
> **SUB-** means *under*
> **UN-** means *not*

Match each word in Column A with its meaning in Column B. Write your answers in the spaces provided.

Column A	Column B
_f_ 1. delousing	a. made worthless
_e_ 2. uncritical	b. undermined or weakened
_d_ 3. absolve	c. not honest; morally wrong
_b_ 4. subverted	d. to take away blame or guilt
_c_ 5. unethical	e. without question or thought
_a_ 6. invalidated	f. removing lice

➤ **Unusual Words/Unusual Meanings**
Use the meanings given below to write a sentence using the underlined word or phrase.

1. If you <u>act your part to the hilt</u> (page 301), you perform it to the maximum degree.

   Your sentence: _____.

2. People who don't like to <u>rock the boat</u> (page 303) do not want to upset a situation or cause a disturbance, as you would if you actually rocked a boat.

   Your sentence: _____.

➤ **H.   SELECTING A LEARNING/STUDY STRATEGY**

Discuss whether outlining, summarizing, or mapping would be the best way to learn the research studies described in this section. Might one strategy be more useful to certain types of learners than others? How does the type of exam for which students are preparing influence this choice?

➤ **I.   EXPLORING IDEAS THROUGH DISCUSSION AND WRITING**

1. Do you think you would have obeyed completely in a situation like the one in the Milgram study? Have you ever been in a situation where you obeyed even though it was against your values? Why do you think you obeyed?

2. Do you think television and film portrayals of prison situations affected the behavior of participants in the prison study?

3. Discuss the quote from C. P. Snow that "more hideous crimes have been committed in the name of obedience than in the name of rebellion" (page 302).

✔ **Tracking Your Progress**

Psychology Selection 1

Section	Number Correct		Score
A. Main Ideas (3 items)	_____	x 4	_____
B. Details (5 items)	_____	x 4	_____
C. Organization and Transitions (2 items)	_____	x 2	_____
E. Inferred Meanings (5 items)	_____	x 3	_____
F. Thinking Critically (5 items)	_____	x 3	_____
G. Vocabulary			
1. Context (8 items)	_____	x 2	_____
2. Word Parts (6 items)	_____	x 3	_____
	TOTAL SCORE		_____%

PSYCHOLOGY SELECTION 2

Identity, Attributions, and Attitudes

(pages 304–311)

To locate a paragraph by number as referred to in an exercise, start counting with the first paragraph on the page, regardless of whether it is an incomplete paragraph continuing from a previous page or a new full paragraph. Please note that page numbers refer to the pages of the textbook chapter, not to the pages of this book.

2   BEFORE READING

> ### PREVIEWING THE SECTION

Using the steps listed on page 5, preview pages 304–311 of Invitation to Psychology. *When you have finished, complete the following items.*

1. What is the topic of this section of the chapter? <u>identity, attributions, and attitudes</u>

2. List five questions you expect to be able to answer after reading this section of the chapter.

   a. <u>What is self-identity?</u>

   b. <u>What are attributions?</u>

   c. <u>Where do attitudes come from?</u>

   d. <u>What is friendly persuasion?</u>

   e. <u>What is coercive persuasion?</u>

 ### MAKING CONNECTIONS

How do you identify yourself? Why?

➤ READING TIP

Be sure to highlight definitions of new terminology that are introduced in this section.

➤ VOCABULARY

caste (page 307) a hereditary social class in Hinduism

cohort (page 307) a generational group as defined in demographics, statistics, or market research

| 2 | **AFTER READING** |

➤ **A.   UNDERSTANDING MAIN IDEAS**

Select the best answer.

__d__ 1. Social identities are the parts of our self-concepts that are based on
   a. nationality and ethnicity.
   b. religion.
   c. social roles.
   d. all of the above

__c__ 2. According to this section of the chapter, *acculturation* is a person's identification with
   a. an ethnic group.
   b. a religious group.
   c. the dominant culture.
   d. his or her gender group.

__c__ 3. In attribution theory, the fundamental attribution error occurs when people attempting to explain someone's behavior tend to
   a. overestimate personality factors.
   b. underestimate the influence of the situation.
   c. both a and b
   d. neither a nor b

__a__ 4. The self-serving bias is a way of explaining one's own behavior by
   a. choosing attributions that are favorable to oneself.
   b. taking full credit for both positive and negative actions.

c. refusing to blame others for the mistakes one makes.

d. attributing every action to factors in the environment.

_d_ 5. An attitude is a relatively stable opinion that contains

a. perceptions about a topic.

b. beliefs about a topic.

c. feelings about a topic.

d. all of the above

_c_ 6. All of the following techniques are effective ways to influence attitudes *except*

a. repeating an idea until it becomes so familiar that it is perceived as valid.

b. using an attractive or admired person to present or endorse an idea.

c. creating a sense of terror and helplessness about a potential danger.

d. associating the message with a good feeling.

➤ B.   IDENTIFYING DETAILS

Indicate whether each statement is true (T) or false (F).

_T_ 1. The area in social psychology that is concerned with social influences on thoughts, beliefs, memories, and perceptions is called social cognition.

_F_ 2. The attribution theory states that people always attribute the causes of the behavior of others to something in the person, such as a trait or motive.

_T_ 3. Westerners are more likely to make the fundamental attribution error than people in countries that are more group-oriented.

_T_ 4. According to the just-world hypothesis, people need to believe that the world is fair in order to make sense out of senseless events.

_F_ 5. A survey of the American population indicated that attitudes formed during the ages of 16 to 24 are not as influential as those formed later in life.

➤ **C. RECOGNIZING METHODS OF ORGANIZATION AND TRANSITIONS**

Select the correct answer.

___a___ 1. In the first three paragraphs on page 307, the authors describe how attributions in Western nations differ from those in other countries, using the organizational pattern called

    a. comparison and contrast.

    b. problem and solution.

    c. time sequence.

    d. enumeration.

___b___ 2. In the first of these same three paragraphs, the transitional word or phrase that indicates the organizational pattern above is

    a. for instance.

    b. unlike.

    c. for example.

    d. of course.

___c___ 3. On page 310, the authors list some of the processes by which individuals can be coerced by cults, using the organizational pattern called

    a. problem and solution.

    b. time sequence.

    c. enumeration.

    d. definition.

___d___ 4. On page 306, in the first paragraph, the transitional word "similarly" suggests the organizational pattern known as

    a. definition.

    b. time sequence.

    c. cause and effect.

    d. comparison and contrast.

___a___ 5. On page 307, in the third paragraph, the two organizational patterns used are

    a. comparison and contrast and example.

    b. comparison and contrast and cause and effect.

    c. time sequence and example.

    d. cause and effect and time sequence.

➤ D.   REVIEWING AND ORGANIZING IDEAS: MAPPING

Complete the following map based on page 305 by filling in the blanks.

Ethnic Identity +	Acculturation =	Outcome
Strong	Strong	Bicultural
Weak	Weak	Marginal
Weak	Strong	Assimilated
Strong	Weak	Separatist

➤ E.   FIGURING OUT INFERRED MEANINGS

Next to each of the following statements, write S if it is an example of a situational attribution and write D if it is an example of a dispositional attribution. The first one has been done for you.

__S__ 1. "Ray is short-tempered because he's trying to meet a deadline for an important project."

__D__ 2. "Agnes won't share her cake with anyone else because she's selfish."

__D__ 3. "That basketball player missed the free throw because he's no good."

__S__ 4. "The new neighbors didn't wave to us because they didn't recognize our car."

__S__ 5. "Santonio flunked the math quiz because he stayed up too late last night."

__D__ 6. "Charlotte bought a box of Girl Scout cookies because she's so kindhearted."

__S__ 7. "I'm grouchy because my car is still leaking oil even after the mechanic said he fixed it."

__D__ 8. "Uncle Lou agreed to give us a loan because he's a generous person."

➤ F.   THINKING CRITICALLY

Select the best answer.

__c__ 1. The authors support the main ideas in this section of the chapter with all of the following types of evidence *except*

a. examples.   c. personal experience.

b. research.   d. facts.

_c_ 2. The authors describe the tension between cultural groups in North America (pages 305–306) in order to

　　a. criticize these groups for not being more willing to assimilate into the dominant culture.

　　b. encourage the U.S. government to eliminate ethnic categories on the census.

　　c. illustrate how difficult it can be for groups to balance acculturation and ethnic identity.

　　d. urge the members of each group to agree on a single term that they would prefer to be used in describing their group.

_c_ 3. Most psychologists prefer the phrase "coercive persuasion" to "brainwashing" because brainwashing

　　a. refers specifically to techniques used on American prisoners during the Korean War.

　　b. is a physical process, whereas coercive persuasion is a psychological process.

　　c. implies that a person has a mysterious and sudden change of mind and is unaware of what is happening.

　　d. is always negative, whereas coercive persuasion is typically a positive experience.

➤ **G. BUILDING VOCABULARY**

➤ **Context**

Using context and a dictionary, if necessary, determine the meaning of each word as it is used in the selection.

_c_ 1. attributions (page 304, paragraph 1)

　　a. excuses　　　　　　　　　　c. explanations

　　b. features　　　　　　　　　　d. arguments

_b_ 2. medley (page 306, paragraph 1)

　　a. background　　　　　　　　c. category

　　b. mixture　　　　　　　　　　d. census

_a_ 3. embedded (page 307, paragraph 1)

　　a. involved　　　　　　　　　　c. opposed

　　b. excluded　　　　　　　　　　d. reformed

_b_ 4. dissonance (page 308, paragraph 3)

　　a. believability　　　　　　　　c. uncertainty

　　b. conflict　　　　　　　　　　d. immorality

___c___ 5. basest (page 308, paragraph 4)

    a. opposite   c. worst

    b. slightest   d. basic

___c___ 6. coercive (page 309, paragraph 5)

    a. persuasive   c. forceful

    b. encouraging   d. polite

___a___ 7. denigrates (page 310, paragraph 7)

    a. discredits   c. requests

    b. supports   d. rewards

___d___ 8. sever (page 310, paragraph 8)

    a. review   c. restore

    b. allow   d. end

___c___ 9. censored (page 310, paragraph 8)

    a. counted   c. suppressed

    b. avoided   d. sought

___d___ 10. dissenting (page 310, paragraph 8)

    a. curious   c. strongly held

    b. suspecting   d. disagreeing

➤ Word Parts

> ### A REVIEW OF PREFIXES
> **BI-** means *two*
> **EXTRA-** means *outside, beyond*
> **MULTI-** means *many*

Using your knowledge of word parts and the review of the prefixes above, fill in the blanks in the following sentences.

1. A <u>bicultural</u> person (page 305, paragraph 2) is a person who has strong ties to _____two_____ cultures.

2. A person who has a <u>multiethnic</u> background (page 306, paragraph 1) has ancestors from _____many_____ ethnic groups.

3. An <u>extraterrestrial</u> (page 310, paragraph 8) refers to a being that has originated from ____outside or beyond____ the Earth and its atmosphere; in other words, a creature from outer space.

➤ H.   SELECTING A LEARNING/STUDY STRATEGY

Discuss methods of learning the new terminology introduced in this section.

➤ I.   EXPLORING IDEAS THROUGH DISCUSSION AND WRITING

1. Discuss the difference between the heads of companies in Japan and in the United States (page 307, paragraph 3). How do these differences reflect the different societies?

2. Have you ever made the dispositional attribution called "blaming the victim" (page 307, paragraphs 4 and 5)? How could this kind of attribution be harmful?

3. How can attributions affect relationships in both positive and negative ways?

4. Think about the major political events and social changes that occurred in your life when you were between the ages of 16 and 24. How have those events helped to form your attitudes? Do you believe those events will be "peak memories" for you later in your life?

5. Think of a situation in which you have experienced cognitive dissonance (page 308). Have you ever had to adjust your attitude about a politician or someone else you admire because of cognitive dissonance?

6. What do you think the Nazis were referring to with the term "the Big Lie" (page 308)?

7. What do the authors mean by the term "love bath" (page 310)? How does this technique influence people to join cults?

✔ Tracking Your Progress

Psychology Selection 2

Section	Number Correct	Score
A. Main Ideas (6 items)	_____ x 4	_____
B. Details (5 items)	_____ x 3	_____
C. Organization and Transitions (5 items)	_____ x 2	_____
E. Inferred Meanings (8 items)	_____ x 2	_____
F. Thinking Critically (3 items)	_____ x 3	_____
G. Vocabulary		
1. Context (10 items)	_____ x 2	_____
2. Word Parts (3 items)	_____ x 2	_____
	TOTAL SCORE	_____%

PSYCHOLOGY SELECTION 3

Individuals in Groups

(pages 311–317)

To locate a paragraph by number as referred to in an exercise, start counting with the first paragraph on the page, regardless of whether it is an incomplete paragraph continuing from a previous page or a new full paragraph. Please note that page numbers refer to the pages of the textbook chapter, not to the pages of this book.

3   BEFORE READING

➤ PREVIEWING THE SECTION

Using the steps listed on page 5, preview pages 311–317 of Invitation to Psychology. *When you have finished, complete the following items.*

1. What is the topic of this section of the chapter? _how individuals behave_

   in groups

2. List four questions you expect to be able to answer after reading this section of the chapter.

   a. _What is conformity?_

   b. _What is groupthink?_

   c. _What is meant by the "anonymous crowd"?_

   d. _What does courage have to do with nonconformity?_

MAKING CONNECTIONS

Has there ever been a time when you behaved in a group in a way you wouldn't have acted on your own? What were the circumstances?

➤ READING TIP

To make the material more meaningful, try to think of situations from your own experience that illustrate the concepts of conformity, nonconformity, groupthink, and anonymous crowd behavior.

➤ **VOCABULARY**

meta-analysis (page 312, paragraph 4) the process of retrieving, selecting, and combining research results from previous separate but related studies

| 3 | **AFTER READING** |

➤ **A. UNDERSTANDING MAIN IDEAS**

Select the best answer.

___b___ 1. The purpose of Solomon Asch's studies of conformity was to determine

    a. what personality traits are associated with highly conforming individuals.

    b. how people would respond when an entire group contradicted an obvious fact.

    c. why conformists and nonconformists behave differently in group settings.

    d. whether women or men are more likely to conform to group behavior.

___d___ 2. Asch's experiments indicated that conformity increases as

    a. the stimulus becomes more ambiguous.

    b. the number of accomplices giving the wrong answer increases.

    c. group members become more alike according to factors such as age, gender, and ethnicity.

    d. all of the above

___c___ 3. According to Irving Janis, groupthink occurs when

    a. a group's need for total agreement overwhelms its need to make the best decision.

    b. the group members' needs to be liked and accepted overwhelm their ability to disagree with a bad decision.

    c. both a and b

    d. neither a nor b

___c___ 4. All of the following features are typical of groups that are susceptible to groupthink *except*

    a. they are highly cohesive.

    b. they are isolated from other viewpoints.

    c. their leader is weak and indecisive.

    d. they feel under pressure from external forces.

_c_ 5. The process called *diffusion of responsibility* occurs when

    a. the responsibility for an outcome is spread among many people.

    b. individuals fail to take action because they assume someone else will.

    c. both a and b

    d. neither a nor b

_b_ 6. The main idea of the section called "Courage and Nonconformity" is that, in addition to personal convictions and conscience, a person's willingness to take independent action is influenced by

    a. the belief that the world is ultimately a fair place.

    b. external factors such as the degree of risk involved in the situation and whether or not the person has an ally.

    c. obedience to a respected authority figure who directs that individual to take action.

    d. the desire to do the right thing.

➤ B. IDENTIFYING DETAILS

Complete each statement by underlining the correct answer in the parentheses.

1. Since the time that Asch's experiments were first conducted in the 1950s, conformity has (increased/<u>decreased</u>) in America.

2. People in individualistic cultures are (more/<u>less</u>) likely to conform than are people in group-oriented cultures.

3. One symptom of groupthink is that there is (<u>direct</u>/indirect) pressure on dissenters to conform.

4. Groupthink can sometimes be counteracted by creating conditions that (<u>encourage</u>/discourage) group members to express their doubt or dissent.

5. Social loafing typically (increases/<u>decreases</u>) when people know their group's performance will be evaluated against that of another group.

6. Deindividuation typically (<u>increases</u>/decreases) in situations that make people feel anonymous.

7. On average, Asians are (more/<u>less</u>) individuated than whites, blacks, and Latinos.

➤ C. RECOGNIZING METHODS OF ORGANIZATION AND TRANSITIONS

Select the correct answer.

___b___ 1. In the last full paragraph on page 312, the three transitional words that indicate the enumeration organizational pattern are

    a. many, many, three.

    b. first, second, third.

    c. in the 1950s.

    d. are less likely.

___c___ 2. On pages 315–316, the organizational pattern used to list the factors that predict independent action is

    a. problem and solution.

    b. definition.

    c. enumeration.

    d. time sequence.

➤ D. REVIEWING AND ORGANIZING IDEAS: SUMMARIZING

Complete the following summary based on item number 1 on page 315 by filling in the blanks with the correct words or phrases.

The individual perceives the need for intervention or help. People have to realize that ___independent___ action is necessary before they will act. Sometimes, however, people deliberately refuse to see the ___need___ for action in order to excuse or ___justify___ their failure to ___act___. During ___World War II___, German residents of Dachau ignored the local ___concentration camp___, and today many ___employees___ ignore illegal actions at work. When people have too many ___demands___ on their attention, at ___work___ or in crowded ___cities___, they tend to ignore the need for action.

➤ E. FIGURING OUT INFERRED MEANINGS

Indicate whether each statement is true (T) or false (F).

___T___ 1. The decisions people make in groups are often different from the decisions they would make independently.

___T___ 2. The pressure that people feel in groups can be real or imagined.

___F___ 3. Group-oriented societies place a high value on individual assertiveness.

___T___ 4. In the example about President Johnson, it can be inferred that Bill Moyers advised against increased bombing in North Vietnam.

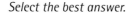 **F. THINKING CRITICALLY**

Select the best answer.

_d_ 1. The suggestion that "conformity reflects prevailing social norms" (page 312, paragraph 4) means that

    a. people tend to become more conforming as they age.

    b. people tend to become less conforming as they age.

    c. conformity is based on rules and conventions that were established centuries ago.

    d. people become more or less conforming depending on current social rules and conventions.

_b_ 2. The authors include the examples about President Kennedy and President Johnson (page 313) in order to

    a. compare a nonconforming president (Kennedy) to a conforming president (Johnson).

    b. provide real-life illustrations of the disastrous consequences of groupthink.

    c. criticize the advisers of both presidents for not being willing to express their dissent.

    d. express admiration for the two advisers who were punished for expressing their dissent.

_c_ 3. Of the following situations, the one in which a person would be most likely to experience deindividuation would be

    a. in a small town where most people know the person.

    b. with an intimate group of old friends.

    c. in a school band uniform identical to a hundred or so other band members.

    d. at a small discussion group meeting with classmates wearing name tags.

_c_ 4. The authors included the study of federal employees and wrongdoing at work (page 316, paragraph 4) in order to

    a. imply that there are many unreported instances of stealing and bribery within the federal government.

    b. reveal that the federal government places pressure on employees not to reveal instances of wrongdoing.

    c. illustrate that people who take some initial step toward involvement typically become committed to taking action.

    d. argue that the cases of wrongdoing at the federal government are typical of those found in any large private corporation.

> ## G.   BUILDING VOCABULARY

> ### Context
Using context and a dictionary, if necessary, determine the meaning of each word as it is used in the selection.

_b_ 1. convened (page 311, paragraph 1)
    a. departed   c. retreated
    b. gathered   d. discussed

_c_ 2. conformity (page 312, paragraph 3)
    a. incompetence   c. following the crowd
    b. variety   d. competing with others

_b_ 3. suppress (page 313, paragraph 1)
    a. achieve   c. release
    b. restrict   d. promote

_c_ 4. presumptuous (page 313, paragraph 5)
    a. cowardly   c. disrespectful
    b. angry   d. imitation

_c_ 5. unanimity (page 313, paragraph 7)
    a. uncertainty   c. complete agreement
    b. unidentified   d. discussion

_a_ 6. counteracted (page 313, paragraph 8)
    a. offset   c. complicated
    b. ruined   d. punished

_d_ 7. abdication (page 314, paragraph 3)
    a. restoration   c. sharing
    b. investigation   d. surrender

_c_ 8. altruism (page 315, paragraph 3)
    a. honesty   c. selflessness
    b. conflict   d. agreement

_d_ 9. inherent (page 315, paragraph 3)
    a. heavy   c. invisible
    b. indirect   d. essential

_b_ 10. flagrant (page 315, paragraph 5)
    a. mild   c. negative
    b. obvious   d. minor

➤ **Word Parts**

Using your knowledge of word parts, fill in the blanks below.

1. If in- means *not* and vulnerable means *susceptible to attack,* then invulnerability (page 313, first item in the bulleted list) means _____not able to be easily attacked_____ .

2. If the suffix -er means *one who* and dissent means *to disagree,* then a dissenter (page 313, the second bullet) is _____a person who disagrees_____ .

3. If the prefix de- means *not,* then the word deindividuation (page 314, paragraph 4) means _____the condition of not being an individual_____ , or *forgetting oneself.*

➤ **Unusual Words/Unusual Meanings**

Use the meanings given below to write a sentence using the underlined word or phrase.

1. The terms <u>hawks</u> and <u>doves</u> (page 313, paragraph 8) refer to attitudes toward war or aggression: a "hawk" is a person who favors military force or action in order to carry out foreign policy, whereas a "dove" is someone who advocates peace rather than armed conflict.

   Your sentence: _____ .

2. To <u>blow the whistle</u> (page 315, paragraph 2) is to try to stop an activity by making it public or by informing a person in authority.

   Your sentence: _____ .

3. A <u>Good Samaritan</u> (page 315, paragraph 6) is a person who compassionately intervenes to help another; the reference is to a New Testament parable about a Samaritan who was the only person to help someone who had been beaten and robbed.

   Your sentence: _____ .

➤ **H.   SELECTING A LEARNING/STUDY STRATEGY**

Evaluate the usefulness of the Quick Quiz on page 317 as a means of reviewing this section. For what types of exam would this quiz be most useful?

➤ **I. EXPLORING IDEAS THROUGH DISCUSSION AND WRITING**

1. Describe a situation in which conformity is important. Next, describe a situation in which nonconformity is more important.

2. Do you think you would feel pressured to go along with the group in Asch's experiment? Describe a situation in which you conformed despite your beliefs or values. Was the pressure in that situation direct or indirect? Real or imagined?

3. Have you ever decided to "blow the whistle" on an activity you felt was unfair or immoral? Have you ever decided to ignore such an activity? Describe how you felt each time.

4. What does the phrase "compassion fatigue" (page 316, paragraph 1) mean?

✔ Tracking Your Progress

Psychology Selection 3

Section	Number Correct		Score
A. Main Ideas (6 items)	_____	x 4	_____
B. Details (7 items)	_____	x 3	_____
C. Organization and Transitions (2 items)	_____	x 2	_____
E. Inferred Meanings (4 items)	_____	x 4	_____
F. Thinking Critically (4 items)	_____	x 3	_____
G. Vocabulary			
1. Context (10 items)	_____	x 2	_____
2. Word Parts (3 items)	_____	x 1	_____
		TOTAL SCORE	_____%

Cross-cultural Relations

(pages 317–331)

To locate a paragraph by number as referred to in an exercise, start counting with the first paragraph on the page, regardless of whether it is an incomplete paragraph continuing from a previous page or a new full paragraph. Please note that page numbers refer to the pages of the textbook chapter, not to the pages of this book.

4   BEFORE READING

➤ PREVIEWING THE SECTION

Using the steps listed on page 5, preview pages 317–331 of Invitation to Psychology. *When you have finished, complete the following items.*

1. What is the topic of this section of the chapter? __cross-cultural relations__

2. List five questions you expect to be able to answer after reading this section of the chapter.

   a. What are stereotypes?

   b. What is prejudice?

   c. What are the origins of prejudice?

   d. What are the varieties of prejudice?

   e. Can cultures get along? (or) How can cultures get along?

MAKING CONNECTIONS

Do you hold any stereotypes about people? If so, describe one.

➤ READING TIP

As you read, look for answers to the questions listed in the "What's Ahead" box on page 317.

➤ **VOCABULARY**

ideology (page 319, paragraph 8) a set of ideas that characterize a particular individual, group, or culture

de facto segregation (page 324, paragraph 4) the actual, albeit unlawful, separation of races with the likely result of discrimination against people of color in a predominantly white society

4   AFTER READING

➤ **A.   UNDERSTANDING MAIN IDEAS**

Select the best answer.

___d___ 1. Ethnocentrism is the belief that one's own culture or ethnic group is
  a. in competition with another.
  b. inferior to another.
  c. equal to all others.
  d. superior to all others.

___a___ 2. People who take a *relativist* position on the differences between cultures argue that we should
  a. not pass judgment on the customs of other cultures.
  b. oppose cultural customs that violate certain human rights.
  c. establish a formal and universal definition of human rights.
  d. adhere to the laws of the majority rather than the practices of the minority.

___d___ 3. Stereotypes may be
  a. positive.
  b. negative.
  c. neutral.
  d. any of the above

___c___ 4. Stereotypes distort reality in all of the following ways *except* by
  a. exaggerating differences between groups.
  b. producing selective perception.
  c. emphasizing traits that are shared by all groups.
  d. underestimating differences within groups.

_d_ 5. The persistence of prejudice can be attributed to each of the following *except*

a. the economic benefits it brings to the majority group.

b. its ability to ward off feelings of doubt and fear.

c. the perpetuation of negative stereotypes in the media.

d. the need to work cooperatively for common goals.

_b_ 6. The purpose of the Robbers Cave study was to

a. reduce ethnic conflict among white, Chicano, and black children in Texas elementary schools.

b. demonstrate the importance of cooperation in reducing competitiveness and hostility.

c. determine how long it would take for conflict to develop between two groups fighting for dominance.

d. make people aware of the discrepancy between their intentions and their actual behavior toward minorities.

_d_ 7. In order for prejudice to decline, both groups must cooperate for a common goal and must have

a. equal status and economic standing.

b. the moral, legal, and economic support of authorities.

c. opportunities to work and socialize together.

d. all of the above

➤ B. IDENTIFYING DETAILS

Complete each statement by underlining the correct answer in the parentheses.

1. Ethnocentrism promotes survival by (<u>increasing</u>/decreasing) people's attachment to their own group.

2. African-American and Mexican students are typically (more/<u>less</u>) concerned about their own weight than are white American students.

3. A prejudice is based on a (positive/<u>negative</u>) stereotype.

4. Studies indicate that prejudice (<u>increases</u>/declines) when economic conditions are poor.

5. Based on expressed attitudes, prejudice toward women and minorities in the United States and Canada appears to be (increasing/<u>decreasing</u>).

➤ C.   RECOGNIZING METHODS OF ORGANIZATION AND TRANSITIONS

Select the best answer.

__a__ 1. On page 319, the authors list the ways that stereotypes distort reality using the organizational pattern called

a. enumeration.

b. problem and solution.

c. comparison and contrast.

d. time sequence.

__b__ 2. The transitional words or phrases that indicate the organizational pattern above are

a. the problem is.   c. odd, unfamiliar, dangerous.

b. first, second, third.   d. all kinds of individuals.

➤ D.   REVIEWING AND ORGANIZING IDEAS: OUTLINING

Complete the following outline based on pages 324–325, paragraphs 4–6, by filling in the blanks with the correct word or phrases.

Approaches to Ending Prejudice

   I. Make ____discrimination____ illegal

      A. Civil ____rights____ and integration

      B. ____Women's____ rights

  II. Increase contact

      A. ____Contact____ hypothesis

        1. Bring both sides together

        2. Let them ____get acquainted____

 III. Increase ____cooperation____ between antagonistic groups

➤ E.   FIGURING OUT INFERRED MEANINGS

Indicate whether each statement is true (T) or false (F).

__T__ 1. Ethnocentrism is based on an "us versus them" philosophy.

__T__ 2. Cultural differences in ideology and values can form the basis for prejudice.

_T_ 3. It can be inferred from the photograph on the lower right of page 320 that Japanese-Americans have been discriminated against in the United States.

_F_ 4. In the years since desegregation laws were passed in the United States, segregation in schools has been completely eliminated.

F. THINKING CRITICALLY

Select the best answer.

_d_ 1. The authors' tone throughout the chapter can best be described as

a. cautionary.

b. critical.

c. angry.

d. objective.

_b_ 2. An example of the concept of ethnocentrism would be the statement that

a. "We're all in this together."

b. "They're not bad, but we're better."

c. "Everyone who goes to that school is a snob."

d. "You just can't trust those people."

_b_ 3. The cartoon on page 318 is intended to illustrate how

a. people in other countries view the United States.

b. countries use negative stereotypes to influence public opinion against the enemy.

c. cartoonists distort the images of other countries to entertain the public.

d. misunderstandings about other cultures are perpetuated through depictions in the media.

_d_ 4. The excerpt from Gordon Allport's book is included on page 320 to show that prejudiced people

a. seek out others with opposing views.

b. use rational argument to convince others of their beliefs.

c. base their beliefs on personal experience and undeniable evidence.

d. refuse to consider rational argument and evidence.

___d___ 5. The authors end the chapter on page 327 with a description of the outcome of the Rodney Peairs case in order to

    a. prove that the case was based on a simple but tragic misunderstanding.

    b. persuade Americans to see the situation from the Japanese point of view.

    c. criticize the Japanese for not trying to understand the American point of view.

    d. illustrate how powerful social norms and cultural differences can be.

➤ G. BUILDING VOCABULARY

➤ Context

Using context and a dictionary, if necessary, determine the meaning of each word as it is used in the selection.

___b___ 1. arbitrarily (page 317, paragraph 2)

    a. calmly

    b. randomly

    c. anxiously

    d. foolishly

___a___ 2. animosities (page 318, paragraph 2)

    a. hostilities

    b. similarities

    c. negotiations

    d. interactions

___c___ 3. reprehensible (page 318, paragraph 3)

    a. believable

    b. understandable

    c. shameful

    d. avoidable

___b___ 4. derogatory (page 321, paragraph 2)

    a. old-fashioned   c. unchanging

    b. insulting   d. complimentary

___c___ 5. depraved (page 321, paragraph 3)

    a. poor   c. wicked

    b. uneducated   d. starving

_c_ 6. overt (page 322, paragraph 4)

　　a. average

　　b. hidden

　　c. expressed

　　d. traditional

_a_ 7. patronizing (page 323, paragraph 4)

　　a. overly proud

　　b. supportive

　　c. expectant

　　d. extremely generous

_d_ 8. aloofness (page 323, paragraph 6)

　　a. shamefulness

　　b. shyness

　　c. kindness

　　d. standoffishness

_c_ 9. reciprocate (page 324, paragraph 1)

　　a. misunderstand

　　b. ignore

　　c. return

　　d. allow

_d_ 10. discrepancy (page 324, paragraph 2)

　　a. importance

　　b. appearance

　　c. resemblance

　　d. difference

_b_ 11. cliques (page 324, paragraph 5)

　　a. trends

　　b. groups

　　c. rules

　　d. ideas

_c_ 12. capitulates (page 326, paragraph 3)

　　a. promotes

　　b. reviews

　　c. surrenders

　　d. changes

➤ **Word Parts**

```
A REVIEW OF PREFIXES
ANTI- means against
DE- means to reverse or eliminate
IN- means not
MULTI- means many
TRANS- means across
UN- means not
```

Match each word in Column A with its meaning in Column B. Write your answers in the spaces provided.

Column A	Column B
_c_ 1. unobtrusive	a. the elimination of separate schools for blacks and whites
_a_ 2. desegregation	b. against homosexual people
_b_ 3. antigay	c. not noticeable
_g_ 4. invariably	d. across the continent
_f_ 5. unapologetically	e. related to many cultural groups
_d_ 6. transcontinental	f. without being sorry
_e_ 7. multicultural	g. always or without fail

➤ **Unusual Words/Unusual Meanings**

Use the meanings given below to write a sentence using the underlined word or phrase.

1. A group that is used as a <u>scapegoat</u> (page 321, paragraph 1) is one that is being made to bear the blame of others.

   Your sentence: _____.

2. If you are guilty of <u>dropping the ball</u> (page 325, paragraph 4), you have disappointed the other members of your team or group by not doing your share of the work.

   Your sentence: _____.

➤ **H. SELECTING A LEARNING/STUDY STRATEGY**

Evaluate the usefulness of the "Summary" on pages 328–330, the "Key Terms" list on pages 328–329, and the "Looking Back" box on page 331. How can you use each to study?

➤ **I. EXPLORING IDEAS THROUGH DISCUSSION AND WRITING**

1. Reread the statement from page 319, paragraph 6 that "difficulties occur when people assume that the grain of truth is the whole seashore." What do the authors mean by this?

2. Discuss the "cycle of distrust" described on pages 323–324. How can such a cycle be broken?

3. What was the "jigsaw method" described on page 325? Was it successful?

✔ **Tracking Your Progress**

Psychology Selection 4

Section	Number Correct	Score
A. Main Ideas (7 items)	_____ x 4	_____
B. Details (5 items)	_____ x 3	_____
C. Organization and Transitions (2 items)	_____ x 2	_____
E. Inferred Meanings (4 items)	_____ x 3	_____
F. Thinking Critically (5 items)	_____ x 3	_____
G. Vocabulary		
1. Context (12 items)	_____ x 1	_____
2. Word Parts (7 items)	_____ x 2	_____
	TOTAL SCORE	_____ %

25

American History Textbook Chapter

Chapter 31

The Post–Cold War
World, 1992–2002

From

THE AMERICAN PEOPLE:
CREATING A NATION AND
A SOCIETY, SIXTH EDITION

Gary B. Nash et al.

31

The Post–Cold War World, 1992–2002

American society became more and more aware of its multicultural past and present in the 1990s. Different groups competed with each other for positions in the marketplace and other public spaces as the gap between rich and poor continued to grow greater. *(Billy Morrow Jackson, Station, 1981–1982, Courtesy of the Artist)*

✦ *American Stories*

AN IMMIGRANT FAMILY STRUGGLES AS THE ECONOMY IMPROVES

In 1997, Marlene Garrett bundled up her three sleepy children—aged four, three, and one—and took them to the babysitter's home every morning at 5 A.M. "Mama has to go to work so she can buy you shoes," she told them as she left for a job behind the counter at a bagel café in Fort Lauderdale, Florida, that began at 6 A.M. This was a new position and she did not want to be late.

Marlene had come to the United States from Jamaica eight years earlier. She and her husband, Rod, had high hopes for a better life in the United States, and they were fortunate enough to be employed. But both of them held entry-level jobs and had to struggle to make ends meet. Rod worked in a factory making hospital curtains and brought home about $250 a week. Marlene had just left a $5.25 an hour job selling sneakers for her $6 an hour job at the bagel café. It was a small improvement, but the $200 she earned made it possible to pay the monthly rent of $400 and buy groceries. With luck, they could repair or replace the car, which had recently died, and perhaps begin to pay off their $5,000 debt from medical bills. They had no health insurance and could only hope that no one got sick.

Marlene was not happy about her babysitting arrangements. Her real preference was to stay at home. "Who's a better caretaker than mom?" she asked. But remaining at home was out of the question. Welfare might have been a possibility in the past, but the United States was in the process of cutting back drastically on its welfare rolls, and, in any event, Marlene was not comfortable with that alternative. "I don't want to plant that seed in my children," she said. "I want to work."

Marlene had few day-care options. She would have liked to have taken Scherrod, Angelique, and Hasia to the Holy Temple Christian Academy—her church's day-care center and preschool—but it cost $180 a week for three children and was beyond reach. Several months before, when she had been earning $8 an hour as a home health aide for the elderly, she had thought she could afford the church center and had even put money down for school uniforms for the kids. Then her car gave out and made it impossible to continue that job.

Instead of the Holy Temple Christian Academy, Marlene took the children to the home of Vivienne, a woman from the Bahamas who worked nights at the self-service laundry where Marlene did her wash. Vivienne's apartment was simple and clean but had no toys or books anywhere in sight. Most days, the children watched television during the 10 hours that Marlene was away.

The Garretts knew how important it was to stimulate their children. Reflecting longingly on the church center and what it offered, Marlene said, "The children play games. They go on field trips. They teach them, they train them. My children are bright. You would be amazed at what they would acquire in a year." But instead of a stimulating center, the Garretts had to settle for a place that was simply safe.

At a time when the administration of Bill Clinton was trying to reconfigure the welfare system, people like the Garretts found themselves left out. Florida, like many states, budgeted most of its child-care money for families moving off of welfare to jobs. People who had never been on welfare received nothing. As the executive director of a Florida child-care referral agency observed, "Many of these parents have no choice but to leave their children in substandard arrangements that are rotting their brains, and jeopardizing their futures."

Marlene refused to give up hope. Her children were on a waiting list for help from the state that might make the Holy Temple Christian Academy accessible. Meanwhile, she took a second job working nights at the local Marriott Hotel. She had to pay Vivienne more money for the extra hours, and she worried even more about the additional time away from the children, but felt she had no choice. "It is temporary," she said. "I am doing what I have to do."

Marlene and Rod Garrett were like millions of poor Americans who found themselves left out of the prosperity that returned to the United States in the mid-1990s. Despite rosy economic indicators, more than 35 million Americans still lived below the federally defined poverty line. Life was hardly easy for the Garretts or for other families who found themselves on the bottom side of the line. Then, soon after George W. Bush succeeded Bill Clinton as president in 2001, the economy faltered. Now even more Americans found themselves in the same straits as the Garretts.

The Garretts' struggle to care for their children—and for themselves—unfolded against the backdrop of the longest period of economic growth in American history. As a deep recession in the early 1990s lifted, the economy went on a tear. American corporations, increasingly operating in a multinational context, dominated the global economy. Though some countries, like Japan, experienced a slowdown in economic growth and became mired in a long-lasting recession, the United States prospered. Taking advantage of remarkable advances in communication technology, corporations found it easy to do business in a world smaller than ever before. With inflation low in the United States, the Federal Reserve Board kept interest rates down, and the easy availability of money encouraged middle- and upper-class Americans to invest in the stock market and mutual funds, often enabling them to realize large gains, at least on paper. The troubling budget deficit that had soared in the Reagan administration disappeared as the government, guided by Democratic president Bill Clinton, ran a surplus for the first time in years. The unemployment level dropped, yet for Americans at the bottom of the economic ladder, many of the jobs now available as a result of the relentless shift toward a service economy paid little more than the minimum wage, and people like the Garretts still found themselves struggling to survive. Conditions became even more difficult when the Democratic party cut back and reconfigured the welfare system to preempt the issue for their own political ends. The loss of that safety net became even more problematical after a tax cut promoted by Republican President George W. Bush cut government income as a troubling recession refused to go away. Corporate fraud shattered investor confidence, and the stock market, which had risen for much of the decade, dropped dramatically.

Meanwhile, the foreign policy scene shifted abruptly. The cataclysmic events in Europe that ended nearly a half century of Cold War required the United States to redefine its international role. This led to substantial debate, as both Republicans, who controlled Congress for most of the 1990s, and Democrats, who controlled the White House for the same period, voiced reservations about playing an activist, and potentially expensive, role abroad. Then, as the new decade began, the United States confronted the menace of terrorism on a scale never known before. The attacks that destroyed the World Trade Center towers in New York City and left a gaping hole in the Pentagon in Washington, D.C., led to a war on terrorism and a fundamental reconfiguration of American foreign policy.

This chapter describes demographic shifts, reflected in the census of 2000, that changed the face of the American people. It highlights the revival of the economy that brought unprecedented prosperity for many but still failed to accommodate the needs of less fortunate Americans like the Garretts, and then records the even greater suffering as the economy fell apart. It examines the political struggle between Democrats and Republicans that brought the second presidential impeachment in American history. It notes the bitterly contested national election of 2000 and its conservative aftermath. Finally, it explores the continuing effort to define the American role in the turbulent and terrorist-dominated post–Cold War world.

THE CHANGING FACE OF THE AMERICAN PEOPLE

The United States changed dramatically in the 1990s, as the continuing influx of new immigrants reshaped demographic patterns. The overall population, as reported in the census of 2000, grew more rapidly than it had in the past several decades and reflected the steady increase in the number of non-white Americans.

The New Pilgrims

The second great wave of immigrants in the twentieth century changed the face of America. The number of immigrants to the United States in the 20-year period from 1981 to 2000 was approximately 17.5 million, making it the most voluminous period of immigration in American history. In the decade of the 1990s, close to 10 million immigrants were counted, just less than the 10.1 million immigrants recorded in the 10 years from 1905 to 1914, which stands as the all-time record for that span of time. Altogether, nearly one-third of the population growth in the 1990s stemmed from immigration.

Immigrants settled in the 1990s in a pattern resembling that of the previous several decades. Whereas most immigrants around the turn of the preceding century remained near the East Coast, or

Immigration, 1970–1998

This chart shows the significant rise in immigration after 1970, as the tightly restricted quotas in force from the 1920s to 1965 were liberalized. The steady rise in the 1970s and 1980s reflected the arrival of Asian and Latin Americans, while the spike in the early 1990s occurred because of the amnesty that legalized the status of many illegal immigrants who were now officially counted.

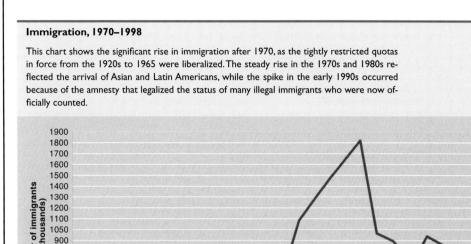

Source: Data from *Statistical Abstract of the United States.*

in contiguous states, in 2000, 39.9 percent of the foreign-born settled in western states, with only 22.6 percent of the foreign-born living in the Northeast. The shift was a result of larger demographic shifts in the United States. As the twentieth century began, the Northeast still dominated the economic and cultural life of the nation. New York City served as a magnet for immigrants, who often ventured no further after getting off the boat at Ellis Island. A hundred years later, the West was increasingly dominant. California had surpassed New York as the most populous state, and Los Angeles International Airport, known as LAX, had replaced Ellis Island as the port of entry for many immigrants.

The sources of recent immigration were similar to those of the 1970s and 1980s. In 2000, just over one-third of all immigrants—legal and illegal—came from Central America, while just over one-quarter came from Asia. The continuing influx was the result of factors that led immigrants to want to leave their home countries as well as factors that drew them to the United States. Faltering economies in many countries in Latin America led people living on the fringe to look toward the United States, where a

better life might be possible. Inhabitants of African nations, equally poor and faced with a crumbling infrastructure—as water and power sources deteriorated and roads sometimes became impassable—likewise saw hope for a brighter future in America, just as earlier immigrants had years before.

Immigration was not confined to the United States. Starting in the 1960s, Europe experienced its own wave of immigration, in a pattern that continued into the new century. Great Britain, France, and the Netherlands all had to deal with immigrants from former colonies. Germany experienced the arrival of people they called *gastarbeiter,* or guest workers, from southern Europe and Turkey, who were supposed to work in the factories and then go home, although many of them ended up staying.

The American influx was spurred by the Immigration Act of 1965, which was aimed at curbing illegal immigration while offering amnesty to aliens who had lived in the United States prior to 1982. Part of Lyndon Johnson's Great Society program, this act authorized the impartial acceptance of immigrants from all parts of the world and was directly responsible for the greater numbers of Asians and Latin Americans. In later years, other legislative measures sought to rationalize the immigration process. In 1986, Congress passed the Immigration Reform and Control Act, aimed at curbing illegal immigration while offering amnesty to aliens living in the United States. The Immigration Act of 1990 opened the doors wider, raising immigration quotas while cutting back on restrictions that had limited entry in the past. It also provided for swift deportation of aliens who committed crimes. Two other measures in 1992 expanded eligibility slightly. In 2001, the United States and Mexico began to talk about how to ease the plight of Mexican immigrants and permit illegal arrivals to stay.

The rise in the number of immigrants fueled anti-immigrant feeling in some quarters. In the 1970s and 1980s, America's efforts to help immigrants coincided with still-intact social-assistance programs of the liberal welfare state. Affirmative action programs aided both legal and illegal arrivals. Bilingual classrooms became more common, and multiculturalism, stressing the different values that made up a larger American identity, became a dominant theme in many schools.

Yet those efforts brought increasing resistance from Americans already here, particularly as the structure of the economy changed and good jobs became more scarce. At the same time, there was a cultural backlash, just as there had been in earlier eras. Opponents to immigration also worried about the challenge to America's character posed by new arrivals who clung to social patterns of their own. Americans were not alone in their fears. Europeans, too, were apprehensive at the threats to their way of

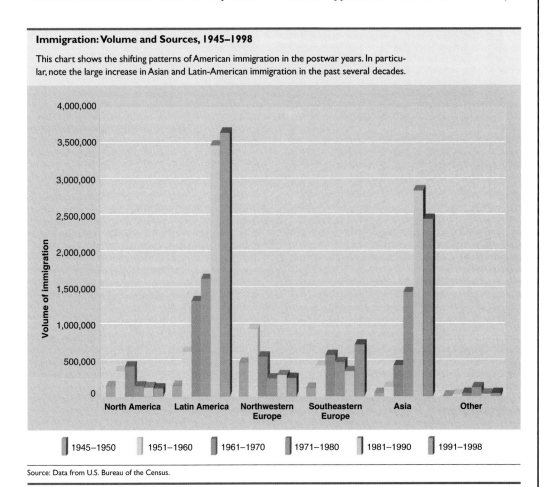

Immigration: Volume and Sources, 1945–1998

This chart shows the shifting patterns of American immigration in the postwar years. In particular, note the large increase in Asian and Latin-American immigration in the past several decades.

Volume of immigration

North America   Latin America   Northwestern Europe   Southeastern Europe   Asia   Other

1945–1950   1951–1960   1961–1970   1971–1980   1981–1990   1991–1998

Source: Data from U.S. Bureau of the Census.

life. Opposition to the German *gastsarbeiter* became a political issue; in the Netherlands, Pim Fortuyn, a right-wing politician who had argued for extreme restrictions on immigration, was assassinated just before the 2002 general election in which his party had expected to do well and he had hopes of becoming prime minister.

That opposition, which echoed the anti-immigrant feeling of the past, included strenuous efforts to restrict illegal immigration. Resistance came to a head in California in 1994, where voters passed Proposition 187, denying illegal aliens access to public education and medical clinics. Just days after the election, a federal judge issued a preliminary injunction to prevent implementation of the ballot measure, which she made permanent several years later. Yet Proposition 187 provided a model for other states to follow and caught the attention of congressional members, especially Republicans, who gained control of Congress in 1994. Two years later, Congress passed legislation barring legal immigrants (who were not yet citizens) from receiving food stamps and disability assistance from the federal government. Meanwhile, toward the end of the decade, California ended its support for bilingual education, mandating English immersion instead and sparking a similar national drive.

Economic improvement, and the move toward full employment in the latter part of the 1990s, brought a political shift in the immigration debate. In 2000, pressure mounted to increase the number of visas for high-tech workers abroad, while a coalition of business groups and immigrant-rights organizations pressed for admitting more unskilled workers who could work in the service sector where there were unfilled jobs. Political considerations also played a part in the shift. Both Democrats and Republicans recognized the voting power of Latinos in particular and wanted to ensure their support.

Immigration issues became headline news at the end of the 1990s in the highly publicized case of six-year-old Elián Gonzales. In November 1999, he was miraculously pulled out of the water near Florida when a group of Cuban boat people trying to reach the United States drowned. His father, still back in Cuba, had not given permission for the boy to leave and wanted him back. Instead, the Immigration and Naturalization Service (INS) placed him in temporary custody with a Cuban cousin in Miami.

Elián became a pawn in a tremendous struggle. The Miami Cuban community, which hated Fidel Castro and his Communist regime, wanted the boy to receive asylum and stay in the United States. Others, including the INS, argued that the boy should be returned to his father in Cuba. In the end,

Attorney General Janet Reno authorized a raid that seized Elián and arranged for his repatriation.

The INS, already unpopular, attracted fierce criticism in the face of the terrorist attacks of September 11, 2001. It had allowed into the country immigrants from Saudi Arabia and elsewhere who had orchestrated the airplane hijackings that shocked the world. Now Americans began to look askance at Arabs or Muslims elsewhere in the country and to condemn the INS for its laxity in screening out potential terrorists.

The Census of 2000

The 2000 census reported a 13 percent increase in the nation's population, as the United States gained 32.7 million people in the 1990s to give a total of 281.4 million inhabitants. This expansion surpassed the previous 10-year record of 28 million people in the 1950s, in the midst of the baby boom after World War II. The rate of growth, which had slowed down over the past three decades, now accelerated in the 1990s as it reflected increased immigration and longer life expectancy.

While every state had a net increase in population, growth was greatest in the West, increasingly important in the economic, social, and cultural life of the nation. Altogether, the West as a whole gained 10.4 million people and expanded by 19 percent. Some areas showed extraordinary expansion. The Phoenix, Arizona, metropolitan area grew by 45 percent, while the Las Vegas, Nevada, metropolitan region expanded by 83 percent.

The United States remained about 69 percent white, with a 12 percent African-American and 11 percent Latino population. Latinos and blacks both predominated in urban centers and immigration entry areas. Latinos continued to flock to southern California, the Texas border region, and the south of Florida, and they also began to congregate in increasing numbers in places like Chicago and Denver, while at the same time settling in small towns all over the United States. Overall, their numbers increased by 38.8 percent. African Americans maintained their dominance in older northern cities such as Detroit and in Washington, D.C., while continuing to move into metropolitan suburbs, where they found changing employment and housing opportunities.

Nationally, the Asian and Pacific Islander population increased by 43 percent. In California, Asians showed the largest increase of any group. They now comprised nearly 13 percent of the state population and maintained their position as the third largest population group, after whites and Latinos. Much of the Asian population growth occurred in the sub-

1078   PART 6 A Resilient People, 1945–2002

Portrait of a Nation

The 2000 census documented changing population patterns and reported where different groups resided in the United States. Note the concentration of African Americans in the Southeast and the concentration of Hispanics in the Southwest. The Asian American population was greatest in the West, while American Indians, who had once roamed the continent, were now confined to a number of much smaller western areas.

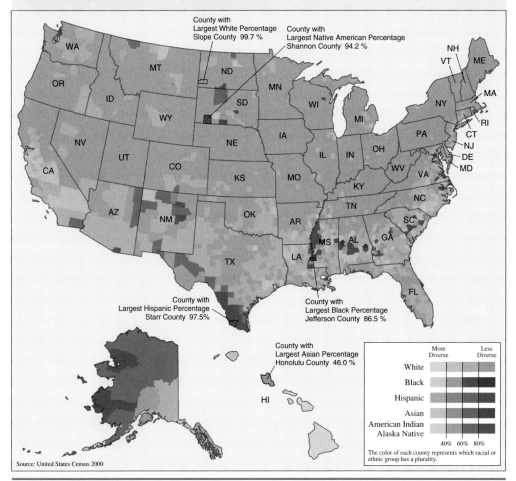

County with Largest White Percentage Slope County 99.7 %

County with Largest Native American Percentage Shannon County 94.2 %

County with Largest Hispanic Percentage Starr County 97.5%

County with Largest Black Percentage Jefferson County 86.5 %

County with Largest Asian Percentage Honolulu County 46.0 %

	More Diverse		Less Diverse
White			
Black			
Hispanic			
Asian			
American Indian Alaska Native			

40% 60% 80%

The color of each county represents which racial or ethnic group has a plurality.

Source: United States Census 2000

urbs, where the more affluent moved, though large pockets of poverty remained in places like Chinatown in Los Angeles and Little Phnom Penh in Long Beach.

The new census revealed that the combination of Latinos, African Americans, and Asians now outnumbered whites in California. This was the first time since 1860, when California began to provide accurate census data, that whites did not have a majority. State politics already began to reflect the shift. In 1998, Cruz Bustamante became the first Latino elected to statewide office in California since 1871, when he became lieutenant governor. This shift had enormous social and political implications. The United States, founded as a white man's country, had now developed into a nation where people of

Population Change for the Ten Largest Cities, 1990–2000

Most American cities grew in the 1990s, although some old industrial centers such as Philadelphia and Detroit lost population.

City and State	Population		Change, 1990–2000	
	April 1, 1990	**April 1, 2000**	**Number**	**Percent**
New York, NY	7,322,564	8,008,278	685,714	9.4
Los Angeles, CA	3,485,398	3,694,820	209,422	6.0
Chicago, IL	2,783,726	2,896,016	112,290	4.0
Houston, TX	1,630,553	1,953,631	323,078	19.8
Philadelphia, PA	1,585,577	1,517,550	−68,027	−4.3
Phoenix, AZ	983,403	1,321,045	337,642	34.3
San Diego, CA	1,110,549	1,223,400	112,851	10.2
Dallas, TX	1,006,877	1,188,580	181,703	18.0
San Antonio, TX	935,933	1,144,646	208,713	22.3
Detroit, MI	1,027,974	951,270	−76,704	−7.5

Source: U.S. Census Bureau, Census 2000; 1990 Census, *Population and Housing Unit Counts, United States* (1990 CPH-2-1).

color were increasingly numerous and soon would be leaving their imprint on public policy in important ways.

One new feature of the 2000 census revealed the desire of large numbers of Americans to identify themselves as part of more than one racial or ethnic group. Nationwide, 2.4 percent of the American people identified themselves as multiracial. In Hawaii, 21 percent of all residents traced their heritage to two or more racial or ethnic groups. At long last, the United States was beginning to embrace its multicultural and multiracial heritage.

ECONOMIC AND SOCIAL CHANGE

In the 1990s, the American economy improved dramatically. Yet despite the revival, millions of Americans remained poor, and homelessness became an increasingly visible problem. Meanwhile, groups pushing for equality made significant gains, but they still faced resistance in their long, continuing struggle for fair treatment in the United States.

Boom and Bust

American economic recovery began in mid-1992, even as other parts of the world found themselves facing industrial problems. In Germany, where extraordinary economic growth had occurred in the post–World War II years, the economy—the largest in Europe—faltered. As the growth rate slowed, the unemployment rate, which reached 5.2 percent in 1990, rose steadily over the course of the decade, hitting 10 percent in 1997 (and going even higher in

the new millennium). Reunification of East Germany and West Germany came at a heavy cost. The Japanese economy, the second-largest in the world (after the United States), likewise encountered trouble. Japan had revived dramatically after World War II, and growth had continued into the 1970s and 1980s, when productivity was higher than in the United States. Then the American productivity rate caught up, and Japan found itself hemmed in with excessive bureaucratic regulation and a system of lifetime employment for workers that made it difficult for companies to retrench in hard times. Recession led to falling prices, and even while the unemployment rate was low (3.4 percent in 1997, 4.1 percent in 1998), the economy remained sluggish.

Against that backdrop, the American revival was even more remarkable. The promotion of big business in the Reagan era (see Chapter 30) spurred investment and led to significant economic expansion as large firms grew larger still and became even more involved in the global economy. The lowering of interest rates by the Federal Reserve Board revived confidence and promoted consumer spending. Productivity rose steadily throughout the decade, though not quite as quickly as it had in the 1950s and 1960s. Similarly, the national economic growth rate began to rise again, reaching 3.9 percent in 1997, while averaging 3 percent in the years since the recovery began. Growth, like productivity, was not as dramatic as it had sometimes been in the golden years of industrial development, but it was sustained in what became the longest expansion in American history. Inflation fell; in 1998, it stood at the lowest rate since 1965. The unemployment rate also declined, dropping from 7.8 percent in 1992 to

4.6 percent in 1997, with monthly rates occasionally even lower in the next several years. Taking credit for the recovery, President Bill Clinton declared that the drop in unemployment was "the latest evidence that our economy is growing, steady and strong, that the American dream is in fact alive and well."

One reflection of the return of prosperity was the soaring stock market. A willingness to invest in the market is often a good indicator of confidence in the nation's economic health. In the 1990s, millions of Americans became emboldened by the positive economic indicators and invested billions of dollars in mutual funds and stocks. This period was marked by a dramatic increase in the number of investors, reaching approximately 50 percent of the population in 2000. Some purchased stocks for themselves, often working on their own computers, without using a stock broker. Others purchased mutual funds, where experts took the money invested and used their expert advice to put together a diversified portfolio. Much of the investment was in the high-tech area, where people poured billions of dollars into start-up companies not yet making a profit, in the hope that they would take off. The market, which had inched upward in past years, now began a dramatic rise. The Dow Jones average topped the once-unimaginable 10,000 barrier in 1999 and quickly moved on past the 11,000 mark. Investors, most from the middle and upper classes, made considerable amounts of money in the market.

An even more important sign of economic health was the dramatic reduction in the budget deficit. A Democratic effort to preempt a Republican issue and hold down spending paid off, particularly as low interest rates encouraged economic expansion. In 1998, the United States finished with a budget surplus for the first time in 29 years. With $70 billion—the largest surplus ever—left over at the end of the fiscal year, Democrats and Republicans began arguing about how the money should be used. President Clinton and most Democrats favored using funds to bolster the social security system, which seemed likely to run out of money, while Republicans, who controlled Congress, preferred a politically attractive tax cut. Forgotten in the euphoria was the fact that the national debt—the total of all past deficits—remained over $5.4 trillion.

In these prosperous times, American companies embarked upon a wave of mergers like those around the turn of the century that created the great oil and steel corporations. In the defense industry, for example, Lockheed and Martin Marietta merged in 1994, while Boeing merged with McDonnell Douglas in 1996. In 1997, a record $1 trillion in mergers involving American companies took place

as huge conglomerates swallowed up smaller competitors in the interests of efficiency and ever-larger profits. One consequence of the mergers, however, was layoffs of workers who duplicated tasks and seemed superfluous. The jobs available to those looking for other work were often positions like those held by Marlene Garrett and her husband, introduced earlier in the chapter, which paid far less.

Then, all too quickly, the economy faltered. The soaring stock market of the 1990s finally reversed course. The bull market reminded some observers of the speculative bubble of the 1920s. Alan Greenspan, chairman of the Federal Reserve Board, warned in 1996 against "irrational exuberance" in the market, but most investors, especially those making millions of dollars, ignored his warning. Yet, as economist John Kenneth Galbraith warned as he studied the Great Crash of 1929, all bubbles must burst some day. In 2000, the stock market began to slide, as investors realized that many of the financial gains did not reflect commensurate gains in productivity. In 2000, the year ended with the major stock indexes—the Dow Jones Industrial Average and the Nasdaq Composite—showing their worst performance in decades, and in 2001 and 2002, the market continued to fall, wiping out the paper gains of millions of large and small investors.

The nation's overall growth rate began to slow as investment declined. Lack of confidence in the market, particularly in the high-tech area that had fueled the boom, led to a corresponding lack of confidence in the economy. As a recession began in 2000, a tax cut, described later in this chapter, further undermined the stability of the economy. Promoted by Republican George W. Bush after his victory in the presidential election of 2000, the tax cut was skewed in favor of wealthy Americans and not only failed to provide a necessary stimulus but contributed to the decline.

By early 2001, it was clear that the economy was slumping. In February, manufacturing fell to its lowest point in 10 years. Economists hoped that it would turn around quickly, but their hopes were shattered as it began to look as though improvement was still in the distant future. Unemployment rolls increased and applications for state unemployment benefits surged. *Newsweek* magazine ran a story asking the question everyone feared: "How Safe Is Your Job?"

Confidence in the economy was further eroded by growing reports of corporate greed and managerial fraud. Emboldened by deregulation in the 1980s, many corporations had taken advantage of lax oversight practices and made huge—and sometimes illegal—profits. Toward the end of 2001, the

Enron Corporation, a company that bought and sold energy, admitted that it had filed five years of misleading reports and declared bankruptcy. As the scandal grew, it became clear that the Arthur Andersen accounting firm had participated in providing cover for financial irregularities, reaping huge financial gains, but in the end losing clients when it faced an indictment for its role in the process. As the corporate empire began to tumble, the top executives cashed in their stock and made millions of dollars, while the company's workers, unaware of the looming catastrophe and prohibited from unloading stock, lost not just their jobs but their life savings as well.

Some people argued that the Enron case was an anomaly—a bad apple in the barrel—and contended that the rest of corporate America was in good shape. As 2002 unfolded, it became clear that many other companies had been falsifying their books and other accounting firms had likewise looked the other way. In the summer of that year, WorldCom, the telecommunications giant whose customers included the 20 million users of the MCI long-distance service, filed for bankruptcy in the largest case in American history. Acknowledging that it had improperly accounted for nearly $4 billion of expenses, it laid off workers and undertook a frantic effort to reorganize its finances. Just as Americans had discovered the abuses of big business during the Progressive period in the late nineteenth and early twentieth centuries, now they found themselves troubled by the corporate scandals in the daily news as the twenty-first century began.

For much of the decade, observers had pointed to the growing gap between rich and poor. Now, as the economy limped along at the start of the twenty-first century, more and more Americans found themselves in economic trouble. Millions who had prospered in the booming market of the 1990s found their gains wiped out, while those who had never had much remained marginalized.

Poverty and Homelessness

Poverty was a problem even in boom times. The Census Bureau reported in 1997 that 35.6 million people in the United States—the richest country in the world—still lived below what was defined as the poverty line of about $16,000 a year for a family of four. The percentage—13.3 percent—had fallen slightly in each of the past few years, but it was still sizable, especially considering that it included one out of every three *working* Americans. Worse still was the fact that in 1998, there were 900,000 more Americans living below the poverty line than in 1990.

Poverty in the United States was different than in other parts of the world, to be sure. People in American slums had more material benefits than many of the residents of Soweto, the huge slum just outside Johannesburg in South Africa. Homeless Americans were more fortunate than Cambodian

The homeless became far more visible in the 1990s. Here a man lies sleeping under a thin sheet of plastic, serving as his blanket, right in front of the White House in Washington, D.C. *(Bettmann/CORBIS)*

beggars who were often incapacitated by the explosions of land mines that still dotted their country years after the Vietnam War. Yet the American poor, like the poor in most other industrialized nations, still found themselves on the fringes of society, unable to cope on their own.

Urban Americans had the toughest time of all. Since the earliest days, the United States had glorified its rural heritage and its impact on national character. Even as population shifts led more and more people to live in cities, government programs often failed to provide fully for urban needs. As cities lost population to the suburbs in the last half of the twentieth century, they lost their tax base at the same time and could not easily meet the demand for services. Near the end of the twentieth century, the poverty rate in New York, Los Angeles, and Chicago hovered around 20 percent. In Cleveland, Detroit, Miami, and New Orleans, it was closer to 30 percent.

The gap between rich and poor increased significantly in the last two decades of the twentieth century. The efforts of the Reagan and Bush administrations in the 1980s and early 1990s to cut back on government spending and eliminate social programs that had provided services for the poor had a powerful effect in causing the growing gap. In 1999, it took 100 million people to equal the wealth of the top one percent. One study of household incomes during the last three economic cycles—in the late 1970s, the late 1980s, and the late 1990s—found that gains in the top 20 percent of families in those periods outstripped gains of the bottom 10 percent in 44 states. In five states—Arizona, California, New York, Ohio, and Wyoming—income of the bottom 20 percent fell, while it rose rapidly in the top 20 percent.

As always, minorities fared worse than whites. The net worth of a typical white household at the beginning of the 1990s was 12 times greater than the net worth of a typical black household and 8 times greater than the net worth of a typical Latino household. Minorities and women continued to lose ground faster than the rest of the population as the decade unfolded.

Just as the United States rediscovered its poor in the 1960s, so it rediscovered its homeless in the 1980s and 1990s. Even as unemployment dropped in the 1980s, the number of homeless quadrupled during that time. Numbers were hard to ascertain, for the homeless had no fixed addresses, but one estimate in 1990 calculated that 6 to 7 million people had been homeless at some point in the past five years. Another study noted that family homelessness in New York had risen between 1990 and 1995, with the largest increase coming among children nine years old and younger. A federal report released by the Secretary of Housing and Urban Development in 2000 noted that approximately 3.5 million people would become homeless at least once during the year, with 1.35 million of those children.

People became homeless for a variety of reasons. Some started life in disturbed families. Others fell prey to alcohol and drugs. Still others had health or learning problems that eroded the possibility of a stable life. For millions of working Americans, homelessness was just a serious and unaffordable illness away. While families in the past had felt a responsibility for taking care of their own, increased mobility in the twentieth century created a fragmentation that led more and more people to fall through the cracks. Though many Americans initially regarded the homeless as "bag ladies, winos, and junkies," they gradually came to realize that the underclass category included others as well.

Red, a homeless man in Las Vegas, Nevada, described his plight in 2000:

> I've been homeless for five years. It's getting worse. All they do at the shelter is give us food and a place to stay. I'm just maintaining. I can't get out of it at this rate. If I find a job and I put down the shelter address, they won't give you a job. At the blood blank, if they find out you're living at the shelter, they won't even let you donate blood. So I can't get money by donating blood.

As the federal government cut back on relief programs in an effort that had begun in the 1980s, private agencies had to pick up the slack. Goodwill Industries International reported a steady climb in the number of people it assisted with incomes well above the poverty line who still could not make ends meet.

Aging and Illness

The American population was older than ever before as the century came to an end. Between 1900 and 1994, when the population of the country tripled, the number of people over the age of 65 rose elevenfold and continued to rise in the next decade, reaching 33 million, or just about 12 percent of the population, in 2001. Underlying the rapid increase was the steady advance in medical care, which in the twentieth century had increased life expectancy in the United States from 47 to 74 years as the elderly were healthier than ever before. People once considered themselves old when they reached the age of 65; now, most 65-year-olds regarded themselves in a different light. Many Americans in their 80s continued to lead productive lives—participat-

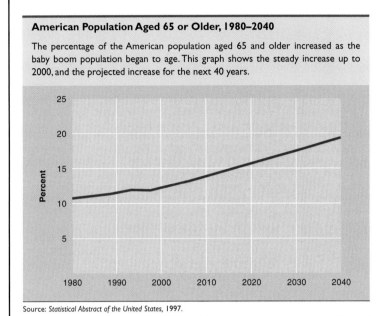

American Population Aged 65 or Older, 1980–2040

The percentage of the American population aged 65 and older increased as the baby boom population began to age. This graph shows the steady increase up to 2000, and the projected increase for the next 40 years.

Source: *Statistical Abstract of the United States*, 1997.

ing in activities such as writing books, teaching classes, and consulting with corporate clients.

Changes in the United States were somewhat different than those elsewhere, particularly in the developing world. According to one estimate, the entire population of the globe 65 years and over was likely to more than double in the 1998–2025 period, while the youth population under the age of 15 would only grow by 6 percent. Even so, most dependents in the world were likely to be children in the coming quarter century. Only in the United States and other developed countries would elderly dependents outnumber those under the age of 15.

One component of the aging revolution in the United States was Viagra, a new drug designed to help men suffering from impotence that came on the market in the 1990s. Whether sexual dysfunction was a result of prostate illness, common among older males, or emotional distress, Viagra helped ailing men enjoy normal sex lives. Americans, including the elderly, now talked frankly about erectile dysfunction, just as they had talked openly about birth control when the birth control pill was introduced three and a half decades before. *Newsweek* magazine noted in 1998 that Viagra was the fastest-selling drug in history.

The elderly raised new issues in a nation suffering periodic recessions. Many wanted to continue working and opposed mandatory retirement rules

that drove them from their jobs. Legislation in 1978 that raised the mandatory retirement age from 65 to 70 helped older workers but decreased employment opportunities for younger workers seeking jobs. In 1986, federal legislation amending the Age Discrimination in Employment Act prohibited mandatory retirement on the basis of age for virtually all workers and created continuing problems for younger employees in the 1990s. The political power of the elderly became increasingly visible.

Generational resentment over jobs was compounded by the knotty problems faced by the social security system, which was established a half century earlier. Other parts of the world—Scandinavia, for example—provided social services out of general revenues and took such expenditures for granted. However, in the United States, contributions to the system were necessary to keep it solvent, and that became a problem as the population aged. As more and more Americans retired, the system could not generate sufficient revenue to make the payments due without assistance from the general governmental fund. In the early 1980s, it appeared that the entire system might collapse. A government solution involving higher taxes for those still employed and a later age for qualifying for benefits rescued the fund for a time, but many Americans in the 1990s wondered whether social security would survive. In 2001, the nation began to

RECOVERING THE PAST

Autobiography

As we reach our own time, the historical past perhaps most worth recovering is our own. Our own story is as valid a part of the story of American history as the tale of Revolutionary War soldiers, frontier women, reform politicians, and immigrant grandparents. In this computerized age, the person we need to recover is ourself, a self that has been formed, at least in part, by the entire American experience we have been studying.

Autobiography is the form of writing in which people tell their own life's history. Although written autobiographies are at least as old as the literature of the early Christians (for example, *The Confessions of St. Augustine*), the word *autobiography* dates from the late eighteenth century, around the time of the French and American revolutions. That is no accident. These momentous events represented the triumph of individual liberty and the sovereignty of the self. *The Autobiography of Benjamin Franklin*, written between 1771 and Franklin's death in 1790 (and excerpted here), is a classic celebration of the American success story. Franklin's work set the standard for one autobiographical form, the memoir of one's public achievements and success. The other brief autobiographical memoir, from the reminiscences of Elizabeth Cady Stanton, also reflects the tone and range of this tradition.

Not all autobiographies are written late in life to celebrate one's accomplishments. The confessional

Autobiographical Memoirs

Benjamin Franklin

DEAR SON,

I have ever had a pleasure in obtaining any little anecdotes of my ancestors. You may remember the enquiries I made among the remains of my relations when you were with me in England and the journey I undertook for that purpose. Imagining it may be equally agreeable to you to know the circumstances of my life—many of which you are yet unacquainted with—and expecting a week's uninterrupted leisure in my present country retirement, I sit down to write them for you. Besides, there are some other inducements that excite me to this undertaking. From the poverty and obscurity in which I was born and in which I passed my earliest years, I have raised myself to a state of affluence and some degree of celebrity in the world. As constant good fortune has accompanied me even to an advanced period of life, my posterity will perhaps be desirous of learning the means, which I employed, and which, thanks to Providence, so well succeeded with me. They may also deem them fit to be imitated, should any of them find themselves in similar circumstances.

Source: *The Autobiography of Benjamin Franklin* (1771).

Elizabeth Cady Stanton

Elizabeth Cady Stanton

It was 'mid such exhilarating scenes that Miss Anthony and I wrote addresses for temperance, anti-slavery, educational and woman's rights conventions. Here we forged resolutions, protests, appeals, petitions, agricultural reports, and constitutional arguments; for we made it a matter of conscience to accept every invitation to speak on every question, in order to maintain woman's right to do so. To this end we took turns on the domestic watchtowers, directing amusements, settling disputes, protecting the weak against the strong, and trying to secure equal rights to all in the home as well as the nation.

It is often said, by those who know Miss Anthony best, that she has been my good angel, always pushing and goading me to work, and that but for her pertinacity I should never have accomplished the little I have. On the other hand it has been said that I forged the thunderbolts and she fired them. Perhaps all this is, in a measure, true. With the cares of a large family I might, in time, like too many women, have become wholly absorbed in a narrow family selfishness, had not my friend been continually exploring new fields for missionary labors. Her description of a body of men on any platform, complacently deciding questions in which women had an equal interest, without an equal voice, readily aroused me to a determination to throw a firebrand into the midst of their assembly.

Source: Elizabeth Cady Stanton, *Eighty Years and More: Reminiscences, 1815–1897* (1898).

Confessional Autobiographies

Black Elk

And so it was all over.

I did not know then how much was ended. When I look back now from this high hill of my old age, I can still see the butchered women and children lying heaped and scattered all along the crooked gulch as plain as when I saw them with eyes still young. And I can see that something else died there in the bloody mud, and was buried in the blizzard. A people's dream died there. It was a beautiful dream.

And I, to whom so great a vision was given in my youth,—you see me now a pitiful old man who has done nothing, for the nation's hoop is broken and scattered. There is no center any longer, and the sacred tree is dead.

Source: *Black Elk Speaks*, as told through John G. Neihardt (1932).

Malcolm X

I want to say before I go on that I have never previously told anyone my sordid past in detail. I haven't done it now to sound as though I might be proud of how bad, how evil, I was.

But people are always speculating—why am I as I am? To understand that of any person, his whole life, from birth, must be reviewed. All of our experiences fuse into our personality. Everything that ever happened to us is an ingredient.

Today, when everything that I do has an urgency, I would not spend one hour in the preparation of a book which has the ambition to perhaps titillate some readers. But I am spending many hours because the full story is the best way that I know to have it seen, and understood, that I had sunk to the very bottom of the American white man's society when—soon now, in prison—I found Allah and the religion of Islam and it completely transformed my life.

Source: *The Autobiography of Malcolm X*, with the assistance of Alex Haley (1964).

autobiography, unlike most memoirs, explores the author's interior life, acknowledging flaws and failures as well as successes; it may be written at any age. The purpose of this type of autobiography is not just to reconstruct one's past to preserve it for posterity, but to find from one's past an identity in order to know better how to live one's future. The story of religious confessions and conversions is an obvious example. This form also includes secular self-examinations such as those by Maxine Hong Kingston in *The Woman Warrior* (1976), Piri Thomas in *Down These Mean Streets* (1967), or Maya Angelou in a series of five autobiographical sketches beginning with *I Know Why the Caged Bird Sings* (1969). The other two excerpts presented here are among the finest examples of confessional autobiography and suggest its variety.

These examples hardly convey the full range of the autobiographical form or how available to all people is the opportunity to tell the story of one's life. In 1909, William Dean Howells called autobiography the "most democratic province in the republic of letters." A recent critic agrees, pointing out:

To this genre have been drawn public and private figures: poets, philosophers, prizefighters; actresses, artists, political activists; statesmen and penitentiary prisoners; financiers and football players; Quakers and Black Muslims; immigrants and Indians. The range of personality, experience, and profession reflected in the forms of American autobiography is as varied as American life itself.

Your story, too, is a legitimate part of American history. But writing an autobiography, while open to all, is deceptively difficult. Like historians, autobiographers face problems of sources, selection, interpretation, and style. As in the writing of any history, the account of one's past must be objective, not only in the verifiable accuracy of details but also in the honest selection of representative events to be described. Moreover, in fiction as well as history, the autobiographer must provide a structured form, an organizing principle, literary merit, and thematic coherence to the story. Many other challenges face the would-be autobiographer, such as finding a balance between one's public life and the private self and handling problems of memory, ego (should one, for example, use the first or third person?), and death.

Reflecting on the Past   To get an idea of the difficulties of writing an autobiography, try writing your own. Limit yourself to 1,000 words. Good luck.

consider establishing private retirement accounts as one part of the solution to the problem, but political agreement proved hard to attain, and the issue became much less compelling when the stock market faltered. Meanwhile, millions of elderly people wondered how they could afford the rapidly increasing cost of prescription drugs.

As Americans lived longer, they suffered increasingly from Alzheimer's disease, an affliction that gradually destroys a patient's memory and brings on infantile behavior. Diagnosis is difficult, and there is no treatment to reverse the ailment's course. The illness gained exposure in 1995 when the family of Ronald Reagan disclosed that the former president was suffering from the incurable disease.

Other illnesses affected old and young alike. The discovery of AIDS (acquired immune deficiency syndrome) in 1981 marked the start of one of the most serious diseases in the history of the United States—

As the AIDS epidemic caused more and more deaths, family members and friends began to create a huge quilt to celebrate the lives of those who had died. Each panel represented a different person. The quilt, shown here in Washington, D.C., was on display around the country and drew millions of viewers who came to remember those lost to the disease. *(Lisa Quinones/Black Star)*

and the world. Some nations found themselves decimated by AIDS. In China, for example, entire villages were infected with HIV (the human immunodeficiency virus that causes AIDS) as a result of unsterile practices in blood stations. In 2002, Russia faced a spiraling rate of infection and had 70,000 full-blown cases of AIDS, compared with 5,500 the previous year. Africa was hit even harder. One estimate from the United Nations, the World Bank, and the World Health Organization found that 34.3 million people in the world had AIDS, with 24.5 million of them in sub-Saharan Africa. Of the 13.2 million children in the world orphaned by the disease, 12.1 million came from the sub-Saharan region. In Kenya, some schools lost a teacher a month to AIDS. In Zimbabwe, estimates of life expectancy were expected to fall from age 61 in 2005 to age 33 in 2010.

While health conditions in the United States were better than those in many parts of the world, AIDS still had a corrosive effect. The sexual revolution of the 1960s had brought a major change in sexual patterns, particularly among the young, but now sexual experimentation was threatened by this deadly new disease. Although it seemed to strike intravenous drug users and homosexuals with numerous partners more than other groups at first, it soon spread to the heterosexual population as well. Babies with AIDS were born to mothers with the illness. AIDS became the leading cause of death in Americans between the ages of 25 and 44. The growing number of deaths—approximately 458,000 in 2001—suggested that the disease would reach epic proportions. That same year, some 800,000 to 900,000 Americans of all ages and ethnicities were living with HIV, which could burst into full-blown AIDS at any time. Advertisements in the national media advised the use of condoms, and the U.S. surgeon general mailed a brochure, *Understanding AIDS,* to every household in the United States. New drugs, taken in combination, extended the lifespan of those with the HIV virus and reduced the death rate in the 1990s, but AIDS remained a lethal, and ultimately fatal, disease. Despite medical advances, a cure remained elusive.

Minorities and Women Face the Twenty-First Century

Americans fighting for equality made gains in the 1990s. For African Americans, home ownership and employment figures rose. The numbers of murders and other violent crimes that involved blacks dropped. A record 40 percent of African Americans attended college in 1997, up from 32 percent in 1991. Yet African Americans faced constant reminders that Martin Luther King, Jr.'s dream of a color-blind America was not yet a reality. Incremental improvements often failed to erode racist ideas that were a legacy of American slavery. Incidents like the beating of black motorist Rodney King in Los Angeles in 1991 and the rioting that occurred the next year made many people wonder just how much progress the civil rights movement had made. A survey in San Diego noted that the police there stopped African-American and Latino motorists more than whites and Asian Americans—a pattern that was common around the country. The 2000 census revealed that the nation was more racially and ethnically diverse than ever before, yet it pointed out that people still lived in neighborhoods inhabited by people like themselves. African-American historian John Hope Franklin, looking back in 1995 at the eight decades of his life, summed up common frustrations when he said: "Just about the time you sit down or sit back and say, 'Oh, yes, we're really moving,' you get slapped back down."

Affirmative action was one area where blacks faced a backlash. Resistance, grounded in continuing racism and reflecting opposition to new arrivals in other parts of the world, began at the state level and spread around the nation. Energized by their political victories in 1994, conservatives launched a powerful attack on the policy of giving preferential treatment to groups that had suffered discrimination in the past. Arguing that government leaders had never intended affirmative action to be a permanent policy, they pushed ballot initiatives and pressured public agencies to bring the practice to an end. The most visible of those was Proposition 209 in California, approved by voters in the election of 1996, which prohibited the use of gender or race in awarding state government contracts or admitting students to state colleges and universities. After victory in California, African-American businessman Ward Connerly, who had spearheaded the effort, established an organization called, ironically, the American Civil Rights Institute to help other states enact similar bans on preferences. When he declared that he wanted to create the kind of color-blind society Martin Luther King, Jr., had sought, black lawmakers and civil rights leaders blasted him for "spitting on the grave" of King's legacy.

The increasingly conservative Supreme Court also waded into the controversy. In 1995, the Court let stand a lower court ruling prohibiting colleges and universities from awarding special scholarships to African Americans or other minorities. In 1996, it declined to hear an appeal of a U.S. District Court decision two years before in *Hopwood* v. *Texas* that prohibited the use of affirmative action in higher education. Meanwhile, other cases moved through the legal system. At the end of 2000, a federal judge ruled that the University of Michigan could use race in undergraduate admissions in the effort to promote diversity on campus. But early the next year, another federal judge ruled that the use of race in admissions at the University of Michigan Law School was unconstitutional. That decision was then overturned on appeal in mid-2002, setting the stage for another Supreme Court ruling, as both proponents and opponents waited anxiously to see what the court would decide.

The booming job market in the late 1990s was the most important factor in fostering better race relations. It provided new opportunities for people who had been unable to find jobs. A survey in 1999 reported that young black men in particular were moving back into the economic mainstream at a faster rate than their white counterparts, and crime levels were falling in areas where joblessness was declining. The jobless rate for young black men was still twice that for young white men, but the improvement was encouraging.

Even so, tensions that had existed throughout the twentieth century persisted. Issues stemming from continuing discrimination in finding jobs and persistent antagonism by the police erupted in the spring of 2001 in Cincinnati, Ohio. When a white policeman killed an unarmed black youth, confrontations around the city provided a bitter reminder of riots in the past. Five months after the riots, *The Cincinnati Enquirer* noted in a large front-page headline: "Races See Two Cincinnatis." The story observed: "In one, many white people feel safe and secure in their homes and neighborhoods, optimistic about their jobs and the futures of their children. In the other, many black people worry about daily survival—about becoming victims of violent crime and being stopped by the police, about being discriminated against in places where they work, eat and shop."

In early 2002, African-American television correspondent Ed Bradley pointed to changes he had seen in the course of his career. "When asked about progress," he said, "I'm often reminded of the old lady sitting in the church who says, 'It ain't what it ought to be, but thank God it ain't what it used to be.'" Bradley was right, but many African Americans wondered when further change would come.

Women likewise made steady progress in the 1990s. They were increasingly involved in academic programs and professions that had been closed to them several decades earlier. In 2001, for example, women made up 49.4 percent of all first-year law students, compared to 10 percent in 1970; that pattern was reflected in other segments of society as well. In the academic world that same year, women held 44 percent of all entry-level college teaching jobs, though they had only 14 percent of the most senior positions, revealing another common pattern. In addition, women worked as pilots on commercial planes and served on the front lines fighting the forest fires that broke out in the West in the summer of 2002. At the same time that there was substantial gender change in nearly every segment of the job market, there was still continuing resistance to inclusion at the top. Women started to become the heads of major firms (such as Carly Fiorina at computer giant Hewlett-Packard) as the glass ceiling, preventing women from rising to the top of the corporate ladder, began to crack in the 1990s, yet most leaders were still men.

Abortion remained a polarizing issue, particularly as anti-abortion activists sought to disrupt abortion clinics. They launched around-the-clock pickets, aimed at frightening away women seeking abortions. Physicians performing abortions found their lives at risk, and Barnet Slepian, a Buffalo doctor, became the latest casualty when he was killed in 1998 in his own home by a sniper shooting through a window. Abortion opponents also took aim at a seldom used, late-term procedure they called "partial birth abortion." Congress passed a measure banning the procedure, but President Clinton vetoed it. When some states passed their own restrictive measure, the courts stepped into the controversy, and in mid-2000, the Supreme Court, by a narrow 5–4 vote margin, declared that a Nebraska law banning the practice (and by implication, similar laws in 30 other states) was unconstitutional. That same year, when the Food and Drug Administration finally approved a drug known as RU-486, the so-called abortion pill, abortion opponents jumped into the controversy and sought—unsuccessfully—to attach conditions that would effectively eliminate its use. Abortion remained one of the issues dividing the American people.

The abortion debate was just one measure that created a backlash against the feminist label, even as men and women both accepted the changes brought by the women's movement. Women hesitated to be associated with what they still considered a radical fringe, and that affected how they identified themselves. In 1998, only 26 percent of working women said "To me, a career is as important as being a wife and mother," down from 36 percent in 1979. While young women took for granted the gains fought for and won by their mothers and grandmothers, fewer wanted to call themselves feminists.

Yet the feminist movement persisted and brought continued improvements in the lives of women. American feminists looked to their counterparts in Europe, where even more advances had taken place. Nations seeking to join the European Union had to accept its equal rights provisions. The government in France considered the issue of gender parity in political representation and in 2000 passed a measure mandating that in certain cases, there needed to be an equal number of male and female candidates. Backlash was much less common in Europe. Progress in the United States did not always come easily, particularly as demographic patterns changed. The 2000 census revealed that the number of families headed by single mothers had risen to 7.5 million, an increase of 25 percent since 1990. Still, despite problems, efforts to bring about equal rights continued.

Latinos likewise pushed for greater equality and had demographic change on their side. The 2000 census and subsequent studies based on the data provided noted that the Latino population spread farther and faster than any previous immigrant wave, even exceeding the influx of eastern Europeans in the early twentieth century. The Latino population increase of 38 percent since 1990 dwarfed the national rise. Metropolitan areas such as New York, Los Angeles, El Paso, and Miami still accounted for the largest numbers of Latinos, but many now gravitated to suburban areas, where they found homes and jobs. In 2000, 46 percent of all Latinos owned their own homes, compared to 42 percent a decade before, though that figure still lagged behind the national number of 66 percent.

The emergence of a sturdy middle class gave Latinos a greater voice in social and political affairs. In 1993, Henry Cisneros became secretary of housing and urban development, and Federico Peña became secretary of transportation in Bill Clinton's administration. At the end of the decade, with Latinos projected to become the nation's largest minority by 2005, Latino political figures became even more numerous and visible. In California, for example, both the lieutenant governor and the speaker of the assembly were Chicano, as was the mayor of San Jose. Democrat Loretta Sanchez, who defeated eight-term congressman Robert Dornan in Orange County, served in the U.S. House of Representatives. In the administration of George W. Bush, White House counsel Alberto Gonzales played a major role in making judicial appointments.

As the nation's overall unemployment rate dropped in the mid-1990s, the rate for the 12 million Latino workers likewise fell—from 9.8 percent in 1992 to 7.3 percent in 1997. Despite that drop, the rate remained higher than the rate for white workers. Meanwhile, median Hispanic household income fell, even as it rose for every other ethnic and racial group. Many Latinos found it difficult to make ends meet.

Latinos nevertheless had a growing impact on American culture. Though Hispanic students were three times as likely as whites, and twice as likely as blacks, to drop out of high school, they made their influence felt in other ways. Merengue music could often be heard in music stores or on the radio. Argentine steakhouses could be found in many cities. Use of the Spanish language became more and more common around the country. President George W. Bush himself used Spanish in appealing to this important electoral bloc.

Even so, Latinos faced many of the same difficulties as blacks. Proposition 209 in California, ending affirmative action at the state level, led to a drop in the percentage of Latino students in the first-year class at the University of California at Berkeley from 13 percent in 1997 to 7 percent in 1998. But aggressive efforts by university administrators to look more carefully at a variety of issues and to minimize the value attached to standardized tests led the percentage to increase in subsequent years.

Native Americans found they had less influence, in part because of their smaller numbers. In the 2000 census, only 4.1 million people, or 1.5 percent of the population, identified themselves as American Indian or Alaska Native. Yet Indians still managed to keep the causes that concerned them before the public.

Indians continued their legal efforts to regain lost land. In 1999, the federal government joined the Oneida Indians in a lawsuit arguing that state and local governments in central New York had illegally acquired 270,000 acres of land from them in the late eighteenth and early nineteenth centuries and wanted restitution. Now it was the turn of 20,000 landowners to be worried about the fate of their property. Meanwhile, Cayugas claimed a substantial section of the northern tip of Cayuga Lake, in upstate New York, while the Mohawks and Senecas fought to regain control over parcels of land they claimed had been wrongfully obtained in the past.

Some of these efforts met with success. In early 2000, the federal government returned 84,000 acres in northern Utah that it had taken from the Utes in 1916 when it sought to secure the rights to valuable reserves of oil shale. "We're trying to do the right thing, returning land to its rightful owners," Energy Secretary Bill Richardson declared.

Native Americans became more politically active in the 1990s. In the election of 1992, Ben Nighthorse Campbell was elected to the Senate from his home state of Colorado. (AP/Wide World Photos)

Indians also pressed successfully for the return of Indian skeletal remains, removed by white scientists and museum officials over the course of the last century. Ever since passage of the Native American Graves Protection and Repatriation Act of 1990, skeletons and sacred objects flowed back to the tribes where they belonged. In 1997, Harvard's Peabody Museum sent back the bones of nearly 2,000 Pueblo Indians in the largest single return of these remains.

Native-American women became increasingly active in the reform effort. Ada Deer, who had successfully fought the government's termination policy in the 1970s, served as Assistant Secretary of the Interior in the 1990s. Winona LaDuke, an environmental activist, directed the Honor the Earth Fund and the White Earth Land Recovery Project, fought needless hydroelectric development, and was singled out by *Time* magazine as one of the nation's 50 most promising leaders under 40 years of age. In 2000, she served as Ralph Nader's vice presidential running mate on the small Green Party ticket.

Many Indians still felt a sense of dislocation, captured by novelist Sherman Alexie in 1993. Asked what

Diminishing Tribal Lands

While Native Americans steadily lost their territory over a period of 200 years, in the 1990s, Indians filed lawsuits to regain tribal lands and were successful in some of their claims. *(Source: New York Times, June 25, 2000)*

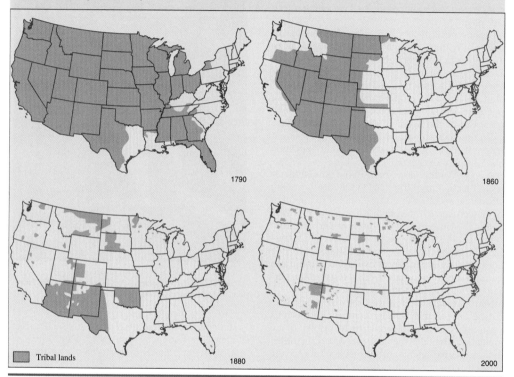

it was like to return from the city to the reservation, he responded through the narrator in one of the stories in *The Lone Ranger and Tonto Fistfight in Heaven:*

> "It's like a bad dream you never wake up from," I said, and it's true. Sometimes I still feel like half of me is lost in the city, with its foot wedged into a steam grate or something. Stuck in one of those revolving doors, going round and round while all the white people are laughing. Standing completely still on an escalator that will not move, but I didn't have the courage to climb the stairs by myself.

An important symbolic gesture occurred in the last months of the Clinton administration. As the Bureau of Indian Affairs celebrated its 175th anniversary, Kevin Gover, head of the agency, reversed the pattern that had been so predominant in the past when he apologized for the nation's repressive treatment of Native Americans. "In truth, this is no occasion for celebration," he said. It was, rather, a time "for sorrowful truths to be spoken, a time for contrition." He spoke of "the decimination of the mighty bison herds, the use of the poison alcohol to destroy minds and body, and the cowardly killing of women and children." The suffering inflicted on the Indians "made for tragedy on a scale so ghastly that it cannot be dismissed as merely the inevitable consequence of the clash of competing cultures." Secretary of the Interior Bruce Babbitt called the bureau "a work in progress" and noted that now most of its 10,000 employees were Indians themselves.

Asian Americans enjoyed real success in the 1990s. With about 11 million people—approximately four percent of the national population—of Asian descent in the United States in 2000, there was a now critical mass. They came from a variety of cultures, to be sure, and Filipinos often had different experiences than Chinese or Koreans or Japanese, yet together they had an increasingly important impact on American society. Many of the children enjoyed remarkable educational achievements, making up a disproportionate share of the students at the most prestigious universities. In 2000, the student body at the Massachusetts Institute of Technology was 28 percent Asian American; at the University of California at Berkeley, the figure was 39 percent. In the middle of that year, President Clinton appointed Norman Y. Mineta as secretary of commerce, making him the first Asian American to hold a cabinet position.

Yet Asian Americans in the 1990s found themselves in an ambiguous position. While they had higher median incomes than whites, due in part to a dedicated work ethic, newcomers faced serious economic problems. Sometimes Asian Americans competed with African Americans and Latinos, as affirmative action programs limited the number of Asians who could be admitted in order to give other groups a chance.

A report in 2000 observed that many Americans still saw Asian Americans as secretive and inscrutable. That kind of reaction was frustrating. "Too many people in this country continue to see us in simple stereotypes," complained Paul M. Ong, a social policy professor at the University of California at Los Angeles.

Asian-American efforts to secure their own rights were complicated by the fact that two-thirds were immigrants, and most came to the United States after 1965. As the leader of one Chinese-American civil rights group noted, "Most don't know civil rights history. They may not understand the struggles of other minorities. But the fact is we are still seen as minorities in this country, no ifs, ands or buts about it."

The struggle for gay rights also continued, and slowly gays began to achieve their demands. In a major change in 2000, the Big 3 automakers— General Motors, Ford, and Chrysler—announced health-care benefits for partners of gay employees, in a move that covered 465,000 workers. That same year, Vermont recognized same-sex relationships through civil unions, though stopped short of permitting gay marriages. In 2002, the American Academy of Pediatricians announced its support of the right of gay men and women to adopt the children of their partners. The definition of a family was becoming broader as a result of gay activism. As the gay rights movement celebrated the 30-year anniversary of the gay rights parade commemorating the riot at the Stonewall Inn in Greenwich Village in 1969 that had sparked gay resistance, proponents noted that the event had changed from a protest to a party, and, as the *New York Times* observed, "that in itself is a sign of success."

Still, there was continuing resistance to gays playing a more visible role in American society. In

Asian Americans followed the example of civil rights activists to demand appropriate treatment. In an effort to counter decades of discrimination— and violence—some marched in 1993 to commemorate the thirtieth anniversary of the March on Washington in which Martin Luther King, Jr., and other activists demanded equality. (© Corky Lee)

1998, 21-year-old University of Wyoming student Matthew Shepherd died after being brutally beaten and tortured by two men troubled by his lifestyle. When actress Ellen DeGeneres came out as lesbian on television, both as a character in her sitcom and in real life, some viewers wondered if her public decision accounted for the eventual canceling of her show. While most American cities had thriving gay communities, there was still deep-seated resistance to gays living openly in some quarters.

The polarization about the acceptance of gays was most visible in a 5–4 Supreme Court ruling in mid-2000 that the Boy Scouts could bar gay troop leaders and even gay boys. The case had begun when the Boy Scouts had ousted James Dale, an assistant scoutmaster, after the organization discovered he was gay. Now, after a series of appeals, the Court declared that forcing the Scouts to accept gays violated the organization's rights of free expression and free association under the First Amendment of the Constitution.

Some Americans supported the ruling. But a growing number began to speak out in opposition. "I think discrimination within the Boy Scouts gets rid of the whole concept of what the Boy Scouts are all about," said Kevin Elliot, a 13-year-old eighth grader who was a scout himself. In the spring of 2001, filmmaker Steven Spielberg, a former Eagle Scout, resigned from an advisory group after 10 years of service, saying he could not serve a group practicing "intolerance and discrimination."

DEMOCRATIC REVIVAL

The 1990s saw a Democratic revival. After the success of conservative Republicans in the 1980s, challenging the assumptions of the liberal welfare state and advancing a more limited conception of the role of government, Democrats regrouped, reformulated their message, and followed the lead of the Republicans in relying on new forms of media to broadcast political appeals. The pattern in the United States reflected similar shifts in the rest of the world as more liberal politicians asserted that government needed to play a greater role in advancing the public welfare. Politicians in a variety of countries tried to recast their appeal in different ways, rather than trotting out tarnished notions from the past, to win office and then implement their plans. In Great Britain, the Labour party headed by Tony Blair took over from the Conservative party of Margaret Thatcher. In Germany, Gerhard Schroeder of the Social Democratic party unseated the more conservative Helmut Kohl of the Christian Democratic Union,

who had served as chancellor for 16 years. But in the United States, for much of the decade, even as the Democrats regained the White House, the Republicans maintained control of Congress and bitter partisan fighting was the result.

Democratic Victory

In 1992, the Democratic party mounted an aggressive challenge to Republican rule. After a fierce primary campaign, Governor Bill Clinton of Arkansas triumphed over a crowded field of candidates. Overcoming allegations of marital instability, marijuana use, and draft evasion, he argued that it was time for a new generation to take command. Forty-six years old, he had reached maturity in the 1960s and stood in stark contrast to President George H. W. Bush, now running for reelection, who had come of age during World War II. The third candidate in what became a three-way race was H. Ross Perot, a billionaire businessman from Texas who had made a fortune in the computer data-processing field. Stressing his independence from both political parties, he declared that he alone could provide the business experience and leadership the nation needed.

This campaign, more than any in the past, was fought on television. In addition to three televised presidential debates, the candidates appeared on

Bill Clinton was an exuberant campaigner who used his musical talent to attract support when he ran for president in 1992. Here he plays his saxophone on nationwide television on "The Arsenio Hall Show" in Los Angeles. *(AP/Wide World Photos)*

Presidential Elections, 1992–1996

Year	Candidate	Party	Popular Vote	Electoral Vote
1992	BILL CLINTON	Democratic	43,728,275 (43.2%)	357
	George Bush	Republican	38,167,416 (37.7%)	168
	H. Ross Perot	Independent	19,237,245 (19.0%)	0
1996	BILL CLINTON	Democratic	47,401,185 (49.2%)	379
	Robert Dole	Republican	39,197,469 (40.7%)	159
	H. Ross Perot	Reform	8,085,294 (8.4%)	0

Note: Winners' names appear in capital letters.

talk shows and interview programs. Perot energized his campaign with appearances on "Larry King Live." Bill Clinton used a post–Super Bowl appearance on "60 Minutes" to answer charges questioning his character and later played his saxophone on the "Arsenio Hall Show" and appeared on MTV. This reliance on the electronic marketplace reoriented American campaign politics. Although Bush's popularity rating was high after the success of the Persian Gulf War, many Americans were turned off when he reneged on his campaign promise of "no new taxes."

On election day, Clinton won 43 percent of the popular vote to 38 percent for Bush and 19 percent for Perot. The electoral vote margin was even larger: 357 for Clinton, 168 for Bush, 0 for Perot. The Democrats retained control of both houses of Congress, with more women and minority members than ever before.

The president-elect wanted to check the cynicism that was poisoning political life. In 1964, three-quarters of the American public trusted the government to do the right thing most of the time. Three decades later, after the deception of leaders in the Vietnam War and the Watergate affair, the number was closer to one-quarter. Clinton sought to shift the nation's course after 12 years of Republican rule with Cabinet nominations that included four women, four African Americans, and two Latinos. He held a televised "economic summit" to explore national options and demonstrated a keen grasp of the details of policy. In his inaugural address, Clinton declared that "a new season of American renewal has begun." He also spoke out on behalf of a "communitarian" initiative, in which Americans would be more concerned with their responsibilities to the larger national community than with their individual and collective rights, as he tried to revive a commitment to participate in public affairs that dated back to the early days of the republic.

Clinton soon found his hands full at home. Although the economy finally began to improve, the public gave the president little credit for the upturn.

He gained Senate ratification of the North American Free Trade Agreement (NAFTA)—aimed at promoting free trade between Canada, Mexico, and the United States—in November 1993 after a bitter battle in which opponents argued that American workers would lose their jobs to less well-paid Mexicans. He secured passage of a crime bill banning the manufacture, sale, or possession of 19 different assault weapons (though a much larger number of semiautomatic guns were not included in this bill). But he failed to win approval of his major legislative initiative: health-care reform. The United States lagged behind most other industrialized countries in the way it provided for public health. A national health-care system in Great Britain provided universal coverage. An even more extensive system in Scandinavia met all health needs. In the United States, people were largely expected to deal with their health needs on their own. Medicare took care of the elderly, and Medicaid provided some relief for the poor, but both were limited when compared to the coverage provided by other nations. "This health-care system of ours is badly broken," Clinton said in September 1993, "and it's time to fix it." Particularly troublesome were escalating costs and the lack of universal medical care, which left 35 million Americans with no medical insurance. Clinton's complicated proposal for a system of health alliances in each state provoked intense opposition from the health-care and insurance industries and from politicians with plans of their own. In the end, he was unable to persuade Congress either to accept his approach or adopt a workable alternative.

Republican Resurgence

Voters demonstrated their dissatisfaction in the midterm elections of 1994. Republicans argued that government regulations were hampering business and costing too much. They challenged the notion that the federal government was primarily responsible for health care and other such services. Capitalizing on the continuing appeal of the leadership of Ronald Reagan in the 1980s, they demanded a scaled-down role for the government. Republicans swept control of both the Senate and the House of Representatives for the first time in over 40 years. In the House, they made the largest gains since 1946, winning more than 50 races against Democratic incumbents. Some of the strongest and most senior Representatives, including Speaker Thomas Foley, lost their seats. At the state level, Republicans picked up 12 governorships and took control in seven of the eight largest states.

The election marked the end of the commitment to the welfare state. The 104th Congress moved aggressively to make good on its promises—outlined during the campaign in the Republicans' "Contract with America"—to scale back the role of the federal government, eliminate environmental regulations, cut funding for educational programs like Head Start, reduce taxes, and balance the budget. Newt Gingrich, as the new Speaker of the House of Representatives, pushed through changes in the House rules that provided him with far greater power in appointing committee members and moving legislation along. Under his leadership, Congress launched a frontal attack on the budget, proposing massive cuts in virtually all social services. It demanded the elimination of three Cabinet departments and insisted on gutting the National Endowment for the Humanities, the National Endowment for the Arts, and the Public Broadcasting System. When, at the end of 1995, the president and the speaker tangled with one another on the size of the cuts and refused to compromise on a budget, the government shut down and 800,000 federal employees found themselves temporarily "furloughed."

While the House of Representatives passed most of the measures proposed in the "Contract with America," only a few of them became law. The Senate balked at some; the president vetoed others. One of the most important ones passed was the unfunded mandates bill, stopping the government from demanding state or local action but failing to provide the funds for implementation. After all the attention it received, voters lost interest in the "Contract with America." As the election of 1996 approached, Newt Gingrich found himself out of favor, as millions of Americans began to realize that they would suffer from the cuts more aggressive Republicans sought.

A Second Term for Clinton

As Bill Clinton sought a second term in 1996, the Republicans nominated Senate Minority Leader Robert Dole as their presidential candidate. The 73-year-old Dole ran a lackluster campaign. His pledge to push through a sweeping 15 percent tax reduction failed to excite voter interest. Even supporters wondered how he would balance the budget at the same time. Stung by Democratic congressional defeats two years before, Clinton reshaped his own image and announced that the "era of big government is over." Like Tony Blair in Great Britain, who spoke repeatedly of a New Labour approach, Clinton co-opted Republican issues, pledging to balance the budget himself and enraging liberal supporters by signing a welfare reform bill that slashed benefits and removed millions of people from the rolls. At the same time, he posed as the protector of Medicare and other programs that were threatened by proposed Republican cuts.

Clinton's strategy worked. On election day, he won a resounding victory over Dole. He received 49 percent of the popular vote to 41 percent for Dole and 8 percent for H. Ross Perot, who ran again, though this time less successfully than four years before. In the electoral tally, Clinton received 379 votes to 159 for Dole. Yet the Republicans kept control of Congress. In the House of Representatives, they lost a number of seats but retained a majority. In the Senate, they added two seats to what they had won in 1994. Around the country, voters seemed willing to support Clinton, but not to give him the mandate he sought.

Partisan Politics and Impeachment

Democrats made small gains in the midterm elections of 1998. They worried about their prospects as election day approached, for Clinton had been accused by an independent prosecutor, appointed by the Justice Department, of having engaged in an improper sexual relationship with Monica Lewinsky, a White House intern. While Clinton denied the relationship at first, the lengthy report presented to Congress left little doubt that such a connection existed, and Clinton finally admitted to the relationship in a nationally televised address.

As Republicans in Congress began to consider impeachment, Americans outside of Washington felt differently. Disturbed at what Clinton had done in his personal life, they nonetheless approved overwhelmingly of the job he was doing as president; in fact, his approval ratings were higher than any of his presidential predecessors in the recent past.

Those sentiments were reflected in the 1998 midterm election. Republicans, who had hoped to score sizable gains in both houses of Congress, maintained their 55–45 margin in the Senate, but lost five seats in the House of Representatives, ending up with a 223–211 margin that made it even more difficult to pursue their own agenda.

Despite that clear signal from the voters, House Republicans continued their efforts to remove the president. Just weeks after the election, a majority impeached him on counts of perjury and obstruction of justice. At the start of 1999, the case moved to the Senate for a trial, where Clinton fought to retain his office, just as Andrew Johnson had done 131 years before. In the Senate, presided over by the Chief Justice of the Supreme Court, a two-thirds vote was necessary to find the president guilty and remove him from office. After weeks of testimony, despite universal condemnation of Clinton's personal behavior, the Senate voted for acquittal. Democrats, joined by a number of Republicans, stood by the president, and with that coalition, neither charge managed to muster even a majority. The count of perjury was decided by a 45–55 vote, while the count of obstruction of justice failed on a 50–50 vote. At long last, the nightmare was over, and the country could deal with more pressing issues again.

Clinton was an enormously successful politician. Not only had he escaped conviction in the highly visible—and embarrassing—impeachment case, but he also managed to co-opt Republican issues and seize the political center. When he moved to reconfigure the national welfare system, to limit the number of years a person could receive benefits and to pare down the number of people on welfare rolls, conservatives were pleased while liberals were furious. Yet in other ways, he quietly advanced liberal goals, with incremental appropriations, even when he was unable to push major programs, such as his medical insurance scheme, through Congress. His administration's antitrust suit against the Microsoft Corporation aroused controversy. Although it was initially successful in court, it was partially overturned on appeal and eventually dropped after he left the White House. Suits against the nation's tobacco companies for deliberately misleading advertising in the face of known health risks were more popular with the public, and led in 1997 to a landmark $368 billion settlement to cover liability claims and provide reimbursement to the states for medical costs related to smoking. Throughout both terms, polls showed that Clinton remained popular (even when people disapproved of his personal conduct) to the end of his term in office.

Overall, in the words of the *New York Times,* Clinton demonstrated "striking strengths, glaring shortcomings." He came into office wanting to be a Roosevelt-like figure, with dreams of reconfiguring the role of government, but after the health-care debacle, he ended up instead quietly endorsing and implementing a variety of more modest causes. He faced more criticism—from the Right—than virtually any other politician, and it led to his impeachment. Yet he brought some of his troubles on himself. James Carville, his political consultant, once asked the president about his propensity for living dangerously, and Clinton replied, "Well, they haven't caught me yet." But that was before the Monica Lewinsky scandal. As he prepared to leave office, Clinton reflected, "I made one mistake. I apologized for it, I paid a high price for it and I've done my best to atone for it by being a good president." Most Americans, except for his virulent opponents, agreed.

Bill Clinton's relationship with Monica Lewinsky affected both the country and his own family. Here he heads off for vacation with wife, Hillary, and daughter, Chelsea, after the painful acknowledgment of the relationship to the nation. *(Brad Markel/Liaison Agency, Inc./Getty Images)*

THE SECOND BUSH PRESIDENCY

Republicans regained control of the White House in the election of 2000. Unable to oust Bill Clinton from the presidency by impeachment, they were determined to win back what they considered to be rightfully theirs in the conservative resurgence of the past 20 years. Texas Governor George W. Bush (son of former President George H. W. Bush—the first father–son combination since John Adams and John Quincy Adams), promised to return morality and respect to the White House, and appealed to those disturbed by Clinton's behavior.

The Election of 2000

The election of 2000 promised to be close. The strong economy gave Vice President Al Gore, the Democratic nominee, an initial advantage. Yet the Republicans, led by the younger Bush, insisted the country needed a change. Reflecting the profound difference in opinion about the overall role of government, the campaign revolved around what the government should do with the federal budget surplus. Republicans argued that much of the money should be returned to the public in the form of a tax cut. Democrats countered that such a tax cut would benefit only the wealthiest Americans, not ordinary workers, and said that the surplus should be used to bolster the ailing social security program and to pay down the national debt.

In the weeks before the election, polls showed that the race was virtually tied. They also showed that many Americans were not very enthusiastic about either nominee.

On election night, returns in several states were so close that the media found it impossible to say who won. As the returns trickled in, neither Bush nor Gore had captured the 270 electoral votes necessary to win the presidency. The electoral vote in Florida, one of the undecided states, was large enough to give the winner a victory. A recount, required by law, began, and Florida became a battleground as lawyers for both sides swarmed to the state to monitor the counting. Democrats and Republicans argued bitterly, in court and in the media, about how the recount should proceed. They also argued about which ballots should be counted. Some punch-card ballots, where a voter punched a hole next to the name of the candidate chosen, proved defective, and the particle of paper—called a chad—failed to drop off. Should such a ballot be counted if the intent of the voter was clear, even if the chad still hung by a thread to the card? And how could that intent be ascertained? Democrats also contended that in certain African-American precincts, voters had been turned away from the

In Florida—and other states—punch card ballots were sometimes defective, and if the little stubs of cardboard—called chads—were not pushed out entirely, the vote might be counted inaccurately. Here Judge Robert Rosenberg looks carefully at a disputed ballot during the manual recount in Florida. *(AP/Wide World Photos)*

polls. That charge was all the more significant since black voters around the country favored Gore by a 9–1 margin.

In December, more than five weeks after the election, after suits and counter-suits by both sides, the case reached the Supreme Court. In *Bush v. Gore*, the justices overturned a Florida Supreme Court decision allowing the recount to proceed, and ruled, by a 5–4 vote, with the most conservative justices voting in a bloc, that the recount should be curtailed, leaving Bush the winner. Although Gore won the popular vote by about 450,000 votes, Bush triumphed in the Electoral

Presidential Election, 2000

Candidates	Parties	Popular Vote	Electoral Vote	Voter Participation
GEORGE W. BUSH	Republican	50,546,002 (47.87%)	271	51.0%
Albert Gore	Democratic	50,999,897 (48.38%)	266	
Ralph Nader	Independent	2,882,955 (2.74%)	0	

Note: The winner's name appears in capital letters.

College by a 271–266 majority. Ill feelings persisted as a result of the partisan ruling. Supreme Court justice John Paul Stevens wrote a scathing dissent, in which he argued: "Although we may never know with complete certainty the identity of the winner of this year's presidential election, the identity of the loser is perfectly clear. It is the nation's confidence in the judge as an impartial guardian of the law." This unusual election, like the disputed election of 1876 at the end of Reconstruction (see Chapter 16), had a profound effect on the course of the country.

The voting in congressional races was equally close. The new Senate was evenly split, with each party holding 50 seats. Republicans organized the chamber and gained all committee chairs, since Vice President Dick Cheney broke the tie. Yet five months after the new session began, Senator James Jeffords of Vermont, frustrated with the approach of the Bush administration, left the Republican party, giving control to the Democrats. Republicans also lost seats in the House of Representatives, leaving them with but a nine-vote majority.

The New Leader

George W. Bush had enjoyed an eclectic career before becoming president. Born into a political family, he had shown little interest in politics himself, gravitating into the Texas oil business and then gaining part ownership of a professional baseball team before running successfully for governor of Texas.

Bush was very different from Clinton. Whereas his predecessor was sometimes called a "policy wonk" who understood all the details of his assorted initiatives, Bush saw himself as a corporate chief executive officer (CEO) who established the broad outlines of policy but then left the details to others. Ronald Reagan had taken that approach, but Reagan used his actor's skill to communicate his vision to the American people. Bush, on the other hand, seemed inarticulate in his comments, stumbling over words and fracturing grammar unless a message was carefully scripted in advance.

Yet Bush had a tenacity that served him well. Author Gail Sheehy observed that "the blind drive to win is a hallmark of the Bush family clan." The new president, she said "has to win, he absolutely has to win and if he thinks he's going to lose, he will change the rules or extend the play. Or if it really is bad he'll take his bat and ball and go home." As president, Bush showed the same determination, driving himself hard then retreating in solitude to his ranch in Crawford, Texas, where he seemed happiest of all.

George W. Bush hoped to follow in the footsteps of his father, though he had much less political and practical experience in the world of public affairs. But Republicans flocked to him, and he triumphed in the disputed election of 2000. *(Suzanne DeChillo/The New York Times)*

Early in his presidency, Bush had to overcome the image of incompetence. On the eve of his first trip to Europe, a senior administration official observed, "The common European perception is of a shallow, arrogant, gun-loving, abortion-hating, Christian fundamentalist Texan buffoon." According to the *Japan Times*, Bush had to persuade Europe's leaders to take him seriously. That first trip went reasonably well, and over the next few years, Bush managed to establish relationships with such counterparts as Vladimir Putin in Russia, Tony Blair in England, and Vicente Fox in Mexico.

Promoting the Private Sector

As president, Bush knew what he wanted to do. He had the interests of corporate America at heart and intended to accommodate business demands. During the campaign, he talked about a tax cut, and this became his first priority. Supply-side economists, who argued successfully in the 1980s that lower tax rates were necessary to promote economic growth, became more influential in his administration. While Bush first promoted the tax cut to give the economy a short-term boost, when Democrats proposed an alternative that would have put money into consumers' hands more quickly, the administration countered that its measure was necessary to provide long-term incentives.

By mid-2001, the tax cut became law. It lowered tax rates for everyone, allowed more tax-free saving for education, and reduced estate taxes. The measure promised to save every taxpayer at least several hundred dollars a year, though top earners in the nation stood to save as much as $4 million a year. Though the administration tried to deny that more than 40 percent of the savings would go to the top 1 percent of American taxpayers, the measure was heavily skewed in favor of the wealthy. Meanwhile, the economy continued to falter as the growth rate slowed and a full-blown recession ensued.

Like his father and Reagan, Bush wanted to reduce the size of government and squelch its intrusions into private affairs, but at the same time, he sought to bolster the military. His first budget, for example, proposed deep cuts in health programs for people without access to health insurance. He argued in favor of private social security accounts, rather than providing federal money to keep the system solvent, even when the downturn in the stock market wiped out the savings of millions of in-

George W. Bush loved the outdoors and spent as much time as he could at his ranch in Crawford, Texas. Here the physically active president is shown clearing cedar logs out of an oak grove. *(Eric Draper/ AP/Wide World Photos)*

vestors. But his proposals for defense called for far greater spending, even before the terrorist attacks of September 11, 2001.

Bush infuriated environmentalists, who had been pleased with Clinton's efforts to protect America's national heritage. Quietly, the new administration moved to allow road-building in national forests, reversed the phasing in of bans on snowmobiles in national parks, and made it easier for mining companies to dig for gold, zinc, and copper on public lands. Under pressure from real estate interests, the administration sought to shrink legal protection of endangered species. And, catering to the interests of oil companies, it fought to promote drilling in the protected Arctic National Wildlife Refuge, even in the face of estimates that there was very little oil there to be found. When his own Environmental Protection Agency (EPA) issued a report in mid-2002 linking the use of fossil fuel (such as coal and oil) to global warming, Bush dismissed the study by declaring that he had "read the report put out by the bureaucracy," making it clear that he had no confidence in the judgments of the scientists working for the EPA.

FOREIGN POLICY IN THE POST–COLD WAR WORLD

As the Cold War ended, the United States had to examine its own assumptions about its international role. The world was now a different place. With extraordinary communications advances, it was more closely linked than ever before. Violence and upheaval in one part of the globe now had an almost immediate impact on other areas. In this setting, new questions arose: What kind of leadership would the United States exert as the one remaining superpower on the globe? How involved would it become in peacekeeping missions in violence-wracked lands? What kind of assistance would it extend to developing nations once the competition with the Soviet Union that had fueled foreign aid was over? How would it deal with the threat of terrorism? These questions, asked in different forms over the course of past centuries, helped shape foreign policy in transitional times.

The Balkan Crisis

In the Balkans, in Eastern Europe, ethnic and religious violence worsened in the mid-1990s. Yugoslavia—a collection of different ethnic constituencies held together by a Communist dictatorship—had collapsed in 1991. Muslims and Croats had fought bitterly with Serbs in the province of Bosnia as the world watched the Bosnian Serbs liquidate opponents in a process that came to be called "ethnic cleansing" during the siege of the city of Sarajevo. Now, brutal killing escalated out of control, rape became commonplace, and civilians suffered most from the uncurbed violence. As the region became increasingly volatile, the United States remained out of the conflict, while the United Nations proved unable to bring about peace. In mid-1995, a North Atlantic Treaty Organization (NATO) bombing campaign forced the Bosnian Serbs into negotiations, and a peace conference held in Dayton, Ohio, led to the commitment of American troops, along with soldiers from other countries, to stabilize the region.

In 1999, a smoldering conflict in Kosovo, another of the provinces of the former Yugoslavia, led to war. In an effort to stop Slobodan Milosevic, the Serbian leader responsible for the devastation of Bosnia, from squelching a movement for autonomy in Kosovo, NATO, now 50 years old, launched an American-led bombing campaign. Milosevic responded with an even more violent "ethnic cleansing" campaign that drove hundreds of thousands of Kosovars from their homes. Even without the introduction of ground troops, this ultimately successful air assault was the largest allied operation in Europe since World War II.

Milosevic finally succumbed. When he refused to recognize the election victory of the opposition leader in 2000, hundreds of thousands of people demonstrated in the streets and declared a national strike. A week and a half after the election, protest-ers set fire to both the parliament and the state television station. Police officers joined the protesters and overthrew the leader who had wrought such havoc. Milosevic was arrested in 2001 and brought to The Netherlands to stand trial for crimes against humanity at the International Court of Justice in The Hague.

The Middle East in Flames

In the Middle East, Clinton tried to play the part of peacemaker, just as Jimmy Carter had done 15 years before. On September 13, 1993, in a dramatic ceremony on the White House lawn, Palestine Liberation Organization leader Yasir Arafat and Israeli prime minister Yitzhak Rabin took the first public step toward ending years of conflict as they shook hands and signed a peace agreement that led to Palestinian self-rule in the Gaza strip. In 1995, Israel and the PLO signed a further agreement, and the Israelis handed over control of the West Bank of the Jordan River to the Palestinians. A treaty between Jordan and Israel brought peace on still another border. While extremists tried to destroy the peace process by continued violence and assassinated Rabin in a move deplored worldwide, the effort to heal old animosities continued.

In 1998, Clinton once again played the role of mediator, this time facilitating an agreement leading to the return of land in the West Bank area to the Palestinians in return for peace between Arafat and Israeli leader Benjamin Netanyahu. As Clinton

President Bill Clinton helped orchestrate this famous handshake between Israeli Prime Minister Yitzhak Rabin and Palestine Liberation Organization Chairman Yasir Arafat in 1993. Though the two men had long been adversaries, they now began to work together to settle the bitter conflicts in the Middle East. *(AP/Wide World Photos)*

Siege in the West Bank

As Middle Eastern violence escalated out of control, Israeli forces in early 2002 responded to suicide bombings by mounting a massive siege of Yasir Arafat's headquarters in the West Bank—that area located on the West Bank of the Jordan River. Though the siege left Arafat unhurt, it undermined his authority and left the question of Palestinian leadership in doubt. **Reflecting on the Past** Why was the West Bank such a volatile area? Why did Israel mount a siege in the West Bank? Why did the siege undermine Arafat's authority?

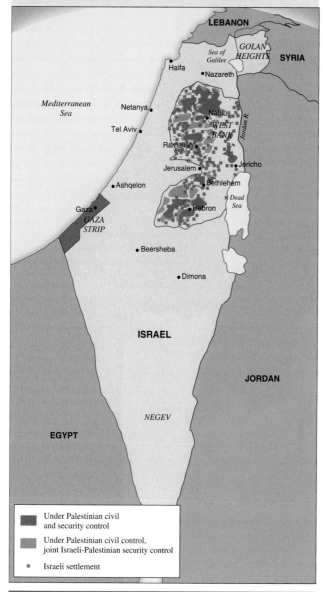

LEBANON

Sea of Galilee

GOLAN HEIGHTS

SYRIA

Haifa

Nazareth

Mediterranean Sea

Netanya

Nablus

WEST BANK

Jordan R.

Tel Aviv

Ramallah

Jerusalem

Jericho

Ashqelon

Bethlehem

Dead Sea

Gaza

GAZA STRIP

Hebron

Beersheba

Dimona

ISRAEL

JORDAN

NEGEV

EGYPT

Under Palestinian civil and security control

Under Palestinian civil control, joint Israeli-Palestinian security control

▪ Israeli settlement

prepared to leave office, he sought to seal a final agreement between the Israelis and the Palestinians, but this time he was not successful, as the Palestinians rejected a generous settlement offer, and the smoldering Middle Eastern tensions burst once more in flames that threatened to engulf the entire region.

The level of Mideast violence in the early twenty-first century was worse than it had ever been before. Arabs and Israelis had fought with each other repeatedly since the establishment of the state of Israel in 1948, and each conflict had left both victors and vanquished raw. Peace efforts culminating in relations with some of the Arab nations had promised to bring stability to the region. But the short-sighted Israeli policy of building settlements in occupied Arab land, and the Palestinian unwillingness to compromise at the negotiating table, culminated in a horrifying escalation of bloodshed following an intrusive Israeli visit to a holy Palestinian religious site in Jerusalem, a city claimed by both sides. Palestinian suicide bombers, some of them adolescents, wrought havoc on Israeli buses and in Jewish shops. A bomb exploded at Hebrew University in mid-2002, killing not just Israelis but Americans as well. Each time a deadly attack occurred, the Israelis counterattacked with equal violence in a never-ending spiral.

Bush was at first reluctant to intervene. Eventually, as the killing cycle continued, he moved from inattention to fumbling attention, becoming increasingly sympathetic to Israel as the suicide attacks continued. He lashed out at Yasir Arafat for not speaking out against the bombings, but was unable to bring the adversaries to the negotiating table. Meanwhile, many of the European nations, feeling that only the United States could help bring peace to the region, voiced dismay at American policy.

African Struggles

Africa also remained a source of concern to American policymakers who struggled to deal with a series of never-ending crises. Left behind as other parts of the world industrialized and moved ahead, the continent was also ravaged by the AIDS epidemic, which infected and killed far more people than in other parts of the world. Meanwhile, most other nations paid little attention to the region. During the Cold War, the United States and the Soviet Union had competed for the allegiance of African nations, but with the end of the conflict, that focus faded. Bill Clinton became the first

American president to travel to Africa, as he sought to dramatize international responsibility for assisting the continent, and he watched with satisfaction as Nelson Mandela handed over power in South Africa to his successor in a peaceful transition. But other areas proved more problematical. Six months after Clinton became president, a firefight with one faction in war-ravaged Somalia, in East Africa, resulted in several dozen American casualties. The United States was trying to promote stability in a region that lacked any central government at all in what was a doomed effort from the start. The shooting prompted some Americans, still haunted by the memory of Vietnam, to demand withdrawal. Reluctant to back down as he groped to define his policy, Clinton first increased the number of U.S. troops, then in 1993, recalled the soldiers without having restored order.

The United States was similarly baffled by a crisis in Rwanda, in central Africa. There a fragile balance of power between two ethnic groups—the Tutsis and the Hutus—broke down. When the Hutu president died in a suspicious plane crash in 1994, hard-line Hutus blamed Tutsi rebels and embarked on a massive genocidal campaign that resulted in the slaughter of hundreds of thousands of innocent Tutsis and moderate Hutus. As the world followed the carnage on television, the United States, like many European nations, debated the possibility of intervention on humanitarian grounds but decided to do nothing. Eventually the killing stopped, although the friction between the rival groups remained.

George W. Bush was much less interested in Africa than his predecessor. He chose not to attend a conference on sustainable development held in South Africa in the summer of 2002, which gave a clear signal that the United States was more interested in its own business interests than in the economic problems of the less-developed world. When Robert Mugabe, the longtime ruler of Zimbabwe, appropriated the land of white farmers to give it to blacks and precipitated a major economic crisis that threatened starvation for many in the country, the United States did little at all.

Relations with Russia

In the area that formerly had been the Soviet Union, the United States continued to try to promote both democracy and free-market capitalism. It worked closely with Boris Yeltsin in Russia, and then with his successor, Vladimir Putin, who assumed power on the last day of the twentieth century and was then elected president in his own right in 2001. But Russia remained unstable, still caught up in the complications of a huge political, social, and economic transformation that was far from over.

George W. Bush recognized the need to work with Putin. In a series of meetings, both in Russia and in the United States, Bush developed a close working relationship with Putin, whose assistance he needed in maintaining European stability. The Soviet Union had ceased to exist, but the component parts still remained important in the larger international scene.

Terror on September 11

On September 11, 2001, three hijacked airplanes slammed into the World Trade Center towers in New York City and the Pentagon in Washington, D.C. The fires in New York from exploding jet fuel

The World Trade Center towers in New York City had dominated the skyline on the Hudson River. As two hijacked commercial airplanes crashed into the tall structures on September 11, 2001, both towers burst into flames and later collapsed, killing most of the people who were still inside. *(Steve Ludlum/The New York Times)*

caused the towers to crumble, altering the skyline forever. Altogether about 3,000 people died in the terrorist attacks. A fourth plane, probably headed for either the White House or the Capital, crashed in Pennsylvania when passengers fought back against the attackers.

The hijackers were Muslim extremists, most from Saudi Arabia, trained at flight schools in the United States, who belonged to the Al-Quaida network headed by a Saudi exile named Osama bin Laden. Osama bin Laden and his organization were headquartered in Afghanistan, led by the extremely conservative Muslim Taliban group that was seeking to impose the law of the Koran, the Muslim holy book, on civil society. Osama bin Laden and his associates were furious at the United States for its Middle Eastern policy of support for Israel, and they also hated its affluent and materialistic values that often conflicted with their religious values and values elsewhere in the world.

The terrorist attacks shattered America's sense of security, at least within its own borders. Irate at the unprovoked strikes, President Bush vowed to find and punish the terrorists. Like his father in the Gulf War a decade earlier, he put together a worldwide coalition to assist the United States, and he quickly launched a bombing campaign to smoke out Osama bin Laden and his network. Although the bombing, followed by attacks by ground troops in Afghanistan, defeated the Taliban and drove its members from power, the campaign failed to find Osama bin Laden. An international coalition attempted to assist in rebuilding Afghanistan, and Bush, who had spoken out vigorously against nation-building in his own electoral campaign, now found himself a reluctant participant in the process. Hamid Karzai became head of a new government, but the instability of his regime was reflected in threats—and attempts—on his life.

Terrorism, the United States discovered, was a complicated enemy. It was, of course, nothing new. For the last couple of decades, terrorism was a constant source of concern as the nation sought to avoid hijackings, kidnappings, and bombings before they occurred. Sometimes these efforts were successful; sometimes (as in a bombing at the World Trade Center in 1993) they were not. But nothing compared to this attack.

As Bush's approval ratings soared to over 90 percent, he vowed a lengthy campaign to root out terrorism wherever it surfaced in the world. He embarked on a massive governmental reorganization to create a new Department of Homeland Security to help prevent future attacks, and he also used terrorism to allow the government to encroach on individual liberties—in the interest of security—more extensively than in the past. Ironically, a president dedicated to smaller government now found himself in the forefront of an effort to give government an even larger role.

American Muslims were often the victims of the government effort. Some faced attacks by Americans angry at the terrorist strikes. Others were held, often without being charged with a crime, on the suspicion that they were somehow involved.

The anti-terrorism campaign escalated. In early 2002, Bush spoke out forcefully against what he called an "axis of evil," as he referred to Iraq, Iran, and North Korea. He was particularly intent on driving Iraqi leader Saddam Hussein from power. Hussein had launched the attack on Kuwait that had led to the Gulf War during the administration of Bush's father. While the United States and the coalition it had put together had won that war, the military had called off the campaign before toppling Hussein. Now Bush, arguing that Hussein was creating weapons of mass destruction, vowed to complete the task. Within his own administration, Secretary of State Colin Powell, inclined to a more restrained foreign policy, fought against Secretary of Defense Donald Rumsfeld and Vice President Dick Cheney, who were eager for an attack. Bush's argument that he could invade Iraq even without the support of Congress aroused a firestorm of protest both in the United States and around the world.

Timeline	
1991–1999	Ethnic turbulence in fragmented former Yugoslavia
1992	Bill Clinton elected president
	Czechoslovakia splits into separate Czech and Slovak Republics
	Riots erupt in Los Angeles
1993	North American Free Trade Agreement (NAFTA) ratified
	Palestine Liberation Organization and Israel sign peace treaty
1994	Nelson Mandela elected president of South Africa
1996	Bill Clinton reelected
1998	Budget surplus announced
	Bill Clinton impeached by the House of Representatives
1999	Bill Clinton acquitted by the Senate
	Stock market soars as Dow Jones average passes 10,000
2000	George W. Bush elected president
2001	Economy falters
	Stock market dips below 10,000
	Tax cut passed
	Terrorists strike New York City and Washington, D.C.
2002	Recession continues and Dow Jones average drops below 8,000

✦ *Conclusion*

THE RECENT PAST IN PERSPECTIVE

In the 1990s, the United States prospered in a period of economic growth longer than any in its history. After weathering a recession at the start of the decade, the economy began to boom, and the boom continued for the next 10 years. Most middle- and upper-class Americans prospered. The budget deficit disappeared, and the government ran a sizable surplus. Yet not all Americans shared in the prosperity. Despite the drop in the unemployment level, many of the available jobs paid little more than the minimum wage, and people like the Garretts, met at the start of the chapter, had trouble making ends meet. Members of minority groups, whose numbers grew throughout the decade, had the toughest time of all.

Meanwhile, Americans worried about their role in the outside world. As they enjoyed their new-found prosperity, some were reluctant to spend money in an activist role abroad. They debated what to do about the defense establishment, which had begun to deteriorate, and were hesitant to become deeply involved in foreign conflicts where they had trouble ascertaining American interests. Then, in 2001, the brutal terrorist attacks on New York City and Washington, D.C., mobilized the nation. Recognizing at long last that terrorism threatened the entire globe, including the United States, they prepared themselves for an extended effort to try to bring it under control and to make the world a safer place. As they had in years past, in both World War I and World War II, the United States again sought to protect the democratic way of life for the American people and for people elsewhere as well.

The Changing Face of the American People

(pages 1072–1079)

This set of questions refers to material from the beginning of the chapter up to the heading "Economic and Social Change." To locate a paragraph by number as referred to in an exercise, start counting with the first paragraph on the page, regardless of whether it is an incomplete paragraph continuing from a previous page or a new full paragraph. Please note that page numbers refer to the pages of the textbook chapter, not to the pages of this book.

1 BEFORE READING

➤ PREVIEWING THE SECTION

Using the steps listed on page 5, preview pages 1074-1079 of The American People. *When you have finished, complete the following item.*

The two major topics discussed in this section of the chapter are _____immigration_____ and _____the 2000 census_____.

MAKING CONNECTIONS

Read the situation described in "American Stories" on pages 1072-1074. Do you know anyone like the Garretts? If so, how have they coped with the current economy?

➤ READING TIP

As you read, take time to study the graphic aids presented in the chapter.

➤ VOCABULARY

recession (page 1074, paragraph 1 of the introduction) an extended period of reduced economic activity

demographic (page 1074, paragraph 3 of the introduction) relating to the characteristics of human populations

infrastructure (page 1075, paragraph 2) the basic facilities and services necessary for the functioning of a community deportation (page 1076, paragraph 1) the act of expelling a person from a country

injunction (page 1077, paragraph 2) a court order prohibiting a party from a specific course of action

1   AFTER READING

➤ A.   UNDERSTANDING MAIN IDEAS

Select the best answer.

___d___ 1. The primary purpose of this section of the chapter is to

  a. compare immigration policies in the United States with those in other countries.

  b. discuss the effects of immigration on the global economy.

  c. explain the process an immigrant must go through to become a U.S. citizen.

  d. describe demographic changes in the United States resulting from recent immigration.

___c___ 2. The chapter's first subheading, "The New Pilgrims," refers to

  a. colonial settlers.

  b. political activists.

  c. recent immigrants.

  d. temporary workers.

___d___ 3. Most immigrants in the latter part of the twentieth century have chosen to settle

  a. on the East Coast.

  b. in the Midwest.

  c. in New York City.

  d. in western states.

___a___ 4. The purpose of the Immigration Act of 1965 was to

  a. limit illegal immigration while offering amnesty to aliens living in the United States.

  b. restrict immigration from certain parts of the world.

  c. provide for immediate deportation of aliens who committed crimes.

  d. establish social-assistance programs for legal and illegal aliens.

___b___ 5. One important finding of the census of 2000 was that

    a. most states had a net decrease in population.

    b. the rate of growth began to accelerate in the 1990s.

    c. the majority of the population was no longer white.

    d. percentages of Latino and Asian immigrants were declining.

► B. IDENTIFYING DETAILS

Indicate whether each statement is true (T) or false (F).

___T___ 1. The 2000 census showed an increase in the number of nonwhite Americans.

___F___ 2. The all-time record for immigration in a ten-year period was set in the 1990s.

___F___ 3. The United States was the only country to experience a wave of immigration in the latter part of the twentieth century.

___F___ 4. The term "guest workers" refers to Americans working abroad in the high-tech profession.

___F___ 5. Proposition 187 in California was intended to ease the plight of Mexican immigrants.

___T___ 6. According to the 2000 census, the combination of Latinos, African Americans, and Asians outnumbered whites in California.

___T___ 7. The 2000 census allowed Americans to identify themselves as part of more than one racial or ethnic group.

► C. RECOGNIZING METHODS OF ORGANIZATION AND TRANSITIONS

Select the best answer.

___c___ 1. In the first section of the chapter (pages 1074-1077), the authors primarily use the organizational pattern called

    a. comparison and contrast.

    b. enumeration.

    c. chronological order.

    d. definition.

___b___ 2. In the last paragraph on page 1074 (continuing on page 1075), the transitional word or phrase that indicates that a contrast will follow is

a. in the 1990s.
    c. as the twentieth century began.

b. whereas.
    d. a hundred years later.

___c___ 3. The Elián Gonzalez case (paragraphs 4–5 on page 1077) is described using the organizational pattern called

a. enumeration.
    c. chronological order.

b. process.
    d. cause and effect.

➤ D. REVIEWING AND ORGANIZING IDEAS: OUTLINING

Fill in the blanks to complete the following outline based on the first two paragraphs of "The Census of 2000" (page 1077).

The Census of 2000

  I. Increased population in 1990s

    A. Gained 32.7 million for total of 281.4 million

    B. Surpassed _previous 10-year record/baby boom record of the 1950s_

    C. Growth rate accelerated

      1. Increased _____immigration_____

      2. Longer _____life expectancy_____

  II. Most growth in _____the West_____

    A. The region as a whole

      1. Gained 10.4 million

      2. Expanded by 19 percent

    B. Specific areas with exceptional growth

      1. _____45 percent growth in Phoenix, Arizona_____

      2. _____83 percent growth in Las Vegas, Nevada_____

➤ E. FIGURING OUT INFERRED MEANINGS

Indicate whether each statement is true (T) or false (F) by making inferences based on the section "American Stories" (pages 1072-1074).

___T___ 1. The Garretts left Jamaica because they believed their life would improve in the United States.

___F___ 2. Marlene Garrett was hoping to qualify for welfare in the United States.

_T_ 3. The Garretts' babysitter was also an immigrant.

_F_ 4. Marlene Garrett was satisfied with her children's day-care situation.

_F_ 5. The Garretts planned to move back to Jamaica.

➤ F.   THINKING CRITICALLY

Select the best answer.

_c_ 1. The chart on page 1075 indicates that the highest number of immigrants in the United States was recorded in the year

    a. 1979.

    b. 1982.

    c. 1991.

    d. 1996.

_b_ 2. The author's tone throughout the chapter can best be described as

    a. critical and cautionary.

    b. objective and informative

    c. pessimistic and anxious.

    d. humorous and lighthearted.

_d_ 3. The introductory story about the Garretts is included to

    a. present factual information about the immigration process.

    b. provide a contrast to the middle-class American lifestyle.

    c. evoke sympathy for the Garrett family.

    d. illustrate the problems immigrants face in the U.S.

_c_ 4. According to the table on page 1079, the city that increased in population by the greatest percent between 1990 and 2000 was

    a. New York.

    b. Houston.

    c. Phoenix.

    d. San Antonio.

_b_ 5. According to the table on page 1079, the city with the smallest change in population (by percent) between 1990 and 2000 was

    a. Los Angeles.

    b. Chicago.

    c. Philadelphia.

    d. Detroit.

➤ G. BUILDING VOCABULARY

➤ Context

Using context and a dictionary, if necessary, determine the meaning of each word as it is used in the selection.

__c__ 1. influx (page 1074, paragraph 1)

    a. assistance   c. arrival

    b. information   d. influence

__b__ 2. voluminous (page 1074, paragraph 2)

    a. loud   c. violent

    b. large   d. insecure

__a__ 3. contiguous (page 1075, paragraph 1)

    a. adjoining   c. separate

    b. urban   d. limited

__a__ 4. amnesty (page 1075, paragraph 4)

    a. pardon   c. negotiation

    b. advice   d. misfortune

__d__ 5. asylum (page 1077, paragraph 5)

    a. institution   c. animosity

    b. retreat   d. protection

__c__ 6. orchestrated (page 1077, paragraph 6)

    a. allowed   c. arranged

    b. restrained   d. captured

__b__ 7. laxity (page 1077, paragraph 6)

    a. formality   c. authority

    b. carelessness   d. strictness

__a__ 8. imprint (page 1079, paragraph 1)

    a. impact   c. presentation

    b. instinct   d. imitation

__d__ 9. embrace (page 1079, paragraph 2)

    a. refuse, deny   c. study, examine

    b. add, supplement   d. accept, welcome

➤ Word Parts

```
A REVIEW OF PREFIXES
ANTI- means against
BI- means two
MULTI- means many
PRE- means before
RE- means back, again
```

Match each word in Column A with its meaning in Column B. Write your answers in the spaces provided.

Column A

<u>e</u> 1. multinational

<u>d</u> 2. preempt

<u>g</u> 3. bilingual

<u>a</u> 4. multicultural

<u>c</u> 5. anti-immigrant

<u>b</u> 6. repatriation

<u>f</u> 7. multiracial

Column B

a. reflecting many diverse cultures

b. sending a person back to his or her country of birth or citizenship

c. against (or hostile to) immigrants

d. to seize upon an issue before someone else can

e. operating in several countries

f. representing various races

g. using two languages

➤ Unusual Words/Unusual Meanings

Use the meanings given below to write a sentence using the underlined word or phrase.

1. In the Introduction (page 1073, paragraph 6) the director of a child-care referral agency says that some substandard arrangements are "<u>rotting their brains</u>." The term rotting, here, does not mean physical decay, but suggests mental abandonment.

   Your sentence: _____.

2. The "<u>rosy</u> economic indicators" (page 1073, paragraph 8) does not refer to the color pink. Instead, it means promising or likely to be characterized by happiness or success.

   Your sentence: _____.

➤ H. SELECTING A LEARNING/STUDY STRATEGY

Predict an essay question that might be asked on this section of the chapter.

➤ I. EXPLORING IDEAS THROUGH DISCUSSION AND WRITING

1. Have you ever experienced or observed the anti-immigrant feelings referred to in this chapter? Describe the situation.

2. Discuss how this chapter may have influenced your feelings toward immigrants. For example, are you more sympathetic toward immigrants than you were before you read the chapter?

3. Discuss the feature on the 2000 census that allowed Americans to identify themselves as part of more than one racial or ethnic group. Do you agree that it will help the United States to "embrace its multicultural and multiracial heritage?" How would you or did you identify yourself on the census?

✔ **Tracking Your Progress**

History Selection 1

Section	Number Correct	Score
A. Main Ideas (5 items)	_____ x 5	_____
B. Details (7 items)	_____ x 2	_____
C. Organization and Transitions (3 items)	_____ x 2	_____
E. Inferred Meanings (5 items)	_____ x 3	_____
F. Thinking Critically (5 items)	_____ x 3	_____
G. Vocabulary		
1. Context (9 items)	_____ x 2	_____
2. Word Parts (7 items)	_____ x 1	_____
	TOTAL SCORE	_____%

HISTORY SELECTION 2

Economic and Social Change
(pages 1079–1092)

This set of questions refers to material from the section titled "Economic and Social Change" up to but not including the section titled "Democratic Revival." To locate a paragraph by number as referred to in an exercise, start counting with the first paragraph on the page, regardless of whether it is an incomplete paragraph continuing from a previous page or a new full paragraph. Please note that page numbers refer to the pages of the textbook chapter, not to the pages of this book.

2   BEFORE READING

▶ PREVIEWING THE SECTION

Using the steps listed on page 5, preview pages 1079–1092 of The American People. *When you have finished, complete the following item.*

In this section of the chapter, the authors discuss several topics in the context of the 1990s. List at least six of those topics.

a. the economic "boom and bust"

b. poverty

c. homelessness

d. aging

e. illness

f. minorities

g. women

 MAKING CONNECTIONS

What changes have you experienced or observed in the treatment of minority groups in your lifetime?

> ► READING TIP

As you read, highlight portions of the text that reveal the major problems various groups have faced during this period in history.

> ► VOCABULARY

inflation (page 1079, paragraph 5) a persistent increase in the level of consumer prices or a persistent decline in the purchasing power of money

bull market (page 1080, paragraph 5) a period of rising stock prices

deregulation (page 1080, paragraph 8) the removal of government controls in economic life

2   AFTER READING

> ► A.   UNDERSTANDING MAIN IDEAS

Select the best answer.

_a_ 1. The primary purpose of this section of the chapter is to
   a. describe the economic and social changes that took place during the 1990s.
   b. compare the patterns of immigration in different parts of the world.
   c. discuss the broadening role of the United States abroad.
   d. identify the factors leading up to the impeachment of President Clinton.

_b_ 2. The authors attribute the American economic revival of the early 1990s to all of the following factors *except*
   a. the promotion of big business in the Reagan era.
   b. a decline in the number of stock market investors.
   c. a steady increase in productivity.
   d. the lowering of interest rates by the Federal Reserve Board.

_c_ 3. The corporate scandals discussed on pages 1080–1081 primarily involved
   a. negligent safety standards.
   b. product recalls.
   c. fraudulent accounting practices.
   d. insider trading.

___b___ 4. In the last two decades of the twentieth century, the gap between rich and poor

    a. increased slightly.

    b. increased significantly.

    c. decreased significantly.

    d. remained about the same.

___b___ 5. All of the following statements about aging in America are true *except*

    a. life expectancy increased in the twentieth century from 47 to 74 years.

    b. all workers face mandatory retirement when they reach the age of 70.

    c. the Social Security system has been strained by an increase in the number of retirees.

    d. elderly dependents will eventually outnumber those under the age of 15.

___b___ 6. The topic of paragraph 3 on page 1086 is

    a. the elderly.

    b. AIDS.

    c. the World Health Organization.

    d. Africa.

___d___ 7. The main idea of paragraph 4 on page 1088 is expressed in the

    a. first sentence.

    b. second sentence.

    c. last sentence.

    d. first and last sentences.

➤ B. IDENTIFYING DETAILS

Complete the following statements by underlining the correct answer in the parentheses.

1. A survey in San Diego indicated that police stopped African-American and Latino motorists (<u>more</u>/less) frequently than whites and Asian Americans.

2. One purpose of California's Proposition 209 was to (allow/<u>prohibit</u>) the use of gender or race in admitting students to state colleges and universities.

3. According to the 2000 census, the number of families headed by single mothers had (<u>increased</u>/decreased) since 1990.

4. Latinos were projected to become the nation's (<u>largest</u>/smallest) minority by 2005.

5. Hispanic students were (<u>more</u>/less) likely to drop out of high school than either whites or African Americans.

6. Native Americans had (more/<u>less</u>) influence than other minorities.

7. Asian Americans in the 1990s had (<u>higher</u>/lower) median incomes than whites.

▶ **C.   RECOGNIZING METHODS OF ORGANIZATION AND TRANSITIONS**

Select the best answer.

___c___ 1. On page 1080, the authors describe the "boom and bust" of the 1990s, primarily using the organizational pattern called
   a. enumeration.
   b. comparison and contrast.
   c. chronological order.
   d. problem and solution.

___b___ 2. In the last paragraph on page 1081 (continuing on page 1082), the authors make a comparison between
   a. poor people and homeless people.
   b. poverty in the United States and other parts of the world.
   c. South Africa and Cambodia.
   d. urban Americans and rural Americans.

___a___ 3. In paragraph 6 on page 1082, the authors discuss homelessness using the organizational pattern called
   a. cause and effect.
   b. chronological order.
   c. process.
   d. definition.

___c___ 4. In the last paragraph on page 1083, a transitional word or phrase that indicates that the authors are making a comparison is
   a. a half century earlier.   c. however.
   b. for example.   d. in the early 1980s.

➤ **D. REVIEWING AND ORGANIZING IDEAS: SUMMARIZING**

Complete the following summary of paragraphs 5-6 on page 1091 and 1-3 on page 1092 by filling in words or phrases from the list below.

civil unions	resistance	children	gay rights
Boy Scouts	Pediatricians	health-care coverage	Supreme Court
family	activism		

The __gay rights__ movement began to make progress. Gay __activism__ led to a broader definition of __family__: partners of gay employees of the three major automakers became eligible for __health-care coverage__, Vermont recognized __civil unions__ for same-sex relationships, and the American Academy of __Pediatricians__ supported the right of gay people to adopt their partners' __children__. But the growing visibility of gays also met with __resistance__. A __Supreme Court__ ruling allowing the __Boy Scouts__ to exclude gays received mixed reactions.

➤ **E. FIGURING OUT INFERRED MEANINGS**

Indicate whether each statement is true (T) or false (F). Refer to the quotation made by each person.

___F___ 1. Red prefers not to work so that he can continue to live at the homeless shelter. (page 1082, paragraph 7)

___F___ 2. John Hope Franklin is satisfied with how the fight for civil rights has progressed during his lifetime. (page 1087, paragraph 1)

___T___ 3. Ed Bradley thinks that there have been some improvements for African Americans. (page 1087, paragraph 6)

___T___ 4. Sherman Alexie believes Native Americans are alienated from and ridiculed by city dwellers. (page 1090, paragraph 1)

___T___ 5. Kevin Gover deplores how Native Americans have been treated throughout the history of the United States. (page 1090, paragraph 2)

___F___ 6. Paul Ong agrees that Asian Americans are secretive and inscrutable. (page 1091, paragraph 3)

➤ **F. THINKING CRITICALLY**

Listed below are the authors of the autobiographical excerpts on pages 1084-1085. Read each excerpt again, then decide which of the two words following each author's name describes his or her tone in the excerpt and underline your choice.

1. Benjamin Franklin: arrogant / proud

2. Elizabeth Cady Stanton: impassioned / docile

3. Black Elk: outraged / <u>tragic</u>

4. Malcolm X: <u>righteous</u> / apologetic

➤ **G.   BUILDING VOCABULARY**

➤ **Context**
Using context and a dictionary, if necessary, determine the meaning of each word as it is used in the selection.

__c__ 1. superfluous (page 1080, paragraph 4)

   a. vital

   b. lazy

   c. unnecessary

   d. shortsighted

__b__ 2. commensurate (page 1080, paragraph 5)

   a. uneven

   b. comparable

   c. critical

   d. sympathetic

__d__ 3. eroded (page 1080, paragraph 8)

   a. reinforced

   b. encouraged

   c. confirmed

   d. weakened

__a__ 4. anomaly (page 1081, paragraph 2)

   a. rare case

   b. prediction

   c. opposite

   d. unknown event

__b__ 5. solvent (page 1083, paragraph 5)

   a. difficult

   b. financially stable

   c. risky

   d. bankrupt

__d__ 6. decimated (page 1086, paragraph 3)

    a. cheated

    b. recovered

    c. identified

    d. destroyed

__b__ 7. restitution (page 1089, paragraph 5)

    a. restriction

    b. repayment

    c. punishment

    d. responsibility

▶ Word Parts

> ### A REVIEW OF PREFIXES
> **DIS-** means *apart, away, not*
> **IN-** means *not*
> **INTRA-** means *within, into, in*
> **PRO-** means *in favor of, for*
> **QUAD-** means *four*

Match each word in Column A with its meaning in Column B. Write your answers in the spaces provided.

Column A	Column B
__e__ 1. incapacitated	a. administered directly into the veins
__d__ 2. quadrupled	b. one who is in favor of something
__a__ 3. intravenous	c. not in proportion to the rest of a group
__f__ 4. inscrutable	d. multiplied by four
__b__ 5. proponent	e. deprived of strength or ability; not capable
__c__ 6. disproportionate	f. not easily understood

▶ Unusual Words/Unusual Meanings

1. The Enron case is described as a "bad apple in the barrel" (page 1081, paragraph 2). This expression means one thing is bad among others that are good. Write a sentence using this expression.

    Your sentence: _____.

2. Black Elk (page 1085, top of page) says he is looking back from "the high hill of my old age." Black Elk is not actually standing on a hill. What does he mean?

    Your sentence: _____.

➤ H.   SELECTING A LEARNING/STUDY STRATEGY

Predict an essay question that might be asked on this section of the chapter and outline your answer to it.

➤ I.   EXPLORING IDEAS THROUGH DISCUSSION AND WRITING

Have you read any autobiographies? Discuss how autobiographies help us to understand history.

1. How do you think corporate scandals such as the Enron case have affected our confidence in corporate America? Explore ways that confidence could be restored.

2. The authors state that many Americans, at least initially, considered homeless people to be "bag ladies, winos, and junkies" (page 1082, paragraph 6). What is your perception of homeless people? Has that perception changed as a result of reading this chapter?

✔ Tracking Your Progress

History Selection 2

Section	Number Correct		Score
A. Main Ideas (7 items)	_____	x 5	_____
B. Details (7 items)	_____	x 2	_____
C. Organization and Transitions (4 items)	_____	x 2	_____
E. Inferred Meanings (6 items)	_____	x 3	_____
F. Thinking Critically (4 items)	_____	x 3	_____
G. Vocabulary			
1. Context (7 items)	_____	x 1	_____
2. Word Parts (6 items)	_____	x 1	_____
	TOTAL SCORE	_____	%

HISTORY SELECTION 3

Democratic Revival, The Second Bush Presidency, and Foreign Policy in the Post–Cold War World

(pages 1092–1103)

This set of questions refers to material from the section titled "Democratic Revival" to the end of the chapter. To locate a paragraph by number as referred to in an exercise, start counting with the first paragraph on the page, regardless of whether it is an incomplete paragraph continuing from a previous page or a new full paragraph. Please note that page numbers refer to the pages of the textbook chapter, not to the pages of this book.

3   BEFORE READING

➤ **PREVIEWING THE SECTION**

Using the steps listed on page 5, preview pages 1092–1103 of The American People. *When you have finished, complete the following item.*

List at least three questions you expect to be able to answer after reading this section of the chapter.

a. How did the democrats stage a revival in the 1990s?

b. What events characterized the second Bush presidency?

c. How has the United States defined its role throughout the world?

 MAKING CONNECTIONS

What events that occurred between 1992 and 2002 are most memorable to you?

➤ **READING TIP**

As you read, keep track of important events by organizing them using a time line.

➤ **VOCABULARY**

capitalism (page 1101, paragraph 7) an economic system characterized by private or corporate ownership of capital goods and by prices, production, and distribution of goods that are determined mainly by competition in a free market

3	**AFTER READING**

➤ **A. UNDERSTANDING MAIN IDEAS**

Select the best answer.

___c___ 1. The primary purpose of paragraph 5 on page 1092 is to

     a. convince readers that Bill Clinton was the best candidate for president in 1992.

     b. describe the allegations that were made against Clinton during his first campaign.

     c. describe the three candidates for president in 1992.

     d. explain the political strategy used by the Democratic party in 1992.

___b___ 2. During President Clinton's first term of office, all of the following occurred *except*

     a. an upturn in the economy.

     b. comprehensive reform of the national health-care system.

     c. Senate ratification of the North American Free Trade Agreement (NAFTA).

     d. passage of a crime bill banning the manufacture, sale, or possession of assault weapons.

___a___ 3. The midterm elections of 1994 resulted in

     a. more control being given to Republicans.

     b. more control being given to Democrats.

     c. a resurgence of the Independent party.

     d. increased funding and support for social services.

___d___ 4. The primary purpose of paragraph 4 on page 1094 is to

   a. describe President Clinton's accomplishments during his second term.

   b. explain the New Labour approach used by Tony Blair in Great Britain.

   c. illustrate the effect of third-party candidates such as Ross Perot.

   d. describe President Clinton's strategy for his re-election campaign in 1996.

___a___ 5. One question that is answered in the section titled "Partisan Politics and Impeachment" (pages 1094–1095) is

   a. How did Americans feel about President Clinton's performance as president?

   b. Why was the Clinton administration's suit against Microsoft controversial?

   c. Why was Andrew Johnson impeached?

   d. Which Republicans supported President Clinton during his trial?

___d___ 6. The main idea of paragraph 4 on page 1096 is that

   a. the media made mistakes in reporting on the presidential election of 2000.

   b. many of the ballots used in the election were defective.

   c. Democrats and Republicans disagreed about how to conduct a recount.

   d. the presidential election was so close that it was impossible to determine the winner on election night.

___c___ 7. The topic of the section titled "The New Leader" (page 1097) is

   a. Bill Clinton.

   b. the Bush family.

   c. George W. Bush.

   d. the Republican party.

___c___ 8. A top priority of the Bush administration was to

   a. increase the size of government.

   b. reduce spending on the military.

   c. cut taxes.

   d. expand environmental protection programs.

➤ B.   IDENTIFYING DETAILS

Indicate whether each statement is true (T) or false (F).

___T___ 1. The 1992 presidential candidates relied heavily on television appearances to promote their campaigns.

___F___ 2. Most of the measures proposed in the "Contract with America" became law.

___F___ 3. President Clinton was impeached for signing a welfare reform bill that removed millions of people from welfare rolls.

___T___ 4. The presidential campaigns in 2000 revolved around what the government should do with the federal budget surplus.

___F___ 5. Ross Perot was the Independent party candidate in 2000.

___T___ 6. Al Gore won the popular vote for president in 2000.

➤ C.   RECOGNIZING METHODS OF ORGANIZATION AND TRANSITIONS

Select the best answer.

___c___ 1. The section titled "Democratic Revival" (pages 1092–1095) is generally organized according to the pattern called
   a. definition.
   b. comparison and contrast.
   c. chronological order.
   d. cause and effect.

___b___ 2. In paragraph 2 on page 1096, the authors make a comparison between
   a. the elections of 1996 and 2000.
   b. the Democratic and Republican campaigns.
   c. wealthy Americans and ordinary workers.
   d. Al Gore and Bill Clinton.

___d___ 3. In paragraph 4 on page 1097, all of the following words and phrases indicate that the authors are making a comparison *except*
   a. different.
   b. whereas.
   c. on the other hand.
   d. in advance.

___b___ 4. In paragraph 3 on page 1098, the authors provide an example to support their main idea in the
   a. first sentence.   c. third sentence.
   b. second sentence.   d. fourth sentence.

➤ **D.   REVIEWING AND ORGANIZING IDEAS: MAPPING**

*Complete the following map based on pages 1098–1102 of the section titled
"Foreign Policy in the Post–Cold War World" by filling in the blanks.*

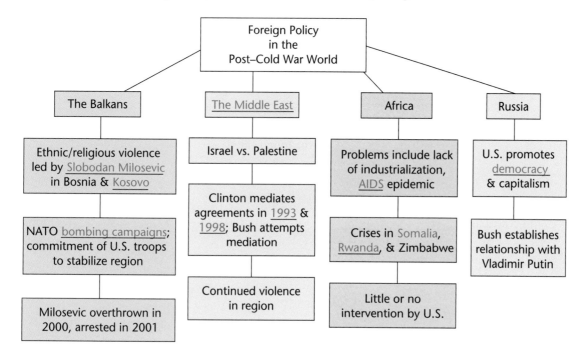

➤ **E.   FIGURING OUT INFERRED MEANINGS**

Indicate whether each statement is true (T) or false (F).

_T_ 1. It can be inferred that the health-care system in America is still in need of reform. (page 1093, paragraph 4)

_F_ 2. When the authors state that 800,000 federal employees were "furloughed" in 1995 (page 1094, paragraph 2), they mean that those workers were fired.

_T_ 3. It can be inferred that President Clinton believed that he was a good president in spite of his impeachment. (page 1095, paragraph 4)

_T_ 4. It can be inferred that if African-American voters hadn't been turned away from the polls, Al Gore might have won the presidency. (page 1096, paragraph 4)

_F_ 5. Environmentalists were supportive of President Bush's policies. (page 1098, paragraph 4)

_T_ 6. The United States has had mixed success in the role of peacemaker in the Middle East and throughout the world. (pages 1099–1101)

➤ **F. THINKING CRITICALLY**

Place a check mark in front of each of the statements below in which the authors use figurative language. Leave the other statements blank.

_____ 1. "On election day, Clinton won 43 percent of the popular vote . . ." (page 1093, paragraph 2)

✓ 2. "Under his leadership, Congress launched a frontal attack on the budget . . ." (page 1094, paragraph 2)

✓ 3. "At long last, the nightmare was over . . ." (page 1095, paragraph 2)

_____ 4. ". . . many Americans were not very enthusiastic about either nominee." (page 1096, paragraph 3)

✓ 5. "Bush seemed inarticulate in his comments, stumbling over words and fracturing grammar . . ." (page 1097, paragraph 4)

✓ 6. ". . . the smoldering Middle Eastern tensions burst once more in flames that threatened to engulf the entire region." (page 1101, paragraph 1)

➤ **G. BUILDING VOCABULARY**

➤ **Context**

Using context and a dictionary, if necessary, determine the meaning of each word as it is used in the selection.

b 1. allegations (page 1092, paragraph 5)

    a. inventions   c. prohibitions

    b. accusations   d. introductions

c 2. reneged (page 1093, paragraph 1)

    a. commented   c. backed out

    b. renewed   d. carried out

a 3. co-opted (page 1094, paragraph 4)

    a. took over   c. isolated

    b. returned to   d. rearranged

d 4. debacle (page 1095, paragraph 4)

    a. achievement   c. event

    b. debate   d. disaster

b 5. virulent (page 1095, paragraph 4)

    a. contagious   c. admiring

    b. bitter   d. enthusiastic

_a_ 6. ascertained (page 1096, paragraph 4)

a. determined

c. allowed

b. predicted

d. avoided

_c_ 7. scathing (page 1097, paragraph 1)

a. unusually mild

c. sharply critical

b. quite timely

d. mildly humorous

_a_ 8. eclectic (page 1097, paragraph 3)

a. varied

c. rough

b. shocking

d. frugal

_d_ 9. tenacity (page 1097, paragraph 5)

a. flexibility

c. severity

b. weakness

d. persistence

_b_ 10. volatile (page 1099, paragraph 1)

a. outspoken

c. tranquil

b. unstable

d. vulnerable

➤ **Word Parts**

Using your knowledge of word parts, fill in the blanks in the following sentences.

1. If re- means *again* and surge means *to rise or increase suddenly*, then resurgence (page 1095, paragraph 5) means _____ a rising again _____ into life, activity, or prominence.

2. If in- means *not* and articulate means *able to express oneself clearly and effectively*, then a person who is considered inarticulate (page 1097, paragraph 4) is _____ not able to express himself clearly and effectively _____.

3. If inter- means *between* and ven- means *come*, then intervene (page 1101, paragraph 3) means _____ come between _____ in order to stop, settle, or modify a situation.

4. If gen- refers to family or tribal *groups* and –cide means *the act of killing*, then a genocidal campaign (page 1101, paragraph 5) refers to the systematic and planned _____ killing _____ of an entire national, racial, political, or ethnic _____ group _____.

➤ **H.   SELECTING A LEARNING/STUDY STRATEGY**

Evaluate the usefulness of the map you completed above. How would you use it to study?

➤ **I. EXPLORING IDEAS THROUGH DISCUSSION AND WRITING**

1. Describe your reaction to President Clinton's "communitarian" initiative (page 1093). Do you believe such an initiative can succeed in the United States and in other parts of the world?

2. Do you believe that President Clinton should have been removed from office after his impeachment? Defend your position.

3. Reread the last paragraph of the chapter (page 1003, paragraph 3). What events would you add to the end of this chapter? Make a list of important events that have occurred since the publication of this chapter.

4. Evaluate the chapter's coverage of the September 11th terrorist attacks. Do you agree with the author's assessment of the effects of the terrorist attacks (page 1102, paragraph 5)?

✔ **Tracking Your Progress**

History Selection 3

Section	Number Correct		Score
A. Main Ideas (8 items)	_____	x 4	_____
B. Details (6 items)	_____	x 2	_____
C. Organization and Transitions (4 items)	_____	x 2	_____
E. Inferred Meanings (6 items)	_____	x 2	_____
F. Thinking Critically (6 items)	_____	x 2	_____
G. Vocabulary			
1. Context (10 items)	_____	x 2	_____
2. Word Parts (4 items)	_____	x 1	_____
		TOTAL SCORE	_____%

Appendix

Assessing Your Reading Progress

This appendix contains a Words-per-Minute Conversion Chart and a Reading Progress Graph.

Use the Words-per-Minute Conversion Chart to calculate your Words-per-Minute Score (WPM) for each reading selection you complete. Locate your selection number across the top of the page. Then locate your reading time in minutes and seconds along the left side of the page. Move down the selection number column and across the minutes and seconds row until they intersect. The number that appears at the intersection is your Words-per-Minute Score. Record it in the Checking Your Reading Rate box that follows the reading selection and on the Reading Progress Graph in this appendix.

Use the Reading Progress Graph to chart your progress as you work through the reading selections in the book. For each reading selection you complete, record the date and the selection number. Then place a dot in the appropriate column to indicate your Words-per-Minute Score from the Checking Your Reading Rate box and your Total Score from the Tracking Your Progress box, both of which follow the reading selection.

Words-per-Minute Conversion Chart

Reading Progress Graph

Words-per-Minute Conversion Chart

Reading Time (Minutes)	Reading Selection												
	1	2	3	4	5	6	7	8	9	10	11	12	13
1:00	630	1358	860	985	2008	1680	1250	1623	634	1028	1101	1420	825
1:15	504	1086	687	788	1606	1344	1000	1298	507	822	881	1136	660
1:30	420	905	573	657	1339	1120	833	1082	423	685	734	947	550
1:45	360	776	491	563	1147	960	714	927	362	587	629	811	471
2:00	315	679	430	493	1004	840	625	812	317	514	551	710	413
2:15	280	604	382	438	892	747	556	721	282	457	489	631	367
2:30	252	543	344	394	803	672	500	649	254	411	440	568	330
2:45	229	494	312	358	730	611	455	590	231	374	400	516	300
3:00	210	453	286	328	669	560	417	541	211	343	367	473	275
3:15	194	418	264	303	618	517	385	499	195	316	339	437	254
3:30	180	388	245	281	574	480	357	464	181	294	315	406	236
3:45	168	362	229	263	535	448	333	433	169	274	294	379	220
4:00	158	340	215	246	502	420	313	406	159	257	275	355	206
4:15	148	320	202	232	472	395	294	382	149	242	259	334	194
4:30	140	302	191	219	446	373	278	361	141	228	245	316	183
4:45	133	286	181	207	423	354	263	342	133	216	232	299	174
5:00	126	272	172	197	402	336	250	325	127	206	220	284	165
5:15	120	259	164	188	382	320	238	309	121	196	210	270	157
5:30	115	247	156	179	365	305	227	295	115	187	200	258	150
5:45	110	236	149	171	349	292	217	282	110	179	191	247	143
6:00	105	226	143	164	335	280	208	271	106	171	184	237	138
6:15	101	217	137	158	321	269	200	260	101	164	176	227	132
6:30		209	132	152	309	258	192	250		158	169	218	127
6:45		201	127	146	297	249	185	240		152	163	210	122
7:00		194	123	141	287	240	179	232		147	157	203	118
7:15		187	118	136	277	232	172	224		142	152	196	114
7:30		181	115	131	268	224	167	216		137	147	189	110
7:45		175	111	127	259	217	161	209		133	142	183	106
8:00		170	107	123	251	210	156	203		129	138	178	103
8:15		165	104	119	243	204	152	197		125	133	172	100
8:30		160	101	116	236	198	147	191		121	130	167	
8:45		155		113	229	192	143	185		117	126	162	
9:00		151		109	223	187	139	180		114	122	158	
9:15		147		106	217	182	135	175		111	119	154	
9:30		143		104	211	177	132	171		108	116	149	
9:45		139		101	206	172	128	166		105	113	146	
10:00		136			201	168	125	162		103	110	142	
10:15		132			196	164	122	158		100	107	139	
10:30		129			191	160	119	155			105	135	

Words-per-Minute Conversion Chart *(continued)*

Reading Time (Minutes)	Reading Selection												
	1	2	3	4	5	6	7	8	9	10	11	12	13
10:45		126			187	156	116	151			102	132	
11:00		123			183	153	114	148			100	129	
11:15		121			178	149	111	144				126	
11:30		118			175	146	109	141				123	
11:45		116			171	143	106	138				121	
12:00		113			167	140	104	135				118	
12:15		111			164	137	102	132				116	
12:30		109			161	134	100	130				114	
12:45		107			157	132		127				111	
13:00		104			154	129		125				109	
13:15		102			152	127		122				107	
13:30		101			149	124		120				105	
13:45					146	122		118				103	
14:00					143	120		116				101	
14:15					141	118		114					
14:30					138	116		112					
14:45					136	114		110					
15:00					134	112		108					
15:15					132	110		106					
15:30					130	108		105					
15:45					127	107		103					
16:00					126	105		101					
16:15					124	103							
16:30					122	102							
16:45					120	100							
17:00					118								
17:15					116								
17:30					115								
17:45					113								
18:00					112								
18:15					110								
18:30					109								
18:45					107								
19:00					106								
19:15					104								
19:30					103								
19:45					102								
20:00					100								

Words-per-Minute Conversion Chart *(continued)*

Reading Time (Minutes)	Reading Selection												
	14	15	16	17	18	19	20	21	22	23	24	25	26
1:00	1660		883	830	1965	2031	1238	968	1001	1179	1616	1062	1089
1:15	1328		706	664	1572	1625	990	774	801	943	1293	850	871
1:30	1107		589	553	1310	1354	825	645	667	786	1077	708	726
1:45	949		505	474	1123	1161	707	553	572	674	923	607	622
2:00	830		442	415	983	1016	619	484	501	590	808	531	545
2:15	738		392	369	873	903	550	430	445	524	718	472	484
2:30	664		353	332	786	812	495	387	400	472	646	425	436
2:45	604		321	302	715	739	450	352	364	429	588	386	396
3:00	553		294	277	655	677	413	323	334	393	539	354	363
3:15	511		272	255	605	625	381	298	308	363	497	327	335
3:30	474		252	237	561	580	354	277	286	337	462	303	311
3:45	443		235	221	524	542	330	258	267	314	431	283	290
4:00	415		221	208	491	508	310	242	250	295	404	266	272
4:15	391		208	195	462	478	291	228	236	277	380	250	256
4:30	369		196	184	437	451	275	215	222	262	359	236	242
4:45	349		186	175	414	428	261	204	211	248	340	224	229
5:00	332		177	166	393	406	248	194	200	236	323	212	218
5:15	316		168	158	374	387	236	184	191	225	308	202	207
5:30	302		161	151	357	369	225	176	182	214	294	193	198
5:45	289		154	144	342	353	215	168	174	205	281	185	189
6:00	277		147	138	328	339	206	161	167	197	269	177	182
6:15	266		141	133	314	325	198	155	160	189	259	170	174
6:30	255		136	128	302	312	190	149	154	181	249	163	168
6:45	246		131	123	291	301	183	143	148	175	239	157	161
7:00	237		126	119	281	290	177	138	143	168	231	152	156
7:15	229		122	114	271	280	171	134	138	163	223	146	150
7:30	221		118	111	262	271	165	129	133	157	215	142	145
7:45	214		114	107	254	262	160	125	129	152	209	137	141
8:00	208		110	104	246	254	155	121	125	147	202	133	136
8:15	201		107	101	238	246	150	117	121	143	196	129	132
8:30	195		104		231	239	146	114	118	139	190	125	128
8:45	190		101		225	232	141	111	114	135	185	121	124
9:00	184				218	226	138	108	111	131	180	118	121
9:15	179				212	220	134	105	108	127	175	115	118
9:30	175				207	214	130	102	105	124	170	112	115
9:45	170				202	208	127		103	121	166	109	112
10:00	166				197	203	124		100	118	162	106	109
10:15	162				192	198	121			115	158	104	106
10:30	158				187	193	118			112	154	101	104

Words-per-Minute Conversion Chart *(continued)*

Reading Time (Minutes)	14	15	16	17	18	19	20	21	22	23	24	25	26
10:45	154				183	189	115			110	150		
11:00	151				179	185	113			107	147		
11:15	148				175	181	110			105	144		
11:30	144				171	177	108			103	141		
11:45	141				167	173	105			100	138		
12:00	138				164	169	103				135		
12:15	136				160	166	101				132		
12:30	133				157	162					129		
12:45	130				154	159					127		
13:00	128				151	156					124		
13:15	125				148	153					122		
13:30	123				146	150					120		
13:45	121				143	148					118		
14:00	119				140	145					115		
14:15	116				138	143					113		
14:30	114				136	140					111		
14:45	113				133	138					110		
15:00	111				131	135					108		
15:15	109				129	133					106		
15:30	107				127	131					104		
15:45	105				125	129					103		
16:00	104				123	127					101		
16:15	102				121	125							
16:30	101				119	123							
16:45					117	121							
17:00					116	119							
17:15					114	118							
17:30					112	116							
17:45					111	114							
18:00					109	113							
18:15					108	111							
18:30					106	110							
18:45					105	108							
19:00					103	107							
19:15					102	106							
19:30					101	104							
19:45						103							
20:00						102							

Words-per-Minute Conversion Chart *(continued)*

Reading Time (Minutes)	Reading Selection												
	27	28	29	30	31	32	33	34	35	36	37	38	39
1:00	1261	1830	1557	659	920	1291	1206	822	898	1335	1128	1374	1499
1:15	1009	1464	1246	527	736	1033	965	658	718	1068	902	1099	1199
1:30	841	1220	1038	439	613	861	804	548	599	890	752	916	999
1:45	721	1046	890	377	526	738	689	470	513	763	645	785	857
2:00	631	915	779	330	460	646	603	411	449	668	564	687	750
2:15	560	813	692	293	409	574	536	365	399	593	501	611	666
2:30	504	732	623	264	368	516	482	329	359	534	451	550	600
2:45	459	665	566	240	335	469	439	299	327	485	410	500	545
3:00	420	610	519	220	307	430	402	274	299	445	376	458	500
3:15	388	563	479	203	283	397	371	253	276	411	347	423	461
3:30	360	523	445	188	263	369	345	235	257	381	322	393	428
3:45	336	488	415	176	245	344	322	219	239	356	301	366	400
4:00	315	458	389	165	230	323	302	206	225	334	282	344	375
4:15	297	431	366	155	216	304	284	193	211	314	265	323	353
4:30	280	407	346	146	204	287	268	183	200	297	251	305	333
4:45	265	385	328	139	194	272	254	173	189	281	237	289	316
5:00	252	366	311	132	184	258	241	164	180	267	226	275	300
5:15	240	349	297	126	175	246	230	157	171	254	215	262	286
5:30	229	333	283	120	167	235	219	149	163	243	205	250	273
5:45	219	318	271	115	160	225	210	143	156	232	196	239	261
6:00	210	305	260	110	153	215	201	137	150	223	188	229	250
6:15	202	293	249	105	147	207	193	132	144	214	180	220	240
6:30	194	282	240	101	142	199	186	126	138	205	174	211	231
6:45	187	271	231		136	191	179	122	133	198	167	204	222
7:00	180	261	222		131	184	172	117	128	191	161	196	214
7:15	174	252	215		127	178	166	113	124	184	156	190	207
7:30	168	244	208		123	172	161	110	120	178	150	183	200
7:45	163	236	201		119	167	156	106	116	172	146	177	193
8:00	158	229	195		115	161	151	103	112	167	141	172	187
8:15	153	222	189		112	156	146	100	109	162	137	167	182
8:30	148	215	183		108	152	142		106	157	133	162	176
8:45	144	209	178		105	148	138		103	153	129	157	171
9:00	140	203	173		102	143	134		100	148	125	153	167
9:15	136	198	168			140	130			144	122	149	162
9:30	133	193	164			136	127			141	119	145	158
9:45	129	188	160			132	124			137	116	141	154
10:00	126	183	156			129	121			134	113	137	150
10:15	123	179	152			126	118			130	110	134	146
10:30	120	174	148			123	115			127	107	131	143

Words-per-Minute Conversion Chart *(continued)*

Reading Time (Minutes)	Reading Selection												
	27	28	29	30	31	32	33	34	35	36	37	38	39
10:45	117	170	145			120	112			124	105	128	139
11:00	115	166	142			117	110			121	103	125	136
11:15	112	163	138			115	107			119	100	122	133
11:30	110	159	135			112	105			116		119	130
11:45	107	156	133			110	103			114		117	128
12:00	105	153	130			108	101			111		115	125
12:15	103	149	127			105				109		112	122
12:30	101	146	125			103				107		110	120
12:45		144	122			101				105		108	118
13:00		141	120							103		106	115
13:15		138	118							101		104	113
13:30		136	115									102	111
13:45		133	113										109
14:00		131	111										107
14:15		128	109										105
14:30		126	107										103
14:45		124	106										102
15:00		122	104										
15:15		120	102										
15:30		118	100										
15:45		116											
16:00		114											
16:15		113											
16:30		111											
16:45		109											
17:00		108											
17:15		106											
17:30		105											
17:45		103											
18:00		102											
18:15		100											
18:30													
18:45													
19:00													
19:15													
19:30													
19:45													
20:00													

Reading Progress Chart

Date
Reading
Selection No.

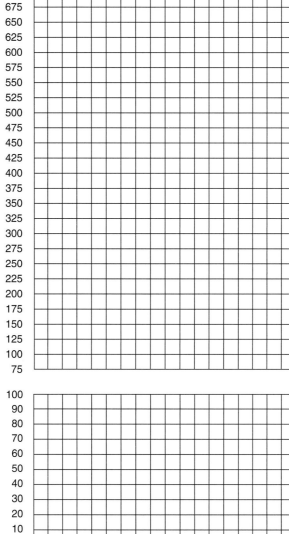

Words-per-Minute Score

800
775
750
725
700
675
650
625
600
575
550
525
500
475
450
425
400
375
350
325
300
275
250
225
200
175
150
125
100
75

Comprehension
Score

100
90
80
70
60
50
40
30
20
10
0

Reading Progress Chart *(continued)*

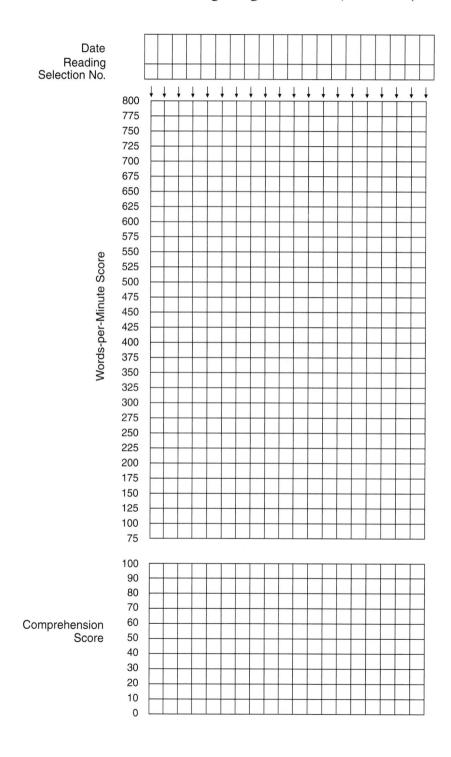

Credits

Text Credits

6: Joseph DeVito, "Ending a Relationship." From *Interpersonal Communication*, Ninth Edition. Copyright © 2001. Boston: Allyn & Bacon. Reprinted by permission of Pearson Education Inc.; **9:** Laura Tangley, "Animal Emotions." In *U.S. News & World Report*, October 30, 2000. Copyright © 2000 Reprinted by permission of U.S. News & World Report.; **20:** F. Philip Rice and Kin Gale Dogin. From *The Adolescent: Development, Relationships and Culture*, Tenth Edition, pp. 250–251. Copyright © 2002. Boston: Allyn & Bacon. Reprinted by permission of Allyn & Bacon.; **22:** Teresa Audeskirk, Gerald Audeskirk, and Bruce E. Byers. From *Life on Earth*, Third Edition, pp. 622–624, 632. Upper Saddle River, NJ: Prentice Hall, Inc. Adapted by permission of Pearson Education, Inc., Upper Saddle River, NJ.; **24:** Mark C. Carnes and John A. Garraty. From *The American Nation*, Eleventh Edition, p. 267. Copyright © 2003. New York: Addison Wesley Longman. Reprinted by permission of Pearson Education, Inc.; **26:** Edward F. Bergman and William H. Renwick. From *Introduction to Geography: People, Places, and Environment*, Second Edition, p. 263. Copyright © 2002. Upper Saddle River, NJ: Prentice Hall, Inc. Adapted by permission of Pearson Education, Inc; **31:** William J. Germann and Cindy L. Stanfield. From *Principles of Human Physiology*, p. 174. Copyright © 2002. San Francisco: Benjamin Cummings. Reprinted by permission of Pearson Education, Inc.; **34:** Jeffrey Bennett, Megan Donahue, Nicholas Schneider, and Mark Voit. From *The Cosmic Perspective*, Second Edition, p. 218. Copyright 2002. San Francisco: Addison Wesley. Reprinted by permission of Pearson Education, Inc.; **38:** Teresa Audeskirk, Gerald Audeskirk, and Bruce E. Byers. From *Life on Earth*, Third Edition, p. 237. Upper Saddle River, NJ: Prentice Hall, Inc. Adapted by permission of Pearson Education, Inc., Upper Saddle River, NJ.; **41:** Leon Baradat. From *Understanding American Democracy*, p. 163. Copyright © 1992. New York: HarperCollins. Reprinted by permission of Pearson Education, Inc.; **42:** Josh R. Gerow. From *Psychology: An Introduction*, Fifth Edition, p. 553. Copyright © 1997 by Addison-Wesley Educational Publishers, Inc. Reprinted by permission of Pearson Education, Inc.; **43:** Joseph DeVito. From *Interpersonal Communication*, Ninth Edition, p. 182. Copyright © 2001. Boston: Allyn & Bacon. Reprinted by permission of Pearson Education Inc.; **43:** Josh R. Gerow. From *Psychology: An Introduction*, Fifth Edition, p. 700. Copyright © 1997 by Addison-Wesley Educational Publishers, Inc. Reprinted by permission of Pearson Education, Inc.; **43:** Robert Wallace. From *Biology: The World of Life*, Sixth Edition, p. 283. Copyright © 1992. New York: HarperCollins. Reprinted by permission of Pearson Education, Inc.; **44:** Josh R. Gerow. From *Psychology: An Introduction*, Fifth Edition, p. 250. Copyright © 1997 by Addison-Wesley Educational Publishers, Inc. Reprinted by permission of Pearson Education, Inc.; **45:** Michael Mix, Paul Farber and Keith I. King. From *Biology: The Network of Life*, p. 532. Copyright © 1996 by Michael Mix. Reprinted by permission of Pearson Education Inc.; **45:** William E. Thompson and Joseph V. Hickey. From *Society in Focus*, Fourth Edition, p. 198. Copyright © 2002. Boston: Allyn & Bacon. Reprinted by permission of Allyn and Bacon.; **46:** Joseph A. DeVito. From *Human Communication: The Basic Course*, Ninth Edition, p. 217. Copyright © 2003. Boston: Allyn and Bacon. Reprinted by permission of Allyn and Bacon.; **46:** Ronald J. Ebert and Ricky W. Griffin. From *Business Essentials*, Fourth Edition, p. 64. Copyright © 2003. Upper Saddle River, NJ: Pearson Education Inc. Reprinted by permission of Pearson Education, Inc.; **46:** Barbara D. Miller. From *Cultural Anthropology*, Second Edition, pp. 144–145. Copyright © 2004. Boston: Allyn and Bacon. Reprinted by permission of Allyn and Bacon.; **47:** Paul G. Hewitt. From *Conceptual Physics*, Ninth Edition, p. 39. Copyright 2002. Boston: Addison Wesley. Reprinted by permission of Pearson Education, Inc.; **47:** Michael R. Solomon and Elnora W. Stuart. From *Marketing: Real People, Real Choices*, Third Edition, p. 108. Copyright © 2003. Upper Saddle River, NJ: Prentice Hall. Reprinted by permission of Pearson Education Inc.; **48:** Nora Newcombe. From *Child Development: Change Over Time*, p. 354. Copyright © 1996. New York: HarperCollins College Publishers. Reprinted by permission of Pearson Education, Inc.; **49:** Michael R. Solomon. From *Consumer Behavior*, Fifth Edition, p. 184. Copyright © 2002. Upper Saddle River, NJ: Prentice-Hall. Reprinted by permission of Pearson Education Inc.; **50:** Jeffrey Bennett, Megan Donahue, Nicholas Schneider, and Mark Voit. From *The Cosmic Perspective*, Brief Edition, p. 40. Copyright 2000. New York: Longman. Reprinted by permission of Pearson Education, Inc.; **50:** Nandy Bandyo-Padhyay. From *Computing for Non-Specialist*, p. 4. Copyright © 2000. New York: Longman. Reprinted by permission of Pearson Education, Inc.; **52:** Roger LeRoy Miller. *Economics Today*, Eighth Edition, pp. 185, 513. New York: HarperCollins College Publishers. Copyright © 1994. Reprinted by permission of Pearson Education, Inc. Publishing as Pearson Addison Wesley.; **53:** Josh R. Gerow. From *Psychology: An Introduction*, Fifth Edition, p. 319. Copyright © 1997 by Addison-Wesley Educational Publishers, Inc. Reprinted by permission of Pearson Education, Inc.; **62:** Michael Mix, Paul Farber and Keith I. King. From *Biology: The Network of Life*, p. 262. Copyright © 1996 by Michael Mix. Reprinted by permission of Pearson Education Inc.; **63:** Barbara D. Miller. From *Cultural Anthropology*, Second Edition, pp. 308–309. Copyright © 2004. Boston: Allyn and Bacon. Reprinted by permission of Allyn and Bacon.; **64:** Elaine Marieb. From *Essentials of Human Anatomy and Physiology*, Sixth Edition, p. 3. Copyright © 2000. San Francisco: Benjamin Cummings. Reprinted by permission of Benjamin Cummings, Inc.; **64:** Gerard Tortora. From *Introduction to the Human Body*, Second Edition, p .56. Copyright © 1991, Biological Sciences Textbook and A&P Textbooks, Inc. Reprinted by permission of John Wiley and Sons.; **65:** Edward Tarbuck and Frederick Lutgens. From *Earth Science*, Ninth Edition, p. 309. Copyright © 2000. Upper Saddle River, NJ: Prentice-Hall, Inc. Reprinted by permission of Pearson Education, Inc.; **66:** Edward Tarbuck and Frederick Lutgens. From *Earth Science*, Ninth Edition, pp. 620–621. Copyright © 2000. Upper Saddle River, NJ: Prentice-Hall, Inc. Reprinted by permission of Pearson Education, Inc.; **67:** Gary B. Nash, et al. From *The American People: Creating a Nation and a Society*, Sixth Edition, p. 1099. Copyright © 2004. New York: Longman. Reprinted by permission of Pearson Education, Inc.; **68:** Gary B. Nash, et al. From *The American People: Creating a Nation and a Society*, Sixth Edition, pp. 611–613. Copyright © 2004. New York: Longman. Reprinted by permission of Pearson Education, Inc.; **69:** R. Jackson Wilson, et al. From *The Pursuit of Liberty: A History of the American People*, Third Edition, p. 493. Copyright © 1997. New York: Longman. Reprinted by permission of Pearson Education, Inc.; **70:** Mark Bishop. From *Introduction to Chemistry*, p. 749. Copyright © 2002. San Francisco: Benjamin Cummings. Reprinted by permission of Benjamin Cummings.; **71:** Rebecca J. Donatelle. From *Access to Health*, Seventh Edition, p. 264. Copyright © 2002. San Francisco: Benjamin Cummings. Reprinted by permission of Benjamin Cummings.; **72:** Alex Thio. From *Sociology*, Fourth Edition, p. 255. Copyright © 1996. Allyn & Bacon. Reprinted by permission of Allyn & Bacon.; **72:** Wilson Dizard. From *Old Media, New Media*, Third Edition, p. 179. Copyright © 2000. New York: Longman. Reprinted by permission of Pearson Education, Inc.; **73:** Michael Mix, Paul Farber and Keith I. King. From *Biology: The Network of Life*, pp. 663–664. Copyright © 1996 by Michael Mix. Reprinted by permission of Pearson Education Inc.; **74:** Gerard J. Tortora. From *Introduction to the Human Body: The Essentials of Anatomy and Physiology*, Second Edition, p. 77. Copyright © 1991. New York: Longman. Reprinted by permission of John Wiley and Sons.; **75:** Alex Thio. From *Sociology*, Fourth

Protect Sacred Site" Indian Country Today (Lakota Times), Vol. 22, No. 48, May 14, 2003, p.1. Used by permission of *Indian Country Today*; **251:** Marvin Harris and Orna Johnson. "Apes and Language" from *Cultural Anthropology*, Sixth Edition, pp. 39–40. Copyright © 2003. Boston: Allyn and Bacon. Used by permission of Allyn and Bacon; **261:** Daniel A. Domenech. "Should Students Attend School Year Round? Yes" *Spectrum: The Journal of State Government*, Fall 1998, Vol. 7, No. 4. Copyright © 1998. Speakout.com. Reprinted by permission of Speakout.com.; **272:** Dorothy Rubin. "Should Students Attend School Year Round? No" *Spectrum: The Journal of State Government*, Fall 1998, Vol. 7, No. 4. Copyright © 1998 Speakout.com. Reprinted by permission of Speakout.com.; **284:** Mayra Rodriguez Valladares. "From the Beginning ... There Needs to be Light!" HispanicMagazine.com, January/February 2003. Reprinted by permission of Hispanic Publishing Group Magazine; **298:** Duane Preble, Sarah Preble, and Patrick Frank. "Shaping Her People's Heritage: Nampeyo (1852-1942)" from *Artforms: An Introduction to the Visual Arts*, Sixth Edition. Copyright © 1999 Addison Wesley. Reprinted by permission of Pearson Education, Inc.; **309:** Panos Ioannides. "Gregory" translated by Marion Byron and Catherine Raizis. From *The Charioteer: A Review of Modern Greek Literature*, copyright © 1989 by Panos Ioannides. English translation copyright © 1989 by Marion Byron and Catherine Raizis. Reprinted by permission from Pella Publishing Company, 337 West 37th Street, New York, NY 10018.; **319:** Linda Hogan. "The Truth Is" from Seeing Through the Sun by Linda Hogan. Amherst: University of Massachusetts Press. Copyright © 1985 by Linda Hogan and published by the University of Massachusetts Press.; **327:** Richard Jerome. "What to Do About Terri?" *People Weekly*, February 14, 2000. Copyright © 2000. All rights reserved. Reprinted by permission of *People Weekly*.; **335:** Christine Mitchell. "When Living is a Fate Worse than Death," *Newsweek*, August 28, 2000. Copyright © 2000 Newsweek, Inc. All rights reserved; 344: Rick Reilly. "Seoul Searching," Time, August 28, 2000. Copyright © 2000 Reprinted by permission of Time Inc.; **358:** Mary Pipher. Excerpts from "The Beautiful Laughing SistersAn Arrival Story" from *The Middle of Everywhere*. Copyright © 2002 by Mary Pipher. Reprinted by permission of Harcourt, Inc.; **370:** Cindy C. Combs. "Profile of a Terrorist" from Terrorism in the Twenty-First Century, Third Edition, pp. 50–54. Copyright © 2003. Upper Saddle River, NJ: Prentice Hall. Reprinted by permission of Prentice Hall.; **382:** John Mack Faragher, Mari Jo Buhle, Daniel Czitrom, and Susan H. Armitage, "American Communities: Los Alamos, New Mexico" from *Out of Many: A History of the American People,* Third Edition, pp. 461–462. Copyright © 2001. Upper Saddle River, NJ: Prentice Hall. Used by permission of Prentice Hall.; **393:** Martha Finney. "Four Simple Words that Guarantee the Job of Your Dreams," Career Magazine, August 24, 1999.; **403:** "McDonald's Makes a Lot of People Angry" from www.mcspotlight.org. Reprinted by permission of www.mcspotlight.org.; **414:** Michael Solomon. "Hispanic Americans: A Growing Market Segment" from *Consumer Behavior* (from chapter entitled "Ethnic, Racial and Religious Subcultures"). Copyright © Prentice Hall. Reprinted by permission of Pearson Education, Inc.; **428:** Anick Jesadun. "Senses on the Net," *Buffalo News,* January 2001, Permission by Associated Press, AP.; **440:** Chris Wood. "A Mania for Messaging," *Maclean's,* November 13, 2000, Vol. 113, No. 46, pp. 58-59. Copyright © Maclean's.; **451:** Hugh D. Barlow. "House Arrest and Electronic Monitoring" from *Criminal Justice in America*. Copyright © 2000. Upper Saddle River, NJ: Prentice Hall. Reprinted by permission of Pearson Education, Inc.; **465:** Bonnie Schiedel. "Use It and Lose It," Chatelaine, July 2000, Vol. 73, No. 7. Copyright © Rogers Publishing Ltd.; **491:** Elaine Marieb. "Athletes Looking Good and Doing Better with Anabolic Steroids?" from *Human Anatomy and Physiology,* Fifth Edition. Copyright © 2000. San Francisco: Benjamin Cummings (Pearson Education Inc.).; **501:** Jonathon Dube. "Baby, Oh, Baby" from "Baby, Oh, Baby: Nothing About 21st Century Will Be Infantile," courtesy of ABCNEWS.com.; **514:** David Bodanis. "Bugs in Your Pillow" from *The Secret Family: Twenty-four Hours Inside the Mysterious World of Our Minds and Bodies* by David Bodanis. Copyright © 1997 by David Bodanis. Reprinted with the permission of Simon & Schuster Adult Publishing Group. All rights reserved.; **524:** Neil A, Campbell and Jane B. Reece. "The Biodiversity Crisis" from *Essential Biology*. Copyright 2001. San Francisco: Benjamin Cummings. Reprinted by permission of Pearson Education, Inc.; **539:** Jeffrey O. Bennett, William L. Briggs, and Mario F. Triola. "Are Lotteries Fair?" from *Statistical Reasoning for Everyday Life*, Second Edition, pp. 266-68. Copyright © 2003. Pearson Education, Inc. Reprinted by permission of Pearson Education, Inc. Publishing as Pearson Addison Wesley.; **549:** Doug McPherson. "Moon Trips and Asteroid Mining Might Be Coming," *Sacramento Business Journal,* January 19, 2001, Vol. 17, issue 45, p. 31. Copyright © 2001, *City Business/USA.* Inc. Originally printed in *Denver Business Journal,* a sister publication. Reprinted by permission of www. scoopreprintscource.com.; **559:** Paul G. Hewitt. "Effects of Radiation on Humans" from *Conceptual Physics*, Ninth Edition, pp. 654-656. Copyright © 2002 Addison Wesley. Reprinted by permission of Pearson Education, Inc.; 570: Courtland L. Bovee, John V. Thill, and Barbara E. Schatzman. "Building Toward a Career" from *Business Communication Today*, Seventh Edition, pp. 543, 544, 545. Reprinted by permission of Pearson Education Inc., Upper Saddle River, NJ.; **582:** Kathy Simmons "Rx For Anger at Work," from *Career Magazine* website.; 594: Dorrit T. Walsh. "The Sandman Is DeadLong Live the Sleep Deprived Walking Zombie" Copyright © Bernard Hodes Group.; **608:** Carole Wade and Carol Tavris. "Behavior in Social and Cultural Context," Chapter 9 from *Invitation to Psychology*, pp. 296-331. Copyright © 1999, Reprinted by permission of Pearson Education, Inc.; **678:** Gary B. Nash, et al. "The Post-Cold War World, 1992-2002" from *The American People*, Sixth Edition, pp. 611, 613, 1099 and 1172, 1106. Copyright © 2004 by Pearson Education, Inc. Reprinted by permission.

Photo Credits

Page 10: Townsend P. Dickinson / The Image Works; **11:** George Holtz / The Image Works; **12:** Daniel J. Cox / NaturalExposures.com; **13 (left):** Thomas H. Brakefield / The Image Works; **13 (right):** Doug Perrine / Innerspace Visions; **93:** Bob Daemmrich Photography, Inc. / The Image Works; **171:** Esbin-Anderson Photography / The Image Works; **182:** SunStaff, *The Baltimore Sun;* **201 (both):** Index Stock Imagery, Inc.; **218:** Jerrican / Photo Researchers, Inc.; **229:** Omni Photo Communications Inc. / Index Stock Imagery, Inc.; **241:** David Melmer; **251:** Dr. Ron Cohn / The Gorilla Foundation / Koko.org; **252:** Georgia State University / Language Research Center; **326:** Joe Walles, *St. Petersburg Times;* **402:** AP / Wide World Photos; **430:** AP / Wide World Photos; **441:** Bayne Stanley Photography; **452:** A. Ramey / PhotoEdit Inc.; **490:** Bob Daemmrich / Stock, Boston, LLC; **503:** AP / Wide World Photos; **515:** Meckes /Ottawa / Photo Researchers, Inc.; **526 (top):** Juan Manuel Renjifo / Animals Animals / Earth Scenes; **526 (bottom):** Gary Kramer; **527:** Reuters / CORBIS; **560:** ©1990 Richard Megna, Fundamental Photographs, NYC; **608:** James W. Terry / SIPA Press; **611:** Ulrike Welsch / Photo Researchers, Inc.; **612 (both):** Copyright 1965 by Stanley Milgram. From the film OBEDIENCE, distributed by the Penn State University Audio / Visual Services; **613:** Mike Greenlar / Black Star; **615:** David Alan Harvey / National Geographic Image Collection; **617:** David Young-Wolff / PhotoEdit Inc.; **618:** AP / Wide World Photos; **621:** Attorney General Canada; **622:** Kim Kulish / CORBIS ; **624 (left):** Alex Webb / Magnum Photos, Inc.; **624 (right):** Guy Marshall Anderson / TimePix / Getty Images; **625:** Sidney Harris; **626:** Phillip G. Zimbardo, Inc.; **628 (left):** AP / Wide World Photos; **628 (right):** Shelly Katz Photographer; **630:** Courtesy National Archives; **631:** Penny Tweedie / Woodfin Camp & Associates; **632 (left):** Julie Marcotte / fotografia / Stock, Boston, LLC; **632 (right):** Courtesy National Archives; **633 (top, left):** Steve Kagan /Photo Researchers, Inc.; **633 (right):** Bettmann /CORBIS; **633 (bottom, left):** Library of Congress; **634 (left):** Courtesy National Archives; **634 (right):** Getty Images; **636:** Don Wright / The Palm Beach Post; **637 (both):** From "Intergroup Conflict and Cooperation: The Robbers Cave Experiment," by Sherif, Harvey, White, Hood, and Sherif. Institute of Group Relations, University of Oklahoma, Norman, 1961. Courtesy Muzafer Sherif; **638:** A. Ramey /PhotoEdit Inc.; **687:** Bettmann/CORBIS; **692:** Lisa Quinones / Black Star; **695:** AP / Wide World Photos; **697:** © Corky Lee; **698:** AP / Wide World Photos; **701:** Brad Markel, Liaison Agency, Inc. / Getty Images; **702:** AP / Wide World Photos; **704:** AP / Wide World Photos; **705:** AP / Wide World Photos.

Index